VENTURE CAPITAL, PRIVATE EQUITY, AND THE FINANCING OF ENTREPRENEURSHIP

VENTURE CAPITAL, PRIVATE EQUITY, AND THE FINANCING OF ENTREPRENEURSHIP:
The Power of Active Investing

Josh Lerner
Harvard Business School
National Bureau of Economic Research

Ann Leamon
Harvard Business School

Felda Hardymon
Harvard Business School

WILEY

John Wiley & Sons, Inc.

VP & EXECUTIVE PUBLISHER	George Hoffman
PROJECT EDITOR	Jennifer Manias
ASSISTANT EDITOR	Emily McGee
EDITORIAL ASSISTANT	Erica Horowitz
ASSOCIATE DIRECTOR OF MARKETING	Amy Scholz
SENIOR MARKETING MANAGER	Jesse Cruz
MARKETING ASSISTANT	Courtney Luzzi
PRODUCTION MANAGER	Janis Soo
ASSISTANT PRODUCTION EDITOR	Elaine S. Chew
EXECUTIVE MEDIA EDITOR	Allison Morris
MEDIA EDITOR	Greg Chaput
COVER DESIGNER	Seng Ping Ngieng
COVER IMAGE	© Kelvin Murray/Getty Images

This book was set in 10/12 Times Roman by Thomson Digital and printed and bound by Courier Westford, Inc. The cover was printed by Courier Westford, Inc.

This book is printed on acid free paper. ∞

Founded in 1807, John Wiley & Sons, Inc. has been a valued source of knowledge and understanding for more than 200 years, helping people around the world meet their needs and fulfill their aspirations. Our company is built on a foundation of principles that include responsibility to the communities we serve and where we live and work. In 2008, we launched a Corporate Citizenship Initiative, a global effort to address the environmental, social, economic, and ethical challenges we face in our business. Among the issues we are addressing are carbon impact, paper specifications and procurement, ethical conduct within our business and among our vendors, and community and charitable support. For more information, please visit our website: www.wiley.com/go/citizenship.

Library of Congress Cataloging-in-Publication Data

Lerner, Joshua.
  Venture capital, private equity, and the financing of entrepreneurship: the power of active investing/
  Josh Lerner, Ann Leamon, Felda Hardymon.—1st ed.
      p. cm.
   Includes bibliographical references and index.
   ISBN 978-0-470-59143-7 (acid free paper)
  1. Private equity. 2. Venture capital. 3. Investments. I. Leamon, Ann. II. Hardymon, G. Felda.
III. Title.
   HG4751.L47 2012
   658.15'224—dc23

                                                                                2011041424

Printed in the United States of America

10 9 8 7 6 5 4 3 2

To Oliver and Bella—the dynamic duo
To Bluesy, Nell, and Hank
To John and to my parents.

Preface

As we will discuss in much greater depth in the introduction, this book stems from a realization that overall private equity—defined in this volume as venture capital and buyouts but excluding hedge funds—has become a vastly more sizable and influential part of the global economic landscape over the past two decades. Yet it is immensely difficult to find a book that clearly describes the players, the dynamics, and the incentives behind the industry.

To be sure, there are books for financial academics, for investment managers, for entrepreneurs, and for people interested in tales from the trenches—many of which are very good indeed. But there seemed a need for a comprehensive introduction to private equity.

Too often, we fear that which we do not understand, or we legislate it in such a way that its benefits become distorted. And private equity does provide benefits, whether through venture capital funding of new technologies or a buyout firm's turnaround of a struggling company. While these are hardly charitable enterprises—and many failed investments have led to private and social losses—knowing how the industry functions can help understand what can go awry.

Here, we hope to present private equity in a clear yet detailed way. This book tells how the fascinating world of private equity works, from start to finish, how it creates value, and where it may destroy value. We then consider various possibilities for its development in the future. With more than sixty years of combined experience as practitioners in and/or academic investigators of private equity, we explain how and why private equity does what it does. We hope you will find it as intriguing as we do.

Acknowledgments

Writing a book involves many people, although only three are listed as authors. Thus, the problem with the acknowledgments section is not deciding whom to include, but rather, worrying about those we have left out.

Our colleagues and students have provided valuable assistance by both asking and answering questions. The partners and managers of many private equity groups, institutions, and companies participated in writing the cases that we refer to throughout this volume. Chris Allen of the Harvard Business School's Baker Library responded to numerous requests for data, often under severe time constraints and always with good humor and close attention to detail. Michael Diverio provided a number of assignment questions and technical assistance on the nuances of buyouts, and who also helped sort out the exhibits. We also thank the many reviewers for their constructive comments and suggestions, which have helped us raise the quality of the book. Theresa Gaignard, Lauren Coughlin Unsworth, and Maurie Sudock managed the many logistical details regarding the writing process—most specifically "Where the devil is Felda, and why isn't his chapter done?"—and provided unflagging administrative support. Lacey Vitetta, Emily McGee, and Jennifer Manias at John Wiley & Sons provided key assistance in the production of the volume.

Finally, Josh thanks Wendy for putting up with his travels on many trips, Ann thanks John and the family for tolerating the summer of the great distraction, and Bessemer Venture Partners for everything they taught her at the Monday meetings, and Felda thanks Dena for her unstinting help and long-suffering support in managing two careers and also his colleagues at Bessemer Venture Partners for their support.

About the Authors

Josh Lerner is the Jacob H. Schiff Professor of Investment Banking at Harvard Business School, with a joint appointment in the Finance and Entrepreneurial Management Units. He graduated from Yale College with a Special Divisional Major that combined physics with the history of technology; he worked for several years on issues concerning technological innovation and public policy at the Brookings Institution, for a public-private task force in Chicago, and on Capitol Hill. He then earned a PhD in Harvard's Economics Department.

Much of his research, which is collected in *The Venture Capital Cycle* (1999 and 2004), *The Money of Invention* (2001), and the *Boulevard of Broken Dreams* (2008), focuses on the structure and role of venture capital organizations. He founded the Entrepreneurship and Innovation Policy and the Economy Groups at the National Bureau of Economic Research. He is a founder and director of the Private Capital Research Institute, a nonprofit body that seeks to encourage research into venture and buyout activity.

In the 1993–1994 academic year, he introduced an elective course for second-year MBAs on private equity finance. In recent years, the Venture Capital and Private Equity course has consistently been one of the top electives at Harvard Business School. In addition, he chairs and conducts private equity executive education courses, teaches several doctoral classes, and plays a variety of administrative roles at the university.

Ann Leamon is a Teaching Fellow at Harvard Business School and a partner at Bella Research Group, a consulting firm providing specialized advisory services to private capital organizations. She came to Harvard after six years as a senior business analyst at L.L. Bean and three years at Central Maine Power Company as a senior economic and load forecaster. Her work in local area load forecasting won an Industry Innovators award from the Electric Power Research Institute, and she has published several papers and addressed conferences on the project.

At Harvard, Ann cofounded the Center for Case Development. She left that position to collaborate with Professors Lerner and Hardymon in the further development of the Venture Capital and Private Equity course, and she has authored more than one hundred cases. Until recently, Ann handled corporate communications for Bessemer Venture Partners. She holds a BA (Honors) in German from University of King's College/ Dalhousie, an MA in Economics from the University of Montana, where she studied urban redevelopment, and an MFA from the Bennington Writing Seminars.

Felda Hardymon is a Professor of Management Practice at Harvard Business School, a career venture capitalist, and recently spent a term as a visiting professor at London School of Economics. Felda joined Bessemer Venture Partners (BVP) in 1981, and he continues there as a general partner. BVP is among the oldest venture firms (founded in 1911) and is a long-standing specialist in early-stage investing.

Felda has led BVP's investments in more than sixty companies in the software, communications, and retail sectors, including Cascade

Communications, Parametric Technology, Staples, Endeca, and MSI. Previously he was a vice president of BDSI, the original venture subsidiary of General Electric Company, where he led investments in Ungermann-Bass, Stratus Computer, and Western Digital. Felda served on the board of the National Venture Capital Association, where he was chairman of the Tax Committee. He received a BSc from Rose Polytechnic Institute, a PhD (mathematics) from Duke University, and an MBA (Baker Scholar) from Harvard Business School. In 2010, Felda received a Lifetime Achievement Award from the National Venture Capital Association (NVCA).

Brief Contents

Table of Contents

Chapter 1

Introduction

During the 1980s, 1990s, and much of the 2000s, there has been a tremendous boom in the venture capital and private equity industries. The pool of U.S. funds of these types—partnerships specializing in venture capital, leveraged buyouts, mezzanine investments, build-ups, distressed debt, and related investments—has grown from $5 billion in 1980 to slightly more than $580 billion at the end of 2009.

The reasons for the spectacular growth of private equity are not hard to see. Many of the companies whose products we use every day—such as Apple, Intel, Google, and Microsoft— were originally venture-backed. Not only did some of these investments have a substantial impact on society as a whole, they also created much value for the entrepreneurs who ran the firms, the institutional and individual investors who invested in the companies, and the private equity investors themselves.

The scale of some of these successes boggles the imagination. In June 1999, Kleiner Perkins paid $12.5 million for 10 percent of Google. (Sequoia Capital made a similar investment at the time.) While the precise value of the shares that Kleiner distributed to its investors after the firm went public in 2004 can be tricky to calculate, the value appears to have been at least $4.3 billion, or some 344 times the original investment.[1] As of August 2009, Google's market capitalization stood at about $141 billion.

Nor have these kinds of successes been confined to esoteric firms sporting technology developed by Stanford doctoral students. Thomas H. Lee Company bought Snapple, the iced tea maker, in April 1992 for roughly $140 million. Eight months later, Lee took the company public. In 1994, only two years after the original acquisition, Lee sold Snapple to Quaker Oats for $1.7 billion. (Quaker Oats subsequently sold the company, which performed poorly under new management, for only $300 million; but that is another story.)[2]

Not only has private equity become more influential in terms of backing world-changing companies, but its influence appears to have spread beyond the industry's immediate boundaries. Many operating corporations, financial institutions, and even governments have emulated venture capitalists and set up their own funds to invest inside and outside their organizations. Established firms have emulated many of the key approaches of buyout funds, such as linking executive compensation to performance, a heavier reliance on debt, and a willingness to sell off under-performing units.

---

[1] For information on the transactions, see Thomson Reuters private equity database, accessed June 14, 2010. For a representative calculation of Kleiner's returns, see http://billburnham.blogs.com/burnhamsbeat/2005/06/just_how_much_d.html, accessed August 16, 2009.

[2] These data are taken from "Thomas H. Lee in Snapple Deal," *New York Times,* April 3, 1992, D3; Barnaby J. Feder, "Quaker to Sell Snapple for $300 Million," *New York Times*, March 28, 1997, D1; and Snapple's various filings with the Securities and Exchange Commission.

Despite this growth, many questions about private equity remain unanswered, and many of its features continue to be mysterious. What do private equity groups really do? How do venture capital and buyout funds create value—do they fundamentally transform the companies they invest in, or is it all simply a financial shell game? What kinds of returns have these funds generated? Maddeningly, private equity is just so . . . private!

In addition to questions about the day-to-day activities of these funds, the patterns of venture capital and buyout fund-raising and investment pose several puzzles. (Figure 1.1 shows the pattern of private equity fund-raising in the United States; Figure 1.2 shows the pattern in the rest of the world.) First, the level of activity today is far greater than in earlier decades—what explains this tremendous growth in these funds? Perhaps even more puzzling is the process of boom and bust that characterizes this industry. There were rapid increases in fund-raising in the late 1960s, mid-1980s, late 1990s, and mid-2000s and precipitous declines in the 1970s, early 1990s, early 2000s, and most recently in the late 2000s. What explains the changing mixture of fund types?

Then there is the global dimension. Private equity, both venture capital and leveraged buyouts, originated in the United States. For much of its history, the industry was concentrated in that nation and the United Kingdom. Over the past decade, however, private equity has become much more global. Not only has the capital disbursed in continental Europe and Asia increased sharply, but emerging markets are becoming far more important in the private equity landscape. Figure 1.3 illustrates this change, comparing the global distribution of private equity investments made in 1995 and 2007. This growth poses several questions. To what extent is the model, developed and refined over the past several decades, likely to be successfully translated to other

FIGURE 1.1   Inflation-adjusted U.S. private equity fundraising, 1969–2009

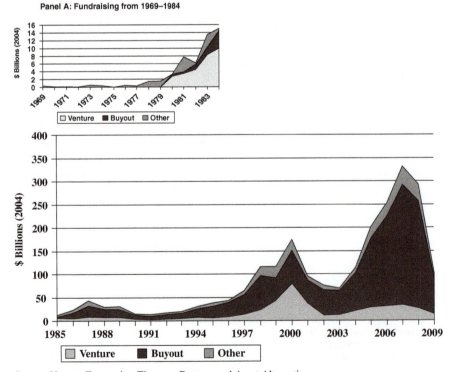

Source: Venture Economics, Thomson Reuters, and Asset Alternatives.

FIGURE 1.2   Private equity fundraising outside the United States, 1989–2009

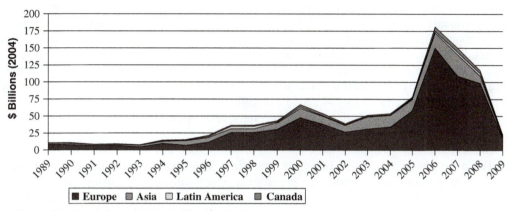

Note: Asian data are investments rather than funds raised.
Sources: Various National PEVC organizations, Preqin, and Thomson Reuters.

countries? Will only buyout funds manage the transition, or will other types of investments, such as venture capital, also make the leap?

While private equity can be said to differ from public investing along a host of dimensions, the most fundamental is its emphasis on activity. Private equity investors across the spectrum are

FIGURE 1.3   Private equity investment by region, 1995 and 2007

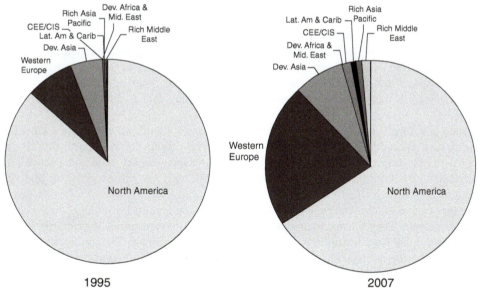

Notes: "Rich Asia Pacific" is Japan, Singapore, Hong Kong, Macao, South Korea, Australia and New Zealand; all other Asia is "Dev. Asia". "Rich Middle East" includes the UAE, Saudi Arabia, Kuwait, Bahrain, and Israel; all other Middle East countries are in "Dev. Africa & Mid. East." CEE/CIS is Central & Eastern Europe and the Commonwealth of Independent States... "Lat. Am & Carib" includes all of Central and South America and all Caribbean islands regardless of nationality. Data from Josh Lerner, Per Strömberg L, and sources Morten Sørensen, "What Drives Private Equity Activity and Success Globally?", *The Global Impact of Private Equity Report 2009,* in *Globalization of Alternative Investments Working Papers Volume 2: Global Economic Impact of Private Equity 2009*, ed. A. Gurung and J. Lerner (New York: World Economic Forum USA, 2009), p. 65-98, available at http://www.weforum.org/pdf/cgi/pe/Full_Report2.pdf.

active investors, deeply involved in managing the companies they invest in. This activity is reinforced through the partnership and deal structures they employ and the way they interact with individuals and institutions at all points of value creation. It is this active involvement that builds companies in the case of venture capital and changes their direction in the case of buyouts. This approach is distinct from the "active management" strategies that managers of hedge funds or mutual funds may use in the public markets. The techniques of active investing make private equity a powerful force not just for growing companies, but for growing economies. But how can its tools—active oversight by investors with a direct interest in the company's success, compensation linked to results, and an emphasis on good governance—best be adopted?

In this textbook, we explore these exciting and important questions, providing a comprehensive overview of the world of active investing. The book follows the cycle of these investments. Raising funds, evaluating investment opportunities, structuring and overseeing transactions, and exiting investments are considered in turn. The focus is not just on the U.S. market, but on the increasingly global nature of these activities. The book also looks at active investors as businesses themselves and introduces the key features of these firms. How groups grapple with questions of scaling and internationalization and the disruptive impact of market cycles are among the topics considered. In addition, we look at the impact of these funds: first at how their investments have performed and then at the broader consequences of these investments. We finally look "into the crystal ball" and project the future of active investing.

WHAT ARE VENTURE CAPITAL AND LEVERAGED BUYOUTS?

A natural first question is what constitutes a venture capital and leveraged buyout fund. Many start-up companies require substantial capital. A company's founder may not have sufficient funds to finance these projects alone and therefore must seek outside financing. Entrepreneurial companies that are characterized by significant intangible assets expect years of negative earnings and have uncertain prospects that are unlikely to receive bank loans or other debt financing. Similarly, troubled companies that need to undergo restructurings may find it difficult to raise external financing.

Meanwhile, large institutional investors, such as pension funds and university endowments, frequently seek illiquid long-run investments such as private equity for their portfolios. They are charged with investing over the longer term, and typically they can set aside some funds for the very distant future. Often, these groups have neither the staff nor the expertise to make such investments themselves.

Venture capital and buyout organizations (in total, private equity) fill the gap between these two sets of players. They finance high-risk, potentially high-reward projects, primarily investing funds that they raise from institutions and high-net-worth individuals. They protect the value of their equity stakes by undertaking careful business and financial due diligence before making the investments and by retaining powerful oversight rights afterward. Ultimately, they sell their stakes in the firms and return the bulk of their profits to their investors.

One of (several) confusing things about private equity is terminology. In Europe, the term *venture capital* is frequently used to refer to the entire spectrum of private equity investment, from seed investments to the largest leveraged buyouts. In the United States, the term *private equity* is sometimes used to refer not only to all these investments (which is the sense we use here) but also to leveraged buyouts, or else to all such investments except for seed venture investing. In yet other cases, private equity refers to transactions that are somewhere between venture capital and buyouts, such as growth equity and mezzanine deals.

WHY IS PRIVATE EQUITY NEEDED?

Private equity plays a critical role in the American economy, and increasingly does so elsewhere around the globe as well. The types of companies financed by private equity organizations—whether young start-ups hungry for capital or ailing giants that need to restructure—pose numerous risks and uncertainties that discourage other investors.

In this section, we first review the risks posed by these companies. We then consider briefly how private equity organizations address the risks. Finally, we discuss why other financiers, such as banks, often cannot address these problems as effectively as private equity firms.

The financing of young and restructuring companies is a risky business. Uncertainty and informational gaps often characterize these organizations, particularly in high-technology industries. These information problems make it difficult to assess these companies and permit opportunistic behavior by entrepreneurs after the financing is received.

To briefly review the types of conflicts that can emerge in these settings, conflicts between managers and investors ("agency problems") can affect the willingness of both debt and equity holders to provide capital. If the firm raises equity from outside investors, the manager has an incentive to engage in wasteful expenditures (e.g., lavish offices) because he may benefit disproportionately from them but does not bear their entire cost. Similarly, if the firm raises debt, the manager may increase risk to undesirable levels. Because providers of capital recognize these problems, outside investors demand a higher rate of return than would be the case if the funds were internally generated.[3]

Additional agency problems may appear in the types of entrepreneurial companies that private equity firms invest in. For instance, entrepreneurs might invest in strategies, research, or projects that have high personal returns but low expected monetary payoffs to shareholders: consider a biotechnology company founder who chooses to invest in a certain type of research that brings him great recognition in the scientific community but provides little return for the venture capitalist. Similarly, entrepreneurs may receive initial results from market trials indicating little demand for a new product, but may want to keep the company going because they receive significant private benefits from managing their own firm.

Even if the manager is motivated to maximize shareholder value, information gaps may make raising external capital more expensive or even preclude it entirely. Equity offerings of companies may be associated with a "lemons" problem: if the manager is better informed about the company's investment opportunities and acts in the interest of current shareholders, then he will issue new shares only when the company's stock is overvalued. Indeed, numerous studies have documented that stock prices decline upon the announcement of equity issues, largely because of the negative signal sent to the market. This "lemons" problem leads investors to invest less in young or restructuring companies than they would otherwise, or even not to invest at all. Similar information problems have also been shown to exist in debt markets.[4]

More generally, the inability of a typical investor to verify actions or outcomes makes it difficult to write contracts that are contingent upon particular events. This inability makes

---

[3] The classic treatment of these problems is in Michael C. Jensen and William H. Meckling, "Theory of the Firm: Managerial Behavior, Agency Costs, and Ownership Structure," *Journal of Financial Economics* 3 (1976): 305–60.

[4] The "lemons" problem was introduced in George A. Akerlof, "The Market for 'Lemons': Qualitative Uncertainty and the Market Mechanism," *Quarterly Journal of Economics* 84 (1970): 488–500. Discussions of the implications of this problem for financing decisions are in Bruce C. Greenwald, Joseph E. Stiglitz, and Andrew Weiss, "Information Imperfections in the Capital Market and Macroeconomic Fluctuations," *American Economic Review Papers and Proceedings* 74 (1984): 194–99; and Stewart C. Myers and Nicholas S. Majluf, "Corporate Financing and Investment Decisions When Firms Have Information That Investors Do Not Have," *Journal of Financial Economics* 13 (1984): 187–221.

external financing costly. Many economic models[5] argue that when investors find it difficult to verify that certain actions have been taken or certain outcomes have occurred—even if they strongly suspect the entrepreneur has followed a certain action that was counter to their original agreement, they cannot prove it in a court of law—external financing may become costly or difficult to obtain.

If the information problems could be eliminated, these barriers to financing would disappear. Financial economists argue that specialized intermediaries, such as private equity organizations, have the skills to address these problems. By intensively scrutinizing companies before providing capital and then monitoring them afterward—essentially, by being active—such organizations can alleviate some of the information gaps and reduce capital constraints. Thus it is important to understand the tools that private equity investors use in this difficult environment because they enable companies ultimately to receive the financing that they cannot raise from other sources. The nonmonetary aspects of private equity are critical to its success. These tools—the screening of investments, the use of convertible securities, the syndication and staging of investments, and the provision of oversight and informal coaching—are highlighted in the middle chapters of the book.

What prohibits other financial intermediaries (e.g., banks) from undertaking the same sort of monitoring? While it is easy to see why individual investors may not have the expertise to address these types of agency problems, one might think that bank credit officers could undertake such oversight. Yet even in countries with exceedingly well-developed banking systems, such as Germany and Japan, policymakers today are seeking to encourage the development of a private equity industry to ensure more adequate financing for risky entrepreneurial companies. Clearly, this falls outside the domain of even skilled bank staff.

The limitations of banks stem from several of their key institutional features. First, because regulations in the United States limit banks' ability to hold shares, they cannot freely use equity to fund projects. Taking an equity position in the firm allows the private equity firm to share proportionately in the upside, guaranteeing that the investor benefits if the company succeeds. Second, banks may not have the necessary skills to evaluate projects with few tangible assets and significant uncertainty. In addition, banks in competitive markets may not be able to finance high-risk projects because they are unable to charge borrowers rates high enough to compensate for the company's riskiness. Finally, private equity firms' high-powered compensation schemes give these investors incentives to monitor companies more closely because their individual compensation is closely linked to the firms' returns. Banks, corporations, and other institutions that have sponsored venture funds without such high-powered incentives have found it difficult to retain personnel once the investors have performed well enough to raise a fund of their own.[6]

At the same time, it is important to emphasize that private equity—especially buyout funds—has stirred considerable fear and uncertainty, which has been manifested in the numerous proposals being considered today by legislators worldwide to tax and regulate the industry. In some cases, this legislation is being prompted by reasonable concerns about an increasingly influential and opaque financial intermediary, which existing rules are not designed to handle. In other cases, however, initiatives seem motivated by a desire by entrenched actors to protect an inefficient status quo.

---

[5] Important examples include Sanford Grossman and Oliver D. Hart, "The Costs and Benefits of Ownership: A Theory of Vertical and Lateral Integration," *Journal of Political Economy* 94 (1986): 691–719; and Oliver D. Hart and John Moore, "Property Rights and the Nature of the Firm," *Journal of Political Economy* 98 (1990): 1119–58.

[6] The limitations of bank financing are explored in such theoretical and empirical academic studies as Joseph E. Stiglitz and Andrew Weiss, "Credit Rationing in Markets with Incomplete Information," *American Economic Review* 71 (1981): 393–409; and Mitchell A. Petersen and Raghuram G. Rajan, "The Effect of Credit Market Competition on Lending Relationships," *Quarterly Journal of Economics* 110 (1995): 407–44.

WHAT IS THE HISTORY OF PRIVATE EQUITY?

In its initial decades, the private equity industry was a predominantly American phenomenon. Of course, fast-growing firms raised financing before the creation of the private equity industry. Banks provided debt in the form of loans, and longer-term, riskier investments often raised funds from wealthy individuals. By the last decades of the nineteenth century and the first decades of the twentieth century, wealthy families had established offices to manage their investments. Families such as the Phippses, Rockefellers, Vanderbilts, and Whitneys invested in and advised a variety of business enterprises, including the predecessor entities to AT&T, Eastern Airlines, and McDonnell Douglas.

But by the time of the Great Depression of the 1930s, there was a widespread perception that the existing ways of financing fast-growing young firms were inadequate.[7] Not only were many promising companies going unfunded, but investors with high net worth frequently did not have the time or skills to work with young firms to address glaring management deficiencies. Nor were the alternatives set up by the Roosevelt administration during the New Deal—such as the Reconstruction Finance Corporation—seen as satisfactory. The rigidity of the loan evaluation criteria, the extensive red tape associated with the award process, and the fears of political interference and regulations all suggested the need for an alternative.

The first formal venture capital firm was thus established with a broader set of goals in mind than just making money.[8] American Research and Development (ARD) Corporation grew out of the concern that the United States, having been pushed out of the Depression by the stimulus of the federal government's wartime spending, would soon revert to economic lethargy when the war ended. In October 1945, Ralph Flanders, then head of the Federal Reserve Bank of Boston, argued that addressing this danger required a new enterprise, founded with the goal of financing new businesses. He argued that the enterprise would not only need to be far more systematic in "selecting the most attractive possibilities and spreading the risk" than most individual investors had been, but would need to tap into the nation's "great accumulation of fiduciary funds" (i.e., pension funds and other institutional capital) if it was to be successful in the long term.[9]

ARD was formed a year later to try to realize this vision. Flanders recruited a number of civic and business leaders to join in the effort, including MIT president Karl Compton. But the day-to-day management of the fund fell on the shoulders of Harvard Business School professor Georges F. Doriot. ARD in its communications emphasized that its goal was to fund and aid new companies to generate "an increased standard of living for the American people." While profitability was a goal of the effort, in the words of Pat Liles, financial returns "were not the overriding purpose of the firms. Instead, they were depicted as a necessary part of the process."[10]

This tension between the broader social goals and financial returns ran through ARD's first two decades. In part, these dual goals reflected the tensions inherent in being a public company. Despite Flanders's emphasis on institutional capital, limited interest had forced ARD to raise its initial $5 million through a public offering. (Most early private equity funds were structured similarly.) Many of the investors—perhaps persuaded by overzealous brokers to buy the shares—had not appreciated the extended time period necessary to realize capital gains or other profits from the early-stage companies that dominated ARD's portfolio. Doriot as a result spent much of the

---

[7] For one discussion of the limitations of public efforts to boost entrepreneurial firms in the 1920s, see Joseph L. Nicholson, "The Fallacy of Easy Money for Small Business," *Harvard Business Review* 17, no. 1 (Autumn 1938): 31–34.

[8] This history of American Research and Development is largely drawn from Spencer Ante, *Creative Capital: Georges Doriot and the Birth of Venture Capital* (Boston: Harvard Business School Press, 2008); and Patrick R. Liles, *Sustaining the Venture Capital Firm* (Cambridge, MA: Management Analysis Center, 1978).

[9] Ralph Flanders, "The Problem of Development Capital," *Commercial and Financial Chronicle* 162, no. 4442 (November 29, 1945): 2576, 2608.

[10] Liles, *Venture Capital Firm*, 32.

1950s and 1960s defending the longer-run objectives of the fund. In *Fortune*'s rather unsympathetic portrait of ARD in 1967, Doriot was quoted: "Your sophisticated shareholders make five points and then sell out. But we have our hearts in our companies, we are really doctors of childhood diseases here. When bankers or brokers tell me I should sell an ailing company, I ask them, 'Would you sell a child running a temperature of 104?'"[11] The ultimate success of ARD's investments ranged widely; almost half of ARD's profits during its twenty-six-year existence as an independent entity came from its $70,000 investment in Digital Equipment Company in 1957, which grew in value to $355 million.

The same tension underlay the next great experiment to promote venture activity, the Small Business Investment Company (SBIC) program. These federally guaranteed risk-capital pools proliferated during the 1960s and accounted for the bulk of all venture capital raised during those years.[12]

The rationale for these entities was similar to that invoked by Doriot: numerous promising entrepreneurs were unable to garner the capital needed to commercialize their ideas. But in one important respect the SBICs were unlike the pioneering efforts of the 1930s: legislators realized that government bureaucrats—no matter how well intentioned—were probably not the right people to make the tricky decisions about which businesses to fund. Instead, this responsibility was put in the hands of the private sector.

As enacted in 1958, the SBICs received two powerful mandates: they could borrow up to half their capital from the federal government, and they also received a variety of favorable tax incentives. In return, the SBICs had to confine themselves to investing in small businesses. More onerously, the investments had to be structured in certain ways; for instance, the SBICs could not hold equity in firms (although the debt could be convertible to equity), and their control over these firms was also limited. Moreover, steps that seem like second nature to venture capitalists—such as offering stock options to employees of the firms—were sharply restricted.

These features of the SBIC program were criticized by knowledgeable observers even before the legislation enabling the funds was enacted. Criticism of the program intensified in the early 1960s, when a large number of SBICs were financed, often with minimal review. The entities receiving charters and loans from the government included some run by inexperienced financiers, who undertook lines of business very different from those originally intended by Congress—such as real estate development—along with corrupt funds determined to make "sweetheart" financings to dubious businesses run by friends, relatives, and, in a few cases, organized crime. Nine out of ten SBICs violated federal regulations in some way.[13] The SBIC program consequently drew extensive congressional criticism for low financial returns and for fraud and waste. Despite some wavering, the officials responsible for the program (and the executive branch more generally) remained committed to it and resisted calls to dismantle it. While the market for SBICs in the late 1960s and early 1970s was strong, incentive problems ultimately led to a rapid decline of activity.

Viewed with the benefit of hindsight, however, the legacy of the program from the 1950s and 1960s looks quite different. Though few of today's significant funds began as part of the SBIC program, it did stimulate the proliferation of many venture-minded institutions in California's Silicon Valley and Boston's Route 128, the nation's two major nurseries of entrepreneurs. These institutions included law firms and accounting groups geared specifically to the needs of entrepreneurial firms. For example, Venture Economics, which originated as the SBIC Reporting Service

---

[11] Gene Bylinsky, "General Doriot's Dream Factory," *Fortune* 76, no. 2 (August 1967): 103–36.

[12] This history of the SBIC program is drawn from C. M. Noone and S. M. Rubel, *SBICs: Pioneers in Organized Venture Capital* (Chicago: Capital Publishing, 1970); Jonathan J. Bean, *Big Government and Affirmative Action: The Scandalous History of the Small Business Administration* (Lexington: University Press of Kentucky, 2001); and Liles, *Venture Capital Firm*.

[13] Bean, *Big Government*, 56.

in 1961, gradually expanded its scope to become the major source of returns data on the entire venture industry. Moreover, some of the United States' most dynamic technology companies—including Apple Computer, Compaq (now part of Hewlett-Packard), and Intel—received support from the SBIC program before they went public. Similar lessons could be drawn from programs modeled after the SBIC program in other nations such as China and Singapore.

The first venture capital limited partnership, Draper, Gaither, and Anderson, was formed in 1958. Despite a few imitators, limited partnerships accounted for a minority of the venture pool during the 1960s and 1970s. Most venture organizations raised money either through closed-end funds or the SBICs described earlier. The annual flow of money into private equity during its first three decades never exceeded a few hundred million dollars and usually was substantially less. During these years, while a few funds made a considerable number of investments in buyouts and other transactions involving mature companies, private equity organizations were universally referred to as venture capital funds.

Activity in the private equity industry increased dramatically in late 1970s and early 1980s. Industry observers attributed much of the shift to the U.S. Department of Labor's clarification of the Employee Retirement Income Security Act's "prudent man" rule in 1979. Before this, the legislation limited the ability of pension funds to invest substantial amounts of money into venture capital or other high-risk asset classes. The Department of Labor's clarification of the rule explicitly allowed pension managers to invest in high-risk assets, including private equity. Numerous specialized funds—concentrating in areas such as leveraged buyouts, mezzanine transactions, and such hybrids as venture leasing—sprang up in response. Another important change in the private equity industry during this period was the rise of the limited partnership as the dominant organizational form.

Meanwhile, another change occurred during the 1980s and affected the buyout industry specifically: creation of the high-yield bond or "junk-bond" market by Michael Milken and Drexel Burnham Lambert. Before this market emerged, private equity firms borrowed primarily through traditional banks. Banks financed companies based on two criteria: cash flow and liquidation value (asset-backed lending). Often banks sought to ensure they had two ways out of any lending situation, in order to limit the loss of their capital (the so-called belt-and-suspenders approach). As a result, private equity groups had limited scope for their acquisition opportunities.

The new high-yield market changed the landscape by greatly enhancing the availability of debt. Complex financial structures with several layers of debt became commonplace: senior bonds were the first to be repaid, junior the second, and so on down to junk, which would be the last to be repaid in the case of distress. The bond's interest rate rose with the risk of loss. Through Drexel, buyout groups were able to structure transactions that frequently involved publicly traded debt, often employing leverage levels that reached as high as 90 or 95 percent of the total capital structure. Buyout firms could thus increase their borrowing capacity and improve or "juice" their return on equity. Using junk bonds, private equity firms could acquire companies of increased scale and size, producing returns on more mature businesses that resembled those of venture capital or growth equity in some cases. Drexel's high-yield market transformed the buyout industry from a cottage industry into an international behemoth with multibillion-dollar funds and facilitated the buyout boom of the 1980s. This culminated in KKR's acquisition of RJR Nabisco (financed by Drexel), which was documented in the book *Barbarians at the Gate*.[14]

The subsequent years saw both very good and trying times for private equity investors. On the one hand, in the 1980s, venture capitalists backed many of the world-changing, high-technology companies, including Cisco Systems, Genentech, Microsoft, and Sun Microsystems. Numerous successful buyouts—such as Avis, Beatrice, Dr. Pepper, Gibson Greetings, and McCall Pattern—garnered considerable public attention during that period. At the same time, new commitments to

---

[14] Bryan Burrough and John Helyar, *Barbarians at the Gate: The Fall of RJR Nabisco* (New York: Harper Collins, 1990).

the private equity industry were very uneven. The annual flow of money into venture capital funds increased by a factor of ten during the first half of the 1980s but steadily declined from 1987 through 1991. Buyouts underwent an even more dramatic rise through the 1980s, followed by a precipitous fall at the end of the decade.

Much of this pattern was driven by the changing fortunes of private equity investments. Returns on venture capital funds had declined sharply in the mid-1980s after being exceedingly attractive in the 1970s. This fall was apparently triggered by overinvestment in a few industries, such as computer hardware, and by the entry of many inexperienced venture capitalists. Buyout returns underwent a similar decline in the late 1980s, due largely to the increased competition between groups for transactions. Moreover, the market for financing dried up in 1989 after Rudy Giuliani, then the U.S. attorney in Manhattan, persuaded a grand jury to indict Drexel's Michael Milken on 89 charges, including racketeering and securities fraud. (In 1990, Milken pled guilty to six lesser charges and served nearly two years in jail. Many of the savings and loans that were large holders of junk bonds failed, leading to an expensive federal bailout.) As investors became disappointed with returns, and the types of highly leveraged deals that had characterized the 1980s became impossible to arrange, capital for the industry dried up.

The 1990s saw several of these patterns repeated on an unprecedented scale. During much of the decade, almost every part of the private equity industry experienced dramatic growth and excellent returns. This recovery was triggered by several factors. The exit of many inexperienced investors at the beginning of the decade ensured that the remaining groups faced less competition for transactions. A healthy market for initial public offerings during the period meant that it was easier for all investors to exit private equity transactions. Meanwhile, the extent of technological innovation—particularly in industries related to information technology—created extraordinary opportunities for venture capitalists. New capital commitments to both venture and buyout funds rose in response to these changing circumstances, reaching record levels by the late 1990s and 2000.

But as is often the case, this growth could not be sustained. Institutional and individual investors—attracted especially by the tremendously high returns enjoyed by venture funds—flooded money into the industry. In many cases, good firms staggered under the weight of capital. In others, firms that should not have raised capital succeeded in garnering considerable funds. Excessive growth led to overstretched partners, inadequate due diligence, and in many cases, poor investment decisions. Moreover, the pressure to put their larger funds to work led to price inflation among potential portfolio companies and reduced eventual returns. The first years of the twenty-first century saw the venture capital industry address this legacy, and appropriately "scaling" the firm has become a major topic of concern.

Meanwhile, the buyout sector underwent a tremendous boom between 2004 and 2007. Fueled by the increased appetite of institutional investors for alternative investments; a greater willing-ness of boards of directors and managers to sell to private equity groups, primarily buyout firms; and, last but not least, a wave of debt on generous terms and with few protective covenants; the industry experienced explosive growth. As in many earlier booms, as the influx of capital continued, valuations rose, and standards for undertaking deals (generally) fell. Due to the sheer amount of money deployed, as well as the dramatic speed with which the global recession arrived, the ensuing downturn was particularly dramatic. Both venture and buyout funds struggled with portfolio companies that had severe difficulties, while investors (whether equity or debt providers) were unwilling to commit additional capital.

Although the booms and busts in private equity investment have attracted the bulk of public attention, the most revolutionary recent changes in the industry have been in the structure of the private equity firms themselves. Private equity organizations, while in the business of funding innovation, were remarkably steadfast in retaining the limited partnership structure between the mid-1960s and the late 1990s. In recent years, however, a flurry of experimentation has occurred as firms try to resolve the question of structure and scale. Among the changes have been the establishment of affiliate funds in different regions and nations and the expansion of the funds to include real estate, mezzanine, distressed debt, and bond funds. The Blackstone Group's decision to offer shares to the public in June 2007 was only the culmination of a period of intensive structural experimentation by private equity groups.

What explains these sudden changes on the part of the major private equity groups in recent years? We believe that the changes reflect a more fundamental shift in the industry, as groups struggle to address the increasing efficiency of their sector. Facing increased competition, they are seeking new ways to differentiate themselves.

Evidence of the private equity industry's increased efficiency abounds. While private equity for much its first decades had the flavor of a cottage industry, with a considerable number of relatively small firms working alongside one another, today it is much more competitive. Industry data show that 4,500 firms worldwide managed $2.3 trillion, and 2,000 of those in the United States managed slightly over $580 billion.[15]

Given this changing competitive environment, the leading firms are increasingly seeking to differentiate themselves from the mass of other investors. They are employing a variety of tools to build up and distinguish their "brands." These steps include strategic partnerships, expansion of international operations, provision of additional services, and aggressive fund-raising as well as many other initiatives to extend and build the firms' visibility in the United States and abroad.

To be sure, private equity is not unique in this transformation. For instance, the investment banking industry underwent a similar change in the 1950s and 1960s, as the top "bulge bracket" firms solidified their leadership positions. The gap between the leading banks and the following ones greatly increased during these years, as the top groups greatly enhanced their range of activities and boosted their hiring of personnel. Similarly, management of the major banks was transformed during these years as procedures were systematized and management structures formalized. Similar patterns appear to be at play in the private equity industry, although it is too soon to tell conclusively.

ABOUT THIS BOOK

This book is based on a course introduced at Harvard Business School in the 1993–1994 academic year. Venture Capital and Private Equity has attracted students interested in careers as private equity investors, as managers of entrepreneurial companies, or as investment bankers or other intermediaries who work with private equity firms and the companies they fund. The materials developed for this course have also been used in a variety of other settings, such as executive education courses at Harvard and graduate and undergraduate entrepreneurship courses at many other business schools.

A natural question for a reader to ask is what he or she will learn from this book. This textbook has four goals:

1. The private equity industry is complex. Participants in the private equity industry make it even more complicated by using a highly specialized terminology. These factors often make the world of venture capital and buyout investing appear impenetrable to the uninitiated. Understanding the ways in which private equity firms work—as well as the key distinctions between these organizations—is an important goal.

---

[15] The number of firms includes only those of "investment grade," that is, those that raise money from outside entities. A large number of entities raise and invest smaller amounts from family and friends. Global numbers are from Preqin; U.S. data from the Private Equity Council and Professor Colin Blaydon, Tuck School, Dartmouth College, cited in Associated Press, "Features of the Private Equity Industry," *The Seattle Times,* August 25, 2009, http://seattletimes.nwsource.com/html/ business technology/ 2009736074_apusbanksprivateequityglance.html, accessed November 5, 2010.

2. Private equity investors face the same problems that other financial investors do, but in extreme form. An understanding of these problems faced—and the ways that these investors solve them—should provide more general insights into the financing process. Thus a second goal is to review and apply the key ideas of corporate finance in this exciting setting.

3. The process of valuation is critical in private equity. Disputes over valuation—whether between an entrepreneur and a venture capitalist or between a private equity firm raising a new fund and a potential investor—are commonplace in this industry. These disputes stem from the fact that valuing early-stage and restructuring companies can be challenging and highly subjective. This textbook explores a wide variety of valuation approaches, from techniques widely used in practice to methods less frequently seen in practice today but likely to be increasingly important in the future.

4. Finally, the private equity industry is going through a period of enormous change. During the recent boom, buyout firms raised funds of $20 billion while the sizes of venture funds rose toward the $1 billion mark. Private equity firms have established international operations on levels previously unprecedented and have experimented with organizational structures such as publicly traded funds. This casebook explores different approaches that firms are using to manage portfolios and offices that are global in scope and imply flows of funds on an international scale that was unthinkable even three years ago.

The book is divided into fourteen chapters. The organization of Chapters 2 through 7 mirrors that of the private equity process, which can be viewed as a cycle. The cycle starts with the raising of a private equity fund; proceeds through investing in, monitoring, and adding value to companies; continues as the private equity firm exits successful deals and returns capital to its investors; and renews itself with the seeking of additional funds. Different instructors, however, may choose to use this book in different ways.[16] Thus it may be helpful to summarize the organization of the book briefly at the outset.

Chapter 2 focuses on how private equity funds are raised and structured. These funds often have complex features, and the legal issues involved are frequently arcane. But the structure of private equity funds profoundly affects the behavior of venture and buyout investors. Consequently, it is as important for the entrepreneur raising private equity to understand these issues as it is for an investor in a fund. Chapter 2 seeks not only to understand the features of private equity funds and the actors in the fund-raising process but also to analyze them. We map out the major investors in private equity firms, the intermediaries who help them, and the nuances of investment structures. We focus on not just understanding the features of these agreements, but the way in which they affect incentives, whether in a positive or problematic manner.

Chapter 3 turns to the investment process. We look here at the way in which transaction opportunities are assessed. We begin with the question of how entrepreneurs can most effectively pitch their businesses. What makes an effective business plan? A three-minute "elevator pitch"? We also consider what entrepreneurs should be looking for as they assess potential investors. Since private equity groups promise to provide "more than money," it is essential to understand the signs of a good investor. We then turn to the other side of the table and consider the perspective of prospective investors. We review the key criteria used during the due diligence process. What key questions are asked? And how is the process managed? We'll review the key steps and decision points as well as the way that private equity groups use others to help them in their decision-making process. We end Chapter 3 with two special situations that are frequently important in the investment process. First, we focus on serial entrepreneurs: individuals who receive funding after

---

[16] While some courses may follow closely the order of chapters in the book, others may deviate substantially. For instance, a course concentrating on entrepreneurial finance may focus on Chapters 3 through 7, 10, and 14.

having run an earlier venture. Many groups favor such investors, even if they have failed, for reasons that we will see are often quite logical. We'll also look at sharing deals with other firms, and whether these syndicated "club deals" can lead to better decisions.

We next turn in Chapter 4 to perhaps the most challenging part of the due diligence process, the question of valuation. We begin by discussing why the valuation of private companies is challenging—the absence of public market indicators, the presence of information gaps, and the dramatic shifts in comparable valuations over the investment period, among other problems, make this a challenging exercise. We then run through the key methodologies employed in practice. Each of the methodologies, from multiples to outcome tables to adjusted present value techniques, has specific strengths and weaknesses. We seek to understand when each makes the most sense, and we argue that in many cases a "big tent" approach employing a variety of methodologies is likely to give the best answer. We end by considering the "methodologies of the future": in many financial markets, sophisticated valuation methodologies employing option pricing and binomial tree approaches have become standard; in private equity, though, these approaches are much less common. In part, this may reflect the inherent difficulty of valuation in this environment, but it also may reflect the practitioners' resistance to change.

In Chapter 5, we explore the structure of transactions. We begin with the building blocks: the key securities that are used in private equity deals and the motivations for them. We then walk through the various covenants found in venture and buyout deals. Throughout, our goal is twofold: to understand how these features actually work—for instance, we'll walk through the workings of the various forms of antidilution provisions—and to explore *why* these various elements have become crucial parts of private equity transactions. One key point is that there are frequently many different ways to achieve the same economic goal. The chapter also explores some of the special terms seen in transactions other than venture and buyouts, for instance, the concept of "warrant coverage" in venture leasing deals, and considers how these terms and the capital structure can evolve over time.

While Chapters 3 through 5 look at different dimensions of the deal-making process, Chapter 6 considers what happens after the money is invested. We begin by considering how firms supervise the companies in which they invest. These governance features range from the formal (board seats and special voting rights) to more informal controls. We also consider the powerful privileges that providing capital in stages gives investors, particularly when financing early-stage companies. We explore what venture and buyout groups are looking for as they oversee investments, and we examine their roles both in normal times and when the unexpected happens (which, sadly, is most often bad news). As we'll see, reworking transactions when the unfortunate tidings arrive is a critical skill for private equity investors.

In Chapter 7, we examine the process through which private equity investors exit their investments. Successful exits are critical to ensuring attractive returns for investors and, in turn, to raising additional capital. But private equity investors' concerns about exiting investments—and their behavior during the exit process itself—can sometimes lead to severe problems for entrepreneurs. We employ an analytic framework very similar to that used in Chapter 3. We seek to understand the key institutional features associated with exiting private equity investments: the choices between going public, trade sales, secondary buyouts, and other deals and the players who facilitate these choices. We also seek to discern the difference between features that increase the overall amount of profits from private equity investments and those that seem to be intended to shift more of the profits to particular parties.

The final part of this section of Chapter 7 looks explicitly at evolution of transactions globally. While our discussion in the prior section frequently draws on examples from outside the United States, the extent of differences across countries suggests the need for a more careful look at the topic. We'll begin by looking at the history of global private equity initiatives, the efforts by governments to encourage these activities, and the many mishaps that befell the pioneers in this arena. The discussion then turns to understanding the key features of and differences between the major markets in which venture firms are active, including Europe, India, China, and the Middle East. We then step back and ask the question, what makes a good market for venture and buyout investors? We highlight the features that have been associated with more activity as well as with more successful deals.

The next two chapters are grouped under the heading of "keeping score," and seek to assess the performance of private equity funds. Chapter 9 looks at the measurement of performance by private equity groups. We begin by discussing why this is a hard problem: because it is difficult to measure the true value of private companies, assessing the performance of funds is problematic until they are wrapped up. But since a fund can take a decade or longer to be fully harvested, the information is of limited usefulness. Having explored the challenges, the chapter considers the evidence on the performance of private equity funds. We compare the performance of public and private equities. In the final part of the chapter, we highlight how investors can go beyond measuring risk to managing it. In particular, we focus on how to create portfolios of funds—how to combine different funds in a way that maximizes performance.

Chapter 10 looks at another way of keeping score and assesses the impact of private equity on society as a whole. Even if private equity firms have generated spectacular returns for their investors, we would have hard questions if there were no benefits to society as a whole. This chapter looks first at venture funding of new companies and discusses the evidence that venture funding allows firms to be more innovative and faster growing. We then turn to buyout investments in more mature firms. This discussion begs the question of what public policies make the most sense when it comes to private equity. While there are few easy answers here, we consider the various arguments in this lively and still ongoing debate.

The next three chapters consider what we term the "business of private equity." From reading media accounts, one might conclude that venture and buyout investors lead glamorous lives, more akin to a rock star than a banker. While there may be a grain of truth here (at least when markets are doing well), it is important to realize that managing a private equity organization, like any professional service firm, is hard work.

Chapter 11 examines this challenging territory. We begin by reviewing the typical career in a private equity firm, from associate to managing general partner. We then explore the challenges associated with building and maintaining a firm. We start with the people issues: the need to retain a team. We also consider the question of strategy, and what constitutes an effective investment approach. Finally, we turn to the special challenges faced by affiliated groups, such as those that are part of an investment bank or manufacturing company. We highlight that while many of the management challenges are similar, affiliated groups also face some daunting issues that are specific to such "captive" funds.

Chapter 12 looks at how firms evolve over time and at the management challenges posed by these changes. As we noted earlier, many private equity groups over the past decade have raised far larger funds than previously and sought to expand their product mix and geographic range. If we look at the history of the industry, rapid expansion has generally not ended well. Far too often, rapid growth has led to deterioration in the returns that investors enjoy, and sometimes to outright disaster. This chapter reviews what the evidence suggests are the likely times when growth proves challenging as well as when the effects are not harmful.

Chapter 13 is particularly timely in light of the dramatic booms and busts that have characterized the buyout market over the past half-decade. Our initial focus is on understanding why the private equity market from its earliest days has been characterized by a stop-start pattern, where an initial period of success leads to too much money being raised and a crash in returns and activity. We then turn to what management strategies can be most effective in this kind of chaotic environment.

In Chapter 14, the final chapter, we consider the future of the private equity industry. Much of the discussion in the book is designed to provide an understanding of the history of the private equity industry's development and the workings of the industry today. Because the studies and cases that these chapters draw on must out of necessity look at events in the past, they provide less guidance about the industry's future. The question of how the venture and buyout industries will evolve over the next decade is particularly critical because the growth in the recent past was so spectacular and the industry's positive effect on the overall economy has become significant. It is natural to ask, in light of the global economic crisis and the downturn in the private equity, whether the increased level of activity seen in the middle part of this decade was an aberration. Will the level of fund-raising and investment rebound to earlier levels? In particular, to what extent will the globalization of the private equity industry continue?

We cover many topics in this volume; but at the same time, it is important to emphasize that beyond its covers are many opportunities for learning about venture capital and private equity. Each of the chapters suggests further readings. These range from trade journals such as the *Private Equity Analyst* and the *Venture Capital Journal* to handbooks on the legal nuances of the private equity process to academic studies. Many information sources exist for readers who wish to explore a particular aspect of the private equity industry in more detail.

WHAT ARE THE KEY THEMES IN THIS BOOK?

Despite the variation across types of private equity (venture capital, growth equity, and buyout) scale, geography and industry sector, seven key common themes emerge from the discussion of the industry in all its forms.

Illiquidity

All private equity deals start out as illiquid (or they would not be private). Therefore, private equity investing is necessarily long-horizon investing and demands that the investor is active in the affairs of the portfolio company. For example, if an investor holding a large public stock, such as General Electric, is dissatisfied with the company's direction, her first option is simply selling the stock. A private equity investor with similar feelings about one of his portfolio companies does not have such an option. But the private equity investor, by the nature of the terms of the investment, nearly always has more direct options to change management either through the board of directors or as a large active shareholder.

The fact of illiquidity also drives decisions about financing and exiting. Since there is no assurance of liquidity at a given time, a private equity investor must always consider his capability to carry an investment for an indeterminate amount of time. Therefore, he may alter a strategic decision to require less capital, force an early exit to avoid financing risk, or invite other private equity firms to join in a syndicate to reduce that risk. Likewise, illiquidity can force hard choices. For example, a venture capital investor may be forced to decide between an unattractive merger option and an unattractive financing.

Illiquidity also motivates the private equity fund structure. Nearly all private equity funds are structured as long-term limited partnerships of ten years or more. They rely on the aligning effect of profit sharing (the carried interest) to keep limited partners and general partners aligned. Illiquidity also motivates structure at the portfolio company level. Most venture capital investments are in the form of preferred stock with liquidation preferences and control provisions, and buyout firms often structure deals to allow for recapitalization with dividends.

Uncertainty and Information Gaps

In private equity, evaluating performance is hard. Valuation is difficult because there is no continuous pricing—as there is with public stocks—and information on portfolio companies is often incomplete. Even when there is information, tools for valuation are limited since most valuation methodologies have been developed for markets with continuous pricing.

Beyond evaluating performance, practitioners must often act on very limited information. In the venture capital setting, the investor may be evaluating an investment with the key features of a new technology being applied to a new market by inexperienced managers. In the buyout setting, an investor may be forced to make a decision on a complex enterprise with global operations in a specific and obscure industry in a compressed time frame.

Given this environment, how can private equity ever succeed? The answer lies in the fact that the investor can influence the result through deal structure (e.g., making failure costly and adding governance), through value-added activities (e.g., contacts and consulting), and through the ability to recontract (i.e., if all else fails, push restart).

Cyclicality

Everything about private equity is cyclical: initial public offerings (IPOs) and trade sales, valuations, and fund-raising. Private equity funds themselves have a long lead time and a long gestation period to realization, so private equity organizations must raise money when they can. Portfolio companies must also follow the same strategy, heightening the industry's cyclicality. Private equity firms must react strategically as the private equity cycles wax and wane. Firms often shift from market to market and must be on the lookout for new niches and new deal structures.

Certification

Information risks can be limited through repeated relationships. For example, while an emerging company may have only one IPO in its life, the venture capital firms that sponsor it regularly deal with the underwriters and the public markets. Private equity firms can also facilitate corporate ties to give their portfolio companies a boost. Even the relationship between limited partners and private equity firms has a strong element of certification, since limited partnerships (LPs) tend to have long relationships with their private equity managers.

But certification can also be abused. Buyout firms can abuse their relationships with their debt providers and over-leverage their companies, and venture capitalists can push problematic companies into the public market too quickly. Reputation, therefore, is a valuable currency to be husbanded in the private equity industry.

Incentives

In an industry fraught with information asymmetries and characterized by illiquidity that handcuffs the participants together, incentive systems keep the interests of the parties aligned. By the nature of the industry, it is very hard to get money out of illiquid investments. At the same time, private equity groups need lots of discretion to pursue opportunities unforeseen at the time of the fund closing: many things cannot be defined in a contractual relationship. For example, the fast rise of the Internet could not be anticipated in the early 1990s, when many of the venture capital funds that participated in its creation were being formed. Similarly, the opportunities for buyout firms in the reinsurance industry that would appear after the September 11, 2001 terrorist attacks would not have been apparent in the late 1990s.

But compensation can be dysfunctional. Management fees and transaction fees—originally designed to cover expenses—have become substantial in their own right at many mega-funds. High fees can encourage asset gathering and excessively safe investment strategies. In an industry with many intermediaries between the limited partners and the private equity firms, rewards to these middlemen are not necessarily tied to results. Clear benchmarks and the power of reputation are important aspects of incentives within the private equity industry.

Deal Context

In this industry, results can differ depending on whether private equity firm A or private equity firm B invests on the same terms in the same company. Not surprisingly, there is no such thing as a "good deal" in absolute terms. Firm- and time-specific environmental attributes, as well as company and industry characteristics, are all inputs to private equity decisions. This is a more fluid and complex world than most investment categories.

Career Management

Private equity has become an attractive career option for a variety of people with business, finance, consulting, and legal backgrounds. Moreover, with the growth of the industry, there is a need for more and better-trained professionals. Throughout this book, we try to highlight some of the career choices participants can make and analyze their consequences.

As highlighted in this introduction and the cases in this book, much is still not yet known about the future of the private equity industry. It seems clear, however, that this financial intermediary will be an exciting and important feature of the global economic landscape in the years to come.

Chapter 2

The Private Equity Cycle—Fund-Raising and Fund Choosing

In the previous chapter, we noted that $1.6 trillion had been raised for U.S.-based private equity funds between 2000 and the end of 2009.[1] Globally, private equity assets under management (including both the value of the current investments and monies raised but not invested) had reached $2.7 trillion by the first half of 2010.[2] This reflects a steady gain from $2.5 trillion in 2008 and $2.0 trillion in 2007, difficulties in the macroeconomic environment notwithstanding. It is completely reasonable to ask, "Where does this money come from?" How do the different parties—investors in private equity funds and investors who invest the funds themselves—find each other? What do they look for in each other? How do they manage their relationship?

In this chapter, we introduce fund-raising, the first step of the private equity cycle. We identify the participants and explore their motivations and the incentives that align the interests of the two groups—private equity firms and the limited partners that invest in their funds. We discuss how partnerships are structured and investigate the different terms in those agreements, how they came to be, and what they tell us about each party's fears and hopes. Next, we consider the actual process of fund-raising. In conclusion, we investigate the intricacies of the ongoing relationship between the entities, how it works in stressful times, and how these behaviors and incentives influence the industry's dynamics overall.

This information will be extremely helpful to anyone involved with private equity, whether directly or tangentially. An entrepreneur seeking private equity investment needs to know the motivations and incentives of her investors, so does the limited partner who considers investing in a fund. A student interested in joining a private equity fund will learn more about the motives and concerns of the limited partners, the nuances of partnership agreements, and the challenges of raising a fund. The need to raise money influences how a fund works, how the partners invest, and how all the parties interact.

Many people dream of "raising a fund," but doing so is one of the ultimate catch-22s: To raise a fund, you must have a track record, and the only way to have a track record is to have raised (and invested) a fund. The founders of Gobi Partners, an early-stage venture capital (VC) firm based in Shanghai, had almost a decade of experience in their target sector, Chinese digital media and information technology, when they started raising $75 million in 2001. Due in part to changes in the macroenvironment—the NASDAQ collapse, the attack on the Twin Towers in

---

[1] Thomson Reuters private equity database, accessed July 1, 2010.
[2] Thomson Reuters private equity database, accessed November 10, 2010.

September 2001, and the SARS virus—it took them two years to raise $35 million, and they did not reach their minimum fund size of $51 million until 2005. During that time, none of the partners took a salary. They debated whether to continue their possibly quixotic quest or to cease their efforts and work with the $35 million they had raised. Not only would this latter course have restricted their ability to invest in and support quality companies, it could be viewed as agreeing with the market's doubts about their fund strategy. For the limited partners, this long and difficult course—and its eventual successful conclusion—guaranteed two things: first, the partners believed in their strategy; and second, the interests of both sides were powerfully aligned because the partners were undoubtedly eager to make money.[3]

DIFFERENT TYPES OF PRIVATE EQUITY

Before exploring who invests in private equity, it is useful to understand some of the details of the asset class. As we mentioned in Chapter 1, the term *private equity* is a large tent with many subgroups. These involve different types of investments, different holding periods, and different investment sizes, ranging from companies that are little more than a stack of PowerPoint slides to fully operational multinational enterprises.

Different types of private equity appeal to different investors. The limited partnership structure is the preferred organizational form to link the suppliers of capital (the **limited partners** (LPs) and the individuals who make and manage the investments—the **general partners** (GPs)). Limited partners (LPs) are so named because their liability for the investment is limited to the amount invested. If they invest in a private equity fund that then invests in a company developing a drug that turns out to have dangerous side effects, the limited partners cannot be sued for damages. They might lose their entire investment in that company and possibly in that fund, but they are legally protected from losing their houses or other assets if the fund is found liable for negligence. The LPs have this protection because they do not directly control the sourcing and management of the portfolio companies. This poses another set of challenges, since no one wants to hand over $10 million or $100 million for 10 years without any strings attached. Later in this chapter, we explore how the LPs can influence the GPs yet still retain their limited status.

The GPs have sole responsibility for sourcing and managing portfolio companies at the cost of unrestricted liability. To protect themselves from this risk, and to handle other legal issues, most U.S. private equity firms create a limited liability corporation (LLC) that bears the liability for product malfunctions and other unfortunate situations. This corporation becomes, strictly speaking, the general partner, and the human investors act as the organization's directors; but for simplicity, this text refers to the individuals who make and manage the investments as the GPs.

Let us quickly review the different sizes, stages, and growth paths of private equity investments. Google and Staples, as examples of venture capital investing, demonstrate situations in which an entrepreneurial team created a start-up on the basis of a better way to do something (search the Internet or sell office supplies). They struggled to attract financing, wrestled with growth, and finally dominated their industries and went public.

Federal Express, also a start-up, created a new industry, overnight delivery. FedEx's founder struggled for years to get his company off the ground. Founded in 1971, FedEx raised $91 million and started overnight delivery services in 1973. Turned down for a loan and desperate to pay the bills, the founder resorted to gambling at Las Vegas. In 1976, FedEx made its first profit. The 1977 United Parcel Service strike gave the fledgling company credibility, and

---

[3] Felda Hardymon and Ann Leamon, "Gobi Partners: October 2004," HBS Case No. 805-090 (Boston: HBS Publishing, 2005). Gobi has since raised a second fund of $151 million.

FedEx went public in 1978 (NYSE: FDX). It has since become an international force in both delivery and document services.[4]

With **growth equity** (or **growth capital**), the company is already established but needs to fund a risky investment for which it cannot get bank debt. A growth equity investor supplies money and guidance and allows the operation to achieve a new growth path, whether by making an acquisition or moving into a new product line. Growth equity investors usually take minority stakes in their companies, in contrast to buyouts, where the private equity investor owns a majority share. While many growth equity investments occur in private companies, public companies can also receive them through a Private Investment in a Public Equity (PIPE) transaction. Growth equity investors in private companies can make money either by having an initial public offering (IPO) or by being acquired, and those in publicly traded companies succeed most often by an increase in the company's stock price due to the improvements that the investment funded.

One example of a growth equity investment is seen in Technology Crossover Ventures (TCV) and its investment in the travel consolidator Expedia. TCV first became involved with Expedia in 2000, when the company acquired Vacationspot, one of TCV's portfolio companies. Expedia had gone public in 1999 (NASDAQ: EXPE), but TCV invested $50 million in it in August 2000 and continued to acquire stock over the next two years. TCV partners served on the board of directors and even helped negotiate Expedia's acquisition by InterActiveCorp (IAC) in May 2003 for $9.4 billion.[5]

In another example, TA Associates, a Boston-based private equity firm, invested $40 million in Lawson Software before its public listing, which occurred nine months later in late 2001 (NASDAQ: LWSN). TA was Lawson's first institutional investor. In addition to the funding, which provided working capital and liquidity for certain shareholders, TA partners joined the board and gave the profitable 25-year-old company advice on governance and the capital markets. Lawson raised $196 million in its IPO, and TA Associates remained involved with the company for several years.[6]

Buyouts, where the investor purchases a majority share of an operating company, have their own peculiarities. Hilton Hotels and Equity Office Properties demonstrate situations where the private equity firm, Blackstone, purchased an entire publicly traded company and took it private to perform operational enhancements without the demands of meeting quarterly stock performance metrics. In contrast, the purchase of the European soft drinks operation Orangina from its corporate parent Cadbury was a corporate spin-off ("spin-out" or "carve-out"),[7] whereby the parent sheds a failing or noncore division. The spin-off may be restructured and reorganized to function as an independent unit or combined with another company to create a larger enterprise. In the case of Orangina, the division was reconstituted as a stand-alone entity. The purchasing syndicate, Lion Capital and Blackstone Group, invested in marketing and product development and participated actively in the new firm's management, to the extent that a GP from Lion served as nonexecutive chairman.[8] Orangina was acquired in September 2009 by Suntory, the Japanese drinks maker, for $3.86 billion.[9]

---

[4] Data from Hoover's Online, FedEx.com, and http://ecommerce.hostip.info/pages/443/Fedex-Corp-EARLY-HISTORY. html, accessed March 13, 2010.

[5] Data from Technology Crossover Ventures' website, http://www.tcv.com/invest/cs.html, accessed December 13, 2009.

[6] Data from TA Associates' website, Thomson Reuters private equity database, and Lawson Software press releases, http://phx.corporate-ir.net/phoenix.zhtml?c=129966&p=irol-newsArticle&ID=480065, accessed December 13, 2009.

[7] Depending on whether existing management is part of the purchasing group, these transactions can also be referred to as "management buyouts" (management is part of the purchasing group) or "management buy-ins" (management is replaced).

[8] In European companies, a distinction is made between "executive" directors, who are employees of the company, and "nonexecutive" directors, who are independent.

[9] Felda Hardymon, Josh Lerner, and Ann Leamon, "Lion Capital and the Blackstone Group": *The Orangina Deal*, HBS Case No. 9-807-005, (Boston: HBS Publishing, 2007); Junko Hayashi and Naoko Fujimura, "Suntory Buys Orangina from Blackstone, Lion Capital (Update3)," Bloomberg.com, http://www.bloomberg.com/apps/news?pid=20601101 &sid=a2yeSW5vtwus, accessed March 16, 2010.

The unique attributes of different types of private equity make each better suited to different LPs. The first consideration is scale. VC firms, which invest in small companies requiring intensive active involvement, raise small funds—less than $1 billion. Hence, they cannot accommodate large checks. Part of that is concern about undue influence from a single LP; but in general, it stems from the goals, approach, and structure of the industry. As Metrick and Yasuda[10] note, the role of a venture capitalist is much less scalable than the **leveraged buyout** (LBO) firm's role of adding efficiency to established operations. In Chapter 12 we discuss at greater length the challenges that scaling presents for VC and LBO firms. LBO firms, which raise funds of at least $1 billion, find it inefficient to provide the intense oversight required by early-stage companies and to deal with many small investors.

Buyouts and VC also differ in terms of the difficulty and importance of access. Multibillion-dollar LBO funds require a lot of investors. In fact, the Preqin *2009 Global Private Equity Review* notes that the only funds that closed in 2008 with more than 100 investors were buyout funds—13 percent of all the buyout funds that year. Just 11 percent of VC funds had more than 50 investors.[11] It is easier for a new entrant to private equity to gain access to the asset class by investing in buyout funds just because the funds are bigger.

In VC, funds are smaller, and there are fewer LPs. In fact, VC funds generally offer their existing LPs the chance to resubscribe before looking to add new entities. This stems in part from the active quality of the investing: if the LP group has worked well, if they have useful contacts or are easy to work with, why change? The LPs are eager to invest if the GP has performed well. Choosing not to participate in a successful firm's next fund may permanently deny the LP access to that firm.

For all of their differences, private equity transactions exhibit four major similarities:

1. **Illiquid assets.** There is no public market for privately held securities. The value of stocks traded on the top ten public markets in 2009 was $69 trillion,[12] a figure that dwarfs the $2.5 trillion of assets managed by private equity funds. The implications of illiquid assets are wide-ranging and inform the very foundation of the interactions between the parties in private equity. Once an institution has invested in a private equity fund, or the fund has invested in a company, it has embarked upon a relationship that will likely be measured in years. Moreover, the methods for measuring financial success, either absolutely or relative to other opportunities, are not intuitive and can supply differing results, as discussed in Chapters 4 and 9.

> The challenge of an illiquid position is shown in the situation of the investors in Dick's Sporting Goods. Founded in 1948, the company has grown to a national chain. A top-tier venture capital firm participated in the company's first private equity financing round in 1992. Although the company did well over time, there appeared to be few opportunities to exit the position; so the GPs had resigned themselves to a long-term illiquid holding. To their surprise, in 2002, a year with only nine venture-backed IPOs, Dick's Sporting Goods went public at $12.25 per share.[13]

---

[10] Andrew Metrick and Ayako Yasuda, "The Economics of Private Equity Funds," *Review of Financial Studies* 23, no. 6 (2010): 2303–41.

[11] Private Equity Intelligence Ltd., *2009 Preqin Global Private Equity Review* (London: Preqin, 2009), 18.

[12] http://www.world-exchanges.org/files/statistics/excel/EQUITY509.xls, accessed November 9, 2010.

[13] Dick's Sporting Goods Inc., company overview, http://moneycentral.hoovers.com/global/msn/factsheet.xhtml? COID=57958.

2. **Long-term relationships.** In part, this is related to the illiquidity mentioned earlier—there is no formal market for selling a privately held position. This means there is no easy way to find a willing buyer. In addition, the process of creating value in private equity, whether building a brand-new company or turning around an established one, requires significant time. Buyout firms routinely create "100-day plans" for their acquisitions, but that merely relates to initial changes; thereafter follows the slow process of fine-tuning the operation. Recent research has found that the median hold time for a company that has undergone a buyout is nine years.[14] For start-ups, the process is commonly estimated at five to seven years as a technology is developed, tested, revised, and retested, and the management team may be recruited, evaluated, upgraded, and so forth.

3. **The general partner participates actively in the governance of the investment.** This is what we mean by "active investing." The GPs routinely attend board meetings, counsel or replace executives, insist on budgets and strategic plans, and monitor the company's performance. The LPs, although not directly involved in investment decisions or company management, may yet provide assistance in indirect ways. This can be in the form of introductions to potential customers or suppliers or simply indicating their faith in the firm. This approach represents a substantial difference between private and public equity: the chairman of General Motors would rarely call a stockholder for introductions.

   In private equity, governance affects an investment's outcome. Google succeeded in part because it was founded by very smart visionaries who created a new approach to search on the Internet and a new way of making money from it. But it was backed by two of the best venture capital firms in the world, Sequoia and Kleiner Perkins, which brought their combined reputation, experience in governance, and networks to assist the emerging company. The person managing the investment affects the results. The source of the money matters.

4. **Access to better opportunities requires active sourcing and negotiation.** Not all investment opportunities are the same. Finding the best ones on a regular basis takes active effort. This is true for the private equity firm, its LPs, and the entrepreneur (whose special situation is discussed in Chapter 3). Private equity firms undertake extensive "road shows" when they raise money; in fact, raising a first fund often takes more than a year. For LPs, finding enough good-quality funds where they can invest enough to reach their goals takes time and effort. For GPs investing a fund, finding good investment opportunities also takes time and effort, as does managing the investment to its conclusion. Having found a desirable investment target—whether a fund or a company—the two must negotiate the terms of the investment, a process that can take weeks or months. In short, private equity investing is a lot of work for everyone.

As a result, the LPs supplying the money need to know it is entrusted to a highly skilled investor. Thus they usually prefer to invest in a firm with a long track record in the industry, where the GPs have developed broad networks and a wide appreciation for the variety of situations that can arise and the best ways to respond. This leads to a second requirement: flexibility. The LPs and GPs must interact in a way that provides the GPs with flexibility in both sourcing and managing the investments. There is no way that LPs, which invest in a host of funds, could provide regular input on the details of thousands of companies, a level of involvement that would also cost them their limited liability status. Given this tension between the need for hands-on involvement by the GPs and hands-off trust by the LPs, the industry has fallen back on the time-honored approach of

---

[14] Per Strömberg, "The New Demographics of Private Equity," in *Globalization of Alternative Investments Working Papers Volume 1: The Global Economic Impact of Private Equity Report 2008*, ed. Anuradha Gurung and Josh Lerner (New York: World Economic Forum USA, 2008), 3–26, available at http://www.weforum.org/pdf/cgi/pe/Full_Report.pdf.

enlightened self-interest, or, as it is called, "alignment of interests." Thus arose the basic profit-sharing agreement of private equity.

In general, the GPs invest funds raised from LPs in portfolio companies, which are managed to an exit. At the exit, the LPs receive the capital that was invested in the company (the cost basis) and the profits are split; the LPs typically receive 80 percent and the GPs 20 percent. The LPs also pay fees to the GPs to cover the costs of doing business. The basic structure is shown in Figure 2.1 and is explained in greater detail later in this chapter.

FIGURE 2.1   The private equity cycle

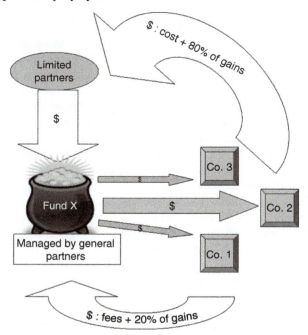

WHO ARE THE LPs?

In Chapter 1, we alluded to the general characteristics of LPs—institutions that are willing to trade anticipated above-market gains for the illiquidity of private equity investments. Let us examine these providers of (usually) patient capital in greater detail.

As discussed in Chapter 1, wealthy families were the first quasi-institutional investors, pursuing high-return opportunities through the investing activities of their family offices. The Rockefellers founded Venrock, the Phipps family had the precursor to Bessemer Venture Partners, and J. H. Whitney established his eponymous firm. These firms have since grown beyond investing just family money, but they were the first organized efforts at venture investing and showed the characteristics that we find in LPs today: large pools of assets, a desire for diversification across asset classes, a willingness to take on risk and illiquidity in exchange for higher returns, and the ability to staff and manage relationships with GPs.

Angel Investors

Angel investors, individuals who invest out of their own net worth, are the closest examples of a pure direct investment model. These are often successful entrepreneurs who were themselves funded by private equity and liked vetting new technologies and teams. Angel investments are usually between $10,000[15] and $200,000[16]— enough to support a start-up after the exhaustion of "friends and family" funds and before the product is proven enough to interest a VC firm. Angels serve an important bridging function,[17] supporting the company as it achieves a proof of concept sufficient to estimate future costs and develop a more detailed business plan. This allows an institutional investor to assess more accurately whether the opportunity offers an adequate return on the time that will be required to shepherd it to maturity.

Individual angels generally invest based primarily on personal relationships, with a secondary interest in a specific market or technology. They may be motivated by a desire to "give back" to the entrepreneurial community or to be part of the excitement of developing new technology without the responsibility of serving as founder.[18]

Angel deals are usually structured very informally. In their study of 182 very early rounds in which angels, VC firms, or a combination invested, Goldfarb et al. found that angel-only rounds tended to have weaker control rights than those with VC participation.[19] This supports the contention that angels tend to play a mentoring and entrepreneur-friendly role. A vast majority of angels receive founder's common stock (discussed in Chapters 4 and 5) rather than the preferred stock of venture capitalists, and they do not receive board seats or specific governance rights (discussed in Chapter 6).[20]

This informal dynamic can create tensions when institutional investors participate in later founds. Angels invest in smaller deals, often on the premise that the company will raise additional money from institutional investors. Yet the angel's close ties to the founders can hinder the venture capitalist's efforts to upgrade management as the company grows. As a result, VC firms may be reluctant to invest in deals with substantial angel participation unless they can structure the new financing to give themselves substantial control of the deal.

In the past few years, sectors such as software and consumer-facing Internet have seen an interesting shift. While previously young companies rarely grew to a meaningful size in a reasonable amount of time without VC support, the advent of infrastructure and tools (cloud-based computing, hyperflexible workforces, and distribution through online stores) has introduced the possibility that a successful company can grow from infancy to a substantial exit funded almost exclusively by angels. The most notable example is Mint.com, the online personal finance website. Turned down by established VC firms, the company was finally funded by a collection of so-called super-angels, small firms focusing on very early-stage investments. In 2009, three years and four rounds after its founding—eventually including an institutional VC firm—Mint.com was acquired by Intuit for $170 million.[21]

Super-angels and angel groups occupy a slightly different place on the funding continuum. First appearing in the mid-1990s, the number of American angel groups exceeded 300 as of 2010 and are thought to contain between 10,000 and 15,000 individual investors.[22] The most famous is

---

[15] Paul Reynolds, *Entrepreneurship in the United States: The Future Is Now* (Miami: Florida International University, 2005); cited in Brent D. Goldfarb et al., "Does Angel Participation Matter? An Analysis of Early Venture Financing" Working Paper No. RHS-06-072, Robert H. Smith School of Business, University of Maryland, College Park, (March 24, 2009), 3 available at http://ssrn.com/abstract=1024186.

[16] Scott A. Shane, *The Illusions of Entrepreneurship: The Costly Myths That Entrepreneurs, Investors, and Policy Makers Live By* (New Haven CT: Yale University Press, 2008), 3; cited in Goldfarb et al., The Goldfarb paper, based on data from a defunct law firm that specialized in VC law, noted an average angel investment of $150,375.

[17] Darian M. Ibrahim, "The (Not So) Puzzling Behavior of Angel Investors," *Vanderbilt Law Review* 61, no. 5 (2008): 1405–47.

[18] Ibrahim, "Angel Investors," 1408.

[19] Goldfarb et al., "Does Angel Participation Matter?" Ibrahim found the same thing.

[20] Ibrahim, "Angel Investors," 1422–23.

[21] Spencer E. Ante, "Mint.com: Nurtured by Super-Angel VCs," *Bloomberg Businessweek*, September 15, 2009, http://www.businessweek.com/technology/content/sep2009/tc20090915_065038.htm, accessed September 29, 2010.

[22] Data from http://www.angelcapitalassociation.org; cited in William R. Kerr, Josh Lerner, and Antoinette Schoar, "The Consequences of Entrepreneurial Finance: A Regression Discontinuity Analysis" Working Paper No. 10-086, Harvard Business School, April 15, 2010, 7.

Silicon Valley's Band of Angels; others, such as Tech Coast Angels and Boston-based Common Angels, are also well known. These groups are composed of individual angels who meet on a regular basis to share deal flow. Sometimes they even team up to split the cost of an analyst, but in general their approach is highly decentralized.

With goals ranging from social to financial, they may raise funds from friends and family. Given their larger size, they invest larger amounts—sometimes as much as $2 million—in a more formal structure than that of the individual angels.[23] They seek a Mint.com-like big return for a small investment.[24] This is a difficult role to play. Prior efforts, such as Zero Stage Capital, have either grown into more classic VC firms with standard fee structures and minimum deal sizes or shrunk into the bridging role typical of standard angels.

In 2009, rough figures estimate that angels disbursed $17.6 billion to 57,225 companies, for an average of $310,000 per company,[25] and studies suggest that the angel market averages $25 billion per year.[26] Reliable data on angel investments is extremely difficult to find because there is a strong success bias. Few organizations track the failure of very young companies that receive small amounts of angel funding. Nonetheless, angels serve two important roles. One is the previously mentioned bridging role; the other involves credentialing the young company and bringing it to the notice of institutional venture firms. Kerr, Lerner, and Schoar, in a study of the companies funded by Tech Coast Angels and Common Angels, found that angel funding by one of these groups positively affected the company's long-run survival and web traffic, although they suggest that the softer benefits of association, such as business contacts and mentoring, were most helpful in its eventual success.[27]

For the purposes of this volume, though, we focus on more institutional investors. Reflecting the origins of private equity in the United States, North America is home to the greatest number of LPs that invest the greatest amount of money in the asset class (in 2008, 49 percent by number; 52 percent by capital). Europe, particularly Western Europe, is home to 32 percent of the LPs, supplying 40 percent of the capital, while Asia and the rest of the world (Australasia, Asia, the Middle East, and South America) have 19 percent and 8 percent, respectively (see Figure 2.2). In 2009, North American LPs had slightly increased their representation in terms of capital, while that of Europe had fallen and Asia/rest of the world had stayed the same.[28] It should be noted, however, that these numbers are likely to shift substantially, given the turmoil in the world financial markets.

LPs, however, are not an undifferentiated mass. Each group has differing motives and constraints and may be interested in different types of private equity.

Endowments

Endowments are the pools of money that typically support universities and foundations. Less constrained by regulatory scrutiny than pension funds, these were among the first institutions to invest in private equity. They generally have very long time horizons and may be managed by individuals with a willingness to implement unorthodox approaches to investment management, as demonstrated by Yale University's David Swensen. In Swensen's book, *Pioneering Portfolio Management*,[29] he argues that less efficient markets with informational asymmetries and

---

[23] Ibrahim, "Angel Investors," 1422–23.

[24] Ante, "Mint.com."

[25] Jeffrey Sohl, "Angel Investor Market Holds Steady in 2009," Center for Venture Research, March 31, 2010, http://wsbe. unh.edu/files/2009_Angel_Market_Press_Release.pdf, accessed November 9, 2010.

[26] Ibrahim, "Angel Investors," 1419, footnote 57.

[27] William R. Kerr, Josh Lerner, and Antoinette Schoar, "The Consequences of Entrepreneurial Finance: A Regression Discontinuity Analysis" Working Paper No. 10-086, Harvard Business School (Boston: HBS Publishing, 2010), 24.

[28] Preqin, *2009 Preqin Global Private Equity Review*, 78, and *2010 Preqin Global Private Equity Review*, databook.

[29] David Swensen, *Pioneering Portfolio Management: An Unconventional Approach to Institutional Investment* (New York: Free Press, 2000).

FIGURE 2.2 The LP universe: 2008 and 2009

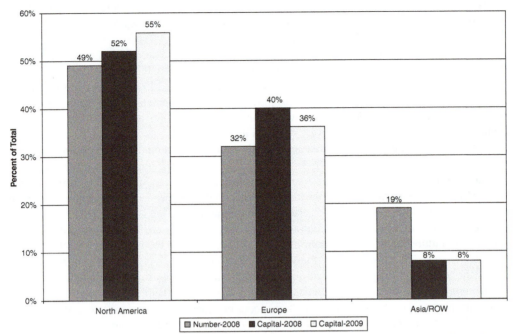

Source: Adapted from Preqin, *2009 Preqin Global Private Equity Review,* (London: Preqin, 2009), 78–79, and *2010 Preqin Global Private Equity Review*, databook.

illiquidity provide the opportunity for above-market returns. As proof, he notes that the difference in performance between U.S. fixed-income managers in the twenty-fifth and seventy-fifth percentiles of their performance universe was 0.5 percent in the decade between 1995 and 2005, while that for venture capitalists was 43.2 percent.[30] Yale invested in its first private equity vehicle in 1973 and its first venture capital partnership in 1976, heralding a long and storied history with the asset class and results that built Yale's endowment to the second largest in the world, lagging only Harvard's. Swensen's private equity philosophy includes backing active managers whose interests are closely aligned with those of the investors. In part because of his evangelism, the endowments—in particular, large universities—became very active in private equity, with allocations to the asset class of 8 percent in 1995, 13.9 percent in 2001, and 15 percent in 2009.[31]

Pension Funds

Sophisticated private pension funds, like those of General Motors and IBM, also understand the trade-off of liquidity for above-market returns. Unlike endowments, though, they are concerned not with supporting a university or philanthropy but with paying promised pensions to their retirees.

---

[30] Yale University Investments Office, *The Yale Endowment 2005* (New Haven, CT: Yale University, 2006), 36–37; cited in Josh Lerner, "Yale University Investments Office: August 2006," HBS Case No. 807-073 (Boston: HBS Publishing, 2007), 4.

[31] Compiled from National Association of College and University Business Officers, *2005 NACUBO Endowment Study* (Washington, DC: National Association of College and University Business Officers, 2006); in Josh Lerner, "Yale University Investments Office: July 2006," HBS Case No. 807-073 (Boston: HBS Publishing, 2007), 18. 2009 data calculated from the *2009 NACUBO Endowment Study* (Washington, DC: National Association of College and University Business Officers, 2009), 28.

Public pension funds came much later to private equity investing, but their huge pools of capital have made them significant forces. After the 1979 Department of Labor clarification, first private pension funds and then public funds with billions of dollars under management moved into private equity. The impact of this can be seen in Figure 2.3, where commitments take a sudden leap upward in 1981, as shown in the inset. In 2008, a year with a relatively normal amount of fund-raising, private and public sector pension funds together accounted for 45 percent of the total capital invested in private equity funds globally.[32] Figure 2.4 shows the positions of the major classes of LPs in 2009, both in terms of their representation in private equity by number and by total capital committed, as well as the capital committed to those funds that closed in 2009. Note that public pension funds' commitments to 2009 funds soared, due to a smaller number of funds raised as well as to their liquidity—they had regular contributions from employees, while endowments, constrained by extra demands for cash (described later), made up a tiny proportion.

FIGURE 2.3   Fund-raising by U.S. private equity firms, 1969–2009

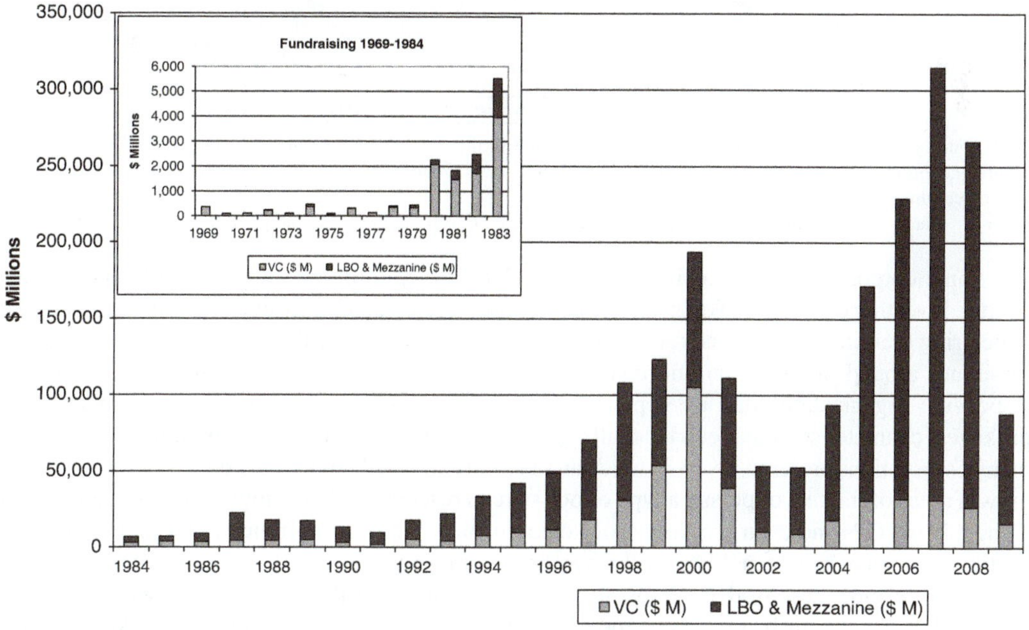

Source: Data from Thomson Reuters private equity database, accessed November 10, 2010.

Corporations

As mentioned in the first chapter, banks, corporations, and insurance companies all have their own reasons for participating in private equity. Insurance companies, like pension funds, invest the fees they receive for insurance products as a way to preserve and increase their assets against future claims. As taxable entities, they have different concerns regarding exits from portfolio companies—as discussed in Chapter 7, tax status affects the desired timing and form of an exit. Interestingly, in the 1960s and 1970s, some insurance companies—Allstate was one—did direct VC investing,[33] but now most act as LPs.

---

[32] Preqin, *2009 Global Private Equity Review*, 80.

[33] "Institutional Investor Profile: Peter Keehn, Head of Alternative Investments, Allstate Investments, LLC," AltAssets. com, June 29, 2006, http://www.altassets.com/private-equity-features/article/nz8835.html, accessed March 17, 2010.

FIGURE 2.4   LPs in private equity

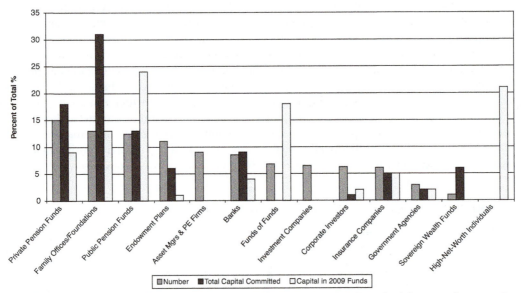

Note: Fund of Funds and Asset Managers are not included in the Total Capital Committed data, out of concerns for double-counting. Superannuation schemes are included in the Private Pension fund data (2% of number and total capital committed).
Source: Data from Preqin, *2010 Preqin Global Private Equity Review* (London: Preqin, 2010), databook.

Some corporations, such as Intel, Siemens, Johnson & Johnson, and Microsoft, have direct venture investing divisions. Like insurance companies, these must be aware of the tax issues around structuring their investments and managing exits. Also difficult for affiliated investment operations are issues around organization and compensation. Traditionally, private equity firms are small, responsive organizations that offer practitioners substantial autonomy and hefty compensation packages, characteristics that can be challenging to implement in a large corporation. As a result, many corporations prefer to invest in funds as LPs. This allows them to track developments in high-growth areas of interest or pursue a type of outsourced research and development. They may invest alongside the GPs and even acquire portfolio companies. This occurs frequently with big pharmaceutical companies, which historically acquire promising start-ups to augment their product development pipelines. And goals of an acquisition-minded LP might conflict with a longer-term institutional LP such as an endowment or pension fund—the first arguing for quicker exits at a lower price as opposed to a longer-term hold with an eventual exit via an IPO.

Commercial banks and investment banks may participate in private equity as GPs, to provide their clients with access to the asset class, or as LPs, as a way to stay abreast of the market. Banks are more likely to participate in buyouts than in VC, often as providers of debt for the transaction.

Sovereign Wealth Funds

Sovereign wealth funds have been investors in private equity for some time and are becoming more active. They are affiliated with governments—Norway, China, Abu Dhabi, Brunei, Singapore, and Qatar, to name a few. Abu Dhabi's fund, the Abu Dhabi Investment Authority (ADIA), is estimated to have $500 billion in assets.[34] Rather like public pension funds, sovereign

---

[34] ADIA does not disclose its assets. This figure comes from a United Nations Conference on Trade and Development report in September 2008; cited in "Abu Dhabi Wealth Fund Unveils First-Ever Strategy," *Middle East Online*, March 15, 2010, http://www.middle-east-online.com/english/business/?id=37836, accessed July 4, 2010.

wealth funds have been moving into more illiquid asset classes to diversify their holdings and ensure a long-term income stream—in fact, Figure 2.4 notes the substantial difference between representation by number (1 percent of the total) and capital committed (6 percent) of the sovereign wealth funds. For instance, China's sovereign wealth fund, China Investment Corporation (CIC), recently purchased 2.3 percent of Apax Partners, a London-based private equity fund, for $956 million, in addition to investments in the U.S. power company AES Corporation and a Russian oil producer.[35]

The recent downturn identified a substantial difference between the various types of LPs. Pension funds, both private and public, were the only ones that received regular infusions of money. Insurance companies could be affected by people canceling policies during a downturn. As their underlying businesses faltered, some corporations reduced their commitments to venture capital funds, both internal and external. Most significantly, endowments and foundations were affected by increased demands from their parent operations and by illiquid positions in their private equity holdings.

The World Turned Upside Down

The financial market downdraft of 2008 shook up the private equity LP world. Traditionally, the endowments like Yale, Harvard, and Princeton had been viewed as top tier: smart, reliable, and rich. Public pension funds, late to the private equity party and dogged by revolving-door management teams, political concerns, and Freedom of Information Act requirements (until legislative clarification), were seen as less desirable. In fall 2008, however, private equity exits froze at the same time that public markets lost 40 percent of their value. Yet operations supported by endowments needed more money. Endowments were stuck: they could fund private equity commitments neither from realizations of former private equity investments nor through sales of public equities. As a result, they tried to sell their private equity positions (a so-called secondary sale) at a deep discount or asked their GPs to slow the rate of investment and reduce capital calls (requests for commitments that had not yet been transferred). Public pension funds, on the other hand, continued to have regular inflows from contributors. As a result, public pension funds received some rare and potentially valuable access to top-tier funds. Whether this rearrangement of the hierarchy will be long lasting is, of course, unclear.

Intermediaries

Intermediaries include a host of organizations that facilitate or inform the interactions of LPs and GPs. Some, like consultants, provide information. Others, like funds-of-funds, raise capital from their own LPs and invest in private equity funds. Interestingly, as much of the rest of the world disintermediates—you buy your airline ticket or trade stocks directly, rather than through a travel agent or a stockbroker—there are more intermediaries in private equity.

The first intermediary organization was created in 1972 by the First National Bank of Chicago. While allowing the client ultimate authority over the investment decision, it commingled smaller investors' assets into "funds of funds" to be invested in private equity funds.[36]

Funds-of-funds, as already noted, play a double role as both LP and GP. Since the 1990s, these have grown and specialized. Many banks offer funds-of-funds to their high-net-worth clients;

---

[35] Li Xiang, "CIC Takes Position in Apax Partners," *China Daily*, February 4, 2010; and Chris V. Nicholson, "C.I.C. Approved to Buy Stake in Apax Partners," *New York Times Dealbook*, ed. by Andrew Ross Sorkin, February 4, 2010.
[36] Paul Gompers and Josh Lerner, *The Money of Invention* (Boston: HBS Publishing, 2001), 95.

independent funds-of-funds have been established to serve small college endowments (the Common Fund), family offices (FLAG), and even to develop customized products for individual clients (Grove Street Advisors). Funds-of-funds solve the problem facing both very large clients (public pension funds) and smaller ones: access to private equity funds is not equal to all, and performance differs across the different managers. Thus funds-of-funds help large clients find, assess their capital across a host of smaller funds, and help smaller clients by serving as something like a mutual fund for their private equity investments, providing access and diversification across a number of funds. Funds-of-funds also provide monitoring services and charge a fee, usually close to 1 percent of capital committed, and a share of the gains, usually 5 percent.[37]

The Debate about Funds-of-Funds

An abundance of academic research[38] has compared the risk and reward of funds-of-funds and concluded that they underperform the average fund—by the size of the extra fees and carried interest.[39] Andrew Ang, Matthew Rhodes-Kropf, and Rui Zhao[40] suggest that funds-of-funds add value for the unsophisticated investor even if they do not outperform the average fund. This is because the randomization strategy that such investors would otherwise employ would encourage the establishment and growth of bad funds. Some researchers have therefore argued that comparing individual fund returns to funds-of-funds returns is misguided since it ignores the poor-quality funds that would have been raised if funds-of-funds did not exist and unskilled investors randomly invested in funds.[41]

Presenting a slightly less favorable view of funds-of-funds, Josh Lerner, Antoinette Schoar, and Wan Wongsunwai[42] found that these managers tended to underperform due not only to fees but also to poor fund selection—on average, the **internal rate of return** (IRR) of an advisor-chosen fund (i.e., a fund-of-funds), before any additional fees, was negative 2 percent. Endowments tended to choose the best funds, those with IRRs of 20 percent. The authors speculate that these results may be due partly to the relative youth of many advisors. Not only are they less experienced, but they may have access only to less experienced funds. In addition, some funds-of-funds are required by their mandate to restrict their field of options, which might require their advisors to suboptimize to achieve a noneconomic goal.[43]

Other intermediaries include pension advisors, also known as gatekeepers, that assess private equity funds for public pension funds; consultants, who help clients determine the optimal

[37] Matthew Rhodes-Kropf and Ann Leamon, "Grove Street Advisors: October 2009," HBS Case No. 810-064 (Boston: HBS Publishing, 2009), 11–13.

[38] Carl Ackermann, Richard McEnally, and David Ravenscraft, "The Performance of Hedge Funds: Risk, Return, and Incentives," *Journal of Finance* 54, no. 3 (1999): 833–74; Francois Lhabitant and Michelle Learned, "Hedge Fund Diversification: How Much Is Enough?" (FAME Research Working Paper No. 52, July 2002), SSRN: http://ssrn.com/abstract=322400 or doi:10.2139/ssrn.322400; G. S. Amin and H. M. Kat, "Stocks, Bonds and Hedge Funds: Not a Free Lunch!" *Journal of Portfolio Management* 30 (2003): 113–20; and William Fung et al., "Hedge Funds: Performance, Risk, and Capital Formation," *Journal of Finance* 63, no. 4 (2008): 1777–1803.

[39] Daniel Hausmann et al., eds., *Dow Jones Private Equity Funds-of-Funds State of the Market*, 2008 ed. (Jersey City, NJ: Dow Jones & Co., May 2008), 51, 54.

[40] Andrew Ang, Matthew Rhodes-Kropf, and Rui Zhao, "Do Funds-of-Funds Deserve Their Extra Fees?" *Journal of Investment Management* 6, no. 4 (2008): 34–58.

[41] Ang et al., "Do Funds-of-Funds Deserve Extra Fees?"; and Andrew Ang, Matthew Rhodes-Kropf, and Rui Zhao, "A New Measure for Measuring," *Institutional Investor's Alpha* (July–August 2006).

[42] Josh Lerner, Antoinette Schoar, and Wan Wongsunwai, "Smart Institutions, Foolish Choices," *Journal of Finance* 62 (2007): 731.

[43] Lerner et al., "Smart Institutions, Foolish Choices," 731.

allocation percentage across various assets depending on their risk tolerance, liquidity needs, and cash flow and may make introductions to private equity groups; and information providers, such as Thomson and Cambridge Associates. These may be compensated based on a percentage of assets under management, a fee-for-service, or through an annual subscription.

An advisory industry has also sprung up to serve GPs. Known as placement agents, these range from investment banks like UBS and Credit Suisse to boutiques like Park Hill Group (owned by Blackstone Group) and Probitas Partners.[44] Such groups keep abreast of the market and the groups that might be interested in investing in a firm's fund. In 2008, more than half (54 percent) of firms that closed a fund used placement agents, and larger funds were more likely to do so, whether to identify investors in specific regions or to find additional investors.[45] Placement agents are usually compensated with a percentage of the capital they help raise.

Now that we have a sense of the different players in the private equity universe, let us explore the structure and the agreement that tries to reconcile their interests. Much can be written down. Much, we will also learn, cannot.

THE LIMITED PARTNERSHIP

LPs and GPs have gradually adopted the limited partnership form, ever since Draper, Gaither, & Anderson pioneered it in 1958. Now, despite a handful of private equity firms that are publicly traded, most groups are limited partnerships. The combination of flexibility and accountability—not to mention the tax and legal benefits—have made it an unusually good match for the demands placed upon it. Even Fortress Investment Group and Blackstone Group chose the Master Limited Partnership structure as a compromise between the flexibility of a limited partnership and the accountability and centralization required by the public markets when they went public in 2007.

Private equity, despite the trillions of dollars entrusted to it, has an unsettlingly opportunistic quality. This is related to the information asymmetries noted earlier. Many decisions can be judged as good or bad only in retrospect, and a good decision in one context, investing in a tele-communications switch company in 1998, can be disastrous in another, investing in a tele-communications switch company in 2000. One of the first institutional investors in Skype, the voice-over-Internet pioneer, announced the company's acquisition by eBay for $2.6 billion (and a 144× return to his firm) with the self-deprecating comment, "I'd rather be lucky than smart."

The opportunism runs in many directions. There is an element of luck in finding a talented entrepreneur with a good idea and a need for money. The active nature of private equity investing requires that the entrepreneur and the investor work well together since the investor will own part of the company and the two will be forced to confront any number of challenges. The choice runs both ways: the GP chooses the entrepreneur and the entrepreneur, should he have a choice, chooses a GP (more on this in Chapter 3).

Opportunism also appears in the relationship between LP and GP. In some cases, the LP chooses the GP. In addition to financial performance metrics, there is a nonstructured element to the choice, based to a certain extent on reputation and prior behavior. In addition, there is an element of timing: the GP must be raising money and the LP must be willing to invest.

Private equity partnerships must allow a degree of flexibility. This is first seen in the "blind pool" that holds the funds raised from LPs. The private equity firm does not specify the companies in which it will invest. Part of this is due to the element of randomness and choice on the part of both GPs and entrepreneurs. Primarily, though, it reflects the uncertainty of the overall asset class. Firms cannot know what opportunities will become available at good prices during the life of the fund.

---

[44] Preqin, *2009 Global Private Equity Review*, 130.
[45] Ibid., 131.

As an example, consider the case of Thomas H. Lee (THL), the Boston-based buyout fund. In the aftermath of the property destruction from the September 11, 2001, attacks on New York City, reinsurance companies—companies that provide insurance to firms that sell insurance policies—looked vulnerable. THL had never done any financial services deals, but the firm decided to buy several reinsurance companies, betting that the markets were mistakenly undervaluing them. It acquired two of these in quick succession,[46] something that was probably a surprise to the LPs.

A firm will raise money based on its preferred stage of investment, target geography, and/or domain expertise—Lion Capital, a mid-market European buyout firm, specializes in acquiring and turning around consumer brands such as Wagamama Noodles, Wheetabix, and Jimmy Choo shoes. But it could not specify when it raised its first fund that it would invest in these companies. When LPs invest in an early-stage VC fund, they are even less assured of the companies that will become part of the portfolio. The prospectus, known as a private placement memorandum (PPM), describes the sector in which the firm expects to invest, such as information technology (IT) or life sciences. But some firms that specialize in IT may invest in a retail operation that uses IT in an innovative way. This occurred when Bessemer Venture Partners, Adler & Company, and the nascent investment program of Bain Capital invested in Staples. Bessemer, a tech-oriented firm, brought in Bain to provide retail expertise. Bessemer's retail practice then expanded to include investments in The Sports Authority, Eagle Lawn and Garden, Domain, and online retailers like Blue Nile and Quidsi.

Compare this imprecision with a public mutual fund managing an S&P 500 index fund. The mutual fund investors have invested precisely to be in the S&P 500. They don't want the manager investing in companies that are not part of the S&P 500—even if other companies may seem more promising.

Unlike the mutual fund managers who are constrained to their stated goal of owning shares of companies listed on the S&P 500 index, GPs in a limited partnership are constrained by the concept of "fiduciary duty" to their LPs. The concept, from the Latin *fides*, meaning "trust," refers to a legal or ethical relationship of confidence or trust, where one partner—the principal (in this case, the GP)—has assets entrusted to it and must act at all times to further the benefit of the other. The fiduciary duty is the counterweight to the flexibility of the blind pool, and both operate within the bounds of the limited partnership agreement (LPA).

Given that the LP trades direct control for limited liability, some mechanism must provide incentives to the GPs to pursue strategies that benefit both parties. The biggest incentive is the profit split. But the interests of both parties are further aligned through a number of terms defined in the limited partnership agreement. In addition, many partnerships have LP advisory boards (also known as LP advisory committees, or LPACs). These bodies vary in terms of their activity and impact on the GPs—some long-time LPs complain that advisory boards have grown excessively large and that many recent investors in private equity insist on seats without providing any useful service.[47] At their best, however, LP advisory boards help the GP develop responses to difficult situations facing the firm. To a certain extent, the advisory board also serves as a training ground for newer LPs, through which more experienced LPs provide a model of best practices for LP behavior.

---

[46] Data from Capital IQ.

[47] Felda Hardymon, Josh Lerner, and Ann Leamon, "Note on Limited Partner Advisory Boards," HBS Case No. 808-169 (Boston: HBS Publishing, 2008).

When one cofounder of a private equity firm had to fire his cofounder, the GP first called a significant LP. The action of terminating the cofounder triggered the "key man" clause, a stipulation in the LP agreement that gave the LPs the right to recall their commitments to the fund in the case of one of the founders ceasing to spend most of his time on it. This would spell the end of the fund and, very likely, the firm. After a long discussion detailing the reasons behind the cofounder's departure and the anticipated changes in the fund going forward, the LP decided to support the GP's move and even rallied his colleagues. The firm survived and developed a top-tier track record in its specialty.

Limited partnership agreements have grown in size and complexity with the institutionalization of the industry. In short, the agreement attempts to assure the LPs that the GPs—fiduciary duty or no— will not run amok for the decade that is the life of most private equity funds. While each agreement has its unique attributes, there are certain similarities, as we explore in the following section.

THE LIMITED PARTNERSHIP AGREEMENT

LPAs agreements define the fund along certain major dimensions: characteristics of the fund, such as its duration and investments; costs and incentives, such as the fees paid by LPs and the way they are calculated, along with the level and basis for the profit share; and the activities of the GPs. Some of these increase the LPs' knowledge of the fund; others define who makes money at whose expense. The relative balance of power indicated by these terms reflects both the demand for and supply of private equity services overall and the market for the services provided by that particular fund.

Characteristics of the Fund

An initial item in the agreement is to specify the minimum and maximum size of the fund and how much the GPs will contribute. LPs want to be sure the GPs can raise a fund of at least a certain size to ensure that it will be viable. If the GPs cannot do so within a certain amount of time (the fund usually has to have a final closing within a certain number of months of the first closing[48]), the LPs would prefer that the fund be disbanded. LPs also want to be sure that the GPs do not raise a fund so large that it strains their investment or management skills. In many cases, the GPs may exceed the maximum size stated in the contract by 10 or 20 percent, as long as they explicitly obtain permission from the existing LPs. The LPs who enter late must usually pay the same initial fees as the original LPs, and they may be restricted from a share of the interest earned on the original LPs' initial capital commitments.

Another feature of the fund is the amount of capital that the GPs must contribute. Prior to the 1986 Tax Reform Act, this was 1 percent of the total fund; since then, it has been left to the discretion of the GPs. Legislation proposed in 2007 would raise this amount to 5 percent. Although the change has not been enacted, roughly 45 percent of funds raised in 2009 had GP commitments in excess of 1 percent (averaging 2.5 percent); more than 30 percent of funds had 1 percent commitments.[49] Rarely, GPs may provide their contribution in noninterest-bearing notes rather

---

[48] Note that in private equity, closing a fund is a good thing. It means that the fund is no longer raising money; it is "closed" to further investors and therefore can begin the work of investing.

[49] SCM Strategic Capital Management, *2009 Annual Review of Private Equity Terms and Conditions* (Zurich: SCM Strategic Capital Management AG, February 2010), 4.

than cash. In the case of first-time funds, the GPs often contribute more than the required percentage to prove their commitment to the endeavor.

The LPA also stipulates the minimum and maximum contribution from each LP. Institutions usually have higher limits than individuals. This part of the agreement reflects several concerns. Without a minimum, GPs might raise funds from a host of small investors and then spend excessive amounts of time on paperwork rather than investing the funds. Without a maximum, one LP might provide a substantial percentage of the capital, possibly allowing it undue influence over the fund's strategy. LPs are also concerned that their total number should be kept at a reasonable level. The Investment Company Act of 1940 requires that funds with more than a few hundred partners (originally one hundred) must register as investment advisors, imposing complex regulatory and disclosure requirements. More generally, the costs of administering a private equity fund increase with the number of LPs.

The minimum may be suspended for a special vehicle called a "side pocket" fund, which is created specifically for friends of the firm—family, people who have been helpful, and/or successful entrepreneurs. This fund invests in deals alongside the primary fund at a certain percentage.

The vast majority of funds have a finite life; the only exception is the evergreen fund that is continuously replenished from recycled gains or a parent investment pool. For LPs, the finite life provides a crucial avenue through which to influence GPs. A VC fund usually has a ten-year life with the possibility of two one-year extensions. The life of a buyout fund is usually shorter: often around seven years, again with possible extensions. Sometimes these extensions require approval of the LP advisory board; in other situations, approval is needed only for additional extensions. During boom times, fund lifetimes are compressed: some VC firms raised three funds between 1997 and 2000 and invested the money as quickly. But the finite life of a fund gives the GPs a horizon date for their investments. While it is possible to transfer investments from one fund to another, possible conflicts of interest make this undesirable, and partnership agreements usually allow it only with approval from the LP advisory board. This system does several things: it encourages the GPs to choose companies that can achieve significant growth in a reasonable amount of time; it encourages the entrepreneurs to undertake aggressive growth strategies rather than create a nice company that maintains a comfortable lifestyle (known as a lifestyle company); and it allows the LPs to assess the GPs' performance in a discrete time period. Admittedly, ten years is a significant amount of time, but it is not infinite. There is liquidity at the end of the decade. The idea of a finite fund life also gives rise to the concept of vintage years, which we discuss at greater length in Chapter 9.

Lastly, the finite life of a fund forces accountability. When the firm goes out to raise another fund, its existing LPs can justifiably ask, "What have you done for me?" The firm must have a convincing answer, by either demonstrating realized returns or making a very good case for their imminence.

Almost all partnerships allow for the fund to be terminated before the ten-year limit under extreme conditions, such as the death or withdrawal of the GPs or the fund's bankruptcy. Most agreements also allow the LPs to dissolve the partnership or replace the GPs if a majority of the LPs—usually a super-majority and sometimes as much as 100 percent—believe that the GP is damaging the fund. Often, however, the parties in these cases end up in court.[50]

There are a few examples of this. In 1996, the LPs in Davenport Group MG, an under-performing buyout fund with $120 million in capital, voted to remove the GP for misuse of certain fees. The firm's performance had been dismal; the portfolio's value decreased by 50 percent in the

---

[50] Articles about such disputes include E. S. Ely, "Dr. Silver's Tarnished Prescription," *Venture* 9 (July 1987): 54–58; "Iowa Suits Test LPs' Authority to Abolish Fund," *Private Equity Analyst* 4 (May 1994): 1, 9; "Madison L.P.s Oust G.P., Legal Skirmish Ensues," *Buyouts* (October 23, 1995): 4; and Andrew S. Ross, "HRJ Capital Gets Saved by Swiss Equity Group," *SFGate.com*, April 3, 2009.

six years since the fund was raised. Davenport sued the LPs, but lost; management of the fund was assumed by a new general partner formed by the LPs.[51] Recently, several firms have removed members of the general partner, often triggering "key man" clauses where LPs can reduce or opt out of their commitments to the fund, or force the firm to stop making new investments. The French buyout firm PAI Partners faced pressure to reduce the size of its €5.4 billion ($7.8 billion) fund after its two most senior executives were forced out under pressure from the firm's largest investor and former parent, BNP Paribas SA. To win support for the new team at PAI, the new CEO had to halt investments for six months and offer the LPs the chance to cut the fund's size by 40 percent. LPs were rumored to want further concessions, such as fee cuts, or even the wholesale return of their committed capital.[52]

Management of the Fund

Understandably, the LPs are concerned about the GPs' management of the fund, especially because limited liability precludes the LPs from active intervention. One of the chief concerns is the amount of the fund invested in a single company. For both VC and buyout funds, the agreement generally stipulates a "concentration limit," or the percentage of the fund (usually based on committed capital) that can be invested in a single company. This limit guards against the possibility that the GPs might focus excessive amounts of time and additional capital on a company in which it had already invested a large amount. Another related concern involves the possibility that GPs might try to offset a large investment in a troubled company by engaging in high-risk strategies with the balance of the fund. This behavior could make sense from the perspective of the GPs, since they typically do not receive a share of profits (their **carried interest**, or carry) until the LPs have been returned their original investment. Consequently, the GPs' share of profits can be thought of as a call option, the right but not the obligation to buy a financial asset at a set price in the future. In this case, the asset is the future value of the portfolio. If the investments collectively lose value, the GPs' carry will be worth nothing, but they will not be responsible for the losses. If the portfolio thrives, they will receive 20 percent of the capital gains. Thus the value of the carried interest option is likely to increase as the risk of the portfolio increases (or, for students of option theory, the volatility of the portfolio grows).[53] One way to accomplish this would be to invest in higher-risk firms; another way (were it not prohibited by the typical partnership agreement) would be to concentrate investment in a single company. Of course, a fund manager who lost the entire fund by putting all the capital into a single risky firm would have a hard time raising another fund, which limits this behavior somewhat.[54] Firms usually can exceed the concentration ratio with approval of the LP advisory board. Another way to handle the situation is to allow the LPs to co-invest in the deal.

The second class of restriction, particularly on venture capital funds, limits the use of debt. Because the GPs' share of the profits can be seen as an option, they may be tempted to increase the variance of their portfolio's returns through leverage. Partnership agreements often limit the ability of private equity investors to borrow funds themselves or to guarantee the debt of their

---

[51] Barry B. Burr, "Pension Funds Oust Partner: Chancery Court Backs Limited Partners' Unusual Move," *Pensions & Investments*, February 5, 1996, http://www.pionline.com/article/19960205/PRINTSUB/602050717.

[52] Anne-Sylvaine Chassany, "PAI's 'Coup d'état' Shows LBO Firms' Feuds Over Power, Strategy," *Bloomberg*, September 28, 2009, www.bloomberg.com, accessed June 30, 2010.

[53] For more on this discussion along with exercises and tools, see Andrew Metrick, *Venture Capital and the Finance of Innovation* (New York: Wiley & Sons, 2007), 231–49.

[54] For a discussion of how the desire to raise another fund can affect behavior, see Ji-Woong Chung, Berk A. Sensoy, Léa H. Stern, and Michael S. Weisbach, "Incentives of Private Equity General Partners from Future Fundraising" (Charles A. Dice Center Working Paper No. 2010-003; Fisher College of Business Working Paper No. 2010-3-003, February 17, 2010), available at SSRN: http://ssrn.com/abstract=1554626.

portfolio companies (which might be seen as equivalent to direct borrowing). If debt is allowed, the agreements may restrict it to a set percentage of committed capital or assets, and in some instances require that all borrowing is short term.[55]

The third restriction relates to investments in the same companies alongside the firm's earlier and/or later funds. Here is another situation that can create opportunistic behavior, since many private equity organizations manage multiple funds, formed several years apart. If a firm's first fund has made an investment in a troubled company, the GPs may want to invest in this company from their second fund, hoping to salvage it. This may also occur if the GPs need to report an attractive return for their first fund as they raise capital for a later one. Many venture funds will write up the valuation of companies in their portfolios to the price paid in the last fund-raising round. By having the second fund invest in one of the first fund's firms at an inflated valuation, they can (temporarily) inflate the reported performance of their first fund. Consequently, partnership agreements for second or later funds frequently contain provisions that the fund's advisory board must review such investments or that a majority (or super-majority) of the LPs must approve them. Alternatively, the earlier fund or an unaffiliated private equity firm may be required to invest simultaneously at the same valuation.

A fourth class of covenant relates to the reinvestment of profits. GPs may have several reasons to reinvest proceeds rather than distribute profits to the LPs. First, many partnerships receive fees on the basis of either the value of assets under management or the adjusted committed capital (capital less any distributions). Distributing profits will reduce these fees. Second, reinvested capital gains may yield further profits for the GPs as well as the LPs.[56] The reinvestment of profits may require approval of the advisory board or the LPs. It may be prohibited after a certain date, or after a certain percent of the committed capital is invested.

Activities of the General Partners

The LPA also regulates the activities of the general partners (GPs). Five restrictions are commonly encountered, and each reflects the concerns of the LPs about the GPs' attention to the specific fund in which the LPs have invested.

Investment of Personal Funds

Co-investing alongside the fund in portfolio companies can be a powerful wealth generator for the GPs. To the LPs, however, this must be managed carefully. If the GPs can choose their investments from among the firm's portfolio companies (known as "cherry picking"), the LPs may worry that partners will be more dedicated to those companies in which they have personal funds invested at the expense of other companies in the portfolio. In addition, the GP may be unwilling to stop funding the company in question. To resolve this, GPs may be limited in the amount they can invest (expressed as a percentage of the deal or, less frequently, the net worth of the GP) or required to obtain permission from the LP advisory board. In some cases, GPs are required to invest the same percentage in each portfolio company, or they may be barred from personally investing in any companies. Another issue relating to co-investment is the timing of the GPs' investments. In some cases, venture capitalists

---

[55] A related provision—found in virtually all partnership agreements—is that the LPs will avoid unrelated business taxable income (UBTI). Tax-exempt institutions must pay taxes on UBTI, which is defined as the gross income from any unrelated business that the institution regularly carries out. If the venture partnership is generating significant income from debt-financed property, the LPs may have tax liabilities.

[56] Another reason private equity investors may wish to reinvest profits is that some investments are unlikely to be mature at the end of the fund's stated life. The presence of investments that are too immature to liquidate is frequently invoked as a reason for extending the partnership's life beyond the typical contractual limit of ten years. In these cases, the private equity investors will continue to generate fees from the LPs (though often on a reduced basis).

involved at a company's founding will purchase shares at a very low valuation and then immediately invest their partnership's funds at a higher valuation. Some partnership agreements require GPs to invest at the same time and price as their fund.

Sale of Partnership Interests by the GPs

A second restriction addresses the reverse problem: the sale of partnership interests by the GPs. In this case, the GPs are selling their share of the fund's profits. While the general partnership interests are not totally comparable to the LPs' stakes (for instance, the GPs typically share in the capital gains only after the LPs' capital is returned), these may still be attractive investments. The LPs may be concerned that such a transaction will reduce the GPs' incentives to monitor their investments. Partnership agreements may prohibit the sale of GP interests outright, or require approval by a majority (or super-majority) of the LPs.

Since the late 1990s, several buyout firms have sold part of the management company to outside groups, thereby sharing the fee stream and the profits. The Carlyle Group sold 5.5 percent of the management company for $175 million to the California Public Employees Retirement System (CalPERS) in 2001 and 7.5 percent to Mubadala, one of the UAE's sovereign wealth funds, for $1.35 billion in 2007;[57] T.H. Lee sold 20 percent to Putnam Investments for $250 million in 1999; and Blackstone Group sold 7 percent to insurer AIG in 1998 for $150 million plus a commitment that AIG would invest $1.2 billion in future Blackstone funds.[58] Starting in 2006, a few LBO firms announced plans to take themselves public—also with the approval of their LPs. Publicly traded private equity groups are more common in Europe but were virtually unknown in the United States until the floatation of the hedge fund Fortress Investment Group in February 2007, followed by Blackstone Group's listing in June of that year.[59] In March 2010, Apollo Management announced plans to move its listing from Goldman Sachs' private exchange to the New York Stock Exchange (NYSE).[60] That same month, Kohlberg Kravis Roberts (KKR) which had listed a fund on the Euronext Amsterdam in 2006, announced that it would take 30 percent of the firm public on the NYSE.[61] The impacts of such transactions are explored at greater length in Chapter 12.

Future Fund-Raising

A third area for restrictions on the GPs is future fund-raising. The raising of an additional fund will increase the management fees that the GPs receive and may reduce their attention to existing funds. Moreover, the activity of fund-raising is tremendously distracting to the partnership and can lead the GPs to embark in suboptimizing exercises, such as the previously mentioned cross-fund investments or a general upward skew in portfolio company valuations.[62] Partnership agreements

---

[57] Jack Ewing, "The New Financial Heavyweights," *BusinessWeek*, November 12, 2007, 52–55.

[58] Josh Lerner, Felda Hardymon, and Ann Leamon, "The Blackstone Group's IPO," HBS Case No. 9-808-100 (Boston: HBS Publishing, 2008), 2–4; and Peter Truell, "A.I.G. Will Put $1.35B into Blackstone," *New York Times*, July 31, 1998, D1 accessed at http://www.nytimes.com/1998/07/31/business/aig-will-put-1.35-billion-into-blackstone.html?scp=1&sq =AIG+blackstone+&st=nyt, March 15, 2010.

[59] For details, see Lerner et al., "The Blackstone Group's IPO."

[60] Data from Megan Davies, "Apollo Proposes Offering $50 Million in IPO: Filing," *Reuters*, March 22, 2010.

[61] In November 2009, KKR had merged with the publicly traded fund and transferred its listing to the NYSE Euronext. The subsequent listing involved a one-for-one trade with shares in the Euronext vehicle. In June 2010, KKR announced that it was delaying the listing a second time.

[62] The question of the value at which an illiquid investment should be held is discussed at greater length in Chapter 4; but for the moment, it is worthwhile to point out that when Peter Wendell of Sierra Ventures was determining how to value his fledgling fund's portfolio, he surveyed a number of his fellow VC firms. All the firms carried their portfolio companies at cost, except for a few quasi-evergreen firms that did not have to worry about fund-raising and generally valued their companies below cost, and those firms out raising money, which were enthusiastic in their valuation estimates. This tendency has implications for the LPs that are determining future asset allocations and internal budgets.

may prohibit fund-raising by the GPs until a set percentage of the fund has been invested or until a given date. Alternatively, fund-raising may be restricted to a fund of certain size or focus (e.g., a venture organization may be allowed to raise a buyout fund, presumably to be managed by other GPs, but is restricted from raising another venture fund until a certain share of capital is invested).

Time Investment by GPs

Some partnership agreements contain a fourth restriction that prevents the GPs from pursuing other projects. Because outside activities are likely to reduce the attention paid to investments, GPs may be required to spend "substantially all" (or some other fraction) of their time managing the partnership's investments. These limitations are often confined to the first years of the partnership, or until a set percentage of the fund's capital is invested, when the need for GP attention is presumed to be the largest.

New General Partners

A fifth class of covenant relates to the addition of new GPs. By hiring less experienced GPs, private equity investors may reduce the burden on themselves, but the cost of bringing on new partners, in terms of introducing the firm's culture to the new hires, can be considerable. Moreover, the LPs have usually signed on to have their money managed by the specific individuals noted in the initial prospectus. As a result, many funds require that the advisory board or a set percentage of the LPs approves the addition of any new GPs. In many cases, rather than run the risk of upsetting the partnership, new hires will come on as "venture partners" until a new fund is raised, and only then become full-fledged GPs. For more on this, see Chapter 11.

Types of Investments

LPs are also concerned about the types of investments the GPs pursue. The first reason is that GPs are paid substantial amounts to invest in specialized areas. Should they choose to, say, invest in public equities rather than managing high-tech start-ups, they would be receiving substantial compensation for a task that someone else—a mutual fund manager, for instance—can do more proficiently and more cheaply. The second concern is that the GPs might choose to invest in other asset classes in hopes of gaining expertise with these types of investments: for instance, during the bubble of the late 1990s, many buyout firms tried to invest in young VC-type companies, only to find that it was not as easy as it looked. VC firms have also attempted buyout investments with similar uninspiring returns. LPs want GPs to devote their expertise to those sectors in which they have made their track records.

Gompers and Lerner, in a 1996 article,[63] explored the role of covenants as indicators of the relative balance of power between GPs and LPs. Based on a sample of 140 venture partnership agreements, the authors determined that the covenants in each contract varied with the difficulty of monitoring behavior and/or the opportunities for opportunism. Moreover, the number of covenants was a function of supply and demand for venture investment services. Over the short term, the supply of VC firms is limited—it takes time to establish a fund, raise money, and develop a track record. Therefore, in the short run, an increased flow of funds into the asset class results in a higher implicit price—that is, VC firms can raise the fees they charge and negotiate contracts allowing them to purse strategies that create gains for the GPs at a cost to the LPs. Gompers and Lerner identified 14 different

---

[63] Paul Gompers and Josh Lerner, "The Use of Covenants: An Empirical Analysis of Venture Partnership Agreements," *Journal of Law and Economics* 39, no. 2 (1996): 463–98.

Table 2.1   Appearance of Covenants in Partnership Agreements

Covenants Relating to	Percentage (%) of Contracts with Covenant in		
	1978–82	1983–87	1988–92
Management of the Fund			
• restriction on size of investment in any one firm	33.3	47.1	77.8
• restrictions on the use of debt	66.7	72.1	95.6
• restrictions on co-investment by earlier or later funds	40.7	29.4	62.2
• restrictions on reinvestment of partnership's capital gains	3.7	17.6	35.6
Activities of the General Partners			
• restrictions on co-investment by general partners	81.5	66.2	77.8
• restrictions on sale of partnership interests by general partners	74.1	54.4	51.1
• restrictions on fund-raising by general partners	51.9	42.6	84.4
• restrictions on other actions by general partners	22.2	16.2	13.3
• restrictions on additions of general partners	29.6	35.3	26.7
Types of Investment			
• restrictions on investments in other funds	3.7	22.1	62.2
• restrictions on investments in public securities	22.2	17.6	66.7
• restrictions on investments in leveraged buyouts	0.0	8.8	60.0
• restrictions on investments in foreign securities	0.0	7.4	44.4
• restrictions on investments in other asset classes	11.1	16.2	31.1
Total number of agreements in sample	27	68	45
Average number of covenant classes	4.4	4.5	7.9
Average number of covenant classes (weighted by fund size)	4.4	4.6	8.4

Source: Paul Gompers and Josh Lerner, "The Use of Covenants: An Empirical Analysis of Venture Partnership Agreements," *Journal of Law and Economics* 39, no. 2 (1996): 485. © *Journal of Law and Economics*, University of Chicago Press, 1996.

types of restrictions in the 140 contracts at their disposal and found that when inflows to VC exceeded the median, LP agreements had four of these. When inflows to VC lagged the median, LP agreements had at least seven, demonstrating a decrease in the effective price of VC services when their supply rises relative to demand.[64] Figure 2.1 shows the percentage of covenant types included in contracts over three different five-year periods. Most notable are the changes in the restrictions on permitted types of investment: while none of the earliest agreements restrict VC firms from investing in leveraged buyouts or foreign securities, 60 percent and 44 percent (respectively) of the latest contracts forbade them.[65] See Table 2.1 for sumary of covenants in LPAs.

ALIGNMENT OF INTERESTS: FEES AND CARRY

Despite the stipulations noted earlier, the typical ten-year life of a fund still gives considerable leeway to the GPs. Given the flexibility implied in a blind pool ("Give us your money, and we'll invest it in promising deals in a given industry"), the illiquidity of unmarketable assets that lack real-time pricing ("We're not sure what it's worth because it's hard to find who would buy it"), and the long-term nature of the investment—with extensions, longer than the average U.S. marriage—

---

[64] Gompers and Lerner, "The Use of Covenants."
[65] Ibid., 485.

FIGURE 2.5 Management fees

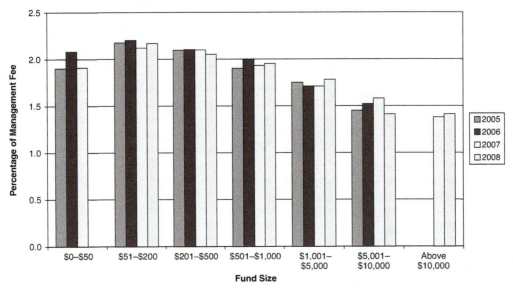

Source: Data from SCM Strategic Capital Management, *2007 Annual Review of Private Equity Terms and Conditions*, (Zurich: SCM Strategic Capital Management AG, February 2008), 8, 17; SCM Strategic Capital Management, *2008 Annual Review of Private Equity Terms and Conditions*, (Zurich: SCM Strategic Capital Management AG, February 2009), 8, 17. Used with permission.

there needs to be some way to ensure that the GPs aren't hiking the Appalachian Trail when they should be doing the hard work of making and managing investments. Yet for an investment officer to monitor the dozens of GPs in which that institution may be invested is impossible.

Moreover, no contract could possibly address every possible contingency. Instead of dictating what the GPs shall and shall not do, the industry has developed an arrangement where the GPs work to the benefit of the LPs, not only due to fiduciary duty but acting in their own interests. On such an alignment of interests rests a multibillion-dollar industry. To understand its dynamics, one must understand the system of incentives—namely, fees and carried interest.

Management Fees

Management fees were instituted to sustain the partnership in its early days, before there were any exits and provided salaries for the GPs and staff. The fees also covered travel, office rent, and salaries for back-office staff. It is important to note that LPs do not write a separate check for management fees; rather, fees are deducted from the funds available to invest. They can be regarded as a tax that reduces the possible gain-creating investments that the GPs could make.

Management fees are set when the firm starts raising its fund and are rarely if ever renegotiated. The classic figure is 2 percent, usually based on capital committed to the fund. It can, however, be calculated based on capital invested or on assets under management. Each of these can create undesired behavior on the part of the GP: basing a fee on committed capital rewards firms that raise larger funds; basing it on invested capital can inspire suboptimal investments; and basing it on assets under management raises issues of valuation. Moreover, the percentage itself can vary: some established firms charge 2.5 percent; some very niche organizations might charge more; and some large buyout firms charge less. First-time funds may charge a lower percentage just to raise money.

Figure 2.5 shows the range of management fees charged at different times by funds of differing sizes. It is clear that 2 percent is typical, although it varies slightly over time and with fund size. Of particular interest is the shift in fund sizes themselves. In 2008, the study did not even report on funds of less than $50 million; in the prior years, the cutoff was funds over $3 billion—let alone $10 billion. In 2008, the most common management fee was between 1.91 percent and 2.20 percent; 2009's level was the same or slightly lower.[66] Larger buyout funds (above $5 billion) averaged fees slightly over 1.4 percent in 2008 and often reduced them over time. Venture capital funds were more likely to charge a 2.5 percent fee, bringing the overall average slightly above 2 percent.[67] Anecdotally, the recent tumult in the fund-raising market, especially among buyout firms, has seen fee reductions or the implementation of other LP-friendly terms.

Management fees often taper off in the later years of a fund's life, on the assumption that the hard work of finding and managing the investments has been done and the GPs are just guiding the companies toward exit. It is also assumed that by then, the firm has raised another fund on which it is collecting the full amount of fees. It is entirely possible that a firm can receive fees from three different funds at a given time: one just beginning, one in midlife, and one that is winding down.

The relative size of low-risk fee streams compared to the performance-based carried interest has long been of concern to LPs. With larger funds, LPs worry that GPs will simply live off the fee streams rather than pursuing above-market returns from investing in risky companies. In response, some GPs established "budget-based fees." In this system, the LPs or the advisory board and the GPs together determine the fee income necessary to cover the firm's expenses—salaries, travel, rent, marketing, and such—and allocate that from the fund. Usually, this was less than 2 percent and left more of the fund available for investment, increasing the opportunities for carried interest gains to both parties. In addition, these arrangements allow more flexibility: if a firm needs additional fee income in a given year to establish offices in emerging markets, for instance, this can be arranged instead of waiting until the next fund is raised. Budget-based fees, adopted by such firms as Menlo Ventures, New Enterprise Associates, and U.S. Venture Partners, are generally favored as a sign of good faith and transparency on the part of the GPs.[68]

Carried Interest

Carried interest, or carry, is the share of the investment gains that goes to the GPs. The traditional percentage share of 20 percent dates from twelfth- and thirteenth-century Venetian and Genovese merchants, who formed syndicates to fund shipping ventures.[69] The merchants supplied the money and hired the captain and crew, who, upon successfully completing their voyage, were compensated with 20 percent of the gains. For private equity partnerships, carry is the performance-oriented portion of pay. A large and growing number of firms, both VC and buyout, use the 20 percent figure. Figure 2.6 compares the levels of carry as reported in 2007, 2008, and 2009 in a survey of global VC and buyout firms[70] to those noted in an earlier study of VC firms only by Gompers and Lerner.[71] The Gompers and Lerner study of partnerships formed before 1992 showed an even longer tail than the more recent data; a few firms reported 25 percent and

[66] SCM Strategic Capital Management, *2008 Annual Review of Private Equity Terms and Conditions* (Zurich: SCM Strategic Capital Management AG, February 2009), 8, 17; and SCM Strategic Capital Management, *2009 Annual Review of Private Equity Terms and Conditions* (Zurich: SCM Strategic Capital Management AG, February 2010), 6.

[67] SCM Strategic Capital Management, *2008 Annual Review*, 8, 17.

[68] George Hoyem and Bart Schachter, "LPs Should Demand to See a Budget . . . ," *Venture Capital Journal*, December 1, 2003, 1.

[69] Metrick and Yasuda offer some other derivations, including the Bible. The account of Italian merchant derivation comes from Raymond Drover, "The Organization of Trade," in *The Cambridge Economic History of Europe: Volume III—Economic Organization and Policies in the Middle Ages*, ed. by M. M. Postan, E. E. Rich, and Edward Miller (Cambridge: Cambridge University Press, 1963); and Robert S. Lopez and Irving W. Raymond, *Medieval Trade in the Mediterranean World: Illustrative Documents Translated with Introductions and Notes* (New York: Columbia University Press, 1955); cited in Gompers and Lerner, *Money of Invention*, 102.

[70] SCM Strategic Capital Management, *2008 Annual Review*, 8, 17; and *2007 Annual Review*, 8, 17.

[71] Paul Gompers and Josh Lerner, "An Analysis of Compensation in the U.S. Venture Capital Partnership," *Journal of Financial Economics* 51 (1999): 3–44.

FIGURE 2.6   Carry levels

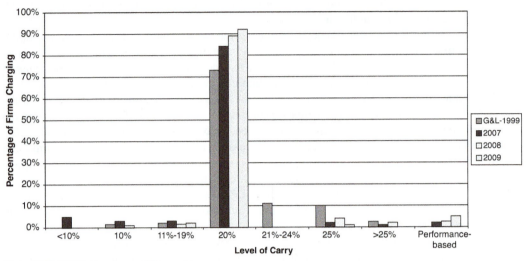

Note: G&L-1999 is Gompers and Lerner data.
Source: Data from SCM Strategic Capital Management, *2007 Annual Review,* 8, 17; SCM Strategic Capital Management, *2008 Annual Review,* 8,17; SCM Strategic Capital Management, *2009 Annual Review,* and Paul Gompers and Josh Lerner, "An Analysis of Compensation in the U.S. Venture Capital Partnership," *Journal of Financial Economics* 51 (1999):15.

30 percent. Interestingly, despite the demand for private equity services since 1992, carry percentages have aligned more closely to 20 percent. A recent development among VC firms has been a wider adoption of hurdle rates (preferred return), or minimum levels of return to the LPs before the GPs share in the gains. The most common approach appears to be 20 percent carried interest with an 8 percent hurdle, rising to a 25 percent carry after a 15 percent return to the LPs.[72]

In short, carry aligns LPs and GPs by ensuring that both share in the gains. LPs, who put up the money, endure the illiquidity, and hope they chose talented GPs, receive the cost basis from the investment and then get 80 percent of the gains. GPs get 20 percent to encourage them to devote themselves to choosing promising companies and guiding them to success. Thus, if a firm has invested $50 million in a company and it sells for $100 million, the LPs get their $50 million back and then receive 80 percent of the $50 million profit, or $40 million. The GPs get $10 million (20 percent of $50 million).

Unlike hedge fund managers, partners in private equity firms receive gains based only on the value of investments that have been exited (rather than incorporating paper gains, due only to value increases while still in the portfolio), and almost universally distribute their gains from deals as they are realized, rather than settling accounts at the end of a fund. Some groups distribute gains annually, others quarterly. This benefits both parties: the GPs start receiving their share of carry earlier, and the LPs receive their cost bases (the money invested in the deal) and their 80 percent share. As we discuss later, deal-by-deal distribution also allows LPs to fund their ongoing private equity commitments from the proceeds of their current holdings.

When the markets decline, though, problems arise because the existing portfolio loses much of its value. If GPs have already received carry payments based on early exits from good deals, they would be said to have "over-distributed to themselves"—the gains already received exceed the level specified in the limited partnership agreement. The LPs, then, might not receive their contractually agreed shares. To address this, LPAs contain the colorfully named **clawback**.

---

[72] SCM Strategic Capital Management, *2009 Annual Review*, 5.

Clawbacks work in the following way: Consider a GP who raised a $100 million fund and made ten investments of $10 million each. Two investments liquidate[73] early, for $50 million each, while the other eight stay in the portfolio and are valued at cost. Assume that this fund employed a standard 80–20 percent split of capital gains between the LPs and GPs and followed the rule that distributions were divided between the GPs and LPs from inception.[74] When the first two investments were liquidated, the $20 million of invested capital was returned directly to the LPs. Of the $80 million in capital gains, $64 million (80 percent) went to the LPs and $16 million (20 percent) to the GPs. These gains are paid out as the first two investments were exited, rather than after the fund reaches the end of its contractual life. If the remaining portfolio drops in value, though, the GPs will have over-distributed to themselves at the expense of the LPs. In our example, if the ultimate value realized from the remaining portfolio is only $40 million (i.e., 50 cents for each dollar invested), the GPs have over-distributed $8 million (20 percent × [$80 million – $40 million])[75] and must repay the LPs that amount, net of any taxes.

This situation can also be complicated by "joint and several" clauses, which specify that each partner can be held responsible for the entire amount of the clawback. If the GPs in the firm are a mix of senior partners who have invested their share of the $16 million, and younger partners who have bought cars and houses, the entire $8 million owed the LPs might not be accessible.[76]

An alternate approach, which was used at the industry's inception, is the "real estate" model. Here, the LPs first receive all of the capital invested *in the fund*, and then the profit is shared. In the example just described, the LPs would have received their $100 million committed capital from the two companies that liquidated early. Any carry would come from liquidating the later companies. Yet this too creates tensions. With such a strong incentive to return capital quickly to the LPs and speed their chance to share in the gains, GPs might choose an immediate but less lucrative offer rather than investing the time and effort to build a company to a longer-term but more substantial exit. In addition, eagerness for short-term exits might incline early-stage funds to invest in later-stage deals promising more certain but less substantial returns.

Although LPAs require clawback to be handled only at the end of a fund's life, firms that are regarded as showing good partnership behavior make amends to their LPs as soon as it appears that the situation is not transitory. After the NASDAQ plunge in 2000, some GPs made immediate restitution by writing checks on their personal accounts. Others cut fees or fund sizes; this approach, by reducing the committed capital, shrank the fee stream.[77]

Within the firm, carry can be shared in two different ways. In the "insurance" model, the partners share carry based on a predetermined percentage regardless of which partner made the investment. This recognizes that "the partner with the hot hand today may have the cold hand

---

[73] Note that in private equity, as opposed to retail sales, "liquidation" is actually a good thing and means that the security is liquid and can be freely traded.

[74] The different rules for liquidating PE portfolios are discussed in Josh Lerner, "A Note on Private Equity Partnership Agreements," HBS Case No. 294-084 (Boston: HBS Publishing, 1994).

[75] Josh Lerner, Felda Hardymon, and Ann Leamon, "Between a Rock and a Hard Place: Valuation and Distribution," HBS Case No. 803-161 (Boston: HBS Publishing, 2003), 6; and Lawrence Aragon and Dan Primack, "Clawback Woes Hit Battery and Meritech," *Venture Capital Journal*, January 1, 2003.

[76] For top-tier firms raising funds after 1998, though, "joint and several" clauses have largely been replaced by "several" clauses, which specify that the partnership as a whole, not each individual partner, is responsible for the clawback. Additionally, the monies are repaid on an after-tax basis, bringing the net nominal value of the clawback to at most 50 percent of its gross amount.

[77] Lerner et al., "Between a Rock and a Hard Place," 6.

tomorrow," as one investor said. The other approach is "eat what you kill." That is, if life sciences endure a long dry spell, the life sciences investors do likewise.

In one of the few papers to study compensation in VC partnerships, Gompers and Lerner[78] found an interesting difference in the responsiveness of new and established firms to compensation. Using evidence from 419 U.S. VC partnerships formed between 1978 and 1992, new and smaller firms tended to have higher fixed base compensation (i.e., from fees), while the compensation of established firms was more variable and more sensitive to performance. The authors ascribe this to a learning model of performance. That is, new VC investors do not know if they will succeed or fail. Therefore, they will work hard simply to prove themselves and build a reputation, with an eye toward higher incentive-based compensation in later funds. This is confirmed by anecdotal evidence that notes the difficulty of assessing a new venture capitalist's performance *a priori*.

Once reputation has been established, firms become motivated by the prospect of financial gains. In general, established firms command higher performance-based compensation and lower fixed compensation. Gompers and Lerner find that these firms receive roughly 1 percent more carry than do newer firms, which can translate into a 4 percent greater increase in the net present value of compensation if the fund is successful. Interestingly, the authors do not find a relationship between incentive compensation and performance.[79]

Other Fees

While the compensation for most VC firms is limited to management fees and carry, buyout firms can receive income from a number of other fees. A major source of such income is transaction fees, which are paid by the acquired company. Anecdotally, these range between 1 and 2 percent of the transaction value; the only published study found an average of 1.37 percent noted in public filings for those transactions where fees were paid.[80] Theoretically, these compensate the acquiring firm for costs of research and expert opinions incurred in pursuing deals that are subsequently lost.

In addition, the acquired company often has to pay an annual monitoring fee to its purchaser. In informal conversations, Metrick and Yasuda[81] learned of annual monitoring fees ranging between 1 and 5 percent of earnings before interest, tax, depreciation, and amortization (EBITDA); larger companies were paying the lower end of the scale and smaller ones the higher end. An LBO fund contracts with the portfolio company to provide these services over a fixed time period. If the company exits before the contracted end date, the fund generally receives a lump-sum payment in compensation for the remaining present value of the contract. In 2006, KKR earned $276 million in transaction fees and $67 million in monitoring fees from its portfolio companies, almost the same amount as the management fees it received from its various funds.[82] A large number of buyout firms offset transaction and monitoring fees against management fees, many of them rebating at least 50 percent of the fees to the LPs. The LPs, however, have expressed growing concern that these fees represent a transfer of wealth from the LPs to the GPs because they reduce the viability of the company itself. The offset, then, would represent a benefit to the LPs but not necessarily to the companies.

---

[78] Gompers and Lerner, "An Analysis of Compensation," 3–44.

[79] Ibid.

[80] Consus Group 2008, "Summary of Deal Fees as Percentage of Transaction Values," downloaded from http://www.consusgroup.com/reports/private_equity_fees/summary.asp; cited in Metrick and Yasuda, "The Economics of Private Equity Funds," 2303–41.

[81] Metrick and Yasuda, "The Economics of Private Equity Funds."

[82] Kohlberg Kravis Roberts, Preliminary S1 Filing, July 3, 2007, http://www.sec.gov, accessed July 15, 2007.

Table 2.2   Fees and Carry Levels and Bases for VC and LBO Funds

Fee Terms	VC	Buyout
% of funds with initial fee level		
– greater than 2%	43	8
– equal to 2%	47	41
– less than 2%	10	51
% of funds changing fee *basis* after investment period	43	84
% of funds changing fee *level* after investment period	55	45
% of funds changing *both* basis and level	16	39
Carry terms		
% of funds with carry level		
– greater than 20%	4	0
– equal to 20%	96	100
– less than 20%	1	0
% of funds with hurdle return	45	92
Of those with hurdles: % of funds with level		
– greater than 8%	12	14
– equal to 8%	67	78
– less than 8%	17	8
Total number of funds	93	144

Source: Adapted from Metrick and Yasuda, "The Economics of Private Equity Fund," 2311.

Metrick and Yasuda's work analyzes the economics of the private equity industry using a data set from a large investor in private equity funds.[83] With detailed information on 238 funds raised between 1993 and 2006, the authors modeled the net present value of expected revenue that managers received. Roughly 66 percent of expected revenue, the authors found, came from fixed components, in particular, management fees. As shown in Table 2.2, almost half of the VC firms, but fewer than 10 percent of the LBO funds, charged management fees in excess of 2 percent. Fewer than half of the VC funds changed the fee basis (i.e., whether the fee was based on invested capital or committed capital) over the fund's life and slightly more than half changed the amount after the investment period, compared to basis changes for 84 percent of the LBO funds and level changes for 45 percent. Among VC funds, 16 percent changed both the basis and the level, and almost 39 percent of the LBO funds did so.

In terms of carry, 20 percent was by far the predominant level; only four VC funds received more, and one received less. All 144 LBO funds in the sample received 20 percent carry. Among the funds that had a hurdle rate (45 percent of VC, 92 percent of LBO), 8 percent was by far the most common.

Capital Calls

Unlike buying shares of a mutual fund and writing a check for the total amount, an LP simply commits to invest in a private equity fund. Often, a certain percentage (10 to 35 percent) of the total commitment must be contributed when the fund "closes," a process that can take place a number of times as the firm gradually raises money. The capital committed is later "called down" as the firm

---

[83] Metrick and Yasuda, "The Economics of Private Equity Funds."

finds and funds investments. An LP, then, may commit $5 million but write a check for only a fraction of that amount when the fund closes. The GPs outline a takedown schedule in the agreement, allowing the LPs to anticipate when the funds will be fully called but rarely specifying exact dates and amounts. In general, private equity funds expect to invest most of their capital by the end of the fourth year, but they also usually reserve an amount for the funding needs of later-maturing companies.

This approach benefits both LPs and GPs. For the GPs, being able to "call" the capital buoys returns by ensuring that funds are immediately invested in high-return opportunities. It also places the onus of liquidity upon the LPs. The GPs do not have to try to balance maturities of various investment vehicles to ensure that funds will be available when a long-negotiated or fast-moving deal closes. Generally, the time lag between a capital call and wiring the money to the investee company is 30 days, but it can be as few as two.

In theory, the process of capital calls allows LPs to let their capital multitask. The uncalled balance of a commitment may come from the proceeds of an earlier private equity investment. As long as the cycle of investment and liquidation is relatively balanced, LPs can fund their future private equity commitments from those made in the past. When exits dip sharply below their historic pace, as occurred in 2008 and early 2009, some LPs suffer severe liquidity constraints. In many cases, the GPs assist their LPs in the nonconfrontational resolution of these issues, whether slowing the investment rate or assisting in secondary sales.

THE LP–GP RELATIONSHIP: STUFF THAT CAN'T BE WRITTEN DOWN

Several key issues are not addressed through partnership agreements. Some of these are handled between the GPs; others arise between LPs and GPs at a later date and must be resolved using "partnership behavior." These latter items reflect the impossibility of creating a contract that covers every contingency.

The internal GP matters concern compensation and retention of GPs, in particular the carry split and the vesting schedule. The carry split, or the division of profits among the GPs, varies among firms and among funds. In some firms, most of the profits accrue to the older GPs, even if the younger investors are providing the bulk of the day-to-day management services. In others, there may be a standard share across the investment staff with additional shares allocated at the end of the year to reward particularly productive individuals.

The vesting schedule details the time over which the GPs earn their share of the profits. A GP who leaves a private equity organization early in the fund's life may forfeit all or some of the carry created. This helps ensure that the GPs stay with the fund during the difficult days of its early life. While these issues are addressed in agreements between the GPs, they are rarely discussed in the contracts between the GPs and LPs.

Much of LP–GP relations depend on the ephemeral notion of "partnership behavior." In all but the most extreme circumstances, the LPs and GPs are stuck with each other. The investments are illiquid, long term, and uncertain, and active investing can make a difference in the situation's outcome. While the LP agreement attempts to regulate certain aspects of the fund's management, there is considerable scope for interpretation.

One of the most significant grey areas involves the valuation of the portfolio. Discussed in greater detail in Chapters 4 and 9, portfolio valuation, especially for VC firms, is highly uncertain. It reflects uncertainties about the companies' progress and prospects—especially for early-stage companies, but even for buyouts undergoing substantial change. Moreover, events might transpire to prove a thoughtful valuation completely wrong: PA Semi, an early-stage semiconductor company, received funding at a very high valuation on the assumption that Apple would adopt its chips. A few months later, Apple decided to use a chip from a different maker. What was PA Semi's value then? The company recovered and adapted its chip to target different markets. Three years later, it was purchased by none other than Apple for $278 million.[84] How many different valuations might PA Semi have had during its odyssey? At every step of the way, the LPs had to trust that the GPs were valuing the company based on their best possible estimate, neither depressing the value to enhance an eventual exit nor boosting it to falsely increase the fund's value.

Another area of uncertainty is the degree of latitude allowed between following the mandate enshrined in the partnership agreement and investing opportunistically. In many cases, a certain percentage of the fund can be invested opportunistically. Sometimes new technologies arise, sometimes new geographies open. In a case of wholesale departure from the agreement—a fund raised to invest in life sciences decides to invest in cleantech—clearly the GP would need to consult with the LP advisory board, but the balance between adhering to the mandate at the cost of returns and incoherent opportunism in pursuit of returns can be difficult to strike.

This raises the more fundamental question of diversification overall, and the level and dimensions at which it should occur. Different GPs treat diversification differently. For instance, Warburg Pincus, a top-tier private equity firm, raises a single fund and invests across a host of stages, geographies, and industries. Sequoia Capital initially raised a number of different funds, some for U.S. early stage, others for India, another for China. To gain access to the U.S. fund, known for investing in Google and PayPal, an LP had to agree to invest in one of the other funds until the fall of 2009, when the firm decided to roll them together. Does an LP choose a GP with faith that the GP will create the best possible returns, regardless of geography and sector? Or does the LP decide to invest in China, U.S. early-stage technology, European growth equity, but not India, and expect the GPs to carry out its wishes? In short, one is asking, "How active should the GPs be? And what sort of activity should be occurring?" The answer varies.

Further complicating the matter, incentives for GPs, powerful though they are, have inexact measures. While "20 percent of the gains" seems very specific, gains can be measured at different times. As is discussed in Chapter 7, distributions are complicated. The value at which a company goes public can differ substantially from that at which the stock is distributed to the LPs and differ yet again from the value it actually generates for the LP when sold. What value should be used in calculating the "gain"? The answer to this question determines whether GPs are incented simply to list the stock, to try to support its value, or to sell the stock and distribute the cash. Furthermore, information is asymmetric. An entrepreneur has different information from the GP, and the GP may have different information from the LP. Information travels winding paths in private equity, and even with the best of intentions, what one person says may not be what another person hears.

In an effort to codify the unwritten aspects of the LP–GP relationship, the LP trade group, the Institutional Limited Partners Association (ILPA), issued the ILPA Private Equity Principles in 2009. Updated in 2011 and endorsed by a substantial number of private equity firms, it set out a list of best practices around alignment of interests, governance, and transparency, shown in Table 2.3. Ironically, one might note that in private equity, where money comes with governance and that governance—active investing—is said to create value, LPs have almost no governance rights at all.

THE FUND-RAISING CYCLE: THE MATING HABITS OF GPs and LPs

A student at a top business school seeking a job with a private equity firm realized, sensibly enough, that he should start with the firms that were raising money. To his vast annoyance, he discovered that there is no central repository for that information. Welcome to the world of *private* equity. The general assumption is that if the firm wants you to know it is raising money, you will know. And if you don't, there's usually a pretty good reason.

---

[84] Erika Brown, Elizabeth Corcoran and Brian Caulfield, "Apple Buys Chip Designer," *Forbes.com*, April 23, 2008, http://www.forbes.com/2008/04/23/apple-buys-pasemi-tech-ebiz-cz_eb_0422apple.html.

Table 2.3 ILPA Best Practices in Private Equity Partnerships

Alignment of Interest	
The agreed profit split in commingled funds has typically worked well to align interests, but tightened distribution provisions must become the norm in order to avoid clawback situations.	The general partners should have a substantial equity interest in the fund to maintain a strong alignment of interests with the limited partners, and a high percentage of the amount should be in cash as opposed to being contributed through the waiver of the management fee.
Clawbacks must be strengthened so that when they are required, they are fully and timely repaid.	Changes in tax law that personally affect members of a general partner should not be passed on to limited partners in the fund.
Management fees should cover normal operating costs for the firm and its principals and should not be excessive.	Fees and carried interest generated by the general partners of a fund should be directed predominantly to the professional staff and expenses related to the success of that fund.
All transaction and monitoring fees charged by the general partner should accrue to the benefit of the fund, including offsetting management fees and partnership expenses during the life of the fund.	

Governance	
General Partners should reinforce their duty of care. The "gross negligence, fraud, and willful misconduct" indemnification and exculpation standard should be the floor in terms of what is agreed to by limited partners. Recent efforts by the general partner to (1) reduce all duties to the fullest extent of the law, (2) demand the waiver of broad categories of conflicts of interests, and (3) allow it to act in its sole discretion even when a conflict exists should be avoided.	A super-majority in interest of the limited partners should have the ability to elect to dissolve the fund or remove the general partner without cause. A majority in interest of the limited partners should have the ability to elect to effectuate an early termination or suspension of the investment period without cause.
Investments made by the general partners should be consistent with the investment strategy that was described when the fund was raised.	A "key person" or "for cause" event should result in an automatic suspension of the investment period with an affirmative vote required to reinstate it.
The general partner should recognize the importance of time diversification during the stated investment period as well as industry diversification within the portfolio.	The auditor of a private equity fund should be independent and focused on the best interests of the partnership and its limited partners, rather than the interests of the general partner.
	Limited Partner Advisory Committee meeting processes and procedures should be adopted and standardized across the industry to allow this sub-body of the limited partners to effectively serve its role.

(*continued*)

Table 2.3 (*Continued*)

Transparency	
Fee and carried interest calculations should be transparent and subject to limited partner and independent auditor review and certification.	Investors in private equity funds should have greater transparency as requested with respect to relevant information pertaining to the general partner.
Detailed valuation and financial information related to the portfolio companies should be made available as requested on a quarterly basis.	All proprietary information should be protected from public disclosure.

Source: Institutional Limited Partners Association, *Private Equity Principles: Best Practices in Private Equity Partnerships*, September 8, 2009, 3–5, http://ilpa.org/ilpa-private-equity-principles/accessed June 30, 2010. Used with permission.

The principal document for fund-raising is a PPM (private placement memo). This is akin to the prospectus for a standard investment fund, but it also has some substantial differences. One of the primary issues for a potential private equity investor is the partnership's track record. While some big mutual fund managers, like Peter Lynch at Magellan, have built mythic reputations, it is the rare mutual fund investor who knows the pedigree of the people handling daily fund management. In private equity, however, there is little on which to judge the team's performance save the past. While any mutual fund prospectus adds a caveat to its information, saying "Past performance is no guarantee of future results," research has found, as we discuss in Chapter 9, that this is less true in private equity.[85]

LPs are keenly interested in track records because they are investing in a blind pool with long holding periods. The GPs affect the results of the portfolio through active investing. Therefore, the LPs want to know what the GPs have invested in, with what results, and how the GPs have interacted with the companies. To what degree do they attract their own deals? (This is known as proprietary deal flow and is discussed in more depth in Chapter 3.) What do they bring to the companies apart from money? What difficult situations have they encountered, and how have they resolved them? The LPs cannot walk away from their investment; they need to know that if the GPs find themselves in a difficult situation, they will use every effort to remedy it.

Another significant LP concern is the experience of the GPs, both individually and as a team. Some firms have specific processes through which they acquire and vet deals; LPs want to know this and GPs want to explain it, as such a process can act as a differentiator. The GPs detail how long they have worked together, the unique skills each brings to the partnership, and how the partnership is more than the sum of its parts. Any changes to personnel must be described.

LPs do not like surprises. Given the multitude of changes that can occur over the decade of a fund's life, they want to control as many uncertainties as possible. One way of doing that is to back a team that has succeeded in the past and plans to continue doing exactly the same thing it has done successfully before.

With this emphasis on history and experience, the situation of a first-time fund is precarious in the extreme. LPs are notoriously unwilling to fund new groups, even groups spinning out on their own after working in a larger organization. This wariness stems from the difficulty of attributing performance. While these individuals may have created stunning results in their former organization, the environment has changed. As a veteran venture capitalist says, "Your partners cannot

---

[85] Steven Kaplan and Antoinette Schoar, "Private Equity Performance: Returns, Persistence, and Capital Flows," *Journal of Finance* 60, no. 4 (2005): 1791–1823.

make you do something smart, but they can keep you from doing something stupid." Perhaps the one person who asked the one question that kept this group from doing something stupid stayed behind or retired. Success, as the proverb goes, has many parents.

To compensate, first-time funds often offer preferential terms to their early investors. They may charge lower fees or carry. They often work hard to attract a "cornerstone" investor, which contributes a substantial portion of the fund in exchange for a share of the fee income.

But all first-time funds, and even many established funds, have horror stories of raising money only after years of meetings. Some top-tier firms can raise funds in weeks or a few months; but by late 2010, firms averaged 19.8 months between the first and final closes of their funds, twice the time needed in 2004.[86]

Some LPs, though, make a specialty of funding first-time funds. A few funds-of-funds, such as Grove Street Advisors and FLAG, consciously seek those organizations that offer promises to be the next generation of top-tier firms, aware that access will be available only in the first few funds. Thereafter, the list of LPs will be set. As a result, these funds-of-funds have staff dedicated to performing the due diligence involved in assessing a firm's desirability. What better differentiator than to turn that skill toward first-time funds, especially if doing so will secure allocations for its LPs in future fund-raising?

DUE DILIGENCE AND ACCESS

We have mentioned that one of the services provided by funds-of-funds and other intermediaries is due diligence. This process of deep questioning stems from the informational asymmetries rife in private equity: there are many different layers of truth, and there are structural incentives to tell one version and not another deeper one. A fund-of-funds may trumpet that it invested its clients' money with Sequoia Capital, but only on deeper questioning will it reveal that this transaction occurred two funds ago. This is simply part of the process. In its way, this is a mating game, and one puts the best possible face on one's history.

The due diligence around a fund investment involves questions from both parties: Is this a good investment for the LP? And is this a good LP for the GP? A similar process of due diligence occurs between the GP and the entrepreneur, as we shall see in Chapter 3.

For the LP, there are two significant concerns: the fit between the fund's objectives and its own; and the GPs' track record. As mentioned earlier, the record is important because the only real guide to future performance is the past, and the only link between the two is personnel. If this group did well in the past, one can hope they will continue to do so in the future.

The question of fit for the LP depends on the institution's goals and size. Many LPs have explicit targets for asset allocation and need to invest a certain amount in a specific type of private equity, whether early stage or international or buyouts. Just as an individual investor seeks to diversify, an LP will do the same, looking for exposure to different industries, geographies, sizes, and stages of investment. The fund's strategy, as detailed in the PPM, must meet this need. LPs will also need a GP that is efficiently sized—a multibillion-dollar pension fund has difficulty managing multiple $50 million commitments to VC funds, and a $100 million family office would be dangerously concentrated if it chooses to put its entire fund with a buyout firm.

Evaluating the fit between a GP and an LP from the GP's perspective is somewhat more nuanced. GPs first seek LPs who are reliable. The permanency of funds is crucial because the GP has to trust that the LP will be able to respond to a capital call. Not only that, but a reliable stable of

---

[86] Preqin data in "Global PE Fundraising Slow But Improving: Preqin," October 1, 2010, http://www.preqin.com/item/global-pe-fundraising-slow-but-improving-preqin/102/3001, accessed November 10, 2010.

LPs reduces the amount of time needed to raise a follow-on fund, thereby benefiting all parties—the GPs, who can get back to investing more quickly, and the LPs, who suffer the GP distraction of fund-raising for less time.

Part of the criteria that LPs and GPs use to assess each other's desirability as partners is reputation. This comes in part from the track record but also from credentialing. A new fund with backing from Yale or Princeton will be considerably more credentialed than one with backing from less prestigious organizations. An experienced LP has its own credentials, and its commitment is a vote of confidence in the GP. For a new LP, to get into an exclusive fund is seen as recognition that one brings "something more than money"—possibly access to technological insight or geographic balance. For a second-tier GP, investment by a respected LP indicates possible elevation in the hierarchy.

Rather than mere brand awareness, the importance of credentials in private equity arises from the themes developed over the course of this chapter: illiquidity and the blind pool. For an LP investing in a long-term asset where the management of the fund is placed so completely in the hands of the GP, reputation informs expectations of future performance. For the GPs, respected LPs help attract prospective entrepreneurs and can even assist in recruiting other GPs, creating a good reputation for the firm. A strong firm reputation allows the partnership to create a platform that extends across generations of partners. Firms that can do this enjoy greater flexibility; they become trusted to find good investments regardless of the PPM, rather than being constrained only to the extent of their mandate.

PATTERNS OF PRIVATE EQUITY FUND-RAISING

The inflows of money into private equity overall and to VC and buyouts specifically have varied dramatically over time, as we saw in Figure 1.1 and will explore in more depth in Chapter 13. In the late 1970s and early 1980s, VC experienced a boom. Attracted by the impressive returns (and the clarification of the "prudent man" rule) money flowed into VC funds. Less experienced VC firms raised funds, which they had to invest, bidding up the prices of companies. With higher cost bases, overall returns to VC fell in the mid-1980s. Meanwhile, buyouts, which had been laboring in relative obscurity, started generating impressive returns. Money that would have gone to VC went to buyout funds instead and was joined by capital from the public pension funds, which found buyouts easier to access because of their larger size. Buyouts boomed in the late 1980s and crashed along with private equity in general in the early 1990s. The later 1990s marked a bubble for VC. Not only did VC firms raise excessively large funds and invest in overpriced, undifferentiated companies, but they took the companies public at an early stage, subjecting them to public market scrutiny while they still needed private market support and funding. After the NASDAQ crash, inflows to VC funds fell to one-tenth of their anomalous peak of $158 billion in 2000. At the same time, buoyed by cheap debt, buyout firms raised almost half a trillion dollars at their 2007 peak, only to have the market collapse in 2008.

Paul Gompers and Josh Lerner[87] explore the forces that influenced VC fund-raising between 1972 and 1994, during the early part of the industry's history. The regulatory changes around pension funds, along with changes in capital gains tax rates, economic growth, R&D spending, and firm-specific performance and reputation all affect fund-raising, along with demand for VC investment services. Some of these forces work in interesting ways: capital gains tax rate reductions, for instance, make it more attractive for an individual to start a company that, if successful, will generate substantial capital gains.

---

[87] Paul Gompers and Josh Lerner, "What Drives Venture Capital Fundraising?" *Brookings Papers on Economic Activity, Microeconomics* 2 (1998): 149–204.

CONCLUSION

In looking forward to the rest of this book, we now have a solid understanding of LPs and GPs, their concerns, and at least some of the nuances of their relationships. We understand how funds are raised and the intermediaries that are involved in that process. We have also presented the themes—the impacts of illiquidity, alignment of interest, asymmetry of information, and the need for activity—that are developed throughout the rest of the book.

Illiquidity means that these actors are stuck. If I own a public stock and don't like what management is doing, I can sell it. I may lose money, but I can get out of the position. Selling my shares in a private equity fund is difficult, costly, and may result in my exclusion from investing with that particular fund ever again. If at all possible, LPs and GPs are motivated to resolve their difficulties. In those situations where LP–GP difficulties become public and acrimonious, the GPs usually suffer significant reputational damage.

Information asymmetry is another major theme. The degree to which something is known or unknown may be as important as the actual fact. A biotech company may tell potential investors that it has certain patents filed. It may take additional investigation, however, before the GPs learn that in this particular domain, patents are relatively easy to avoid and therefore provide far less secure protection than one might assume. Many of the terms in the LP agreement are attempts by the LPs to reduce the information asymmetries that accompany their limited liability.

To manage both the information asymmetry and illiquidity, interests have to be aligned. It is to everyone's benefit to share as much information as possible and to resolve difficult situations amicably. When the GPs work to their own best interest, which also benefits the LPs, powerful incentives are created. This explains the intuitive appeal of carried interest (even though, as Gompers and Lerner describe, in the early stages of a fund's life, mere reputation building outweighs financial gains as a driver). The power of interest alignment explains the challenges behind building corporate venture capital departments and public pension fund investment departments, where the investors are compensated through salary rather than carried interest. Throughout the remainder of this book, interest alignment is an important lens to use when considering a situation. If interests are not aligned, note the ways in which a situation can be turned to a particular party's advantage, and try to determine ways in which the misalignment could be corrected.

Private equity has many gaps—in information, in communication, and in knowledge. Activity is required to resolve these gaps. One cannot wait for a PPM to fall in one's lap; the student cannot look up a list of the GPs raising funds. LPs seeking GPs with good track records need to make calls, hire intermediaries, and talk with other LPs and GPs. They need to sell themselves as good LPs to be allowed to invest in a top-tier GP fund, odd though that may seem. GPs seeking reliable LPs need to use all of their resources—placement agents, other GPs, friends, alumni at their university. The portfolio—whether the LP's portfolio of GPs or the GP's portfolio of companies—requires active management. One can even argue that GPs need to manage their portfolio of LPs, by having frequent meetings, supplying information, and generally exhibiting the kind of partnership behavior that inspires the LP to think the better of the GP in the inevitable difficult situations.

As we move into Chapter 3, discussing the due diligence and evaluation of deals, we will observe that many dynamics of the LP–GP relationship also play out between the GPs and entrepreneurs. Here again, illiquidity, alignment of interests, information asymmetry, and activity play important roles in influencing behavior.

QUESTIONS

1. What are the major subcategories of private equity, and how do their investment approaches differ?
2. What are the advantages of setting up a private equity firm as an LLC?
3. What are the four major similarities for private equity transactions?

4. How might a GP be successful in raising a first-time fund without a track record?

5. Why would a corporation, like Intel, want to invest in private equity?

6. Which type of LP might be inclined to increase its private equity investment allocation going forward? Why?

7. What is the primary role of a fund-of-funds, and what type of investor is likely to invest in one?

8. Why have funds-of-funds received criticism?

9. In the LPA, how are the interests of the LP and GP aligned?

10. What is the purpose of a "concentration limit"?

11. How does the use of leverage vary among the different types of private equity firms?

12. Why have larger private equity firms (in terms of assets under management) come under scrutiny regarding their management fee structure?

13. If a firm with a $5 billion fund charges a 2 percent management fee for eight years, and 20 percent carried interest on all profits, and earns a 3× return on its investments, what is the true multiple of investment and IRR for the LP? (Assume that investments are made equally at the beginning of the first through fifth years, the holding period of each investment is five years, and there are no transaction fees.)

14. In question 13, what if the fund is structured so that instead of having to return drawdown capital, the manager needs to return only the capital that was actually invested in companies (i.e., not including management fees). How would the investment multiple and IRR change?

Chapter 3

Deal Sourcing and Evaluation—Not as Easy as it Looks

The second part of the private equity cycle involves investing. At first, one might ask how hard this part of the process really is—according to Figure 3.1, the number of companies receiving private equity each year has averaged more than 4,500 annually for the past decade in the United States alone. In addition, average investment per company also trends upward. Clearly, investors are finding deals and entrepreneurs are finding investors. Venture capital (VC) lore is replete with stories of "the next big thing" found in a garage or a dorm room. Michael Dell did indeed build computers in his dorm room before Joel Adams, then at Fostin Capital, invested $750,000 in the first outside funding Dell Computer ever raised. This investment was worth $470 million in 2000.[1] Intel, Apple, eBay, Compaq, and Google all received VC funding and became block-busters. How hard can it be?

The short answer is, very. Intel, Apple, eBay, Compaq, and Google are listed in the "anti-portfolio" maintained by Bessemer Venture Partners (BVP), employer of one of the authors of this volume. BVP was offered the chance to invest in each of these—and others, including PayPal, A123 Systems, and Federal Express. For one reason or another, the partners turned them down. In the case of Google, the anti-portfolio recounts:

> A friend of David Cowan's [a BVP partner] was renting her garage to Sergey and Larry [Google's cofounders] and told David he should really look into these smart Stanford students building a new search engine. Students? A search engine? David made anti-portfolio history by asking his friend, 'Is there any way to leave your house without going anywhere near the garage?'[2]

In the case of Federal Express, the BVP partners turned down the opportunity seven times. Six times, one can argue that they were right. That is the difficulty—you can be right six times in refusing a deal and then wrong. Deal selection is a dynamic process.

The account of "the ones that got away" from a top-tier VC firm emphasizes the difficulty of evaluating deals. Information gaps (asymmetries) are widespread. Determining a venture's

---

[1] Felda Hardymon, Josh Lerner, and Ann Leamon, "Adams Capital Management: March 2002," HBS Case No. 803-143 (Boston: HBS Publishing, 2003), 2–4.

[2] www.bvp.com/antiportfolio, accessed March 20, 2010.

FIGURE 3.1   Number of companies funded, 1989–2009

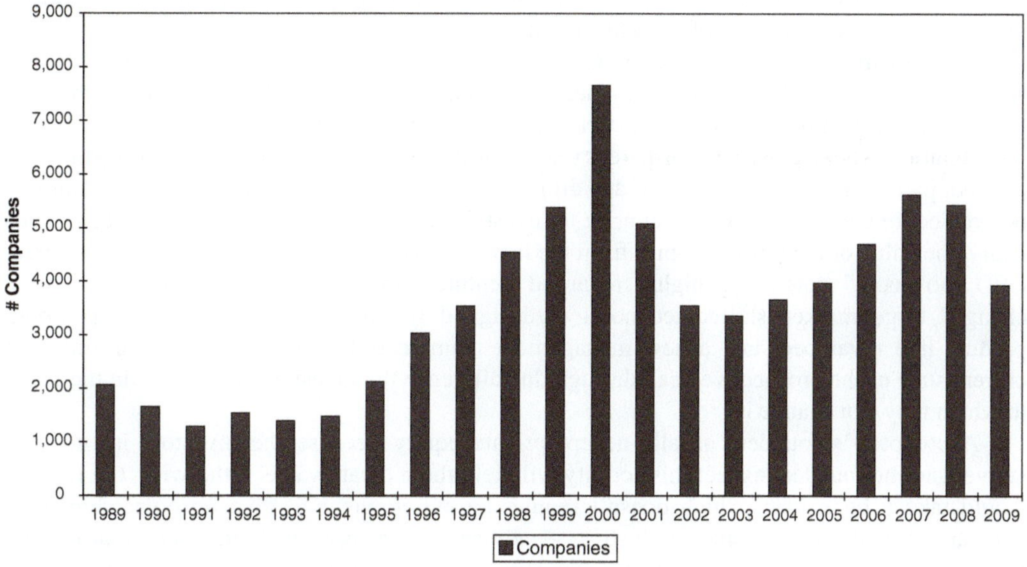

Source: Thomson Reuters private equity database, accessed September 10, 2010.

promise is fraught with difficulty. In an early-stage deal, the team may never have worked together, the technology is unproven, and the market is unknown. The founding team is buoyant with optimism. The VC investor may not have the same amount of information or optimism.

These asymmetries are not confined to early-stage deals. In a buyout, the depth of a target's malaise is hard to determine. With a corporate divestiture, the parent has an incentive to paint the future in rosy hues. Even with the best of intentions, it is challenging to determine the underlying profitability of a division that will be spun off as a stand-alone entity. Management, with future incentives based on meeting or surpassing various goals, may have an incentive to "sandbag," or suppress expectations. Whom does the investor believe?

The private equity firm must not just *find* a deal, but also assess it and become comfortable with the facts, the unknowns, and its ability to influence the outcome. For the entrepreneur, finding an investor is difficult. Moreover, an investor must provide more than just money: here again, we encounter the importance of activity and the real difference in outcome that an investor can create.

To source a deal successfully, the private equity investor must develop a view of the industry, the sector, and the company's place in it and then begin a conversation that uncovers the beliefs and fears of the other parties. The entrepreneur must convey her own information clearly and be honest about the areas of uncertainty. It helps the process if the entrepreneur has led other successful start-ups or knows the private equity firm. The entrepreneur needs to research potential investors and approach an appropriate one—an early-stage biotechnology project should not approach a later-stage IT investor for funding. After a period of investigation and negotiation, the investor may issue a term sheet (or in some cases, a letter of intent, or LOI) that proposes a deal addressing each party's concerns.

When several firms are contesting the deal, the entrepreneur will have the happy experience of choosing an investor. During the process, the private equity firm will be trying to position itself to win the deal by convincing the management team that it can best complete the transaction and/ or add value to the company. Winning a deal sometimes involves managing an auction or a syndicate of investors, sometimes with differing amounts of capital and levels of expertise. Finally, especially in VC, an existing deal may need additional funding. This chapter explores all these matters from both sides of the table, the investor and the entrepreneur.

Many of the themes introduced in Chapter 2—illiquidity, information gaps (asymmetries), and the importance of hands-on governance—continue to be developed here. Not everything can be written down—this is another long-term relationship in which the participants face numerous uncertainties. There must be transparency and partnership behavior. Information asymmetries abound, particularly in the process of due diligence, as the investing team examines the company before deciding whether and at what price to invest. Finally, part of the uncertainty and, paradoxically, the value of the process comes from the investor's activity and governance. "I never fired a CEO too soon," noted one highly regarded venture capitalist. Management teams can be changed, target markets shifted, technology redesigned. In buyouts, a division can be spun out, a product line revamped, and a new management team recruited. Along with determining the current state of the prospective deal, through due diligence the investors also ascertain the degree to which they can change it.

A company's founders usually accept private equity because the investors intend to be active, and the founders expect this activity will help them create value. Otherwise, the founders would take a bank loan, which doesn't require an entrepreneur to give up ownership in the company. Private equity comes with strings—advice, governance, meddling—and that is where the value lies. Part of the importance in choosing the right investor (and company) is this very advice: different individuals have different skills and different approaches, so one investor or firm will have a different impact on a company's outcome than will another.

The chapter is organized as follows: first we consider how private equity firms find a deal and how an entrepreneur finds an investor. We then explore the due diligence process through which the investors determine whether they want to do the deal that they have found. We discuss the internal process that firms use to make decisions about both new deals and, in VC, subsequent financings. Finally, once a firm has decided that this is a good deal, we examine how they go about winning the deal.

FINDING THE DEAL

As with so much in private equity, there are several sides to finding a deal. The investor must find an entrepreneur looking for funds, and the entrepreneur must find an investor looking to invest. There are multiple supporting parties to the search as well, as we describe in this section.

Where to Look—Specialization vs. Diversification

Private equity firms look for investment opportunities in sectors that fit their expertise, reputation, and charter from the limited partners (LPs). Early-stage VC firms often focus on areas undergoing discontinuous change, such as information technology and life sciences. Leveraged buyout (LBO) firms may target companies undergoing generational transitions or seeking to reorganize to improve their competitive position. For a first-time fund, the inaugural deals should demonstrate the themes from the private placement memorandum (PPM) that the firm used to raise money. Yet what if a really promising deal in a different sector becomes available? How closely should a firm stick to its strategy? Isn't the whole point good returns?

The question of specialization as opposed to diversification is thorny. As we discussed in Chapter 2, LPs usually plan to allocate their assets across investment opportunities to achieve their particular goals. If their early-stage, IT-focused VC fund suddenly decides to pursue later-stage Asian investments, the LPs would be rightly concerned. Not only might they wonder whether the venture capitalists have sufficient expertise to succeed, but they may then find themselves with more Asian exposure than they wish. In the worst case, the LP might be in two funds that are competing for the same asset. Yet if an industry endures a prolonged period of poor performance—buyouts during the VC boom; life sciences during the IT boom—its practitioners may reasonably wonder whether sticking to their strategy is a sound choice.

Two papers illustrate how firms think about specialization versus diversification. Edgar Norton and Bernard Tenenbaum[3] surveyed ninety-eight VC firms about the degree of specialization in their investment strategies. Diversification is a well-known strategy for reducing unsystematic risk, or the risk specific to a company or an industry. This study, though, found that early-stage firms tended to *specialize* (thereby increasing risk) in order to share information, networks, and deal flow with other venture investors. Rather than diversifying the portfolio across different investment stages, the firms in the sample focused on a single stage or several adjacent stages, such as start-up and early stage or expansion and later stage. This makes intuitive sense, not only in terms of information sharing but also when one considers time constraints: advising emerging companies and their teams in one sector is demanding enough; doing so in two would be extremely difficult. Additionally, the authors found that specialization helped firms build their reputations and enhanced their standing in information and deal flow networks.

An earlier article by Anil K. Gupta and Harry J. Sapienza[4] examined 169 U.S.-based VC firms (27 percent of the 1987 total) to explore preferences regarding industry diversity and geographic scope in investments. The firms in the sample closely resembled the industry average at the time. Results showed that early-stage VC firms tended to prefer less industry diversity and a narrower geographic scope; corporate VC firms (the investing arms of corporations) preferred less diversity but a wider geographic scope; and larger VC firms preferred greater diversity and a wider scope. This supports the popular image of an early-stage VC firm that invests in a narrow range of companies within an hour's drive of the home office and that of a larger firm with a larger fund that must be allocated across a wider range, both in terms of industry and geography. The authors argued that VC firms must focus their portfolio strategies to attract LPs and must also offer added services and domain knowledge to attract top entrepreneurs. As we will develop in Chapter 6, entrepreneurs must consider the benefits of accepting funding from a particular VC firm based on its portfolio, reputation, and the help that the firm can be expected to provide.

The Special Role of Reputation in Private Equity

In private equity, reputation comes up repeatedly. When a company gets a loan from a bank, no one really cares which bank or which company is involved in the transaction. Not so with private investment. The importance of reputation was first identified by General D'Oriot, founder of American Research and Development (ARD) corporation, the first recognizable venture capital firm, who realized the intertwined importance of selecting the best investment opportunities, providing careful control (governance); and credentialing, or providing a reputational halo effect. In essence, an outside investor known for doing good deals created a reputation for itself that the companies in its portfolio could share. Having a well-regarded investor means that the company is well regarded. While this phenomenon is particularly evident in venture capital deals, which are so new that the only metric is

---

[3] Edgar Norton and Bernard H. Tenenbaum, "Specialization versus Diversification as a Venture Capital Investment Strategy," *Journal of Business Venturing* 8 (1993): 431–42.

[4] Anil K. Gupta and Harry J. Sapienza, "Determinants of Venture Capital Firms' Preferences Regarding the Industry Diversity and Geographic Scope of their Investments," *Journal of Business Venturing* 7, no. 5 (1992): 347–62.

the quality of its investors, it also can occur with buyouts, where investment by top-tier firms can give a struggling company breathing space as it turns itself around and then builds its own reputation.

Reputation works in a self-reinforcing cycle. A company backed by firms with good reputations has access to higher-reputation customers and service providers. It can attract higher-quality managers. This makes it more likely that the company will succeed, burnishing the reputation of its backing firms and management. The other arena in which firms earn a reputation is in their interactions with limited partners. Acting honorably toward LPs, which have entrusted their money over a long period to a blind pool on the basis of interest alignment and fiduciary duty, is a crucial aspect of a firm's reputation as well. The combination of good returns and good relationships with LPs creates a top-tier firm's reputation, which the firm then guards carefully, reinforcing careful company choice and good practices toward both companies and LPs. As Harvard Management Company's Peter Dolan has said, "Trust and reputation are the glue that keeps the private equity industry together."

For private equity firms overall, a further reason for establishing and adhering to a set of investment themes—apart from making themselves attractive to LPs and entrepreneurs—is efficiency. Each fund has a limited amount of money to be invested over a defined period, as noted in Chapter 2—usually ten years. The truly scarce resource, though, is partner time. Adhering to broad themes allows a firm to develop expertise in the efficient discovery, assessment, and management of companies. As Norton and Tenenbaum note, such specialization helps the firm unearth and assess the best opportunities for that fund as well as develop a reputation and a network.

Even if a company fits a firm's investment themes, it must also fit the firm's current needs, resources, and portfolio composition. Is it invested in a close competitor? The firm is likely to avoid the deal unless it anticipates merging the two. Does the partner who would manage the deal have time? Some firms limit their partners to a certain number of companies, and the skill sets are not particularly transferrable; the life sciences partner would not be very effective on an IT company's board.

Some buyout firms use particular approaches to deals to differentiate themselves. TPG (formerly Texas Pacific Group), for instance, is known for buying and restructuring once-great brands like J. Crew, Ducati Motorcycles, and Beringer Wines, while Bain Capital often draws on the consulting background of many of its partners to create strategic improvements. Thoma Bravo (formerly known as Golder Thoma and then GTCR) is known for platform deals.

Platform Deals

When founded in 1980 as Golder Thoma, the firm would purchase a leading company in a fragmented industry and, with management support, embark on a program of strategically acquiring competitors to consolidate the market. The company would later be taken public or sold. A representative deal was the 2002 acquisition of Prophet 21, a provider of enterprise software and services (software employed company-wide). After the investors helped it improve operating margins and acquire seven companies, Prophet 21's revenue doubled and earnings rose fourfold in less than three years. In September 2005, Prophet 21 was sold to Activant Solutions Inc.; Thoma Bravo made five times its investment on the deal.[5]

---

[5] www.thomabravo.com/about/history and www.thomabravo.com/portfolio/all/prior_investment#prophet, accessed June 14, 2010.

While specialization helps build reputations and domain expertise, it can be taken too far. Too much exposure to one sector and stage can make a firm vulnerable to market fluctuations, as many technology VC firms learned to their regret when the Internet bubble collapsed. Excessive concentration can also spread partner expertise over too many companies, reducing the assistance that can be provided and hence the company's success. Firms must guard against the fact that it is easier to add companies to a portfolio than investors to a partnership.

The concern with partner workload reflects the ongoing theme of illiquidity. All private equity deals are long term. The value of active investing depends on time spent monitoring, assisting, and managing the portfolio. The entrepreneur has accepted money from this particular firm in part because of the value that a specific general partner (GP) can bring. Once again, the source of one's money matters.

Attracting vs. Finding Deals

Once a firm has decided its general strategy for deals—sector, stage, geography, strategy—it must then find and evaluate them. Firms use two different approaches to finding deals: attracting and finding them. The choice is a matter of both philosophy and necessity.

Every firm would like to attract deals. As noted earlier, top firms attract top entrepreneurs because of the greater likelihood of success due to association with those firms. In fact, top-tier firms attract not just top deals, but a great majority of all available deals, thus giving them a broader pool to choose from. Increased deal flow is a function of a firm's record. Accel, Benchmark, Bessemer Venture Partners anti-portfolio and all, Greylock, Kleiner Perkins, MPM Capital, New Enterprise Associates (NEA), Sequoia, and Sprout are among the VC firms that attract deals. Among buyout groups, Apollo, Bain Capital, Blackstone, Carlyle, Kohlberg Kravis Roberts (KKR), and TPG attract the largest deals; the smaller market is more fragmented. Firms with good records in well-defined niches—Lion Capital in European consumer goods; Montagu Private Equity in European family-owned businesses; Brazos Private Equity Partners in family-owned businesses in the U.S. Southwest—attract deals in that sector. In general, though, being a deal attractor is a status to be striven for but rarely achieved. Especially in buyouts, most deals are done through auctions, which are described later.

The other approach is finding deals. If attracting deals is having apples fall in your lap, finding deals is shaking the tree. As this analogy indicates, finding deals is more difficult but also more proactive, which can convey some important benefits. We explore both approaches here, starting with proprietary deals.

Proprietary Deals

With a proprietary deal, the entrepreneur comes directly to the firm or GP. The GP is intimately involved with the deal as it develops. Said one investor, "Ah, proprietary deals. Everything is advantageous—provided they work out."

The advantages of proprietary deals are familiarity, differentiation, and, often, price. Because the entrepreneur has chosen the investor, the GPs come to know the deal intimately. Proprietary deals occur in both the VC and buyout spheres. A brand-new "seed" stage company—one that is just developing its technology—can present itself to a firm, as can a late-stage buyout. Sometimes a GP will create a company to develop a technology, recruiting and funding the initial team. A later-stage company may specifically ask a firm to lead or invest in a financing. Entrepreneurs decide to approach a firm because their research shows it has expertise in a particular area, a strong reputation, or there is a personal connection with the GP.

The GPs working on a proprietary deal have the benefit of time because the deal usually is not contested. They can become well acquainted with the technology or the company's business, reducing uncertainty. This may allow them to better price the deal and manage it more effectively.

Moreover, there is a public relations factor—if the deal succeeds, there is no doubt about the firm that backed it.

Proprietary deals are easily as important to buyout firms as they are to VC operations. Many buyout transactions are widely broadcast, leading to auctions that are very efficient and leave little chance for easy gains. While an auction might produce the highest price to the seller, it also presents risks to all parties. Buyout firms worry that they might spend large amounts of time, personnel, and money doing due diligence on a company up for auction, only to have someone else win the deal.[6] The seller worries that the auction will fail, causing embarrassment and generally setting the company back due to the management team's distraction during the process.

A further concern is the degree to which information is dispersed. Qualified buyers, often competitors, can receive full access to the company's internal information through both the material created by the investment bank (called a bank book or a confidential information memorandum, or CIM) and the data room, an absolute trove of corporate detail. In 2008, the Chinese subway media company Digital Media Group (DMG) went up for sale. The two most assiduous suitors were its major competitors. After the sale fell through, DMG had to compete with both of them in bidding for Shanghai's subway advertising contract.[7]

Firms try to limit this problem by using "tiered" auctions. In these, an auction occurs over several rounds—for instance, initially bids must be over $100 million, then $150 million, and so on. As the field of acquirers is winnowed down, the remaining firms receive access to greater detail about the company's performance and prospects.

The embarrassment of a failed auction makes the management or owner of a buyout target eager to avoid one, even at some reduction in price. The owners may approach an individual buyout firm either directly or through an investment bank, providing a proprietary deal.

Just as with VC firms, proprietary buyout deals allow the firm time to become familiar with the company and give it influence over the eventual price. But with buyouts, the purchaser does not have free rein, since the seller can always decide to turn the deal over to an auction or not sell at all. Chris Masterson of Montagu Private Equity, a London-based mid-market buyout firm, described the process of negotiating a deal with a family-owned business:

> Most of the time, you've got the founder who wants to get some liquidity, some of the family wants to be involved, some doesn't. You don't know what they want. So we ask them, right up front. And it's disarming for them. They know everything about their industry, but then they come down here to London and into our building that looks like the Sistine Chapel, and they're nervous. They've never done a buyout before. And for us to ask them what they want—and it's very rarely just money—is extremely powerful. It puts the ball in their court. We position our offer that, as long as it's reasonable, we'll give them what they want. And we usually can do it.[8]

Beyond pricing power, proprietary deals have a powerful demonstration effect to many constituencies, most importantly LPs. Most firms' fund-raising documents mention the number of proprietary deals or the initiatives under way to develop them. These also distinguish a firm to potential employees (of both the firm and the portfolio companies) and to other private equity firms. The allure of reciprocal invitations to proprietary deals can give a firm access to another firm's deals, possibly at a favorable price. We explore the dynamics behind such deal sharing

---

[6] Traditionally, if the negotiations reached a certain point and the target chose a competing bid, it had to pay the jilted suitor a "break-up fee" to compensate for those incurred expenses.

[7] For details, see Josh Lerner, Felda Hardymon, and Ann Leamon, "Digital Media Group: The Shanghai Bid," HBS Case No. 810-097 (Boston: HBS Publishing, 2010).

[8] Felda Hardymon, Josh Lerner, and Ann Leamon, "Montagu Private Equity (A)," HBS Case No. 804-051 (Boston: HBS Publishing, 2005), 8.

(syndication) later in this chapter. Finally, a reputation for attracting proprietary deals enhances a firm's reputation with service providers such as investment banks and other deal brokers.

As one might expect with such substantial benefits, proprietary deals involve a large amount of risk. The reputational risk is sufficient that many VC firms keep their extremely early deals under wraps (in industry jargon, "in stealth") until they raise their first outside financing. For buyouts, the advantages of avoiding an auction, along with the greater understanding of the seller's motivations and situation, outweigh most of the risk of a proprietary buyout. A string of bad proprietary deals, however, would lead LPs to question the firm's sagacity.

Proactive Deal Sourcing

Most firms also have a proactive deal-sourcing effort. This requires that the GPs develop an in-depth knowledge of their sector of interest, often by creating a so-called road map.

In a road map, GPs describe the future they anticipate in sectors that match their expertise—biotech and health care, software and telecoms, energy and clean technology, for instance—and the potential for innovation. They develop a deep knowledge of the opportunities and potential pitfalls in the sector. For instance, they may believe that Indian real estate is a good opportunity, but only in the residential sector, because the industrial space may be prone to higher regulatory risks.

They then look for companies in myriad ways—attending conferences and trade shows, reading industry journals, and developing relationships with thought-leaders in the field. Sometimes they may hire industry experts either as consultants or as entrepreneurs in residence (more on these in Chapter 11) for access to their expertise and networks. Mostly, they ask questions and listen. Few dinner companions are more engaging than private equity practitioners.

Some firms have institutionalized the deal-sourcing process. Two Boston-based growth equity firms, TA Associates and Summit Partners, use an approach of "dialing for deals." They hire smart recent college graduates, who learn about an industry's sizable privately held companies. The analysts then cold-call the CEO or CFO and ask if the company would consider taking private equity financing. To the astonishment of all shy people, this technique has been effective; both of these firms are regularly ranked in the top quartile. Many private companies never consider taking private equity for any number of reasons—the founders may not have thought of it, they don't think they qualify, or they have been too busy building and managing the operation. Having someone approach them, though, opens up the possibility. This is, however, an approach suited only to companies that have reached a size sufficient to generate publicly available information on their business, prospects, and financials.

A more widely used approach in finding deals is intermediaries, such as banks, stock-brokers, friends, accountants, lawyers, and business development officers within the companies. Each has a different set of motivations and incentives, which the GP and the entrepreneur must keep in mind.

Friends are perhaps the most transparent. A friend of the VC may be motivated by sheer altruism—"Here's this neat company/founder, and my VC friend should learn about it"—like David Cowan's friend whose garage he avoided at such cost. Others may be more self-interested; they may have invested in the company already as an angel or may receive a finder's fee, usually a percentage of the capital raised. Another possible motivator is the validation that VC investment conveys, or the possibility that the institutional investor will buy out the positions of earlier investors, giving them liquidity at a gain. With buyouts, friends can play similar roles.

Commercial bankers know of interesting companies across the spectrum of size and viability. Start-ups need banking services, and a bank is eager to contribute to its client's success. A bank may also refer a company to a private equity provider if the client wants a loan that is beyond the scope of the normal banking services or would violate standard lending practices.

Banks may also want to increase their credibility with venture capitalists to expand their list of VC-backed customers. Although private equity is an illiquid asset to investors, it provides liquidity to a bank. A company raises several million dollars and places it in a checking or money market account. It then gradually draws down the money as it develops the product/technology, only to raise another round before the money is exhausted. This offsets the less liquid assets (loans) on the bank's balance sheet.

Banking on (and for) Start-Ups

Silicon Valley Bank (SVB) in California is the largest technology lender in the world. SVB maintains good relations with the leading venture capitalists and offers venture debt to their early-stage start-ups, receiving interest and principal payments along with warrants, the right to purchase stock at a set price in the future. Sometimes SVB also receives the right to invest in future rounds. Traditional banks usually shy away from lending to start-ups due to their risk of failure, but SVB protects itself in two unique ways. First, the bank knows that top-tier VC firms almost always fund several rounds for their portfolio companies, increasing the likelihood that the bank loan will be paid off before the company runs out of money. SVB's long history of interactions with VC firms makes it a respected partner whose interests the investors protect. Secondly, if the company fails, its intellectual property can be sold as a second means of repayment, and SVB knows how to monetize these assets. This allows the bank to conform to the classic belt-and-suspenders requirement that a loan must have two means of repayment. For SVB, it is an equity infusion or sale of the intellectual property; with more conventional banks, it is operating cash flow or the value of the underlying assets.[9]

Investment bankers facilitate mergers, acquisitions, buyouts and initial public offerings (IPOs). Their role in exits is described in Chapter 7; they also, however, help source investment opportunities especially for buyout firms. The owner or management of a company in play often chooses an investment bank to represent it, typically following a "beauty contest." In these meetings, a number of banks present their strategies for representing the company and the price they would expect to set. The chosen investment bank then creates the bank book described earlier and makes introductions to interested groups.

Investment banks do not receive a fee for introducing a target to a buyout firm. When a transaction occurs, though, it receives payment through a variety of fees, including arrangement fees for creating financing packages, commitment fees for providing the loan (commercial banks can also receive commitment fees), and syndicate fees if it leads a group of banks that provide financing. All of these are contingent upon the deal's closing, but longer-term relations follow if the bank invests in the transaction through its own private equity affiliates or has recommended that its high-net-worth clients invest in those funds. In addition, it will want to maintain good relations with the GPs, in hopes of additional business.

Stockbrokers, which follow various companies and industries, may have insights into companies that are seeking to sell divisions. They must be careful to maintain the necessary regulatory distance to ensure they do not profit from inside information.

Service providers such as accountants and lawyers are another source of deals. These individuals often know good people with promising concepts because would-be entrepreneurs

---

[9] Felda Hardymon, Josh Lerner, and Ann Leamon, "Silicon Valley Bank," HBS Case No. 800-332 (Boston: HBS Publishing, 2000), 4.

often consult lawyers and accountants before founding a company. Moreover, as a company grows and starts generating cash or needing it, entrepreneurs may discuss the situation with their accountants and lawyers, who tend to suggest contact with a private equity firm.

Unlike the external intermediaries already listed, **business development officers** are executives at the company itself. Usually responsible for creating relationships with suppliers, distributors, or partner firms, they can also present the company to the private equity community as an investment opportunity.

In each case, understanding the intermediaries' motivation is important. A commercial bank may want to add clients in a certain sector. The investment bank is looking for fees and future opportunities. Lawyers and accountants want the company to survive and continue consuming their services. Business development officers may see successful contacts with an investor as a way to enhance their careers. Many intermediaries may regard successful referrals as a way to burnish their credentials in the private equity industry.

The intermediary, the entrepreneur, and the private equity firm must all understand the truly scarce resource: partner time. By suggesting deals that fit the firm's profile and screening out those that do not, the intermediaries become important allies.

Yet the entrepreneur is not passive in this process. Through research and preparation, she can have a profound effect on finding not just any investor or acquirer, but the right one. Here too, the quality of the fit can profoundly affect the company's outcome.

The Entrepreneur's Perspective

Before seeking private equity investment, the entrepreneur must decide whether he is ready to raise this type of funding. If the company concept is still embryonic, the entrepreneur might be better advised to seek funding from technology development groups or angels, take out a second mortgage, or use credit cards. While it is possible to get funding with an idea and a stack of PowerPoint slides, many investors prefer to see a more developed concept. Developing the idea on one's own also emphasizes the entrepreneur's commitment, and more advanced concepts tend to be worth more money, thus allowing the entrepreneur to retain more equity.

In a growth equity or buyout situation, the owner or management team must be ready to contend with the due diligence process, to be described later, and the reality of meddlesome equity-owning investors. In the case of family-owned businesses, family dynamics and self-identity issues may appear. A company with prior investors may have complicated ownership structures and motivations to resolve.

Entrepreneurs seeking funding must develop a so-called elevator pitch—a brief (between one and three minutes) summary that describes the idea or the company, the team, and the market in just enough detail to intrigue the potential investor. Guidelines for a pitch are found in Table 3.1.

Next, the entrepreneur must decide which firms and partners to target. Everything from firm reputation and location to a specific GP's reputation and network should be considered. A sample of relevant questions to consider is listed in Table 3.2. In addition to research in databases and news articles, the entrepreneur should consult the entrepreneurs leading the firm's current and prior portfolio companies. Online references such as TheFunded.com provide opinions. In addition to the partners themselves, the availability of "helpers" should also be considered. Many private equity firms maintain operating partners who can parachute into a company and act as anything from interim CEOs through chief marketing officers. If part of the company's future value rests upon the use of these resources, their availability will have to be understood.

To meet an investor face-to-face, an entrepreneur must be active, attending conferences and workshops, and becoming involved in local- and state-level entrepreneurship programs. The owner of a buyout target usually needs access through an investment bank or service provider—or those analysts at TA and Summit.

Table 3.1   Rules for Elevator Pitches

1. Start with energy and excitement. The first sentence must grab the listener by highlighting the enormity of the problem. "Corporate databases are growing by XX percent per year, costing corporations $YY millions."

2. Make it easy. Explain in simplified form what the company does (or will do). "Our data compression system reduces the size of data warehouses while increasing the speed and efficiency of searches by 100 percent."

3. Avoid scientific details and jargon. Because the entrepreneur is often the technical founder, she wants to explain exactly how the technology works. This tends to overwhelm and turn off the audience. Instead, describe the solution without going into the details. "We use an innovative, superfast compression technology . . . "

4. Establish credibility. If the product or the problem it solves has been mentioned in a major news outlet or a noted expert is involved, use that! "Our product was developed by a professor at MIT and used in the NASA Mars program."[10]

Once the pitch has aroused interest, more information is required. The business plan can be helpful, but usually the entrepreneur must give a presentation that summarizes the plan. To do this, experts[11] recommend a set of no more than twelve PowerPoint slides, as shown in Table 3.3. If the slides are effective, the investors will want to know more—and then the process of due diligence will begin.

Table 3.2   Questions Entrepreneurs Should Ask

1. Does this firm/partner have expertise in my sector?

2. Where is the firm located? VC tends to be local; LBO transactions less so, but being nearby is still useful.

3. Has it backed companies similar to mine? Similar to those that would be my customers? My acquirers? Knowledge of the greater business ecosystem and strong networks within it help the investors guide a company.

4. How many companies has the firm/GP taken public? Greater experience means that the firm has better networks among investment bankers and the other experts involved in this process.

5. How recently did it raise a fund? Recently closed funds have longer time horizons than those that are nearing the end of their lives, when the GPs will be looking to harvest gains to show good returns when they raise their next fund.

6. What do other entrepreneurs say? A firm should be happy to supply a list of entrepreneurs it has backed, and it usually lists its portfolio on the website. Databases such as Thomson Reuters or Capital IQ can also provide a list of a firm's current and former portfolio companies with their executives.

7. What other resources can a firm supply? Some firms have dedicated human resources experts who can help portfolio companies recruit executives; some offer marketing or public relations help. While these can always be hired from outside, internal resources may be more responsive.

---

[10] Adapted from David Cowan, "Practicing the Art of Pitchcraft," *Who Has Time for This?*® January 23, 2006, http://whohastimeforthis.blogspot.com/2006/01/practicing-art-of-pitchcraft.html, accessed April 25, 2010.

[11] See for instance, Matt Cutler, mcutler@alum.mit.edu, *VC Pitch Template v1*, www.bvp.com/downloads/VC-Pitch-Template-v1.0.ppt; Brad Feld, Mobius Venture Capital, "The Torturous World of PowerPoint," www.feld.com/wp/archives/2004/06/the-torturous-world-of-powerpoint.html; Guy Kawasaki, Garage Technology Ventures, "The Zen of Business Plans," http://blog.guykawasaki.com/2006/01/the_ zen_of_busi.html #axzz0sYISXXE7; and David Cowan, Bessemer Venture Partners, "How Not to Write a Business Plan," http://whohastimeforthis.blogspot.com/2005/11/how-to-not-write-business-plan.html; all accessed August 28, 2009.

Table 3.3   The Twelve-Slide Company Presentation

1. Front slide
   a. Company name, phone number, e-mail address
   b. One line that captures what the company does

2. Market being addressed: "How big is it?"

3. Why is this market in pain?

4. Why the current solutions aren't adequate.

   a. How your solution will ease their pain.

5. Why it is ten times better than the previous solutions.

6. Who is the team that is going to build this business?

   a. How are they credible for the solution you're building? (sometimes this is slide 2)

7. What early proof points do you have?

   a. Prototypes, testimonials, early revenues, contingent purchase orders, nonrecurring engineering revenues

8. How are you going to sell it? How are you going to get leads?

9. A two-by-two matrix that shows your company and the competition on axes of your choosing such that your company is in the upper right quadrant

10. How fast can this grow?

11. Show basic financials: projections by quarter for three years for:

    a. Revenue, expenses, cash, head count

12. How much capital do you need to raise now?

    a. What milestones will you hit before you need to raise more?

Source: Chris Risley, serial CEO of seven VC-backed companies and Operating Partner at Bessemer Venture Partners, in a speech given to the Maine Center for Enterprise Development's Top Gun Program, November 9, 2009. Used with permission.

DEAL EVALUATION

Finding a deal is not enough. The investor must also assess it. As noted at the beginning of the chapter, a good deal is not always obvious; and different venture capitalists, with very successful records, differ on the importance they give various deal attributes.

Regardless, the deal will undergo scrutiny in the due diligence process, and, almost simultaneously, an internal process of partnership approval. Due diligence involves the process of reviewing the team, technology, market, distribution method, competition, and customers of the opportunity. In the internal process, the partner looks to the partnership for input, questions, and concerns. The outcome of both of these processes is the eventual decision to invest or to pass on the opportunity at that time.

Exactly what makes a VC investor decide to invest has mystified practitioners and researchers for decades. Tyebjee and Bruno[12] described venture capitalists as following an orderly process of

---

[12] Tyzoon Tyebjee and Albert Bruno, "A Model of Venture Capital Investment Activity," *Management Science* 30, no. 6 (1984): 1051–66.

FIGURE 3.2   Entrepreneur assessment criteria by venture capitalists

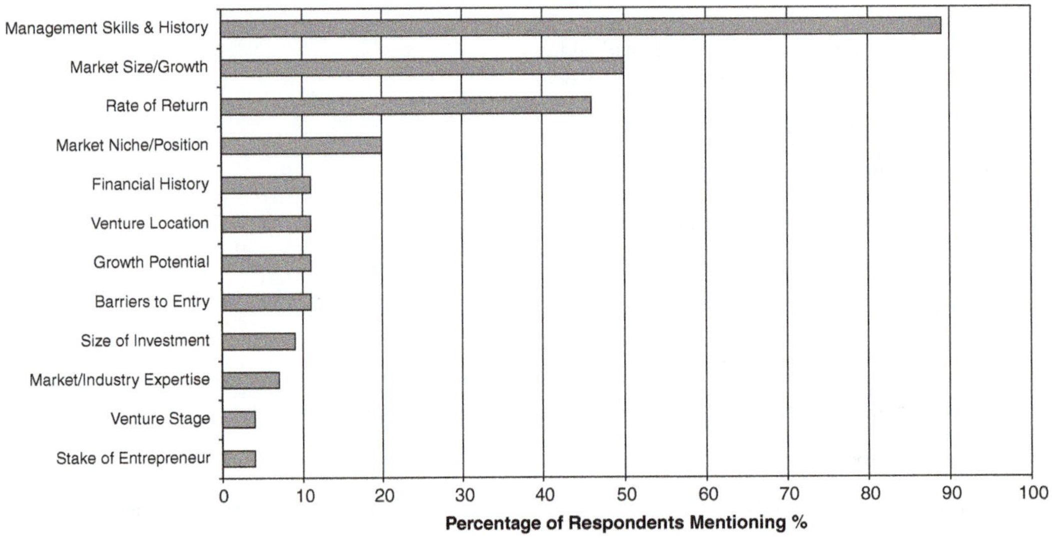

Source: Adapted from Tyzoon Tyebjee and Albert Bruno, "A Model of Venture Capital Investment Activity," *Management Science* 30, no. 6 (1984): 1045. © Management Science, 1984.

five sequential steps in finding, screening, evaluating, structuring, and managing a deal. Using data on forty-one deals from ninety venture capitalists, the authors gathered information on the factors that determined a venture's attractiveness. From these, shown in Figure 3.2, they developed five dimensions along which a deal was evaluated: Market Attractiveness (size, growth, customers); Product Differentiation (uniqueness, patents, technical edge, profit margin); Managerial Capabilities (skills in marketing, management, finance, and the entrepreneur's references); Environmental Threat Resistance (technology life cycle, barriers to entry, robustness given business cycles, downside risk protection); and Cash-Out Potential (possibilities for a merger, acquisition, or IPO). In their analysis, the expected return was determined by Market Attractiveness and Product Differentiation, while perceived risk was determined by Managerial Capabilities and Environmental Threat Resistance. The seven venture capitalists who reviewed the model and findings noted that the importance of management had been understated. The issue of management's relative importance to a venture's attractiveness is a long-standing debate.

Due Diligence

Through the process of due diligence, a GP assesses the qualities that Tyebjee and Bruno describe. The partner, often supported by at least one other individual, pursues a structured, multifaceted process of learning everything possible about the deal. This includes identifying strengths and risks, understanding the unknowns, and determining the milestones that would trigger either additional funding or corrective measures. The team must decide whether it can live with the answers it finds and the unknowns that cannot be resolved. For many teams, part of the answer derives from their ability to influence or control the uncertainties.

One of the ongoing debates among venture capitalists has been whether to back "the jockey"—the management team—or "the horse"—the business idea. Ian C. MacMillan, Robin Siegel, and P. N. Subba Narasimha surveyed one hundred venture capitalists to determine the criteria they used in deciding to invest in a new venture. Corroborating Tyebjee and Bruno's findings of the importance of management, six of the top ten most important criteria involved the entrepreneur's experience or personality. Two involved returns, and one each involved the product

Table 3.4 Entrepreneur Evaluation Criteria

Characteristic	Applies to	Percentage Naming
Capable of sustained effort	CEO	64
Thoroughly familiar with the market	CEO/Market	62
Return of at least 10× in 5–10 years	Returns	50
Demonstrated leadership previously	CEO	50
Evaluates/reacts to risk well	CEO	48
Investment can be made liquid	Returns	44
Significant market growth	Market	43
Relevant track record	CEO	37
Articulates venture well	CEO	31
Proprietary protection	Technology	29

Source: Adapted from data in Ian C. MacMillan, Robin Siegel, and P. N. Subba Narasimha, "Criteria Used by Venture Capitalists to Evaluate New Venture Proposals," *Journal of Business Venturing* 1 (1985): 121, 123.

and the market, as shown in Table 3.4. The most important qualities were the entrepreneur's ability to manage risk, work hard, and have familiarity with the market. The authors concluded, "It is the jockey (entrepreneur) who fundamentally determines whether the venture capitalist will place a bet [on the start-up], irrespective of the horse (product), horse race (market), or odds (financial criteria)."[13]

Some venture capitalists agree. Arthur Rock, who backed Intel and Apple, comments, "Nearly every mistake I've made has been because I picked the wrong people, not the wrong idea."[14]

The opposing view, however, also has its adherents in the profession and its own research support. Don Valentine, whose firm Sequoia Capital backed Google and PayPal, says, "I would invest almost exclusively based on market size and momentum and the nature of the problem being solved by the company."[15]

Weighing in on Valentine's side is an article by Steven N. Kaplan, Berk A. Sensoy, and Per Strömberg.[16] They studied the evolution of fifty venture-backed companies from business plan to their IPOs in 2004 and their further development three years later. The business lines as described in the business plan changed very little; only one company changed its core business. If anything, companies might increase their offerings within the original market segment. Yet over this period, the management teams changed substantially, as did the emphasis placed on "expertise," which can be interpreted as human talent. In the business plan, half the companies stressed expertise; at IPO and three years later, only 16 percent did so. Only 72 percent of the CEOs identified in the business plan were CEO at IPO, and only 44 percent survived three years thereafter. Founders (defined as the four executives just below CEO) had an even lower survival rate: only 50 percent

[13] Ian C. MacMillan, Robin Siegel, and P. N. Subba Narasimha, "Criteria Used by Venture Capitalists to Evaluate New Venture Proposals," *Journal of Business Venturing* 1 (1985): 119.

[14] J. Merwin, "Have You Got What It Takes?" *Forbes* 128 (August 3, 1981): 61; cited in Josh Lerner, *Expert Testimony*, October 2, 2008, 13.

[15] U. Gupta, *Done Deals: Venture Capitalist Tell Their Stories* (Boston: HBS Publishing, 2000), 167.

[16] Steven N. Kaplan, Berk A. Sensoy, and Per Strömberg, "Should Investors Bet on the Jockey or the Horse?" (CRSP Working Paper No. 603, August 2007), available at http://ssrn.com/abstract=657721.

made it to IPO, and only 25 percent survived three years later. To address concerns that the sample might be anomalous, the authors then tested all nonfinancial start-up firms that went public in 2004 for changes in core business, top management, and ownership, and the results held. Thus it appears that while a talented (expert) management team may be attractive, human talent is more readily changed than is the market or business concept. This may, of course, be a side effect of growth: a company that targets the right market and grows often requires different skills in its management team, leading naturally to management turnover.

Part of the difficulty in selecting a good deal are the information gaps (asymmetries)—one party, usually the entrepreneur, knows more than the other—and moral hazard—one party has a limited risk of loss and therefore behaves differently than it would if fully exposed. Raphael Amit, Laurence Glosten, and Eitan Muller[17] explored the types of entrepreneurs that would accept VC investment. They contend that high-quality entrepreneurs will have a preference *not* to take VC investment, because they can then keep the full returns of their deal. This would lead to an adverse selection problem: only less talented entrepreneurs would accept the need to share profits and endure the interference that accompanies VC involvement. Untalented entrepreneurs, because they accept venture funding, would not bear the full cost of their losses. To make money, venture capitalists must back talented entrepreneurs that are uncomfortable with risk (risk averse). The problem for venture capitalists, then, is to distinguish between untalented entrepreneurs and talented ones that are risk averse.

Although this view is extreme, it does indentify a real problem. Private equity investors *can* add value even to firms run by talented entrepreneurs. Were it not so, the analysts at TA and Summit would never find prospects, because there would be no talented entrepreneurs with good companies that would be willing to share their gains with an investor. Yet because entrepreneurs never approach an investor and say, "I'm really untalented," careful due diligence is essential. Let us explore how this is done.

The Due Diligence Checklist

In due diligence, the investors explore the management team, the customers, the sales pipeline, the financials, and the product. There may not be answers to all of the questions that come up, but even no answer identifies an area of concern. While each firm is likely to have a slightly different template, in this section we list the major areas of investigation.

The Management Team

A chief source of uncertainty in an investment is the management team. Early-stage investments endure for years, and management is a vital partner. Replacing elements of the management team is costly and delicate, even though it is not uncommon, as Kaplan et al. described. Changing a sales VP, for instance, can hamstring all sales efforts until the sales force assesses the threat to their jobs and the possible changes to their compensation framework and settles into the new reality. It is not unusual for the entire team to leave along with the departing executive. Thus the cost of replacing an executive may be not just the costs of severance, retainers for the recruiter, and signing bonuses and associated expenses with a new hire but also reduced effectiveness of the organization during and immediately after the search, if not additional costs to replace other departing employees. When a CEO must be recruited, the upheaval can be more profound since the organization's entire direction may be revised. At the same time, an interim CEO may be so well liked that the team resists any replacements.

---

[17] Raphael Amit, Laurence Glosten, and Eitan Muller, "Entrepreneurial Ability, Venture Investments, and Risk Sharing," *Management Science* 36, no. 18 (1990): 1232–45.

Executive changes can be disruptive even in leveraged buyouts, where the operation may be more stable. Some buyout firms replace the executive team with a team of in-house operational experts as a matter of course, recruiting a permanent team later. Others, especially those that specialize in management-friendly transactions, retain the existing team. Even so, the company will suddenly be operating in a different environment, suffering a different set of stresses, and coping with previously hidden weaknesses. A classic tale is the aftermath of KKR's takeover of RJR Nabisco for $25 billion in 1988, the largest buyout then and for more than fifteen years thereafter. The CEO at the time, Ross Johnson, left after the transaction and was replaced by American Express's Lou Gerstner, then Charles Harper from ConAgra, and finally Steve Goldstone from the Davis Polk & Wardwell law firm.[18] While this revolving door of CEOs was not the only reason RJR Nabisco struggled with declining market share and profitability, it certainly did not help.

Private equity investors—whether VC or buyout—must have a solid understanding of management's strengths and weakness before executing the transaction. Initially, one hopes that the existing team will perform. If not, it is hoped that they will be self-aware enough to accept replacement. As start-ups grow, their leaders require different skills. The scientist who develops a breakthrough technology may not wish to continue in the CEO position when it involves more mundane but still crucial daily management tasks, and he or she often becomes the chief technology officer (CTO). An early controller steps aside for a CFO. But sometimes a charismatic founder fights fiercely to retain control, forcing an ugly battle. The GPs may have to invest a significant amount of time in building board resolve to change the team and then in finding a replacement and calming the employees who remain. The investors must understand the skills, personalities, and motivations of the executives so they can factor any financial and time-related costs of replacement into the price of the deal.

To do this, the investors perform extensive reference checks on the team. This exercise encompasses three aspects:

1. What are management's strengths and weaknesses now?

2. What does the company need now?

3. What will the company need in the future, and will this team/individual be able to provide it? ("Will the team scale?")

Here the investing team must use its experience in pattern recognition. The GPs have seen different types of CEOs—the salesperson, the technologist, the strategist—and know when they are effective and when they fail. All types can build successful companies, but they must acknowledge their strengths and weaknesses and compensate by hiring a complementary team and devolving the necessary authority to them.

The CEO–Company Match

Mark Leslie began his career as a programmer with IBM in the 1960s and then moved to sales positions in Scientific Data Systems and Data General. He founded Synapse Computer in 1980 and raised $26 million from a host of VC firms. He focused intently on sales and had set up the marketing organization before the product was even ready to ship. His venture backers removed him in 1984 as the price of investing the final $8 million.[19] The company failed.

---

[18] John Helyar, "RJR Goes from Ashes to Ashes," *Fortune*, October 13, 2003, http://money.cnn.com/magazines/fortune/fortune_archive/2003/10/13/350888/index.htm, accessed June 15, 2010.

[19] Cheryll Aimee Barron, "Silicon Valley Phoenixes," *Fortune*, November 23, 1987, http://money.cnn.com/magazines/fortune/fortune_archive/1987/11/23/69875/index.htm, accessed May 6, 2010.

> After a difficult job search, Leslie landed at Rugged Digital Systems, a struggling supplier of military computers. Leslie slashed sales projections and spending; and by 1987, revenues had risen from $2 million to a projected $20 million.[20] He left the company in 1989,[21] and the following year became involved with Veritas software. This company repackaged technology that had been developed by Tolerant Systems, which had gone out of business after raising $50 million from the local VC firms.[22] Despite few demonstrable successes—Rugged Digital was acquired by DataMetrics a few years later for an unspectacular amount[23]—Leslie became CEO of Veritas. He benefited from being in Silicon Valley, which values the humility of prior failures. As Sequoia's Don Valentine said, "The sadder- but-wiser and humbled 35- to 40-year-old will take a lot of risk out of the situation, whereas the inexperienced 30-year-old with his ego-driven insensitivity is so cocky that he won't even listen to warnings."[24] Veritas needed a sales-oriented CEO—and Leslie excelled at sales. He was well aware of his earlier mistakes. Investors who had funded Synapse were impressed with Leslie's account of his lessons from that experience and backed the new venture. Under Leslie's leadership, Veritas went public in 1993 (NASDAQ: VRTS) and was acquired by Symantec in 2004 for $13.5 billion.[25] Leslie stepped down from the CEO position in 2000.

A thorough set of reference checks on the management team is produced by talking with former colleagues, investors, and the like. Entrepreneurs should expect such due diligence and provide a list of individuals who can be called. People who are not on the list will also be contacted, particularly if they worked with the candidate in a difficult situation. The investing team will base its expectations for working with management on the output of this process, possibly broaching the idea of replacing certain executives at the time of the investment, sometimes with the help of special compensation arrangements.

The Reference Check Checklist

A veteran venture capitalist creates a list of all his questions and asks them in an open-ended way. Instead of "Is he a good communicator?" he asks "How are his communication skills?" As the conversation progresses, answers to some questions will also cover others, and the interviewer checks them off. Toward the end of the conversation, the venture capitalist goes back through the list and directly asks those questions that have not been answered in the process. "It's very telling, what doesn't come up in general conversation," he observes. "You have to pay attention to that."

As with much in private equity, reference checks should not be one way. The entrepreneur should do reference checks on the investors. The management team needs to understand their

---

[20] Ibid.

[21] "Who's Where, Who's Where," *Aviation Week & Space Technology* 131, no. 11 (1989): 6.

[22] Data from Mark Leslie; cited in Javier Rojas, "Opinion: Conversation with the Founder: Mark Leslie," *Sandhill.com*, March 3, 2010, http://www.sandhill.com/opinion/daily_blog.php?id=62&post=609, accessed May 6, 2010.

[23] Reuters, "Datametrics Completes Rugged Digital Merger," *Reuters News Service*, August 10, 1993.

[24] Barron, "Silicon Valley Phoenixes."

[25] http://www.fundinguniverse.com/company-histories/Veritas-Software-Corporation-Company-History.html and "Veritas and Symantec Affirm Marriage Vows," *Information Age*, February 26, 2006, http://www.information-age.com/articles/285131/veritas-and-symantec-affirm-marriage-vows.thtml.

motivations and methods. How much do they micromanage? How good are their contacts? How good is their advice? How do they act when there's a crisis? The best way to learn this is to ask managers who have faced crises with them. Good investors expect that entrepreneurs will ask such questions.

Customer Checks

Investors also need to talk with customers. Getting unbiased information here is particularly difficult since the customers have a unique set of concerns that are unaligned with those of the investors. First, the customers want an uninterrupted supply of the technology or service that the company provides. As a result, a major customer is unlikely to say it is evaluating options, because the customer wants to keep its options open. On the other hand, a customer may take this opportunity to give candid feedback on the product's shortcomings—but only as the customer applies it. The product may do X very well, but the customer wants it to do Z. Thus the investor must filter the information carefully since it may be too broad and positive or too narrow and specific to the customer's needs. Many GPs have a network of executives who will provide a more balanced assessment of the customers' commitment. These trusted sources may have personal experience with the product/technology or have a variety of sources themselves that can provide unbiased information. Often a private equity firm's chief information officer (CIO) maintains a network of fellow CIOs who will share their experiences with various technologies.

There is an ongoing discussion about the value of intermediaries in due diligence, particularly for VC deals. In LBO transactions, teams of intermediaries are routinely used due to the complexity of assessing large operations with multinational operations and historical liabilities. VC firms encounter these situations less often. Many VC investors prefer to do as much of their own interviewing as possible to get a firsthand impression. Even so, consultants will be used where specialized knowledge is needed, often with customers and product reviews. In customer checks, a domain expert "speaks the interviewee's language" and can interpret or follow up on the feedback to create a rounded and informed report. Similarly, GPs will ask their firm's CIO to contact other CIOs for detailed technical information on the market's response to various products and technologies.

When Orangina was acquired by Blackstone Group and Lion Capital, the market insights came from Javier Ferrán, a Lion GP with extensive experience at Bacardi. He knew the drinks industry intimately—not just business models but people, personalities, and the nuances of European drinking habits and regulations. He knew, for instance, that *La Casera*, an effervescent lemon-flavored drink, was an absolute requirement for any Spanish bar and thus faced an inelastic price curve. With his deep contacts in the industry, Ferrán could discover the real situation in the company.[26] This is a key part of due diligence, especially in buyouts, where one is dealing with existing products and organization. Everything that needs to be known to make a good investment decision exists somewhere in the company, but finding it often requires making contact deep within the organization.

The Sales Pipeline

Performing due diligence on the sales pipeline is among the most difficult and critical parts of assessing a deal. Like Heisenberg's uncertainty principle, the act of measuring the sales pipeline affects its quality. The prospect of having the company receive any sort of private equity

---

[26] Felda Hardymon, Josh Lerner, and Ann Leamon, "Lion Capital and the Blackstone Group: The Orangina Deal," HBS Case No. 805-007 (Boston: HBS Publishing, 2005).

investment—whether a VC injection or a buyout—can raise fears among the sales prospects that the product will materially change and reduce their willingness to purchase.

It might seem preferable to question the sales force, but that too can be misleading. Salespeople are by nature optimists. To keep their energy up, they must tell themselves that the *next* sale is just about to close. The graveyard of private equity investors' hopes is filled with sales about to close.

The only way to adequately assess the sales pipeline is to think through the sales process step-by-step. Is there evidence of need? Has the product been adopted in proof of concept? Has the sales force made contact with the right decision maker? How do we know that this is the right decision maker? Has the product been taken into the lab for testing? Are there competitors? Has a request for proposal/quotation been issued? Has the company been asked to participate? Have the finalists been named? Are we among them? Have we received notice of a design win? Have we received a purchase order?

In this exercise, the investor actually assesses the quality of the sales process and whether it produces the information necessary for decision makers to assess the company's future demand. This is vital, since that information informs the financial plan. It is also important that the sales force is following the process, regardless of its quality.

Evaluating Financials

This aspect of due diligence is very sensitive to the stage of the company. Start-ups have different amounts of existing data and must focus on different parts of the financial story than do buyout targets. An investor who tries to take a buyout checklist into a start-up deal is doomed; likewise the one who tries to do the opposite.

- *Start-ups.* Any start-up should have a set of basic financial projections. This provides estimates of the progress it expects to make by the time it raises more money and gives the GPs a sense of the entrepreneur's understanding of the business and its future cash needs. In addition, this information can help the team target sectors, develop sales processes, and refine distribution methods. It may, for instance, be more cost-effective to sell through partners initially, to delay the cost of hiring and training a sales force while also perfecting the product, even though the partners may receive a share of revenues.

- *Buyouts.* A buyout target is usually an operating entity, but its financials may be indecipherable. If a collection of brands, a group of country-specific operations, or a division is being sold, they may never have operated as a unit. In such a case, the investor must reconstitute the financials of an entire company.

Reconstituted Financials

This was the case when Apax Partners, the European buyout firm, purchased BTR Paper Technology (BTRP). A global maker of consumables for the paper industry, BTRP ran a very decentralized operation with 38 plants and 18 offices in 17 countries. In 1998, it merged with Siebe, eventually renaming itself Invensys. When Apax began to examine BTRP's financials in 1999, it discovered, in the words of Michael Phillips, the GP involved in the deal:

> [BTRP] wasn't really a company but a group of separate operating units. BTRP Canada ran Canada; BTRP Argentina ran Argentina. There were no groupwide control systems, just a collection of individual country accounts. The headquarters made pro-forma statements as if a company existed. . . . We had to take the pro forma, disaggregate it to the country level, and then reaggregate it. There were big exchange movements during the three years

that constituted history, so even merging accounts or standardizing them in a single currency during the period was complex.

This very complexity, however, created a competitive advantage for Apax. Although the team incurred $3 million in legal and financial costs, their dedication made them stand out from the competition and gave them a better understanding of the amount they could bid and the efficiencies they could create.[27]

Another challenge for LBO funds occurs when a company does a "carve-out" or spin-out. In these cases, all the corporate overhead tasks—leadership, strategic planning, human resources, tax planning, purchasing—were done in the central office. How to account for these presents a real challenge. If a potential carve-out has borne a share of central costs in excess of its true need and usage, it can appear less profitable than it actually is. On the other hand, the division may be neglecting the positive impact of synergies, which might include shared advertising expenses, lower-priced supplies due to bulk purchases, tax offsets, or favorable prices from service providers that hope to do business with the larger entity.

Many mega buyout funds differentiate between accounting and financial checklists. The accounting checklists record the standard data that supports a company's accounts in the annual audits and are viewed as more confirmatory than explanatory. The financial diligence checklists, on the other hand, differ for each deal and have more explanatory power. The answers to one set of questions may inspire additional questions. While the target company's systems and data structures might not provide the information required to answer some of the more detailed questions, answers to the most significant questions are essential for the deal to proceed. In acquiring a syndicated cable program provider, the questions might involve subscriber fees (e.g., name of cable operator, number of subscribers, price per subscriber, price escalator, term of the contract); advertising revenues (e.g., ratings, cost per thousand, proportion sold in advance vs. spot market vs. direct response, sellout); and a detailed cost structure.

For start-ups, information is rarely available at such granularity, but the team must have some idea of the metrics that are important and how they will go about finding them. For instance, a seed-stage company planning to create a function that retrieves abandoned Internet banner ads and re-serves them to the user might refine its proposed cost structure by testing customer uptake. Understanding first, that this is important; and second, what this test would cost are important ways of judging both the leadership's vision and the idea's viability, in addition to obtaining financial data.

With most early-stage companies, the biggest concern must be that the financials are presented with transparency and good-faith fidelity to Generally Accepted Accounting Principles (GAAP). The GPs' domain expertise and pattern recognition skills—the general sense of what a company's financials at a particular stage in its development should look like and how they will progress over time—is essential. The issue becomes deciding which numbers are material and how to understand them.

As industries evolve, these change. In the Internet boom, "eyeballs" became a short-lived valuation metric.[28] Another valuation metric from that era has endured, however. In the late 1990s, as Internet companies doubled in revenue from quarter to quarter, investors changed from looking at the classic trailing twelve months (TTM) financial data to a shorter-term "revenue run rate," in which the most recent quarter's performance was extrapolated into the future. The Software as a

---

[27] Felda Hardymon, Josh Lerner, and Ann Leamon, "Apax Partners and Xerium S.A.," HBS Case No. 804-084 (Boston: HBS Publishing, 2005), 5.

[28] While a number of loss-making Internet companies did go public at astronomical valuations and large numbers of eyeballs (traffic to their sites), their long-term sustainability depended on the far more pedestrian concept of profits.

Service (SaaS) sector focuses not on the metric of bookings (expected revenues from accepted sales) that is commonly used in software firms, but on Committed Monthly Recurring Revenue (CMRR)— ongoing revenues net of cancelations—to help gauge the immediate cash flow of a growing company.

Not only do meaningful metrics shift over time and industries, they also change with the stages of a company's life. For early-stage companies, cash flow is essential. The balance sheet is relatively meaningless since most assets are intangible human knowledge—"they wear sneakers and walk home at night." Cash flow determines how much progress the company can make before it has to raise money again, and that progress will determine the value at which it can do so. At this point, a young company and its team should be developing good habits around accounting, with a focus on cash efficiency. As the company grows, other aspects of its financials become more important. Once a company has revenues, the income statement becomes important, followed by the balance sheet.

In buyouts, the balance sheet is very important; it helps the investor and banks determine the company's ability to handle the debt. The income statement, on the other hand, can be changed through operational improvements. Cash flow is critical because it reflects funds available to pay off the debt. Here again, accounting must be transparent so the investment and management teams receive accurate actionable information.

One theme we observe is the importance of domain knowledge. Venture capitalists need to have a general sense of how the financials should look and how revenue and expenses will evolve over time. Buyout practitioners must have a framework for interpreting the data, determining the company's stability under debt payments, and anticipating operational improvements. This can be developed into a competitive advantage. ABRY Partners, a top-tier, late-stage firm investing in media-related industries, used its deep understanding of the industry's dynamics to act quickly on emerging trends and identify improvement opportunities in underperforming assets. The founders' backgrounds in media industry consulting allowed them to assess opportunities and quickly determine their attractiveness.[29] Knowing the questions to ask and how to follow up on the answers is a key skill.

Product Evaluation

Product evaluation is another area in which domain expertise is extremely important. Often, a firm will hire a consultant or an outside expert of some sort if they lack internal expertise. While this makes sense on one level, it can also create a question of alignment of interests. The consultant is paid for the job; the GP is rewarded based on results. In addition, the partnership's budget may constrain the consultant's ability to dig into the details of the product and its fundamental technology. With in-house expertise, the matter can be investigated as deeply as necessary.

In-house domain expertise is easier to maintain for VC firms, which have a narrower focus. For LBO firms, the number and size of deals and the breadth of product portfolios often precludes this, although many will use outside experts who are closely aligned with the firm. Even for VC firms, there is an opportunity cost—the partner's time might be better spent on another project— but if a more promising project appears, it is almost costless for the partner to switch from the old prospect to the current one. In fact, the information gained on researching the first may increase the efficiency with which the second is assessed.

There is a significant advantage in domain expertise when it comes to asking follow-up questions. While an investor at BDSI, GE's VC division, Felda Hardymon backed Stratus Computer, an early fault-tolerant computer. He recalled:

> *Because I'd run computer systems earlier in my career, I could do the due diligence myself. I talked to the computer guys at GE about the technology, what might work, what might not.*

---

[29] For more on ABRY Partners, see Josh Lerner and Darren Smart, "ABRY Partners LLC: WideOpenWest," HBS Case No. 806-116 (Boston: HBS Publishing, 2007).

I invested in the company's first two rounds, then came to Bessemer, which had invested in one of Stratus' competitors on the advice of a consultant. I had looked at that company but thought its approach was too costly. The difference, I believe, is that I could ask the follow-on questions. A consultant will ask the questions he's been told to ask, but doesn't necessarily have the charter to dig as deeply as someone who has to stake their money and their reputation on the product working and working better than competitors.

Execution Risk

Part of the challenge when evaluating new products is that much of the technology risk is execution risk. The product may work and fill a real need, but its market success will depend on how well it is executed. For instance, the company Miasole designed a new approach to making solar panels by using less exotic (and thus less costly) materials deposited on a flexible substrate. In the lab, this achieved conversion efficiencies of almost 20 percent.[30] With huge demand for solar power (particularly for, of all things, garden lights), Miasole received backing from Kleiner Perkins and many other VC firms. Management predicted reaching profitability and shipping substantial amounts of product in 2007; but by late that year, the company had released its founding CEO along with forty other employees and was not yet shipping in quantity.[31] Not until two years later, with $300 million in venture funding, did the company begin shipping product.[32] Investors must be aware that executing the best design may be difficult and success may go to a suboptimal but more tractable product that is earlier to market.

Execution and technology risk are often combined as "product risk," but managing it requires separating the two. In Miasole's example, the problem was not the technology but the production process, which could not consistently produce large amounts of product at the advertised efficiency.[33] With a new production-oriented CEO, the company resolved its issues.

Important as execution is for a product using a new technology, it is even more crucial for a service. Terra Firma's buyout of EMI Records, the label of the Beatles and the Rolling Stones, has been struggling with those issues. In August 2007, the buyout group paid £3.2 billion ($5.2 billion) for the company (including debt), after its stock price plunged. Guy Hands, the founder of Terra Firma, planned to streamline EMI's business, cut marketing and administrative costs, and scrutinize the advances paid to artists. These worthy strategies ran afoul of cultural norms in the industry.[34] Hands' focus on financial efficiency alienated many of the label's most important assets—the bands.[35] The Rolling Stones departed—as did Radiohead and, in May 2010, the band Queen.[36] As brand-name bands left, sales fell and EMI violated the terms of its debt, which stipulated that the company maintained certain amounts of equity and cash. In September 2009, Terra Firma invested an additional £84 million ($137 million) followed by £105 million ($154.8 million) in May 2010 to keep the company in compliance.[37] At the same time, the private equity firm wrote down the company's value to zero,[38] and at this writing, the deal's outcome is still uncertain. Guy Hands certainly paid a high price for lunch with Mick Jagger.

---

[30] http://www.miasole.com/pgs-products/tech-cigs.shtml, accessed April 14, 2010.

[31] Jennifer Koh, "Miasolé; Layoffs Raise Questions About Technology," *Greentech Media*, December 21, 2007.

[32] Ucilia Wang, "MiaSolé Breaks the Silence, Moves into Production," *Greentech Media*, December 16, 2009.

[33] Michael Kannelos, "New Solar Technology Hits Snags," *CNET News*, May 22, 2007, http://news.cnet.com/New-solar-technology-hits-snags/2100-11392_3-6185572.html, accessed May 5, 2010.

[34] Sarah Arnott, "EMI: No Background Music," *The Independent*, July 8, 2008.

[35] Aaron O. Patrick, "EMI Deal Hits a Sour Note," *Wall Street Journal*, August 15, 2009.

[36] Pete Paphides, "Can EMI Pick Up the Pieces?" *Times Online*, June 20, 2010, http://entertainment.timesonline.co.uk, accessed July 1, 2010.

[37] Data from "Owner Averts EMI's Default on Citi, Loan," *NYTimes.com*, May 14, 2010.

[38] Dana Cimilluca, "Terra Firma to Help EMI Avoid Default," *Wall Street Journal*, May 12, 2010.

Legal Risk

Legal risk, of course, attends many new ventures. In addition to patent protection, entrepreneurs must consider the legal aspects of their planned business model,[39] and the investors must be aware of the legal structures of various agreements. In the early days of e-commerce, Internet sales of wine ran into a thicket of legal issues governing interstate transport of liquor. PayPal, the online payments processor, had to sort out the regulatory and legal issues of its business. Companies that provided electronic funds transfers for online gaming sites encountered significant legal problems in 2006 with the passage of the Unlawful Internet Gambling Enforcement Act in the United States, which severely hampered the U.S. portion of their business. An investor must identify these risks and understand how they can be managed. Some VC firms and most buyout firms have a lawyer on staff to assist with the myriad legal details of investments, exits, and partnership agreements. In large or specialized transactions, the investors may use outside legal experts managed by the in-house team, which is more aware of the materiality of various issues. Just because there are legal risks does not mean that the investment should be declined; however, those risks need to be considered and, sometimes, folded into the deal's pricing or return expectations.

A subset of legal concerns involves tax issues. In many buyouts, these are a key part of the investment calculus. Because the interest on debt is tax deductible, the company can shelter its profits. In addition, LBO acquirers can restructure their companies to take advantage of various tax benefits—sale-leasebacks of real estate, overseas incorporation, or product transshipment—and thus increase the company's profitability.

What to Do with All This Stuff?

Given the length of the previous discussion, it is clear that due diligence is both exhaustive and exhausting. A single investor rarely has all the expertise necessary to assess a deal completely—and then there is the matter of time. The investor must come to a conclusion fairly quickly, both to lock up a desirable deal and to honor the entrepreneur with a speedy reply. One angel investor estimates that it takes 35 to 40 hours to evaluate an early-stage deal.[40] Yet only a small percentage of the deals that private equity investors source are actually funded—one study found a range of 0.6 to 4 percent and another estimated 1 percent.[41] While outside experts—accountants, academic researchers, consultants, and others—can provide critical insights and extend the partners' time, the GP must determine the importance of any indentified risks and their impacts on the overall investment—that is, their materiality. But not all risks can be resolved.

But which of these risks are the most important? Based on investment memos from eleven VC firms for sixty-seven companies, Kaplan and Strömberg[42] explored the relative importance of three classes of risk in assessing a deal's desirability. Risks were classified as internal, external, and execution related. Internal factors—where the entrepreneur knows more than the investor, usually about her own behavior, willingness to work hard, and ethics—are named reasons to invest as often as they are noted as risks. This occurs, for instance, if a GP is impressed with an

---

[39] Constance Bagley and Craig Dauchy, *The Entrepreneur's Guide to Business Law*, 3rd ed. (Mason, OH: South-Western College/West, 2003, 2008), provides a comprehensive and accessible guide to everything from how to leave one's employer through vesting founder's stock, incorporation, and avoidance of fraud.

[40] Andrew Blair of Business Angels International, cited in Expert Testimony of Josh Lerner, October 2, 2008, 10.

[41] W. A. Wells, "Venture Capital Decision Making" (PhD dissertation, Carnegie-Mellon University, 1974), 47; and G. W. Fenn, N. Liang, and S. Prowse, "The Economics of the Private Equity Market," Federal Reserve Board, 1996; referenced in Expert Testimony of Josh Lerner, October 2, 2008, 10.

[42] Steven N. Kaplan and Per Strömberg, "Characteristics, Contracts, and Actions: Evidence from Venture Capitalist Analyses," *Journal of Finance* 69, no. 5 (2004): 2177–2210.

entrepreneur's technical knowledge but uncertain about management ability. External factors—matters equally unknown to both parties, such as market size or adoption rate—are noted as reasons to invest *more frequently* than they are noted as risks. This might be because they can be externally assessed or because the uncertainty is shared between entrepreneur and investor. Execution-related factors—aspects not wholly internal nor external, such as whether the strategy can be implemented or if the technology will work—are also significant but were not noted as quite as frequently as the other two. To address this uncertainty, investors structure the deal using the techniques and securities described in Chapter 5. Another way to control these uncertainties is good governance, implemented through a talented board of directors, and interests aligned through equity allocations, as discussed in Chapter 6. These are important not just at the time of investment, but over the deal's life span.

The Procedure of Due Diligence

Firms use a variety of approaches when performing due diligence on a deal. Some LBO firms "swarm" the deal with a large team, each individual charged with a particular task. Others send small teams that work closely with a number of consultants. When LBO firms do a deal together, they may split the work and rely on one team's environmental consultants and another's accounting consultants. In other situations, both teams will create their own set of models and use separate consultants. No wonder transaction fees are so high! VC firms, with smaller staffs, tend to have the GP lead the work, with help from an associate and external experts as necessary.

It is important to understand that due diligence is never complete. If given infinite time, the deal team can always chase down another question. Part of the art of the deal is becoming comfortable with the questions that can be answered only "in the fullness of time." While the best due diligence could not have predicted 2008's turmoil in the world financial markets, proper diligence around the team would allow the investors to anticipate the management team's reactions to the situation. If the answers to the diligence questions only lead to more questions—beyond a certain point—the deal team is learning something. Some teams use the phrase "getting comfortable" with the deal. The stakes are high, because fixing surprises in a committed deal is usually expensive. More damning, missing items in diligence reveals a gap in the team's domain knowledge. This is one of the reasons that LPs like GPs to stay within their areas of expertise.

Due diligence involves shifting perspective from precise detail to the big picture. Findings from due diligence must be fit into the whole picture of the deal, and the team must be aware of the materiality of additional information with respect to the overall decision. Like the blind men looking at the elephant,[43] excessive focus on the details of the unknown creates a picture that is false when viewed as a whole. The key to successful use of due diligence is to create an understanding of the entire deal, complete with uncertainties, and proceed from that.

Excessive detail focus can lead to false positives (i.e., each individual aspect of the company is good *enough* although the entire opportunity should be declined) and false negatives (i.e., the team declines a deal based on piecemeal information). Many private equity opportunities have a few drawbacks; otherwise, they'd qualify for much cheaper bank debt. A deal team can become so fixated on those drawbacks that they forget the power of active investing to change them.

---

[43] The story relates that a group of blind men (or people in the dark) trying to define an elephant based on touching only one part. They variously assert that the elephant is like a pot (the head), basket (ear), ploughshare (tusk), plough or water spout (trunk), granary (body), pillar (leg), mortar (back), pestle (tail), or brush (tip of the tail). Of course, an elephant is different from all of these.

Managing the investment helps address some of the inevitable unknowns. Unlike a Fidelity account manager, the GPs do not simply hold a position after they invest. Rather, they manage the investment, a process that can begin during the initial negotiations. DMG (Digital Media Group), an operator of mass media in China's transport networks, approached Tom Tsao of Gobi Partners for funding in 2002 with only a diagram of the product. Tsao made the deal contingent on DMG's winning a contract and hiring a business-oriented CEO to replace the technical founder. After this occurred in 2003, Gobi led the Series A and participated actively in guiding the company until its 2009 acquisition by Vision China.[44] Similarly, Apax's purchase of BTRP/Invensys was influenced by its ability to add value to a motley amalgam of operations.[45]

The Role of the Partnership

Due diligence findings must be viewed in context—and this context includes the deal's fit with the firm itself. This applies to both VC and LBO transactions. Does the deal raise the firm's profile in a desired area? Does the partner with domain expertise have sufficient time to manage it? Many questions asked at the start of the process are not simply answered and forgotten, but revisited. The GP who embarks on a due diligence process may suddenly have problems with a current portfolio company and find it impossible to add a company that requires monthly board meetings in Eastern Europe. Alternatively, an overtaxed GP may sell a company or resolve a difficult deal, freeing time for a promising deal.

And if the due diligence inclines the team toward no? Instead of refusing deals with which it cannot become comfortable, one VC firm responds, "Not yet."[46] A company with too many unresolved questions in an early round may be more favorably considered later, or the firm may invest in the entrepreneur's next venture. "Hanging around the net" of a VC deal that just does not fit the firm at that moment is a time-honored tradition, and such interested but uncommitted, firms often participate in or even lead a subsequent fund-raising. Many buyout shops have taken knowledge gained in an unsuccessful contest and put it to good work in a later acquisition in the same industry.

SERIAL ENTREPRENEURS AND SUCCESSFUL DEALS

Entrepreneurs who pursue multiple ventures—known as serial entrepreneurs—and succeed in them are a special case.[47] In an industry rife with uncertainty, serial entrepreneurs have a track record. Even with failed projects, as seen earlier with Mark Leslie, the investors know what to watch for and can better match the company's needs to the entrepreneur's talents. This knowledge is often widely shared, given the small size of the VC community.

The phenomenon of serial entrepreneurs has inspired a number of researchers. Paul Gompers, Anna Kovner, Josh Lerner, and David Scharfstein[48] explore how serial entrepreneurs succeed by reviewing data on companies that were founded, funded, and had an IPO between 1975 and 2000. Only 5 percent of entrepreneurs have led a company before, but those who were successful in the past are considerably more likely to succeed again (30 percent) than those who failed in their prior effort (20 percent) or first-time entrepreneurs (18 percent).

Success, the researchers determine, has two aspects: timing—that is, choosing to found a company in a sector poised for growth—and managerial skill, or the ability to build a successful company regardless of the sector's health. Entrepreneurs with *timing success* are more likely to

---

[44] Lerner et al., "Digital Media Group: The Shanghai Bid."

[45] Lerner et al., "Apax-Xerium," 4.

[46] Josh Lerner, Felda Hardymon, and Ann Leamon, "Best Practices: Decision Making Among Venture Capital Firms," HBS Case No. 804-176 (Boston: HBS Publishing, 2004), 7.

[47] Entrepreneurs who found multiple companies that uniformly fail are called . . . well, we won't go into that.

[48] Paul A. Gompers, Josh Lerner, David Scharfstein, and Anna Kovner. "Performance Persistence in Entrepreneurship and Venture Capital." *Journal of Financial Economics* 96, no. 1 (April 2010), Abstract.

succeed in subsequent ventures than those with managerial skill alone. The authors propose that the entrepreneur with timing skill can attract talented staff and has more credibility with customers; in short, timing skill is both necessary and sufficient for persistently good performance. GPs keep track of these gifted entrepreneurs and try to invest in their companies when they seek funding.

Interestingly, support from a top VC firm does not appear to influence the success of a company started by a previously successful entrepreneur. For companies started by first-time entrepreneurs or those who failed in a past venture, however, the involvement of a top VC firm does increase the odds of success. In explanation, the authors refer to the New England Patriots' star quarterback, Tom Brady. Chosen in the sixth round of the football draft, Brady required a top-quality coaching staff to assess his latent ability and help him achieve it. When Brady was at the top of his game in 2004, anyone could assess his ability; he needed little assistance to reach his potential. Hence, a strong entrepreneur can be expected to succeed regardless of the quality of the investor team.

Serial entrepreneurs also affect returns to the VC firms that back them. Lower-tier firms seem to be willing to pay a premium for previously successful entrepreneurs, but top-tier firms do not (due, perhaps, to nonmonetary terms that are not reflected in pre-money valuations). Top-tier firms do appear to be willing to pay more for new ventures overall, perhaps expecting better results given the firm's demonstrated skill. The analysis found no support for the idea that a higher pre-money valuation indicated a greater likelihood of success, further supporting the idea that *a priori* evaluation of deals is extremely difficult. There is, then, a coterie of successful entrepreneurs whose track record is not reflected in the pricing of their subsequent deals. The authors propose two explanations for this. First, given their ability in anticipating market growth, the new venture founded by a serial entrepreneur with timing skill may be seen as a risky bet in a new and uncertain sector. Secondly, their prior success may make the investors question the entrepreneur's commitment to the new venture's success.

Success appears more likely not only when the founder is experienced, but even when any member of the founding team has previously been involved in a successful start-up. Some companies, of which a recent example is PayPal, have spun out a surprising number of subsequent entrepreneurs.[49] For some VC firms, a serial CEO whom they have backed in the past becomes "their" CEO and they are predisposed to invest in subsequent projects, even to the point of giving a successful prior CEO a position as entrepreneur in residence with the firm as she charts her next venture. Research has found, though, that the relationship between VC firms and the serial entrepreneurs they back is less straightforward than one might think. Ola Bengtsson[50] analyzed the relationships between members of entrepreneurial management teams (all of which he called "entrepreneurs") and the first two companies that any of the group (executives or founders) established. He found that only 22 percent of almost five thousand serial entrepreneurs used *any* of the VC firms that had backed them previously, and only 5 percent used the same lead firm.

Entrepreneurs who had failed previously, the author found, were twice as likely as successful entrepreneurs to repeat with their lead VC firm, and the relationship was more likely to repeat if the new company was in the same industry as the prior one and located outside of California. Finally, the relationship was more likely to repeat with experienced VC firms.

The apparent fickleness of the successful serial entrepreneurs can be blamed on public signaling, as noted earlier by Gompers et al. Like Tom Brady in 2004, the world knows that the founder of a successful company has talent. The VC team backing a failed venture, on the other hand, has learned the strengths and weaknesses of the entrepreneur and may see the new venture as

---

[49] In fact, Founders Fund is a VC firm established by some PayPal alumni to fund their colleagues' ventures. For more information, see Paul Gompers and Emily Weisburst, "Founders Fund III," HBS Case No. 211-040 (Boston: HBS Publishing, 2010).

[50] Ola Bengtsson, "Repeated Relationships between Venture Capitalists and Entrepreneurs," (Working Paper, Cornell University, March 2007, unpublished) 1–38, http://www2.binghamton.edu/som/pdf/Ola%20Bengtsson%20March%202007.pdf, accessed May 2, 2010.

a chance to make money on that painful experience, especially (once again corroborating Bengtsson's findings) if the learning can be employed in a similar industry. The relative rarity of repeat relationships in California probably stems from the sheer number of VC firms in that state, which means there is more information available on both firms and entrepreneurs and more pressure for deals. The persistence in relationships between old VC firms and their entrepreneurs may stem from familiarity and comfort between the two. On the other hand, serial entrepreneurs may see a new venture as a chance to "trade up" to a more prestigious investor and exchange a lower valuation (per Gompers et al.) to do so. At the same time, first-time entrepreneurs that are backed by top-tier VC firms are more likely to start a subsequent company than are those backed by lower-tier firms—4.8 percent probability if funded by a lower-tier firm versus 5.7 percent for a higher-tier firm. While this number may appear low, the small number of serial entrepreneurs overall makes it significant.

The Serial Entrepreneur

Rubin Gruber founded four successful venture-backed companies. His first, Cambridge Technologies, the first company to incorporate microprocessors in communications equipment, was founded in 1974 with backing from Adler & Co. and Henry Burkhardt. After its acquisition by GTE, he founded Datavox (renamed Davox and then Concerto), which developed the first data and voice system, with backing from Hambrecht & Quist in its first round.[51] Gruber and one of his executives not only had prior experience in the industry but had been partners in a previously successful company.[52] This is music to a venture capitalist's ears. Davox went public in 1987 (NASDAQ: DAVX). Gruber followed Davox with VideoServer, a multimedia communications company, which was backed by several of his former investors and went public in 1995 (NASDAQ:VSVR). In 1997, Gruber founded Sonus Networks, again with many of the same VC firms, and took it public in 2000 (NASDAQ: SONS) at a $2.2 billion market cap.[53]

THE DECISION

Very little has been written about the process a private equity firm uses to decide upon a deal. In general, the same steps are followed:[54]

1. The GP learns of the deal and does enough due diligence to be interested.
   a. The GP may approach the partnership to obtain resources (money and people) for additional diligence.
2. The GP assembles a deal team to continue diligence and meets with the company.
3. The GP socializes the deal within the firm informally (this often starts with step 1a).
4. The company meets with the partnership (formal socialization),
5. The partnership approves or declines the deal or requests additional information.

---

[51] Data from Thomson Reuters.

[52] Personal communication with Felda Hardymon, May 2, 2010.

[53] Data from Thomson Reuters private equity database, accessed May 2, 2010; Hoovers; and material from the Sonus Networks' website, www.sonusnetworks.com, accessed May 2, 2010; Reuters, "Sonus Networks' Shares Jump 55 Percent in IPO," May 25, 2000, http://www.crn.com/it-channel/18834019m, accessed May 2, 2010.

[54] Josh Lerner, Felda Hardymon, and Ann Leamon, "Best Practices in Private Equity Decision Making," HBS Case No. 804-176 (Boston: HBS Publishing, 2004).

6. The GP issues a term sheet (or letter of intent).

7. The term sheet is negotiated.

8. The deal is signed.

Sometimes the order diverges slightly from that just described—the GP may issue a preliminary term sheet before the company presents to the partnership—and some firms skip some steps. A formal partnership meeting may not occur; the company may instead come in several times, meeting with small groups that are interested in the technology or market. At Warburg Pincus, a particularly decentralized firm, the deal socialization is almost entirely informal, as we discuss in depth in Chapter 12. Almost every firm requires some written record of the reasoning behind the transaction. Most require it before the partnership considers the deal; a few request it after the deal is approved as a record of the assumptions the firm has made.

The method of approving the deal varies by firm.[55] Some vote; some use a strong consensus (everyone must say yes); others have a weak consensus (no one says no), as shown in Figure 3.3. Some of the voting firms use a numerical system of 1 to 10; some give more weight to the votes from senior partners. In some firms, a partner is allowed to do a deal he is passionate about even if no one else likes it. This is rare even in concept and even more rarely occurs, given the huge reputational risk shouldered by the sponsoring partner.

The deal must be approved in the context of the overall portfolio in terms of what it brings to the firm and what the firm can provide it. Does the company under consideration reinforce the firm's position in the sector? What have we learned from other portfolio companies that we can bring to this one?

Another concern must be the other firms that are investing in the deal. Deal sharing (syndication) occurs in both venture and buyouts for a number of reasons. We explore this issue

FIGURE 3.3   Methods of decision making

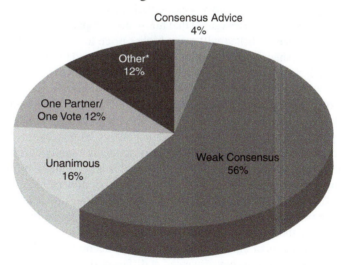

Notes: "Consensus Advice" involves the decision-making group providing input to the sponsor, who makes the final decision. "Other" includes ranking a deal, assigning a rank from which the sponsor makes the final decision, and situations where certain partners have "super-votes."
Source: Data from Josh Lerner, Felda Hardymon, and Ann Leamon, "Best Practices in Private Equity Decision Making," HBS Case No. 805-167 (Boston: HBS Publishing, 2005), 14.

---

[55] For details, see Lerner et al., "Best Practices in Private Equity Decision Making."

in the next section; but in short, additional firms share the risk and work, and they can help fund the deal while also validating the price and the investment thesis.

NETWORKS AND SYNDICATES

As mentioned earlier, private equity exhibits an interesting tension between individual and collective action, seen perhaps most vividly in the syndication of deals. While firms compete ferociously for deals, they also share them. In fact, they often rely on competitor firms to help bring companies to maturity or, in the case of buyouts, to fund the purchase price. Is this a case of institutionalized schizophrenia?

Syndicates started in VC as a response to the small average fund sizes in the industry's early days. Having multiple pockets to support a company increased the likelihood that there would be enough money to take it to maturity. In addition, partners helped to advise the growing company and expanded the networks of possible customers, advisors, and acquirers. As VC funds grew, they were less likely to need financing help with their companies and anecdotally, VC firms are indeed syndicating fewer deals.

There are, however, other reasons for syndication. Teaming up with an investor that specializes in an unfamiliar sector or geography eases a firm's entry into unfamiliar territory and can help expand its reach. In addition, there is the matter of public relations. LPs want to invest in firms that have companies in the headlines. This makes it worthwhile for a GP to invest in a company poised for success even at a later, high-priced round when outsized returns are unlikely.

Josh Lerner[56] discovered this dynamic when he explored deal syndication between VC firms, looking at a sample of 651 financing rounds for 271 biotechnology companies. In the first rounds of early-stage companies, established firms tended to syndicate with one another. This likely reflects interest in reciprocity (I'll let you into my deal if you'll let me into yours) as well as the lead firm's desire for outside support of its decision to invest. In later rounds, the established firms typically syndicated with lower-tier firms—possibly seeking their funding without expecting much help, or exploiting informational asymmetries (gaps) that allow the company to raise money at an inflated price.[57] Firms that are less established will pay a higher price to be involved in a deal backed by firms that are more established. Interestingly, established firms tend to invest in later rounds after a spike in valuation. This supports the idea of "window dressing"—that is, regardless of the cost, the firm wants a position in a company that has demonstrated its success.[58]

Yael Hochberg, Alexander Ljungqvist, and Yang Lu[59] explored how networks between VC firms improve deal flow and decision making. VC firms will share promising deals not just to ensure future reciprocity, which might be expected, but also to reduce uncertainty. Another firm's interest in a deal confirms its attractiveness, essentially acting as a sanity check. An additional VC firm increases the available expertise regarding both sector and location, allowing both firms to expand their knowledge bases.[60] While sector expertise is understandable, location is also important since VC tends to be a local business. Investing alongside a firm that has an office in an area where the other operation does not can increase the nonlocal firm's geographic reach.

At the same time, though, experience shows that syndication can have drawbacks. The dynamics among the members of the board of directors can become complicated as the number of firms increases. When various firms have invested at different stages in a company's development

---

[56] Joshua Lerner, "The Syndication of Venture Capital Investments," *Financial Management* 23, no. 3 (1994): 16–27.

[57] Ibid., 16.

[58] Ibid., 25.

[59] Yael Hochberg, Alexander Ljungqvist, and Yang Lu, "Whom You Know Matters: Venture Capital Networks and Investment Performance," *Journal of Finance* 58, no. 1 (2007): 251–301.

[60] Ibid., 252.

FIGURE 3.4   Average prices of LBO club deals and average LBO fund sizes

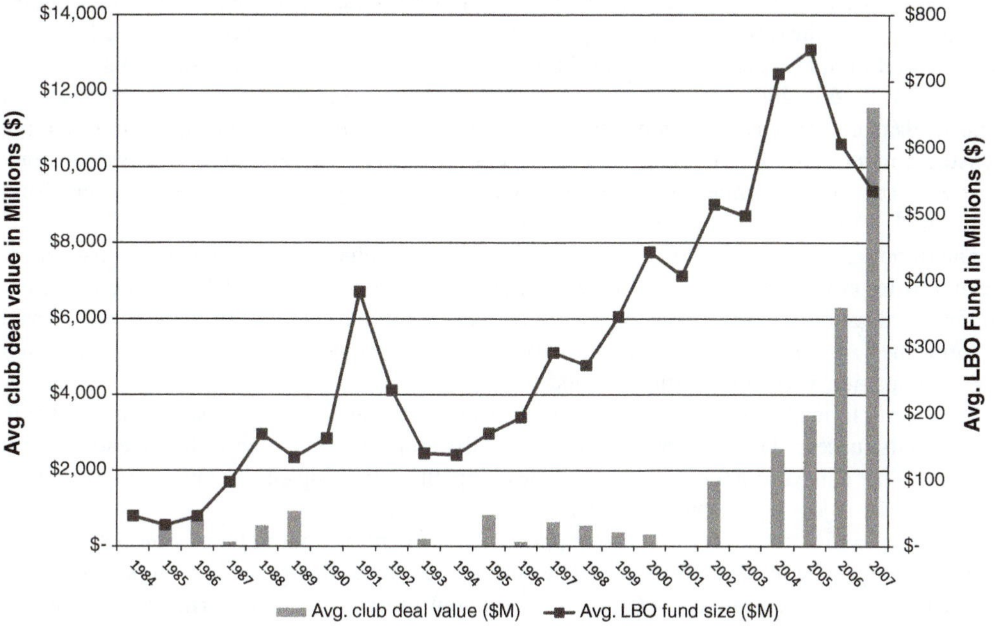

Source: Data from Thomson Reuters private equity database, accessed July 12, 2011, and Micah S. Officer, Oguzhan Ozbas, and Berk A. Sensoy, "Club Deals in Leveraged Buyouts," *Journal of Financial Economics* , Vol. 98 no. 2, November 2010, 214–240.

with different securities issued at different prices and with different rights, the board relationships can become complex indeed, as we discuss in Chapter 6.

Syndicating plays a role in buyout transactions as well. So-called club deals came later to that industry as very large deals outstripped fund sizes. The size of the average LBO club deal waxes and wanes with the amount of money in the industry, as seen in Figure 3.4. Club deal prices soared in 2007; even the large funds raised in the years before could not keep pace as deal sizes soared above $20 billion (Alliance Boots at $20 billion, Alltel at $27.5 billion, and TXU at $32 billion are just a few examples).

The possibility that club deals might reduce competition for buyout targets aroused the interest of the U.S. regulators in 2006. The data were intriguing: between 2004 and 2006, "buyouts of companies worth $100 million to $1 billion (typically deals that did not involve clubs) had an average premium of 27.4%; deals over $1 billion (which usually involved clubs) had a premium of only 16.5%," noted one journalist.[61] This may simply reflect the structural fact that there are fewer mega buyout firms and hence less competition for a deal of that size, although Officer et al. found a worrisome impact.[62] Using a sample of the buyouts of U.S. publicly traded companies between 1984 and September 2007, the authors analyzed the pricing and characteristics of buyouts involving two or more firms. These club deals produced roughly 10 percent less pre-bid firm equity value, or 40 percent lower premiums, compared to sole-sponsored buyouts. By reducing prices, such behavior shortchanges the target company's shareholders.[63]

---

[61] Data from Dealogic, cited in Andrew Ross Sorkin, "Colluding or Not, Private Equity Firms Are Shaken," *New York Times,* October 22, 2006, http://www.nytimes.com/2006/10/22/business/yourmoney/22deal.html?_r=1, accessed April 23, 2010.

[62] Micah S. Officer, Oguzhan Ozbas, and Berk A. Sensoy, "Club Deals in Leveraged Buyouts," *Journal of Financial Economics (JFE)* (Forthcoming), available at http://ssrn.com/abstract=1128404, accessed May 5, 2010.

[63] Another study found the opposite effect—see Audra L. Boon and J. Harold Mulherin, "Do Private Equity Consortiums Facilitate Collusion in Takeover Bidding?" (paper presented at AFA 2009 San Francisco Meetings, February 2, 2009), available at SSRN: http://ssrn.com/abstract=1104224.

Regardless of any pricing impact, clubbing in buyouts also plays the same information sharing and credentialing role we observed in VC. One example appears in the experience of London-based Lion Capital, the reborn European operations of Hicks Muse, a formerly top-tier U.S. buyout fund. Focused on mid-market buyouts in the consumer goods industry, the group raised its first €820 million fund in 2005. After participating with Blackstone in an aborted attempt to buy an alcoholic drinks company, the two teamed up successfully in the acquisition of Orangina. Blackstone, investing from its $21 billion Fund V, did not need Lion's money; it needed Lion's sector insights. At the same time, working with Blackstone increased the younger firm's reputation.[64]

The importance of syndication exceeds mere reputation enhancement. Syndicates also can be expected to improve company outcomes by increasing the resources available to the company, both financial and advisory.[65] An expanded network improves access to specialized service providers, such as recruiters or investment banks; possible customers, partners, or acquirers; and, for VC companies, investors in future rounds.

In the article mentioned earlier, Hochberg et al. also consider the impact of a VC firm's network on its success. The authors measure the relative importance, or centrality, of each actor in a network. After controlling for fund size and the competitive funding environment, VC firms with better networks enjoy significantly better fund performance.

Research by Sorenson and Stuart[66] supports the contention that networks help a VC firm expand the geography in which it invests. The authors determine that geographical proximity and social networks help determine a VC firm's investment preferences. New firms or new venture capitalists without a trusted network will tend to invest in nearby companies because they must monitor and advise the companies in person. More experienced venture capitalists (i.e., those with wider networks) and older firms (which have also developed wider networks through successful investments and prior coinvestment) tend to invest in farther-flung companies, especially if a member of the syndicate with whom the firm has previously invested has an office nearby. The likelihood of a VC investing in a state where it has previously invested is also higher—even controlling for the state in which the firm is located. The issue for states seeking to increase VC activity thus becomes attracting the first VC firm.

A well-networked VC firm provides advantages for the portfolio company as well. Hochberg et al.[67] determine that a small increase in the importance of the lead investor in the industry network (centrality) increases the company's likelihood of surviving to its next financing round from 66.8 to 72.4 percent. Obviously, there may be biases—the more networked VC firm may have better sources of information and thus choose better companies initially. Yet the authors conclude that well-networked VC firms perform better because they provide better services to their portfolio companies, not just because the network provides better companies in the first place.

This creates the dynamic through which the private equity industry separates into tiers. Better-networked firms prefer to network with similar firms, rather than having to do all the heavy lifting of company governance. This further demonstrates the impact of activity on outcomes. Good VC firms can attract good companies because their strong networks increase the chances of the company's success, and thus their own. This reinforces the theme of credentialing—a company backed by a top-tier firm has a greater chance of success simply by dint of being chosen.

---

[64] Hardymon et al., "Lion Capital and the Blackstone Group: The Orangina Deal."

[65] By providing access to their networks of service providers, such as recruiters, attorneys, investment bankers, and the like, as described in Michael Gorman and William Sahlman, "What Do Venture Capitalists Do?" *Journal of Business Venturing* 4 (1989): 231–48 and William Sahlman, "The Structure and Governance of Venture Capital Organizations," *Journal of Financial Economics* 27 (1990): 473–521.

[66] Olav Sorenson and Toby E. Stuart, "Syndication Networks and the Spatial Distribution of Venture Capital Investments," *American Journal of Sociology* 106, no. 6 (2001): 1546–88.

[67] Hochberg et al., "Whom You Know Matters," 253.

WINNING THE DEAL

Once the due diligence is done and the syndicate arranged, how does a team win a deal? Partly, this occurs through the interactions around the due diligence. Being friendly and patient, asking good questions, making helpful introductions even before the deal is completed—all of these help a firm stand out as a good partner for the long haul.

At the same time, the GP needs to create a situation where people want to share information. This can be done in a number of ways. Some GPs attract others due to personality, others through domain expertise. There is also the community-building aspect of information sharing. GPs in one firm reach out to those in another, knowing that their counterparts will do the same. Even now, with 2,700 private equity firms in the United States,[68] it is a small industry and practitioners frequently encounter one another throughout their careers.

It is to an investor's benefit to keep as many options open as long as possible. A term sheet or an LOI may be couched in ranges of valuation, contingent upon the outcome of due diligence. The deal may be revised depending on the number of firms in the final syndicate. How this is resolved depends on the investors' assessment of the company's need for future financing or guidance in various areas of expertise.

Part of the information flow involves creating a sense of partnership among all the participants, particularly with people in the company. A GP is on the board of directors, not running the company. Investors need to understand the important players in the company's existence and form fruitful relationships with them. These players may be management, vendors, or customers, and it will be a long-term relationship—five to seven years in the case of early-stage deals. The participants must have some degree of partnership behavior, respect, perhaps even liking to make the interactions run smoothly.

Of course, the GPs are also being evaluated as potential partners. The firm's brand and the individual GP's track record create the first impression. An investor is as good as his (or her) platform and biggest-name deal. A firm may send its most renowned deal maker to wow the team, only to have the board seat and the actual work done by a more junior partner; but the implication persists that in difficult times, the firm's overall expertise will be brought to bear.

With LBO firms, the multiple auction rounds that we mentioned earlier winnow down the field of acquirers. In the example of Lion and Blackstone's purchase of Orangina, the number of interested entities (some combined to form syndicates) went from 40 to 7 to 2 in the auction's rounds. The seller had several concerns beyond simply getting a good price. Regulators had blocked Coca-Cola, the winner of an earlier auction, from acquiring the entire Orangina operation. This had left Cadbury, Orangina's owner, managing a subscale operation that it had earlier tried to sell, after its primary competitor had taken a good look at the financials. More than anything, Cadbury wanted to get the soft drink division off its hands. Thus, one of the chief requirements was that the potential acquirer could provide certainty that the deal would occur.

The various rounds of an auction narrow the field based on the bidders' characteristics and their willingness to pay. Often, the bank will inform the bidders of an expected price. Those that do not value the company at that level, or cannot become comfortable with a given price by the deadline, will fall out of contention. As the field narrows, other matters, especially the ability to arrange financing, become more important. LBO firms must convince the company or its parent that they can buy the equity and raise the necessary tiers of debt. A target's vendors and customers want to know that the acquirer can get the deal done, marshaling all the moving parts and concluding the transaction in a reasonable time frame. Little distresses a company's ecosystem more than the uncertainty of having it in play.

---

[68] Data from National Venture Capital Association, *NVCA 2009 Yearbook* (New York: Thomson Reuters, 2010), 10; and *Pitchbook*, cited in Private Equity Growth Capital Council, http://www.pegcc.org/, accessed November 12, 2010.

Finally, the company's management team needs to know that the purchaser can help them create value. In their acquisition of Orangina, Lion Capital and Blackstone met extensively with the management team and planned to increase spending on marketing and product R&D and welcomed strategies for management.[69] The management team's compensation rides on its ability to meet targets for revenue and earnings before interest, tax, depreciation, and amortization (EBITDA) growth and to pay off the debt (the debt is assumed not by the acquiring LBO firm, but by the company), so concrete plans for strategies that will help it do so are essential.

In VC deals, too, the prospective investors must add value. The entrepreneur and any current investors want investors with a reputation for smart engagement and a strong and effective network. Domain knowledge, so important in due diligence, is also important in building trust with the management team. The entrepreneurs seek experienced VC investors who understand how new companies can manage their sales processes,[70] bring a product to market, sequence product development, consider an acquisition, and find a really good executive when necessary.

Two attributes here are the most significant: reputation and domain knowledge. Reputation tends to stay with the platform. As we noted earlier, while only one investor at Kleiner Perkins did the Netscape deal, everyone at Kleiner Perkins benefits from the aura of being smart, forward-thinking investors. Domain knowledge, especially in VC, and operational enhancement expertise in buyouts enhances the platform's reputation—not only are these guys smart, but they're also helpful. These attributes differentiate firms and made one more desirable than another.

FOLLOW-ONS

Much of the previous discussion considered new deals. A situation where a current portfolio company needs additional investment poses different challenges. This frequently occurs in the VC context; in fact, the entire VC model is predicated on funding that matches the achievement of milestones. This is far less frequent with buyouts.

Usually, the diligence process on a follow-on deal is considerably less detailed than that for a new one. The GP on the board is assumed to have a thorough knowledge of the company's progress, limiting diligence to a summary write-up on changes and progress since the last financing. When a company has hit its milestones and met its plan, a follow-on financing request is approved almost automatically. Companies that have not hit their milestones and, worse yet, those that have not but just might, are more difficult. The firm's name is attached to the company, and the GPs often have some level of emotional commitment (GPs use phrases like "You're married to it," "You're in love with it," "You're emotionally tied to it"[71]). Moreover, success is often just one quarter away.

VC firms use several approaches to resolve this tension, as shown in Figure 3.5. In some cases, they create an entirely new deal team to assess the problematic follow-on. In others, they add a new person to the existing team, assigning that individual the role of "devil's advocate" to question all assumptions. Some hold all follow-ons to a higher bar than a first-time deal. In the majority, the GPs trust their partner to manage the deal in the best possible way. The difficulty of the decision is demonstrated in the belief among most firms that their follow-on decision process needs improvement—regardless of the process currently in use.[72] The implications of follow-ons, particularly when the company has fallen short of its goals and the entire deal may be open to recontracting, are discussed in Chapter 6.

---

[69] Lerner et al., "Lion Capital and the Blackstone Group: The Orangina Deal."

[70] Mark Leslie and Charles Holloway, "The Sales Learning Curve," *Harvard Business Review*, July 1, 2006. HBS Publishing product number R0607J-PDF-ENG.

[71] Lerner et al., "Best Practices in Private Equity Decision Making," 8.

[72] Ibid., 9.

FIGURE 3.5   Approach to follow-on decisions

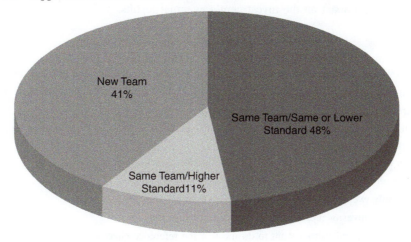

Source: Data from Josh Lerner, Felda Hardymon, and Ann Leamon, "Best Practices in Private Equity Decision Making," HBS Case No. 805-167 (Boston: HBS Publishing, 2005), 15.

CONCLUSION

An approach to deal sourcing and approval forms a central part of a firm's culture. How deals are found, whether proprietary, proactive, or reactive, varies substantially. One firm may do intensive white papers on prospective sectors or create a network; another looks through the mail. How a deal is socialized, how it is approved—whether by a vote or a consensus, whether one person has a super-vote or each vote has the same weight—all become woven into the firm's mystique. A person who fits well in one decision system may not fit in another.

The entire process attempts to use the power of active investing to identify and resolve areas of uncertainty. No one method suits everyone. Don Valentine backed technology; Arthur Rock backed people. What mattered was that they chose based on the best information they had at the time. The constraint upon due diligence is time; the investors make the best decision they can with uncertainty and limited time. Activity crucially informs how the investors consider the eventual gains that can be created.

It is important for an entrepreneur to understand that decisions are made in the context of the firm's realities. As the early examples in this chapter demonstrate, top-tier firms have passed over excellent companies. They have invested in middling companies that succeeded wildly or slightly or failed miserably. Today's "most promising" company in an investor's portfolio may be tomorrow's utter disaster.

The process of due diligence is accretive, not only to the investment decision on the company in question but to the firm itself. Sources of information develop over time, as do reputation, trust, and a series of reciprocating relationships. Questions, checklists, and methods all evolve to fit the needs and sensibility of the particular firm. This process becomes ingrained, unique to the firm, and part of the process through which the industry separates into tiers. A high-reputation firm usually has access to better or more responsive sources of information in its diligence process, thus facilitating the decision making. But none of this drops in the investor's lap; it all requires action.

Of course, winning a deal is only part of the process. From that point, the team will structure it, as we discuss in the next chapters, and then manage it, as we explore in Chapter 6. In each of these steps, we contend with the ongoing themes of illiquidity and informational asymmetry that the industry tries to allay through the alignment of interests and the tools of active investing. And all of these steps have an impact on the investment's eventual results.

QUESTIONS

1. Why do investors prefer proprietary deals? Why would an entrepreneur or a seller prefer these deals?

2. How might a sector or geographic focus for a fund be beneficial in attracting a proprietary deal?

3. What are the key points to include in a pitch to a potential investor?

4. What are the disadvantages and potential risks of an auction process for both the investors and the seller? How might either party mitigate them?

5. What are the channels for an investor to seek out an investment opportunity?

6. How does an entrepreneur find an investor?

7. Why use only twelve slides in a company presentation?

8. Why might an investor prefer a CEO who had failed in the past?

9. Why would a general partner want to do most of the reference checks himself?

10. What are the three risks that Kaplan and Strömberg describe? Why would external risks be viewed as reasons to invest more often than reasons not to?

11. Discuss the impact of timing success and managerial skill in entrepreneurial success. Why would the price of a venture started by a serial entrepreneur with timing success tend not to be particularly high?

12. Why would an entrepreneur backed by a top-tier firm be more likely to start another venture?

13. Give three reasons why a private equity firm would syndicate a deal. How do the reasons differ for VC and buyout firms?

14. Why do so many VC firms think their follow-on decision process needs to be changed? What do you think would be the best approach?

Chapter 4

Assigning Value

While we have spoken thus far about the difficulty of finding and deciding upon deals, we have not yet visited the thorny issue of assigning a value to them. The valuation of private companies, especially those in the earlier stages of their life cycle, is a difficult and often subjective process. Early-stage companies typically forecast a period of negative cash flows with highly uncertain—but tantalizing—future rewards. Even the more mature firms in buyouts can be challenging to value, since the value depends critically on the ability to make improvements to the operations. In both cases, the valuation will be very sensitive to the assumptions made.

In addition to uncertainty, other challenges also make the valuation of private firms difficult. Often there are information problems: the entrepreneurs may know far more about progress within the firm's laboratories than do the venture capitalists, who in turn know much more than outsiders. Many young firms have few hard assets. Instead, the primary assets of a start-up are likely to be its employees (who can always go work elsewhere) and its ideas (which often are difficult to protect adequately through patents and other means). Such intangible assets are particularly tricky to value. Finally, turbulent markets may mean that a valuation that was plausible one quarter is nonsensical the next.

Moreover, the **capital structures** of these companies evolve over time. Early-stage companies raise money at various times throughout their lives to fund their growth and minimize their investors' exposure. Companies that have been acquired by leverage buyout (LBO) firms pay down the accompanying debt over time. All of these characteristics, along with the sheer difficulty of finding data, can complicate the application of standard financial approaches to valuation.

These challenges can lead to very different valuations of the same firm, particularly during periods where market conditions are changing rapidly. For instance, in 2002, Santera Systems was one of many struggling telecommunications equipment makers. Its advanced telephone switching technology, which offered significant cost savings and technical advances, had been developed by its 250 employees with the help of more than $200 million in private equity financing. But the entire telecommunications sector was mired in a deep recession. This period saw key industry players (and major potential customers) like Lucent and Nortel experience huge losses, massive cutbacks, and numerous questions about their viability.

Perhaps reflecting these disparate views of the company and the industry (and possibly their own circumstances), the venture investors who held shares in Santera valued it very differently. In its report in the second quarter of 2002, Austin Ventures valued its Series A preferred stock (see Chapter 5 for details of types of securities) at $4.42 per share, reflecting the valuation assigned to Santera in its last financing round. (The July 2001 Series C financing, led by Austin Ventures, implied a valuation of the firm of $365 million.) Sequoia Capital valued the same share of Series A preferred at just 46 cents. With the benefit of hindsight, Sequoia's more skeptical view was justified because Tekelec acquired Santera for $75 million in a complex multistep deal between 2003 and 2005. (Perhaps even this valuation was optimistic, since Tekelec sold Santera and two other companies in 2007 in exchange for stock and a minority stake in a private firm w1orth about $26 million.)[1]

This is challenging territory indeed. But through the rigorous application of various methodologies, it is possible to get a reasonable sense of how much firms are worth. In this chapter we discuss a variety of valuation techniques that can be used in private equity settings. Our intention is to provide a practical tool kit to be used when tackling these issues.

Two limitations should be acknowledged up front. First, since this is only one of fourteen chapters, we gloss over the background theory: our focus here is on the essential underlying mechanics of each method and a discussion of strengths and weaknesses. Fortunately, the theory is covered in many corporate finance texts. A second limitation is that we focus largely on approaches that are in common use today. For more advanced applications of option pricing techniques, the reader is referred to Andrew Metrick's brilliant book.[2] The suggestions for further reading at the end of this chapter provide more detailed information on the various valuation techniques discussed.

We begin with the building blocks: the concepts of pre- and post-money valuation. We then turn to the question of how valuations are derived. We explore the comparables, net present value, adjusted present value, venture capital, and options valuation methods. We also discuss the use of Monte Carlo simulation employing the software package Crystal Ball to enhance these valuations. In the final section, we attempt to put all this information together and discuss how these differing approaches can be reconciled.

THE BUILDING BLOCKS: PRE- AND POST-MONEY VALUATIONS

Before we turn to how to value private-equity-backed firms, it is worth considering how valuations in transactions are typically assigned. To do this, we need to understand the concepts of pre- and post-money valuation.

In many buyouts, this process is relatively straightforward because investors will purchase all the equity of the firm. Thus, when Blackstone, Carlyle Group, Permira, and TPG agreed to purchase Freescale Semiconductor in September 2006, they acquired all the company's shares. Freescale, Motorola's semiconductor division, had been spun out as a public entity in July 2004. The company agreed to be purchased at $40 per share. This translated into the sum of $17.6 billion for the equity, plus another $1.3 billion of assumed debt. Thus the transaction set the company's enterprise value at $18.9 billion.[3]

Venture capital (VC) transactions are more complex. For instance, GENBAND (Santera's ultimate acquirer) had its tenth financing round in April 2007.[4] Its large stable of venture investors included old-line groups like Oak and Venrock; newer groups like SVM Star and Trellis, Siemens' corporate venture affiliate; and secondary buyer Cipio (which acquires shares in private

---

[1] This account is based on Ann Grimes, "Little VC Secret: Value Lies in the Eye of the Beholder," *Wall Street Journal*, November 4, 2002; Thomson Reuters private equity database, accessed August 29, 2009; Tekelec Systems, Amended 8-K Filing, October 3, 2005, http://www.sec.gov/Archives/edgar/data/790705/000095012905012059/v15468e8vkza.htm, accessed August 29, 2009; and Tekelec Systems, 8-K Filing, March 20, 2007, http://www.sec.gov/Archives/edgar/data/790705/000095012407001744/v28652e8vk.htm, accessed August 29, 2009.

[2] Andrew Metrick, *Venture Capital and the Finance of Innovation* (New York: John Wiley & Sons, 2007).

[3] This account is based on Matt Andrejczak, "Freescale Semi Agrees to $17.6 Billion Buyout," *MarketWatch*, September 15, 2007, accessed at www.marketwatch.com/story/freesacle-semiconductor-agrees-to-176-billion-buyout and Freescale Semiconductor, Form 8-K, September 15, 2006, http://www.sec.gov/Archives/edgar/data/1272547/000118143106053300/rrd130605.htm, accessed August 29, 2009.

[4] GENBAND's financial history is taken from Thomson Reuters private equity database, accessed August 29, 2009.

companies from owners, usually private equity firms, that no longer want to or can hold them). In the April 2007 financing, the group invested $13.56 million, in exchange for **preferred stock** that would convert into 10.43 percent of the common stock.

What did this transaction imply about GENBAND's value? The simplest answer can be computed by dividing the amount invested by the share of the company's **common stock** this will translate into. Venture capitalists call this the **"post-money" valuation**:

$$\text{Post-Money Valuation} = \text{Amount Invested/As-Converted Ownership}$$
$$= \$13.56 \text{ million}/10.43\% = \$130 \text{ million}$$

(Alternatively, this value can be computed as the product of the price per share in the transaction and the total number of shares of common stock that will be outstanding, once all the preferred shares are converted into common stock.)

In some contexts, however, this value may not be what we want to measure. In particular, we may want to measure how much the transaction implied the firm was worth *before the new money went into the firm*. This concept, the **"pre-money" valuation**, is computed as

$$\text{Pre-Money Valuation} = \text{Post-Money Valuation} - \text{Amount Invested}$$
$$= \$130 \text{ million} - \$13.56 \text{ million} = \$126.44 \text{ million}$$

The difference between pre- and post-money valuation can perhaps best be thought about in real estate terms. If you buy a run-down house for $500,000 and then spend another $250,000 renovating it, the pre-money value can be defined as $500,000 and the post-money as $750,000. In the case of GENBAND, the one certainty is that whatever valuation we use is certainly a lot lower than the company's third financing in August 2000, when many of the same investors invested $48.3 million in exchange for 19.43 percent of the equity on an **as-converted basis**.

It should be noted that in most cases, this methodology gives only a misleading (and sometimes very misleading) impression of a company's value. This calculation assumes that the private equity investors get shares like any other investor. But as we discuss in depth in the next chapter, this is most definitely not the case in the typical deal. Rather, the private equity group gets preferred shares, which have numerous special rights that range from the ability to be repaid first to the right to veto key decisions. These rights are, as one can imagine, potentially quite valuable.

Thus, when a venture capitalist invests a million dollars and gets preferred shares that would convert into 10 percent of the **common equity**, the investor is actually receiving shares that are likely to be worth more than the common shares (exactly how much more will depend on the terms and conditions of the preferred shares). As a result, our calculation of a $10 million post-money valuation ($1 million/10 percent) is misleading. In reality, the venture capitalist has gotten *more* than 10 percent of the company's value, and the post-money valuation implied by the transaction is less than that calculated by the simple post-money method.

COMPARABLES

In this section, we explore the most commonly used ways to value private-equity-backed companies. (The strengths and weaknesses of each method are summarized in Table 4.1.)

The use of comparables often provides a quick and easy way to obtain a "ballpark" valuation for a company. When searching for comparables, we need to find companies that display similar "value characteristics" to the company of interest. These value characteristics include risk, growth rate, capital structure, and the size and timing of cash flows. Often, these are driven by other

Table 4.1 Strengths and Weaknesses of Various Valuation Methods in Private Equity Settings

Method	Strengths	Weaknesses
1. Comparables	• Quick to use • Simple to understand • Commonly used in industry • Market based	• Private company comparables may be difficult to find and evaluate • If using public company comparables, need to adjust resulting valuation to take into account private company's illiquidity
2. Net Present Value (NPV)	• Theoretically sound	• Cash flows may be difficult to estimate • Private company comparables (β and capital structure) can be difficult to find and evaluate • Weighted average cost of capital (WACC) assumes a constant capital structure • WACC assumes a constant effective tax rate • Typical cash-flow profile of outflows followed by distant, uncertain inflows is very sensitive to discount and terminal growth rate assumptions
3. Adjusted Present Value (APV)	• Theoretically sound • Suitable (and simple to use) in situations where the capital structure is changing (e.g., highly leveraged transactions such as LBOs) • Suitable in situations where the effective tax rate is changing (e.g., when there are net operating losses—NOLs)	• More complicated to calculate than the NPV method • Same disadvantages as NPV method except it overcomes the shortfalls of the WACC assumption (i.e., constant capital structure and tax rate)
4. Venture Capital	• Simple to understand • Quick to use • Commonly used	• Relies on terminal values derived from other methods • Oversimplified (large discount rate "fudge factor")
5. Asset Options	• Theoretically sound • Overcomes drawbacks of NPV and APV techniques in situations where managers have flexibility	• Methodology is not commonly used in industry and may not be understood • Real-world situations may be difficult to reduce to solvable option problems • Limitations of Black–Scholes model

underlying attributes of the company, which can be incorporated in a multiple. For example, the anticipated cash flows for a new health maintenance organization (HMO) might be accurately predicted by the number of members it has enrolled (see Example 4.1.)

There are, however, many potential problems with the use of comparables for private companies. First, it is often difficult to ascertain the valuations assigned to other privately held companies. Consequently, it may be impossible to compare our company to the companies that are most similar. Second, because accounting and other performance information on private

EXAMPLE 4.1 *Sample Valuation Using Comparables*

The fifty-year-old chairman and major shareholder of Private Health, a private regional HMO, is considering selling his stake in the company and retiring. He has asked Private Health's chief financial officer (CFO) to calculate the value of the firm by the following morning. He is entertaining two main options: the sale of his interest to an employee stock ownership plan (ESOP) or to one of the firm's publicly traded competitors. The CFO regularly receives research reports from investment bankers eager to take the company public. From these reports, she is able to compile the following information for Private Health and two public HMOs operating in the same region. Data for the 2009 financial year is in Table 4.2 (amounts in millions of dollars unless indicated).

Table 4.2   Inputs to Comparables Analysis ($ Millions)

	Private Health	Happy Healthcare	Community Health
Balance Sheet			
Assets	160	300	380
Long-Term Debt	5	100	0
Net Worth	80	120	175
Income Statement			
Revenues	350	420	850
EBITDA	45	55	130
Net Income	30	20	75
Market Data			
Earnings per Share ($/share)	3	0.67	2.14
Price-Earnings Ratio (times)		21	14.5
Shares Outstanding (M)	10	30	35
Number of Members	500,000	600,000	1,100,000

From this information, the CFO calculated the multiples and implied valuations for Private Health shown in Table 4.3. The CFO believed that overall, the multiples gave a good indication of the value of Private Health, but that it was overvalued on a price-to-earnings (P/E) multiple basis. She thought this was because Happy Healthcare (long-term debt to total assets of 33 percent) was substantially more leveraged than Private Health (3 percent). Valuing Private Health using Community Health's P/E ratio of 14.5 gave an implied valuation of $435 million. Based on her analysis, she was confident that the value of Private Health was in the range of $360 to $435 million if sold to a public company. If the shares were sold to an ESOP she believed that, because of the company's private status, it would be appropriate to assume a discount of 15 to 20 percent, or a valuation of $290 to 360 million to reflect the stock's illiquidity.

Table 4.3 Comparables Analysis ($ Millions)

	Happy Healthcare	Community Health	Average	Private Health Implied Equity Value ($M)
Price-Earnings Ratio	21.0	14.5	17.8	533
Market Value/Book Value of Equity	3.52	6.21	4.86	389
Enterprise Value/EBITDA*	9.49	8.35	8.92	397
Enterprise Value/Revenues	1.24	1.28	1.26	436

*EBITDA = earnings before interest, tax, depreciation, and amortization.

companies are often unavailable, key ratios may not be calculable, or other important impacts on valuation may be missed. Finally, the valuations assigned to comparable companies may be misguided. Periodically, whole classes of companies have been valued at prices that seem unjustifiable on a cash flow basis, as seen in the dot-com boom of the late 1990s.

Consequently, sound judgment should drive the use of comparables. One must search for potential measures of value that can be sensibly applied from one company to the next. In public markets, common ratios are (1) the share price divided by the earnings per share (the P/E ratio), (2) the market value of the company's equity divided by total revenue, and (3) the market value of the company's equity divided by the shareholder's equity on the balance sheet (market-to-book ratio). These ratios, however, may be misleading. Consider the price-earnings ratio. The earnings (profit after tax) reflect the capital structure of the company, since earnings are calculated after interest expenses and taxes. Common sense would tell us that when comparing two companies with similar characteristics but substantially different capital structures, it would be more appropriate to use a multiple based on **earnings *before* interest and taxes** (EBIT). By using this latter comparable, which ignores the different levels of interest expense each incurs, we compensate for the different capital structures of the two entities. (Of course, using EBIT ignores the interest tax shields associated with these capital structures, which we may wish to factor into the comparisons.)

Accounting-based comparables, such as those mentioned earlier, are clearly less suitable in a private equity setting where companies are often unprofitable and experiencing rapid growth. One must therefore look for other sensible measures of value. For example, in an Internet business, a good indicator of value may be the number of subscribers enrolled by a company. A valid proxy for the value of a biotechnology firm may be the number of patents awarded. In a gold exploration company, a typical measure of value is the number of ounces of gold indicated by initial drilling results. These are just a few examples of nonfinancial, industry-specific measures that can be used to estimate the value of a firm.

Interestingly, a study by Kim and Ritter[5] suggests that industry-specific multiples have strong explanatory power for the offering prices of initial public offerings (IPOs). In contrast, accounting-based multiples, such as the price-earnings ratio and the ratio of the market-to-book value of equity, were found to have little predictive ability. The reason is that among young, publicly traded firms in the same industry, accounting-based multiples vary substantially. Table 4.4 summarizes the key results.[6] The astute reader will note that, although the market-to-book ratio appears to have the most predictive power, it succeeds (defined as a result within 15 percent of reality) only one out of five times.

Using public market comparables to value private companies is further complicated by the equity's marketability. Here again we encounter the issue of illiquidity. Because shares in private

---

[5] M. Kim and J. Ritter, "Valuing IPOs," *Journal of Financial Economics* 53 (1999): 409–37.
[6] Ibid.

Table 4.4   Key Results from Kim-Ritter Analysis

	Percentage of Predicted Valuations within 15% of Actual Multiple Using:	
	Offer Price (%)	Market Price (%)*
Price/Earnings	12.1	11.1
Market/Book	21.6	21.6
Price/Sales	16.2	12.0

*Market price is the first closing market price.
Source: Adapted from M. Kim and J. Ritter, "Valuing IPOs," *Journal of Financial Economics* 53 (1999): 421.

companies are less marketable than those of typical public firms, it may be appropriate to apply a discount for illiquidity. The size of the proper discount will depend on the particular circumstances. Surveys have determined that the discounts for lack of marketability used in practice fall within a fairly narrow band, usually between 25 and 30 percent.[7]

THE NET PRESENT VALUE METHOD

The **Net Present Value** (NPV) method is one of the most common methods of cash-flow valuation. (Others include the Equity Cash-Flow and Capital Cash-Flow methods. The Adjusted Present Value (APV) method discussed in the next section is a variation on the Capital Cash-Flow method.) This section briefly visits the basics of the NPV method.

The NPV method incorporates the benefit of tax shields from tax-deductible interest payments in the discount rate (i.e., the **weighted average cost of capital**, or WACC). In calculating the WACC, each type of capital, whether common or preferred stock, bonds or long-term debt, is included with the appropriate weights. Increases in the WACC usually reflect higher risk.

To avoid double-counting these tax shields, interest payments must not be deducted from cash flows. Equation 4.1 shows how to calculate cash flows (subscripts denote time periods):

$$CF_t = EBIT_t^*(1 - \tau) + DEPR_t - CAPEX_t - \Delta NWC_t + other_t \qquad (4.1)$$

where:

$$
\begin{aligned}
CF &= \text{cash flow} \\
EBIT &= \text{earnings before interest and tax} \\
\tau &= \text{corporate tax rate} \\
DEPR &= \textbf{depreciation} \\
CAPEX &= \textbf{capital expenditures} \\
\Delta NWC &= \text{increase in net working capital} \\
other &= \text{increases in taxes payable, wages payable, etc.}
\end{aligned}
$$

Next, the **terminal value** should be calculated. This estimate is very important because most of the value of a company, especially one in an early-stage setting, may be in the terminal value. A common method for estimating the terminal value of an enterprise is the perpetuity method.

Equation 4.2 gives the formula for calculating a terminal value (TV) at time T using the perpetuity method, assuming a growth rate in perpetuity of g and a discount rate equal to r. The cash flows and discount rates used in the NPV method are typically nominal values (i.e., they are

[7] S. Pratt, *Valuing a Business: The Analysis and Appraisal of Closely Held Companies* (Homewood, IL: Dow Jones-Irwin, 1996).

not adjusted for inflation). If forecasts indicate that the cash flow will be constant in inflation-adjusted dollars, a terminal growth rate equal to the rate of inflation should be used:

$$TV_T = [CF_T * (1 + g)]/(r - g) \tag{4.2}$$

Other common methods of TV calculation used in practice include price-earnings ratios and market-to-book value multiples, but these short-cuts are not encouraged.

The NPV of the firm is then calculated as shown in Equation 4.3:

$$NPV = [CF_1/(1 + r)] + [CF_2/(1 + r)^2] + [CF_3/(1 + r)^3] + \ldots + [(CF_T + TV_T)/(1 + r)^T] \tag{4.3}$$

The discount rate is calculated using Equation 4.4:

$$r = (D/V) * r_d * (1 - \tau) + (E/V) * r_e \tag{4.4}$$

where:

r_d = discount rate for debt
r_e = discount rate for equity
τ = corporate tax rate
D = market value of debt
E = market value of equity
$V = D + E$

If the firm is not at its target capital structure, however, the target values should be used for D/V and E/V.

The cost of equity (r_e) is calculated using the capital asset pricing model (CAPM) shown in Equation 4.5:

$$r_e = r_f + \beta * (r_m - r_f) \tag{4.5}$$

where:

r_e = discount rate for equity
r_f = risk-free rate
β = beta, or degree of correlation with the market
r_m = market rate of return on common stock
$(r_m - r_f)$ = market risk premium

When determining the appropriate risk-free rate (r_f), one should attempt to match the maturity of the investment project with that of the risk-free rate. Typically, the ten-year rate is applied. Estimates of the **market risk premium** can vary widely: for simplicity, 7.5 percent can be assumed.

For private companies, or spin-offs from public companies, betas can be estimated by looking at comparable public firms. The **beta** for public companies can be found in a beta book or on the Bloomberg machine. If the firm is not at its **target capital structure**, it is necessary to "unlever" and "relever" the beta. This is accomplished using Equation 4.6:

$$\beta_u = \beta_t * (E/V) = \beta_t * [E/(E + D)] \tag{4.6}$$

where:

β_u = unlevered beta
β_t = levered beta
E = market value of equity
D = market value of debt

An issue arises if there are no comparable companies, as often occurs in entrepreneurial settings. In this situation, common sense is the best guide. Think about the cyclical nature of the particular company and whether the risk is systematic or can be diversified away. If accounting data is available, another approach is to calculate "earnings betas," which have some correlation with equity betas. An earnings beta is calculated by comparing a private company's net income to a stock market index such as the S&P 500. Using least squares regression techniques, the slope of the line of best fit (the beta) can be calculated.

A sample NPV calculation is shown in Example 4.2.

EXAMPLE 4.2 *Sample Valuation Using the Net Present Value Method*

Lo-Tech's shareholders have voted to cease its diversification strategy and refocus on its core businesses. As part of this process, the company is seeking to divest Hi-Tech, its start-up high-technology subsidiary. The management team of Hi-Tech, which wants to purchase the company, has approached George, a venture capitalist, for advice. He decides to value Hi-Tech using the NPV method. George and Hi-Tech management have agreed on the projections in Table 4.5 (all data are in millions of dollars).

Table 4.5   Inputs to Net Present Value Analysis ($ Millions)

	Year 1	Year 2	Year 3	Year 4	Year 5	Year 6	Year 7	Year 8	Year 9
Revenues	100	140	210	250	290	380	500	650	900
Costs	230	240	260	275	290	310	350	400	470
EBIT	−130	−100	−50	−25	0	70	150	250	430

The company has $100 million of net operating losses (NOLs) that can be carried forward and offset against future income. In addition, Hi-Tech is projected to generate further losses in its early years of operation that it will also be able to carry forward. The tax rate is 40 percent. The average unlevered beta of five comparable high-technology companies is 1.2. Hi-Tech has no long-term debt. Treasury yields for ten-year bonds are 6 percent. Capital expenditure requirements are assumed to be equal to depreciation. The market risk premium is assumed to be 7.5 percent. Net working capital requirements are forecast as 10 percent of sales. EBIT is projected to grow at 3 percent per year in perpetuity after Year 9.

As shown in Table 4.6, George first calculated the WACC:

$$WACC = (D/V) * r_d * (1 - t) + (E/V) * r_e = 0 + 100\% * [6.0 + 1.2 * (7.5)] = 15\%$$

Table 4.6   Net Present Value Analysis ($ Millions)

Calculating the WACC	
Tax Rate	40%
Rm − Rf	7.5%
E*N*	100%
β_u	1.2
Ten-Year Treasury Bond	6.0%
WACC	15.0%
CASH FLOWS	
Terminal Growth Rate	3.0%

Year	0	1	2	3	4	5	6	7	8	9
Revenues		100	140	210	250	290	380	500	650	900
Less: Costs		230	240	260	275	290	310	350	400	470
EBIT		−130	−100	−50	−25	0	70	150	250	430
Less: Tax		0	0	0	0	0	0	0	26	172
EBIAT (Earnings Before Interest After Taxes)		−130	−100	−50	−25	0	70	150	224	258
Less: Ch. Net Working Capital		10	4	7	4	4	9	12	15	25
Free Cash Flow		−140	−104	−57	−29	−4	61	138	209	233
Discount Factor		0.870	0.756	0.658	0.572	0.497	0.432	0.376	0.327	0.284
Present Value (Cash Flow)		−122	−79	−37	−17	−2	26	52	68	66
Present Value (Cash Flows)	(44)									
Terminal Value										2000
Present Value (Terminal Value)										569

Net Present Value and Sensitivity Analysis

						WACC		
Present Value (Cash Flows)	(44)					13%	15%	17%
Present Value (Terminal Value)	569		Terminal Growth Rate	2%	699	476	323
Net Present Value	525			3%	778	525	355
				4%	876	583	391

Tax Calculation

EBIT		−130	−100	−50	−25	0	70	150	250	430
NOLs Used		0	0	0	0	0	70	150	185	0
NOLs Added		130	100	50	25	0	0	0	0	0
Tax		0	0	0	0	0	0	0	26	172
Beginning NOLs		100	230	330	380	405	405	335	185	0
Ending NOLs		230	330	380	405	405	335	185	0	0

Net Working Capital (10% sales)

Beg NWC		10	14	21	25	29	38	50	65
End NWC	10	14	21	25	29	38	50	65	90
Ch. NWC	10	4	7	4	4	9	12	15	25

He then valued the cash flows, which showed the company had an NPV of $525 million. As suspected, all the value of the company was accounted for in the TV (the present value of the cash flows was −$44 million and the present value of the TV was $569 million, giving a NPV of $525 million).

The TV was calculated as follows:

$$\text{TV}_T = [\text{CF}_T * (1 + g)]/(r - g) = [233 * (1 + 3\%)]/(15\% - 3\%) = \$2,000$$

George also performed a scenario analysis to determine the sensitivity of the value of Hi-Tech to changes in the discount rate and the terminal growth rate. He developed a scenario table,[8] also shown in Figure 4.6.

George's scenario analysis gave a series of values ranging from $323–$876 million. Clearly, this large range did not provide precise guidance as to Hi-Tech's actual value. He noted that the profile of negative early cash flows followed by distant positive cash flows made the valuation very sensitive to both the discount rate and the terminal growth rate. George considered the NPV method a first step in the valuation process and planned to use other methods to narrow the range of possible values for Hi-Tech.

Strengths and Weaknesses of the Net Present Value Method

Estimating company values by discounting relevant cash flows is widely regarded as technically sound. Relative to comparables, the values produced should be less subject to the distortions that can occur in public and, more commonly, private markets.

Given the many assumptions and estimates that have been made during the valuation process, however, it is unrealistic to arrive at a single, or "point," value for the operation. Different cash flows should be estimated under "best," "most likely," and "worst" case assumptions. These should then be discounted using a range of values for WACC and the terminal growth rate (g) to give a likely range of values. If you can assign probabilities to each scenario, a weighted average will determine the expected value of the firm.

Even with these adjustments, the NPV method still has some drawbacks. First, we need betas to calculate the discount rate. A valid comparable company should have similar financial performance, growth prospects, and operating characteristics to the company under consideration. A public company with these characteristics may not exist. On a similar note, the target capital structure is often estimated using comparables—and using comparable companies to estimate a target capital structure shares many of the same drawbacks as finding comparable betas. Third, the typical start-up company's cash-flow profile of large initial expenditures followed by distant inflows leads to much (or even all) of the value residing in the TV. TVs are very sensitive to assumptions about both discount rates and terminal growth rates. Finally, recent finance research

---

[8] Sensitivity analyses can be easily undertaken using the Microsoft Excel command *Data Table*.

has raised questions regarding the suitability of beta as the proper measure of company risk. Numerous studies suggest that firm size or the ratio of book-to-market equity values may be more appropriate.[9] Few have tried to implement these suggestions, however, in a practical valuation context.

Another drawback of the NPV method is in the valuation of companies with changing capital structures or effective tax rates. Fluctuating capital structures are often associated with highly leveraged transactions, such as leveraged buyouts. Effective tax rates can change due to the consumption of tax credits, such as NOLs, or the expiration of tax subsidies sometimes granted to fledgling firms. Under the NPV method, the capital structure and effective tax rate are both incorporated in the discount rate (WACC) and assumed to be constant. For this reason, the APV method is recommended in these cases.

Monte Carlo Simulation

When calculating values using spreadsheets, we arrive at a single, or "point," estimate. Even when undertaking sensitivity analysis, we simply alter variables one at a time and then determine the change in the valuations. Monte Carlo simulation is an improvement over simple sensitivity analysis because it considers all possible combinations of input variables. The user defines probability distributions for each input variable, and the program generates a probability distribution describing the possible outcomes.

One such package, which is described here, is Crystal Ball.[10] The first step is to set up the base case spreadsheet. We then define the assumption and forecast variables and determine the effect of changes in the assumption cells on the value contained in the forecast cell. Assumption cells contain variables such as the discount rate, terminal growth rate, and cash flows, entered as numerical values, not formulas or text. Probability distributions define the way in which the values in the assumption cells vary. Crystal Ball has a suite of probability distributions from which to choose in describing the behavior of each variable. The user needs to select an appropriate distribution and estimate the key parameters (e.g., mean and standard deviation).

Assumptions can be defined by highlighting one variable at a time and using the command *Cell Define Assumption*. Similarly, the forecast is defined by highlighting the cell with the valuation calculation and using the command *Cell Define Forecast*. A simulation is then generated using the command *Run Run*. To create a report, use the command *Run Create Report*. A summary of the report for the NPV valuation performed in Table 4.6 is shown Figure 4.1, describing the probability distribution for the value of the subsidiary, Hi-Tech. The report also indicates that the assumptions were defined as normal distributions with means equal to the values initially contained in the cells, and standard deviations set at +10 percent of the mean.

The availability and simplicity of simulation packages make them a useful tool. Simulation allows a more thorough analysis of the possible outcomes than does regular sensitivity analysis. An additional benefit is that simulation packages allow the user to consider the interrelationships between the different input variables, and it is easy to define correlations between the various explanatory variables. One must remember, however, that in reality the shapes of distributions, and interrelationships between variables, can be very hard to discover. As sophisticated as the output reports look, the old adage about a model being only as good as the assumptions behind it still applies.

---

[9] For an overview, see Eugene F. Fama and Kenneth R. French, "The Cross-Section of Expected Stock Returns," *Journal of Finance* 47 (1992): 427–65.

[10] Crystal Ball is a personal computer simulation package produced by Decisioneering, Inc., which is located at 1515 Arapahoe Street, Suite 1311, Denver, CO 80202. The company's phone is 800-289-2550 or 303-534-1515; its fax, 303-534-4818; and its URL http://www.decisioneering.com.

FIGURE 4.1 Simulation report produced by Crystal Ball using data from NPV example

Statistics	Value
Trials	500
Mean	562
Median	535
Mode	—
Standard Deviation	194
Variance	37,485
Skewness	0.89
Kurtosis	4.05
Coeff. of Variability	0.34
Range Minimum	162
Range Maximum	1,296
Range Width	1,134
Mean Std. Error	8.66

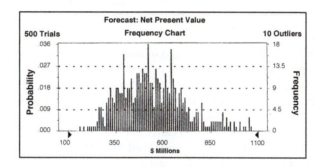

Assumptions: WACC

Normal distribution with parameters:
Mean   15.0%
Standard deviation   1.5%

Assumptions: Terminal Growth Rate

Normal distribution with parameters:
Mean   3.0%
Standard deviation   0.3%

Assumptions: Free Cash Flow (Year 1)

Normal distribution with parameters:
Mean   −140
Standard deviation   14

THE ADJUSTED PRESENT VALUE METHOD

The APV method is a variation of the NPV method. APV is preferred over the NPV method where a firm's capital structure is changing or has NOLs that can be used to offset taxable income. (An example demonstrating the APV method can be found in Example 4.3.)

EXAMPLE 4.3   *Sample Valuation Using the Adjusted Present Value Method*

Vulture Partners, a private equity organization specializing in distressed company investing, was interested in purchasing Turnaround. Mr. Fang, a general partner at Vulture, used the projections in Table 4.7 to value Turnaround (all data are in millions of dollars):

Table 4.7   Inputs to Adjusted Present Value Analysis ($ Millions)

	Year 1	Year 2	Year 3	Year 4	Year 5
Revenues	200	210	220	230	240
Costs	100	105	110	115	120
EBIT	100	105	110	115	120
ΔNWC	3	3	4	4	5

Turnaround had $220 million of NOLs available to offset future income. At the beginning of Year 1, the company had $75 million of 8 percent debt, which was expected to be repaid in three $25 million installments beginning at the end of Year 1. The tax rate was 40 percent. Mr. Fang believed an appropriate unlevered beta for Turnaround was 0.8. The ten-year Treasury bond yield was 7.0 percent and the market risk premium 7.5 percent. Net cash flows were forecast to grow at 3 percent per year in perpetuity after Year 5. Mr. Fang performed the following steps.

As shown in Table 4.8, Mr. Fang employed the APV method to value Turnaround and, as such, used the cost of equity as the discount rate:

$$\text{Cost of Equity} = r_f + \beta_u * (r_m - r_f) = 7.0 + 0.8 * (7.5) = 13\%$$

Cash flows and the terminal value were both calculated in the same manner as under the NPV method. Mr. Fang arrived at a terminal value of $690 million using the perpetuity method (assuming a growth rate of 3 percent per annum).

Mr. Fang then calculated the interest tax shields by multiplying the interest expense for each period by the tax rate of 40 percent. The interest expense was calculated using the debt repayment schedule. The present value of the interest tax shields, equal to $4.2 million, was determined by discounting each year's interest tax shield at the pretax cost of debt.

To value the tax shields from the NOLs, Mr. Fang first determined the taxable earnings for each period and hence the rate at which the NOLs would be utilized. By subtracting the interest

Table 4.8   Adjusted Present Value Analysis

Discount Rate Calculation			
Tax Rate	40%	Rm − Rf	7.5%
Ten-Year Treasury Bond	7	βu	0.8
Discount Rate (Unlevered)	13		
Step 1: Value Cash Flows			
Terminal Growth Rate	3		

Year	0	1	2	3	4	5
Revenues		200	210	220	230	240
Less: Costs		100	105	110	115	120
EBIT		100	105	110	115	120
Less: Tax		40	42	44	46	48
EBIAT		60	63	66	69	72
Less: Ch. NWC		3	3	4	4	5
Net Cash Flow		57	60	62	65	67
Discount Factor		0.885	0.783	0.693	0.613	0.543
Present Value (Cash Flow)		50	47	43	40	36
Present Value (Cash Flows)	217					
Terminal Value						690
Present Value (Terminal Value)						375

Step 2: Value Interest Tax Shields

Beginning Debt		75	50	25	0	0
Repayment (End of Year)		25	25	25	0	0
Ending Debt		50	25	0	0	0
Interest Expense		6.0	4.0	2.0	0.0	0.0
Interest Tax Shield		2.4	1.6	0.8	0.0	0.0
Discount Factor	8.00%	0.926	0.857	0.794	0.735	0.681
Present Value		2.2	1.4	0.6	0.0	0.0
Net Present Value	4.2					

Step 3: Value NOLs

EBIT		100	105	110	115	120
Interest Expense		6.0	4.0	2.0	0.0	0.0
EBIT less Interest Expense		94	101	108	115	120
NOLs Used		94	101	25	0	0
Beginning NOLs		220	126	25	0	0
Ending NOLs		126	25	0	0	0
NOLs Used		94	101	25	0	0
NOL Tax Shield		38	40	10	0	0

(continued)

Table 4.8   (*Continued*)

Discount Rate Calculation							
Discount Factor	8.00%	0.926	0.857	0.794	0.735	0.681	
Present Value (NOL)		35	35	8	0	0	
Net Present Value (NOLs)	77						

Step 4: NPV and Sensitivity Analysis				WACC			
Present Value (Cash Flows)	217				12.0%	13.0%	14.0%
Present Value (Terminal Value)	375		Terminal	2%	692	635	589
Present Value (Tax Shields)	4		Growth	3%	739	673	619
Present Value (NOLs)	77		Rate	4%	798	718	655
Net Present Value	673						

expense on debt from taxable earnings (EBIT), he determined the amount of NOLs that would be used each period. The NOL tax shields were then calculated by multiplying the NOLs consumed each period by the tax rate. Mr. Fang discounted the NOL tax shields at the pretax cost of debt. The present value of the NOLs was equal to $77 million.

The sensitivity analysis showed the likely valuation range for Turnaround to be in the order of $650 to $750 million. The range of values indicated the valuation was reasonably sensitive to both the discount and terminal growth rate assumptions.

The NPV method assumes that the capital structure of the firm remains constant at a prespecified target level. This is inappropriate in situations such as LBOS, where the high leverage of the initial capital structure is reduced as the debt is repaid. In this case, the "target" capital structure changes over time. A way of illustrating this issue is by considering a company that has undergone an LBO and has an ultimate target capital structure of zero; that is, after a certain period, it aims to have paid off all its debt. Under the NPV method, the discount rate (WACC) would be calculated using an all-equity capital structure. This ignores the company's current leverage load. APV overcomes this drawback by considering the cash flows generated by the company's assets while ignoring its capital structure. The savings from tax-deductible interest payments are then valued separately.

The NPV method also assumes that the firm's effective tax rate, incorporated in the WACC, remains constant. This is inappropriate where a firm's effective tax rate changes over time. For example, a typical start-up company incurs NOLs before it attains profitability. Under certain circumstances, these NOLs can be carried forward for tax purposes and netted against taxable income. APV accounts for the effect of the company's changing tax status by valuing the NOLs separately.

Under APV, the valuation task is divided into three steps. First, the cash flows are valued, ignoring the capital structure. The cash flows of the firm are discounted in the same manner as under the NPV method, except that a different discount rate is used. Essentially, it is assumed that the company is financed totally by equity. This implies that the discount rate should be calculated using an unlevered beta, rather than the levered beta used to compute the WACC used in the NPV analysis. The discount rate is calculated using the CAPM shown in Equations 4.5 and 4.6.

The tax benefits associated with the capital structure are then estimated. The NPV of the tax savings from tax-deductible interest payments is valuable to a company and must be quantified. The interest payments will change over time as debt levels rise or fall. By convention, the discount rate often used to calculate the NPV of the tax benefits is the pretax rate of return on debt. This amount will be lower than the cost of equity because the claims of debt holders rank higher than those of ordinary shareholders and therefore are a safer stream of cash flows.

Finally, NOLs available to the company also have value that must be quantified. NOLs can be offset against pretax income and often provide a useful source of cash to a company in its initial years of profitable operation. For instance, if a company has $10 million of NOLs and the prevailing tax rate is 40 percent, the company will have tax savings of $4 million. (Note, however, that this ignores the time value of money. The NPV of the NOLs will be only $4 million if the firm has taxable income of $10 million in its first year. If the NOLs are utilized over more than one year, then discounting will reduce their value to some amount less than $4 million.)

The discount rate used to value NOLs is often the pretax rate on debt. If you believe that the realization of tax benefits from the NOLs is certain (i.e., the company will definitely generate sufficient profits to consume them), then use the risk-free rate. If, however, there is some risk that the company will not generate enough profits to use up the NOLs, then discounting them by the pretax rate of corporate debt makes sense.

THE VENTURE CAPITAL METHOD

The Venture Capital method is a valuation tool commonly applied in the private equity industry. As discussed, private equity investments are often characterized by negative cash flows and earnings as well as highly uncertain but potentially substantial future rewards. The Venture Capital method accounts for this cash-flow profile by valuing the company, typically using a multiple, at a time in the future when it is projected to have achieved positive cash flows and/or earnings. This "terminal value" is then discounted back to the present using a high discount rate, typically between 40 and 75 percent. (We discuss the rationales for these very high discount rates later.)

The venture capitalist uses this discounted terminal value and the size of the proposed investment to calculate her desired ownership interest in the company. For example, if the company's discounted terminal value is $10 million, and the venture capitalist intends to make a $5 million investment, she will want 50 percent of the company in exchange. This assumes, however, that there will be no dilution of the venture capitalist's interest through future rounds of financing. This is an unrealistic assumption, given that most successful venture-backed companies sell shares to the public through an IPO.

The underlying mechanics of the Venture Capital method are demonstrated by the following four steps. (Example 4.4 demonstrates the Venture Capital method.) The method starts by estimating the company's value in some future year of interest, typically shortly after the venture capitalist foresees taking the firm public. The terminal value is usually calculated using a multiple; for example, a price-earnings ratio may be multiplied by the projected net income in the exit year. (See the earlier discussion of comparables.) The terminal value can of course be calculated using other techniques, including discounted cash-flow methods.

As Example 4.4 demonstrates, the Discounted Terminal Value of the company is determined by, not surprisingly, discounting the Terminal Value calculated in the first step. Instead of using a traditional cost of capital as the discount rate, however, venture capitalists typically use a Target Rate of Return. The Target Rate of Return is the yield the venture capitalist feels is required to justify the risk and effort of the particular investment. Equation 4.7 provides the formula for

---

EXAMPLE 4.4   *Sample Valuation Using the Venture Capital Method*

James is a partner in a very successful Boston-based venture capital firm. He plans to invest $5 million in a start-up biotechnology venture and must decide what share of the company he should demand for his investment. Projections he developed with company management show net income in year 7 of $20 million. The few profitable biotechnology companies are trading at an average price-earnings ratio of 15. The company currently has 500,000 shares outstanding. James believes that a target rate of return of 50 percent is required for a venture of this risk. He performs the following calculations:

Discounted Terminal Value = Terminal Value$/(1 + $Target$)^{\text{years}} = (20 * 15)/(1 + 50\%)^7 = \$17.5$ million
Required Percent Ownership = Investment/Discounted Terminal Value $= 5/17.5 = 28.5\%$
Number of New Shares $= 500{,}000/(1 - 28.5\%) - 500{,}000 = 200{,}000$
Price per New Share $= \$5$ million$/200{,}000$ shares $= \$25$ per share
Implied Pre-money Valuation $= 500{,}000$ shares $* \$25$ per share $= \$12.5$ million
Implied Post-money Valuation $= 700{,}000$ shares $* \$25$ per share $= \$17.5$ million

James and his partners believe that the company will need to hire three more senior staff. In James's experience, this number of top-caliber recruits would require options amounting to 10 percent of the common stock outstanding. Additionally, he believes that, at the time the firm goes public, additional shares equivalent to 30 percent of the common stock will be sold to the public. He amends his calculations as follows:

Retention Ratio $= [1/(1 + 0.1)]/(1 + 0.3) = 70\%$
Required Current Percent Ownership = Required Final Percent Ownership/Retention Ratio
  $= 28.5\%/70\% = 40.7\%$
Number of New Shares $= 500{,}000/(1 - 40.7\%) - 500{,}000 = 343{,}373$
Price per New Share $= \$5$ million$/343{,}373$ shares $= \$14.56$ per share

---

calculating the Discounted Terminal Value:

$$\text{Discounted Terminal Value} = \text{Terminal Value}/(1 + \text{Target})^{\text{years}} \qquad (4.7)$$

Third, the venture capitalist calculates the Required Final Percent Ownership (Equation 4.8). The amount of the proposed investment is divided by the Discounted Terminal Value to determine the ownership necessary for the venture capitalist to earn the desired return (assuming that the investment is not subsequently diluted):

$$\text{Required Final Percent Ownership} = \text{Investment/Discounted Terminal Value} \qquad (4.8)$$

Finally, the investor estimates future dilution and calculates the required current percent ownership. Equation 4.8 would be the correct answer if there were to be no subsequent "rounds" of financing to dilute the venture capitalist's interest in the company. Venture-backed companies, though, commonly receive multiple rounds of financing, followed by an IPO. Hence, this assumption is usually unrealistic. To compensate for the effect of dilution from future rounds of financing, the venture capitalist must calculate the retention ratio. The retention ratio quantifies the expected dilutive effect of future rounds of financing on the investor's ownership. Consider a company that intends to undertake one more financing round, in which shares representing an additional 25 percent of the company's equity will be sold, and then to sell shares representing an additional 30 percent of the company at the time of the IPO. If the venture capitalist owns

10 percent today, after these financings her stake will be $10\%/(1+0.25)/(1+0.3) = 6.15\%$. Her retention ratio is $6.15\%/10\% = 61.5\%$.

The Required Current Percent Ownership necessary for the venture capitalist to realize her Target Rate of Return is then calculated using Equation 4.9:

Required Current Percent Ownership = Required Final Percent Ownership/Retention Ratio   (4.9)

Strengths and Weaknesses of the Venture Capital Method

A major criticism of the Venture Capital method is the use of very large discount rates, typically between 40 and 75 percent. Venture capitalists justify the use of these high target returns on a number of grounds. First, they argue that large discount rates compensate for the illiquidity of private companies. As discussed earlier, the equity of private companies is usually less marketable than public stock, and investors demand a higher return in exchange for this lack of marketability. Second, venture capitalists view their services as valuable and consider the large discount rate as compensation for their efforts. Finally, venture capitalists believe that projections presented by entrepreneurs tend to be overly optimistic. They submit that the large discount rate adjusts for these inflated projections.

Financial economists suggest that although the issues raised by venture capitalists may be valid, they should not be addressed through a high discount rate. They propose that each of the "justifications" should be valued separately using more objective techniques. First, they argue that the discount for lack of marketability makes sense, but that the estimated premium is far too large: numerous investors—including endowments, foundations, and individuals—have long-run time horizons but receive nothing close to such extra performance for being willing to live with illiquidity. Second, financial economists contend that the services provided by the venture capitalist should be valued relative to the cost of acquiring equivalent professional services on a contract basis. Once the fair market value of the services provided was determined, the venture capitalist could be granted shares equal to this. Finally, financial economists maintain that discount rates should not be inflated to compensate for the entrepreneurs' overly optimistic projections. They argue that unbiased estimates of the company's future cash flow could be assessed by applying judgment to determine the likely values and probabilities of various scenarios.

The use of high discount rates suggests an element of arbitrariness in the venture capitalist's approach to valuing a company. A better process is to scrutinize the projections and perform reality checks. This involves asking a number of questions. What has been the performance of comparable companies? What share of the market does the company need to meet its projections? How long will it take? What are the key risks? Are contingency plans in place? What are the key success factors? This type of analysis is far more meaningful than just taking the entrepreneur's pro forma financials and discounting them at a very large rate.

OPTIONS ANALYSIS

In some cases, it is appropriate and desirable to use option pricing techniques to value investment opportunities. Discounted cash-flow methods such as NPV and APV can be deficient in situations where a manager or investor has "flexibility." Flexibility can take many forms, including the ability to increase or decrease the rate of production, defer development, or abandon a project. These changes all affect the value of the company in ways that are not accurately measured using discounted cash-flow techniques. One form of flexibility that is of particular interest to the venture capitalist is the ability to make "follow-on" investments.

Private-equity-backed companies are often characterized by multiple rounds of financing. Venture capitalists use this multistage investment approach to motivate the entrepreneur to "earn" future rounds of financing and also to limit the fund's exposure to a particular portfolio company. Often, the first right of refusal for a later stage of financing is written into the investment contract.

The right to make a follow-on investment has many of the same characteristics as a call option on a company's stock. Both comprise the right, but not the obligation, to acquire an asset by paying a sum of money on or before a certain date. As we shall see, this flexibility is not readily accounted for by discounted cash-flow techniques. By way of contrast, option pricing theory accounts for the manager's ability to "wait and then decide whether to invest" in the project at a later date.

To illustrate the drawback of using NPV flow methods when pricing options, consider the following simplified example. A project requiring an investment of $150 today is equally likely to generate revenues next year, that—discounted to today's dollars—total $200, $160, or $120. Consequently, the project will have a net present value of $50, $10, or −$30. The expected return is $10 [= (1/3) ∗ (50 + 10 − 30)].

Now consider an investor who has the ability to delay his investment until period 1.[11] By delaying investing until he obtains further information, he can avoid investing when revenues will be only $120. Essentially, by waiting and gathering more information, the investor modifies the expected return profile from [$50, $10, −$30] to [$50, $10, $0]. The option to delay investing is worth $10, the difference between the new expected NPV of $20 [= (1/3) ∗ (50 + 10 + 0)] and the earlier $10 expected value.

This section introduces a developing area in finance. For brevity, a basic knowledge of option pricing theory (at the level, for instance, of Brealey and Myers[12]) is assumed. Readers are referred to the suggested reading list at the end of this chapter for further literature on option pricing techniques.

Valuing Firms as Options

The Black-Scholes model values European options[13] by using five variables as inputs. For an option on a stock, these comprise the exercise price (X), the stock price (S), the time to expiration (t), the standard deviation (or volatility) of returns on the stock (σ), and the risk-free rate (r_f). Using these variables, we can value the right to buy a share of stock at some future point. We can evaluate a firm's decision to invest in a project using a similar framework. The equivalents are shown in Table 4.9.

Once the input variables have been estimated, the value of the option can be calculated using a Black-Scholes computer model or a call option valuation table.

Reducing Complex Problems to Options Analyses

Real-world decisions can be difficult to reduce to problems that can be mathematically solved. There is often great value, however, in attempting to simplify these types of problems. For example, the right to abandon the development of a gold mine is similar to a put option. A finance lease gives the lease holder both the right to cancel the lease by paying a fee (a put option) and the right to purchase the asset for a fixed price at the end of the lease (a call option). This section

---

[11] We assume the NPV of the investment in today's dollars is still $150, whether the investment is made in period 0 or period 1.

[12] R. Brealey and S. Myers, *Principles of Corporate Finance* (New York: McGraw-Hill, 1991).

[13] European options can be exercised (i.e., the stock can be purchased) only on the option's expiration date. American call options can be exercised at any time during the life of the option.

Table 4.9   Financial and Firm Option Variables

Variable	Financial Option	Firm Option
X	Exercise price	Present value of the expenditures required to undertake the project
S	Stock price	Present value of the expected cash flows generated by the project
t	Time to expiration	The length of time that the investment decision can be deferred
σ	Standard deviation of returns on the stock	Riskiness of the underlying assets
r_f	Time value of money	Risk-free rate of return

considers only the solution of call options using the Black-Scholes formula for European options (which can be exercised only at the end of the period).

In Table 4.9, we described the five inputs necessary to value an investment option held by a firm. The approximation of four of the variables (X, S, t, r_f) is fairly intuitive and is illustrated in Example 4.5. The process of estimating the fifth variable, the standard deviation (σ), merits further discussion. One way to estimate the standard deviation is to look at the stock price volatility for businesses with assets comparable to the project or company under consideration. These are, for instance, available on the Bloomberg machine. An important point is that volatilities estimated using this method will require adjustment to account for the leverage of the comparable company. Remember that leverage amplifies risk, and hence comparable companies with higher leverage than the project under consideration will have higher risk. As a guide, volatilities of 20 to 30 percent are not unusually high for most companies, and many small technology companies have volatilities of between 40 and 50 percent.

EXAMPLE 4.5   *Sample Valuation Using Option Pricing*

Sharon Rock, a famous venture capitalist, was considering whether to invest in ThinkTank, Inc., a company owned and managed by Mr. Brain. ThinkTank's new product was ready to be manufactured and marketed. An expenditure of $120 million was required to construct research and manufacturing facilities. Rock was of the opinion that the projections shown in Table 4.10 that were developed by Mr. Brain and his associates were justifiable (all data are in millions of dollars):

Table 4.10   Data for Option Pricing Analysis ($ Millions)

	Year 0	Year 1	Year 2	Year 3	Year 4	Year 5
Cash Flow Except Capital Expenditures	0.0	0.0	0.0	10.0	25.0	50.0
Capital Expenditures	−120.0	0.0	0.0	0.0	0.0	0.0
Total Cash Flow	−120.0	0.0	0.0	10.0	25.0	50.0

Rock performed an NPV valuation using a discount rate (WACC) of 25 percent and a terminal growth rate of 3 percent. She was unimpressed with the resulting valuation of −$11.55 million.

After thinking more carefully, Rock realized that the investment could be broken into two stages. The initial investment, which would need to be made immediately, would be $20 million for R&D equipment and personnel. The $100 million expenditure on the plant could be undertaken any time in the first two years. (Whenever the project would be undertaken, the present value of the plant construction expenditures would total $100 million in today's dollars.) Rock decided that the option to expand should not be valued using discounted cash-flow methods, since she would pursue the opportunity only if the first stage of the project were successful. The expansion opportunity could more validly be considered as an initial $20 investment bundled with a two-year European call option and priced using the Black-Scholes model.

The easiest variables to estimate were the time to expiration (t) and the risk-free rate (r_f): two years and 7 percent, respectively. The "exercise price" (X) was equal to the present value of the investment to build the plant, or $100 million. The "stock price" (S) was estimated by discounting the expected cash flows to be generated by the underlying assets associated with the expansion opportunity. Using a discount rate of 25 percent and a terminal growth rate of 3 percent per year, S was calculated as being worth $108.45 million in Year 0. The only Black-Scholes input variable remaining to be calculated was the standard deviation (σ). Rock found this difficult to estimate but proceeded to look at some comparable companies. She estimated that the value of σ was likely to lie in the range of 0.5 to 0.6.

Using this data, Rock then calculated the Black-Scholes European call option to be worth between $38.8 and $43.7 million. The total NPV of the project, equal to the cost of the first-stage investment and the value of the call option (the stage 2 opportunity), was therefore between $18.8 and $23.7 million [= −$20 million + $38.8 to $43.7 million].

Based on this analysis, Sharon Rock decided to invest in ThinkTank on the provision that she would be granted first right of refusal on any subsequent rounds of financing.

Strengths and Weaknesses of Using Option Pricing to Value Investment Opportunities

Option pricing theory is useful in situations where there is the "flexibility" to wait, learn more about the prospects of the proposed investment, and then decide whether to invest. As discussed, opportunities that incorporate flexibility will consistently be undervalued using discounted cash-flow techniques.

At least three concerns are associated with the use of option pricing methodology:

1. First, this methodology is not well known to many businesspeople, particularly in the private equity community. As with most "new technologies," it may be difficult to convince associates and counterparties that its use is valid.

2. A second drawback of the option pricing methodology is the difficulty of reducing real-world opportunities to simple problems that can be valued. While the models can accommodate cases where the firm pays dividends or where the option can be exercised early, the calculations may be more complex. Option pricing used inappropriately can inflate values achieved using other methods, thereby falsely justifying projects that would otherwise be rejected.

3. Finally, some situations may not be appropriate for the Black-Scholes formula. For instance, the exact pricing of a series of call options that are nested (i.e., where one cannot be exercised before the other one) is a difficult problem. In these cases, it may be best to use simulation techniques.

Using Option Pricing to Price Private Equity Securities

Option pricing can also be used to price private equity securities. Many of the rights associated with preferred stock (discussed in Chapter 5) can be seen as either call or put options that the private equity investor can exercise. In this way, the differential of value between common and preferred stock that we discussed earlier can be quantified.

This discussion may seem quite theoretical. But in fact, these rights can be valuable. For instance, in October 2007, Microsoft paid $240 million for 1.6 percent of Facebook.[14] A quick calculation shows that the implied valuation of this social networking site was an astronomical $15 billion. But like any venture investor worth its salt, Microsoft insisted on various protections in its preferred share. An internal Facebook calculation, which took into account the many rights that Microsoft received, computed the true value of the firm after the transaction as $3.75 billion.

This calculation might have remained an interesting academic exercise were it not for Facebook's dispute with ConnectU. The founders of the defunct Harvard dating site claimed that Facebook's founder (and Harvard classmate) Mark Zuckerberg had absconded with their intellectual property. As part of the settlement of its lawsuit against Facebook, the unsuccessful entrepreneurs agreed to accept a set number of Facebook shares. But once ConnectU's founders realized that the value of Facebook was considerably less than $15 billion (and the value of the stock they received in the settlement—in addition to $20 million in cash—was worth far less than the $45 million its lawyers claimed), they sought to renegotiate the settlement. Despite a flurry of litigation, the hapless ConnectU founders were unable to extract a larger settlement. Maybe they'll need to look around the next alumni reunion to find some other classmate to sue.

While these issues are fascinating, correctly accounting for the preferences that private equity investors enjoy can be a challenging exercise. The reader who is interested in figuring out how the features of preferred stock agreements affect the valuations of ventures is referred to Chapters 13 through 18 of Metrick's book, *Venture Capital and the Finance of Innovation*.

PUTTING IT ALL TOGETHER

Given this variety of approaches, what is the right way to think about valuing firms? Not only can each methodology be sensitive to the assumptions behind it, but different methodologies can give widely varying valuations. These are important questions, given that institutions rely on the valuation of companies to assess the performance of private equity groups to which they are or might be committed as well as to make their own budgetary decisions (for instance, a university may spend 5 percent of its endowment each year, making that figure of keen interest).

In this section, we first review the ongoing efforts to bring systematic practice to the valuation of private companies. We end the chapter with a few items of advice about the best ways to approach these issues.

Efforts to ensure that private equity groups are consistent in their valuation practices can be traced back to 1990, when a committee of the National Venture Capital Association (NVCA) proposed guidelines reproduced in Figure 4.2. Although never formally adopted, these became the industry's de facto standard. In short, they suggested that as private companies became more like public entities— generating revenues and profits, for instance—they could be valued at discounts to

---

[14] This account is drawn from Facebook, "Facebook and Microsoft Expand Strategic Alliance," press release, October 24, 2007, http://www.facebook.com/press/releases.php?p=8084, accessed August 30, 2009; Brad Stone, "What Is Facebook Worth? (Part 37)," New York Times Bits Blog, July 3, 2008, http://bits.blogs.nytimes.com/2008/07/03/what-is-facebook-worth-part-37/, accessed August 29, 2009; Brad Stone, "ConnectU's 'Secret' $65 Million Settlement With Facebook," New York Times Bits Blog, February 10, 2009, http://bits.blogs.nytimes.com/2008/07/03/what-is-facebook-worth-part-37/, accessed August 29, 2009; and Owen Thomas, "When ConnectU's Founders Won, They Still Lost," ValleyWag, February 16, 2009, http://gawker.com/5153955/when-connectus-founders-won-they-still-lost, accessed August 29, 2009.

their public comparables. Until then, companies were held at their book cost because "investment cost is presumed to represent value."[15] If a VC firm had participated in one round at 50 cents per share and a second round, led by a sophisticated unrelated party, at $2.00, the entire holding could be marked up to the latter round's price. The rule of thumb became "higher of cost or market unless impaired," where market was the most recent independent round. Valuations should be reduced if "a company's performance and potential have significantly deteriorated."[16] In general, the guidance provided by the standards was quite vague but emphasized looking at historical cost.

FIGURE 4.2   Proposed valuation guidelines of the national venture capital association

---

venture capital funds are required by generally accepted accounting principles to account for their investments in portfolio companies at value. there can be no single standard for determining value because value depends upon the circumstances of each investment. these valuation guidelines are intended to aid venture capital fund general partners in estimating the value of their investments.

Private Companies

1. Investment cost is presumed to represent value except as indicated otherwise in these guidelines.

2. Valuation should be reduced if a company's performance and potential have significantly deteriorated. Such reduction should be disclosed in the notes to the financial statements.

3. Valuation should be adjusted to equate to a subsequent significant equity financing that includes a sophisticated, unrelated new investor. A subsequent significant equity financing that includes substantially the same group of sophisticated investors as the prior financing should generally not be the basis for an adjustment in valuation.

4. If substantially all of a significant equity financing is invested by an investor whose objectives are in large part strategic, it is presumed that no more than 50% of the increase in the investment price compared to the prior significant equity financing is attributable to an increase in value of the company.

5. Valuation of a company acquired in a leveraged transaction should be adjusted if the company has been self-financing for at least two years and has been cash flow positive for at least one year. The adjustment should be based on P/E ratios, cash flow multiples, or other appropriate financial measures of similar companies, generally discounted by at least 30% for illiquidity. Such adjustment should occur no more frequently than annually and should be disclosed in the notes to the financial statements.

6. Warrants should be valued at the excess of the value of the underlying security over the exercise price.

7. The carrying value of interest bearing securities should not be adjusted for changes in interest rates.

Public Companies

8. Public securities should be valued at the closing price or bid price except as indicated otherwise in these guidelines.

9. The valuation of public securities that are restricted should be discounted appropriately until the securities may be freely traded. Such discount should generally be at least 30% at the beginning of the holding period and should decline proportionally as the restrictive period lapses.

10. When the number of shares held is substantial in relation to the usual quarterly trading volume, the valuation should generally be discounted by at least 10%.

Source: "*U.S. 1989 Valuation Guidelines*," unpublished document obtained from John Taylor, Vice President for Research, National Venture Capital Association. Used with permission.

---

[15] "Proposed Venture Capital Portfolio Valuation Guidelines (1989/1990)," National Venture Capital Association (unpublished).

[16] Ibid.

But because the NVCA guidelines were never formally adopted, VC firms could use any valuation method that the partnership agreement allowed. A study by the Tuck School at Dartmouth found that roughly a third of the 561 firms that responded followed the proposed NVCA guidelines closely.[17] A larger number used some aspects of the guidelines.[18] However, a small group of the surveyed firms indicated that "inefficiency and lack of transparency are good for the industry. . . . [A] standard would either be restrictive or uselessly vague."[19]

Meanwhile, in the early 1990s, the British Venture Capital Association (BVCA) launched its own efforts to address venture fund valuation in response to the industry's declining performance in that nation. With backing from a group of powerful limited partners (LPs), the BVCA introduced measures designed to develop a set of performance benchmarks and a consistent set of valuation standards. While these standards had more authority—from 1997 onward, firms were required to use them by the industry's regulatory body, the Financial Services Agency (FSA)—they followed the same template as the American effort.

In 2002, the BVCA proposed a new set of valuation guidelines that moved from the U.S. reliance upon cost to an approach based on fair value, or "the amount for which an asset could be exchanged between knowledgeable, willing parties in an arm's-length transaction."[20] The precise methodology to be used was defined over sixteen pages and was to be "appropriate . . . generally accepted . . . and [based] on market-based measures of risk and return. . . . Methodologies are to be applied consistently from period to period except where a change would result in a better estimate of Fair Value."[21] Preferred methodologies for valuing privately held companies included earnings multiples, the price of a recent investment, and net assets. Public companies could be held at their market price but discounted by 10 to 30 percent based on factors that would reduce liquidity, such as large holdings relative to the market or trading restrictions.[22] The European Venture Capital Association (EVCA) adopted very similar guidelines.

The backlash after the accounting scandals of the early 2000s, such as Enron—which involved, among other shenanigans, the use of wildly misvalued off-balance-sheet partnerships—led to increased scrutiny. As the Securities and Exchange Commission (SEC) moved to regulate hedge funds, the U.S. private equity industry sought to head off regulation by adopting a self-policing strategy. In February 2002, a group of LPs, GPs, buyout funds, and advisors created the Private Equity Industry Guidelines Group (PEIGG) and released a set of recommendations in December 2003.[23] Like the BVCA, the PEIGG urged GPs to comply more closely with the use of "fair value" in valuation.[24] The U.S. Generally Accepted Accounting Principles (GAAP) defined *fair value* as "the amount at which an investment could be exchanged in a current transaction between unrelated willing parties, other than in a forced liquidation sale."[25] This meant, essentially, that GPs should determine the value of their companies based on the amount a willing purchaser would pay for them today. While the GP still determined the valuation, which was to be reported on a quarterly basis, it was no longer automatically "cost or last round."

---

[17] Colin Blaydon and Michael Horvath, "GPs Say Valuation Standard is Important but Can't Agree on One," *Venture Capital Journal*, October 1, 2002, 1.

[18] Ibid.

[19] Ibid.

[20] Lisa Bushrod, "New Valuation Guidelines for BVCA," *European Venture Capital Journal*, December 1, 2002, 1.

[21] "New Reporting and Valuation Guidelines Exposure Draft," BVCA, www.bvca.co.uk, 37, accessed February 11, 2003.

[22] Ibid.

[23] Jerry Borrell, "Hedge Fund Regulators Set Sights on PE Funds," *Venture Capital Journal*, September 1, 2004, 1.

[24] This discussion informed by PEIGG, "U.S. Private Equity Valuation Guidelines" and "U.S. Private Equity Valuation Guidelines: Frequently Asked Questions," *December 2003*, http://www.peigg.org, accessed August 30, 2009; and PEIGG, "U.S. Private Equity Valuation Guidelines," *September 2004*, http://www.peigg.org, accessed August 30, 2009.

[25] PEIGG, "U.S. Private Equity Valuation Guidelines."

The guidelines aroused a great deal of comment, much of it about the ability of GPs to write up investments independent of a financing. Some LPs were concerned that without an independent third-party review, GPs would write up investments across the board,[26] although the guidelines gave fairly specific instructions regarding this move. Other observers noted that establishing fair market value was as much art as science and used no single approved methodology. One observer commented, "The PEIGG blessed just about all known valuation approaches as appropriate in some circumstances. . . . It is hard to see how this would ever get us to the goal of consistency."[27]

Despite the initial response, pressures to adopt fair value accounting only grew as accounting regulators turned to private equity in the mid-2000s. In Europe, the relevant guideline was International Accounting Standard (IAS) 39; in the United States, it was Financial Accounting Standards Board (FASB) Statement 157, known as FAS 157. While both attempted to make valuation more transparent, their application was fraught with complexity. FAS 157 (and to a lesser extent, IAS 39) focused on the "exit" price of a security, a complete change from the industry's historic emphasis on "cost or last round"—essentially, entrance price. The FASB defined *fair value* as "the price that would be received to sell an asset or paid to transfer a liability in an orderly transaction between market participants at the measurement date."[28] The PEIGG clarified this definition as "the exchange price at which hypothetical willing marketplace participants would agree to transact in the principal market, or lacking a principal market, the most advantageous market." The group went on to explain that while a public market might not exist for most private equity transactions, such an exchange could and did take place between willing participants "at arms' length" and would be applicable, as long as the securities were substantially the same.[29] Given the variation between securities in different financing rounds, such situations might arise less frequently than one could wish.

The FASB established three levels of inputs to the fair value calculation, where lower numbers corresponded to more transparent data. Thus a Level One input was the price of a public stock; Level Three was an "unobservable" input, often the output of a model or "the reporting entity's own expectations about the assumptions that market participants would use in pricing the asset in a current transaction . . . even if the market participant assumptions are different than the reporting entity's own expectations."[30] Level Two inputs combined elements of both. Critics claimed that "fair value represents an attempt by ivory tower academics to shoehorn everything into a single neat methodology without regard for the messiness of the real world,"[31] and implied the existence of "willing buyers and sellers"[32] even if the firm had no intent or desire to sell the security.

Unlike earlier efforts, the power of the accounting standards organizations—and the need for limited and general partners alike to produce financial statements that were approved by major accounting firms—made these standards widely adopted. Many groups, from private equity organizations to major financial institutions to university endowments, struggled with how to put them into practice. Accounting experts were trying desperately to do the right thing, only to be told "there is really no right way" to determine fair value.[33] "Valuation issues are more difficult than

[26] Carolina Braunschweig, "NVCA Balks at Valuation Standards," *Buyouts*, January 5, 2004, 1.

[27] Susan Woodward; quoted in Braunschweig.

[28] FASB 157 Paragraph 5; quoted in PEIGG, "2007 Updated Private Equity Valuation Guidelines: Frequently Asked Questions," http://www.peigg.org/images/2007_March_Updated_US_PE_Valuation_Guidelines_FAQ.pdf, 1, accessed August 30, 2009.

[29] PEIGG, "2007 Updated Private Equity Valuation Guidelines," http://www.peigg.org/images/2007_March_Updated_US_PE_Valuation_Guidelines.pdf, 4, accessed August 30, 2009.

[30] Center for Audit Quality, "Measurements of Fair Value in Illiquid (or Less Liquid) Markets," (white paper, October 3, 2007) 6, http://www.aicpa.org/caq/download/WP_measuruement_of_FV_in_Illiquid_Markets.pdf, accessed August 30, 2009.

[31] Jennifer Hughes, "Concept of 'Fair Value' Ignores Stench of the Real World," *Financial Times*, February 14, 2008, 16.

[32] Ibid.

[33] "FASB Fair Value Standard Remains Confusing," *Operations Management*, November 2007, 1.

I can ever remember," one senior banking auditor admitted.[34] Said the CFO of a top-tier VC firm, "I am doing nothing but FAS 157."

FINAL THOUGHTS

This chapter has dealt with the challenging area of assigning value to the companies in the private equity group's portfolios. We have first highlighted how hard it is to find their appropriate value: the special circumstances of private companies, and in particular the types of private companies in which private equity groups typically invest, make this a daunting challenge.

We then reviewed the tool kit that private equity groups employ. We began with the math of pre- and post-money valuation: how the firms' equity stakes can be translated into valuations. We then ran through the key methodologies, such as comparables, net and adjusted present value, the "venture capital" method, and the use of option pricing techniques. Along the way, we considered how simulation software can augment these approaches.

One point that came through in these discussions was the challenges involved in employing each of these methodologies, not to mention the possibility that they might produce very different answers. These challenges might lead us to anticipate that any effort to mandate valuation standards, no matter how well intentioned, may end up in ineffective confusion.

At the same time, we believe it is possible to draw some real conclusions about the valuations of private-equity-backed companies:

- Approximating reality is the best we can hope for.
- Valuations are only as good as the projections they are based on. Think long and hard about whether the projections reflect the expected outcomes and not an unrealistically rosy view.
- Explore the sensitivity of the valuations to changes in assumptions.
- Take a "big tent" approach and use a variety of approaches. If different methodologies give similar answers, confidence rises that the valuation is reasonable.
- Resist the temptation to stick to the tried-and-true approaches. We are still at an early stage in the valuation of private companies, and the development and diffusion of more advanced techniques will likely be ultimately rewarded.

FURTHER READING

BREALEY, R., and S. MYERS. *Principles of Corporate Finance.* New York: McGraw-Hill, 1991.

COPELAND, T., T. KOLLER, and J. MURRIN. *Valuation: Measuring and Managing the Value of Companies.* New York: John Wiley & Sons, 1991.

European Venture Capital Association. "The EVCA Performance Measurement Guidelines." Zaventum, Belgium: EVCA Venture Capital Special Paper, 1994.

FAMA, E., and K. FRENCH. "The Cross-Section of Expected Stock Returns." *Journal of Finance* 47 (1992): 427–65.

FENSTER, S., and S. GILSON. "The Adjusted Present Value Method for Capital Assets." Note 9-294-047. Cambridge, MA: HBS Publishing, 1994.

GREENWOOD, R., and D. SCHARFSTEIN. "Calculating Free Cash Flows." Note 9-206-028. Cambridge, MA: HBS Publishing, 2005.

HIGGINS, R. *Analysis for Financial Management.* New York: Irwin, 1992.

KAPLAN, S., and R. RUBACK. "The Valuation of Cash Flow Forecasts: An Empirical Analysis." *Journal of Finance* 51 (1995): 1059–93.

KIM, M., and J. RITTER. "Valuing IPOs." *Journal of Financial Economics* 53 (1999): 409–37.

LUEHRMAN, T. "Capital Projects as Real Options: An Introduction." Note 9-295-074. Cambridge, MA: HBS Publishing, 1995.

---

[34] Jennifer Hughes, "Valuation is the Big Issue for Auditors Twitchy over the E-Word," *Financial Times,* November 8, 2007, 19.

METRICK, A. *Venture Capital and the Finance of Innovation.* New York: John Wiley & Sons, 2007.

PRATT, S. *Valuing a Business: The Analysis and Appraisal of Closely Held Companies.* Homewood, IL: Dow Jones–Irwin, 1996.

RUBACK, R. "An Introduction to Capital Cash Flow Methods." Note N9-295-155. Cambridge, MA: HBS Publishing, 1995.

SIEGEL, D., J. SMITH, and J. PADDOCK. "Valuing Offshore Oil Properties with Option Pricing Models." *Quarterly Journal of Economics* 103 (1988): 473–508.

QUESTIONS

1. What are the difficulties and challenges that investors face in valuing early-stage companies?

2. Describe the difference between pre-money and post-money valuation. In what settings are investors most likely to focus on pre-money valuation, and when on post-money valuation?

3. What were the pre-and post-money valuations for GENBAND's August 2000 financing?

4. What are the potential shortfalls of using comparables to value a private company?

5. What are appropriate multiples to use when comparing two companies with different capital structures and varying levels of capital expenditures? Which are not?

6. Calculate the WACC using the following assumptions:

$$D = \$200 \text{ million}$$
$$r_d = 4\%$$
$$r_f = 3\%$$
$$E = \$400 \text{ million}$$
$$\tau = 30\%$$
$$\beta = 1.9$$
$$(r_m - r_f) = 7.5\%$$

7. Recalculate the NPV of Hi-Tech using the data in Table 4.6; but assume that the company is currently not at its target capital structure, which is 30 percent debt and 70 percent equity. Also assume the firm's cost of debt is 8 percent.

8. What are the drawbacks of the NPV method?

9. Under what circumstances is it more useful to use the APV method than the NPV method?

10. Calculate the APV for Hi-Tech using the assumptions in Table 4.6 and assuming the firm takes on $100 million debt at the time of the sale. At the end of each subsequent year to the sale, $25 million of this debt is retired.

11. Suppose a venture capitalist owns 20 percent of a company today, and the company intends to undertake three additional rounds of financing, selling additional shares of its equity of 20, 25, and 20 percent. Calculate her retention ratio.

12. What are the criticisms of using high discount rates for the Venture Capital method? How do venture capitalists justify their use?

13. Under what circumstances is using the option pricing model more useful than the discounted cash-flow method?

14. What are some of the difficulties regulators face regarding portfolio company valuations?

15. Compare and contrast how FASB and PEIGG define *fair value*. Which definition do you agree with? Why?

Chapter 5

Deal Structuring—
Private Equity Securities
and Their Motivation

After a firm has decided to invest in or purchase a company, the GPs do not simply write a check and walk out with a stack of stock certificates under their collective arms. Private equity, be it venture capital (VC) or growth or leveraged buyout (LBO) financing, requires deal structures that allow for active intervention and protect the investors against loss while encouraging the entrepreneurs or management team to strive for the greatest possible gain from the investment. While there are general similarities among these, we do encounter some differences in deal structuring between minority investing (venture capital and growth equity) and majority investing (buyouts), as well as differences caused by the use of debt (mezzanine and buyout transactions).

The key feature common to all private equity securities is the illiquidity of these investments. When a public securities trader buys stock in IBM and becomes dissatisfied with the company's direction, he can simply sell the stock. That is not true for the private equity investor. Consequently, private equity securities are designed to take into account the active investor's need to stay and fix the situation rather than simply sell the securities.

As emphasized in the previous chapters, the challenge of illiquidity is compounded by the information gaps between the company's management and the active investors. In general, management or the entrepreneur knows more than the investor. Hence, the investors want to be sure that the entrepreneur is encouraged to do the right thing, and that their own investment is protected.

Private equity securities, therefore, are designed to protect the investors on the downside—that is, from losing money—and enable them to intervene by changing the company's management and strategy when necessary. The party that funds a project does not have day-to-day control over execution, but gets some degree of protection from loss (downside protection) in case the management team that is responsible for execution fails to perform.

In the example of the start-up of eDOCS,[1] a company that provided document and image management systems, Kevin Laracey, the founder and CEO, received a term sheet that prominently featured a liquidation preference, the vesting of management stock, and, in the cover letter, the possibility of bringing in a new CEO. The liquidation preference, discussed later in this chapter, protected Charles River Ventures (CRV), the investor, should eDOCS fail to meet its

---

[1] Paul Gompers, "eDOCS Inc. (A)," HBS Case No. 200-015 (Boston: HBS Publishing, 2001).

117

expectations. This term allowed CRV to receive its money first from any sale or liquidation of the business. Vesting of stock—the practice by which an employee only gradually earns full ownership of a stock grant—allowed the firm to consider replacing members of the management team in the event of the company's underperformance, since some portion of their stock would be returned to the company, and that in turn could be used to hire and incentivize new executives. In addition, because the CEO and other managers did not own their entire stock grants outright, each had an incentive to pursue strategies that created long-run value in the company.

This chapter explores in some depth the key securities used in private equity transactions and the nature of their terms, along with examples of how these terms are used. More important, since all financing negotiations are in fact a conversation between the investor and the company's management, terms act as a signaling device to exchange information in a very precise way regarding what each party expects and fears. We discuss this signaling aspect in some detail.

The terms and securities used in the venture capital setting are similar to those used in the LBO setting. Buyouts differ along two dimensions: because the deal structure includes debt securities, we must understanding how the debt interacts with the equity securities; and because buyouts are majority control investments, they may be structured with less specific control provisions. Mezzanine investing is a type of later-stage minority investing and uses a variety of flexible debt and equity securities that we will deal with separately. Therefore, this chapter begins with basic private equity securities using the VC model and then expands to consider other terms used in the mezzanine and buyout setting. We then walk through a term sheet and finally create a capitalization table.

BASIC PRIVATE EQUITY SECURITIES

In the beginning there was common stock . . .

Common stock is the basic unit of ownership.[2] It carries no special rights beyond those described in the company charter and bylaws. It is the security that is typically bought when putting in an order for a publicly listed stock at a broker. It gives the holder ownership that is subordinated to (1) all government claims (read "taxes"), (2) all regulated employee claims (e.g., pension obligations), (3) all trade debts (accounts receivable), (4) all bank debt, and (5) all forms of preferred stock. Specifically, were the company to be liquidated—or sold in an asset sale—the common shareholder stands behind all those other stakeholders before getting the residual value, that is, what's left after all other obligations are satisfied.

Typically, venture capitalists do not buy common stock. The fundamental reason is illustrated by the following example: Sam Flash has a great idea for a new Internet company and goes to his local venture capitalist, Max Finance. Sam and Max agree that $1.5 million will fund the project to the next big value accretion point, and they further agree on a 50.05/49.95 split, with Sam holding the majority stake. But contrary to standard venture practice, due likely to intense competition to finance Sam's deal, Max agrees to a structure involving all common stock. Therefore, immediately after the closing, the company has an implied enterprise value of $3 million (since the market price that Max paid was $1.5 million for 49.95 percent), one employee (Sam), and one class of tangible assets (cash), and some intangible assets (Sam's PowerPoint slides and a business plan).

---

[2] This section draws from Felda Hardymon and Josh Lerner, "Note on Private Equity Securities," HBS Case No. 200-027 (Boston: HBS Publishing, 2000).

FIGURE 5.1 Payout chart for all common structure

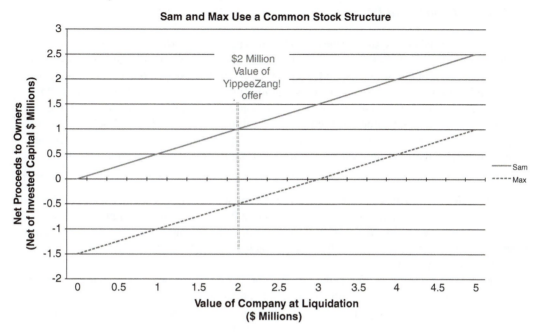

On the day of the closing, as they walk out of the lawyer's office, Sam bumps into his old friend, Isabel Amazing, who is vice president for business development of YippeeZang!, a public Internet company valued in the market at just over $12 billion. YippeeZang! needs ideas and talent to maintain its stock price, so Isabel pulls Sam aside and offers him $2 million for the new company. Seeing a quick return on the hours he put into writing his business plan and concerned that YippeeZang! will use its considerable resources and market clout to enter the market ahead of him should he decline, Sam accepts the offer.

How is the pie divided? (See the payout chart in Figure 5.1 and the payout table in Table 5.1.)

Sam and Max each get $1 million from YippeeZang!, so in a matter of minutes Sam's investment goes from zero (sweat equity) to $1 million, while Max's investment goes from $1.5 million (cash) to $1 million. Max was powerless through the whole process because Sam held slightly more shares and therefore could vote the majority for the sale. Note that YippeeZang! recruited Sam and his idea for a mere $500,000, since they end up with the $1.5 million, less the legal fees, that was in Sam's company. How could Max have avoided this disaster?

Table 5.1   Net Payout Table for All-Common Structure

	Max invests $1.5M for 49.95 percent		
	Common Stock Structure		
	Transaction Value		
Payout Net of $1.5 Million Invested	$2 Millions	$5 Millions	$10 Millions
Max	$(0.501)	$0.998	$3.495
Sam	$1.001	$2.503	$5.005

Payout Tables and Charts

Payout tables and charts, such as the ones shown in this chapter, show the proceeds that each investor or class of securities would receive at the time of a company's sale or liquidation. Generally, payout charts are shown for a range of possible valuation outcomes. In our case, the chart shows the payout for company valuations ranging from zero to $5 million that Max and Sam would each receive in the event they both hold common stock. We show the *net* payout—the amount returned to each *net* of the dollars invested. In this book we use net payout charts as a convention since from an investors' point of view, the *total* proceeds are less important than the proceeds *net of invested dollars* (i.e., the gains and losses).

Most venture securities contain three features, any one of which would have saved Max from having to explain to his partners how he lost $500,000 in an afternoon: (1) preferred stock; (2) vesting of shares owned by the founder, management, and key employees; and (3) covenants and super majority provisions. We briefly discuss each feature, highlighting the major variations commonly used in practice.

These three features reinforce the reward for performance principle. That is, the active investor is trading day-to-day control for downside protection (preferred stock), and the management team is rewarded for high performance and given an uncapped potential if they capture the opportunity. However, there are contingent controls (board seats, covenants) that allow the active investor to intervene and get the project back on track should it go awry. The exercise of these governance powers is discussed in Chapter 6.

Key to all of these structural features is the concept of the entrepreneur earning equity through value creation. In the preceding example, Max valued Sam's company based on its potential value, not its current tangible value. In a perfect, frictionless world, Max's money might be metered into Sam's company precisely in proportion to the value being created and expenses incurred; but in the real world, entrepreneurs need to finance ahead of their expenses—a vice president of Sales usually receives some of the agreed-upon salary before sales increase. Moreover, value is created in lumps coincident with important events like the first proof of product feasibility, the first customer shipment, and major successes in the marketplace. VC bridges such value accretion events; at the same time, the entrepreneur should not be able to truly own his or her stake until the company has delivered on the promised value. This is the basis of the typical deviations from common stock used by private equity investors. In the example, Sam had not *earned* his equity interest at the time of the YippeeZang! buyout, and that violated the principle of reward for performance. Max had valued Sam's company based on its potential future value, and the immediate sale stopped value accretion before it started.

In the case of common stock, control in the form of voting on the board of directors, changing the company bylaws, and even selecting management is coincident with economic interests. If one party owns 30 percent of the common stock, then that party has not only 30 percent of the economic interest but also 30 percent of the voting rights that control the company. In the classic private equity deal structure, economic interests are separated from control features. In fact, the goals of deal structure in a private equity setting are to (1) align the interests of both parties to add value, (2) signal commitment from both sides (this is usually through vesting, performance guarantees, and benchmarks), (3) anticipate the needs for future financing, and (4) streamline the transfer of value to both parties as the company itself becomes more valuable. That is, in nearly all private equity deal structures, the upside is uncapped for both the equity investors and management.

The notion of alignment of interests is important in private equity securities, just as it has been in fund-raising and investment. For securities, the alignment of interest comes about from both terms and the split of the company's underlying equity. On the one hand the equity split is based in part on the perceived potential of the business, its future cash flows, and the progress made to date—all of which combine to attract investment if the split gives the investor a large enough share of the future value to compensate him for the risk he perceives. On the other hand the equity split needs to put enough future value in the hands of the entrepreneur to ensure that the entrepreneur has enough incentive to continue to work hard. We will see that the terms of private equity securities can change the split of future value between the investor and entrepreneur based on the value of the exit, thus tuning the equity split to reduce the risk of the investor losing all his money while keeping the potential of uncapped reward for the entrepreneur.

PREFERRED STOCK AND ITS VARIATIONS

Particularly in the most developed markets, such as the United States and Europe, private equity investors (especially venture capitalists) typically purchase not common stock but preferred stock. This security has a *liquidation preference* over common stock; that is, if the company is sold or liquidated, the preferred stock gets paid first, ahead of the common stock. Preferred stock therefore has a face value, which is the amount that the preferred stockholders receive before the common stock is paid. Generally the face value of preferred stock in a private equity transaction is the cost basis—the amount that the investor pays for the stock. If in the original example Max had invested his money in Sam's company in the form of preferred stock, then when YippeeZang! purchased Sam's company, Max's $1.5 million would have been returned to him through redemption of the preferred stock. But that leaves a $500,000 remainder. How would that have been divided? Answering that question leads to a discussion of the variations of preferred stock.

Redeemable Preferred

Redeemable preferred, sometimes called "straight preferred," is preferred stock that cannot be converted into common equity. Its intrinsic value is therefore its face value plus any dividend rights it carries. Dividends are discussed in detail later in the chapter.

In most ways, redeemable preferred behaves like deeply subordinated debt (i.e., if the firm gets into trouble, the redeemable preferred stock is paid off only after the banks and other lenders are repaid). But there are some twists. Redeemable preferred stock always carries a negotiated term specifying when it *must* be redeemed by the company—typically the earlier of a public offering or five to eight years. The term of five to eight years coincides with the notion that private equity investors invest from funds that have a limited life and provides some assurance to the general partners (GPs) that a liquidity event will occur before the fund's life ends.

Redeemable preferred stock is used in private equity transactions in combination with common stock or warrants. (A warrant is like the call option discussed in Chapter 4: it gives the holder the right but not the obligation to buy a share at a preset price. The key difference is that a warrant is typically issued by the same company that would issue the stock the warrant holder would purchase. As a result, warrants issued by the company are dilutive: when the warrant is exercised, the company issues new shares of stock, so the number of outstanding shares increases.) Let's see what would have happened had Max agreed with Sam to the same 50.05/49.95 split, but specified that his investment would be in the form of units of redeemable preferred stock. In this case, the redeemable preferred would have a face value of roughly $1.5 million face value (so Max would get his money back) and Max would also have 49.95 percent of the common stock bought for pennies (in our example, we have Max paying $1,000 for the entire 49.95 percent worth of common). In the YippeeZang! acquisition, the straight preferred stock would be redeemed first —$1.499 million to Max—and the remaining $500,000 would have been split proportionally to the ownership of common stock (approximately $250,000 each to Max and to Sam, as shown in Table 5.2).

Table 5.2 Net Payout Table for Redeemable Preferred (Pfd) and Cheap Common Structure

		Max Invests $1.5M for 49.95 Percent		
		$1.499 Million Redeemable Preferred + $1,000 Common Structure		
		Transaction Value		
		$2 Millions	$5 Millions	$10 Millions
	Max	$0.249	$1.748	$4.245
	Sam	$0.251	$1.752	$4.255

(Left side vertical label: Payout Net of $1.5 Million Invested)

Had the company gone on to a successful public offering, Max could have expected his initial $1.5 million investment to be returned through redemption of the redeemable preferred without affecting his basic ownership position held in common stock. He would in effect be getting his money back *and* keeping his investment in the common equity of the company. As observed in the accompanying charts, the redeemable preferred plus common stock structure means that once Max is paid back, Max and Sam share essentially equally (due to their equity split of 50.05/49.95) in returns higher than $1.5 million, as shown in Figure 5.2. However, Sam might be troubled by the lack of a catch-up once Max's initial investment has been returned: while Sam and Max receive the same net returns, the gross amount is greater for Max (due to the return of his investment through the redemption of preferred stock). Sam might feel it more reasonable that the gross payout be shared equally after Max is assured of getting his cost basis back.

One possible solution to the problem of an entrepreneur's slow recovery after the return of the investor's capital could be to assign more value to the common stock. For example, Max could have invested his $1.5 million by buying a $750,000 redeemable preferred stock and then paid an

FIGURE 5.2 Payout chart of redeemable preferred plus cheap common structure

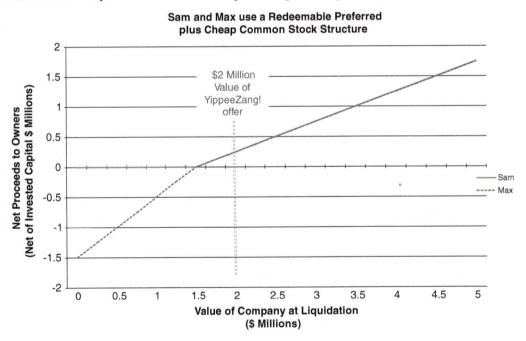

Table 5.3   Net Payout Table for Redeemable Preferred and Expensive Common Structure

		Max invests $1.5M for 49.95 percent	
	$750,000 Redeemable Preferred + $750,000 Common Structure		
		Transaction Value	
	$2 Millions	$5 Millions	$10 Millions
Max	$(0.126)	$1.373	$3.870
Sam	$0.626	$2.127	$4.630

(Left margin label: Payout Net of $1.5 Million Invested)

additional $750,000 for the 49.95 percent of common stock. In that case the payout chart would have been more favorable to Sam. But note that in the $2 million YippeeZang! transaction, Max first would have received his $750,000 back and then split the remaining $1.25 million with Sam, for a total return of $1.375 million and a loss of $125,000 in an afternoon. While better than losing $500,000 in the all-common deal, this is hardly a successful VC investment. Sam would have made $625,000 in the deal, as if he had "earned" his payout, but Max would have still lost money on the investment before Sam did anything (see Table 5.3 for the outcomes table in this case, and Figure 5.3 for the payout chart).

For several reasons, it is accepted practice to assign as much value as possible to the redeemable preferred and very little to the common stock in these redeemable preferred plus common stock structures:

FIGURE 5.3   Chart for a $75,000 redeemable preferred and expensive common structure with $75,000 in the common

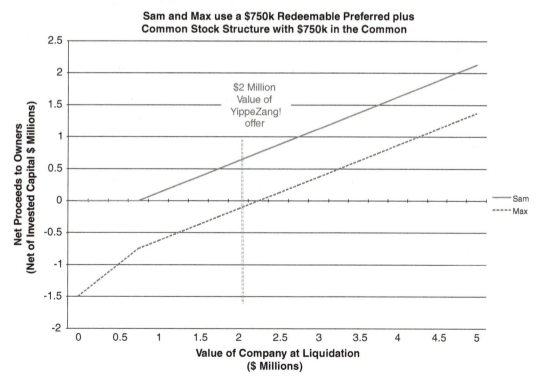

1. *Downside protection.* Using preferred stock means that the common stock, in essence, does not receive value before it is earned—as described in the previous examples. From the investor's perspective, it makes sense to put as much value in the preferred as possible to encourage the entrepreneur to create as much value as possible in the company so that at the exit, the preferred will be easily repaid with lots of money left over for the common. Note that this structure helps resolve one of the sources of uncertainty in the deal—that the investor does not know how hard the entrepreneur will work. If the initial example had not been structured with all-common stock but instead was redeemable preferred plus common with nearly all of the investment in the preferred, Sam would have had to repay Max's $1.499 million preferred before he got any money from this venture. No quick $1 million payday for Sam! Such a structure makes it easy for Max to believe that Sam is going to work really hard. Max is protecting $1.499 million with a priority payout and exposing only $1,000 to being paid out last with the common stock.

2. *Pricing employees' incentive shares.* To purchase the shares for which they have been granted options, employees have to write a check on their own accounts. They may have more pressing things to purchase (like food). To encourage employee stock ownership, which aligns employee interests with the company's success, the board of directors wants the share price for common stock to be as low as possible. This practice has two outcomes: it makes the shares affordable and increases the likelihood that any liquidity event, whether a sale or an initial public offering (IPO), will occur at a price that creates a gain for the employees—consider the difference between a sale at $5 per share when the employees have paid 5 cents per share as opposed to $8 per share. The prospect of creating wealth for themselves will encourage employees to stay with the company and work hard. The board can use the "cheap common" precedent of the transaction as the basis of a low share price. For example, if the board can issue employee incentive shares at 1 cent per share rather than at $1 per share, each incentive share has 99 cents *more* embedded value, assuming the same eventual sale price. The price at which boards may issue incentive shares to employees without running afoul of tax issues[3] is controlled by the "market value" of the underlying common stock, set by the valuation established in the financing round. This dynamic creates a further reason to price the common as low as possible.

3. *Tax deferral.* Investors pay taxes when they realize gains from selling their stock. The gain, of course, is the difference between what they paid for the stock (the "cost basis") and the amount they received for it. As a general principle, investors want to defer taxes—that is, pay taxes later rather than sooner—because of the time value of money. In the case of a redeemable preferred plus common stock structure, the investor is holding two securities: preferred stock and common stock. When the preferred stock is redeemed, the investor receives the face value, which is usually the cost basis. Because redemption of preferred stock is simply return of capital with no associated gain, there is no tax on redemption.[4] Moreover, since the preferred is much more likely to be redeemed before the common is sold, putting more value in the preferred portion of the unit defers tax. In our example, Max paid $1.499 million for a redeemable preferred stock and $1,000 for the 49.95 percent of common stock. If the company later goes public, Max could redeem the preferred stock and thereby get nearly all of his money back. Since redemption is a return of capital for tax purposes, there would be no tax consequences at that time. Max would be deferring taxes on

---

[3] The tax laws around incentive compensation plans are complex, though in many cases, companies are able to maintain very low prices for their common stock. For more on such issues, see Constance E. Bagley and Craig Dauchy, *The Entrepreneur's Guide to Business Law*, 3rd ed. (Mason, OH: South-Western College/West, 2007).

[4] Note that in the case of multiple liquidation preferences described later in this chapter, there would be a gain on redemption of redeemable preferred stock because the face value for which it is redeemed exceeds the cost basis.

the gain from his investment in Sam's company until he sells his common stock with the low tax cost basis of $1,000.

Yet problems also arise if the preferred has too much value—as in the case just described, where Max has $1.499 million in preferred and only $1,000 in common. In an IPO, the redeemable preferred stock usually carries a term that stipulates it should be redeemed out of the proceeds of the public offering. Since public investors don't like to buy stock in a company at the same time that the old investors are taking money out of the company, the company's public market value can be adversely affected when a substantial portion of the IPO's proceeds is used to redeem out the venture capitalists' preferred stock. These issues of redeemable preferred, in particular, the slow catch-up for the entrepreneur and the issues around pricing the common, have led to the use of *convertible* preferred stock in many private equity transactions.

Convertible Preferred Stock

Convertible preferred stock is preferred stock that can be converted *at the shareholder's option* into common stock. This forces the shareholder to choose between taking returns through the liquidation feature or through the underlying common equity position. Clearly, if the value being offered for the company exceeds the implied total enterprise value at the time of the investment, then the shareholder will convert the preferred stock to common stock in order to realize her portion of the gain in value. Table 5.4 presents the payout for Max and Sam in the event of different exit values if Max owns convertible preferred stock.

Conceptually, convertible preferred allows the entrepreneur to catch up to the investor after the investor's initial investment is secured. Compare the net payoff chart for convertible preferred stock (Figure 5.4) with the previous net payoff chart for redeemable preferred stock (Figure 5.3).

If Max had held convertible preferred stock in our example, YippeeZang!'s offer to buy the company would have forced him to decide whether to convert. Recall that on conversion, Max owns basically half the company's stock. If he had converted to the common, he would have received 49.95 percent of the proceeds (about $1 million), which would have left him in a loss position. Therefore, he would *not* have converted, instead receiving his original $1.5 million investment from the redemption of the unconverted preferred, and Sam would have gotten the residual $500,000. On the other hand, if YippeeZang! had chosen to pay more than $3 million for Sam's company, Max would have had an incentive to convert to common stock in order to enjoy his portion (49.95 percent) of whatever premium over the $3 million implied enterprise value that YippeeZang! was offering. If, for instance, YippeeZang! had offered $4 million, Max would have happily converted and received $2 million.

One result of the convertible preferred structure is that Max gets each dollar from the sale of the company up until the sale price is equal to his $1.5 million preference. After that, Max must decide whether to convert or take his preference. Until the sale price reaches $3 million, he is better

Table 5.4   Net Payout Table for Convertible Preferred Structure

		Max invests $1.5M for 49.95 percent		
Payout Net of $1.5 Million Invested		**Convertible Preferred Structure**		
		Transaction Value		
		$2 Millions	$5 Millions	$10 Millions
	Max	$ —	$0.998	$3.495
	Sam	$0.500	$2.503	$5.005

FIGURE 5.4   Net payout chart for convertible preferred structure

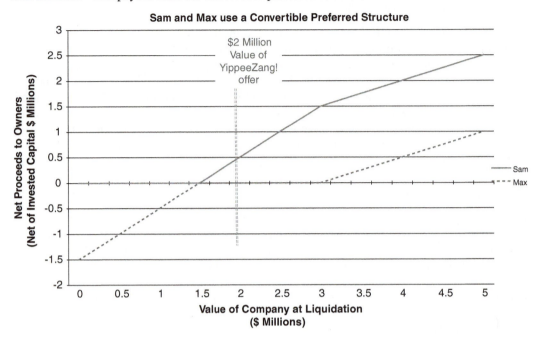

off taking the $1.5 million preference. Thus there is a "flat spot" in Max's payout chart between selling the company for $1.5 million and for $3 million. In that range, Max always receives $1.5 million and Sam gets the incremental value of the company's increasing sale price. This is the catch-up, where Sam catches up to Max once Max receives all his money back. By the end of the catch-up phase, the gross (not net) amounts of the payouts the two individuals receive are about equal.

Why don't we see any of these types of preferred stock in young *public* companies? In short, because preferred structures are somewhat complex, younger public companies eschew them.[5] The public markets generally expect companies to have a simple capital structure that uses only common stock and debt. Underwriters nearly always insist that *all* preferred stock be converted at the time of an IPO. To avoid a round of negotiations where investors demand to be compensated for their conversion to common, convertible preferred stock routinely contains a mandatory conversion term that allows the company to force conversion as part of an underwritten IPO of a certain (negotiated) size and price. The minimum size necessary to trigger such a conversion is usually large enough to ensure a liquid market, and the minimum price is usually two or three times the level at the time of the investment, high enough to ensure the investors' keen interest in converting.

Participating Convertible Preferred Stock

Participating convertible preferred stock is convertible preferred stock with the additional feature that in the event of a sale or liquidation of the company, the holder has a right to receive the face value *and* their equity participation *as if* the stock were converted; that is, it *participates* in the equity even after conversion. Like convertible preferred stock, these instruments carry a mandatory conversion term triggered on a public offering. The net result is an instrument that acts like redeemable preferred while the company is private and converts into common stock on a

---

[5] Mature public companies, especially financial service companies, often have several layers of preferred stock in many forms.

Table 5.5   Net Payout Table for Participating Convertible Preferred Structure

	Max Invests $1.5 Million for 49.95 Percent		
	Participating Convertible Preferred Structure		
	Transaction Value*		
	$2 Millions	$5 Millions	$10 Millions
Max	$0.249	$1.748	$4.245
Sam	$0.251	$1.752	$4.255

Payout Net of $1.5 Million Invested (row label, vertical)

*Unlike a redeemable structure, participating convertible preferred reverts to a common stock structure after the IPO.

FIGURE 5.5   Net payout chart for participating convertible preferred structure

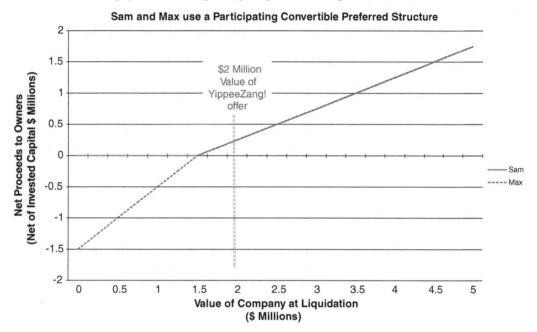

public offering, as shown in Table 5.5. The payout chart in Figure 5.5 is identical to the chart for the redeemable plus preferred structure.

Indeed, the mandatory conversion feature is the primary reason for using participating convertible preferred stock over a redeemable preferred stock and cheap common structure. The participating convertible preferred stock does not have the awkwardness of forcing a payout to the private investors at the public offering, something underwriters often discourage since it is easier to sell a new public offering if all the proceeds will be used to further the company's business rather than pay out existing shareholders.

Details of Participation: The Change of Control

A key companion term to a participating convertible preferred security specifies when the participation term is in effect. Usually the term reads "in the event of sale or liquidation" and often defines *liquidation* as any merger or transaction that constitutes a change of control. As a result, a merger transaction between two private firms may trigger this clause if the private surviving merged company issues new stock in exchange for the preexisting preferred stock of the acquired company. The holders of the participating convertible preferred may then demand both new stock equal in face value to the old preferred stock *plus* a participation in the common equity of the new company equivalent to the conversion of stock for the common shareholders. This in turn can lead to problems in valuing the securities involved since the participation feature calls for receiving private stock that is *valued* the same as the face value of the preferred stock. Note that this transaction does not generate any true liquidity (no cash changes hands) because it is an exchange of private, illiquid securities.

Multiple Liquidation Preferences

The difference in the net payoff curves of the participating convertible preferred stock and convertible preferred stock suggests that these terms are simply a function of each party's expectations. In our example, Max may doubt Sam's eventual success and insists on a participating convertible preferred structure in order to capture a larger share of the proceeds once the company is worth more than his $1.5 million investment. That is, depending on the market, the negotiation between the entrepreneur and the private equity firm may dictate that one or the other has better treatment in the lower exit values—the downside.

For example, the convertible preferred clearly favors the entrepreneur compared to the participating convertible preferred because it requires a catch-up to the level of investment before both parties share in the gains. The chart in Figure 5.6 compares the two for Sam in our example.

FIGURE 5.6   Comparison of convertible preferred and participating convertible preferred structures from the entrepreneur's point of view

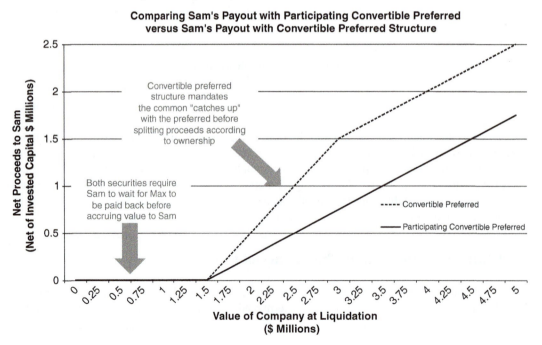

Table 5.6   Net Payout Table for 2× Convertible Preferred Structure

	Max Invests $1.5M for 49.95 Percent		
	2 × Convertible Preferred Structure		
	Transaction Value		
	$2 Millions	$5 Millions	$10 Millions
Max	$0.500	$1.500	$3.495
Sam	$ —	$2.000	$5.005

Payout Net of $1.5 Million Invested

In the nonparticipating case, Sam's share increases much faster after Max gets all of his money back. In fact, Sam gets *all* of the proceeds after $1.5 million (i.e., the amount Max invested) until he too has $1.5 million. At that point, Sam and Max share proportionally to their ownership (50.05–49.95 percent). However, in the participating preferred case, Sam and Max share proportionally as soon as Max has his investment back, which shifts the gains from Sam to Max.

The difference between the catch-up seen in convertible preferred and participating convertible preferred is one way of responding to different expectations of the entrepreneur and the investor regarding exits at low values. If the investor is concerned about low-value exits, participation gives him an extra turn on his capital compared to having no participation. Another way to adjust for the risk of low exit values is by modifying the liquidation preference. All of our previous examples have assumed a liquidation preference of one; that is, Max gets his cost basis back and then the sharing begins. But multiple liquidation preferences allow for finer adjustment of different expectations. For example, convertible preferred can be specified to have a *2 × liquidation preference*; that is, the security holder will get twice the face value of the preferred before starting to share with the entrepreneur. If Max had a 2× liquidation preference in our earlier example, he would have received the entire $2 million when YippeeZang! bought Sam's company for $2 million. In fact, with a 2× liquidation preference, Max would have received all of the proceeds of any sale up to $3 million (i.e., twice the $1.5 million that he has put in), as shown in Table 5.6. At values higher than $3 million, Sam would receive every additional dollar of exit value up to $6 million, as shown in Figure 5.7. That is, there is still the concept of a catch-up for the entrepreneur, even though there are multiple liquidation preferences.

By comparing the payout charts, you can see that these terms (i.e., multiple liquidation preference and participation) are simply pricing mechanisms that alter the net payoff between the entrepreneur and the investor in the lower ranges of exit values. Table 5.7 shows how multiple liquidation preferences of 3× and 5× change our example.

In Figure 5.8, we compare the payout charts for Max in our example for convertible preferred stock with various liquidation preferences.

As shown in the chart, Max gets the first $1.5 million in a 1× liquidation preference. Then he has to wait for Sam to catch up, so he doesn't share in the gains until the company's payout reaches $3 million. Thereafter he receives 49.95 percent. At 2× liquidation preference, Max gets $3 million back ("2×" his $1.5 million liquidation preference) and then has to wait until Sam receives $3 million before sharing, which requires an exit value of $6 million. A 3× liquidation preference gives Max $4.5 million ahead of Sam and then $4.5 million to Sam, and sharing starts after $9 million. Finally, a 5× liquidation preference requires a very large exit value just to pay Max, let alone leave any reward for Sam. In this case, Max gets the first $7.5 million and then the next $7.5 million goes to Sam. Only after the company has paid out $15 million would Max convert his preferred into common and the two would split the proceeds based on their 50.05/49.95 percent equity split.

FIGURE 5.7   Net payout chart for 2× convertible preferred structure

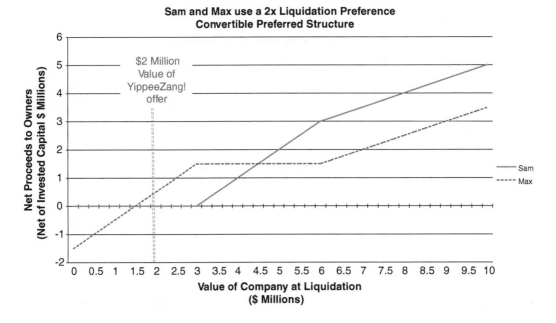

Use of the various liquidation preferences can be a reaction to market conditions as much as a price negotiation. For example, in the VC market in the post-2000 bubble crash, it was not unusual for later rounds of struggling companies to be priced with liquidation preferences of 6× or even higher. In these cases, investors usually were trying to save a failing company and expected to get their return entirely from the multiples of liquidation preference. By using high multiples of liquidation preferences, they could leave previous preferred stock in place and simply make the

Table 5.7   Net Payout Table for 3× and 5× Convertible Preferred Structure

		Max Invests $1.5M for 49.95 Percent		
Payout Net of $1.5 Million Invested		**3 × Convertible Preferred Structure**		
		Transaction Value		
		$2 Millions	$5 Millions	$10 Millions
	Max	$0.500	$3.000	$3.495
	Sam	$ —	$0.500	$5.005
Payout Net of $1.5 Million Invested		**5 × Convertible Preferred Structure**		
		Transaction Value		
		$2 Millions	$5 Millions	$10 Millions
	Max	$0.500	$3.500	$6.000
	Sam	$ —	$ —	$2.500

FIGURE 5.8 Net payout charts for max with different liquidation preferences on a convertible preferred structure

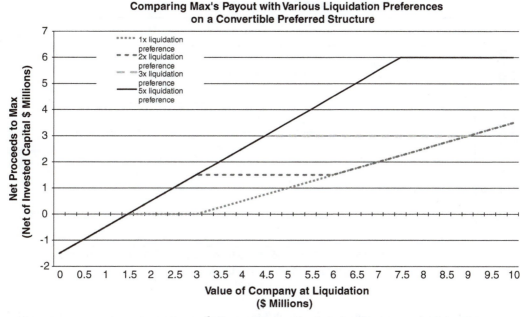

new securities senior to the old ones.[6] This strategy often streamlined the deal negotiations with the holders of the old securities, largely because it did not force the prior investors to write down their old securities—first because the old securities were not being replaced; and second, because there was a (very remote) chance that the old securities could have value.

Note that as multiples of liquidation become greater, the securities beneath them[7]—that is, the ones that get paid later, such as common stock or preferred stock—that lack this term, lose value. This can make it more difficult to retain and provide incentives for the management team, which is responsible for creating any value in the company at all, as noted later in this chapter.

Exotic Securities ("Gingerbread")

But why stop just with multiple liquidation preferences? An enterprising investor can incorporate multiple liquidation preferences *with* participation to create a number of effects to accommodate market conditions. Securities that have a basic structure loaded with a number of terms are often referred to as gingerbread. If Max insisted on a participating convertible preferred stock with 2× liquidation preference, then not only would he have received all $2 million from the YippeeZang! sale, but had there been a sale at more than $2 million, he would have shared in the outcomes above his $3 million in liquidation preference (2 × $1.5 million = $3 million) without Sam having a catch-up. Figure 5.9 shows the net payoff curve for this kind of security.

Not only can terms be combined, but certain terms can be active only under certain conditions. For example, Max could have insisted on participating preferred stock with 2× liquidation preference where the 2× liquidation is in force up to a $7 million exit. After that, the security reverts to a participating preferred structure with standard liquidation preference. Such a security

---

[6] The notion of *seniority* of securities is discussed extensively later in this chapter, in the section titled "Exotic Securities."

[7] Less senior securities are referred to as being "beneath" more senior ones, not only conceptually (they get paid later), but also in terms of their position in the capitalization tables, which list the more senior securities farther up on the list. The position of securities with respect to their relative preferences is sometimes called the "preference stack."

FIGURE 5.9 Net payout chart for a 2× participating convertible preferred structure

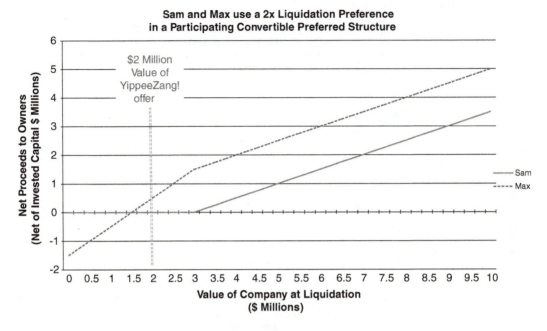

might result from a close negotiation in which Max views the investment to be high risk with a relatively low potential outcome (e.g., less than $7 million) and Sam views the investment as more likely to have a very high outcome, as shown in Figure 5.10.

In such a circumstance, Sam may be trading off the costly gingerbread terms for a larger common equity share that will pay off handsomely if—as he expects—the company is worth much

FIGURE 5.10 Net payout chart for a changing liquidation preference

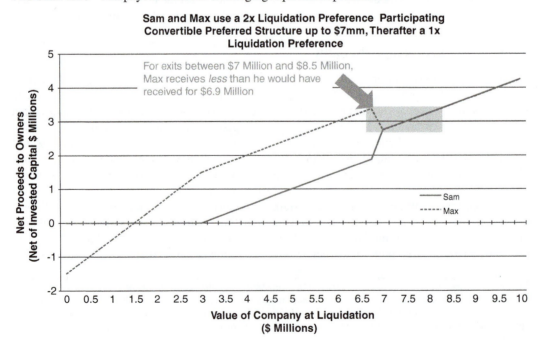

more than $7 million. A problem with such conditional securities (in this case, the security is based on the proceeds from the company's liquidation) is that they create anomalies in the payout chart. Notice in Figure 5.10 that for the case of exit values between $7 million and $8.5 million, shown in the grey rectangle, Max would receive *less* than he does at values just below $7 million. Max would be willing to do this if he believed that such a situation is unlikely—that the company will either have a low outcome, in which case the 2× liquidation preference protects his interests, or a very high one, which he is happy to share with Sam.

Not only are preferred structures used for pricing deals, but they also directly affect incentives. Note that in our examples, a participating convertible security with 2× liquidation preference means that Sam receives his first $1 million only when the exit value reaches $5 million, whereas with convertible preferred, Sam reaches that first $1 million when the company is sold for $2.5 million. Again, Max may be investing in Sam's company with a focus on the upside and is using this structure—participation with 2× liquidation preference—to encourage Sam to reach for the higher exit values. It is also possible that Max is simply very risk averse or very skeptical about the likelihood of Sam's success and is using terms to protect himself at the lower end.

Finally, Sam may simply be trading terms for price, seeking to receive a much larger share of the economic benefit in the upside in return for giving away a lot of protection on the downside. One can picture a conversation where Max offers Sam the $1.5 million in exchange for two-thirds of the company in common stock; but Sam, confident in his project, counters by offering to give Max much of the benefit in the downside outcome in return for half, rather than one-third, of the upside.

Most investors believe they don't make money on terms, but think of terms as a way of adjusting price to get an acceptable balance of risk and return to both parties. Indeed, the securities discussed in this chapter allow for fine-tuning the price by adjusting who gets what based on the price and conditions at the sale or liquidation of the company, and also allow for midcourse corrections based on company performance and market conditions.

Aligning Interests: Management Carve-Outs

Since management stock is almost always held as common shares or options on common shares, making the common shares less likely to pay off by adding very high liquidation multiples creates management incentive problems. If the company has to be sold for an unreasonably high price before the common stock is worth anything, the board of directors often resorts to a *management carve-out* to incent management to stay and create value. A management carve-out is a contractual agreement between the management and the investors that promises management a certain bonus based on the company's successful sale (not unlike a commission). Often the bonus is tied to the price and paid in kind, or the same currency that is used to buy the company, which is usually cash or shares in the acquiring company. Unfortunately, management carve-outs are treated as current income for tax purposes, whereas stock-based management incentive plans receive capital gains tax treatment since they make management into owners. Thus management carve-outs typically are used only when the regular management incentive plan has been devalued by such things as high liquidation multiples on preferred stock.

Such a midcourse correction appeared in the case of Ellacoya, a communications company that was founded during the bubble in 1999 and subsequently struggled. It was recapitalized in 2002 because some of the investors, notably Lightspeed Partners, believed that Ellacoya's technology could be repurposed and repackaged into a viable business. Other investors, such as Goldman Sachs Private Equity, were less enthusiastic about the company's prospects and declined to participate because Ellacoya had already consumed $111 million, almost all invested as preferred securities. A few new investors led by Lightspeed invested $14 million to enable Ellacoya to shift direction.[8] For the new investors and the ongoing management to have enough incentive to carry on, they needed to have the lion's share of the economic interest in Ellacoya. Because the old investors held preferred stock, the new investors had to reach an accommodation with them since leaving the old preferences in place would have forced any exit to clear $111 million before the new investors and management received substantial returns. The old investors and the new investors, therefore, negotiated an agreement that allowed the old investors to have some return in the case that Ellacoya met great success but in other outcomes devalued the old position relative to the new securities.

Note that holding preferred stock did not guarantee returns to the old investors but did mean the old investors had to be dealt with before a substantial new investment could be made, even though they did not intend to continue investing in Ellacoya. The subsequent negotiation allowed each side, the new investors and the old, to find an acceptable balance of risk and return in their Ellacoya investment. The old investors put nothing new at risk and gained the possibility of a small return should things work out well. The new investors received the incentive of a big potential return in exchange for investing new money in Ellacoya's turnaround.

It is a characteristic of private equity investing that a new investment can result in the "recontracting" of an existing investment, as occurred with Ellacoya. The nature of the private equity preferred securities ensures that existing investors—not just the company—have a big say in the new investment. Not unfrequently, when a private-equity-backed company hits unforeseen issues, the economic and control interests of the company are redivided in a multisided negotiation resulting in a new capitalization for the company. In the venture setting, this is referred to as "re-capping" a company and is discussed in more detail in Chapter 6.

In our example, if Sam feels his company surely will be successful and be sold for at least $20 million, it is reasonable for him to trade the first $3 million in returns in the form of a 2× liquidation preference for a greater share of the underlying ownership. After all, at a $20 million exit, Max will convert his preferred stock into common and his liquidation preferences won't mean a thing. The preferred share structure with all of its variations, then, can be used to adjust risk and potential return, allowing one party to trade away downside protection for more potential upside return.

Seniority and the Interplay of Multiple Securities

Many private-equity-backed companies receive multiple rounds of investment. This is particularly true of early-stage companies, because each round of investment is designed to take the company to the next value accretion point. Because the company and the investors have different risk and reward levels at each of these rounds, the investments may have different terms and structures. How do these interact?

Much is defined in the description of the securities. The liquidation preferences of preferred stock from multiple rounds always explicitly define their seniority relative to other rounds. Preferred securities are designated in two possible ways: one security can be *senior to* the other, or they can have equal, or *pooled* seniority. When one security is senior to the other, and when the company is sold for an amount that brings the liquidation preferences into play, the junior security has the same relationship to the senior security as common stock has to preferred stock in our previous discussion. In short, the senior securities are paid first; if there is money left, the junior

---

[8] Scott Denne, "Bubble Survivors: Ellacoya Reinvents Itself Yet Again," http://66.162.125.247/News/Stories/ LSVP_20070918a.pdf, accessed August 8, 2010.

Table 5.8   Net Payout Table for a Convertible Preferred Structure with Pooled Liquidation Preferences

Max Invests $1.5 Million for 49.95 Percent in Series A
and then AVP Invests $2 Million for 25 percent in Series B*

		Convertible Preferred Structure with Pooled Liquidation Preferences		
			Transaction Value	
		$2 Millions	$5 Millions	$10 Millions
	AVP	$(0.857)	$ —	$0.500
	Max	$(0.643)	$ —	$2.246
	Sam	$ —	$1.500	$3.754

Payout Net of $3.5 Million Invested

*Max's position is diluted to 37.5 percent by the Series B round.

securities are paid, and only last does the common stock receive any proceeds. If, instead, the preferred stock preferences are pooled, each stock's liquidation amount is calculated proportionately (pro rata) by face value to the total liquidation preferences in the pool.

An example is in order. Suppose Sam's company successfully completed its product and needed an additional $2 million financing to fund marketing, sales, and general operating costs. The company might raise that money from a private equity investor, perhaps a VC or growth equity firm depending on the exact circumstances and market conditions. Assume that Sam and Max convince Acme Venture Partners (AVP) to invest $2 million for 25 percent of the company in a second-round financing ("Series B").[9] After the AVP financing, Sam and Max will each own 37.5 percent.[10] Moreover, assume that Sam and Max did their original financing ("Series A") by using a convertible preferred structure and AVP also agreed to a convertible preferred structure. Table 5.8 shows the net payout.

How does the ultimate payout to Max's Series A, AVP's Series B, and Sam's common differ when the Series A and B have pooled preferences versus the Series B having seniority over Series A? Let's consult the tables and charts.

Figure 5.11 and Table 5.8 present the payout for both series of preferred as well as the common in the case that the Series A and Series B preferred stock have pooled preferences. Note that the interplay of the conversion points causes some interesting inflection points in the chart. Max will convert when 37.5 percent ownership is worth more than $1.5 million; AVP will convert when 25 percent ownership is worth more than $2 million. At first thought, Max should want to convert at prices above $4 million (37.5 percent × $4 million = $1.5 million). However, at $4 million, AVP will *not* want to convert (25 percent × $4 million = $1 million, which is less than AVP's $2 million cost basis) and will therefore use the Series B liquidation preference to redeem its preferred stock for $2 million (clearly, there is enough money in the sale to pay the preferences; $4 million is greater than the $3.5 million total amount invested in the company). When AVP takes

---

[9] Multiple private securities issued by the same company are often labeled with successive letters of the alphabet. Thus Series A is the first such financing, Series B the second, and so on indicating each round of financing even though the investors may be largely the same in each round. In LBOs, multiple preferred securities often are issued as part of a single large financing to acquire the company. In that case, the different series of securities (also designated A, B, and so on) indicate a difference in terms such as seniority, conversion price, or voting rights. In the LBO case, each series may be designed to sell to a different type of investor.

[10] AVP will own 25 percent, leaving the remaining 75 essentially split equally between Sam and Max; thus, 37.5 percent each.

FIGURE 5.11   Net payout chart for a convertible preferred structure with pooled liquidation preferences

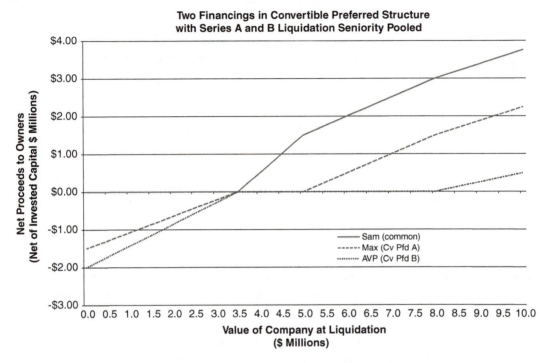

its $2 million in preferences, only $2 million remains to be divided between the Series A and the common shareholders. So Max will *not* convert and will use his preferences to take his $1.5 million, leaving $500,000 for Sam. This situation exists until the company sells for more than $5 million. With AVP's position already redeemed, Max and Sam are back to their old split of 49.95/50.05 percent; and so at $5 million, Max is again incented to convert to common rather than use his preferences ($5 million − $2 million = $3 million × 50 percent = $1.5 million). At values from $5 million to $8 million, Max will convert his preferred into common stock and take his payout based on his half of the ownership while AVP continues to use its Series B liquidation preference. Above $8 million, both Series B and Series A have more value in their underlying economic ownership than in the preferences of the preferred stock, so all owners will convert to common and split the proceeds 37.5 percent, 37.5 percent, 25 percent among Sam, Max, and AVP respectively.

Now consider the case where AVP buys exactly the same convertible preferred stock, but with one difference: the Series B is senior to the Series A. Now AVP can expect to have its full $2 million investment back first, ahead of all other investors, as shown in Figure 5.12 and Table 5.9. After the preferences are paid out (i.e., above $3.5 million), the payout charts for all the securities are identical.

Seniority often is a major issue in the case where a new investor is buying shares at a considerably higher price than the current investors' cost basis. If the first financing is one dollar per share (that is, one dollar per *common equivalent share*—the price of the convertible preferred divided by the number of shares into which it converts), and the later financing is at five dollars a share, then the early-round investors, as well as management, would be delighted to sell the company for four dollars a share. Unless the later-round investor had a liquidation preference *over the previous round of shares*—that is, seniority—he or she would lose money in such a transaction, just as Max lost money in our starting example where Sam had a cost basis of zero and was delighted to take the offer from YippeeZang! even though Max would lose money.

Table 5.9   Net Payout Table for Convertible Preferred Structure with Series B Senior to Series A

Max Invests $1.5 Million for 49.95 percent in Series A
and then AVP Invests $2 Million for 25 percent in Series B*

		Convertible Preferred Structure with Series B Senior to Series A		
		Transaction Value		
		$2 Millions	$5 Millions	$10 Millions
	AVP	$ —	$ —	$0.500
	Max	$(1.500)	$ —	$2.246
	Sam	$ —	$1.500	$3.754

Payout Net of $3.5 Million Invested (row label on left)

*Max's position is diluted to 37.5 percent by the Series B round.

Dividends

In public markets, dividends are often associated with preferred stock. In private equity, dividends play a different role. In the case of VC, dividends are generally avoided or deferred considerably into the future because venture capitalists are capital gains oriented—in fact, carried interest may not even be paid on gains produced by dividends. Moreover, dividends can limit the ability of a growing company to raise capital because potential investors wonder why the company is returning cash to its shareholders when it needs that cash to grow. Finally, dividends create an asymmetry of rewards between the preferred shareholders (the investors) and the common

FIGURE 5.12   Net payout chart for convertible preferred structure with Series B senior to Series A

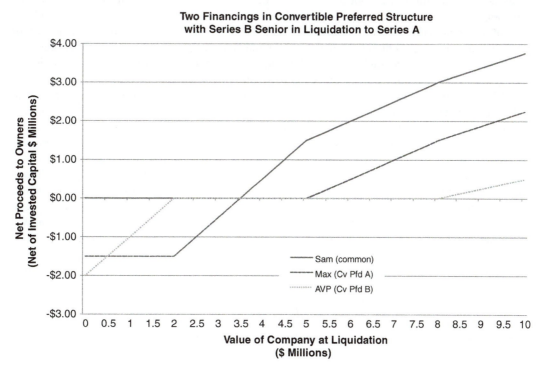

shareholders (typically the founders, management, and key employees), which in turn leads to a misalignment of incentives between investor and company.

To attract certain classes of investors who want high income streams, large public companies often issue preferred stock with high dividends that are preferential to common stock dividends. In the same way, dividends appear in certain classes of preferred stock used in the structures of buyouts and growth financings to attract investors who want dividends. This practice can allow the company to sell shares at a higher price than they would otherwise, because the investor who wants dividends is willing to pay more. For example, Securicor Wireless Networks (SWN), a maker of telecommunications equipment originally financed by Bessemer Venture Partners (BVP) and Securicor, Ltd., a large publicly traded, service-oriented business with thin margins, sold a Series A and a Series B redeemable preferred stock packaged with common shares simultaneously to Securicor and BVP, respectively.[11] The only difference between Series A and Series B was the dividend policy: Securicor's Series A paid a current dividend; BVP's Series B did not. While the price per share of the two series was the same, BVP received more rights regarding board seats and control over future financing in return for giving up a dividend. In other circumstances, the dividend-yielding shares likely would have been sold for a higher price. This arrangement occurred because Securicor was a strategic investor rather than a financial investor. With its thin margins, Securicor's internal policies forbade investments that did not have some form of current income associated with them.

In buyouts, dividends are often in the form of payable in kind (PIK) dividends, particularly during markets where financing is readily available, such as in 2006–2007. These dividends are not paid in cash but in the form of additional amounts of preferred stock. Typically, preferred stock with a PIK dividend is used in the mezzanine, or middle layer, of a buyout's financing. The mezzanine layer is senior in preference to the main equity layer but junior to the bank debt (hence the notion of "middle layer" since it fills the space between the bank debt and the highest-risk equity). Because the mezzanine layer involves more risk than the bank debt, its investors require a higher return on capital, which is provided by the equity it represents[12] and often supplemented by a dividend. Companies often opt to pay a PIK dividend rather than a cash dividend since the company's cash flow is first needed to pay off the bank debt. In some ways, the PIK dividend in a buyout's mezzanine layers acts as both a return enhancement for the holders and as an incentive for the company's management to buy out the mezzanine layers as soon as possible. This is because a PIK can, over time, considerably increase the value of the security it is attached to. We provide an example of a PIK security later in this chapter when discussing buyout securities.

LBO investors often use one-time special dividends to get an early return of capital and enhance their returns. When a company acquired in an LBO is operating successfully—paying down the debt incurred when it was first purchased and enjoying an increasing enterprise value— the investors have the option of refinancing some or all of the debt. With an enhanced cash flow and increased asset value, the new debt is cheaper and the company can borrow more. In such a circumstance, the investors may choose to have the company increase its level of borrowing and then use the additional cash to pay a one-time dividend to the equity investors. Thus they return some of their invested capital while still holding their stock in the company. Refinancing and paying a dividend (in the buyout setting, this is called re-capping—not to be confused with the VC recapitalization, which is rarer) has two disadvantages: (1) the company takes on more risk as it

---

[11] Felda Hardymon and Bill Wasik, "Securicor Wireless Networks February 1996," HBS Case No. 899-134 (Boston: HBS Publishing, 1999), 11.

[12] The form of the equity portion of such a mezzanine security depends on the security itself. If it is a convertible preferred stock, the equity portion is the common stock into which it may be converted. If it is a straight redeemable preferred stock, the equity portion may take the form of warrants or common stock that is purchased at the same time. Some mezzanine securities are in the form of debt with interest payable by issuing more debt (a PIK debt security); the equity is often warrants to buy cheap common stock.

increases debt, making the investment riskier than it was before the re-cap (see, for instance, the story of Simmons Mattress, discussed at the beginning of Chapter 13); and (2) returns in the form of dividends may be taxed at higher rates than returns in the form of capital gains.[13] This transaction puts a company at increased risk. As such, management often dislikes re-caps in the buyout setting because the company not only ends up with more debt, but in so doing incurs additional fees from issuing more debt. If re-caps are too large or too frequent, they can lead to a misalignment of incentives.

TERMS

Thus far, we have described private equity securities and their properties. We now consider the terms under which these securities are bought. Private equity securities are governed by terms set out in a purchase agreement, and often these terms have as much effect on payout as the securities themselves. We discuss the most common private equity terms in this section.

Vesting

The concept of vesting is simple. It holds that a manager's stock is not "owned" until that individual has been with the company for a period of time, or some value accretion event occurs (e.g., the sale of the company). Typically, vesting is implemented over a period of time (typically three to five years in the United States; although periods are shorter on the West Coast than on the East Coast, indicating that vesting reflects activity in the market) and the stock "vests" (i.e., the manager obtains unqualified ownership of the shares or options) proportionally over that time. For administrative purposes, stock vesting usually occurs quarterly, occasionally annually, and sometimes even monthly.

In our example, suppose Max had eschewed preferred stock entirely but insisted that Sam's shares vest proportionally over four years (one-sixteenth per quarter). In a typical common stock transaction, the mechanism of such a vesting arrangement includes the right for the company to buy back Sam's stock for what he paid for it. Since Sam is a founder, he would have paid very little for the stock. When the YippeeZang! transaction occurred, Max could have insisted the company buy back Sam's stock at cost and theoretically received the entire $2 million of proceeds. Why? Because Sam had been an employee for only a few hours, none of his stock would have vested. Thus Max would own 100 percent of the company and would therefore receive 100 percent of the sales proceeds. Since Sam likely would have objected to receiving nothing from the sale to YippeeZang! and since YippeeZang! wanted to acquire Sam's talent and wanted Sam to be a happy YippeeZang! employee, the transaction may have been called off under those conditions.

Having foreseen this situation and because he might want Sam to approach him to finance his next company, Max may have agreed to a partial acceleration of Sam's vesting in the event of acquisition—that is, the vesting schedule would speed up in the case of a change of control of the company. If the agreement called for 25 percent acceleration, then 25 percent of Sam's shares

---

[13] The tax disadvantage can be resolved by creative structuring if the investors anticipate they will be able to re-cap the company. When Apax bought Xerium, a supplier of consumables to the papermaking industry with very strong cash flow, the investors issued common equity to themselves in an arrangement where they loaned the company money in addition to buying stock for pennies per share (similar to the redeemable preferred stock plus cheap common discussed earlier). Management could also buy the common part of the security for pennies per share, thus increasing the incentive value of the management's common shares. When Apax later re-capped the company with more (and cheaper) debt, the partners returned capital to themselves by paying down the shareholder loan, which was a nontaxable return of capital. Of course the investors had to get the senior debt holders' agreement to allow the paydown of deeply subordinated shareholder debt. Information from Felda Hardymon, Josh Lerner, and Ann Leamon, "Apax Partners and Xerium S.A.," HBS Case No. 804-084 (Boston: HBS Publishing, 2004).

would have been vested. Because he owned 50.05 percent of the company, he would have received 12.5 percent of the proceeds (i.e., 25 percent of the 50.05 percent of his total ownership) and the remainder would go to Max. In this case, rather than $0 with no acceleration or $1 million from an all-common structure with no vesting, Sam would get $250,000.

Often, venture term sheets allow for a 25 to 50 percent acceleration of vesting for certain managers in the event of an acquisition, based on the theory that (1) many managers lose their jobs in an acquisition, and it is unreasonable for those who have created the value to lose a big portion of it by the very act of realizing that value for the shareholders; and (2) it is better to have the cooperation of management and key employees in the event of a potential acquisition, and acceleration acts as an incentive to get the deal done. In particular, the vesting period for a chief financial officer's stock frequently accelerates on change of control to resolve a substantial conflict of interest: the CFO's help is critical to completing the deal, yet acquiring companies generally have their own finance departments and terminate much of the acquired company's finance department in an acquisition. Acceleration rewards the CFO for active participation and support of a transaction that very likely renders him or her jobless.

Of course, acceleration acts *against* the interests of the acquiring company, which may have to spend stock option shares to re-incent the acquired employees who have had the benefit of acceleration. It also acts against the interests of nonmanagement shareholders by effectively adding shares to the pool of shares to be bought, thus diluting their interests. The fixed negotiated share price is therefore divided among more shares. For these reasons, acceleration usually is restricted to a few employees and often accelerates only a portion of each employee's position.

In general, preferred stock structures do a better job of implementing the principle of reward for performance than does a structure of vesting with common stock, since preferred stock structures rely on the investment's value at acquisition or IPO. Furthermore, vesting is contractual; that is, potential events and situations must be anticipated and written down if vesting is to do the same job as preferred stock. Vesting does, however, perform the important function of preventing an employee from leaving and taking along value disproportionate to the time of employment at the company. Vesting creates the "golden handcuffs" that inspire an employee to stay when other opportunities call. If a company is doing well, and a key employee holds valuable options or stock that would be lost if the employee left before a certain date or event, the possibility of an early departure is greatly diminished.

Vesting also performs a function of returning shares to the incentive stock pool from employees who in some sense "haven't finished the job," and, in turn, provides incentive stock for their replacements. This allows companies to budget their incentive stock by position or task with some assurance that they are somewhat protected from turnover. Similarly, vesting protects morale by assuring employees that those who leave will not benefit as much as those who stay behind and create value.

Covenants

Perhaps the best way private equity investors pave the way to be active in the governance of their investments is through covenant provisions. Covenants are contractual agreements between the investor and the company and fall into two broad categories: positive covenants and negative covenants. Positive covenants are the list of things the company agrees to do, such as producing audited reports, holding regular board meetings, paying taxes on time, doing annual budgets, and so forth. Negative covenants limit behavior by the entrepreneur and/or management that is detrimental to the investor by either expressly forbidding certain actions or requiring that they receive the approval of investors. For instance, the sale of assets is often restricted, and any disposal of assets above a certain dollar value or above a certain percentage of the firm's book value may be forbidden without the investors' approval. This prevents the entrepreneur from increasing the risk profile of the company or changing its activities from the intended focus without consent of the investors. It also prevents the entrepreneur from making "sweetheart" deals with friends.

In addition, the private investors are often concerned about changes in control. The covenants may state that the founders cannot sell any of their common stock without investor approval or without first offering the securities to the investors. Restrictions on transfer of control are important because venture capitalists invest in people, and buyout investors often invest in a specific management team. If the management team decides to remove its human capital from the deal or to reduce the degree of its investment (through its share ownership), investors would want to approve the terms of the transfer. Similarly, restrictions may prevent a merger or sale of the company without approval of the investors because such an action might hurt the position of the private equity investors.

Details of Covenants

Covenants can come in many forms and be expressed in many different ways. Following are three examples of how covenants can be used and where they may appear.

The eDOCS term sheet mentioned at the start of the chapter, contained a typical list of negative covenants. eDOCS was a 1999 high-technology VC start-up, and in the term sheet the venture investor, Charles River Ventures, asked that at least 60 percent of the outstanding preferred stock (which in effect meant the two VC investors in the company) must approve the company's decision to (1) pay dividends on common stock; (2) repurchase preferred or common stock; (3) make loans to employees; (4) provide guarantees; (5) merge, consolidate, sell, or dispose of substantially all of the properties or assets; (6) mortgage, pledge, or create a security interest; (7) incur debt senior to the Series A preferred stock; (8) change the principal business of eDOCS; (9) invest in third parties; or (10) make capital expenditures of $250,000 in a single expenditure or an aggregate of $500,000 in a twelve-month period.

Obviously, if eDOCS were to take on any additional risk by financing through pledges, debt, or new equity, the management would *have* to obtain the investors' approval. Moreover, the capital expenditures of a large amount were raised to the level of shareholder approval as a way of maintaining operating boundaries on the founding team at eDOCS. In Chapter 6, we discuss the governance aspects of these covenants in greater depth.[14]

A second example of negative covenants is seen in the case of Incept, a health care technology producer that invested in start-up companies that adopted its technologies. Incept invested rights to patents in lieu of dollars in these start-ups, and in turn used the business plan built around the patents to attract outside capital to the start-ups. A major feature of the patents that Incept invested in these spin-out companies were covenants that limited the markets in which those patents could apply. When Incept spun out Confluent Surgical in 1999, the new company received Incept's hydrogel technologies; but the use of those technologies was restricted by covenant to the fields of adhesion prevention, vascular access closure, and vascular embolization only in abdominal and gynecological situations. Incept could therefore take those same patents and provide them to a different company that could use them only for some other part of the body.[15]

---

[14] Gompers, "eDOCS Inc. (A)."

[15] Bhaskar Chakravorti, Toby Stuart, and James Weber, "Incept LLC and Confluent Surgical (A)," HBS Case No. 809-062 (Boston: HBS Publishing, 2009).

A third example of the use of covenants was the promise by Yieldex to bring in a new CEO shortly after raising venture money in 2007. Such a positive covenant (the company promised to do something, although the change may be seen as negative for the existing CEO) protects the investor in several ways. First, it retains the current (albeit clearly imperfect) CEO for the short term, which is tremendously helpful for the investors and the company given the difficulties in recruiting a CEO midway through a fund-raising process and before anyone knows how much money the company would be able to raise and from whom. Second, the stipulation ensures that the current CEO is under no illusions about the future. Often a founding CEO becomes an executive officer other than CEO (such as chief technology officer, VP Engineering, VP Sales) after the company reaches a certain size, in recognition that the skills required to handle a company engaged in the marketing and sales of a product are different from those required to build a brand-new product in the first place. The founding CEO, then, can begin to envision a future as CTO of the current operation or as founder of an entirely new company, possibly with backing from this same investor group.[16]

The purchase of major assets above a certain size threshold may also be forbidden without the private equity investors' approval. This restriction may be written in absolute dollar terms or as a percentage of book value, in wording broad enough to cover purchases of assets and the merger of the company. Restrictions on purchases may help prevent radical changes in strategy or wasteful expenditure by the entrepreneur. Many such strategy changes could have detrimental effects on the value of the private equity investors' stake by taking the company into areas where the team has little expertise—for instance, should a biotech company decide to move from developing a drug into providing a health management service.

Finally, the contracts usually contain some provision for restricting the issuance of new securities. Almost all contain a provision that restricts the issuance of senior securities without the approval of the previous investors, requiring that the holders of a majority of preferred shares vote in favor. Restricting security issuance—especially of securities senior to existing securities—prevents the unapproved transfer of value from current shareholders to new ones.

Often negative covenants are coupled with super-majority voting provisions, in which the company agrees not to do certain things without the approval of some percentage greater than 50 percent of the shareholders or, more commonly, the board. For example, if Max had insisted in the original deal that the company could be sold only if two-thirds of the common shares agreed in a shareholder vote, he would have had a veto over the YippeeZang! transaction and could have insisted on an acceptable deal.

A few frequently encountered covenants are somewhat different from the positive and negative ones considered earlier. One of these is the right of mandatory redemption. This covenant involves the rights of the private equity investor to "put" or sell, at a predetermined price, the preferred stock back to the company. Essentially, the venture capitalist can force the firm to repay the face value of the investment at a given time in the future—five or eight years hence. This mechanism can in theory be used to force the liquidation or merger of the firm. The mandatory redemption provisions are often included for two reasons: (1) most private equity partnerships have a limited life, so they must have some mechanism to force a liquidity event before the partnership expires; and (2) mandatory redemption clauses help prevent "lifestyle companies," or

---

[16] Toby Stuart and Alison Berkley Wagonfeld, "Yieldex (A)," HBS Case No. 809-090 (Boston: HBS Publishing, 2009).

companies that exist only to provide a good living to the management but do not accrete value to the investors. By demanding redemption, investors can get their money back—or, should the company lack sufficient funds, they can force a negotiation to create a liquidity event. A mandatory redemption term is often more valuable as a negotiating lever than as an actual way of getting money out of an investment. The process of actually fulfilling such a put option would be extremely challenging to the typical entrepreneurial firm and would likely destroy much of the entity's value.

The reasons that motivate mandatory redemption rights also motivate inclusion of *registration rights* in minority investments. Registration rights give the holder the right to demand that the company register its shares for sale in the public markets. In concept, this gives investors the right to create a liquidity event even over management's objections. This term, too, has limited practical applicability. An IPO is a serious and complex undertaking and requires the active and enthusiastic support of management to succeed. Moreover, the registration rights often require that the shareholders be able to offer a significant number of shares for sale in the IPO. If they cannot, public investors in the IPO may be unwilling to buy the stock. In any case, the rights themselves often cannot be exercised until a specified number of years have passed since the investor made the investment.

While detractors of registration rights point out that a management team resistant to the idea of an IPO can easily thwart the provision's intent, proponents note that the mere existence of registration rights provides leverage that investors can use with management and other investors in getting the company to create liquidity options for shareholders.

There is a form of registration right called *piggyback rights* where the shareholder has a right to sell shares into any public registration of shares that the company is already undertaking. Piggyback rights are considered to be fairly valuable because the company *has already decided* to make a public offering, which means this right does not rely on forcing a company to go through a complex process just to allow shareholders to exercise their registration rights.

A purchase agreement[17] for a private equity transaction usually contains a covenant describing the size and composition of the board of directors. These board covenants typically state the explicit number of board seats that private equity investors can elect, which is a special form of a covenant. Board composition is a key matter for negotiation in nearly all private equity term sheets, be they venture capital or buyout, because governance is at the heart of value accretion in private equity settings (Chapter 6 includes much more about governance). Typically, in companies that are venture-backed from the beginning, investors control the board; or at least the board has a majority of outside (i.e., nonmanagement) directors, and the board is required to approve various critical actions (such as an acquisition or a major capital expenditure) with a super-majority. Even if the investors do not own more than 50 percent of the equity, the contract may allocate control of the board to the venture capitalist. Board control serves as an important check on management teams that may try to exploit minority shareholders. Similarly, in any future IPO, an outside board (i.e., a board of directors composed mostly of nonmanagement directors) lends credibility to the firm. A board election covenant is another clear example of the principle of

---

[17] Generally in the process of negotiating a private equity transaction, the investor and the management (or seller) agree on terms in the form of a *term sheet*. A term sheet describes all major terms and acts as a road map for the actual legal documents that complete the transaction. The main transaction document is the *purchase agreement*, which is the contract under which the securities are bought. Other legal documents include the company charter, which describes the securities being issued, the securities themselves, and the shareholder agreements. In general this text describes the business decisions involved in private equity investing. Therefore, in the case of deal structuring we describe transactions at the level of a term sheet. For a description of the legal documents, see Bagley and Dauchy, *Entrepreneur's Guide to Business Law*. The most comprehensive source is Michael J. Halloran, *Venture Capital & Public Offering Negotiation* (New York: Aspen Publishers, 2010).

separating economic interest from control interest in private equity securities, as noted in the discussion of preferred stock.

Another typical set of covenants are those granting *information rights.* Unlike public companies, private companies are under no obligation to disclose business results to a certain standard at specified times (e.g., quarterly, annually, when securities are issued, etc.). These rights are negotiated by the private equity firms at the time of investment. They may range from simply disclosing year-end audited financial statements to making covenants that grant the investor the right to visit and inspect the company's books at any time. They may pertain to specific documents, such as requirements that an annual budget shall be available sixty days before the start of the fiscal year, or to the availability of logs of stock issued to employees. In some cases, such covenants grant *board observation rights*—that is, the right of the investor to send a representative to observe the board when it meets, but not to vote.

Often covenants must expire when the company becomes publicly listed. Stock exchanges have rules designed to make sure all investors receive the same rights, which conflict with the information rights and covenants designed to allow an active investor to be effective in a private company setting. So, like many private equity terms, information rights and board control covenants typically expire automatically when the company goes public.

All in all, covenants are most frequently used to effectively disconnect control on important issues from owning a majority of the equity. The deal's price and control of the company then become separate items for negotiation. Control issues implemented through covenants and super-majority voting provisions can be settled quite specifically to address each side's concerns. For example, management often has stronger concerns about operational matters than financing ones, while investors' concerns are typically the reverse. A negotiated set of covenants can leave investors minimally involved in determining operating policy on a day-to-day basis but intensely consulted and involved in financial strategy.

Antidilution Provisions

A term that is similar to a covenant is an antidilution provision. Convertible preferred stock, as noted earlier, naturally led to the idea that the conversion ratio need not be fixed. Many convertible preferred stocks contain antidilution provisions that automatically adjust the conversion price[18] down if the company sells stock below the share price paid by the current investor. The rationale for these provisions is that the company is presumably selling stock at a lower price (a "**down round**") because of underperformance. If the stock has an automatic adjustment, the investor is less likely to oppose or forestall a dilutive financing that will allow the company to raise capital when most needed (if the company is underperforming) or when the private equity markets are difficult. Moreover, antidilution provisions reflect the fundamental reality of private investing—illiquidity. When public stock investors are dissatisfied with the performance of a company whose stock they own, they simply sell the stock. No such opportunity exists for the private investor, who must stay invested until a liquidity event occurs. Antidilution provisions act as a cushion and therefore create an incentive for investors to take on such risk.

Often, antidilution provisions come into effect only if the investor holding them participates in the new down round. This prevents "free riding," which can occur when there are multiple investors in a company that is struggling to raise financing and only some choose to invest in the new round. If the antidilution provisions have a "pay or play" term, those investors who

---

[18] Antidilution provisions are not limited to convertible preferred structures. Even in a structure using all common stock, the purchase agreement may specify that the company must issue more shares to the investor if the company sells common shares at a price below that at which the investor bought them. Issuing more common shares has the same effect as changing the price at which a convertible preferred security converts into common.

Table 5.10   Initial Cap Table for Sam and Max's Deal

	Price/Share	Amount	C.E. Shares*	% Owned
Sam	$ —	$ —	5,005	50.05
Max	$300.30	$1,500,000	4,995	49.95
Total		$1,500,000	10,000	100.00

*C.E. stands for "common equivalent," which is either the number of common shares owned or the number of common shares that the investor would own upon conversion.

participate in the down round receive the antidilution protection, while those who do not lose this price adjustment and suffer more. This is seen as an incentive for all investors to participate in difficult financings, should they occur.

The exact adjustment mechanism for antidilution is a negotiated term and can range from a complete adjustment to the new price (**full ratchet**) to one based on the size of the round and the size of the price decrease (**weighted average**). Some antidilution provisions apply only below a certain negotiated price level, and some exclude smaller financings and shares issued to employees.

The full-ratchet calculation works in this way: let's go back to our original example and assume Max and Sam do their original deal in a convertible preferred structure, setting the base number of common shares at 10,000. Sam therefore owns 5,005 common shares and Max owns Series A Convertible Preferred Stock convertible at $300.30 per share into 4,995 common shares.

We can capture what the ownership looks like by developing a simple **capitalization table**, or "cap table," that shows the division of the firm's securities. After the first round, the ownership is as shown in Table 5.10. The ownership is graphed in Figure 5.13.

Now assume that building the product proves to be more difficult than expected, and Max and Sam find themselves running out of money. The project is still promising enough to attract the interest of Acme Venture Partners (AVP), which agrees to invest $2 million. AVP insists on a price of $150 per share, and Sam and Max accept it. How does the relative ownership of the three parties differ across the various antidilution provision scenarios?

Had Sam and Max agreed during the first round to have no antidilution provision, then both would be diluted equally by AVP's second-round investment. The revised capitalization is shown in Table 5.11, and the ownership situation is depicted in Figure 5.14.

FIGURE 5.13   Post-first-round ownership

Table 5.11   Post-Second-Round Cap Table with No Antidilution

	Price/Share	Amount	C.E. Shares*	% Owned
Sam	$ —	$ —	5,005	21.45
Max	$300.30	$ —	4,995	21.41
AVP	$150.00	$2,000,000	13,333	57.14
Total			23,333	100.00

*C.E. stands for "common equivalent," which is either the number of common shares owned or the number of common shares that the investor would own upon conversion.

FIGURE 5.14   Post-second-round ownership with no antidilution

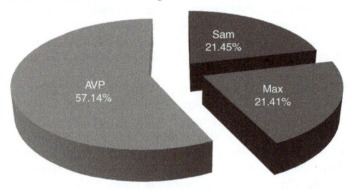

Now let's consider the case where Sam and Max agreed that the Series A will have a full-ratchet antidilution provision. That is, if Sam's company sells stock at a lower price, Max's Series A stock price will be adjusted, or "ratcheted" down, to the new price. In our example, Max's Series A would be adjusted from $303.30 per share to $150 per share, which is the new, lower, price per share that AVP is paying. Ownership after the second round differs considerably from the case of no antidilution provision, as the revised cap table shows in Table 5.12. The ownership is graphed in Figure 5.15.

Weighted average antidilution responds to the concern, noted earlier, that a full-ratchet reduction in price may impose an excessive cost on management and other common shareholders. In this case, the price is adjusted more if the diluted down round is larger or at a substantially lower price. Conversely, if it is a small down round at a slight down increment, the adjustment is smaller. Therefore, the adjustment converges to a price that is the average of the old price and the new price, and each price is weighted by the size of the round. In our example, the old $1.5 million round was done at $300.30 per share and the new $2 million round was done at $150 per share. All of the shares in the old round would be adjusted to a price calculated to be the weighted average of $150 and $300.30, as weighted by $1.5 million (M) and $2.0M, respectively:

New Price = (Old Price × Old Amount + New Price × New Amount) ÷ (Old Amount + New Amount)

In our example:

$$\$214 = [(\$300.3 \times \$1.5\,M) + (\$150 \times \$2.0\,M)] \div (\$1.5\,M + \$2.0\,M)$$

Table 5.12   Post-Second-Round Cap Table with Full-Ratchet Antidilution

	Price/Share	Amount	C.E. Shares*	% Owned
Sam	$ —	$ —	5,005	17.66
Max	$150.00	$ —	10,000	35.29
AVP	$150.00	$2,000,000	13,333	47.05
Total			28,338	100.00

*C.E. stands for "common equivalent," which is either the number of common shares owned or the number of common shares that the investor would own upon conversion.

FIGURE 5.15   Post-second-round ownership with full-ratchet antidilution

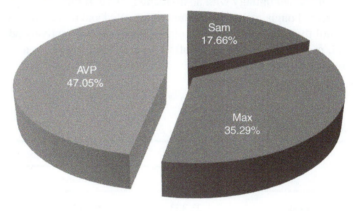

Antidilution and Valuation

Note that the presence of an antidilution provision affects the valuation of the company, as shown in Table 5.13. With antidilution, the company is effectively issuing an option that entitles some of the shareholders to receive more shares in certain future cases. This option is valuable to the shareholders and will reduce the price that an incoming investor is willing to pay for the company.[19]

The implications are clear. If AVP's partners have determined that they will not pay more than a certain company valuation, they will factor in the antidilution shares when making their offer. If the value is such that antidilution is triggered, the company will then receive a lower per-share offer than if it did not have antidilution provisions in its previous rounds. In this situation, the interests of common shareholders diverge from the interests of the first-round investors because the common shareholders want the company to raise funds

---

[19] For a series of calculations of the different types of antidilution and their impact on the pre-money and post-money valuations of a company, see Andrew Metrick, *Venture Capital and the Finance of Innovation* (New York: John Wiley & Sons, 2007), 173–76.

at the highest prices possible, regardless of the impact on existing investors. On the other hand, Max may have been unwilling to receive only 50 percent of the company without some form of antidilution protection. Terms have a cost, and that cost is often conditional on what happens in the future.

As a result of weighted average antidilution, Max's price is adjusted to be between the old price and the new price. As the size of the second round increases, the adjusted price moves closer to the second-round price. Table 5.14 shows the revised cap table, and the impact on ownership is depicted in Figure 5.16.

Although antidilution provisions were developed to adjust the conversion ratio of convertible preferred stock, investors have applied the concept to the redeemable preferred structure by having the company issue free common shares in a down round using similar formulas. Other antidilution structures include the use of PIK dividends when the company misses its targets. For example, a preferred stock could be issued initially with no dividend feature. If the company misses an annual plan by a certain amount, though, a dividend feature is activated and the stock gets a 10 percent per year PIK dividend until the company is back on plan. This practice effectively adjusts the price of the stock downward, presumably acting as an offset against the company's low performance by giving the investors greater ownership. Antidilution provisions based on targets are often included in growth equity and mezzanine investing.

Table 5.13   The Cost of Antidilution

		Type of Antidilution	
	None	Full Ratchet	Weighted Average
Number of shares post Series B	23,333	28,338	25,334
AVP's $2M buys (%)	57.14	47.05	52.63
Valuation after Series B ($ Millions)*	$3.50	$4.25	$3.80
Number of antidilution shares issued	0	5,005	2,001
Value of antidilution shares ($ Million)	$ —	$0.75	$0.30

*Value is $2 million divided by AVP's percentage after the deal (see Chapter 4).

Table 5.14   Post-Second-Round Cap Table with Weighted Average Antidilution

	Price/Share	Amount	C.E. Shares*	% Owned
Sam	$ —	$ —	5,005	19.76
Max	$214.41	$ —	6,996	27.61
AVP	$150.00	$2,000,000	13,333	52.63
Total			25,334	100.00

*C.E. stands for "common equivalent," which is either the number of common shares owned or the number of common shares that the investor would own upon conversion.

FIGURE 5.16   Post-second-round ownership with weighted average antidilution

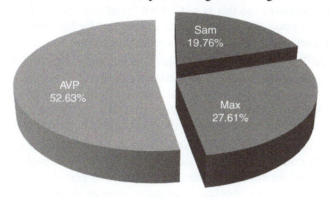

A TOUR OF A TERM SHEET

All of these securities, terms, and covenants are described in a term sheet that is presented to a company when a VC investor proposes an investment. All term sheets cover essentially similar material, but the language may differ—as will the actual concerns and priorities of the parties. If a new firm is proposing an investment in a company that already has venture investors, additional issues will arise involving differences in seniority and other rights. In Appendix 1, we compare two term sheets. Both of these were presented to Endeca Technologies,[20] an IT company that was raising a Series C round in 2001. Its existing investors, Venrock and Bessemer Venture Partners, had submitted a term sheet already, and a new deal was proposed by an outside investor, Ampersand Ventures. Comparing these two term sheets provides insight into how terms adjust a deal to reflect the concerns and anticipations of both new and old investors in general and these firms in particular. Following are some notable differences in the term sheets (the letters *A–G* refer to the annotations in Appendix 1):

A. While both deals were nominally for an $18 million round, the insiders were willing to close on $10 million from themselves and then attempt to find investors to fill out the round afterward. The outsider, on the other hand, specified that the deal would not be funded until the full $18 million had been raised, including the $10 million from the insiders. The insiders were already committed and presumably had better knowledge of the company, so it is not surprising that they would be willing to go forward with less capital. Of course the insiders' price per share was 20 percent less than the outsider's, so they were being compensated for being willing to take this risk

B. The outsider's term sheet asked for a mandatory redemption schedule that would have returned its money no later than years 5 through 7. The insiders suggested redemption further out, in years 7 through 9. This request may suggest that the outside investors were more concerned about the time to liquidity, while the insiders were more focused on getting the company financed in the short term.

C. Not surprisingly, the insiders wanted the liquidation preference for the new Series C investment to be pooled with the existing Series A and B stock, whereas the outside investor wanted the Series C shares—the only class they would hold post-financing—to have seniority.

---

[20] Felda Hardymon, Josh Lerner, and Ann Leamon, "Endeca Technologies (A)," HBS Case No. 802-141 (Boston: HBS Publishing, 2002).

Of course, the $10 million of Series C stock that the insiders would hold in the outside-led deal would *also* have seniority, so this is not a hard "give" for the insiders. They might worry, however, that such a concession could create a precedent for further rounds where they might not be a major participant, thus gradually eroding their control.

D. Insiders want the less onerous weighted average antidilution since it is their original position that will be diluted by any additional protection for Series C. The outsider prefers full ratchet since it holds none of the Series A and B shares and is offering to pay 25 percent more per share than the insiders. Both term sheets exempt shares issued to employees and very small issuances from antidilution adjustment to preserve the company's flexibility.

E. While written in different styles, the negative covenants are essentially the same. One requires 66 percent of the combined preferred stock (i.e., all series A through C voting together) to approve a waiver of the covenants; the other requires 60 percent. The two proposals likely differ very little because in either case, two out of three of the main investors have to agree. Often, difficult negotiations involve situations where one investor out of many holds a right to block the waiver of a negative covenant, which does not appear to be the case here.

F. The term sheets include typical information rights for a venture investment. The outsider's specification is more detailed, reflecting the uncertainty connected with investing in the company for the first time. Both groups require that the company will budget ahead and share that planning with the investors—a key governance provision. Also, both restrict this sensitive information to only the largest shareholders.

G. The two proposals present several differences in registration rights. The insiders are content to pool the rights with the other classes of securities that they already hold. But they would be the dominant holders in that pool and so would control the process. Moreover, if there were a limit to the number of shares being registered ("cutbacks"), the insiders would have a proportionally greater share. The outsider ties the registration rights to the Series C only, and while allowing that the other two investors could block its right to a registration, the outsider would be in a stronger position—especially with respect to cutbacks. The outsider also wants to prevent the issuance of any new registration rights by specifying that 40 percent of the Series C can block this—and the new investor would hold 44 percent (8/18) of the Series C.

VENTURE AND MEZZANINE DEBT SECURITIES

Mezzanine financing is the provision of capital, usually in the form of subordinated debt,[21] structured to have greater return than straight debt and a lower risk than straight equity. In buyout financings, the mezzanine layer fills the gap between senior bank lending and the higher-risk equity. Providers of mezzanine debt are often growth investors that provide capital to growing companies at a lower cost than equity. In return for their investment, the mezzanine investors receive not only the repayment of debt with interest, but an "equity kicker," typically warrants[22] to purchase the firm's common stock. While these investments do not offer the higher returns that equity investors enjoy, the protection provided by the company's cash flows and liquid assets limits the potential for substantial losses.

---

[21] Subordinated debt is debt that has lower liquidation preference than senior debt; but being debt, it is still senior to the equity. Senior debt is usually bank debt and is secured by the assets of the company. Subordinated debt is often either unsecured or has a second lien on the company's assets.

[22] Common terminology refers to "warrants" (plural) to purchase shares in a company. Technical correct legal terminology refers to a warrant (singular) to purchase shares (i.e., one warrant could confer the right to purchase a million shares). We use the common terminology in this book.

One characteristic of mezzanine lending is its flexibility in structuring transactions. Based on the company's projected cash flows, the interest rate and timing of repayment can vary substantially and even conditionally. For example, when the firms Lion Capital and Blackstone Group bought the soft drink maker Orangina from Cadbury Schweppes, some of the funds came from a €278 million mezzanine bridge facility, which the controlling investors intended to pay down within a year of closing through the sale of certain company assets and the expansion of senior bank debt. The PIK interest rate was 5 percent over the London Interbank Offered Rate (LIBOR).[23] The interest rate margin would increase to 5.5 percent over LIBOR if the bridge facility was still outstanding after one year. By using a variable pricing mechanism, Lion and Blackstone were able to tailor the bridge facility to match their intention to pay it off with one year.[24]

Occasionally, complex call-and-put provisions are part of a mezzanine tranche of financing. These enable the company to buy back the outstanding warrant within certain time windows, either at a price set in advance or at fair market value, thus giving an incentive to the management and private equity owners to repay the mezzanine debt early and minimize dilution to their equity. In some cases, as further downside protection, the terms allow the mezzanine investor to force the company to repurchase the debt.

Venture debt is similar to mezzanine debt, except that it appears in venture settings. Whereas mezzanine debt investors count on the cash flow of the company to service and ultimately repay their debt, venture debt investors rely on the VC backers to continue to finance the company until the debt can be serviced from operating cash flow. Venture debt and mezzanine debt are very similar in form, but they are priced quite differently. Venture debt typically commands a high interest rate in absolute terms (8 to 14 percent depending on the market), whereas mezzanine debt is usually priced by using variable market rates such as LIBOR.

Warrant Coverage Details

The concept of *warrant coverage* reflects the notion that the "equity kicker" should be proportional to the amount of debt and be priced at the current market. In private equity, the current market is usually the price paid by the private equity investors for the stock. When a mezzanine debt provider negotiates 6 percent warrant coverage for a $200 million loan as part of a buyout where the private equity investors are paying $2 per common equivalent share, the total exercise price of the warrant will be equal to 6 percent of $200 million. That is, the number of warrants issued is $12 million divided by the $2 per share. The debt holder, then, has a warrant for 6 million shares exercisable at $2 per share. Conceptually, the debt holder is getting the effect of investing 6 percent of his $200 million investment in equity with no cost basis. Usually, warrants issued as part of mezzanine or venture debt coverage are for purchase of common stock. That is because the warrants are a reward for success and would be exercised only when the stock price is higher than the price at the time of issue. The debt holder's principle is protected in the downside cases by the seniority of the debt, which has a liquidation preference higher than the equity and is often secured by company assets (albeit behind the senior bank debt).

The notion of warrant coverage is strange from a finance perspective. The Black-Scholes model (see Chapter 4) teaches us that the value of an option (or a warrant) is greater

---

[23] LIBOR is a daily reference rate based on the interest rates at which banks borrow unsecured funds from other banks in the London wholesale money market. It often acts as the base rate for pricing interest rates, since LIBOR varies from day to day with the general cost of funds and thus any interest rate tied to LIBOR also varies with the cost of funds.

[24] Felda Hardymon, Josh Lerner, and Ann Leamon, "Lion Capital and the Blackstone Group: The Orangina Buyout," HBS Case No. 807-005 (Boston: HBS Publishing, 2007).

if, for instance, the underlying company's valuation is more variable. The notion of warrant coverage does not capture this point. Thus the warrants involved in two different transactions with the same amount of warrant coverage may have very different valuations. The prevalence of this "rule of thumb" reflects the surprising lack of financial sophistication seen in some parts of the private equity industry.

The warrant coverage—that is, the number of shares under warrant that are granted for making the loan—for venture debt is usually considerably greater than it is for mezzanine debt. Typically mezzanine debt warrant coverage is in the 4 to 8 percent range, and venture debt warrant coverage ranges between 8 and 14 percent (see the sidebar for details). The warrants themselves are issued at an exercise price based on the price the equity investors have paid in the most recent round. Due to the inherent risks associated with start-up companies, venture debt is considerably riskier than mezzanine debt despite the similarities.

STRUCTURING A BUYOUT

Leveraged buyouts are designed to make the best use of existing cash flow. As a result, the many layers of debt and equity are structured to match the price with the risk and minimize the overall cost of capital while also allowing the deal makers to pay off or refinance the company in more manageable transactions.

This concept is usually shown in a *sources and uses table*. Here the private equity firm sets up the deal structure by identifying how capital will be used—purchase of the company, fees to complete the transaction, and so on—and how the transaction will be financed. That is, the private equity firm identifies precisely how many different loans the investors will take out and what equity securities they will sell to themselves (and possibly to others, including management) to make the acquisition. In contrast to term sheets issued to buyers, which describe the terms and conditions of buying the company, and those issued to the seller, which describe the specifics of the debt securities agreed to with banks and assorted debt providers, the sources and uses table provides an overview of the total financing structure and is the transaction's single most important document.

This roles played by the sources and uses table and terms sheets in a buyout are somewhat different from the way we typically describe growth financing and VC deals, which are usually minority ownership deals. There, the term sheet plays an important role in describing the terms of the equity purchase for a minority investor whose rights need to be explicitly spelled out for purposes of protection and control (remember our discussion of Max and Sam). In a buyout, the private equity firm is typically the majority investor, and the terms between the private equity firm and the company are less important than in the minority investor case.

An example of a simple buyout with a simple sources and uses table is Brazos Partners' purchase of Cheddar's,[25] a restaurant chain in the southwest United States. Brazos, in conjunction with management, agreed to buy the assets of Cheddar's for $60.5 million. With $3.5 million in fees and other transaction costs, the total transaction would cost $64 million. Brazos negotiated a $39 million bank loan secured by all the company's assets. The Brazos investors asked the management group that remained with the company to buy $2 million worth of equity.[26] This

---

[25] Felda Hardymon, Josh Lerner, and Ann Leamon, "Brazos Partners and Cheddar's Inc.," HBS Case No. 806-069 (Boston: HBS Publishing, 2006).

[26] Since members of management were already owners, their $2 million purchase could be funded from the proceeds of the sale of Cheddars to Brazos.

Table 5.15   Sources and Uses of Funds for 2003 Cheddar's Transaction[27]

Uses	$ Millions	Sources	$ Millions
Purchase Assets	$60.5	Senior Debt	$39.0
Fees and Expenses	$3.5	Total Debt	$39.0
Total Uses of Funds	**$64.0**	Brazos Equity	$23.0
		Management Equity	$2.0
		Total Equity	$25.0
		Total Sources of Funds	**$64.0**

ownership would serve as both an incentive to increase the company's value and as "skin in the game" to align management's interests with those of the investors. Brazos had to buy the remaining $23 million in equity. The investors structured the transaction as all common stock because Brazos owned 92 percent of the company ($23 million owned by Brazos out of the $25 million in total equity), and management paid for the shares with cash alongside Brazos. Table 5.15 is the sources and uses table.

Larger private equity deals are rarely as straightforward as that just depicted, where one bank, one private equity firm, and management simply divided up the capital structure. When Lion and Blackstone bought Orangina, they forecast that earnings before interest, tax, depreciation, and amortization (EBITDA) would increase from €184 million to over €230 million in the five years following the acquisition, due to the operational improvements and changes in distribution strategy that the investors planned to make. EBITDA in this case closely approximated cash flow. Moreover, the investors planned to sell off some nonstrategic assets within the first year and use those proceeds to pay down some debt. With those parameters in mind, Lion and Blackstone structured the senior debt (all sourced from commercial banks) as shown in Table 5.16.

Lion and Blackstone broke the €935 million senior debt into four tranches. Three of the tranches (labeled A through C in the table) differed modestly in maturity—the shorter the maturity, the lower the interest rate. The last tranche had a very short maturity and was designed to be paid

Table 5.16   Senior Debt Structure in the Orangina Transaction

	Senior (1st lien) Debt Structure, Orangina Transaction		
	Amount (€ Millions)	Margin over LIBOR	Maturity (Years)
Senior Debt A	245	2.25	7
Senior Debt B	270	2.75	8
Senior Debt C	270	3.25	9
Senior Debt D	150	2.25	2.5
Total	935	2.68	7.1
		Weighted Average	

---

[27] Hardymon et al., "Brazos Partners and Cheddar's Inc.," 22.

by the planned asset sales. The net effect is that the investors borrowed €935 million at a weighted average maturity of 7.1 years and a weighted average price of 2.68 percent over LIBOR. Had the investors borrowed that much in a single syndicated loan, the maturity likely would have been shorter and the price higher (consider that the eight-year tranche B cost 2.75 percent over LIBOR). Moreover, the investors likely had an easier time selling the four tranches to different banks with varying risk profiles than they would have had when selling a single €935 loan.[28]

Furthermore, with the stratified structure of senior debt, the Orangina investors established the possibility of paying off the most expensive tranches first as cash flow increased. This would further increase cash flow and create a virtuous cycle of decreasing the average interest rate while also decreasing the total amount of debt.

The principles that the Orangina investors applied to the senior debt section of their balance sheet can be applied across the whole balance sheet. Senior debt is less risky than mezzanine (or subordinated) debt, which in turn is less risky than preferred equities, which are less risky than common stock. Consequently, the price (cost of capital) increases from senior debt to subordinated debt and so on. The cost of capital associated with each type of security includes the mandated interest or dividend payments as well as the return that the holders expected to receive from the equity associated with the security. Thus, in the Orangina transaction, the less risky securities required a current cash payout in the form of interest or dividends and had very little equity participation.

In general, if a target company has more cash flow, it can take on (and comfortably pay off) more debt, which means that the private equity firms will have to contribute less cash in the form of equity to the transaction. The structure of a leveraged buyout, then, involves balancing three factors: (1) the cash flow available for debt service (CFADS) with (2) the least costly securities possible while (3) maintaining enough control for strong value-creating governance.

Because CFADS is a less familiar notion than EBIT, EBITDA, or net income, it is worth a moment's discussion. CFADS would normally be defined as the firm's earnings before interest and taxes (EBIT); plus the noncash items in the income statement; less taxes, working capital increase, and required financing payments for more senior securities. Thus depreciation, as a charge against earnings, would be added to the EBIT figure. Other payments that do not involve a charge against earnings—such as an increase in accounts receivable and inventory and anticipated capital expenditures—would be subtracted. When making this calculation, providers of junior securities also typically net out required interest and principal payments due to the more senior debt. (Therefore, the calculation for the purposes of a mezzanine lender would typically look at payments after required payments on the bank loans.) This measure is very closely related to the cash-flow measures used in the discounted cash-flow analysis described in Chapter 4, but it may also reflect the impact of required payments to other sources of capital.

Lenders emphasize CFADS rather than the EBITDA more commonly discussed in press accounts because the former term more closely measures the actual cash-flow characteristics of the company; and ultimately, cash flow services the debt. EBITDA and CFADS are often the same, but they differ in cases where there are noncash earnings (from subscription products, for example) or where pools of cash must be reserved for other uses (e.g., for a major factory upgrade).

In structuring a buyout, the private equity investors will naturally want to contribute as little cash as possible. There are limits, though, to the amount of debt that a company in a buyout can comfortably assume. These limits are expressed by debt covenants.

Debt Covenants

In a buyout, the private equity firm typically owns a super-majority of the company's shares. It might be thought that the private equity investors have all the governance rights too. But the debt

---

[28] Hardymon et al., "Lion Capital and the Blackstone Group."

providers need to protect their interests as well. In the same way that a bank adds language to a mortgage that prohibits a home owner from tearing down the house, debt holders (banks, insurance companies, debt funds, etc.) will employ debt covenants to protect their interests.

Debt covenants take many forms. Many of these resemble those in the agreements between venture capitalists and entrepreneurs that we discussed earlier. On the positive side, the company will be required to provide timely information to the banks, to comply with the laws and pay its taxes and to maintain property (whether physical equipment and intellectual property). On the negative side, the firm is likely to face restrictions on its ability to take on new debt, sell off existing assets, undergo a change in control, make dividend payments to shareholders, and undertake new acquisitions (often above a certain size limit). The rationale for these provisions is the same as that encountered earlier: the senior claim holder does not want management (or other claim holders) to do anything that will reduce the value of its stake.

More unique to the LBO setting are financial covenants: rules that define the financial strength of the company to which the lenders have agreed to provide debt. These set minimum levels of financial performance that the firm must maintain (expressed either as an absolute level or as a ratio). They might take the form, for instance, of a minimum coverage ratio (e.g., of CFADS as a proportion of required interest and principal payments), a maximum level of total indebtedness (expressed, for instance, as a ratio of total indebtedness to CFADS or EBITDA), and/or an absolute minimum level of EBITDA or net worth. If these financial covenants are breached, the lending documents give the lenders certain control rights that can eventually allow them to take over operating control or even force the company into bankruptcy, wiping out the equity holders. Thus even a company that remains current on its required interest and principal payments can find itself in default.

These covenants reflect banks' concerns about getting repaid. Balance sheet ratios (e.g., an upper limit on the amount of debt) reflect a concern about whether the underlying assets can cover the debt, whereas coverage ratios reflect a concern for the cash available to pay off the debt's principal and interest. Because lenders have few governance rights, they typically require two sources of repayment: cash flow and asset sales (referred to earlier as "belt and suspenders"). If their debt cannot be paid off from cash flow, the lenders expect to recoup their money through asset sales. In the post-recession period of 2009 and 2010, many lenders added a third source of repayment: taking over the equity positions of private equity firms and managing the deals themselves.[29] Time will tell whether this approach is a successful alternative to simply forcing a company sale and taking the proceeds.

Private-equity-backed companies are naturally concerned if they fall "out of covenant," which means that they have to raise cash, pay down debt, or somehow increase cash flows (e.g., by cutting important R&D programs) in order to keep lenders from seizing control. Note that in the buyout case, the interests of the private equity firm and the debt holders are aligned as long as the company is performing well. But should problems arise that are sufficient to breach the debt covenants, these interests diverge. The main debt covenants are coverage ratios and balance sheet ratios.

Market conditions as well as company-specific characteristics limit the amount of debt that private equity firms may use in a transaction by dictating the *coverage ratio*, or the ratio of CFADS to debt payments. In markets where debt is cheap, as in 1987–1989 or 2003–2007, coverage ratios are low: in some cases, the required levels were as low as 1.1:1—the lenders required only 10 percent more CFADS than the cash for debt service. These markets also are characterized by generous covenants regarding the ratio of debt to EBITDA. The loans made with such easy terms are called "covenant-lite." In the post-recession market of 2008 and 2009, the coverage ratios required by lenders were often 2:1 and more; that is, debt providers insisted that companies have twice as much CFADS as their debt service costs. In a market where liquidity is so highly valued, the lenders are less interested in equity—which is a pricing mechanism to give them upside—than in higher coverage ratios, which provide a safety net against operational risk in the company. We discuss these cycles in considerably more detail in Chapter 13.

CONCLUSION

Private equity securities and the terms that accompany them have developed as a targeted response to many of the characteristics of the asset class. The primary security, preferred stock and its variations, addresses the long-term nature of these investments and the many accompanying uncertainties. Interests are aligned through liquidation preferences, vesting, and the use of covenants. Antidilution and other terms included in the covenants for both VC and buyout transactions reflect concerns about the long time frame and the illiquidity of the asset. Covenants also help buyout firms allay the concerns of lenders.

An important feature of deal structures overall is the way they set the company up for governance. As we discuss in the next chapter, governance is the process whereby the investors help the company create value, through anything from developing a product and adopting clear reporting systems and transparent financials to restructuring struggling operations. The powers that the investors negotiate at the time of investment, along with the management incentives included in the deal structure overall, set the stage for concentrated and aligned efforts to create value and eventually position the company for a profitable exit.

QUESTIONS

1. Why do venture capitalists use preferred stock?
2. If you were an entrepreneur, how would you think of the difference between a preferred-plus-cheap-common structure and a convertible preferred structure?
3. How does the concept of fiduciary duty play into the use of preferred stock?
4. Why is vesting used in venture capital deals? Why do managements agree to it?
5. Why would Kevin Laracey of eDOCs agree to a transaction that included a liquidation preference, vesting of the management team's stock, and the possibility of his replacement? Why would Charles River Ventures have suggested it?
6. Ever the risk taker, Max has invested in another of Sam's companies. This time, he pays $3 million for 30 percent of SpecialStuff (SS). Calculate the payout table and draw the graphs for Sam and Max in the following situations:
   a. The deal is structured as all-common, and PredatoryPurchaser (PP) offers Sam $3.5 million for the company.
   b. The deal is structured as redeemable preferred with cheap common, and PredatoryPurchaser offers Sam $3.5 million for the company.
   c. The deal is structured as convertible preferred, and PredatoryPurchaser offers Sam $5 million for the company. At what price will Max convert to common?
   d. SpecialStuff goes public at a valuation of $20 million, and Max owns participating convertible preferred.
   e. OtherStuff, a private company, buys SpecialStuff for $7 million. Max owns participating convertible preferred.
7. Why would an investor even fund a company that would accept a 5× liquidation preference?
8. Consider that you hold securities in a company that has just accepted an investment of $10 million with 6× liquidation at $3 million pre-money. How would you value this company if you were the "new money"? The previous investors?

9. SpecialStuff needs another $3 million. Acme, happy with its returns on Sam's first company, eagerly agrees to participate, investing $4 million for 20 percent of the company. Assume the first round was as in question 6 and that Sam and Max each own convertible preferred stock.

   a. How much do Max and Sam now own?

   b. Create payout tables for exit values at $4 million, $8 million, $12 million, and $20 million for each participant assuming pooled seniority

   c. . . . with Acme senior to Max and Sam.

10. How does antidilution make sense?

11. Calculate the difference in Max's ownership in the following scenarios: SpecialStuff raised its A round at $1.50 per share. Max invested $1.5 million for one million shares and 30 percent ownership. Now SpecialStuff is raising a B round, but the market has turned against it and Acme will pay only $1.00 per share for 1 million shares. (Assume that Max doesn't participate at all and allows Acme Ventures to take the whole round.)

   a. What if Max has full-ratchet antidilution?

   b. Weighted average?

   c. If Max participates pro rata to his ownership, how will parts 11a and 11b change?

12. If a mezzanine investor has received warrant coverage for 5 percent of a $3 million loan where the equity investors are paying $2.50 per share, how many shares will she be able to buy and at what price?

13. Assume Max and Sam are negotiating their first round in SpecialStuff. Sam is sure that $3 million is all that will be needed, but Max believes it will take at least twice that. Max is willing to invest $3 million in this round for ownership somewhere between 25% and 40%. What do you think the final deal will look like and why?

APPENDIX 1
A TOUR THROUGH COMPETING VENTURE TERM SHEETS[30]

Item	Insiders		Outsider
	Venrock/BVP Term Sheet		**Ampersand Ventures Term Sheet**
Amount and Security	Up to $18,000,000 in Series C Convertible Preferred Stock (the "Series C," together with Endeca's Series A Convertible Preferred Stock, the "Series A," and Series B Convertible Preferred Stock, the "Series B," the "Preferred") Minimum closing: $10,000,000. Later closings allowable for up to 60 days from initial closing.		$18 million for Series C Convertible Preferred Stock (the "Series C Stock"), at a purchase price of $1.25 per share, convertible into shares of Common Stock of the Company.
Purchasers			The investment will be made by the following entities or their affiliates (the "Purchasers") in the amounts indicated: – Ampersand Ventures: $8M – Current Investors: $10M – Total: $18M
Price	The Series C will be sold at $0.985 per share. Each share of Series C converts into one share of common stock (subject to antidilution adjustment and stock splits) at the holders' option.		
Redemption	The Preferred Stock shall be redeemed in equal quarterly installments from January 1, 2008, through December 31, 2010. *NB: Series B will be modified to conform to Series C mandatory redemption.*		Each holder of Series C Stock may elect, at such holder's option, to have the Company redeem up to a maximum of 33.3%, 50.0%, and 100% of the outstanding shares of Series C Stock held by such holder on each of the fifth, sixth, and seventh anniversary dates, respectively, of the Closing, at a price of $1.25 per share, plus any accrued but unpaid dividends. If any shares are eligible for redemption in one year and the holder of Series C Stock chooses not to have such shares redeemed in that year, he may elect to have them redeemed in a later year, provided that such election must be made not later than the seventh anniversary of the Closing.

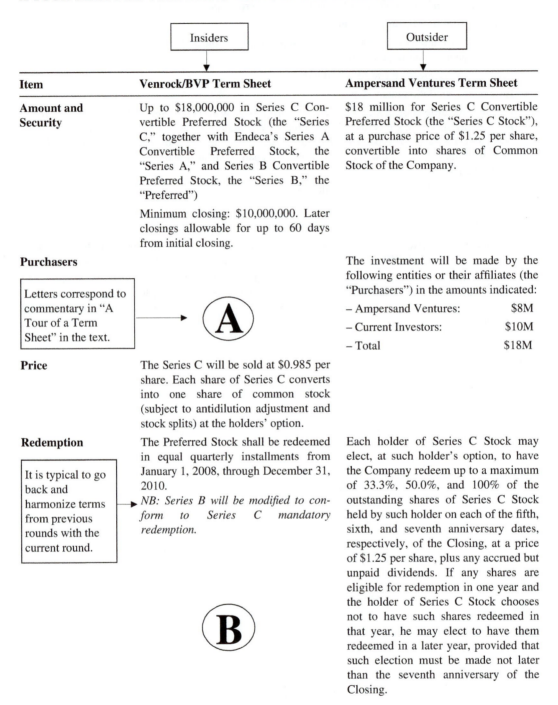

Letters correspond to commentary in "A Tour of a Term Sheet" in the text. →

It is typical to go back and harmonize terms from previous rounds with the current round.

---

[30] Adapted from Felda Hardymon, Josh Lerner, and Ann Leamon, "Endeca Technologies (A)," HBS Case No. 802-141 (Boston: HBS Publishing, 2002), 17–22.

Item	Venrock/BVP Term Sheet	Ampersand Ventures Term Sheet
Voting Rights	The Preferred votes as if converted.	On all matters submitted to a vote of holders of Common Stock generally, holders of Series C Stock shall be entitled to exercise a number of votes equal to the number of shares of Common Stock into which shares of Series C Stock then held by such holders are convertible on the appropriate record date. Holders of Series A, Series B, and Series C Preferred Stock (together, the "Preferred Stock") shall vote with holders of Common Stock as a single class on all matters submitted to a vote of the Common Stockholders.

> Two very different ways of saying the same thing!

Item	Venrock/BVP Term Sheet	Ampersand Ventures Term Sheet
Liquidation Preference	The Series C has a liquidation preference equal to its original purchase price, payable upon a merger, sale, or liquidation of Endeca. *NB: Series A and B will be modified so that the Series C ranks on parity with Series A and Series B.*	In the event of any liquidation, dissolution, or winding up of the Company, the holders of Series C Stock shall receive an amount per share of Series C Stock equal to its purchase price, plus any accrued but unpaid dividends, before any payments to holders of the Series A, Series B, Common Stock, or other capital stock of the Company. If the assets of the Company available for distribution upon liquidation are not sufficient to pay to each holder of Series C Stock $1.25 per share plus any accrued but unpaid dividends, such assets shall be distributed pro rata among the holders of Series C Preferred Stock on the basis of the number of shares held by each holder thereof. The merger or consolidation of the Company into or with another corporation or the sale of all or substantially all of the Company's assets shall be deemed to be a liquidation of the Company unless the holders of 60% of the shares of Series C Preferred Stock then outstanding elect otherwise by giving written notice thereof to the Company at least 15 days before the effective date of such event.

(continued)

Item	Venrock/BVP Term Sheet	Ampersand Ventures Term Sheet
Mandatory Conversion	Series C must convert to Common Stock upon consummation of an underwritten public offering of at least $10,000,000 at a price of at least $____ per share (split adjusted). *NB: Series A and Series B will be modified to conform to Series C on mandatory conversion.*	Each share of Series C Stock will be convertible, at any time, at the option of the holder, into shares of Common Stock, at a conversion price of $____ per share (subject to adjustment as described below), plus the payment of all accrued but unpaid dividends. The Company may require the conversion of all (but not less than all) of Series C Stock in the event of a firm commitment underwritten public offering of Common Stock of the Company at a price that equals or exceeds $____ per share in which the net proceeds received by the Company equal or exceed $____ million.

> Essentially the same; both adhere to the principle of converting on a legitimate public offering. The only question is the definition of "legitimate" by price and offering size. Note the need to keep earlier Series A and Series B conforming to Series C.

Item	Venrock/BVP Term Sheet	Ampersand Ventures Term Sheet
Antidilution	Broad weighted average protection (i.e., adjustment to conversion price) for issuance of shares at a price below Series C common equivalent share price (except to employees *or* under a Board-approved stock incentive plan) in a financing of at least $200,000 for the holders of Series C on a common equivalent basis in future offerings only if investor participates pro rata to common equivalent position. Existing Series B will be price adjusted to convert at $0.985 per share and will be modified to have weighted average antidilution identical to Series C.	The Series C shareholders shall be entitled to full-ratchet antidilution protection only if that shareholder participates pro rata to their common equivalent position in that financing. The conversion price and the number of shares of Common Stock into which shares of Series C Stock are convertible shall also be appropriately adjusted to reflect stock splits, stock dividends, reorganizations, reclassifications, consolidations, mergers or sales, and similar events. There will be no adjustment in the conversion price upon the issuance of up to____ shares of Common Stock (or options to acquire such shares) to employees of the Company under the Company's Incentive Stock Plan. Concurrent with this financing, the conversion price of Series B Stock will be adjusted to Series C share price of $1.25 per share.
Negative Covenants (Venrock/BVP) **Covenants and Restrictions (Ampersand Ventures)**	The approval of 66% of face value of the Preferred is required for the following: (1) organic changes outside the normal course of business; (2) the sale, liquidation, or merger of Endeca; (3) any increase in Board seats or a change in election procedures; or (4) the issuance of any equity security senior to Series C.	The Purchase Agreement for Series C Stock will contain customary covenants and restrictions and will specify certain actions that may be taken by the Company only with the consent of the holders of 60% of the outstanding shares of Preferred Stock (except that altering, changing, or amending the preferences or rights of any individual

Item	Venrock/BVP Term Sheet	Ampersand Ventures Term Sheet

series of preferred stock will require the consent of 60% of the outstanding shares of that series) including, without limitation, authorizing, creating, or issuing any debt or equity securities (except for the issuance of shares (or options to purchase the same) reserved for issuance to employees of the Company); merging with or acquiring another entity or selling substantially all of the assets of the Company; paying dividends on or making other distributions with respect to any securities other than the Preferred Stock; engaging in any business other than the business engaged in by the Company at the time of the Closing or described in the Business Plan or otherwise making any substantial deviation from the business strategy contained in the Business Plan; increasing or decreasing the number of directors constituting the Board of Directors; repurchasing or redeeming any securities, except for repurchases under restricted stock agreements with employees previously approved by the Board of Directors; transferring, by sale, license, or otherwise, any intellectual property rights of the Company.

Representations and Warranties

Standard.

The Company will make representations and warranties in the Stock Purchase Agreement customary in transactions of this kind including, without limitation, representations regarding due incorporation, quali-fication and standing, charter documents and bylaws, corporate power, enforceability of the Stock Purchase Agreement and related agreements, subsidiaries, capitalization, authorization, due issuance, use of proceeds, litigation, contracts and commitments (including contracts between key employees and prior employers), financial statements, subsequent developments, title to assets, proprietary information, and environmental matters.

> Representations and warranties are often described as "standard," meaning they include all of the appropriate legal boilerplate to assure ownership is transferred legally and the company is in good standing with all tax and regulatory requirements. Occasionally, when a well-established company is involved, the investors will require certain warranties from existing management about the state of the company and attesting to their confidence that there are no hidden liabilities.

(continued)

Item	Venrock/BVP Term Sheet	Ampersand Ventures Term Sheet
Financial Statements	Annual audit by a nationally recognized firm plus monthly actual vs. plan and prior year, plus annual budget 60 days before beginning of fiscal year to holders of more than 3,000,000 split-adjusted shares. All recipients of financial statements must execute a nondisclosure agreement acceptable to Endeca's counsel.	The Company will submit unaudited financial statements to holders of at least 3,000,000 shares of Preferred Stock not later than 60 days after the close of each fiscal quarter and not later than 30 days after the end of each month, including income statements, balance sheets, cash flow statements, summaries of bookings and backlogs, and comparisons to forecasts and to corresponding periods in prior years. Audited annual financial statements shall be provided not later than 90 days after the end of each year. Not later than 30 days after the start of each fiscal year, the Company shall provide an annual Operating Plan prepared on a monthly basis and, promptly after preparation, any revisions to such Operating Plan. The Company will promptly provide other customary information and materials, including, without limitation, reports of adverse developments, management letters, communications with stockholders or directors, press releases, and registration statements.
Registration Rights	Pooled with Series A and B. Two (2) demand registrations, subject to $5 million *and* 100,000 share trigger, unlimited piggybacks, and evergreen S-3 if requested and possible. All of the above shall be at Endeca's expense.	1. The holders of Series C Preferred Stock shall be entitled to two demand registrations on Form S-1 or S-2, or any successor forms, at the Company's expense, exercisable upon request of holders of not less than 50% of the outstanding Series C Preferred Stock. A registration will not count for this purpose (a) unless it becomes effective and holders are able to sell at least 50% of the shares sought to be included in the registration, or (b) if the Company elects to sell stock pursuant to a registration statement at the same time. There will be no piggybacking on such registrations without the consent of the participating Preferred Stock stockholders. 2. The holders of Series C Preferred Stock shall be entitled to unlimited registrations on Form S-3, or any successor form.

Item	Venrock/BVP Term Sheet	Ampersand Ventures Term Sheet
		3. The holders of Series C Preferred Stock shall have unlimited piggyback registration rights at the Company's expense, with priority over all other selling stockholders.
		4. The Company shall not grant registration rights to any other party without the consent of 60% of the holders of Series C Preferred Stock.
Dividends		Dividends shall accrue on each share of Series C Preferred Stock when and as declared by the Company's Board of Directors, and shall be payable before the payment of any dividends with respect to any other Series of Preferred or Common Stock and in the event of a liquidation, dissolution, or winding up of the Company.
Options and Vesting	Additional pool for future employees of ___ shares set aside with vesting of four (4) years straight line with a one-year blackout. Endeca will have a right of first refusal on all employee shares vested prior to a public offering. Employees may transfer shares to immediate family, trusts, and the like.	<div style="border:1px solid">Often financing triggers consideration of the adequacy of option pools. Adding shares to the pool can be the subject of close negotiation since it in effect increases the company's valuation (e.g., adding 200,000 shares in this case would raise the post-money valuation by $250,000 in relation to the Ampersand deal).</div>
Employee Agreements	Proprietary Information Agreements must be obtained from all employees, and Noncompete Agreements must be obtained from all key employees. The agreements must be in a form satisfactory to the Board. <div style="border:1px solid">Venture capitalists almost always require key employees to be bound by these agreements to protect their investment. In this case the terms are identical.</div>	The Founders and Key Management of the Company shall enter into agreements in a form satisfactory to the Purchasers, (1) not to compete with the Company and (2) not to induce, directly or indirectly, employees of the Company to terminate their employment with the Company, during the term of their employment and for a period after termination of their employment. All employees and consultants of the Company shall execute standard Nondisclosure and Assignment of Inventions Agreements with the Company in form satisfactory to the Purchasers.

(*continued*)

Item	Venrock/BVP Term Sheet	Ampersand Ventures Term Sheet
Closing	ASAP subject only to completion of definitive legal documents acceptable to all parties.	On or before September 14, 2001. The Stock Purchase Agreement will contain customary closing conditions, including satisfactory completion of legal due diligence review.

> Note that Ampersand, being an outsider, leaves room for more due diligence before closing while the insiders are willing to close as soon as legal documentation can be finalized.

Chapter 6

After the Money Arrives

Once the term sheet has been signed, the investment does not run itself. Rather, the investors join the board and embark on deal management, an essential, fascinating, and unsung part of private equity investing. It is deal management that distinguishes active equity investing from most other types of investing: the gains of equity investment are predicated on creating value. If the entrepreneur took a bank loan, no one would show up at the next board meeting looking expectant. Value is created through active deal management and governance—a company with its value fully developed does not just fall in one's lap. Whether the transaction is a buyout or a seed-stage investment, the entrepreneur and the investor have, in the words of Robert Frost, "miles to go/before [we] sleep."[1]

One person's activity is another person's meddling; but in this book, we call it governance. Governance provides the discipline, transparency, accountability, and outside perspective that ensures the items described in a strategic plan are executed. "Ideas are cheap, execution is dear" goes the maxim. Many great plans have gathered dust on the shelves of struggling companies; the power of private equity is that the plan comes along with governance from experienced investors with tightly aligned interests in seeing it successfully executed.

It seems intuitively obvious that a start-up company would require governance; after all, venture capital (VC) is billed as "money with strings attached." Those strings—advice, recommendations, processes, reports—are part of the reason an entrepreneur is willing to part with a chunk of the company.[2] In 1982, Ben Rosen of the firm Sevin-Rosen invested in Lotus Development Corporation, the creator of Lotus 1-2-3, an early market-leading spreadsheet program. As part of the closing conditions, Rosen challenged the fledgling company to exhibit at the upcoming industry trade show, Comdex. No one at Lotus knew what Comdex was or what was involved in exhibiting there,[3] but the Lotus 1-2-3 debut at Comdex in November 1982 generated orders of $1 million at the show itself.[4] The software's first-year sales in 1983 were $53 million, $50 million over budget.[5] While founders Mitch Kapor and Jonathan Sachs had made prescient structural decisions and created a fast, intuitive product that interacted perfectly

---

[1] Robert Frost, "Stopping by Woods on a Snowy Evening," *The Poetry of Robert Frost*, ed. Edward Connery Lathem, (New York: Henry Holt & Co., 1969), 224.

[2] The other reason is that the entrepreneur usually cannot raise enough money through less expensive bank loans.

[3] Private communication with Sonia Dettmann, employee 8 at Lotus Development Corp.

[4] William Asprey, "Oral History of Mitch Kapor," Computer History Museuem Reference No. X3006.2005, November 19, 2004, 16, http://archive.computerhistory.org/resources/text/Oral_History/Kapor_Mitch/Kapor_Mitch.oral_history.2006. 102657943.pdf, accessed July 15, 2011.

[5] Ibid., 13.

with the just-released IBM PC,[6] Rosen's industry knowledge and marketing advice vaulted them into the big leagues.

Yet governance is also important in buyouts. The investors put in place not just a plan to achieve improvements but the governance systems that ensure execution and accountability. Some of aspects of the system—incentive alignment, bonus payments, stock ownership—help extend an ownership mentality to employees.

Creating value in buyouts takes many forms. Sometimes, the investors simply assist the management team in better implementing an existing strategy. When Brazos Partners invested in the Cheddar's restaurant chain,[7] the partners knew they were backing a skilled entrepreneur and a proven model. To increase the company's growth rate, the partners expanded the management team by recruiting a talented CFO and setting up more centralized systems. Aubrey Good, the 70-year-old founder and CEO, was eager to take on new risks now that he had a broader perspective and had diversified his personal wealth. The company became more corporate; rather than meeting in a back booth at one of the restaurants, the CEO rented simple, no-nonsense office space in an unpretentious building, thus sending the message that this was a real company. The private equity partners did not change expansion strategy as much as accelerate it.

In other cases, the investors change the company's strategy. When Blackstone Group bought Equity Office Properties (EOP) in 2007 for a then record $39 billion, the firm used its combined expertise in private equity and real estate to rationalize EOP's portfolio of properties. Instead of its former strategy of undifferentiated growth, EOP changed its approach and kept core, high-margin properties while selling off the rest. This also, as we learned in Chapter 5, allowed Blackstone to pay down much of the debt it took on in the initial acquisition.[8]

The governance that leads to value creation flows from the board of directors. Private equity boards are composed of investors, management, and a few outsiders. The details of board power, membership, and even some voting procedures are negotiated along with the deal. In most cases, investors control the board either through sheer numbers or special voting rights that we discussed later. The board itself has a fiduciary duty to the shareholders, most of whom are directly represented. This stands in sharp contrast to public company boards, which have a dispersed and—for the most part—passive shareholder base. Private equity is active investment; ergo, the board is active.

Let's consider the continuum of corporation governance, as shown in Figure 6.1. In a single-person proprietorship, there is one person with total responsibility. Governance is totally integrated; there is no disconnect between the shareholder, the board of directors, and the

FIGURE 6.1 Continuum of governance

Sole Proprietor   Private Equity-Backed   Public Company
                                      Company

---

[6] Ibid. and Christopher Hartman, Carole Gunst and Gil Press, "History of Lotus 1-2-3," *High Tech History*, January 26, 2010, http://hightechhistory.com/2010/01/26/history-of-lotus-1-2-3/, accessed July 15, 2011.

[7] Josh Lerner, Felda Hardymon, and Ann Leamon, "Brazos Partners and Cheddar's," HBS Case No. 806-069 (Boston: HBS Publishing, 2006).

[8] Dan Levy and Hui-yong Yu, "Blackstone to Sell 10 Buildings to Morgan Stanley (Update1)," *Bloomberg.com*, February 23, 2007, www.bloomberg.com/apps/news?pid=newsarchive&sid=aRxhPzTdizs8&refer=home, accessed November 15, 2010.

management. One must hope that the one person is smart enough to grow Moe's Garage into Moe's World-Dominating Garage. On the far right lies a public company. The public company's shareholder base is very distant from its board of directors, which is also separate from management. Sometimes the company seems to be run for the benefit of management, not shareholders, as in situations where top executives at underperforming companies receive surprisingly generous pay packages.[9] In the middle is the private-equity-backed company with perhaps the strongest governance. It has a professional, active investor (or a small number of them) with control and a keen interest in the company's success, for the achievement of which it chooses strategy, marshals resources, and aligns management. There is little discontinuity between the shareholder and board (which are often, or to a large extent, the same) and management.

With early-stage companies, value creation means setting company direction, deciding how big it can get, how fast it can grow, how the products will evolve, and how much money to raise and when. In buyouts, value creation may mean growth by acquisition or subtraction, when various divisions are sold to focus on the core. In all cases, the idea is to create value.

In this chapter, we examine what happens after the money arrives. We focus on the board level, where governance occurs, and consider the structure, powers, and decision making involved. We explore how the staging of financing affects the company's progress. Next we spend some time on case studies of good and bad deal management—where value is created and destroyed. We then investigate the roles of private equity firms in overall deal management, both formal and informal. Finally, we consider what happens when the entire deal is re-contracted.

As we proceed, note the linkages between a deal's structure, from the type of security to the number of board seats, and its governance. Items that might seem minor at the beginning of an investment's life can end up having a huge impact on the eventual outcome or require great effort and distraction to change.

BOARDS—THE SEAT OF GOVERNANCE

Boards of directors represent all the company shareholders and make decisions for the company's overall good. The deal structures put power in the hands of the investors in exchange for the money they invest. Through the negotiated deal terms, the investors do not have to own a majority of the company to have effective control.

Management implements the board's decisions in the company's day-to-day operations. The senior executives report to the board, but the board does not intervene directly in most aspects of corporate life. If the company is falling short of revenue due to inadequate performance of the sales force, the board may fire the vice president of sales, but it will not fire specific salespeople. On the other hand, board-recommended changes in strategy might mean the salespeople use a different sales approach.

The size of a board varies. It may be as small as two or three people for a seed-level start-up; between five and seven is common for many private companies; and buyouts may have seven to nine directors. The investors often have a majority of seats—in some buyouts, the firm may have four of five seats, and the CEO holds the last. In the vast majority of situations, private equity investors either have a majority of seats or the majority of votes in crucial matters.

---

[9] Among others, Alice Gomstyn, "Top Five Highest-Paid, Worst-Performing CEOs," *ABCNews.com*, September 22, 2005, http://abcnews.go.com/Business/top-highest-paid-worst-performing-ceos/story?id=8642794, accessed July 20, 2010.

Not all investors have seats on the board, though. Sometimes this is from preference: the firm may have the right to appoint a representative and choose an outside expert or a co-investor to take the seat due to that person's geographical proximity or expertise. In other cases, an investor may not have invested enough or negotiated hard enough to receive a seat (this is known as being a passive investor). A few firms make a practice of taking observer seats, in which their representative does not have a vote. Some observers have information rights that allow them full access to board information; others can attend the full board meetings but are excluded from executive sessions and the material considered there. Microsoft's IP Ventures, for instance, specializes in helping to found companies that commercialize technology that the computer giant has developed but chooses not to pursue. Because Microsoft has deep knowledge of the technology and a share of the equity and provides marketing and public relations services to the new operation, it wants to remain informed of the firm's progress; but it does not want the control that a voting position would confer.[10]

The number of board members often grows over time; more investors join as additional firms invest. An excessively large board is unwieldy, but it can be difficult to dislodge an existing investor because board membership is seen as a mark of advancement during the early stages of an investor's career. A successful mid- or later-career investor may want to reduce board responsibilities just when reputation and industry contacts make that person most valuable. How firms handle this tension is part of their internal structure, discussed in Chapter 11.

In the case of a buyout, the firm controls the majority of board seats because it owns the majority of the company. The CEO holds one of the remaining seats. The rest, if any, may be held by cofounders, an additional high-ranking officer, or an independent who may be a material customer or a well-regarded industry expert or manager. The CFO is usually an observer. Although these companies and the buyout firms strive for good relationships with their lenders, it is extremely rare to have a bank representative on the board. If a limited partner (LP) has co-invested in the deal, it might have board representation; but in general the board is composed of just the buyout firm and management, which simplifies the decision making process. When a consortium of firms has executed the buyout, competing goals can complicate board function, just as can occur in VC deals.

Board Composition and Responsibilities

In a seminal paper, Michael Gorman and William A. Sahlman[11] considered board membership and responsibilities in private equity settings. In late 1984, they sent questionnaires to 100 VC firms, receiving 49 responses from firms that had roughly 40 percent of the industry capital under management. Board members averaged seven years of experience in the VC industry and the average firm was twelve years old, so these were individuals and firms with some longevity. As shown in Figure 6.2, most of the respondents spent more than half their time monitoring their nine portfolio companies and sitting on five boards. Each board seat required eighty hours of on-site time and thirty hours of phone conversations per year, or roughly two hours of direct attention per week. The investors most often helped the company raise funds and build the investor group; the next most frequent tasks included strategic analysis and management recruiting, as shown in Table 6.1.

The time requirements were far lower if the investor did not lead the deal. Non-lead VC investors reported that they spent 45 minutes per week with their companies. The lead investors, on

---

[10] For more on IP Ventures, see Josh Lerner and Ann Leamon, "Microsoft's IP Ventures," HBS Case No. 810-096 (Boston: HBS Publishing, 2010).

[11] Michael Gorman and William A. Sahlman, "What Do Venture Capitalists Do?" *Journal of Business Venturing* 4, no. 4 (1989): 231–49.

FIGURE 6.2 Time spent by venture capitalists

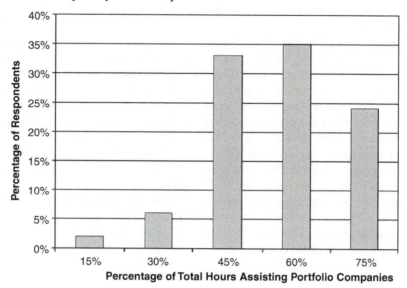

Source: Adapted from Gorman and Sahlman, "What Do Venture Capitalists Do?" 236.

average, visited the company nineteen times per year, spending five hours at the company at each visit. Non-lead investors came barely once a month and stayed for only three hours. An investor who had funded the company at a later stage in its life and did not lead the round attended one four-hour meeting per quarter.

Table 6.1 Company Assistance

Type of Assistance	Importance	Percent of Companies Receiving
Help with additional financing	1	75.0
Strategic planning	2	67.5
Recruiting management	3	62.5
Operational planning	4	55.0
Introductions to potential customers and suppliers	5	52.5
Resolving compensation issues	6	55.0
Serving as CEO's confidante	7	NA
Introductions to service providers	8	NA
Managing the investor group	9	NA
Recruiting board members	10	NA

Source: Adapted from Michael Gorman & William A. Sahlman, "What Do Venture Capitalists Do?" 237. The items where "Percent of Companies Receiving" is listed as "NA" are those that were written in and cited by only one or two respondents; the true frequency with which companies received these services is unknown.

Gorman and Sahlman then explored reasons for the high failure rate of early-stage VC-backed businesses. But if the board members are providing real services, why don't more early-stage businesses succeed?

The authors provided three possible explanations. First, early-stage businesses by their nature pose questions (about technology function and customer adoption) that can be resolved only by going forward. Without investing in technology development, no one can tell if it will work. Second, because venture investors funded to milestones and the entrepreneur knew that raising more money occurred only at the expense of personal dilution, the companies were thinly staffed and thus less resilient when something went awry. Third, there was a lemming-like tendency to crowd into popular market sectors. In a study by Sahlman and Stevenson,[12] forty-three start-ups entered the disk drive market segment over six years, even though the sector was highly unlikely to support more than four companies. Note that this was in 1984, far before the 1999 dot-com boom and the proliferation of doomed online pet food emporia.

Intriguingly, the venture capitalists tended to blame senior management for company failures—largely, Gorman and Sahlman surmised, because board members interacted mostly with the senior management. In difficult times, the interests of the venture capitalist to preserve capital and provide a good return on the scarce resource of time could diverge from those of the entrepreneurial team, which wanted the company to survive. On average, the investors replaced a CEO every 2.4 years during their careers.

In a later paper, Josh Lerner[13] examined 271 early-stage biotechnology firms between 1978 and 1989, studying both the composition of the boards and the changes that ensued when a CEO was removed. Table 6.2 shows that the number of board members grows with additional funding rounds, from slightly over four for the first round to almost six by the later rounds. On average, venture capitalists controlled 1.4 seats in the first round, rising to 2.12 seats in the fourth or later round. As a company grows, two things happen. Often, additional firms join in supporting the company and want board representation. Also, the board may want to bring on domain experts (defined in the table as "Other Outsiders"), or additional executives ("Insiders"). A founder who

Table 6.2   Board Membership by Round in Private Biotechnology Companies

Financing Round	Mean Number of Board Members			
	Venture Capitalists	Other Outsiders	Insiders	Quasi-Insiders
First	1.40	0.86	1.28	0.52
Second	1.87	0.86	1.40	0.56
Third	2.09	1.02	1.61	0.67
Later	2.12	1.27	1.73	0.54

Note: This sample reflects 653 financing rounds of 271 biotechnology companies between 1978 and 1989, reduced to the 362 rounds where membership can be determined. *Venture capitalists* include general partners, full-time affiliates, or associates of VC organizations. *Other outsiders* include corporate investors, investors who at some point were part of an organization that held at least 5 percent of the company, were not officers of the company, and were not affiliated with organizations that partnered with the company, and did not have any other relationship with the company. *Insiders* are senior or junior managers who work directly for the company. *Quasi-insiders* are individuals who do not work directly for the company but have an ongoing relationship with it.
Source: Josh Lerner, "Venture Capitalists and the Oversight of Private Firms" *Journal of Finance* 50, no. 1 (1995): 308.

---

[12] William A. Sahlman and Howard Stevenson, "Capital Market Myopia," *Journal of Business Venturing* 1, no. 1 (1985): 7–30.

[13] Josh Lerner, "Venture Capitalists and the Oversight of Private Firms," *Journal of Finance* 50, no. 1 (1995): 301–18.

Table 6.3   The Professional Affiliation of Board Members at the Last Financing Round

	Percent of Total
Outside Directors	
Venture capitalist	36.2
Corporate partner	6.4
Other investor	3.1
Executive in other health-care/biotech firm	3.5
Retired health-care/high-tech executive	3.6
Academic without firm affiliation	0.9
Lawyer, consultant, or investment banker without firm affiliation	1.4
Other/unidentified	5.1
Inside Directors	
Senior manager	20.3
Junior manager	7.1
Quasi-Inside Directors	
Academic with firm affiliation	8.9
Lawyer with firm affiliation	0.5
Investment/commercial banker with firm affiliation	1.0
Former manager of firm	0.6
Relative/other	1.3

Source: Josh Lerner, "Venture Capitalists and the Oversight of Private Firms," 308.

has moved from CEO into a chief technology officer (CTO) role may still retain a seat on the board even as the new CEO joins. Lerner also found that serving on a board had a strong geographic component: if the firm's office was within five miles of the company, the investor was twice as likely to be on the board than if the firm was five hundred miles away. Most venture capitalists sat on the boards of companies located within sixty miles of their offices.

Lerner also explored the composition of boards at the companies' last financing rounds before going public or being acquired. Table 6.3 shows that a substantial number of venture investors remain (although these often leave the board at the time of an initial public offering—IPO). The companies have also added a number of outside experts from the biotech industry, reflecting a change in focus from typical early-stage growth issues to more industry-specific challenges.

Lastly, Lerner observed forty instances of CEO replacement, as distinct from retirement, in his sample. Here it became clear that replacing a CEO extracted a huge toll on the venture investors. On average, if a CEO was replaced in the interval between financing rounds, 1.75 venture capitalists joined the board of directors in the next round. If the CEO stayed constant, 0.24 did so. This suggested that the failure of a CEO was seen to require more investor intervention, whether by increasing the size and expertise of the board or by adding VC firms to a funding round and thus increasing the amount of money available to support a company that might be experiencing growing pains or changing direction.

Baker and Gompers[14] supported Lerner's findings on board size in the later stage of a venture-backed company's life, determining that VC-backed companies on the verge of an IPO had 1.7 venture capitalists on a board that averaged six people. In their analysis of IPO prospectuses for 1,116 firms that went public between 1978 and 1987, they suggested that board composition was the outcome of a bargain between the CEO and investors wherein the skill of the CEO and the reputation of the VC firm both influenced the result. A longer-serving CEO or one with more voting control could reduce the number of board seats controlled by the VC investors, while the number of investor-controlled board seats rose with a higher-reputation VC firm (proxied by the age of the firm in question). As the VC firm's reputation rose, the probability of the founder remaining as CEO at the time of the IPO fell. The reason for this, the authors suggested, was that a high-reputation VC firm had a stable of talented CEO candidates from prior investments. Because the firm's reputation made it a desirable funder and established a record of success, the CEO was willing to accept less control and a greater risk of replacement.

Note that we earlier discussed the impact of VC firm's reputation on its ability to obtain favorable terms from LPs; later, we explore the impact of reputation on returns to those LPs. This is part of the underlying dynamic—high-reputation firms can often create board situations that allow them greater control.

Compared to the boards of other companies in the sample, Baker and Gompers found that those with VC backing were 27 percent smaller and had 20 percent fewer "instrumental" directors—outside advisers such as consultants, investment bankers, lawyers, and accountants. The VC directors added value, then, by monitoring and advising management, and increased the board's efficiency by reducing its size.

There are fewer analyses of buyout company boards. In one of these, Robert Gertner and Steven Kaplan[15] analyzed detailed board structure and director data for fifty-nine companies that underwent reverse leveraged buyouts (LBOs; they were taken private in a buyout and then relisted by their owner) between 1987 and June 1993 and where the owners continued to hold a position after the IPO. This background—the company was acquired, improved, and then succeeded in the public markets while the owners continued to be involved—indicated that the operation was structured to maximize value, given the fiduciary duties of the buyout firms. Compared to other companies that went public at the same time, the boards of the LBOs tended to be smaller: they had 8.19 directors, slightly fewer insiders, and the directors owned larger equity stakes. While formal meetings occurred less frequently (5.73 times per year compared to 6.62), the authors posited that informal communication played a larger role in monitoring and advising of buyout companies.

In general, then, private equity boards tend to be smaller, more dominated by investors, and more oriented toward providing monitoring and advisory services. This all creates value. The directors are knowledgeable, deeply invested (in all senses of the term), and provide both formal and informal guidance. In the next section, we examine how boards get their powers.

BOARD POWERS

Board powers—seats, voting rights, and the like—are negotiated as part of the deal structure. They are not merely proportionate to investment ownership, although that may play a part. Recall Baker and Gompers' idea that board representation results from a bargain between the CEO or founder and the venture backers, where the relative power and reputation of each helps to determine the outcome. A superstar technologist-founder can sometimes use his reputation to structure a board to

---

[14] Malcolm Baker and Paul Gompers, "The Determinants of Board Structure at the Initial Public Offering," *Journal of Law and Economics* 46, no. 2 (2003): 569–98.

[15] Robert Gertner and Steven N. Kaplan, "The Value-Maximizing Board," December 1996 (unpublished), http://faculty.chicagobooth.edu/steven.kaplan/research/gerkap.pdf, accessed July 13, 2010.

his liking. If he is negotiating with two inexperienced and starstruck investors, he may get his way, resulting in an unwieldy board structure dominated by the founder and individuals he controls. Usually, though, private equity investors can create boards that are more investor-friendly.

One of the ways that private equity investors control boards is through voting rights. Some boards use "one vote per director"; others weight votes by the percentage ownership; still others vote by class. Moreover, there can also be special voting rights, in which certain representatives' votes carry more weight than others in specific situations. For instance, the investors may control two of the five seats, but both must approve matters like a budget or the hiring of a senior executive. In other situations, these two investor directors are just two votes.

Rather than giving some representatives special rights, specific matters such as a new CEO, a budget, an acquisition, adding debt, or being acquired may require approval from more than a simple majority, possibly a super-majority or even a unanimous vote. Different classes—the shares issued in different rounds of financing—may also have special voting rights. This is particularly common if a start-up has progressed to a late stage and therefore has a board composed of investors with very different share prices. In such a situation, the later-stage investors want to be sure that the early-stage directors cannot approve an acquisition offer at a price that makes a nice return on the less expensive shares but loses money for those holding higher-priced stock. Hence, the later investors might insist that their class has approval rights or veto powers over such transactions.

Every VC deal stipulates that the holders of preferred stock must vote to allow the issuance of preferred stock senior to itself. That is, you have to agree to displace yourself in the capital structure. The board must also approve any change to its own structure.

The degree to which these situations actually occur depends on the company's performance. If it is doing well, financing rounds tend to be uncomplicated and relations among investors are usually smooth. Any challenges then involve strategy, which we will explore. When things don't go according to plan and the company runs out of money, the powers conferred by special voting rights can create extremely contentious situations. As we have mentioned previously, there are opportunities to behave in ways that expand the pie and ways that simply claim bigger pieces of it (rent seeking). Different classes of stock with different rights in a difficult company situation set the stage for rent-seeking behavior.

Staging of Financing

Different classes of stock in the VC environment generally arise from different rounds of financing. For buyouts, financing occurs through bank loans and staging is usually a decision regarding different maturities and interests rates and which loans should be paid first. Additional financing is rare and usually accomplished by renegotiating loans with the banks.

In VC, however, staged financing—financing to milestones—is a central part of the process. It provides a means of control for the investors and also provides value for the founders by allowing them to avoid excessive dilution. Let's walk through an example.

Suzy Smartyboots has a great idea for a company. She believes that bringing it to fruition will cost $10 million. Victor Ventureguy will invest at a $3 million pre-money valuation (i.e., as we discussed in Chapter 4, the value of the company before funding: the product of the shares outstanding before the financing and the price per share in the new financing round). If Suzy raises the $10 million all at once (assuming Victor would be willing to do such a harebrained thing and that his partners would let him), the company's post-money valuation (the value of the company immediately after the investment occurs) would be $13 million and Suzy would own 23 percent of it, assuming no fancy terms. If, on the other hand, Victor's partners convince him to see reason, Suzy might raise a first round of $2 million at a $3 million pre-money valuation, with a $5 million post-money valuation. That gives Victor 40 percent of the company; she keeps 60 percent. Two years later, having developed a proof of concept that's being tested with four customers, Smartyboots Software raises $3 million at $12 million pre-money valuation ($15 million post-money). Victor gets $3 million/$15 million, or 20 percent, of this round. After the financing, Suzy and her team own 48 percent of the company. A year later, with the product widely released, she raises $5 million at $25 million pre-money ($30 million post-money). The team now owns 40 percent of the company, having raised $10 million; Victor owns 60 percent.

While the second scenario leaves the entrepreneur with a higher ownership percentage, it also benefits the investor. First, the investment can be timed to meet milestones—note that the second round occurs after the software is deployed at customers and the third after general release. This de-risks the deal for Victor in terms of technology, market, and execution and adds flexibility. If he really likes the company's prospects, he can offer a higher price in exchange for greater ownership. He can bring in additional investors if he thinks the company will need more money or expertise. In addition, the entrepreneur is fully aligned in making as much progress as possible on each financing round to preserve equity. The investor and entrepreneur can check in and correct progress over time. Before subsequent fund-raisings, the company is expected to address any problems. Staged financing keeps the entrepreneur in touch with the investors and the market because the product, the company, and its progress toward goals are being constantly assessed.

On a practical level, staging of financing supports governance because the board and management cooperate within the context of aligned goals. The mantra of venture-backed CEOs runs: "When you're losing money, the venture investors control you because you have to ask for more. When you're making money, nobody bothers you." All parties know the goal and work to achieve it as effectively and economically as possible, knowing that if the company succeeds, it will be able to raise additional money at a higher valuation, which reduces dilution for the existing shareholders.

The staging of financing has received a substantial amount of attention from researchers. Paul Gompers[16] noted that the role of staged capital infusions can be compared to that of debt in highly leveraged transactions since both keep the management team tightly focused on creating value. Staged financing, Gompers determined, helped reduce the possibility that entrepreneurs might use the investors' money to pursue strategies that provided private benefits but did not contribute to the investors' financial return. This spared investors the expense of maintaining a constant monitoring presence. By staging the investment, the investors could check in periodically but preserved the option to abandon the project.

The option to abandon was critical to convincing venture capitalists to invest in the first place. Using data on 2,143 funding rounds and amounts for 794 randomly chosen VC-backed companies between 1961 and 1992, Gompers concluded that venture capitalists used their monitoring skills and industry knowledge (the pattern recognition noted in Chapter 3) to finance highly uncertain projects. Monitoring occurred more frequently, he determined, in three situations: as the company became more valuable; as more research and development occurred; and as the assets became less tangible—that is, less amenable to discrete measurement, as might be the case with a company developing intellectual-property-rich technology or life sciences products. The difficulty of measurement increased the scope for conflicts of interest, in particular the possibility that entrepreneurs might find it personally beneficial to continue running the company despite questionable financial returns to their investors.

Gompers provided two examples of venture capitalists using staged investment and the resulting price per share to reflect their assessment of a company's progress.[17] Apple Computer

---

[16] Paul A. Gompers, "Optimal Investment, Monitoring, and the Staging of Venture Capital," *Journal of Finance* 50, no. 5 (1995): 1461–89.

[17] These examples are discussed in greater length in Gompers, "Optimal Investment, Monitoring, and the Staging of Venture Capital," 1465.

FIGURE 6.3   Percent of early-stage and late-stage investments, 1980–2009

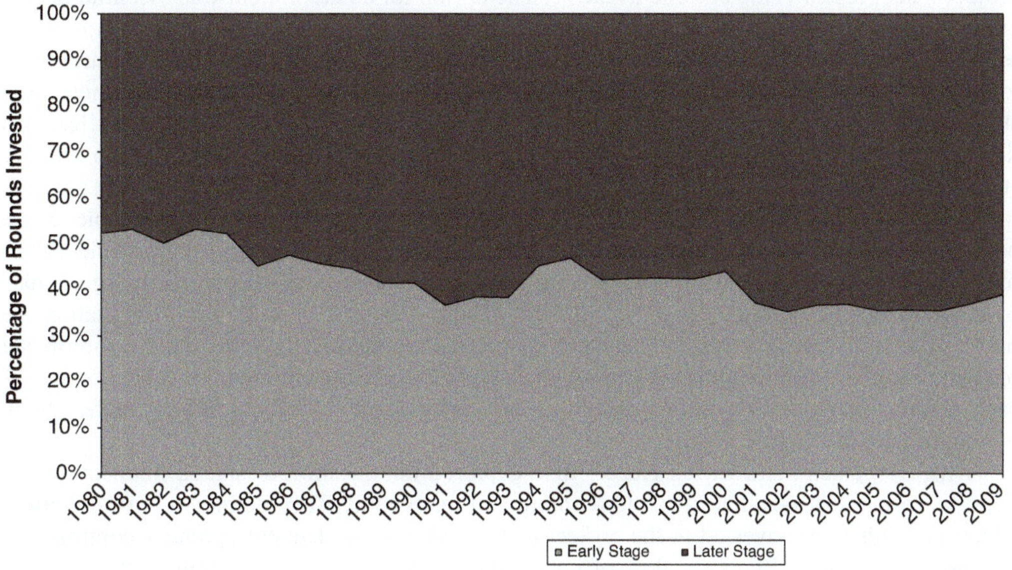

Note: Early stage is Seed, Start-up, and Early Stage. Later stage is Expansion and Late Stage.

Source: Data from Thomson Reuters private equity database, http://banker.thomsonib.com/ta/?Express Code=harvard university, accessed November 8, 2010.

raised its first round of financing in January 1978 at $0.09 per share. In September 1978, the second round occurred at $0.28 per share. In December 1980, the final round occurred at $0.97 per share, reflecting the gradual reduction in uncertainty about Apple's prospects. Federal Express, the overnight delivery company, presented a more tumultuous example. Its first round occurred in September 1973 at $204.17 per share, an eye-popping figure even today. The price had plummeted to $7.34 per share in March 1974, when the company had to raise a second round in light of poor performance. The third round, which occurred in September 1974, was priced at $0.63 per share, reflecting the company's continued deterioration. When the company went public in 1978, the share price had recovered to $6.00 per share, a good return for the third-round investors. Unless the investors in the earlier two rounds had strong antidilution protection, Federal Express would not have ranked as one of their better investments.

It is interesting, building on this work, to observe variations over time in the percentage of investments in early-stage companies that needed the intense work of monitoring, as shown in Figure 6.3. Note that during boom periods, such as in the early 1980s and the late 1990s, VC firms add large numbers of work-intensive early-stage companies to their portfolios. During the downturns, they tend to invest in later-stage companies. In part, this reflects the composition of their portfolios at the time—in bust cycles, they are still working hard but are often trying to save a struggling company rather than steer a new company to success.

From these fairly applied examples, we now move to some more theoretical work that examines how the interests of the two parties, the entrepreneur and the investor, are aligned in staged investments. One of the principal methods by which these interests are aligned is convertible stock.

Writing in 2003, Francesca Cornelli and Oved Yosha[18] explored the dynamics between the entrepreneur and investors in a staged investment situation. Investing capital over time, they

---

[18] Francesca Cornelli and Oved Yosha, "Stage Financing and the Role of Convertible Debt," *Review of Economic Studies* 70, no. 1 (2003): 1–32.

determined, provided the venture capitalist with the option of abandoning the venture if the project's net present value became negative. The option for abandonment was essential because entrepreneurs would never give up on a company funded by someone else's capital. The possibility that the investor might abandon the project provided incentives for the entrepreneur to maximize value and meet goals. The concern here, though, was that the entrepreneur might sub-optimize over the short term by focusing excessively on achieving a short-term milestone at the expense of the company's long-term goals in an effort to convince the investor to support a struggling project.

A crucial tool for preventing this, the authors maintained, was the use of a convertible security because it guarded against future financings based on bad information. The convertible security offset the entrepreneur's expected gain from getting funding for an underperforming company with the increased likelihood that the investors would convert the stock upon liquidation (i.e., participate as common and dilute the entrepreneur's returns). Although this short-term sub-optimization made low-performing projects harder for the investor to identify, it backfired in the case of strong performers by artificially enhancing performance and would making higher-quality projects easier to identify.

Dirk Bergemann and Ulrich Hege[19] also explored the question of staged financing and its importance in situations that involved learning and innovation. They defined a tension between releasing funds to be invested in the project and abandoning it. The entrepreneur controlled the allocation of funds and thus the flow of information to the investor, who could not observe the investment effort. If the entrepreneur diverted the money for personal use, the investor would downgrade the company's prospects because progress had not occurred and would prematurely cancel an effort that would otherwise have succeeded.

To resolve this issue, the entrepreneur must be offered a sufficiently large share of the returns to ensure that the funds were invested according to expectations. The venture capitalist received control rights to monitor and change out the management team, but the optimal timing for this change was difficult to determine.

The authors decided that monitoring, although costly, provided an accurate signal about the use of funds, which eliminated the moral hazard problem—that is, the likelihood that the entrepreneur would do something for personal benefit because he did not bear the entire cost. Moreover, monitoring had a temporal benefit—monitoring in one time period meant that misallocation of funds in prior periods would also be discovered. Staged financing thus is the optimal way of funding uncertain efforts because the information arrives sequentially and triggers additional investment.

Erik Berglöf's article[20] examined the role of convertible securities in restraining an entrepreneur from running amok. He posited that parties to VC investments designed the company's capital structure to reduce issues regarding the distribution of gains from the company's eventual sale. In VC, Berglöf maintained, control and incentives could not be separated; the entrepreneur's private benefits formed an important part of his incentive scheme, and assets were difficult to protect through contracts. Convertible securities offered the best way of structuring a contract contingent upon nonverifiable but observable information—that is, if the investor observed that the company was making progress but could not verify it, the convertible feature allowed her to hold the security until such time as she could verify the improved performance and then convert to common to share in the gains. Lastly, the need for future financing provided an opportunity for the investor to change the type of shares owned and thus increase the amount of control exerted on the investment.

---

[19] Dirk Bergemann and Ulrich Hege, "Venture Capital Financing, Moral Hazard, and Learning," *Journal of Banking and Finance* 22 (1998): 703–35.

[20] Erik Berglöf, "A Control Theory of Venture Capital Finance," *Journal of Law, Economics, and Organization* 10, no. 2 (1994): 247–67.

While staged financing makes theoretical and practical sense, there are practical limits to it. Enacting these agreements imposes transactions costs—the legal documents are more complex and often take longer to negotiate and close. In addition, each round (or tranche, which occurs when a round is broken into further chunks that are released upon reaching a step to a milestone) imposes a burden on the venture firm's back office as it manages the supporting paperwork. For companies themselves, raising funds is a tremendous distraction for the management team, one that everyone—investors and entrepreneurs alike—tries to minimize.

Generally, investments are predicated on three or four rounds of financing. As the rounds of financing increase beyond that, several things can happen. First, the initial investors get tired. They may lose interest or the company's champion may leave the firm, adding the company to the portfolio of a former colleague who lacks the background and enthusiasm of his predecessor. Another challenge occurs if an investor's fund reaches the end of its life. If the company is not performing well, transferring it to a successor fund will be extremely difficult. The firm may try to get out of the investment, whether through an early exit, selling shares to other investors, or a round that it does not participate in. To raise additional money, investors may have to agree to hard terms. Any of these can create tensions with other investors and management, as shown in Metapath's situation.

Metapath

The founder of the high-tech start-up Metapath believed it was on the verge of an IPO.[21] To sustain it until then, the company raised an $11.75 million Series E round at $6.00 per share from two late-stage investors, Robertson Stephens Omega Fund and Technology Crossover Ventures. The earlier investors, VC firms and Metapath's corporate parent, held shares priced between $1.05 and $1.62 each. As a condition of investing in the company, the Series E firms insisted upon receiving participating convertible preferred stock, which in the case of a liquidity event allowed them to receive the value of their investment back first as preferred and then as if converted to common stock, as discussed in Chapter 5. In the case of an IPO, this feature disappears because all stock is converted to common. The Series E investors (and later Series F) received not only seniority and participation but also the right to declare any change of control a liquidation, triggering the participation feature.

Metapath did not go public. In 1998 it merged with a private company, MSI, for stock. This was a change in control. The Series E and F holders exercised their right to declare the transaction a liquidation and received the face value of the MSI stock in addition to the common equivalent—that is, their stock was treated like participating convertible preferred stock in an acquisition rather than an IPO. When the merged company was acquired by Marconi in 1999, the Series E and F holders received three times their investment—funds that came directly from the proceeds that would have otherwise been shared with the earlier investors and management.[22]

Metapath teaches many lessons, among them the perils of running out of money, excessive optimism, and the impact of staged financing. Metapath's A to D rounds were all raised at less than $2 per share. The large E round occurred at a higher price to reduce the dilution to existing

[21] Felda Hardymon and Bill Wasick, "Metapath: September 1997," HBS Case No. 899-160 (Boston: HBS Publishing, 1999).

[22] Felda Hardymon, Josh Lerner, and Ann Leamon, "Metapath: September 1997—Teaching Note," HBS Case No. 5-802-051 (Boston: HBS Publishing, 2002), 7–8.

shareholders and reflect the company's progress. But management had to trade terms for price: the higher price came with the harsher terms because the company was still losing money. Once those terms were embedded in the capital structure for the holders of the E shares, they had to be extended to the F investors. These were later-stage firms that wanted to generate relatively reliable, lower-risk returns for their investors. Therefore, at the first opportunity—the MSI merger—they exercised their participation rights. This was completely understandable for them, but a shock to the entrepreneur.

This underscores an issue we raised in Chapter 3, the fit between the entrepreneur and the firm. Metapath had started as a very early-stage company. Two early-stage technology firms backed it. Adding later-stage firms was a risky move. It is important that both entrepreneurs and investors understand and seek to align the motivations of different parties. We discuss later what happens when different motivations impede an exit.

THE BUSINESS OF BOARDS: CREATING VALUE

Boards use their power to create value. Value creation does not start with the arrival of the money and the first board meeting. The investors begin thinking about how they will do this as soon as they start evaluating the deal. Every private equity deal has risks. In the process of performing due diligence on the opportunity, developing an investment thesis, and negotiating the deal, investors create a road map for adding value.

Achim Berg and Oliver Gottschalg[23] explore the phases of value creation in their paper. During the holding period after the money arrives, the planned value-adding strategies are put in place. They develop along several dimensions. Some are external to the company's operating performance—conditions in the specific sector or the market overall might improve and increase the valuations of all companies. We might see this in the clean tech industry, for instance, as regulatory changes and increased oil prices make companies in that sector more attractive. A generally rising stock market, reflecting investor confidence and good earnings performance, buoys sentiment overall ("a rising tide lifts all boats"). Thus a private equity firm might buy a company that rises in value simply because the sector or market does so. Figure 6.4 shows the NASDAQ index over the past three decades—clearly, it would be easier to buy a company in 1996 and sell it in 1999 for a gain, even without implementing specific value-creating strategies.

Another type of external improvement comes from arbitrage across various securities due to the buyout firm's abilities or insights. If, for instance, a firm specializing in distressed situations invests in a distressed company's debt at a substantial discount, and the company then recovers and repays the debt in full, the firm will have created value simply because it better understood the debt's true value, not because of any improvements.

A final source of external improvements can be the firm's deal-making ability, through which it obtains a better purchase price. This ability can include a network that develops proprietary deals, or the firm's insight that a target would be more efficient if it were broken up (also called "optimization of corporate scope").

Opportunities to create value internally are those methods that directly affect the company's financial performance. These include financial engineering that optimizes debt and equity levels or provides a tax shield and strategies that improve operating performance, reduce the cost of capital, decrease the fixed or current asset base for operations, and increase the company's operating effectiveness or strategic distinctiveness. A final category involves "reduced agency costs," or

---

[23] Achim Berg and Oliver Gottschalg, "Sources of Value Generation in Buyouts," *Journal of Restructuring Finance* 2, no. 1 (2005): 9–37.

FIGURE 6.4 NASDAQ index, January 1980–June 30, 2010

Source: Data from Global Financial Data, https://www-globalfinancialdata-com.ezp-prod1.hul.harvard.edu/platform/
Mainform.aspx, accessed October 12, 2010.

increased incentive alignment between management and shareholders, along with the mentoring of management.

The final phase of value creation is the exit, which we discuss in Chapter 7. Of course, none of these phases operates in isolation. Feedback from the company's operating performance informs the decision about the exit avenue; but even as early as the investment thesis, the general partner (GP) will note whether the company is likely to be an acquisition target or an IPO. In buyouts, the proposed exit is more likely to affect strategies chosen during the deal management period; for an early-stage VC investment, the first few years are devoted to getting the product to market. The idea of an exit does figure into a VC investment thesis, but does not affect deal management strategy until later.

For our use in analyzing sources of value creation in buyouts, we will adapt Berg and Gottschalg's framework, as shown in Table 6.4. We classify financial arbitrage—known as "riding the multiple"—as external to the company. Choosing an undervalued company in a good sector is a perfectly acceptable strategy for making good returns, but it does not create value intrinsic to the company. It is nonetheless a source of value for the firm and its LPs, so we want to consider it. The next group includes those changes that occur internally and improve the company's financial performance. Financial engineering, the optimization of the company's capital structure, cannot be said to increase its operational effectiveness, which is why it sits alone. Such changes do, however, help the company reduce its cost of capital, which should allow it to make more expenditures (e.g., acquiring new equipment) and in turn increase its operational effectiveness. Strategic repositioning, increased scale (making more stuff), increased scope (making stuff for more consumers), and management recruitment all improve operational efficiency. We have split Berg

Table 6.4 Value Creation Framework

	Governance								
	Internal								
External	Directly Increase Operational Effectiveness						Indirectly Increase Operational Effectiveness		
Financial Arbitrage	Financial Engineering	Cost Reduction	Strategic Repositioning	Increased Scale	Increased Scope	Management Recruitment	Increased Alignment	Outsourcing	Mentoring

Source: Adapted from Achim Berg and Oliver Gottschlag, "Sources of Value Generation in Buyouts," *Journal of Restructuring Finance* 2, no. 1 (2005): 13.

and Gottschalg's rather broad category of "reduced agency costs" into increased alignment and outsourcing, which—along with mentoring—make up the category of changes that indirectly increase the company's operating effectiveness.

With VC investments, value is created in a more straightforward way. Gorman and Sahlman noted that the board members most frequently reported helping their companies raise funds; the next most frequent tasks included strategic analysis and management recruiting. Considering this more broadly, venture capitalists are involved in arranging financing for the company, developing strategy, and building the team, which we can decompose into management recruiting and mentoring. Some of the debate in Chapter 3 regarding the "jockey" (entrepreneur or, in the case of LBOs, manager) or the "horse"— the technology—reflects the question about which of these is more important to have in place when the company is young or, conversely, the investor can provide more easily: management recruitment and mentoring or strategic direction. We do not include financial arbitrage here, because while choosing a good sector is important, few early-stage companies are purchased at a gain without any operational improvements whatsoever.

In both the buyout and VC frameworks, the sufficient condition is the governance that ensures all of this actually happens. It may be through hourly e-mails, daily phone calls, or weekly, monthly, and quarterly meetings. But this personal involvement by investors who are risking substantial money and reputation on this deal and also have a history in the business, which provides pattern recognition, brings a unique sense of urgency. Moreover, since their guidance will not be provided in perpetuity, the private equity investors assist the company in developing the necessary systems and reporting functions to internalize accountability and good governance.

We now examine a number of case studies on both early-stage and buyout investments to see how the investors have managed them and where they have (and have not) created value. Where they failed, we can perhaps assess what levers were not pulled or were pulled with excessive force. Although we may not mention it explicitly, note how governance infuses the environment where these changes take place.

VALUE IN VENTURE

Creating value in VC-backed companies is usually synonymous with helping them develop their management teams and addressable markets as well as their products. In addition, VC-backed companies typically need to institutionalize, which involves developing systems for goal setting, accountability, and governance.

Most VC-backed companies already have a strategy for their first product, on which they raise their initial investment. The investors typically become involved as that product is being released to the market. By their nature, early-stage companies address niche markets, or niche needs in large markets. Few early-stage companies have a product or service substantial enough to take it to maturity.

If the first product is successful, the company must achieve the next milestone, which requires adding a product or expanding the market served. The board determines the next big area that the company can pursue and assembles the necessary resources. It assesses the company's financial performance and the management team's ability, and it determines any necessary changes. It plans and orchestrates the next financing. Eventually, it determines the best exit strategy. These build upon each other iteratively. In the section below, we explore the ways in which boards and investors have worked with companies for good and, sometimes, for ill.

Avid Radiopharmaceuticals

Avid is a biotech company that develops imaging agents, molecules that act as markers to illuminate various disease processes.[24] Its most advanced compound helps diagnose Alzheimer's disease in living patients. In January 2005, the company raised $1.5 million from a state-linked biotech start-up fund and RK Ventures,[25] a very early-stage venture financing firm. Matthew Rhodes-Kropf, from RK Ventures, is a current board member and also served as interim CFO in the company's early years, providing assistance with financing and mentoring in a very hands-on way. In late 2005, Avid raised a $9.8 million B round from the venture funding arms of pharmaceutical heavyweights Eli Lilly and Pfizer. Here we see concrete examples of value creation—the participation of these investors signaled that the industry at large saw value in this start-up. RK Ventures undoubtedly helped the company's CEO find a CFO to replace Rhodes-Kropf and fill out the team. In addition, other top scientists in the field were recruited. The company gradually developed a high-quality candidate compound that indicated Alzheimer's and others addressing Parkinson's disease and diabetes. One of the decisions in this industry is often "buy or build"—does a company develop an indicator on its own or license it in from a university lab? Strategic direction on this would have come from the investors.

By September 2008, Avid faced the challenges of growth in a financially constrained environment. With three high-potential products (biomarkers for Alzheimer's, Parkinson's, and diabetes) going through various stages of Food and Drug Administration (FDA) testing, the company needed more space and money. The CEO was in constant contact with the board members as he thought through the risks and advantages of various approaches. He could shut down all but the Alzheimer's product and stretch the company's current cash, or figure out some way to raise more money (ideally after the results from the latest clinical trials had increased the company's share price) and move forward. With the board's guidance, Avid's CEO negotiated a venture debt package from Lighthouse Capital Partners.

Note the role of the board here. Avid's product suite grew from one indicator to three. The board had to balance the costs and benefits of various strategies for proceeding: delay offers deep-pocketed competitors the chance to catch up; raising equity before the trials results arrive dilutes the investors; raising venture debt extends the runway without dilution but at a cost. In late 2010, Eli Lilly agreed to acquire Avid for up to $800 million.[26]

---

[24] For more, see Matthew Rhodes-Kropf and Ann Leamon, "Avid Radiopharmaceuticals & Lighthouse Capital Partners," HBS Case No. 810-054 (Boston: HBS Publishing, 2010).

[25] www.avidrp.com/aboutus/aboutus_boardofdirectors.html, accessed July 19, 2010.

[26] Peter Loftus, "Lilly to Acquire Avid Radiopharma," *Wall Street Journal*, November 8, 2010, http://online.wsj.com/article/SB10001424052748703514904575602241265151042.html, accessed November 15, 2010.

Endeca Technologies

Founded in 1999, Endeca first focused on e-commerce search applications.[27] From there, it expanded to become a more complete e-commerce platform and then moved to providing an integrated business information product for large organizations like the U.S. Defense Intelligence Agency, Boeing, Sigma-Aldrich, and Raytheon. Since the company's first funding, the investors were intimately involved in Endeca's strategy and growth. The founding CEO Steve Papa, on the guidance of his board, stretched his Series B funds for 18 months during the downturn of 2000.

Raising the C round,[28] though, was very difficult and the board was deeply involved. In March 2001, when the fund-raising began, the board suggested that Papa raise $10 million at $90 million pre-money, reflecting the fact that the company had hit every milestone, attracted a top-quality management team (with the help of the board's contacts), and achieved good traction with major customers. The technology market, though, was in a tailspin and the board had overestimated the appetite of VC investors for young software companies, even those with Endeca's record. Three months later, the board cut the pre-money valuation to $60 million, then $40 million, and finally $25 million, even though the $8 million B round had been raised at $27 million pre-money. When AOL offered to invest $2 million as long as Endeca could find an outsider (i.e., a firm that is not currently invested in the company) to lead the round, the board members called their network to generate the required term sheet. Finally, ABS Ventures submitted a term sheet that valued the company at less than its Series A price. The board then submitted an inside term sheet at friendlier terms, as seen in Chapter 5. The Series C round led by Ampersand Ventures eventually closed at an effective pre-money valuation of $32.5 million.

The board then worked on building the team. In early 2005, it promoted a professional manager, James Baum, from president to CEO. Papa became chairman and head of business development. Less than a year later, though, Baum was "benched" and Papa returned to the CEO role to help the company pursue more aggressive growth.[29] In 2007, Endeca announced revenues in excess of $100 million.[30] While this result makes the decisions seem obvious, Endeca's changes in strategy and personnel were high-risk moves. Papa had not led a large company before!

Recently, the board began to consider exit options. Rumors circulated that Microsoft had considered purchasing the company[31] and that it was looking to present an IPO.[32] As of mid-2010, it had yet to file the paperwork to do so, although it had expanded the board to include the types of high-profile directors often associated with public companies.[33]

Both Endeca and Avid demonstrate value creation and governance in growing, successful companies. But companies that are floundering also need governance and intervention that either

---

[27] For more on Endeca's strategic evolution, see Paul Gompers and Kristin Perry, "Endeca Technologies: New Growth Opportunities," HBS Case No. 206-041 (Boston: HBS Publishing, 2006).

[28] For more on Endeca's Series C fund-raising, see Felda Hardymon, Josh Lerner, and Ann Leamon, "Endeca Technologies (A) and (B)," HBS Case Nos. 802-141 and 802-142 (Boston: HBS Publishing, 2002).

[29] Scott Kirsner, "As It Turns Out, You Can Go Home Again (If You're a CEO)," *Boston Globe*, January 14, 2008. In August 2006, Baum became CEO of Netezza, a data warehousing company.

[30] "Endeca Reports 19th Consecutive Quarter of Year-over-Year Growth," press release, November 15, 2007, www.endeca .com/799133b2-f822-49c8-a162-3d629aa6e804/news-and-events-press-releases-2007-details.htm, accessed November 15, 2010.

[31] Wade Roush, "Microsoft Passed Over Cambridge Enterprise Search Firm Endeca Before Acquiring Norway's Fast," *Xconomy*, January 10, 2008, www.xconomy.com/boston/2008/01/10/microsoft-passed-over-local-enterprise-search-firm-endeca-before-acquiring-norways-fast/, accessed July 17, 2010.

[32] Tim Mullaney, "Searching for an 07 IPO," *Bloomberg BusinessWeek*, March 31, 2006, www.businessweek.com/ the_thread/dealflow/archives/2006/03/searching_for_a.html, accessed July 17, 2010.

[33] www.endeca.com, accessed July 16, 2010.

creates value or reduces losses. Management may be replaced (one former entrepreneur and current venture capitalist maintains that firing the CEO is the only tool at the investors' disposal[34]) and product strategy changed.

The biggest challenge when a company is not meeting its plan often becomes financing. With staged financing, the current investors usually assume that the company will need more money; but the question becomes whether its prospects warrant the investment. Proper governance, of course, can detect problems with the company's progress and correct issues early. The decision hinges on what the investors believe about the team, the product, and the market, as noted in Chapter 3 with follow-on financings. If the company is making progress in raising additional money but the round has not yet coalesced, the current investors (insiders) might advance part of their share as a bridge that gets folded into the eventual financing, sometimes at a lower share price or with warrants.

If the company has struggled for some time, it may not be able to raise money at all. In that case, the insiders must decide whether to recapitalize the enterprise (i.e., finance it as if it is completely new) or shut it down. For all that growing companies require guidance, the companies in distress or going sideways—always one quarter or one customer away from profitability—take most of an investor's time.

Ellacoya Networks, mentioned briefly in Chapter 5, is a classic example of this. Between 1999 and 2002, the company raised $111 million to produce technology that enabled local telephone companies to deliver on-demand broadband services. But over that period, two-thirds of its customers went out of business.[35] In February 2001, the board brought on a new CEO to replace the founder, who became the CTO; in March, the vice president of sales resigned. The company was six months late in delivering products to customers for testing. Ellacoya was said to be burning $2 million to $3 million per month.[36] Over the course of 2001, the company—undoubtedly prodded by the board—cut its workforce twice, eventually to 50 percent of its level in late 2000, and raised an insider-only round of $25 million.[37] The company changed its focus and targeted cable providers. In 2002 Ellacoya's board recapitalized the company, and investors who did not participate were converted to common. Just after the recap, the board brought in a new CEO and shifted the target market from cable providers to top-tier phone companies. In addition, the technology changed from providing on-demand services to doing deep-packet inspection of network traffic, helping the service provider prioritize delivery based on specific requirements for bandwidth and speed.[38]

Even in mid-2007, the company was not yet profitable.[39] It had raised $26.5 million since the recap, and the investors noted that "a public offering is still possible," although they also suggested that an acquisition by a large network company like Juniper or Cisco would be acceptable. In January 2008, Ellacoya, which had by then raised $158 million over its nine years, merged with Arbor Networks, another venture-backed technology company. The two had complementary products: Arbor's equipment monitors security events across a network, while Ellacoya's

[34] Jeffrey Bussgang; quoted in Kirsner, "As It Turns Out, You Can Go Home Again."

[35] Scott Denne, "Bubble Survivors: Ellacoya Reinvents Itself Yet Again," *VentureWire*, July 3, 2007, accessed July 16, 2010.

[36] Marguerite Reardon, "Ellacoya Loses Sales VP," *LightReading*, March 30, 2001, http://www.lightreading.com/document.asp?doc_id=4518; accessed July 16, 2010.

[37] Marguerite Reardon, "Ellacoya Snags Third Round," *Light Reading*, November 26, 2001, www.lightreading.com/document.asp?doc_id=9465; accessed July 16, 2010.

[38] "Ellacoya Networks Attracts New Investors in $13.5 million Financing," *BusinessWire*, July 18, 2005, accessed July 16, 2010.

[39] Denne, "Bubble Survivors: Ellacoya Reinvents Itself."

identifies the needs of individual messages.[40] The investors still held out hope for an IPO. Two of Ellacoya's competitors, which had raised far less money, had already gone public.[41]

In summary, Ellacoya was founded to provide a product to customers which disappeared. The product itself became obsolete. Most of the early venture investors left in the refinancing—only one, Lightspeed, supported the company through all seven rounds. With the recapitalization, the company restarted with new management, new technology, and new customers. That worked just well enough to land occasional large customers like British Telecom, but the company could not become profitable. Finally the company merged with another private company, leaving the investors still illiquid.

Has value been created? Should the board have shut down the company? Clearly the board was slow to cut the company's burn rate, as indicated by the $2 million to $3 million figure even in early 2001—especially after missing a milestone. When the CEO finally cut, it wasn't enough, as noted in the reference to *two* rounds of layoffs. Here again the board can be faulted. It hired a veteran of 3-Com, a big public company; he was not someone who could make quick, effective decisions in an environment resembling a train wreck. The directors had forgotten pattern recognition, or they had come of age during the tech bubble and were not familiar with difficult times.

What about the investors who were converted to common in the recap? They may have had other companies that needed their scarce partnership resources of time and money. Perhaps they believed that Ellacoya would be a harder slog than the others, or that they would simply never get a return on their share of the $111 million already invested. Even Barry Eggers of Lightspeed was quoted as saying, "There were a few times when it was a tough decision whether to keep funding or not. But the company was always resilient in its ability to grab new customers."[42] These new customers, though, had not made Ellacoya profitable.

If the merged entity of Ellacoya and Arbor can eventually go public or be acquired for liquid securities (cash or public stock), the current investors will at least get some money back. They will not have lost everything, whereas the investors who were converted to common back in 2002 have lost every penny. Lightspeed clearly believed that its LPs were better served by supporting Ellacoya than by closing it down.

As demonstrated by Lightspeed with Ellacoya, investors may sometimes choose to put more money into a company in hopes of getting at least something back. An early online platform dedicated to the exchange of political ideas was close to collapse in mid-2001, despite backing by top-tier VC firms. When one of the board members told his partners that they had not only lost their entire investment but needed to pay another few hundred thousand dollars for cartage fees (removing garbage and cleaning out the offices), the partners said, "What if we put in another million? Could you find someone to buy it?" This is the difference between venture investing and bank loans: the bank would have wanted to close it down when there was still enough money to pay back the loan. Venture investors are willing to put in more money if there is a chance to get something back.

BOARD STRATEGY FOR BUYOUT INVESTMENTS

Several major differences between buyouts and VC-backed companies are glaringly obvious from the first: buyouts are already operating entities, and the private equity firm owns a majority

---

[40] Scott Denne, "Bubble Survivors Arbor Networks and Ellacoya Combine," *VentureWire*, January 18, 2008, http://www.lightspeedvp.com/News/releases/LSVP01182008.pdf, accessed July 16, 2010.

[41] Denne, "Bubble Survivors: Ellacoya Reinvents Itself." Sandvine had raised $38 million since its founding in 2001. It was profitable and its 2006 revenues were $32 million; its market capitalization in 2007 was $725 million. Ellacoya's other competitor was the Israeli company Allot, which was struggling.

[42] Denne, "Bubble Survivors: Ellacoya Reinvents Itself."

share. As noted in our framework, there are more levers to pull but some aspects become more complicated. In the following brief studies, we discuss different ways of creating (and destroying) value.

Montagu Private Equity

Montagu Private Equity, a U.K.-based mid-market buyout group, acquired Dignity Caring Funeral Services[43] in early 2002. The company's American parent needed to raise cash quickly, and Montagu could move fast because it was familiar with the management team and the industry's dynamics. Death's predictability made the cash flows from Dignity, the UK's largest provider of funeral services, very leveragable.[44] In December 2002, less than a year after the £235 million ($352.5 million) transaction, the investors refinanced the company, raising £250 million ($375 million) on "very attractive terms"[45] that allowed the investors to recoup 97 percent of their investment.[46] The board therefore created financial engineering improvements and reduced Dignity's future financing costs. Montagu gave the management team an equity incentive along with power to run the business and the support to make small acquisitions. Dignity pursued a roll-up strategy of acquiring small local funeral operators that continued to operate under their own names, thereby retaining local connections while the parent provided back-office infrastructure and investment in such items as limousines.[47] The company also offered prepaid funeral plans and crematorium services. In 2004, the company went public at a value of £394 million ($721 million) and a share price of £2.30 ($4.21). By late July 2010, it traded at £6.64 ($10.56).

In addition to financial engineering, we can assume that Dignity increased its scale through its acquisitions, although it did not increase its scope. Note that Montagu provided management incentives and equity ownership and advice, which was part of the firm's stated acquisition strategy. Said Christopher Masterson, the firm's managing general partner:

> Who better to build a company and take it to the next level than the driven guy with a business plan who's been constrained from implementing it by a distant and uninvolved head office? But the plan isn't enough—execution is the key. We have developed this into a laser focus. . . . We just look at whether the business is leveragable—at no more than 65% debt-to-equity—and that it's a mature Northern European business in our price range. And then the rocket fuel is an equity-owning CEO.[48]

Montagu's board strategy, then, was to clear the runway, ensure that all the incentives are aligned, and get out of the way.

Clayton & Dubilier

Clayton & Dubilier (C&D, later Clayton, Dubilier & Rice) purchased O.M. Scott & Sons,[49] the maker of lawn care products, in 1986. Like Dignity, the company was part of a corporate parent that wanted to divest noncore divisions and wanted the best price for its asset.

---

[43] Material from Montagu Private Equity, Video Case Studies, Dignity Funeral Services, www.axisto.com/webcasting/montagu/casestudies-230306/dignity-en/index.htm, accessed July 7, 2010.

[44] "Funeral Services Provider Dignity Sees Double-Digit Growth," *Times Online*, May 14, 2009, http://business.timesonline.co.uk/tol/business/industry_sectors/need_to_know/article6289055.ece, accessed July 20, 2010.

[45] Material from Montagu Private Equity, Video Case Studies, Dignity Funeral Services.

[46] "Dignity Caring Funeral Services," *Montagu Private Equity*, www.montagu.com/portfolio/?id=807, accessed July 20, 2010.

[47] "Funeral Services Provider Dignity Sees Double-Digit Growth."

[48] Felda Hardymon, Josh Lerner, and Ann Leamon, "Montagu Private Equity," HBS Case No. 804-051 (Boston: HBS Publishing, 2004), 8.

[49] George Baker and Karen Wruck, "Creating Value in Leveraged Buyout: The Case of O.M. Scott," *Journal of Financial Economics* 25 (1989): 163–90.

FIGURE 6.5 Ownership of O.M. Scott after buyout

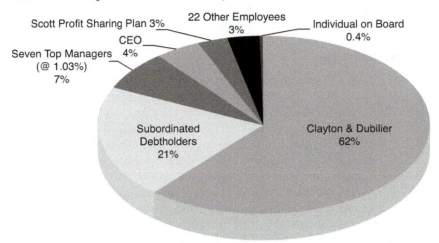

Source: Adapted from George Baker and Karen Wruck, "Creating Value in Leveraged Buyout: The Case of O.M. Scott," *Journal of Financial Economics* 25 (1989): 174.

In their careful study, George Baker and Karen Wruck detailed the changes that occurred at Scott under private equity ownership. Because 91 percent of the purchase price was funded with debt, the organization had little margin for error. Although management was not part of the initial transaction, senior managers were strongly urged to purchase equity using their own funds. Figure 6.5 shows that management and employees ended up owning 17.5 percent of the company's equity. In addition, C&D changed the bonus system to reward managers with as much as 100 percent of their base pay, based on the achievement of corporate, divisional, and individual goals. C&D relied on the managers' firm-specific knowledge to achieve the operational changes necessary to make the debt payments. The compensation package helped retain them and, by making the bonus contingent on achieving earnings before interest and taxes (EBIT) and working capital goals, brought home to them the importance of cash generation. The high level of equity ownership also aligned the interests of the employees with those of the investors in avoiding default, which would hurt their reputations and their ownership positions, given the dilution that would occur should Scott be refinanced.

The board composition merits attention. The CEO was the only member of management to have a voting seat on the board, because the board evaluated management and the CEO could hardly be evaluated by a subordinate. Initially, the board consisted of three C&D partners, the CEO, and an outsider. Before Scott went public in 1988, C&D added three directors: a turf researcher, an individual with consumer products expertise, and the CEO of Hyponex, another C&D acquisition in a similar sector. The full board met quarterly; the executive committee (two C&D partners and the CEO) met monthly to deal with policy, personnel, and provide advice to the CEO.

C&D also designated an operating partner to serve as an executive coach for the CEO. This individual helped the CEO make the transition from being part of a large conglomerate, where the emphasis was on meeting the budget, to being involved in a private equity operation, where he had great latitude in choosing strategies as long as they improved the business. The difference was stark: any divisional vice president (the CEO's former title) who needed advice from headquarters would not long be in his or her position; seeking advice from C&D's operating partner was encouraged.

Scott's operational results improved dramatically between late 1986, when the transaction closed, and September 1988. EBIT rose 56 percent and sales by 25 percent. Moreover, expenses for research and development climbed 7 percent, marketing 21 percent, and capital spending by 23 percent. Working capital requirements fell by half, to 18.4 percent of sales. Employment fell but due to attrition rather than wholesale layoffs.

These improvements were due to improved incentive and management control systems. The direct feedback from the operating partner and the incentive of equity ownership and bonuses created an environment in which improvements were encouraged. Both cash and inventory management improved; the company expanded into the professional turf care market and then into the mass merchandiser channel by acquiring Hyponex.

The combination of incentives and monitoring, along with the change in governance stemming from the LBO, clearly created enormous value. By eighteen months after the buyout, Scott addressed different markets (change in scope and scale), had made an acquisition (financial engineering), and reduced costs for working capital and inventory.

TPG

TPG's 1997 acquisition of the privately held clothier J. Crew[50] provides a more tumultuous example. This was a classic organic growth transaction in which the buyout firm believed that its financial, strategic, and operating resources would transform the family-run catalog business into a multichannel retailer that could announce an IPO by 2000. The transaction valued the company, which included three entities—J. Crew, Popular Club Plan, and Clifford & Wills—at $528 million or 9.8 times the earnings before interest, tax, depreciation, and amortization (EBITDA). The board included three TPG partners, the cofounder (who also invested), and six outsiders.

TPG had a standard approach for turning around battered brands by bringing in operations experts and developing an operations "playbook" to set clear direction for strategy, operational priorities, key performance indicators (KPIs), and goals. The "100-day" plan for the company included analyzing product-line profitability and reengineering the process of building new stores. Goals were set around growth, EBITDA, and the number of stores. The process review targeted design efficiency and cut 10 percent of the workforce, revamped the markdown process, and increased merchant accountability for designing popular clothes and planning proper inventory. The number of product variations fell, reducing overhead and production costs, improving inventory efficiency, and streamlining the story told to customers.

By 2002, though, J. Crew had not announced an IPO. In fact, TPG was having substantial difficulties with the investment. There had been three CEOs in five years. Retail sales contracted sharply in the aftermath of the NASDAQ crash. The Popular Club Plan division had been sold for $42 million, but no buyers appeared for Clifford & Wills, which was shut down. J. Crew, at TPG's direction, had introduced beauty products, golf wear, and a line of active outerwear, to lukewarm customer response. TPG tried to sell the company; but two of three potential buyers lost interest on closer inspection and the last steadily dropped its offer, finally reaching $500 million.[51]

As of late 2002, TPG had not created value in J. Crew. Attempts to increase scope had failed, as had attempts to recruit management. TPG had mistaken the general upswell of catalog sales in the late 1990s for unique qualities of J. Crew. In its pursuit of operational efficiency, TPG degraded the product and brand. The lead designer noted that she "had been told to create clothing primarily

---

[50] Mike Roberts, William Sahlman, and Lauren Barley, "Texas Pacific Group—J. Crew," HBS Case No. 808-017 (Boston: HBS Publishing, 2008).

[51] Ibid.

on the basis of price. 'We'd get a list—six $55 pants, seven $70 pants. . . . It completely stifled creativity.'"[52] Attempts to increase scale had targeted the product to younger customers who could not afford it and alienated core customers.[53]

But then TPG's luck turned. In January 2003, with the company's debt on the brink of being downgraded, the firm recruited Millard (Mickey) Drexler, the impresario who had remade The Gap and Ann Taylor, and gave him free rein to reinvigorate the company. Drexler not only came on as CEO, but invested $10 million in the company. He revamped the clothes, added a children's line, and reduced the number of stores—and performance improved. When J. Crew went public on June 28, 2006, TPG bought $73.5 million worth of stock.[54]

TPG did one thing right—it hired Mickey Drexler—and then the rest fell into place. Certainly its operational improvements helped, but if no one wants to buy the clothes, the fact that they are designed, produced, and shipped efficiently is beside the point. Eventually—but in a much longer time frame than originally anticipated—TPG did create value.[55]

Kohlberg Kravis Roberts

When Kohlberg Kravis Roberts (KKR) purchased Beatrice,[56] home of Meadow Gold milk, Avis Car Rental, Fisher's Nuts, and more, it created value almost entirely through financial arbitrage. Since its founding in 1890, Beatrice had made four hundred acquisitions, which it ran with a decentralized strategy. KKR understood that Beatrice was worth more in terms of its constituent parts than its $9.3 billion price tag. In a single year, divestitures generated enough cash to pay off Beatrice's entire bank debt, and administrative cuts saved an additional $100 million. The total proceeds of Beatrice's breakup created $11.06 billion in value.[57]

Value Destruction

In May 1998, KKR and Hicks, Muse, Tate & Furst, both top-tier buyout groups at the time, acquired Regal Cinemas,[58] the third-largest theater chain (by number of screens) in the United States, for a price roughly twice industry norms.[59] The investors believed they would benefit from the industry trend toward megaplexes, which had become a roll-up strategy as small operators could not find the funds to upgrade their facilities, and from Regal's cost-conscious management philosophy.

After the buyout, Regal's board adopted a strategy of acquisition, new facility construction, and megaplex innovation that almost doubled Regal's total screen count in eighteen months. Many of the acquired theaters were converted into "entertainment centers," some with IMAX 3D players. The company's debt soared during a period when Hollywood produced an unusual scarcity of blockbuster films. Moreover, the small headquarters staff—a key part of Regal's

---

[52] Meryl Gordon, "Mickey Drexler's Redemption," *New York Magazine*, May 21, 2005, http://nymag.com/nymetro/news/bizfinance/biz/features/10489/index1.html, accessed July 15, 2010.

[53] Roberts et al., "Texas Pacific Group—J. Crew."

[54] Aaron Pressman, "J. Crew's Tidy Turnaround Story," *BusinessWeek*, June 20, 2006, www.businessweek.com/investing/insights/blog/archives/2006/06/j_crews_tidy_turnaround_story.html, accessed July 15, 2010.

[55] In late November 2010, a fascinating postscript to this transaction occurred as TPG and Leonard Green & Partners, along with Micky Drexler, proposed a $3 billion deal to take J. Crew private again.

[56] George P. Baker, "Beatrice: A Study in the Creation and Destruction of Value," *Journal of Finance* 47, no. 3 (1992): 1081–119.

[57] Ibid., 1109.

[58] Malcolm Salter and Daniel Green, "Regal Cinemas (A)," HBS Case No. 902-019 (Boston: HBS Publishing, 2002).

[59] Allen R. Myerson and Geraldine Fabrikant, "2 Buyout Firms Make Deal to Acquire Regal Cinemas," *New York Times*, January 21, 1998.

competitive advantage while independent—was overwhelmed with the pace of growth.[60] In November 2000, the company admitted it had breached the covenants of its lending agreements and was technically in default.[61] Although KKR and Hicks Muse tried to recapitalize the company, they could not reach agreement with the bondholders and the company ended up in bankruptcy. It was subsequently bought out of bankruptcy by one of those recalcitrant bondholders.

While its demise was certainly due in part to external factors—the dreadful lineup of Hollywood films—the Regal Cinema deal may have failed because the board did not understand that the true source of the company's value was its cost-conscious management approach and the steady pace of growth. Although the investors implemented increases in scale and, to a certain degree, scope, and helped management do financial engineering to acquire other locations, the underlying cost structure was already so lean that operational improvements could not generate the necessary cash to pay off the debt.

Recent Studies

Little work has been done on value created from buyout transactions executed during the recent buyout boom—which is not surprising, given the short time frame in which to measure those results. In the one careful examination of these issues, written by Shourun Guo, Edith S. Hotchkiss, and Weihong Song,[62] the authors can look only at deals done through the beginning of the "buyout bubble" (2006); but the results are intriguing and sobering for private equity investors. The sample of 192 buyouts completed between 1990 and 2006 and valued at more than $100 million appeared to be more conservatively priced and less levered than their predecessors in the 1980s—60 percent by the end of the period, while O.M. Scott's 91 percent debt load was not unusual for its era. The more recent deals frequently involved more than one equity sponsor, and the operations often underwent substantial restructuring (asset sales or acquisitions) while private.

For the ninety-four sample deals that had post-buyout data available, the authors found that due to publicly traded debt or an IPO, gains in operating performance were either comparable to or slightly greater than those in benchmark companies that did not undergo buyouts. Cash flow actually increased less than in the 1980s deals. External improvements (gains in industry and market valuation multiples) and financial engineering (tax benefits due to the shields on debt) appeared to be as important as operating performance improvements in terms of creating value. Given the post-2007 recession and the consequent decline in equity values, the authors caution that private equity firms may no longer be able to consistently exit from their investments with substantial gains.

GOVERNANCE TECHNIQUES

We have discussed the value created by the components of our framework—financial arbitrage, financial engineering, cost reduction, increased scale and scope, and management recruitment, incentivization, and mentoring. The governance environment has been a constant theme throughout all of it. In the next section, we discuss the tools that investors use to make all of this happen.

---

[60] Bruce Orwall and Gregory Zuckerman, "Box Office Blues," *Wall Street Journal*, September 27, 2000, A1; referenced in Salter and Green, "Regal Cinemas (A)," 8.

[61] Malcolm Salter and Daniel Green, "Regal Cinemas (A) and (B)," HBS Case Nos. 902-019 and 902-020 (Boston: HBS Publishing, 2002).

[62] Shourun Guo, Edith S. Hotchkiss, and Weihong Song, "Do Buyouts (Still) Create Value?" *Journal of Finance* 66, no. 2 (2011): 479–517.

Information Gathering and Monitoring

A persistent theme in deal management concerns the investors' difficulty in assessing the management team's performance. The board needs to sustain a constant flow of information to guide the company accurately. Whether overseeing Endeca's growth strategy or Beatrice's divestiture program, boards need to receive constant feedback about the performance against plan. If Ellacoya's board had been able to convince the CEO to cut costs more decisively earlier, perhaps it would have become one of the happier investment stories. How do boards implement their directives? And how do they ensure that they are creating the desired results? Boards have a number of feedback points that help determine the company's progress before things get so bad that the firm must be abandoned.

The Budget

For all private-equity-backed companies, the budget (or the plan) is a vital document. The management team and the board must agree on both the budget and its KPIs, whether the company is a brand-new start-up, a once publicly traded behemoth recently taken private, or a spun-out division. The KPIs trickle down throughout the company, even to personal goals and assessments.

Many buyouts have a 100-day plan, like the one TPG created for J. Crew. This sets the company's goals and direction under its new owners and contains a series of indicators that measure progress. Venture investors rarely use these, because the timeline is longer.

With so much riding on the budget, the items it measures and how it does so must be intuitive and understandable. The goals and reporting metrics must be transparent, allowing executives and investors—whether current or prospective—to easily determine the company's performance against plan. This helps everyone understand what needs to be done. Clear, straightforward definition and tracking of goals is essential.

The board participates in creating the budget, approves it, and then reviews performance against it. The board also helps create strategies for responding to performance that differs from expectations. Early knowledge through transparent reporting and good communication is critical. A budget shortfall sends a signal, and the board needs to respond. What caused it? Did the world economy crash, as occurred in 2008? The best marketing plan in the world would not have helped Realogy,[63] a provider of real estate and relocation services. When taken private by Apollo Global Management in an $8.5 billion deal that closed in April 2007, Realogy had to renegotiate its debt. In the end, Apollo had to invest additional capital in the company, which also took on additional debt.

Yet even growth can be troublesome if it is unforeseen. Growth is expensive, requiring additional staff and raw materials. The board of directors must start thinking about all of this as soon as revenues exceed the budget. Is this a one-time blip or the start of the hockey stick? The board can react to unexpected growth in one of four ways: (1) invest more money; (2) limit growth by raising prices or changing the target market; (3) sell the company sooner than expected; and (4) raise money from other sources. When Avid's board was faced with managing its growth, it chose option four and raised venture debt.

Key Performance Indicators

KPIs help the board break down budget goals into more granular items, ensuring that the company makes progress not only in the right direction, but by focusing on the right things. If, for instance,

---

[63] Andrew Ross Sorkin, ed. "Realogy, Owned by Apollo, Sells Debt in Deal with Icahn," *New York Times Dealbook*, September 30, 2009, http://dealbook.blogs.nytimes.com/2009/09/30/apollos-realogy-sells-debt-in-deal-with-icahn/, accessed June 29, 2010.

Dignity Caring Funeral Services wants to expand its presence in the cremation market, its board needs to know what percentage of revenues comes from funerals as opposed to cremations and track the growth in each.

Milestones

The budget and the KPIs show progress toward the achievement of board-approved milestones. These often span several budgets in a row and may be tied to fund-raising, in the case of VC-backed companies, or debt maturation dates, in the case of buyouts. For VC-backed companies, milestones may stipulate that ten customers should be testing the product, a chief marketing officer should be hired, or the drug should be in Phase III trials. They may also set targets for reaching cash-flow breakeven or starting conversations with investment bankers. A buyout may need to have sold some assets or achieved higher operating margins. The Scott team, for instance, achieved the milestone of reducing working capital needs by 42 percent in two years.[64]

Management Performance Review

Because management reports to the board, the board must assess its performance. Board members may personally review senior management or hire consultants to do so. Buyouts and VC companies that hope to go public will have a compensation committee that both produces formal reviews and sets overall compensation strategy, just as they will also have an audit committee to oversee financial matters. The board does not review the performance of more junior staff, but it may be involved in setting general wage increase bands.

CEOs may have an incentive to inflate their own performance, which makes it important for board members to have a network throughout the organization that will mention concerns. For example, the incentives and monitoring established by C&D in the Scott transaction made it almost impossible (and counterproductive) for the CEO to inflate his performance.

Independent Accounting Audits

Part of a board's role in early-stage companies is creating a set of replicable, transparent processes. One of these is an annual audit by an independent accounting firm. The board must ask the accounting firm to produce a management letter that provides its opinion on controls and management. While often dry and formal, it provides an important comparison to other similar-sized companies by an objective, outside organization. This opinion may recommend that the company upgrade its controller to a CFO to handle more complex financials, for instance, or that the firm change its approach to revenue recognition, which is a common challenge for young companies in emerging industries as they try to figure out how their unique financial situation fits within Generally Accepted Accounting Principles (GAAP).[65] Endeca's financial reporting function would have evolved as the company's revenues rose above $100 million and it established international operations.

Regular Strategy Reviews

Strategy reviews are a substantial part of the value that a board of directors adds to a company, regardless of its stage of development. The multiday off-site strategic review is held by any

---

[64] Baker and Wruck, "Creating Value in Leveraged Buyouts."

[65] Revenue recognition for software companies has always been a thorny issue since payment generally occurs up front and the delivery over a period of time, sometimes complicated by product customization or staff training.

well-run private-equity-owned company. These meetings provide important opportunities to align interests and expectations, describe goals and strategies, and create an appropriate culture.

DEAL MANAGEMENT: THE NITTY GRITTY

In this section, we discuss the actual in-the-trenches aspects of deal management. The boards that created the most value, Gertner and Kaplan[66] noted, did so through substantial communication outside the formal board meeting. According to practitioners, such informal interaction creates strong bonds; and the stronger these informal bonds are, the more effective the formal mechanisms will be. Understanding how these informal bonds develop is important in considering the mechanisms whereby various strategies are chosen and eventually create value.

As we have mentioned throughout the chapter, an investment often has a lead firm, which arranges the deal and manages the firms involved, and some firms that are non-leads. Even if there are co-lead firms with equal amounts invested, one GP is often the entrepreneur's "first call" due to reputation, domain expertise, early contact, or personality. This individual is the entrepreneur's trusted advisor. In the Scott transaction, this person was the C&D operating partner. Such access is important both for the investors and the CEO, providing insight and supplying direction. The formal information supplied to the board and the decisions or strategies the board considers are likely to be the product of many conversations between the entrepreneur and certain trusted advisers; it is important to exert influence on the process before the arrival of a polished recommendation at the board meeting. If the investor is not the first call, she or he should identify the director who is and present desirable actions in that way.

Relationships in private-equity-backed companies are complex because these organizations are experiencing great change. The earlier the entrepreneur feels comfortable just picking up the phone and calling the investor, the earlier the investors will know about potential challenges. This gives the board more time to create contingency plans. In a healthy board situation, information sharing goes deep in the organization. In a bad one, the board deals only with the CEO. Unfortunately, when CEOs feel overwhelmed, they tend to hide, rather than share information that could ultimately help the company recover. These situations rarely end well for anyone.

A classic situation of poor communication was seen in an early-stage investment when the CFO called the lead investor to say he lacked the funds to cover payroll for that Friday. The CEO was vacationing in Vietnam. Matters like payroll are entirely foreseeable; the fact that the CEO had not alerted the board to the situation spoke volumes about corporate dysfunction. While the investors did provide enough funds to cover payroll, the CEO returned to find himself jobless.

Just as the entrepreneur must understand the investors, the investors must understand the entrepreneur and the team, the amount of risk the team can tolerate, and how to read their reactions. One start-up CEO sends e-mails at 2 a.m. and calls his chief marketing officer at 7 a.m. He lives, dreams, and breathes his company. He scales back goals only because the board convinces him to spare his employees. "I love to invest in his companies," notes one of his investors, "and I'd sure hate to work for him." Another equally successful CEO proceeds more cautiously. Rather than setting lofty goals and trying to meet them, he prefers to set reasonable goals and exceed them. The same investor may sit on boards of companies run by many different CEOs and must understand how each entrepreneur thinks.

Another critical skill is the ability to build consensus. Even if most of the investors on the board are from the same firm, ideas must be sold to one's colleagues. In growth equity or venture capital, the investors may individually have minority positions in an overall minority position,

---

[66] Robert Gertner and Steven N. Kaplan, "The Value Maximizing Board" (December 1996). Available at SSRN: http://ssrn.com/abstract=10563 accessed July 13, 2010.

further emphasizing the need to build consensus around the board as well as with the management team.

Consensus becomes more difficult, of course, with multiple investors. We have noted the differing motivations between investors in Metapath's different rounds, but that can happen even among investors in the same round. Different firms may value a company differently depending on the health of their portfolios. For one investor, this company may be the most promising opportunity in a weak portfolio. She wants to support it. It may be the worst company in another investor's portfolio, and he wants to exit it at any price. An investor with a fund that needs to raise money may want to maintain the company's value or get rid of it at any cost to avoid cross-fund investments. An investor who was invited into the deal by another firm may defer to the "host." A firm running out of money wants to participate as little as possible. While the board should always act in the best interests of the company (and its LPs), these priorities can conflict. Knowing such motivations and concerns can help a board member create consensus even for difficult changes.

With buyouts, managing the board of a syndicated deal is also complex. Whether seeking to refinance the company, pay a dividend, change an executive, or accept an acquisition offer, the investors have to create a shared understanding of how the move creates value. From the start, the investor must constantly be selling concepts to the other members of the board and the management team to create consensus. These coalitions get things done, and getting things done (we hope!) creates value.

WHEN THE UNEXPECTED HAPPENS: RE-CONTRACTING

Sometimes, though, creating value looks a lot like turning lemons into lemonade. The staged financing discussion earlier assumed that the investor had two options: to continue funding or to abandon the project. In real life, though, there's a third option: the investors can renegotiate the existing contract. Sometimes this is done through consensus, but it can also occur through the application of the private equity golden rule: The Person with the Gold Makes the Rules. If a company is in a sufficiently difficult situation, a new investor can often extract any number of concessions in exchange for putting in more money—as occurred with Ellacoya in the 2002 recapitalization.

Re-contracting occurs most frequently in VC, although it is not unknown for buyouts, where it tends to be more contentious because it is less common. In buyouts, any deal revision involves the banks, which usually want the firm to invest more money before they will renegotiate any loans.

Re-contracting means that classic sunk-cost economic theory does not apply. Sunk costs— that is, historic costs that cannot be recovered—theoretically should not affect a decision on whether to invest more money in a project. That decision should be predicated solely on prospective gains. Humans, though, tend to be loss averse, which means that we *do* consider sunk costs. In a re-contracting situation, the terms of the old deal are renegotiated, which changes the relationship and cost structure going forward. A re-contracting firm can reprice its existing investment to increase its ownership. The reward is increased while the risk has supposedly been reduced due to the progress already made. The most extreme form of this repricing is the recapitalization (sometimes called a cramdown because the positions of firms that do not participated are "crammed" down to common) we saw with Ellacoya. Thus Lightspeed's previous investment in Ellacoya was repriced and preserved because it continued to support the company; the positions of the other investors were deeply subordinated in the capital structure if not converted to common. Lightspeed therefore had a larger position in a company where the technology was already functioning and installed at a handful of customer sites. Its original investment had been in a start-up with undeveloped technology, an unproven management team, and an uncertain customer base. The firms that dropped out had subsidized the development of technology from which Lightspeed would benefit—if it succeeded. If not, the other firms would have lost less than Lightspeed.

Whether a firm is willing to participate in re-contracting that reprices its old position depends on what it believes about the management, the product, and the market—and the options it has for its time and money. Clearly, Lightspeed thought Ellacoya had sufficiently favorable prospects to continue with the deal.

Re-contracting—The Situation at Summit

Summit Microelectronics makes fault-tolerant, power-efficient semiconductors. Founded in 1997, it raised four institutional rounds between 1998 and 2001[67] and developed a product aimed at the data communications and telecommunications industries.[68] When the market crashed in 2001, Summit had just raised $18 million from five VC firms. In 2005, the company seems to have changed its direction substantially. The website noted a different target market, described as "the communications, computing, automotive, consumer, and military markets."[69] In May of that year, the company's new CEO, Patrick Brockett, a 20-year veteran of National Semiconductor, said "The Summit board asked if I would be interested in moving the company into the consumer market."[70] A year later, Summit raised almost $10 million in debt and equity. The board changed, likely to reflect a changed investor consortium, and added representatives of two previously unrepresented firms.[71] Summit has since won several industry awards[72] and, in 2007, raised a $10 million equity round led by Nokia's venture arm.[73]

Re-contracting can also occur in exits, most commonly venture backed. Recall that management owns common stock, while investors own preferred that has liquidation preferences. These liquidation preferences can be more than $1\times$, especially if the capital was raised in a difficult time and the investors wanted downside protection. Sometimes the investors will receive an acquisition offer for a company that is insufficient to pay the full amount of the preferred plus preferences. To encourage management to accept the offer, the investors may forgo some amount of their contracted preference rights. This may be done to reward management for a good job done under difficult circumstances or to encourage them to work for these investors in the future.

Brian Broughman and Jesse Fried[74] explored this phenomenon. Examining fifty VC-backed companies based in Silicon Valley that were acquired between 2003 and 2004, the authors

---

[67] All information on fund-raising, timing, amounts, and participants from Thomson Reuters private equity database, Summit Microelectronics company profile, http://www.summitmicro.com, accessed April 22, 2010.

[68] Data from Summit Microelectronics, http://www.summitmicro.com, as of November 11, 1999, available at www.waybackmachine.org; accessed July 8, 2010.

[69] http://www.summitmicro.com as of February 2005 via www.waybackmachine.org, accessed July 8, 2010.

[70] "Summit Appoints Patrick Brockett as President and Chief Executive Officer," press release, May 12, 2005, http://www.summitmicro.com/comp_info/press/051205/SummitPR_051205.pdf, accessed April 22, 2010; and Paul Rako, "Voices: Summit Micro's Pat Brocket [sic]," *EDN*, March 15, 2007, http://www.edn.com/article/461528-Voices_Summit_Micro_s_Pat_Brocket.php, accessed April 22, 2010.

[71] http://www.summitmicro.com/comp_info/company.htm

[72] EN-Genius Products of the Year, February 2010, http://www.en-genius.net/site/static/EN-Genius_Products _of the_Year_2009, accessed April 22, 2010.

[73] John Walco, "Nokia Investment Arm Backs Summit Microelectronics," *Dr. Dobb's*, February 5, 2007, http://www.drdobbs.com/197003346;jsessionid=MUKQOAILZPFAPQE1GHRSKH4ATMY32JVN, accessed April 22, 2010.

[74] Brian Broughman and Jesse Fried, "Renegotiation of Cashflow Rights in the Sale of VC-Backed Firms," *Journal of Financial Economics* 95 (2010): 384–99.

examined hand-collected data from the entrepreneurs and investors on the details of the acquisition transaction. In eleven of the fifty cases, the investors re-contracted their liquidation preferences to benefit the common shareholders. The average carve-out (the amount by which the preferences were reduced) was $3.7 million, or 11 percent of the venture capitalists' cash-flow rights. The authors suggest that this was due to the "hold-up" powers of the common shareholders in situations where the venture capitalists lack a majority on the board or the state corporate law gives shareholders more leverage (California law requires acquisition offers to be accepted through a vote by class, including common).

The time frame of this study is interesting, coming as it does after the NASDAQ crash. Many firms had tried to ensure returns from struggling companies by investing with multiple liquidation preferences. VC firms were eager to sell companies at almost any price to return at least some money to LPs. This may have made the investors unusually willing to part with some of the proceeds in exchange for an exit, so this study may overestimate the hold-up powers of the common shareholders.

Buyout firms can also re-contract their deals if necessary. As with a VC investment, the question becomes what the investors believe about the market, company, prospects, and alternate uses of time and money. The bank, which has a vested interest in closing down the company while it is still solvent enough to repay the loan, will urge the investors to increase their equity investment. The investors may offer to do so if the bank eases covenants or restructures the loan— perhaps by accepting interest-only payments for a time or reducing the interest rate. Because banks are regulated, they have limited flexibility. Moreover, because banks tend to be more risk averse than venture investors (banks want principal and interest; venture investors are interested in gains), they may be more resistant to changes regardless of any benefits to the underlying company. For instance, Freescale Semiconductor, noted in Chapter 4 as one of the major buyouts of 2006, struggled through the credit crunch of 2008. In March 2009, the company proposed to exchange up to $3 billion of junior notes (the riskier slice of debt, which pays higher interest rates but would receive less in a bankruptcy) for $1 billion of additional senior debt. This would substantially reduce its interest payments. The institutions that held the company's senior debt (the least risky type, which had first claim on any assets should Freescale go bankrupt) took the owners to court over this, unhappy that their own share of the proceeds of any eventual bankruptcy would be diluted by the new notes.[75]

Despite the unhappiness of the senior debt holders, the exchange did go ahead, reducing the company's annual interest payments by $140 million, down to $560 million per year, and the overall level of long-term debt by $1.9 billion.[76] In May 2010, however, Moody's Investor Services, one of the rating agencies, reported that Freescale might again need to take drastic measures to reduce its debt[77]—and who knows what that might entail.

CONCLUSION

Private equity is focused on creating value, and it is through deal management and governance that this occurs. Whether the investment is $ 2.5 million or $25 billion, it is long-term and illiquid. The only way to be sure that this investment can generate the returns that the firm needs to raise another

---

[75] Steven Davidoff, "Freescale's Debt War with Its Noteholders," *The New York Times Dealbook,* April 2, 2009, http://dealbook.blogs.nytimes.com/2009/04/02/freescales-debt-war-with-its-noteholders/, accessed June 18, 2010.

[76] David Manners, "Freescale Reports Operating Loss: To Close Two Fabs," *ElectronicsWeekly.com,* April 23, 2010, http://www.electronicsweekly.com/Articles/2009/04/23/45952/freescale-reports-operating-loss-to-close-two-fabs.htm, accessed July 5, 2010.

[77] Michael J. de la Merced, "Troubled Borrowers May Need New Round of Debt Exchanges," *The New York Times Dealbook,* ed. Andrew Ross Sorkin, May 18, 2010, http://dealbook.blogs.nytimes.com/2010/05/18/troubled-borrowers-may-need-new-round-of-debt-exchanges/#more-227967, accessed July 5, 2010.

fund is to be actively involved. Deal management, by being on the board, setting strategy, being involved, and creating consensus with management and the other board members, all within the context of creating good governance, is at the heart of private equity.

As with much in private equity, deal management is in the details. Understanding the covenants is important. What can the company do? What is prohibited? Understanding the motivations of the other shareholders is crucial.

The framework we developed helps define the general approach toward creating value in a financial, operational, and management framework. The overall setting, though, must include governance. Mickey Drexler could ignore the TPG board when it came to determining J. Crew's color palette, but he had to make sure that the company could service its debt. He had invested in the company after all, and his interests were aligned with those of the investors. We saw the same thing with O.M. Scott. At Endeca, the board replaced the CEO with the founder; and the following year, Endeca's revenues exceeded $100 million. People see their reputation and compensation tightly linked to the company's performance.

But all the alignment in the world fails in a situation like Regal Cinema, where there was no blood to be squeezed from the turnip. Whether the board members were not told or did not heed the signals, the deal faced significant challenges.

Creating value is the product of a multiphase process. Information gathered throughout the deal assessment and structuring process influences the strategies enacted and the ways they are measured. Board-level governance blends flexibility with interest alignment. Board structure stems from and reinforces deal structure. The eventual exit influences how the deal evolves. Everyone wants this company to succeed; but if necessary, we can re-contract. Where interests diverge, problems can arise.

Again we see credentialing at work. Firms with higher reputations have more leverage on the boards because they are perceived to have stables of talented CEOs-in-waiting. That allows them greater control, due merely to the potential for replacing the CEO. With more experience around the partnership, pattern recognition should improve, providing better advice and more informed governance. Every truly talented board member of a successful private equity investment always uses the plural pronoun *we* in referring to the project, because no one person does it all; every board member can describe in excruciating detail the mistakes and what they cost.

An ongoing question for private equity is the degree to which value creation for the firm equates to value creation for society as a whole. Whether these companies are better run and generate benefits—jobs, innovation—for the greater good has been the subject of much consideration and is discussed in Chapter 10.

In the next chapter, we consider the final stage of the private equity cycle, the exit, whether through IPO, merger, secondary sale, or bankruptcy. All boards must confront the question of exit. The company's ability to reach a happy conclusion, and the board's ability to consider the options in a productive and collaborative way, speaks to the skills and dedication of everyone involved.

QUESTIONS

1. How do venture capital boards differ in composition from the boards of companies that have been bought out?

2. Hardy Smith, a noted venture capitalist, sits on the board of Walt's Widgets. When widget sales fall consistently short of expectations, which of the following (there may be several) would Hardy be mostly likely to do and why?

   a. Get on the road himself to sell them.

   b. Suggest different sales channels and pricing strategies.

   c. Redesign the product, suggesting different cases and colors.

    d. Fire the vice president of sales.

    e. Present a term sheet that triggers his antidilution protection.

3. Why would a board have special voting rights? How do these address some of the basic tenets of private equity?

4. Calculate the final ownership for Walt if he raises $12 million at $8 million pre-money, as opposed to the following in two-year increments: (a) $3 million at $3 million pre-money; (b) $3 million at $9 million pre-money; and (c) $6 million at $24 million pre-money.

5. From the venture capitalist's viewpoint, what are three reasons for staged financing?

6. Consider the value creation framework (Table 6.4). Why are changes in the external market not included?

7. How does value creation differ between venture capital and buyout investments? Why?

8. How can a situation like KKR's break-up of Beatrice be said to create value?

9. Was TPG's successful IPO of J. Crew a matter of good deal management or luck? Why? Why do you think TPG might want to take J. Crew private again?

10. As best you can from the material in the text, explain how different deal management styles contributed to the success of O.M. Scott and the failure of Regal Cinemas.

11. Why would the board of Endeca Technologies have thought a professional manager was a good replacement for the founder? Why might that manager have then succeeded with another company? What sort of company would have matched his skills?

12. Why is consensus building such an important part of a board member's work?

13. How does staged financing complicate the management of a venture deal? How could a board member from an early round resolve some of these issues?

14. Why would limited partners countenance their GPs putting more money into a struggling company? How does that differ from a bank's response to a company's difficulties? How does that help explain the differences between the sorts of companies that take VC investment as opposed to those that take bank debt?

15. If you were one of Freescale's junior noteholders, what would make you take the offered deal? As one of Freescale's senior noteholders, how could you be convinced to agree to the new deal?

Chapter 7

Achieving Liquidity—
Exits and Distributions

The eventual aim of governance is to create enough value in the company that its investors can exit. Exiting is the crucial last step in the private equity cycle of raising funds, investing them, and creating value, because without an exit, there are no returns. A firm that goes too long without returns cannot raise another fund. In the end, there is the beginning—"We must enter the [deal] with our eyes on the exit sign," said Allan Gillespie of CDC Capital Partners, the precursor to today's Actis.[1]

Exits can occur in a number of ways. A company can list on a public market (an initial public offering, or IPO), be acquired by another company or another private equity firm, buy back the investors' shares, or be shut down. Some of these exit strategies may not yield gains to the investors, but they are all important, because sometimes the best gain is simply freeing up resources to invest in more promising efforts.

Exits are another one of those maddening situations in private equity where multiple sets of interests converge. In the first place, the company has to be ready to be exited, valuable enough to attract an acquirer, or capable of existing independently in the public markets. There are cases of companies going public too early, as seen in the momentary madness of the Internet bubble or quick flips of leveraged buyouts (LBOs). In general, though, the exit occurs after the real long-term value-creation work of private equity has run its course. But there must also be an avenue for achieving the exit. "Companies are bought, not sold," runs the dictum. Someone has to want to buy it; or, for an IPO, the markets must be willing to welcome a new company. Thus supply and demand conditions must both be right.

The private equity firm's internal needs can also affect an exit. If the investment firm needs to create liquidity to raise a new fund, the company may be hustled out the door at an earlier stage of development and thus at a lower price than it would otherwise warrant. Tensions may arise between different firms on the same company's board—some may want to take an early sale offer at a lower price simply to show some gains, while others want to hold out for a higher-priced alternative farther in the future. In other cases, some may want to shut down a company, as opposed to those who are desperate to keep it going and are willing to "double down." In an IPO, the choice of an exchange on which to list can create issues between the management and the investors or the investors and limited partners (LPs), which may not want stock that trades on a little-known or volatile exchange. A final set of concerns around exits

---

[1] Josh Lerner, Felda Hardymon, and Ann Leamon, "CDC Capital Partners," HBS Case No. 800-133 (Boston: HBS Publishing, 2000).

involves LPs, which may have preferences about the timing of the exit and the form in which they receive their payments.

An interesting set of challenges arose when Warburg Pincus decided to exit EMGS,[2] a Norwegian oil detection company, in 2007. EMGS was a bit of a hybrid because it had developed technology (essentially the use of radar through water and rock to determine the location and amount of oil in a seabed deposit) but used it to conduct studies for the traditionalist oil industry, which was famous for its reluctance to adopt new techniques. Oil stocks were popular at the time. EMGS had made good progress in the three years since the Warburg Pincus investment and needed to invest in new equipment, which could be funded either by additional funds from Warburg Pincus, its majority owner, or by going public. The reputational advantages of being publicly traded would be helpful to the young company and liquidity was attractive to Warburg Pincus, even though the firm would retain much of its ownership.

The biggest question came down to the choice of exchange. New York's exchanges, with the greatest liquidity and the most sophisticated analysts, would probably generate the best price for the company. Arguing against New York were the costs involved in the listing process and ongoing compliance. Norway's Børs was notoriously cyclical, given its preponderance of oil-related listings. It was less liquid than New York; there were fewer tech analysts who could explain the nuances of EMGS's business; and Warburg Pincus had less of a network. But EMGS's managers were Norwegian. They did not want to move to New York, and there was pride in being listed on the home market. Because it would be retaining a large share of the company and needed to keep the managers on board, Warburg Pincus took EMGS public on the Børs.

Alnara Pharmaceuticals[3] demonstrates the dynamics around the acquisition of a venture-backed life sciences company. In 2010, just two years after Alnara's founding, Eli Lilly purchased the company for $180 million and an additional $200 million contingent upon reaching certain goals.[4] Alnara's venture backers had invested only $55 million in the company—a modest amount for a life sciences venture—which was marketing liprotamase, a drug that had been developed by an earlier venture-backed company that went public and then failed. Liprotamase treated a condition common to cystic fibrosis: patients could not digest fat, protein, and carbohydrates and thus suffered malnutrition. The drug was proceeding well through Food and Drug Administration (FDA) trials, and approval was expected in early 2011. Alnara thought the small target market could be reached with a niche sales force but then learned that the drug was applicable to a number of other conditions, including diabetes and pancreatic cancer. The small company would have been unable to target such large markets without a partner; Eli Lilly's sales force was ideal for taking liprotamase to its new target market. For Lilly, buying Alnara was another way of doing research and development.

Exits resolve the illiquidity of private equity. As in much of private equity, the choice of an exit in terms of both method and timing lies in the hands of a few people with interests that are largely aligned with those of management. While interests can diverge, many of the securities described in earlier chapters mitigate this problem. Interests of the LPs and GPs can diverge as well. Resolving these issues involves yet more partnership behavior.

[2] Felda Hardymon and Ann Leamon, "Warburg Pincus and EMGS: The IPO Decision (A)," HBS Case No. 807-092 (Boston: HBS Publishing, 2007).

[3] Trista Morrison, "Alnara's Late-Sage Pancreatic Enzyme Drive Lilly Acquisition," *BioWorld Today*, July 6, 2010.

[4] Such provisions are known as "earn-outs." "Eli Lilly Completes Alnara Pharma Purchase," *PEHub*, July 21, 2010, http://www.pehub.com/77832/eli-lilly-completes-alnara-pharma-purchase/, accessed July 22, 2010.

Other themes of the book persist as well. Information asymmetries and/or gaps mean that the selling or listing party usually has more information than the buyer, whether an acquiring company or the institutions buying shares in an IPO. Bodies of research explore the implications of these differences. Market cyclicality determines whether IPOs are even possible. Finally, credentialing again appears, helping to certify the company in the eyes of the market or an acquirer and even helping to improve its chances of good long-run performance.

This chapter begins by considering how firms think about a company's exit. When is a company deemed ready? How do investors choose whether to sell a company or to take it public? What role does the entrepreneur have in the decision? What impact does the private equity investor have? We then explore the different exit methods already introduced and describe the actual mechanics of the process. Lastly, we look at the exit—rather, the proceeds of the exit—from the LPs' perspective, considering the difficulties of stock distribution and the complications of cash.

THE DECISION TO EXIT

When the general partners (GPs) in a private equity firm assess their portfolio companies, they invariably consider the length of time until liquidity—and what form it will take. Some acquisition offers appear out of the blue; some shutdowns occur abruptly in response to a missed milestone or a technological roadblock. Most exits, though, require a lot of work to create the opportunity and then to convince the other investors and management to accept it. Many factors—the company's performance, the state of the public markets, the sector's prospects, and conditions internal to the private equity firm itself—affect the exit decision and avenue.

The company's performance plays a substantial part in the decision. Companies accrete value in specific steps, ascending a growth curve that looks like the one in Figure 7.1. Eventually, they reach the point where the gains due to additional time under the current investors flatten out; or, as

FIGURE 7.1   S-Curve growth

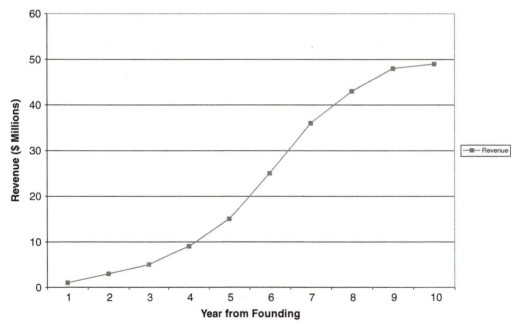

Douglas Cumming and Jeffrey MacIntosh phrase it, "when the projected marginal value added as a result of the VC's efforts, at any given measurement interval, is less than the projected cost of these efforts."[5] Assuming that the investors on the board all agree with this assessment, they must then decide on the best exit avenue: IPO; merger or acquisition (often called for M & A **merger and acquisition**, although mergers, a situation in which the two companies combine and issue new stock in the new merged company, are much less common than acquisitions, in which the acquiring company absorbs the acquisition wholesale and pays for the other company in its own stock or in cash) partial exit through dividends; secondary sale; or shutdown. If a difference of opinion arises, investors may try persuasion; some may sell their shares to other investors; or they may resort to the special voting rights enshrined in the term sheets. In the following discussion, though, we assume that the board has agreed to exit; and simply consider the implications of each method they might use.

IPO OR ACQUISITION?

Going public has typically been viewed as the gold standard of exits. Historically, the most successful investments—whether Kleiner Perkins' and Sequoia's investment in Google or Ripplewood's purchase of the Long-Term Credit Bank of Japan (later renamed Shinsei Bank)—have been exited this way. Yet acquisitions provide most of the exits, as shown in Table 7.1. In their 2009 study, Lerner, Sørenson, and Strömberg[6] assessed global exit strategies and determined that more than 75 percent of the known exits between 1995 and 2005 came through acquisition (78.2 percent for venture capital [VC], 75.1 percent for growth capital, and 83.6 percent for LBOs). A far smaller proportion of companies went public (3.5 percent of VC, 10.4 percent of growth capital, and 7.1 percent of LBOs). Failures made up 18.2 percent of the VC exits, 14.6 percent of growth capitals, and 9.3 percent of LBO exits. In North America, acquisitions accounted for 72.6 percent of all known private equity exits, IPOs for 11.7 percent, and failures for 15.7 percent. By comparison, Western Europe had slightly more acquisitions (75.1 percent), fewer IPOs (10.4 percent), and fewer failures (14.6 percent). A substantial number of the companies (more than half) had unknown exits or were still private.

The preponderance of acquisitions holds true even for more recent data. The Thomson Reuters data in Table 7.2 shows that every year since 2000, there have been more acquisitions than

Table 7.1   Exit Avenues from Global Private Equity Deals (%)

	Venture Capital	Growth Capital	LBO	Overall
Acquired	78.2	75.1	83.6	78.7
IPO	3.5	10.4	7.1	6.0
Failed	18.2	14.6	9.3	15.3

Source: Data from Josh Lerner, Morten Sørenson, and Per Strömberg, "What Drives Private Equity Activity and Success Globally?" in *Globalization of Alternative Investments Working Papers*, Volume 2: *The Global Economic Impact of Private Equity Report 2009*, ed. Anuradha Gurung and Josh Lerner (New York: The World Economic Forum USA, 2009), 111, available at http://www3.weforum.org/docs/WEF_IV_PrivateEquity_Report_2009.pdf.

[5] Douglas J. Cumming and Jeffrey G. MacIntosh, "A Cross-Country Comparison of Full and Partial Venture Capital Exits," *Journal of Banking and Finance* 27 (2003): 512.

[6] Josh Lerner, Morten Sørenson, and Per Strömberg, "What Drives Private Equity Activity and Success Globally?" in *Globalization of Alternative Investments Working Papers Volume 2*: *The Global Economic Impact of Private Equity Report 2009*, ed. Anuradha Gurung and Josh Lerner (New York: The World Economic Forum USA, 2009), 81–112, available at http://www3.weforum.org/docs/WEF_IV_PrivateEquity_Report_2009.pdf.

Table 7.2   Acquisitions vs. IPOs of U.S. Venture-Backed Companies

	No. of Acquisitions	No. of IPOs
2000	8,920	385
2001	6,544	99
2002	6,045	92
2003	6,576	85
2004	7,359	248
2005	8,026	214
2006	8,942	209
2007	9,571	229
2008	7,751	33
2009	5,643	62

Source: Data from Thomson Reuters private equity database, http://banker.thomsonib.com/ta/?ExpressCode=harvarduniversity, accessed July 29, 2010.

IPOs for VC-backed deals in the United States and, except for 2004, the same has been true for LBOs.

Exiting a company via IPO as opposed to an acquisition has a number of different impacts on the entrepreneur and the investors. In an IPO, the entrepreneur keeps her position; in an acquisition, the entrepreneur may be let go or become the head of a division within the acquirer, but will not retain her former prestige. An IPO tends to provide a higher valuation than an acquisition—studies[7] have found a 22 percent valuation premium in IPOs as opposed to acquisitions. Yet an IPO is more uncertain. The markets and the price the company can command may change during the filing process and even afterward, during the "lock-up" period when the major investors and the management team ("insiders") are barred from selling much of their stock.

Several studies explore the choice to go public or be acquired. Douglas Cumming[8] identified a preference among VC-backed entrepreneurs for IPOs because, in short, they kept their jobs. Whether this occurred, though, was very much due to the relative power of the VC investors and the entrepreneur, as negotiated in the initial term sheets. Using data from 223 European VC-backed companies with exits between 1996 and 2005, Cumming determined that VC investors chose the exit method that created the greatest gain while the CEOs preferred an IPO due to the private benefits of running a public company. He found that stronger control rights for the VC investor were associated with a higher probability of exit via acquisition and a lower probability of IPO or write-off. When the venture investors had board control and the right to replace the founder, the chance of an acquisition rose by 30 percent and the chance of a write-off fell by the same amount—possibly indicating operational improvements driven by the venture capitalists. In cases where the entrepreneur had more control, the venture investor was less experienced, or the investor's shares were held in common stock rather than convertible preferred (clearly, someone didn't know about Max and Sam), IPOs were 12 percent more likely.

---

[7] James Brau, Bill Francis, and Ninon Kohers, "The Choice of IPO versus Takeover," *Journal of Business* 76, no. 4 (2003): 583–612.

[8] Douglas Cumming, "Contracts and Exits in Venture Capital Financing," *Journal of Financial Studies* 21, no. 5 (2008): 1947–1982.

Part of the decision between an acquisition and an IPO, then, may be a question of return on personal investment. The entrepreneur may start only one company (only 5 percent of entrepreneurs start multiple companies[9]); the venture capitalist invests in several every year. Thus, even if the return from an IPO is higher, the venture capitalist may prefer a relatively predictable exit via acquisition, whereas a risk-seeking entrepreneur might prefer a higher-risk approach to hit the "jackpot" in his or her one chance. A growing economic literature adds to this, suggesting that entrepreneurs may be excessively optimistic about their chances, which may lead them to hold out for an IPO even if the option is unrealistic.[10]

Yet there is more to the choice than relative control rights and personal ambitions. The characteristics of a company that goes public differ from those of a company that is acquired. These differences have become a subject of interest to researchers.

Onur Bayar and Thomas J. Chemmanur[11] created a theoretical model of exit choice. Larger companies with more dominant products, they predicted, would tend to go public while companies that were less likely to succeed in the face of market competition would be acquired. Like Cumming, they determined that companies would go public more readily if management enjoyed particular benefits from control; but the choice was also influenced by whether market valuations were high, if further product development required substantial investment, and if potential acquirers had significant bargaining power, which would drive down the price of an acquisition. The likelihood of acquisition rose if the industry had a dominant player (leaving a smaller market for others to contend) and if potential acquirers could provide important synergies such as marketing or distribution help.

Bayar and Chemmanur predicted that a company would go public at a higher average valuation than the price it would achieve if it was acquired. In part, this was because larger firms with more stable revenue streams went public. Furthermore, because the IPO market had greater information asymmetry, investors might overestimate the company's prospects; but a potential acquirer would do more exhaustive due diligence, resulting in a price that more closely approximated the company's true value.

In addition to firm-specific factors, macroeconomic conditions play a role in the decision. In 2008, twelve private-equity-backed companies exited via IPO in the United States; it was the lowest number in two decades. This means that thousands of companies backed by private equity investors—particularly skilled at taking companies public—did not do so due to the markets' inhospitality. James Brau, Bill Francis, and Ninon Kohers[12] explored the impact of macroeconomic factors along with industry-level characteristics in a private company's choice of acquisition or IPO. Using two samples, one of companies that went public and the other of companies that were acquired, all between 1984 and 1998, they considered the effect of liquidity, ownership, and control along with the condition of the stock market, the cost of debt, and specific industry issues. IPOs were more likely, they found, if the companies were in a highly concentrated industry (antitrust issues might preclude mergers) or in the high-tech industry, if debt was expensive (which might otherwise finance an acquisition), if the IPO market was "hot," if the company was large (due to the high fixed costs of an IPO), and if there was substantial insider ownership. Acquisitions were more likely if the company was in a highly leveraged industry (presumably, the acquirer would find it easier to borrow) or in the financial services industry

[9] Paul Gompers, Anna Kovner, Josh Lerner, and David Scharfstein, "Performance Persistence in Entrepreneurship," *Journal of Financial Economics* 96 (2010): 18–32.

[10] Augustin Landier and David Thesmar, "Contracting with Optimistic Entrepreneurs: Theory and Evidence," *Review of Financial Studies* 22 (2009): 117–50.

[11] Onur Bayar and Thomas J. Chemmanur, "IPOs or Acquisitions? A Theory of the Choice of Exit Strategy by Entrepreneurs and Venture Capitalists" (Working Paper, December 2006, unpublished), http://www.eu-financial-system.org/fileadmin/content/Dokumente_Events/ninth_conference/Chemmanur.pdf, accessed August 2, 2010.

[12] Brau et al., "The Choice of IPO versus Takeover."

Table 7.3   Descriptive Statistics for IPOs and Acquisitions, 1995–2004

	Median		Mean		
Firm Characteristics	Acquisition	IPO	Acquisition	IPO	Significance
$ Millions					
Revenues before transaction	$36.5	$26.9	$100.3	$196.9	0.0005
Total assets before transaction	$27.7	$26.3	$79.1	$159.5	0.0001
Value of transaction	$127.4	$171.5	$234.9	$412.0	0.0038
EBITDA before transaction	$4.0	$1.6	$7.8	$15.7	0.0021
Capital expenditures	$1.5	$1.9	$8.2	$27.8	0.0019
R&D expense	$ —	$1.7	$2.2	$6.0	0.0001
Intangibles	$ —	$ —	$10.0	$29.5	0.0081
Years of operation	7	6	15.6	10.1	0.0001
Number of employees	269	235	996.4	1,449.2	NS
Venture backing (%)	41.4	55.5	41.4	55.5	0.0001
Insider ownership before transaction (%)	75.4	65.1	68.4	64.5	NS
Insider ownership after transaction (%)	0.0	50.1	5.6	49.4	0.0001

Note: NS = not significant.
Source: Adapted from Annette Poulsen and Mike Stegemoller, "Moving from Private to Public Ownership," *Financial Management* (Spring 2008): 90.

(reflecting the rapid industry consolidation that followed the sector's deregulation). They were also more likely if the insiders wanted more immediate liquidity—although the average exit price was lower, the target company owners received on average 60 percent of the deal's value in cash, while the cash received by insiders in an IPO averaged 11 percent of the financing raised.[13]

Using industry- and macroeconomic-level data, Annette Poulsen and Mike Stegemoller[14] investigated firm-specific characteristics that determined the choice of IPO or acquisition. Using two data sets, 1,074 private firms that underwent IPOs and 735 that were acquired, all between 1995 and 2004, along with a subsample of companies matched by assets, industry, and time, they found that the company's size was an important factor. The predominant exit method for small companies in their sample was through acquisition; only larger companies had the choice of IPO or acquisition.

Table 7.3 shows the differences between acquired companies and those that went public. For the companies that went public, the dollar value of the transaction was higher, they were younger, and the median firm had fewer employees. More had venture backing. Note how much stock the insiders still owned even after the IPO transaction—because a fairly small amount of stock is sold, insiders cannot simply get out of their positions.

These companies, the authors concluded, tended to have higher growth and higher valuations, and they needed access to nondebt sources of funding to continue their growth path. They had

---

[13] Ibid., 600.

[14] Annette Poulsen and Mike Stegemoller, "Moving from Private to Public Ownership," *Financial Management* (Spring 2008): 81–101.

fewer intangible assets—that is, less goodwill and fewer patents as a percentage of assets. Theoretically, highly technical patents and goodwill would be harder to explain to a large number of public investors; companies that had such assets would find it easier to explain their value to a single sophisticated acquirer.

In some cases, the choice between IPO and acquisition is muddy—a company may file for an IPO only to pull it for an acquisition or be acquired shortly after completing an IPO. James Brau, Ninon Sutton, and Nile Hatch[15] suggest that the first course of action is a response to the increased availability of information as part of the pre-IPO process. With information easier to obtain thanks to Securities and Exchange Commission (SEC) filings and with market excitement around the impending offering, the acquirer can offer a higher price because it is more confident of having accurately assessed the company's value. The process of filing the IPO also provides evidence of a level of corporate development that may be attractive. The quasi-public nature of the pre-IPO process may also attract multiple potential acquirers, creating competition that increases the price of the deal.

The other option, where a company goes public and is acquired within a few years, is counterintuitive. After all, the process of an IPO is quite expensive. Here too, though, information asymmetry fails—the potential acquirer can follow the company's progress through regular public reports and a public stock price. The company often enjoys a rising stock price once the acquirer makes an offer and then has the option of acquiescing to the deal or staying public. Either course improves the gains to investors and management. The companies that filed for an IPO but opted for acquisition before listing, the authors found, received a premium of 22 to 26 percent compared to simply being acquired; those that went public and then were acquired earned a premium of 18 to 21 percent compared to an acquisition when private.

In general, research indicates that IPOs are preferred if the company occupies a significant role in the market, is a high-growth operation, and needs nondebt funding for continued investment. Companies also tend to choose IPOs if the CEO has particularly strong control rights or the investors plan to maintain their position. Companies will tend toward acquisitions if they have complicated assets, high levels of debt, or investors that want immediate liquidity.

Going public gives companies several other advantages. Being publicly listed enhances a company's reputation, providing an aura of reliability and trustworthiness. This can be a competitive advantage because established companies may be unwilling to entrust mission-critical systems to young start-ups lest they go out of business and deprive the customer of maintenance and updates. If a company has developed to the point of being a public entity, it has a longer anticipated life span.

A public company also has added visibility in the market. As we commented earlier, this can lead to the phenomenon of an acquisition shortly after the IPO, but it also helps with market awareness and the ability to raise additional financing. For a foreign company, a listing on the NASDAQ or New York Stock Exchange (NYSE) allows it to tap new capital markets and raises its profile with analysts, institutional investors, and even potential customers.

Of course, there are drawbacks to an IPO. The process is expensive—just the direct fees (underwriter commissions; legal, printing, and auditing expenses; and other out-of-pocket costs) can easily reach 10 percent or more of the total amount raised.[16] The ongoing disclosure and scrutiny associated with being public can be emotionally unsettling for a company accustomed to being private—not to mention expensive, to the point that an increasing number of companies are choosing to list on London's Alternative Investment Market (AIM) rather than comply with the requirements of the Sarbanes-Oxley Act in the United States.

---

[15] James Brau, Ninon Sutton, and Nile Hatch, "Dual-Track versus Single-Track Sell-Outs: An Empirical Analysis of Competing Harvest Strategies," *Journal of Business Venturing* 25 (2010): 389–402.

[16] Jay Ritter, "The Costs of Going Public," *Journal of Financial Economics* 19, no. 2 (1987): 269–81.

Lastly, the market's appetite for new issues varies dramatically over time. During the periodic dips, investors and management may be forced to pull the transaction, imposing reputational consequences on all parties. This is less likely to happen if the company is backed by an experienced venture capitalist, as Josh Lerner[17] demonstrated in his study of 350 venture-backed biotech companies between 1978 and 1992. Venture investors, he found, seemed quite skilled at reading the markets. They took companies public when equity valuations were high and raised private financing when values were low. In addition, seasoned venture capitalists (as measured by the age of the firm) appeared to be particularly adept at taking companies public near market peaks.

The interest of VC firms in IPOs is understandable since IPOs tend to produce better returns than the next-best option, acquisitions. An older *Venture Economics* study of VC exits[18] reported that a $1 investment in a company that went public yielded an average net cash return (in addition to the amount invested) of $1.95 in gains with an average holding period of 4.2 years. The same amount invested in a company that was acquired generated a cash return of only 40 cents with a 3.7-year mean holding period.

Returns—A Note

The average IPO creates greater returns than does the average acquisition, due in part to the impact of selection effects. Companies that go public tend to be larger, more successful, and more ready to be independent. Acquisitions, on the other hand, provide exits for two sorts of companies: those that are doing well and those that are struggling but have created some value and are sold for results ranging from a small gain to a significant (but not total) loss. Being sold "for a peppercorn" serves two purposes: it provides some modicum of return and, more importantly, frees the firm of further investments of time and money. The number of such small-return acquisitions is hard to determine since the price of an acquisition need not be publicly announced. While some acquisitions create huge returns, like eBay's $2.6 billion acquisition of Skype or Google's acquisition of AdMob for $750 million, others may provide their greatest benefit to the venture capitalists by simply removing the company from the portfolio. The lower return for acquisitions comes in part from such transactions involving disappointing companies.

The credibility conferred by IPOs extends beyond the company to the investor. The fact that Kleiner Perkins and Sequoia backed Google is well-known; but Google's purchase of Accel-backed AdMob may not generate the same "buzz," because AdMob becomes absorbed in its acquirer. Taking a company from a raw start-up to a public presence demonstrates remarkable value creation by the investors. These reputational benefits appear to affect the way a VC firm thinks about an exit and even how it executes an IPO.

Using data on 433 venture-backed IPOs between 1978 and 1987 and augmenting it with information on the first IPO brought to market by 62 VC firms, Paul Gompers[19] explored the reasons driving venture capitalists' IPOs. These appeared to differ depending on the age of the VC firm. Young VC firms (those under six years old) took their first company public when it was more immature, apparently using it as a fund-raising device. As shown in Table 7.4, venture capitalists from young firms had been on the company's board fourteen months less than those from older

---

[17] Joshua Lerner, "Venture Capitalists and the Decision to Go Public," *Journal of Financial Economics* 35 (1994): 293–316.

[18] "Exiting Venture Capital Investments," in *Venture Economics* (Needham, MA: Venture Economics, 1988); cited in Lerner, "Venture Capitalists and the Decision to Go Public."

[19] Paul Gompers, "Grandstanding in the Venture Capital Industry," *Journal of Financial Economics* 42 (1996): 133–56.

Table 7.4   Characteristics of IPOs for Companies Backed by Young and Old VC Firms

	VC Firm Less than Six Years Old		VC Firm More than Six Years Old	
	Mean	Median	Mean	Median
Time from IPO date to next follow-on fund (months)	16	12	24.2	24
Size of next follow-on fund ($ millions)	44.2	55.9	120.4	99.9
Age of VC-backed company at IPO (months)	55.1	42	79.6	64
Duration of board representative for lead VC firm (months)	24.5	20	38.8	28
Underpricing at IPO date (%)	13.6	6.7	7.3	2.7
Offering size ($ millions)	16.1	11.5	21.8	16.8
Carter and Manaster underwriter rank	6.26	6.5	7.43	8
Number of prior IPOs	1	0	6	4
Fraction of equity held by all VC investors before IPO (%)	32.1	28.7	37.7	37.1
Fraction of equity held by lead VC investor before IPO (%)	12.2	10.0	13.9	12.0
Market value of lead VC's equity after IPO ($ millions)	8.4	3.79	12.93	7.65

Source: Adapted from Paul Gompers, "Grandstanding in the Venture Capital Industry," *Journal of Financial Economics* 42 (1996): 140.

firms, owned less of the company at the IPO, and took their companies public almost two years earlier than did the older firms. They managed this by offering the companies at a lower price— that is, the price of the shares offered to the initial public investors was substantially lower than the price at which they traded later in the day they went public (later in this chapter we explore this practice, known as "underpricing," at length). Intriguingly, these younger VC firms often raised an additional fund close to the time of the IPO. The average time between a young firm's first IPO and raising a subsequent fund was sixteen months, but the median was just twelve, indicating that a substantial number of these firms raised a fund within less than a year of that IPO. The IPO, then, can be a credentialing event for the private equity investors as well as the company. Both are disadvantaged when the VC firm does so, because the company raises less money than it could have had the firm held the company longer and created more value or priced it higher. For the venture firm, the money forgone represents the cost of the certification from having taken a company public. For more experienced venture capital firms, on the other hand, another IPO is no big deal. The experienced firms take their companies public at a more mature age, after more involvement, and at a higher price. For these firms, the IPO's timing has little impact on the timing of the next fund. Peggy Lee and Sunil Wahal[20] extended Gompers' analysis and found that these patterns also held true for the period of 1980 to 2000. Younger firms and those that had done fewer IPOs tended to do more underpricing.

But when is a company ready to go public? The papers cited earlier note that many companies that went public were already profitable, in fact, more so than those that were acquired. Yet that is not always the case. As Poulsen and Stegemoller determined, access to nondebt financing can be a

---

[20] Peggy Lee and Sunil Wahal, "Grandstanding, Certification and the Underpricing of Venture Capital Backed IPOs," *Journal of Financial Economics* 73 (2004): 375–407.

significant part of the decision to go public. This has been a long-standing approach in life sciences companies, where an IPO is viewed less as an exit than as a financing event; it was also true for Tesla Motors.

Tesla—No Profits, No Problem, We're Public!

When Tesla, the maker of high-end electric sports cars, went public on June 28, 2010 (NASDAQ: TSLA), its share price rose 41 percent from the opening price of $17, which was itself above the expected range of $14 to $16. The company sold 11.1 million new shares, and its current owners sold 2.2 million.[21] The company, though, has shown a profit only once, for the month of July 2009. It lost $25 million in the first quarter of 2010 and $55.7 million in 2009 overall. Since its founding in 2003, the company has raised $300 million from investors that include Capricorn Management, Compass Technology Partners, Draper Fisher Jurvetson, and individuals like the Google cofounders and the serial entrepreneur (and Tesla CEO) Elon Musk. Tesla went public as a financing event—it needed to raise money for its more affordable Model S. "It gives them some cash that they desperately need," said John O'Dell, senior editor at Edmunds GreenCarAdvisor.com.[22]

Tesla had a successful IPO based on its prospects, not its current situation. In addition, the market was favorable. Venture capitalists often talk about the "IPO window," or the time when investors are willing to consider buying the stock of new companies. Tesla was fortunate in that its prospects, its clean-tech sector focus, and the market all came together.

It's important to understand that exiting an investment through an IPO is really a two-stage process. In the initial offering, the company typically sells mostly "primary" shares, that is, new shares that raise money for the company to invest in the enterprise's further development. This is particularly true in VC and in the United States, as seen in the case of Tesla. Even if some of the shares sold are "secondary" ones—existing positions owned by the investors and management—the investors usually continue to retain a substantial position in the company (according to Poulsen and Stegemoller, the average ownership of all insiders, including managers and directors, falls from 65 to 50 percent[23]). Rather than becoming instantly liquid, the private equity investor's position is typically unwound only after an extended period, through additional secondary sales and stock distributions, as described later. "An IPO is not an exit," said several experienced venture investors. "But it creates the opportunity to exit."

THE PROCESS OF EXITING

Having discussed the choice of IPO and acquisition, we think it is useful to get a sense of how these exits actually occur. The process demonstrates many of the enduring private equity themes: illiquidity, concerns about reputation, cyclicality, and information asymmetries. It is interesting to observe the techniques employed in responding to each issue.

---

[21] Lynn Cowan and Matt Jarzemsky, "Tesla Roars Out of the Garage," *Wall Street Journal*, June 30, 2001, http://online.wsj.com/article/NA_WSJ_PUB:SB10001424052748704103904575336853549268476.html, accessed July 30, 2010.

[22] Chuck Squatriglia, "Tesla IPO Raises $226.1 million," *Wired.com*, June 29, 2010, http://www.wired.com/autopia/2010/06/tesla-ipo-raises-226-1-million/, accessed July 30, 2010.

[23] Annette Poulsen and Mike Stegemoller, "Moving from Private to Public Ownership," *Financial Management* (Spring 2008): 81–101.

The IPO Process

Once management and the board have decided to take the company public, several things happen. First, the company must prepare itself to become public. It must have the right financials. Not only must the reports follow accepted national standards—U.S. Generally Accepted Accounting Principles (GAAP), UK GAAP, or International Financial Reporting Standards (IFRS)—but the company must also produce the steadily improving financial results that public markets expect. This does not mean that the company "manages" its financials in some nefarious way—in fact, research has shown that VC-backed companies going public are less likely to engage in earnings management (e.g., by manipulating accounting items like inventory and accounts receivable) than their non-VC-backed peers[24]—but that the company would take steps to ensure that its revenues and earnings show a compelling growth story.

In addition, the management team must be suitable. In some cases, a founder (for instance, a technologist) may be appropriate for a firm's early years, but not for a role as a spokesman frequently interacting with analysts and institutions. A talented private company CFO may be uncomfortable with the demands of public company scrutiny and decide to resign to embark on another project.

Lastly, the board may be reconstituted. Because the sale of stock owned by board members is often restricted by securities laws, private equity investors sometimes leave the board at the time of (or just before) the IPO to allow their firm to sell the position more quickly. The lead investor, though, often remains. A substantial number of directors will need to be outsiders to satisfy the frequently encountered rules about corporate governance. Often, the investors try to attract some marquee directors, such as thought leaders in the company's sector or individuals with expertise in large public companies. In addition, there may be specific national requirements, as in Norway, where a certain percentage of directors must be women.

Here again we see the impact of the investor's reputation on the company's results. A higher-quality private equity firm has access to higher-quality board members. In addition, as the company continues through the process, higher-quality backers provide other important benefits including contacts with higher-quality investment banks, which will represent the company, and accounting firms. Megginson and Weiss,[25] in a study of 640 companies that went public between 1983 and 1987, matched 320 VC-backed companies with 320 in similar industries and of similar offering size and found that the presence of venture capitalists on the board conferred some advantages. First, as shown in Table 7.5, the venture firms had brought several firms to market in the past and concentrated their business with a small number of investment banks. This experience with and knowledge of high-reputation players allowed the process to move more smoothly. Because they knew the process and wanted to safeguard their reputation and relationships, the VC firms produced accurate information in a timely manner. There was less underpricing, which meant that the company and its investors kept more of the value that the market assigned. Venture-backed issues also attracted more attention from institutional investors, which were less prone to fad-driven behavior than retail investors and contributed to a stable share price. VC-backed companies also went public at a younger age than their peers, and often with slightly lower profits but a higher growth rate, as shown in Table 7.6. The market apparently accepted this because the VC investors continued to hold a significant position in the company's shares after the IPO.

Once the company is positioned with the right sort of board and the right sort of earnings, the IPO process begins. First, the board selects an investment bank to serve as underwriter. There may be a **beauty contest** involving several interested investment banks that describe their plans for

---

[24] Yael V. Hochberg, "Venture Capital and Corporate Governance in the Newly Public Firm" (paper presented at AFA 2004 San Diego Meeting, December 8, 2003), available at SSRN: http://ssrn.com/abstract=474542, accessed July 30, 2010.

[25] William L. Megginson and Kathleen A. Weiss, "Venture Capitalist Certification in Initial Public Offerings," *Journal of Finance* 66, no. 3 (1991): 879–903.

Table 7.5   Characteristics of Venture Capitalists in IPOs

Firm Name	Number of IPOs, 1983–1987	% of IPOs with VC on Board of Directors	Most Frequent Underwriters
Kleiner, Perkins, Caulfield & Byers	22	50	Robertson, Colman (9); Morgan Stanley (7)
Citicorp Venture Capital (now Court Square)	15	40	Alex. Brown (4)
Mayfield Funds	15	80	Robertson, Colman (9)
Venrock Associates	14	86	Robertson, Colman (5)
Greylock Partners	13	77	Hambrecht & Quist (8); Morgan Stanley (5)
Oak Investment Partners	13	69	Alex. Brown (7)
Advent Funds	11	82	L. F. Rothschild (3)
TA Associates	11	55	L. F. Rothschild (3)
Bessemer Venture Partners	10	70	Robertson, Colman (3); L. F. Rothschild (3)
New Enterprise Associates	10	90	Alex. Brown (5)
Charles River Ventures	9	44	Hambrecht & Quist (3); Roberson, Colman (3)
Sequoia Capital	9	67	Hambrecht & Quist (4)
Norwest Growth Fund	8	63	Alex. Brown (2)

Source: Adapted from William L. Megginson and Kathleen A. Weiss, "Venture Capitalist Certification in Initial Public Offerings," *Journal of Finance* 66, no. 3 (1991): 888–89. © *Journal of Finance*, 1991.

marketing the company to investors, what comparable companies it has taken public and how they have performed, what analysts will cover it once it goes public, and the price it is likely to command. Analyst coverage is extremely important; an investment bank with respected analysts in the company's sector definitely has an advantage.

Table 7.6   Mean and Median Statistics for VC-Backed and Non-VC-Backed IPOs

Firm Characteristics	VC-Backed		Non-VC-Backed	
	Mean	Median	Mean	Median
Amount offered ($ millions)	$19.7	$15.0	$13.2	$9.2
Offering price ($ millions)	$11.2	$10.5	$10.2	$10.0
Prior year's revenue ($ millions)	$37.1	$16.2	$39.4	$13.0
Growth in EPS per year (%)	76.8	61.1	65.5	42.1
Years from incorporation date to offer date	8.6	5.3	12.2	8.1

Source: Adapted from William L. Megginson and Kathleen A. Weiss, "Venture Capitalist Certification in Initial Public Offerings," *Journal of Finance* 66, no. 3 (1991): 886. © *Journal of Finance*, 1991.

The fee charged by investment banks for their services varies little: at least in the United States, it is almost always 7 percent of the capital raised[26] in addition to legal and other costs that the listing company bears. In total, the cost of a typical IPO approaches 10 percent of the funds raised.[27] A very few very large offerings may be charged 5 percent; and in some cases, low-caliber banks managing very small offerings will insist on warrants in addition to a 7 percent fee. In a sign of its market power, Blackstone Group (NYSE: BX) negotiated a super-low fee of 3.75 percent in its June 2007 IPO.[28]

Often, multiple banks underwrite the offering with one bank serving as lead or "book" underwriter. A smaller institution that specializes in the company's market segment or industry may work with a larger bank, such as Goldman Sachs or Morgan Stanley, that can reach many institutional buyers. The lead underwriter will be responsible for the most critical function, managing the records that list the institutions wanting shares in the offering and then allocating the shares among them. The managing or comanaging banks recruit other banks and brokerage houses to form a syndicate that sells the offering to their clients. While only one to three banks actually underwrite the offering, a much larger number of financial institutions are involved in the sales process.

Choosing a prestigious underwriter (the most reputable are termed "bulge bracket") signals a company's credibility to the market.[29] Because institutional investors have only scarce resources to assess an unknown company entering the market, they rely on the underwriter's own research and its reputation to certify the investment as being low risk. The willingness of a high-reputation bank to work with a new company sends a positive signal to the market and reduces some of the information asymmetry that would make the investors normally assign a lower valuation to the new offering. As noted in Megginson and Weiss, a private equity investor's ability to recruit a high-reputation investment bank to underwrite the offering is a substantial advantage to the company.

The underwriter does several important tasks before the offering is marketed. Among others, it does due diligence on the company to ensure no unhappy accounting or operational surprises, determines the offering size, and prepares the marketing material. Along with the law firm representing the company, the underwriter also helps prepare the regulatory filings.

In most major industrialized nations, a company going public requires permission from at least one regulatory body. In the United States, the critical role is played by the SEC. The SEC review focuses on whether the company has disclosed all material information; it does not evaluate the offering's price. Since 1996, all offerings listed on the major U.S. exchanges have been exempt from state-level scrutiny. Previously, however, states did their own reviews, which sometimes led to peculiar outcomes. In 1980, for instance, Massachusetts regulators initially prohibited the marketing of Apple Computer's IPO in the state, arguing that the price was too high—even though the company was profitable and its proposed market capitalization in the IPO was $1.6 billion (in August 2010, Apple's market capitalization was $238 billion).

The extent of the required disclosure varies with the size of the offering and the company. Many countries allow smaller companies or those listing on smaller exchanges to file simpler statements. In the United States, if a company going public has revenues of less than $25 million, it can use SEC Form SB-2 as opposed to the exhaustive S-1; those raising less than $5 million can file using Regulation A, which requires even less disclosure.

---

[26] For details, see Hsuan-Chi Chen and Jay R. Ritter, "The Seven Percent Solution," *Journal of Finance* 55 (2000): 1105–31.

[27] According to Jay Ritter, "The Costs of Going Public," *Journal of Financial Economics* 19, no. 2 (1987): 269–81, there are substantial economies of scale in the direct costs of going public. Direct costs for transactions above $10 million averaged 9.3 percent; for the smallest transactions (raising less than $2 million), they were close to 20 percent.

[28] Joseph A. Giannone, "Goldman, JP Morgan Take Minor Blackstone IPO Roles," *Reuters*, June 13, 2007, http://www.reuters.com/article/idUSN1339631720070613, accessed July 28, 2010.

[29] Richard Carter and Steven Manaster, "Initial Public Offerings and Underwriter Reputation," *Journal of Finance* 45, no. 4 (1990): 1045–67.

Companies must conform to other regulations as well. In the United States, the SEC designates the weeks before and after the IPO as the "quiet period." The rules governing the quiet period in the past severely restricted the company from communicating with potential investors, aside from distributing the offering material, called the prospectus, and conducting formal investor presentations (road shows). In 2005, the SEC amended this rule to allow executives to speak to the media as long as the statements were accurate and copies had been filed with the SEC. Electronic road shows are now also permitted as long as they are available to an unrestricted audience; otherwise, the company will have to file the material with the agency.

Marketing the Offering

The investment bank markets the offering by circulating a preliminary prospectus to the institutional investors that might purchase substantial blocks of stock. The preliminary prospectus is known in the United States as a **red herring** (due to the disclaimers printed in red on the cover) and in other countries as a preliminary or pathfinder prospectus.[30] A prestigious underwriter will know more sophisticated investors; recall that Megginson and Weiss found that venture-backed IPOs had greater institutional holdings. Because institutions tend to be better informed and have longer time horizons, they are more likely to be long-term holders of the stock, contributing to a stable price in the market. This gives the company itself a reputation for stability.

In many situations, the company's management goes on a **road show** to make presentations that describe the company and its prospects to institutional investors. In addition to answering questions about the company, road shows provide the investment banks with information on how investors regard the company and its prospects.[31] During the difficult market of 2008, the credit card processor Visa went public on the New York Stock Exchange. Along with its investment banks, J.P. Morgan and Goldman Sachs, the company engaged in a road show that had three teams traveling across three continents to conduct 36 group investor meetings (a total of 1,700 investors) in 10 countries and 24 cities.[32] Visa listed at $44 per share in March 2008, raising $17.9 billion.[33] Generally, the executives will visit the recognized financial centers in the company's major markets. If the company is located in a second-tier city, it might also visit regional hubs; a company based in Phoenix, Arizona, might visit Salt Lake City and Tucson.[34]

Pricing the Offering

The method used to determine the price of the offering varies. In the United States, the most common method is "book building." In this case, the investment bankers use their preliminary research to establish a price range for the shares and publish it in the red herring. In the **book-building** process, potential investors submit bids to the underwriter for the number of shares they would purchase at a given price. If demand appears particularly strong or weak, the price may be revised and investors revisited to get their new bids. Essentially, the underwriter gathers information to create a demand curve for the company's shares.[35] The lead underwriter compiles a central "book" in which all indications of interest are recorded. If there is insufficient interest in the company in the established price range, the company and the investment bank will have to

---

[30] Tim Jenkinson and Alexander Ljungqvist, *Going Public*, 2nd ed. (Oxford: Oxford University Press, 2000), 13.

[31] Ibid., 14.

[32] http://www.imagination.com/work/casestudy/visa/; accessed August 9, 2010.

[33] Katie Benner, "Visa IPO Prices at Record $17.9 Billion," *CNNMoney.com*, March 19, 2008, available at http://money.cnn.com/2008/03/18/news/companies/visa_ipo.fortune/index.htm, accessed August 9, 2010.

[34] Ross Geddes, *IPOs and Equity Offerings* (Burlington, MA and Oxford: Butterworth-Heinemann, 2003), 167.

[35] For more on book building, see Jenkinson and Ljungqvist, *Going Public*, 18.

decide whether to drop the price or delay the offering—that is, whether the lack of interest is due to characteristics of the company at that price or to the market at that time.

In some countries, such as Singapore, Finland, and the United Kingdom,[36] the share price is set before gathering information about demand. This is called a "fixed price" approach. During the marketing period, the underwriter learns how many shares would be demanded at that price. Shares are then allocated across the interested investors. If the listing is oversubscribed, many countries allocate shares proportionately across the investors, sometimes requiring payment up front to reduce strategic overbidding. Another approach is to allocate shares randomly.[37]

Lately, auctions have been tested in the United States. They were widely popular in the United Kingdom until the mid-1980s, when they suddenly ceased; they have also been used in France, Israel, and many other countries (though in many places they have subsequently been abandoned). As opposed to book building, where, as Christine Hurt noted, "the lead underwriter [has] all of the control, all of the time,"[38] in an auction, stock is offered equally to all bidders. The investment bank creates a demand curve as investors submit bids for certain amounts and prices. The price is set at the highest price that will sell all the stock.[39]

Fees for auctions are usually 3 to 4 percent of the total money raised,[40] thus making them more economical to the company; but the approach has yet to be widely adopted in the United States and has struggled in many markets. Proponents of auctions claim that they include more small investors. Detractors of the process have cited the possibility that small investors are less likely to educate themselves about the company and thus may overpay for the stock, leading to a post-offering price drop. These concerns have led to a possible "lemons" problem—that auctions are thought by some to be the IPO avenue for companies that cannot go public in more conventional ways.[41]

The Morningstar Auction

While perhaps the most widely known auction IPO in the United States was that of Google, a more successful one is that of Morningstar, the investment-research company. With the boutique firm WR Hambrecht + Co. as underwriter, Morningstar's auction raised $162 million, and 8.75 million shares sold at prices at or above $18.50. The price rose 8.4 percent on the first day of trading.[42] While the post-IPO price rise is common, the average amount is 18.4 percent,[43] indicating that Morningstar suffered less underpricing than was customary and therefore could keep more of its value. Interestingly, the big institutional investor Fidelity, which usually receives substantial allotments from IPOs, received no Morningstar shares because its bid of $17.50 was lower than the market-clearing price.[44]

---

[36] Bruno Biais and Anne Marie Faugeron-Crouzet, "IPO Auctions: English, Dutch, French, and Internet," *Journal of Financial Intermediation* 11, no. 1 (2002): 9–36 cited in Christine Hurt, "What Google Can't Tell Us About Auctions (And What It Can)," *University of Toledo Law Review*, 403 (2006): 403–438, accessed July 28, 2010.

[37] Jenkinson and Ljungqvist, *Going Public*, 16.

[38] Christine Hurt, "What Google Can't Tell Us About Auctions".

[39] Randall Smith, "Heard on the Street," *Wall Street Journal*, July 6, 2005, C1, http://schwert.ssb.rochester.edu/f423/WSJ050706_IPO.pdf, accessed August 2, 2010.

[40] Ibid.

[41] Nayantara Hensel, "Are Dutch Auctions Right for Your IPO?" *Harvard Business School Working Knowledge*, April 11, 2005, http://hbswk.hbs.edu/archive/4747.html, accessed July 28, 2010.

[42] Smith, "Heard on the Street."

[43] Jay R. Ritter, "Differences in European and American IPO Markets," *European Financial Management* 9, no. 4 (2003): 421–34.

[44] Smith, "Heard on the Street."

Well-regarded investment banks in the United States typically undertake only "firm commitment" offerings. In these, unlike "best efforts" offerings, the investment bank commits to sell the shares to investors at a set price. The price is not set, though, until the night before the offering; so the investment bank runs only a small risk of not being able to sell the shares. At the "pricing meeting," the investment bank and the company combine all the available information about demand to determine the price at which the company goes public. In making this decision, the bankers are also likely to factor in the valuation of comparable companies, along with discounted cash-flow analyses of the company's projected cash flows. In the situation of Tesla described earlier, the final share price was $17—outside the $14 to $16 range because of general enthusiasm for the company. The shares to be sold are then allocated to the purchasers. Some may receive particularly generous allotments based on the quality of the pricing information they supplied.

The Day of the Offer . . . and Beyond

Regardless of the price set at the time of the offering, the share price is likely to rise on the next trading day—in fact, even the first trade usually occurs at a substantial premium to the IPO price. Figure 7.2 shows the average amount of **underpricing** calculated in a wide variety of studies over a host of time periods. Many of the most outrageously underpriced IPOs in the United States—such as the 900 percent underpricing of the TheGlobe.com—occurred during the dot-com boom. Nor is underpricing unique to the U.S. exchanges—research on IPOs on exchanges from Austria to Greece to Nigeria to the United Kingdom corroborates the phenomenon.[45] The median firm on a U.S. exchange experiences only a minor price jump, although a small but significant number of firms have seen substantial increases.

FIGURE 7.2 Average share price increases

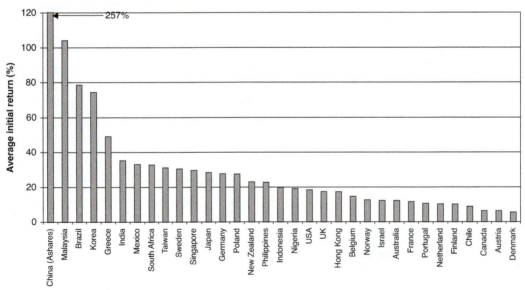

Source: Adapted from Jay R. Ritter, "Differences in European and American IPO Markets," *European Financial Management* 9, no. 4 (2003): 423–24.

---

[45] Ritter, "Differences in European and American IPO Markets."

Underpricing represents a substantial cost for the companies and their investors because it "leaves money on the table"; that is, the investment bank could have set a higher price, allowing the company and investors to raise more money. As noted earlier, investment banks with better reputations and private equity investors that are more experienced are associated with reduced underpricing. At the same time, it persists.

The effect has generated a host of academic research. A whole set of explanations, ranging from fear of legal action to the nature of the book-building process, have been proposed. Three leading explanations are as follows:

1. *Compensation for Information Gaps* If the company is a young technology operation that no one has ever heard of, investors may need a discount to be persuaded to purchase its stock.[46] Uninformed or unsophisticated investors might fear that investors with more information will purchase the more desirable stocks—and leave them with the less attractive ones. This could be summarized as the Groucho Marx approach to IPOs—I wouldn't want to hold shares in any IPO that I could buy. To entice these prospective investors to buy, they must be given a discount, and hence, underpricing. The initial "pop" that the investor gets may serve as compensation for any subsequent price drop.

2. *The Bandwagon Effect*[47] Economists have become increasingly interested in "cascades," where individual actors make decisions based on what others do rather than on their own information. IPOs may be another example of this. In the context of IPOs, if the offering seems to be doing well, other investors may rush in; if it encounters weak demand, investors will shy away. To cause such a cascade, investment banks may sell IPO shares at a lower price to sophisticated investors. Seeing this activity, less sophisticated investors will rush in and buy the shares in the secondary market at a higher price.

3. *Investment Bank Market Power* This hypothesis maintains that investment banks deliberately set prices too low to transfer wealth to select clients who are permitted to participate in the IPO. These investors repay the banks for this favor by steering business their way. This is not without merit, as the litigation about the "spinning" of IPO shares to favored clients of investment banks has demonstrated.[48]

In the immediate period following the IPO (often 30 days), underwriters in the United States commit to stabilizing the price of the stock and try to keep it above the offering price. To do this, the bank will almost always use the "Green Shoe" option, a complex feature named for the 1963 offering where it was introduced. In essence, the bank reserves the option to sell 15 percent more shares than the stated offering size. That is, if the offering was 2 million shares, the bank will sell 2.3 million. If the price rises after the offering, the bank will declare that the offering was 15 percent larger than the size initially projected. If the price drops below the offering price, however, the banks will buy back the additional 15 percent of the shares. This activity, it is hoped, will drive up the price, allowing the bank to fulfill its obligation to support the price. At the same time, the bank will make a profit on the difference between the selling price of the IPO shares and the price at which it buys them back. If the bank is particularly worried about the share price falling, it may sell even more than the 15 percent allowed by the Green Shoe option. This puts the

---

[46] This theory is proposed in Kevin F. Rock, "Why New Issues are Underpriced," *Journal of Financial Economics* 15, nos. 1–2 (1986): 187–212.

[47] This idea was first laid out in Ivo Welch, "Sequential Sales, Learning and Cascades," *Journal of Finance* 47 (1992): 695–732.

[48] For a comprehensive study of the impact of this practice, see Xiaoding Liu and Jay Ritter, "The Economic Consequences of IPO Spinning," *Review of Financial Studies* 23, no. 5 (2010): 2024–59.

Spinning the IPO

In the late 1990s whirl of tech stock IPOs, investment banks became known for spinning stocks to preferred clients. That is, the banks allocated stock in a hot IPO to executives in a different company, sometimes providing shares at the IPO price after they had begun trading and risen in value. In one example,[49] Robertson Stephens, a reputable investment bank, allocated 100,000 shares of Pixar Animation's IPO to Joseph Cayre, CEO and majority owner of GT Interactive Software. Cayre's Pixar stock appreciated 77 percent on the first day. A month later, GT Interactive Software went public, using Robertson Stephens as its lead underwriter, and later hired the bank to advise it on some acquisitions. Robertson Stephens made more than $5 million in fees from GT Interactive Software work. Unlike the typical allocation of IPO shares to institutional investors, these "spin" shares went to individuals at corporations that might do business with the investment bank. Some observers called the practice bribery; others viewed it as a marketing technique akin to golf outings. Whatever one's view, the technique was effective, as shown in Liu and Ritter's study[50] of fifty-six companies that went public between 1996 and 2000 where top executives received stock from other hot IPOs: only 6 percent of stock issuers whose executives received spun shares changed investment banks in a subsequent issue, while 31 percent of other issuers switched. Moreover, Liu and Ritter found that these offerings also had more severe underpricing than others that were not spun—on average, 23 percent more than the market average for the period.

bank in a "naked short" position, where it will have to buy back the shares regardless of the price movement. If the share price continues to fall, the bank again supports the price and also profits from the price differential; but if the price rises, it will have to purchase the shares at a loss.[51]

Underwriters continue to interact with the company going forward, by providing analyst coverage, serving as the primary market maker to ensure orderly daily trading, and, often, continuing to supply financial advice. The relationship appears to be long-lasting. Roughly 70 percent of companies completing a follow-on offering in the United States in the three years after the IPO used the same underwriter as they did for the IPO.[52]

The Impact of Private Equity on IPOs

We have noted the impact of VC backing on the selection of underwriters and on the certification of the companies. In addition, VC support appears to influence the company's performance at the time of the IPO and thereafter. Several studies have shown that the involvement of VC investors who hold significant amounts of stock at the IPO and continue to do so helps reduce the

---

[49] Michael Siconolfi, "The Spin Desk," *Wall Street Journal*, November 12, 1997, A1.

[50] Liu and Ritter, "The Economic Consequences of IPO Spinning."

[51] For a discussion of the role of investment banks in market making, see Katrina Ellis, Roni Michaely, and Maureen O'Hara, "When the Underwriter is the Market Maker: An Examination of Trading in the IPO Aftermarket," *Journal of Finance* 55 (2000): 1039–74.

[52] Laurie Krigman, Wayne H. Shaw, and Kent L. Womack, "Why Do Firms Switch Underwriters?" *Journal of Financial Economics* 60, nos. 2–3 (2001): 245–84.

underpricing that the company suffers and then helps it perform better in the years after the offering. Yet private equity firms sometimes rush companies to market. Let us examine some studies that assess the overall contributions from private equity firms to their newly public portfolio companies.

Barry et al.[53] examined 433 IPOs by VC-backed companies between 1978 and 1987 and found that the value of this continuing involvement and its accompanying governance varied with the quality of the VC firm. Underpricing fell with the number of venture capitalists invested in the company and the amount of equity they owned, perhaps because the investment banks wanted to maintain good relationships with them. It also fell with the length of time the lead venture capitalist had served on the board; the age of the lead VC firm; and the number of past IPOs among the lead investor's portfolio companies—all indicators of VC quality. Corroborating the findings of Megginson and Weiss, Barry et al. found that VC-backed IPOs had a higher median value than non-VC-backed ones and tended to be sold by more prestigious underwriters. In addition, VC firms tended to take companies public at an earlier stage of development, as indicated by a higher likelihood of continued negative earnings in the first year after the IPO. They were able to do this because, as noted earlier, the venture investors stayed on the board to continue to provide monitoring and advisory services.

But what happens in the long run? If VC backing has a positive impact on the IPO (by reducing underpricing), might it reverse itself after the VC firms sell their positions and leave the board? Are VC-backed companies better prepared to succeed in the public arena, or does their early entry make them burn out, like a child prodigy? And how does the market respond to the continued negative earnings that often occur with young, high-growth companies?

A body of research has established that IPOs overall have tended to underperform the market significantly over the past twenty years. This might imply that public market investors are too optimistic about the performance of such newly public firms.[54] In that case, we might ask ourselves whether VC backing exacerbates this tendency.

In comparing the performance of a sample of 934 VC-backed IPOs from 1972 to 1992 and 3,407 non-VC-backed IPOs from 1975 to 1992, Alon Brav and Paul Gompers[55] determined that VC-backed companies outperformed those without VC backing over a five-year period if the returns were weighted equally (i.e., not weighted by the company's market value). Weighting by value improved the performance of the non-VC-backed stocks and narrowed the performance gap. After examining the question further, the authors found that the underperformance of IPOs in general was due to the smaller non-VC-backed companies, and that this poor performance endured regardless of whether the company had recently gone public. In short, VC-backed IPOs did not underperform the market; rather, IPO performance data was dragged down by the inclusion of offerings from very small, non-VC-backed companies.

Moreover, as with so much else in private equity, the venture capitalists involved make a difference. Using data on investments made between 1991 and 2001, Rajarishi Nahata[56] determined that companies backed by more reputable venture capitalists tended to outperform the market for at least four years after the IPO. Not only were the companies more promising initially, but the VC firm also created operational improvements. Nahata developed a reputation factor that he called the "IPO capitalization share," based on the cumulative market capitalization of IPOs

[53] Christopher B. Barry, Chris J. Muscarella, Josh W. Peavy III, and Michael R. Vetsuypens, "The Role of Venture Capital in the Creation of Public Companies," *Journal of Financial Economics* 27 (1990): 447–71.

[54] Documented in Jay Ritter, "The Long-Run Performance of Initial Public Offerings," *Journal of Finance* 42 (1991): 365–94; and Tim Loughran and Jay Ritter, "The New Issues Puzzle," *Journal of Finance* 50 (1995): 23–52.

[55] Alon Brav and Paul Gompers, "Myth or Reality? The Long-Run Underperformance of Initial Public Offerings: Evidence from Venture and Nonventure Capital-Backed Companies," *Journal of Finance* 52, no. 4 (1997).

[56] Rajarishi Nahata, "Venture Capital Reputation and Investment Performance," *Journal of Financial Economics* 90 (2008): 127–51.

backed by a given VC firm. Companies backed by firms with a higher IPO capitalization share were less likely to fail and more likely to have an IPO. The top VC firms (rated by IPO capitalization share) were associated with more IPOs, medium VC firms with more acquisitions, and the least reputable VC firms with more shutdowns. Not only were companies backed by the top venture investors more likely to go public, but they went public at an earlier stage in their lives, and these offerings performed better.

IPOs as Exits from LBOs

Although we have been talking thus far about IPOs from VC investments, buyout firms also use IPOs to exit from their companies. For investments that use the platform roll-up strategy, an IPO often becomes the only exit available, due to regulatory concerns.

Jerry Cao and Josh Lerner[57] authored one of the few papers dealing with recent LBO IPOs (called **reverse LBOs**, or RLBOs). Using a database of 526 RLBOs between 1981 and 2003, they determined that an average of 12.7 percent of LBOs were exited via RLBO over that period, although the percentage varied from 0 percent in 1982 to a high of 30.7 percent in 1992.[58] Table 7.7 shows that firms undergoing RLBOs had usually been private for almost 3.5 years before the IPO. Again, private equity ownership appeared to certify the company by reducing the amount of underpricing relative to comparable companies. The buyout group held, on average, 59 percent of the company's shares before the IPO but was diluted to 40 percent thereafter. Given the size of

Table 7.7   Characteristics of RLBOs

Characteristic	Mean
Years private after LBO	3.46
Buyout group capital raised before RLBO ($ millions)	$4,452.13
Buyout group ownership before IPO	58.9%
Buyout group ownership after IPO	40.5%
Director/management ownership before IPO	54.6%
Director/management ownership after IPO	38.0%
Board share of buyout group	44.0%
Comparison to Non-Buyout-Backed IPOs	
Gross proceeds: RLBOs ($ millions)	$105.73
Gross proceeds: non-buyout-backed IPOs ($ millions)	$55.52
Underpricing for RLBOs	12.88%
Underpricing for non-buyout-backed IPOs	22.18%

Note: Sample consists of 526 RLBOs and 5,706 other IPOs between January 1981 and December 2003.
Source: Adapted from Jerry Cao and Josh Lerner, "The Performance of Reverse Leveraged Buyouts," *Journal of Financial Economics* 91, no. 2 (2009): 144, Tables 2 and 3.

[57] Jerry Cao and Josh Lerner, "The Performance of Reverse Leveraged Buyouts," *Journal of Financial Economics*, 91, no. 2 (2009): 139–57.
[58] Ibid., 144.

this position, the firm still had a vested interest in the company's continued performance. The authors concluded that RLBOs tended to be larger in size and were backed by more reputable underwriters (as also noted in the venture IPO certification literature). While the companies carried more leverage than other IPOs, they were more profitable.

In addition, Cao and Lerner determined the RLBOs in general performed slightly better than other IPOs and comparable companies in most cases. There were differences across offerings, though: in particular, "quick flips"—those taken public within a year of the LBO—perform significantly worse than others. The authors speculated that poor performance may reflect the fact that the "flipped" firms had not spent enough time under private equity ownership to adopt many operational improvements. With added leverage and few improvements, their performance is, unsurprisingly, poor.

Acquisitions

As we discussed earlier, acquisitions are another viable exit route from private-equity-backed investments. In fact, since 1990, they have made up roughly 65 percent of the exits from U.S. private-equity-backed companies.[59] Acquisitions play an important role in both gain maximization and loss minimization—unlike IPOs, where the company almost invariably has positive prospects.[60]

Mergers and Acquisitions

Often, acquisitions are referred to as mergers and acquisitions (M&A). Although similar—an exit achieved by combining two companies—each term has a specific definition. In an acquisition, one company simply buys the other for stock, cash, or a combination of the two. Management of the acquired company may be retained in various roles within the acquirer; but the acquired company's board is dissolved, and the shareholders receive either cash or shares in the acquirer. In a merger-of-equals transaction, the two companies become one in a stock-for-stock trade. The board contains directors from each company; the CEOs work out a power-sharing arrangement. Merger-of-equals transactions have become fairly rare—a recent one was the TicketMaster-LiveNation merger in 2009 following the Sirius and XM satellite radio transaction announced in 2007. In the late 1990s, though, several leviathan merger deals occurred, including the mergers of Morgan Stanley and Dean Witter, and Travelers and Citigroup.[61]

Growth by acquisition is a common strategy. Companies may buy others to acquire technology, products, customer groups, geographic presence, brands, or distribution channels. During the Internet boom, large telecoms companies purchased start-ups both to acquire their technology and to keep it away from competitors. In a thoughtful analysis of the reasons behind

---

[59] Data from Thomson Reuters.

[60] There are, of course, numerous examples of private-equity-backed companies with positive prospects that went public and then went out of business due either to being rushed to market or to external events. Among them are eToys, WebVan, and Pets.com (see "20 Worst Venture Capital Investments of All Time," *InsideCRM*, November 19, 2007, http://www. insidecrm.com/features/20-worst-vc-investments-111907/, accessed July 30, 2010). For LBO examples, Thomas H. Lee purchased Refco, Inc., a financial services company, in 2004 for $500 million and took it public in August 2005; two months later, the company filed for bankruptcy protection; other companies such as Regal Cinemas and Simmons Bedding filed for bankruptcy before IPOs.

[61] Steven M. Davidoff, "The Return of the Merger of Equals," *Deal Blog—The New York Times*, February 17, 2009, http:// dealbook.blogs.nytimes.com/2009/02/17/the-return-of-the-merger-of-equals/, accessed July 31, 2010.

acquisitions among public companies, Gregor Andrade, Mark Mitchell, and Erik Stafford[62] determined that this activity is clustered by industry, often in response to external shocks. The most dramatic shock they noted was deregulation, although others included technological innovations and supply shocks such as oil price increases.

We are, however, more concerned with acquisitions of private companies. The challenge of an acquisition exit for a private equity investor is that it takes two to tango. Finding an acquirer can be difficult. Not even the tactic of listing the company on a billboard with the slogan, "If You Don't Buy This Company, We'll Shoot This [small furry creature],"[63] assures success. Much of the effort of an acquisition is simply finding the acquirer.

When investors and management agree to sell a company, an investment bank often is retained to represent it. Again, the investors' reputation influences the quality of the investment bank and thus its knowledge of potential acquirers. The two parties, the bank and the board of directors, will define the sales process strategy—are they trying to get rid of the company or get top dollar for it? The bank will prepare a preliminary write-up and the more detailed offering memorandum (known as a **bank book** or a confidential information memorandum—CIM, among other things). The bank often performs a valuation exercise, putting a rough price on the company for internal use only, and creates a list of possible buyers. Depending on the company's size, it may create a (physical or electronic) data room where financial information is made available to potential buyers.

After receiving a "teaser" with high-level information, interested potential buyers contact the bank. They usually have to sign confidentiality agreements before receiving the bank book and the process overview. The bank arranges initial meetings between buyers and the company and, in concert with the company, responds to due diligence questions. A series of meetings between the company and various potential buyers (it is hoped) ensues. After an initial round of bidding, the company management makes presentations describing the company's business and prospects to those parties whose initial bids fell within the acceptable range. These are followed by additional due diligence. As the field of buyers narrows, each has access to more detailed information.

Once buyers have sufficient information, they typically submit indications of interest and/or letters of intent (LOIs), along with term sheets. These are negotiated by the board and the buyer, with assistance from the investment bank. Finally, the preferred deal will be accepted.

Once the deal has been agreed in principle, there are many points for negotiation. The acquirer may buy the company in a stock deal, acquiring the whole entity including possible future liabilities, or in an asset deal, purchasing only the company's assets. (These choices may also have differing tax implications.) Timing may be an issue, along with the positions of the management team in the new company. The currency, whether cash or stock in the acquirer, is always a concern. Investors in the acquired company are likely to prefer the immediacy of cash to a large block of stock that may take many quarters to sell, while the buyer may prefer to make the purchase with stock rather than deplete its cash holdings. This assumes that the acquirer is public; we discuss the implications of a private-to-private acquisition later. There may be an earn-out, where part of the payment is conditional on the achievement of certain operating metrics. On average, the acquisition process takes slightly over six months.[64]

Private-to-private acquisitions can be more complex since they involve valuing two illiquid assets. Sometimes they are cash transactions; often, especially if the acquirer has made substantial progress, the acquiring firm uses its own stock. Usually the board of the acquired company is

---

[62] Gregor Andrade, Mark Mitchell, and Erik Stafford, "New Evidence and Perspectives on Mergers," *Journal of Economic Perspectives* 15, no. 2 (2001): 103–20.

[63] With apologies to *The National Lampoon*, January 1973 cover. For clarity, this approach has never been tried—at least to the authors' knowledge.

[64] Hamilton Lin, CFA "M&A Process Timetable," http://www.wallst-training.com/WST_M_and_A_Process_and_Timetable.pdf, accessed August 4, 2010.

disbanded; but occasionally, members will join the acquirer. Selling a company to another private company for stock is often a loss-minimizing strategy since the investors not only continue to hold illiquid securities, but have a smaller position in a company where they have little if any influence.

Even at the end, the buyer does final due diligence. Deals can be scuttled at the last minute, as with the aborted merger of Continental and United Airlines in 2008 (which was revived in 2010), but that is rare. The definitive agreement is negotiated, the necessary forms are filed with the appropriate regulatory bodies, and the deal is announced.

Some acquisitions, though, can be consummated much more quickly. In September 2009, the Japanese beverage company Suntory purchased Orangina from Lion and Blackstone for $3.82 billion, because it wanted to diversify its portfolio and use Orangina's distribution system to enter the European market.[65] Eager to avoid an auction, Suntory set a condition that Orangina's management and investors could not shop the company, a time-honored strategy for increasing interest in a deal and raising its eventual price. Also unusual was the fact that the two sides—the lead partners of the private equity firms, along with Lion's GP Javier Ferrán (who served as chairman of Orangina's board) and Suntory—agreed on the terms of the transaction before the negotiations began.

The process took an unusually quick two months because Suntory, with substantial cash on its balance sheet and Japanese banks willing to underwrite the deal, was a credible acquirer.[66] In restricting the private equity investors' ability to shop Orangina, Suntory acquired a significant advantage in the negotiations. Recall, however, when the transaction occurred—in September 2009, when liquidity was a rare commodity for any private equity firm and investors were particularly skeptical about "mega-funds." In addition, Blackstone was raising its sixth private equity fund, which had been cut from $20 billion to "$10 to $15 billion" since the global economic crisis began. A liquidity event would help the firm convince investors of its continued investment savvy.

In choosing to acquire a private company in its own industry (beverages), Suntory corroborated the findings of Laurence Capron and Jung-Chin Shen.[67] Using a multinational sample of 92 acquisitions by public firms of public (52) and private (40) companies, Capron and Shen explored the role of information in the acquirer's choice between a public and a private target. They found that an acquirer will purchase a private company in a familiar industry because of the difficulty of finding and accurately assessing information about the operation. Therefore, the acquirer's private knowledge allows it to value the company more precisely (and with more scope for its own value creation) than would another firm without this information. Public companies are to be preferred when the acquirer wants to expand beyond its area of expertise, because information is readily available. While this argument is interesting, there are many examples of companies making disastrous acquisitions of or mergers with public companies in industries they did not know well, such as Time-Warner's merger with AOL in 2000.

A private company can take steps to signal its value long before putting itself up for acquisition by taking investment from a corporate venture capital (CVC) operation[68] or creating a strategic alliance. Research thus far has shown that these strategies have differing impacts on the company and the acquirers in an exit.

---

[65] Marietta Cauchi, "Suntory of Japan Makes Binding Offer to Acquire Orangina," *Wall Street Journal*, September 23, 2009, http://online.wsj.com/article/NA_WSJ_PUB:SB125360946080930345.html, accessed July 29, 2010.

[66] David Rothnie, "Suntory Adds Fizz to Orangina Takeover," *Institutional Investor*, November 2009.

[67] Laurence Capron and Jung-Chin Shen, "Acquisitions of Private vs. Public Firms," *Strategic Management Journal* 28 (2007): 891–911.

[68] CVCs are the divisions of corporations that pursue investments in private companies, usually with an eye toward more strategic than financial return. Intel Capital, Microsoft's IP Ventures, Eli Lilly Ventures, and Johnson & Johnson Ventures are a few examples of CVC programs.

Intuitively, it seems to make sense for a CVC entity to invest in a start-up before the parent's acquisition of that company. In a "try before you buy" approach, information gathered by the investment professionals presumably reduces the information asymmetry that would otherwise exist. David Benson and Rosemarie Ham Ziedonis[69] studied 431 entrepreneurial companies (less than twelve years old and with fewer than a thousand employees) acquired by the parents of CVCs between 1987 and 2003, of which 81 had received an earlier CVC investment. They found an interesting pattern: the market reacted positively to acquisitions of non-CVC companies, increasing the parent firm's valuation on a net-of-market basis (i.e., adjusting for the overall return of the market) by +0.76 percent. The market reacted to the acquisition of CVC companies (i.e., the acquisition of the investee company by the CVC's parent), however, with a negative return of −1.01 percent. One possible explanation is that the CVC parent is likely to overpay if its subsidiary has invested in the firm, perhaps because it has "fallen in love" with its investment.

These results differed substantially from those of Matthew Higgins and Daniel Rodriguez.[70] Their study focused on 160 acquisitions in the life sciences industry made between 1994 and 2001, where the companies had been in alliances with the acquirer. The market responded *more* favorably to the acquisition of former alliance partners than non-alliance partners, and the response was particularly positive when the acquirer's product pipeline was especially thin. Given that life sciences companies made up only 12 percent of Benson and Ziedonis's sample, the difference between these two studies may reflect the differing dynamics between industries. In particular, pharmaceutical companies may be able to more readily incorporate acquired products in a seamless manner and may be more reliant on such external research and development efforts.

One example of a CVC-parent acquisition was that of Playdom, a social gaming company that Disney acquired in July 2010 for $563.2 million plus a possible $200 million earn-out. Playdom had closed a $33 million financing round from a consortium of investors that included Disney's Steamboat Ventures the month before at a $345 million post-money valuation.[71] In total, the company had raised $76 million since its founding in early 2008. Disney had decided that it needed to have a presence in the social gaming industry, and Playdom was one of the top three in the sector. Compared to the market leader, Zynga, which was valued at a rumored $5 billion, Playdom was attractively priced.[72] In addition, Disney already had substantial information about the company. Whether the timing and price of the acquisition had anything to do with the information that Disney acquired through the Steamboat Ventures staff, we cannot be sure.

It is interesting to consider whether alliances create different dynamics among acquirers than do CVC investments. Both certainly help bring a company to the attention of others. Using data on a cross-section of industries and both public and private firms that created alliances between 1987 and 2001, Laura Lindsay[73] described the impact of venture capitalists in creating strategic alliances and noted that allied portfolio companies linked by a common venture capitalist were more likely to have a successful exit, whether it was an acquisition or an IPO. She posited

---

[69] David Benson and Rosemarie Ham Ziedonis, "Corporate Venture Capital and the Returns to Acquiring Entrepreneurial Firms," *Journal of Financial Economics* (forthcoming).

[70] Matthew J. Higgins and Daniel Rodriguez, "The Outsourcing of R&D through Acquisitions in the Pharmaceutical Industry," *Journal of Financial Economics* 80, no. 2 (2006): 351–83.

[71] Michael Arrington, "Playdom Pulls Down $33 Million More in Funding," *Techcrunch.com*, June 21, 2010, http://techcrunch.com/2010/06/21/playdom-steamboat-bessemer-venture-round/, accessed July 30, 2010.

[72] Michael Arrington, "Playdom Acquired by Disney for up to $763.2 Million," *Techcrunch.com*, July 27, 2010, http://techcrunch.com/2010/07/27/playdom-acquired-by-disney-for-up-to-763-2-million/, accessed July 29, 2010; and Tomio Geron, "Playdom Investor Jeremy Liew on Why Disney Stepped Up," *Wall Street Journal—Venture Dispatch*, July 28, 2010, http://blogs.wsj.com/venturecapital/2010/07/28/playdom-investor-jeremy-liew-on-why-disney-stepped-up/, accessed August 9, 2010.

[73] Laura Lindsay, "Blurring Firm Boundaries: The Role of Venture Capital in Strategic Alliances," *Journal of Finance* 63, no. 3 (2010): 1137–68.

that the venture capitalists' monitoring role ensured that all alliance members respected intellectual property (IP) rights and generally "played fair."

Another aspect of an acquisition is the currency in which it occurs. Sometimes—as with Orangina and Playdom—the acquisition price is paid in cash. In other situations, the acquisition is partly or entirely funded by the parent's stock. Andrade et al. found that stock-funded acquisitions of public companies resulted in negative net-of-market returns to the acquirer and positive net-of-market returns to the (publicly traded) acquisition. This result would suggest that the acquirer is thought to be overpaying for the acquisition.

A Special Kind of Acquisition—The Secondary Buyout

Secondary buyouts, where a buyout firm acquires a company from the portfolio of another buyout firm, have become more common recently—in fact, secondary buyouts in the United Kingdom reached £4.8 billion ($7.3 billion) in the first half of 2010, and the number of secondary buyouts in those six months, 21, was higher than the 14 recorded in all of 2009.[74] In the United States, too, secondaries are playing a larger role, accounting for one-third of the buyout activity in the first quarter of 2010.[75] Overall, Per Strömberg determined that 30 percent of buyouts exited between 2000 and 2007 had done so through secondary buyouts.[76]

Let's look at just two examples. In July 2010, BC Partners and Silver Lake Partners agreed to purchase MultiPlan, a U.S. health-care manager, from Carlyle Group and Welsh, Carson, Anderson & Stowe, the buyout firms that purchased it in 2006. The transaction valued the company at $3.1 billion; Carlyle was expected to make more than three times its initial investment.[77] At the same time in Europe, Lion Capital announced its acquisition of Picard, a French frozen-food maker, from BC Partners.[78] The value was rumored to be close to $1.94 billion, or almost twice BC's initial equity investment. BC Partners itself had bought Picard in a secondary buyout for €1.3 billion ($1.16 billion) from Candover in 2004. In 2001, Candover had purchased the company as a spin-out of Carrefour for €920 million ($791 million).[79]

LBO firms maintain that these transactions are "win-win." The company's new owners are specialized firms acquainted with the peculiarities of a buyout structure. Moreover, the new owners may have knowledge and contacts that suit the needs of the company at its current stage of development. In the Picard transaction, Lion's focus on customer brands and food companies (its portfolio includes Jimmy Choo shoes, Wheatabix, and Wagamama restaurants) might support Picard as it implements plans to open three hundred more stores in France and streamline merchandising and supply chain operations.[80] BC Partners provides MultiPlan with a European network, although the extent of its usefulness in such a nationally idiosyncratic industry as health care is unclear.

---

[74] "UK Buyout Value Overtakes 2009 by 45% in First Half of 2010," *Centre for Management Buyout Research*, June 28, 2010, http://www.nottingham.ac.uk/business/cmbor/Press/28June2010.html, accessed July 29, 2010.

[75] Data from Dealogic, cited in Selina Harrison, "Uptick in Private Equity Secondary Buyouts," *Financier Worldwide*, June 2010, http://www.financierworldwide.com/article.php?id=6721, accessed July 29, 2010.

[76] Per Strömberg, "The New Demographics of Private Equity," in *Globalization of Alternative Investments Working Papers, Volume 1: The Global Economic Impact of Private Equity Report 2008* ed. Anuradha Gurung and Josh Lerner (New York: World Economic Forum USA, 2008), 3–26. Available at http://www.weforum.org/pdf/cgi/pe/Full_Report.pdf.

[77] Peter Lattmann, "Buyout-Shop Swap MultiPlan in $3.1 Billion LBO," *Wall Street Journal*, July 9, 2010, http://online. wsj.com/article/NA_WSJ_PUB:SB10001424052748703609004575355392787558722.html, accessed July 29, 2010.

[78] Quentin Webb and Victoria Howley, "Lion to Buy Picard in Biggest French LBO since 2008," *Reuters.com*, July 26, 2010, http://in.reuters.com/article/2010/07/26/us-picard-idINTRE66P27B20100726, accessed July 8, 2011.

[79] Marietta Cauchi, "Lion Buys BC Partners' Picard," *Dow Jones Newswires*, July 27, 2010, http://www.efinancialnews. com/story/2010-07-27/lion-picard-bcpartners, accessed August 1, 2010; and "Candover Realizes Investment in Picard for Euro 1.3 Billion," *PR Newswire UK Disclosure*, October 24, 2004.

[80] Webb and Howley, "Lion to Buy Picard in Biggest French LBO since 2008."

To a certain degree, different buyout operations with different skill sets may indeed add value as sequential owners of a developing company. This argument has long been used in VC—an early-stage company is backed by a firm with a smaller fund that specializes in managing the growth of young companies, only to graduate to the portfolios of larger firms with deeper pockets that can support the company's more expensive merchandising and sales efforts later in its life. In the VC case, though, the new group typically buys additional shares offered by the company, diluting the existing owners, rather than purchasing the original investor's stake. Lion's expertise with consumer brands might well help Picard create additional value. For the sellers in a secondary buyout, the transaction creates gains for their investors. Liquidity-starved LPs might be delighted to receive returns of any sort, and earlier returns help the GPs create good performance figures for use in raising another fund. Lastly, secondary transactions can be executed more easily than either sales to strategic buyers, which may have to go through protracted negotiations, or public offerings, which are prey to market conditions.[81] For the firms that purchase the company, prior backing by a private equity firm may indicate a clean bill of financial health.

LPs, however, have some concerns with secondary buyouts. First, the same LP may be invested in a number of big buyout funds. Thus the LP receives a check from one firm at the same time that capital is called down by another—for the same company. What does one firm know that the other does not? Second, it is questionable in some instances whether there is scope for additional value generation or whether all the "low-hanging fruit" has been plucked.[82] The biggest issue, though, involves the fees. A company purchased in a secondary buyout has had to pay two sets of transaction fees: once to its initial buyer and then again to the second buyer based on its higher cost basis. In addition, the company often has to pay a termination fee to the selling firm because it will no longer purchase its advisory services, even though the firm is making a gain on the deal.[83] The LPs can argue that this is rent-seeking behavior that transfers value from the company (and the LPs who want returns) to the GPs by reducing the company's value, regardless of any fee offset[84] to the LPs.

OTHER WAYS TO THE EXIT

In addition to exits via acquisition and IPO, there are other types of exits. Some return only part of the investors' funds—through dividends, for instance. Others, like shutdowns, return very little but cut off the private equity firm's continued investment of time and money in a regretted opportunity.

Partial Exits: Dividends

With dividends, the company pays money back to its investors. Dividends constitute a type of partial exit: the company is still in the private equity firm's portfolio and requires guidance and monitoring, but the firm has reduced the deal's risk by reducing the money invested. In some cases, a company may pay a dividend because it lacks the cash to redeem the preferred stock. In other situations, buyout firms may have their companies pay them a dividend that returns much of their equity value while keeping their ownership unchanged. For instance, Hertz Global Holdings, the car rental company, issued new debt to pay its private equity owners (Clayton, Dubilier and Rice;

---

[81] Lattmann, "Buyout-Shop Swap MultiPlan in $3.1 Billion LBO."

[82] Very little research has been done on this question to date. Stefan Bononi's "Secondary Buyouts" May 15, 2010 (unpublished), available at SSRN: http://ssrn.com/abstract=1571249, accessed July 23, 2010) suggests, based on a small sample, that while primary buyouts do create value, secondary buyouts are much less likely to do so.

[83] This situation has become less common since the 2008 financial crisis.

[84] As noted in Chapter 2, some transaction fees are shared between the GPs and the LPs. The LPs usually receive them as offsets against the management fee.

Carlyle; and Merrill Lynch Private Equity) a $1 billion dividend during the fourteen months that they owned it. These payments, though, had a dark side: Hertz's interest costs doubled as a result.[85] In the first quarter of 2010, companies controlled by LBO firms raised $10.8 billion in debt to fund such dividend payments, compared to $1 billion for all of 2009.[86]

As noted in Chapter 5, dividends set up a divergence of interests between the entrepreneur and the investors—the entrepreneur wants to keep the money in the company, and the investors who receive the dividend want it paid to them. Yet dividends can serve some useful purposes. As described in Michael Jensen's classic article,[87] free cash flow—cash flow in excess of that required to fund projects that have a positive net present value at the relevant discount rate—can create conflicts of interest between managers and shareholders, primarily if managers fund wasteful projects and reduce the company's efficiency. In such a situation, using free cash flow to pay a dividend increases corporate efficiency while rewarding shareholders.

Thus dividends have two faces. As a way to return capital to LPs, they can benefit all parties as long as the funds are not needed for the company's underlying operations. If, on the other hand, they are funded not out of free cash flow but by sharply increasing the company's debt or slashing valuable long-run investments or depleting essential financial reserves, they can make the company more vulnerable to external shocks and substantially weaker in the long run.

Loss-Minimizing Exits

The investors in Orangina and Playdom definitely made money when their companies were acquired. So did those on the selling ends of the secondary buyouts described earlier. In some cases, though, exiting through acquisition offers a strategy to minimize losses. The acquisition of Ellacoya by Arbor Networks, as mentioned in Chapter 6, represented the efforts of both companies' investors to create an entity with sufficient market presence to go public or become an interesting acquisition for a larger company. The actual transaction was not a liquidity event at all, because the investors in both companies received stock in the new merged—and still private— company. While an IPO is not an exit but creates the *opportunity* for one, a private-to-private merger creates the *hope* for an exit.

Every portfolio includes companies that never quite fail and never quite succeed. They miss milestones, but only by a quarter; they are just one customer away from cash-flow breakeven; a very interested potential acquirer is just about to initiate the transaction. At some point, the investors determine that the marginal value of investing more time or money in the company will not yield a positive return. The board must decide whether to close the company down and write off the investment or "put lipstick on the pig" and find someone who will buy it. Ideally, the transaction creates some amount of liquidity, even at a loss; but most important, it frees up time and money for more promising opportunities.

For instance, after the NASDAQ crash, many VC firms ended up with struggling high-cost companies that had lost many of their potential customers. Selling them for the value of the technology already developed, often at pennies on the dollar invested, was preferable to either closing them down and losing everything or continuing to invest large amounts. As one investor said, "At that time, having me on the board of a private technology company with no revenues was akin to hanging a big 'For Sale' sign out front."[88]

---

[85] Chris Kirkham, "An IPO in Overdrive," *Washington Post*, November 14, 2006, http://www.washingtonpost.com/wp-dyn/content/article/2006/11/13/AR2006111301295.html, accessed August 5, 2010.

[86] Tim Catts, John Detrixhe, and Kristen Haunss, "LBO Firms Extracting Dividends as Blackstone's Apria Sells," *Bloomberg*, April 15, 2010.

[87] Michael C. Jensen, "Agency Costs of Free Cash Flow, Corporate Finance, and Takeovers," *American Economic Review* 76, no. 2 (1986): 323–29.

[88] Private communication with Felda Hardymon, 2003.

When an acquisition is proposed to the board, as noted earlier, the prices and terms will have to be negotiated. Particularly with a struggling company, we may see the interplay of different investors with different voting rights as discussed in Chapters 5 and 6. An early investor with a low share price who needs to show gains to raise a fund may be willing to sell at a very low price. If it also has seniority, it may be able to force the transaction on other investors with higher cost bases. This behavior is rare, though, because VC is a small industry; firms will often encounter each other in later deals, and dealing badly with a co-investor is never a good idea.

Selling companies that have little recognition or market traction is hard work. Here again the venture capitalist's reputation and the quality of its network makes a difference. Investment banks that have worked with the investors before and hope to do so again on more successful exits will represent struggling companies to possible acquirers and share in the eventual proceeds. Managers who have worked with the investors previously may be at companies or know of companies with an interest in the current company's technology. At some price, some companies may find an acquirer or may be split into its assets—essentially, the IP that is acquired—while the shell of the company is shut down. This is one of the situations where the initial capitalization structure is likely to be renegotiated to carve out a reward for the management.

Selling the Shares Back

Sometimes, an investor avails itself of the "put" that was mentioned in Chapter 5 and sells its position back to the company. The term, of course, usually has to be negotiated as part of the initial agreement; but it can apply to start-ups or to LBOs.

A put allows the investor to sell his or her share back to the company, sometimes at a premium that allows the private equity group to realize a modest rate of return. Usually these transactions are allowed only five to eight years after the original investment, and only if the company has not achieved a liquidity event. Motilal Oswal Financial Services,[89] an Indian stock broker and financial advisory company, took an investment in 2006 from a hedge fund and a U.S.-based early-stage investor. The hedge fund insisted on a term that allowed it to put its shares back to the company at stated minimum rate of return if Motilal Oswal had not gone public within five years. The hedge fund wanted to protect itself from the downside of being stuck with an illiquid holding. As it was, the company went public in 2007, providing a much more lucrative exit.

Sometimes an investor can sell its shares back to the company even without a formal put. One start-up company was operating at cash-flow breakeven but, despite several offers, the founder-CEO refused to sell. Moreover, the founder loathed one particular VC investor, who had assumed the board seat from a colleague who left the firm. In the end, a third investor from the VC firm (note: three investors, one VC firm, one company) managed to negotiate an agreement. The founder-CEO bought back that investor's shares for roughly half their cost, and the annoying director left the board. For the VC firm, retrieving half its cost basis was a good outcome, largely because the board member could now devote himself to companies with much more potential. In many start-ups, though, it is difficult to sell shares back to the company or exercise a put because the company lacks sufficient funds to buy back the stock.

Another type of partial exit occurs when one investor sells its shares to other investors. This can happen in the course of raising a round, or when an investor has reached the end of its fund or needs an exit for some other reason, ranging from the investor's health to the investment firm's change of focus. A corporation's decision to abandon a corporate VC program may trigger such a sale. Often the transfer occurs at the cost basis of the round at which the shares were purchased.

---

[89] For more on this, see Felda Hardymon, Josh Lerner, and Ann Leamon, "Motilal Oswal Financial Services: An IPO in India," HBS Case No. 807-095 (Boston: HBS Publishing, 2008).

Sometimes there is an agreement that allows the initial owner to share in an eventual exit to some degree. This mechanism is much more likely to simply provide an exit rather than a gain.

Shutdowns

Of course, some companies have to be closed down. Like Tolstoy's unhappy families, every company that fails does so in its own way. Amp'd Mobile, the mobile content company, raised $360 million from Highland Capital Partners, Columbia Capital Equity Partners, and others, only to go bankrupt when it targeted high-risk customers and discovered that half of them could not pay their bills.[90] Coghead Inc., a Web application company, made some progress on developing IP but could not raise the money to repay its venture loan. The company sold its IP to one of its investors, SAP, and shut down.[91] Sequoia Communications, a developer of transceivers for mobile phones, had the market pass it by. Founded in 2001, the company could not compete with larger operations like Qualcomm that produced a host of mobile phone parts complying with the requirements for specific countries. Having already invested $64 million in the venture, the investors were unwilling to invest more—and the company was a year away from breaking even. A firm that specialized in winding down companies planned to sell the company's assets and IP in an auction.[92]

But not all shutdowns end so civilly. Terralliance Technologies, an oil and gas exploration company, raised $300 million in equity and $150 million in debt from a consortium that included Kleiner Perkins, Goldman Sachs, Dubai-based Ithmar Capital, and several others. After issues with financial accounting and questions about the technology's accuracy torpedoed a $1.1 billion financing from Temasek Holdings of Singapore in August 2008, the board demoted the founder-CEO and fired him in May 2009. A few months later, the board sued the founder for misuse of the company's IP when starting two competing companies. After extensive involvement by Kleiner's star deal maker, John Doerr, the company was restructured (with an additional $54.2 million invested) as TTI Exploration, doing surveys for clients on a project basis.[93]

The saying that "You can only lose 100 percent of your money" in private equity is not precisely correct. When VC investors close down a company, they may have to invest additional money for any applicable severance pay, payroll taxes, or vacation compensation that might be owed, to pay off long-term leases, and even to remove trash from the offices (cartage fees). It is a traumatic experience for everyone involved.

Even though LBO deals involve companies with real operations, they too can get in trouble. In such a situation, the company cannot pay the interest on its debt or falls out of compliance with its loan covenants. At that point, the investors and lenders (banks and bondholders) try to renegotiate the agreement. The lenders will want the LBO firm to put in more money, increasing its equity position in the company and reducing its returns. The LBO firm will want the lenders to relax the covenants, agree to an interest grace period (e.g., a period during which the company need not pay interest), or engage in a debt swap. In some cases, an agreement is reached. In other instances, the

[90] Matt Marshall, "What Were They Thinking? Amp'd Mobile's Mad Credit Strategy," *Venturebeat.com*, July 20, 2007, http://venturebeat.com/2007/07/20/what-were-they-thinking-ampd-mobiles-mad-credit-strategy/, accessed July 29, 2010.

[91] Timothy Hay, "Turning Out the Lights: Sequoia Communications," *Wall Street Journal—Venture Capital Dispatch*, August 20, 2009, http://blogs.wsj.com/venturecapital/2009/08/20/turning-out-the-lights-sequoia-communications/, accessed July 29, 2010.

[92] Ibid.

[93] Adam Lashinsky, "How a Big Bet on Oil Went Bust," *Fortune.com*, March 29, 2010, http://money.cnn.com/2010/03/26/news/companies/terralliance_tech_full.fortune/index.htm, accessed August 3, 2010; and Zoran Basich, "Let's Hope Joe Lacob's Golden State Warriors Is No Terralliance," *Wall Street Journal–Venture Capital Dispatch*, July 15, 2010, http://blogs.wsj.com/venturecapital/2010/07/15/lets-hope-joe-lacobs-golden-state-warriors-is-no-terralliance/, accessed August 3, 2010.

negotiations break down and the private equity group walks away with a total loss. Let's explore a few examples.

Harrah's, the casino operator, was purchased by Apollo Investment Management and TPG in December 2006 in a transaction valued at $27.8 billion. In November 2008, struggling with the slowdown in consumer discretionary spending, the casino and its private equity owners asked the holders of bonds maturing between 2010 and 2018 to exchange them at prices ranging from 40 cents to 100 cents on the dollar. The newer security had seniority over the older one in a bankruptcy, but carried a lower yield (10 percent compared to 40 percent on the earlier notes) and later redemption. The bondholders were not eager to make the exchange, but finally, in March 2009, notes worth $5 billion were exchanged for $2.8 billion of the new notes due in 2018.[94]

Some buyouts, on the other hand, end up in Chapter 11 bankruptcy rather than in an out-of-court restructuring. In the United States, this gives the owners a chance to restructure the company's debts, shed onerous leases or other long-term agreements, and emerge leaner and more competitive. The buyout firm may have had to inject additional equity as well.

In the worst cases, the company cannot reorganize and goes out of business. This happened with Linens 'n Things, a home furnishings retailer taken private in February 2006 by a consortium led by Apollo Management. At the time of the transaction, Linens 'n Things was the second-largest home goods retailer in the United States, with 17,500 employees and 589 stores in the United States and Canada. Apollo's group paid $1.3 billion in total, $28 per share, which was 6 percent above the closing price the day before.[95]

Covenants from the lenders required that the retailer meet certain financial targets, including earnings before interest, tax, depreciation, and amortization (EBITDA) of at least $140 million and store sales not below 94 percent of the prior quarter.[96] Over the following two years, though, Linens 'n Things struggled, made some ill-fated strategic changes, and confronted the slowdown in consumer spending. In April 2008, the company's $650 million of senior notes were trading at 35 to 39 cents on the dollar, indicating that even the most secured noteholders expected to get only one-third of their money back. The $648 million in equity contributed by the investment consortium looked in trouble—and the investors had not paid themselves any special dividends.

In May 2008, after trying to negotiate with creditors and find a buyer, the company missed an interest payment and filed for bankruptcy. It announced plans to close 120 stores and lay off 2,500 workers. In October 2008, after being unable to find a buyer in the face of the deepening global financial crisis, Linens 'n Things sold its remaining $500 million of inventory to a group of liquidators for 95 cents on the dollar (approximately $475 million). The company had $650 million in debt. In February 2010, because the remaining corporate entity could not come to an agreement with its bondholders, the company filed for Chapter 7 and ceased to exist.[97]

In Europe, there is evidence that banks are increasingly refusing to negotiate with private equity firms and are ending up owning companies as a result. Derek Sach, head of the global restructuring group for Royal Bank of Scotland, was quoted as saying, "If private equity wants to stay in the game, they have to be willing to invest more equity. Otherwise we are happy to go ahead

---

[94] Caroline Salas, "Harrah's Bondholders Get as Low as 40 Cents in Swap," *Bloomberg*, November 17, 2008, http://www.bloomberg.com/apps/news?pid=21070001&sid=apPgoV5YfmwA, accessed August 4, 2010.

[95] Jonathon Keehner and Jason Kelly, "Apollo's Linen 'n Things Unit Files for Bankruptcy," *Bloomberg*, May 2, 2008, http://www.bloomberg.com/apps/news?pid=newsarchive&sid=aIibQcTFLkgY, accessed August 9, 2010.

[96] "Linens 'n Things Agrees to $1.3B Buyout," *USAToday.com*, November 8, 2005, http://www.usatoday.com/money/industries/retail/2005-11-08-linens_x.htm, accessed August 9, 2010.

[97] Material from Andrew Ross Sorkin, "Linens 'n Things Lands in Chapter 11," *New York Times DealBook*, May 2, 2008; Andrew Ross Sorkin, "Linens 'n Things: Don't Expect a Soft Landing," *New York Times DealBook*, April 11, 2008; Andrew Ross Sorkin, "Linens 'n Things to Liquidate After Failing to Find a Buyer," *New York Times DealBook*, October 14, 2008; and Ajay Kamalakaran, "Linens 'n Things Plans Bankruptcy Exit: Report," *Reuters.com*, August 18, 2008, http://www.reuters.com/article/2008/08/18/us-linensnthings-plan-idUSBNG24752420080818, accessed July 8, 2011.

without them." In the 1990s, after the last LBO boom, banks adjusted the terms of the loans. Since the start of 2009, though, an estimated €50 billion ($66.5 billion) worth of companies had been partially or completely acquired by banks due to default.[98]

One such case was the Swedish maker of interior fittings for travel trailers and pleasure boats, Dometic. Lenders took control of the company from BC Partners following a debt-for-equity swap.[99] BC Partners bought Dometic for €1.1 billion ($1.6 billion) in a secondary buyout from the Scandinavian firm EQT in 2005.[100] BC Partners then returned 100 percent of its equity investment through a dividend recapitalization that left the company with a debt load of €1.3 billion. The reduction in demand due to the global recession meant that convenants were breached in January 2009. In September 2009, the twenty-five-bank syndicate took control of the company, wrote down the debt to €780 million and reduced interest payments by 70 percent in exchange for 70 percent of the equity. Top management received 25 percent of Dometic's equity, and the remaining 5 percent went to the board of directors.[101] Whether the banks can create value, of course, is another question.

Is value created when investments end in distress? Steven Kaplan argues that Robert Campeau's acquisition of Federated Department Stores created value even though Campeau overpaid for the company and it could not meet its interest payments.[102] Kaplan compares Federated's value before its purchase by Campeau Corporation to its post-bankruptcy value. After the bankruptcy, Federated's assets in inflation-adjusted dollars were $3.1 billion greater than before. This calculation, though, may not fully account for the plight of many stakeholders, such as the bondholders who lost their money and the employees who lost their jobs. The overall impact of private equity ownership is a topic we consider in Chapter 10.

THE DETAILS OF DISTRIBUTIONS

Once a company becomes public or has been acquired, the private equity firm has to distribute the proceeds to its LPs.[103] These "distributions" can be in the currency of the transaction (cash or stock). A variation on this is a cash distribution made not because the transaction occurred in cash, but because the firm sold stock received for the company and conveyed the cash to the LPs. A number of competing interests make distributions complex indeed. The process has frustrated LPs for decades, as noted in a *Venture Economics* article from 1987: "There are few venture capital fund management issues that evoke so much controversy as the timing and execution of stock distributions. Venture capital managers [and investors] differ in their philosophy as to when stock should be distributed and how those distributions should be handled."[104]

---

[98] Toby Lewis, "Banks Seize €50 Billion Worth of Private Equity-Backed Companies," *Financial News*, August 2, 2010, http://www.efinancialnews.com/story/2010-08-02/banks-seize-private-equity-backed-companies, accessed August 4, 2010.

[99] Paul Hodkinson, "Large Buyout Restructuring to Last through Summer," *Financial News*, July 31, 2009, http://www.efinancialnews.com/story/2009-07-31/large-buyout-restructuring-to-last-through-summer, accessed August 9, 2010.

[100] Mark Leftly, "BC Loses Control of Dometic in Equity Deal with Lenders to Ease £1.1Bn Debt," *The Independent*, September 6, 2009, http://www.independent.co.uk/news/business/news/bc-loses-control-of-dometic-in-equity-deal-with-lenders-to-ease-16311bn-debt-1782297.html, accessed August 9, 2010.

[101] "Dometic: Banks Take Control," *IBI Magazine*, September 6, 2009, http://www.ibinews.com/ibinews/newsdesk/20090807153729ibinews.html, accessed August 9, 2010.

[102] Steven N. Kaplan, "Campeau's Acquisition of Federated," *Journal of Financial Economics* 25, no. 2 (1989): 191–212; and "Campeau's Acquisition of Federated: Post Bankruptcy Results," *Journal of Financial Economics* 35, no. 1 (1994): 123–36.

[103] This section is based on Josh Lerner, Felda Hardymon, and Ann Leamon, "Between a Rock and a Hard Place: Valuation and Distribution in Private Equity," HBS Case No. 803-167 (Boston: HBS Publishing, 2003), 14–18; and Felda Hardymon, Josh Lerner, and Ann Leamon, "The Plummer Endowment: The Distribution Question," HBS Case No. 802-174 (Boston: HBS Publishing, 2001).

[104] "Stock Distributions—Fact, Opinion and Comment," *Venture Capital Journal* 27 (1987): 8.

FIGURE 7.3 Cash and stock distributions in U.S. private equity exits

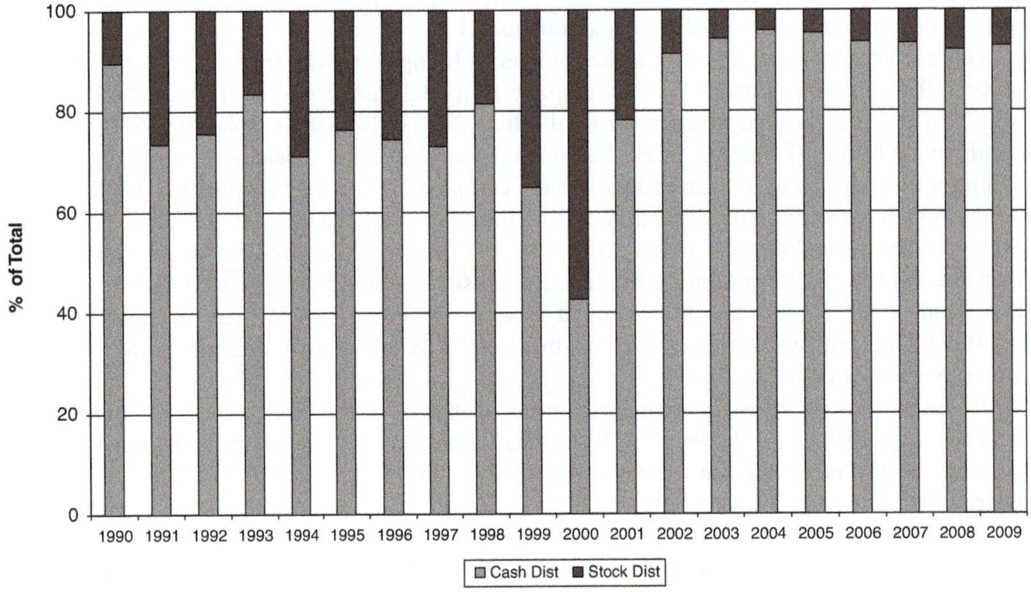

Source: Data from Thomson Reuters private equity database, accessed August 10, 2010.

The form that distributions take varies over time and with the type of investment. In 2000, stock accounted for almost 60 percent of all private equity distributions; in 2009, it was 7 percent,[105] as shown in Figure 7.3. Stock has made up an average of 46 percent of VC distributions between 1990 and 2009, peaking at 72 percent in the boom year of 2000. For buyouts, stock is a much smaller percentage, averaging 5 percent between 1990 and 2009 with a peak of 20 percent in 1994. Whether the investors choose to distribute cash or stock depends on the nature of the exit transaction and, often, on the prevailing attitudes of the moment. Distributions in any form pose challenges for LPs who must decide whether to hold or sell the securities—if the distribution occurs in stock—and how to handle the tax implications of cash. Especially after the recent dearth of distributions, this dilemma would be welcome; but the decision still has extremely high stakes.

Distributions follow a winding road from the announcement that a company has gone public to the arrival of money in the LP's pocket. First there is the **lock-up period** (often 180 days), which is a standard feature of underwriting agreements between investment banks, companies that are going public, and their investors. During this period, all executives and most private equity investors, depending on their ownership and amount of inside information, are typically required to hold onto their shares.

Upon the lock-up's expiration, or later, the GPs send a distribution notification to the LP. These notices detail the amount of stock being distributed, the cost basis, the distribution value, and the restrictions to which it is subject. These might include limits on the volume that can be sold in a single period if the distribution is more than 1 percent of the outstanding shares, if it has been held for less than two years, or if it needs to have the legend removed (the term of art is "de-legended").[106] The GP will have opened an account with a distributing broker (broker-dealer)

---

[105] Data from Thomson Reuters private equity database, accessed August 10, 2010.

[106] The stock of private companies is stamped with a legend that prohibits it from being traded. Before it can be traded, each certificate must be traded in for one without the legend.

and deposited the shares in it. The notification letter asks the LP to contact the broker with instructions—sell, transfer to a custodian or distribution manager, or await instructions from another party. Brokers provide this service because they receive the fee for executing a trade, which LPs frequently request.

If the LP wants the broker to sell the shares, there is a delay as the physical certificate goes to the transfer agent, who, with lawyers and the GP, coordinates splitting large blocks of shares into smaller holdings for each LP. There might even be an additional delay—six weeks or more during the Internet bubble—while the physical stock certificates make their way to the broker. If the stock is subject to SEC restrictions, the necessary paperwork must arrive at the broker's office when the sell order is given. Brokers then execute the trade, but settlement may be delayed. Many banks will offer the service of executing the trade in advance of finishing the paperwork, in effect loaning the proceeds to the LP for a fee. Predictably, the LPs are not exactly enthusiastic about this service. The process is particularly complex if companies go public and then are acquired or have stock splits during the lock-up period, as occurred in 1999 and 2000. Since 2000, LPs have tended to sell any stock distributions as quickly as they arrive. A few LPs, though, pursue a strategy of selectively managing some of their post-distribution stocks.

Why Distribute Stock?

Stock distributions occur for three reasons. First, SEC rules restrict the size of sales by corporate affiliates (officers, directors, and holders of 10 percent of the firm's equity). Private equity investors often qualify as affiliates because of their role on the board and the size of their equity holdings. For VC investors, selling a significant stake in a young, thinly traded company could take a long time. By distributing the shares to LPs (who are not considered affiliates and can therefore sell their shares freely), the investor can quickly dispose of a large holding. This is a concern primarily in IPOs; with acquisitions, the investors in the acquired company are far less likely to hold substantial positions and can usually sell their shares freely.

Second, tax motivations provide an incentive for the partners to distribute shares. If GPs sell the shares and distribute cash, the LPs and the GPs themselves may be subject to immediate capital gains taxes. The LPs often include a mix of tax-exempt entities (e.g., pension funds, endowments, and foundations) and others that are not (individuals and corporations). These investors might have different preferences regarding the timing of the share sale. Furthermore, the GPs themselves might wish to postpone paying personal taxes by selling their shares at a later date.

Finally, the investor might want to distribute stock to avoid the suggestion that any drop in the stock price was due to its own share sales. GPs have two reasons to worry about reducing the share price of a portfolio company that has gone public. As we discuss in Chapter 9 on returns and performance, outside fund trackers (e.g., Venture Economics and Cambridge Associates) and many LPs compute a fund's returns based on the closing price of the distributed stock on the day of distribution.[107] If a firm waits to sell shares and return cash, the fund's return is based on the dollars realized from the sale, which may be less than the market value at the time of the stock's distribution. The distributed price might not be the actual price received (or even near it) when the LPs sell their shares. The shares can take two or three days, or even longer, to reach the LPs after a distribution is declared. If the market reacts negatively to the distribution, or if the price falls due to increased supply, actual returns to the LPs may be substantially less than calculated returns. In response to the LPs' desire that GPs' performance numbers correspond more closely to the actual performance of the stock, many GPs have adopted five-day average pricing—that is, the average share price over the previous five days—in their reports. Some LPs have started evaluating

---

[107] Many distributions are declared at 5 p.m. after the stock market has closed.

their GPs on the realized price (i.e., what the LPs receive) rather than the price at distribution, further encouraging the GPs to handle the sales themselves if they feel they can receive a better price.

The second reason for concern about the share price is related to the GPs' compensation. Distributing higher-valued stock, rather than realized cash, returns more of the LPs' capital, at least on paper, and hastens the day that GPs can start collecting carried interest without fear of clawback.

One of the biggest challenges in maximizing post-distribution value, the LPs agree, is that most GPs distribute the stock on a single day. Almost all firms aspire to distribute into strength; but the converse is that they may hold a weakening stock, hoping to distribute once it stabilizes. One LP complained:

> One of our GPs had a substantial position in a company that came off lock-up at 100. We received about 25% of it at 95. Sure, we'd rather have it at 100, but it's not a huge deal. Then they held the balance as it fell. It finally stabilized at 80. When we received the rest of the distribution, the price was 81. They said they didn't want to distribute a falling stock. Part of it was pride, but part was that they priced it at the 10-day average price before the distribution or the price at distribution, whichever was lower. The price had been falling when they first distributed it. My point is that I'd rather have it falling at 95 and maybe get out of the whole position at 90 than stable at 81. Who'd rather have 81 than 90? Not me!

Many institutional investors can relate stories of shares that fell sharply in value after distribution, especially during the bubble. For example, the Internet toy retailer eToys was valued at over $10.3 billion at its peak in October 1999, and its shares traded at $84. In December, when the IPO lock-up expired, the shares were still over $50. Several of the VC backers began distributing stock, much to the annoyance of the CEO.[108] Within two months the stock had fallen to less than $20 per share, a drop of over 60 percent in sixty days. In March 2001 the company declared bankruptcy, and the equity was worthless. The CEO and Sequoia Capital, eToys' lead investor, stood on the sidelines watching their shares lose value. Sequoia was still holding its eight million shares when eToys declared bankruptcy.[109]

Crosspoint Venture Partners and Institutional Venture Partners (IVP) pursued different strategies when dealing with distributions from their portfolio company, Foundry Networks, a maker of Internet switching gear, after its IPO in early 2000. Crosspoint distributed its sixteen million shares to investors as quickly as possible in October 2000, when the price averaged $87. IVP distributed half its shares at $100 but in February 2001 still held four million shares valued at $10 each.[110]

Some private equity firms, both LBO and VC, make a point of holding shares in their companies for the long term. They argue that they are demonstrating their belief that an IPO is just another financing event and that the company will continue to increase in value. GPs may also continue to hold stock in their now-public companies to avoid signaling to LPs and short sellers. Often, the GPs still have substantial holdings; and if the LPs interpret sales by insiders as lack of confidence in the company's prospects, downward pressure on the stock will reduce the GPs' returns.

The difficulty is that private equity investors often do not want to manage a publicly traded security. The skill sets in correctly timing the market are very different from those involved in creating value in a private firm. GPs frequently prefer to turn the securities over to the LPs to keep

---

[108] Michael Sokolove, "How to Lose $850 Million—And Not Really Care," *New York Times Magazine*, June 9, 2002, http://www.michaelsokolove/michael_sokolove/howtolose850million.htm, accessed July 22, 2010.

[109] Luisa Kroll, "In the Lurch," *Forbes*, April 2, 2001, 54.

[110] Ibid.

FIGURE 7.4   Stock price patterns around distribution

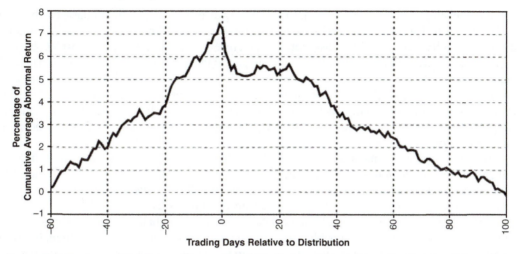

Source: Paul Gompers and Josh Lerner, "Venture Capital Distributions: Short- and Long-Run Reactions," *Journal of Finance* 53, no. 6 (1998): 2174.

or sell as they wish. GPs do, however, urge their CEOs to sell stock, worrying that concentrating their wealth in a single company is a poor financial strategy. To reinforce alignment of interests, the GPs might establish a system of future share grants.

GPs naturally want to distribute stock that is increasing in value, not just to burnish their internal rates of return (IRRs) but also to reduce the possibility that increasing the supply of a falling stock will trigger a downward spiral. Yet the rules of economics dictate that increased supply, all things being equal, reduces price. Distributing stock can compound the increased supply–reduced price dynamic if much of that stock finds its way into the hands of LPs who promptly sell it. Gompers and Lerner's 1998 study[111] of nearly eight hundred distributions showed more systematic evidence about the relationship between distributions and stock prices. The stock price falls steadily after distribution, and the results support the view that the venture capitalists do time stock distributions. Figure 7.4 shows the average stock price of firms, net of market returns,[112] for the period of three months before to three months after distributions by VC funds. The findings are robust even when the authors control for characteristics including companies financed by older and younger private equity organizations; companies taken public by high-, medium-, and low-reputation investment bankers; companies where the private equity investor did and did not leave the board at the time of the distribution; and the size of the distribution.

The distribution of shares poses a substantial administrative burden to all parties, particularly with respect to record-keeping and tax calculations. Also, it is often difficult for the LPs to decide what to do with the shares. Private equity investors typically give little notice of a share distribution; they claim that, under SEC regulations, LPs are safer that way. In addition, the GPs try to avoid providing information to hedge fund managers, who might short the stock and drive the price down before the distribution. This means, however, that the stock of a young company is often distributed with little supporting information and few recommendations. To address this, some GPs arrange to have CEOs meet with groups of LPs, to provide them with more information about their new holdings.

---

[111] The results are presented in more detail in Paul Gompers and Josh Lerner, "Venture Capital Distributions: Short- and Long-Run Reactions," *Journal of Finance* 53, no. 6 (1998): 2161–83.

[112] Adjusted for the shift in the relevant stock index.

Dealing with Distributions

LPs have developed a number of strategies for handling distributions. Several of these can be seen in the evolution of approaches taken by the manager of a major university endowment.[113] Initially, the private equity manager sold all distributions upon receipt because the value of most VC-backed stocks drops immediately after distribution, due in part to the modest size of the float (the share of the company that is actually available for trading before the distribution).[114] The next approach involved watching the stock's behavior and selling on the upswings. While this performed better, it involved a longer hold period, which reduced returns to the portfolio. Eventually, the manager adopted a third, hybrid approach to private equity stock distributions by selling the position immediately on its receipt but in smaller increments over (typically) five days.

Another major endowment has a number of possible rules: "We may push out pieces, maybe sell 25 percent a week in four weeks. We may accelerate if we're nervous, relax if we're not. We keep an eye on the [trading] volume; if that shrinks, we'll pull back. We don't want to impact the market in a negative way, and we have to be aware of who else is out there."[115]

If the LP is large enough that it also has a public portfolio, it might use yet another approach, in which the analysts responsible for public small-cap stocks assess each distribution. Often, it is sold immediately, either because it is viewed as undesirable or because the position is too small to warrant attention. If it is attractive, however, the private portfolio managers "sell" it to their public counterparts at the prevailing price.

Smaller LPs may use stock distribution managers. These intermediaries receive distributions from LPs and decide, with the LPs' input, whether to sell or hold them. Examples of such firms include Shott Capital Management, S-Squared Technologies, J.P. Morgan, and T. Rowe Price. The enduring issue with using stock distribution managers is the problem of finding the appropriate benchmark to use in measuring their performance. Since the manager does not choose which security to buy but only which security to hold, there is no natural comparison. Moreover, the use of such managers adds fees to the private equity portfolio.

During the late 1990s, these firms became significant players in the distribution field. Despite their fees, one distributing broker credited distribution managers with saving millions if not billions of dollars for LPs simply by maintaining a sense of objectivity about the company. In addition, distribution managers tracked the distributions, splits, and mergers that occurred during the lock-up period and managed the attendant complexities for the client. Even in a down market, when the watchword was liquidation, distribution managers prided themselves on managing portfolios to maximize returns rather than minimize losses.

One hotly debated issue is hedging. Yale University's endowment started hedging the stocks in its private equity firms' portfolios, or companies similar to them, before distribution, apparently with considerable success.[116] This is abhorrent to GPs, who do not want selling pressure on their stocks—*especially* from LPs, who are ostensibly on their side. On the other hand, some LPs wonder if such a strategy would be particularly effective for them.

CONCLUSION

As with so much in private equity, exits are not clear-cut. They depend on everything from the terms of the initial investment to the amount of value created to the market conditions. A very

---

[113] This is drawn from Hardymon et al., "The Plummer Endowment: The Distribution Question."

[114] One phenomenon that is not fully captured here is that in the days after the distribution, the bid-ask spreads will often become very wide for these stocks.

[115] Lerner et al., "Between a Rock and a Hard Place: Valuation and Distribution in Private Equity," 18.

[116] Josh Lerner, "Yale University Investments Office: July 2000," HBS Case No. 201-048 (Boston: HBS Publishing, 2000).

small number of people with concentrated ownership in the company make the decision regarding timing and method of exit. Multiple parties are engaged in the process, and interest alignment becomes more difficult to achieve—the investment bank wants to be sure that it can sell all the stock it has underwritten in an IPO so it has an incentive to underprice; the company wants to raise as much money as possible from the transaction; the private equity firm wants to be sure it can raise another fund. Sometimes the private equity firm would prefer an acquisition, but the CEO wants to remain in his position and would prefer an IPO. In an acquisition, the sellers may have to trade off speed or certainty for price.

As we have reviewed the process of exits, it should become clear how much each phase of the private equity cycle depends on the earlier ones. The cycle of fund-raising and the priorities of LPs may influence an exit's timing. The terms discussed in Chapter 5 influence whether an acquisition offer is accepted. The value creation from Chapter 6 affects the price. The governance methods position the company for IPO or make it appealing to an acquirer. The exit influences the firm's ability to raise another fund.

To a great extent, private equity plays its familiar role here. Its investors are extremely active regardless of the exit method chosen. First, they must make the choice; then, they must execute it. That can range from finding a good investment bank and going on a road show to putting in the additional money to wind down the firm. Just being involved in the company sends signals. Shutting down a company is a sad but crucial step because it allows the investors to focus on the next investment. Bankruptcies provisions—the ability to stop funding a flailing company—are an important part of a private-equity-friendly environment. Exits are created; they are very rarely found. Most exits involve many telephone calls, much networking, and, eventually, some liquidity. Even then, as we discussed, the process of distributing gains takes substantial time and involves many parties.

Without exits, private equity is a nonprofit endeavor. As we saw in 2008 when exits stopped, much else stops too—building programs at universities, funding for the arts, development of new technology, and turn around efforts for struggling operations. The process of private equity doesn't stop with an exit; exits create gains; the LPs spend some and invest some; the CEO starts another company; the firm raises another fund.

In the next section of the book, the focus shifts. Rather than examining the private equity cycle in ever closer detail, we look at its broader applications and related issues. We move to its application internationally; the evaluation of firm performance; its broader implications; the ways private equity firms manage themselves and grow; private equity's cycles; and the future. We hope that these first seven chapters have given you a good sense of the underlying rhythms, incentives, and personalities of the players involved. Now we will observe them in different contexts.

QUESTIONS

1. Exits are ultimately how private equity firms realize returns on their investments. Describe the various ways for a private equity firm to exit an investment.

2. What are some of the key considerations in determining whether to take a company public?

3. What are some of the possible explanations for why acquisitions account for a greater percentage of exits than IPOs?

4. What are some of the characteristics of a private company that may increase the likelihood of an IPO?

5. What are some of the characteristics of a private company that may prevent it from going public?

6. Why might the pursuit of an IPO elicit higher interest and/or offers from strategic acquirers?

7. What are some of the key advantages of being a public company? What are the disadvantages?

8. Why would a public company prefer institutional holders to comprise a large portion of their investor base? Who is responsible for attracting these investors?

9. Explain the phenomenon of underpricing as it relates to IPOs.

10. What is a "Green Shoe" and why does it exist?

11. What is a possible explanation for why a VC-backed company outperforms the market for several years after its IPO?

12. What purpose does corporate VC serve? What are the potential advantages?

13. What are some of the reasons for avoiding an auction process?

14. What are some of the potential issues associated with a secondary buyout?

15. Under which circumstances might it make the most sense to shut down a distressed business rather than inject additional capital or engage in a sale process?

16. What are some of the key issues with distributing stock directly to LPs in conjunction with an IPO? What would LPs prefer?

Chapter **8**

The Globalization of Venture Capital and Private Equity

Thus far we have discussed private equity as a general phenomenon, without focusing much on the differences across nations. In this chapter, we look at the spread of private equity around the world. David Rubenstein, cofounder and managing director of the Carlyle Group, noted that even as early as 2004, private equity capital, including the leverage involved in buyout transactions, was the United States' fourth-largest export.[1] Nor are buyout funds going overseas alone—according to the National Venture Capital Association's 2009 survey, 52 percent of the 725 venture capital firms that replied were already investing outside their home country.[2]

Although much of this international expansion has only occurred since the late 1990s, some firms are veterans at investing around the globe. One of the earliest international private equity firms was Actis. Founded in 1948 as an arm of the U.K. aid agency with a focus on lending for project finance, it moved entirely to equity investments in the late 1990s and then spun out as an independent private equity partnership.[3] Actis' Mumbai team led India's first successful private-equity-backed privatization in 2003 when it purchased 23.5 percent of Punjab Tractors from the State of Punjab. Actis' approach to the deal was similar to that of any investor in any market: the firm had followed Punjab Tractors for years and knew the management team and the company's competitive advantages. The only issue that differed from a typical growth equity investment was the regulatory constraint on the ability of Actis, as a foreign entity, to borrow domestically.[4]

In 2007, four years after winning the deal, Actis sold its stake to Mahindra & Mahindra, India's largest tractor manufacturer. Actis had helped Punjab Tractors expand its worldwide presence by introducing it to global distributors. It also helped with operational and procurement process improvements and new product development. The value of the entire company had risen

---

[1] David Rubinstein, "Is America's Burgeoning Export of Private Equity Capital a Plus or Minus for the Global Economy?" (speech to the Peterson Institute for International Economics, December 6, 2005), http://www.iie.com/publications/papers/rubenstein1205.pdf, accessed July 11, 2011.

[2] National Venture Capital Association, *Results from the 2009 Global Venture Capital Survey*, June 2009, http://www.nvca .org, accessed May 29, 2010.

[3] For more on Actis, see the series of cases by Josh Lerner, Felda Hardymon, and Ann Leamon, "CDC Capital Partners," HBS Case No. 801-333 (Boston: HBS Publishing, 2001); "CDC Capital Partners: December 2002," HBS Case No. 803-167 (Boston: HBS Publishing, 2003); and "Actis: January 2008," HBS Case No. 808-130 (Boston: HBS Publishing, 2008); and Felda Hardymon and Ann Leamon, "Actis and CDC: A New Partnership," HBS Case No. 805-122 (Boston: HBS Publishing, 2005).

[4] Information from Actis website, http://www.act.is/732,49/punjab-tractors, accessed May 26, 2009.

from INR 9.48 billion ($204 million) at the time of Actis' investment to INR 22.09 billion ($542 million) at the time of its exit.[5]

On the venture capital (VC) side, Accel Partners, a U.S.-based, early-stage VC firm, set up its London office in 2000. The London team's first investment occurred in 2001 when it backed Cape Clear Software, an Irish software company founded by veterans of IONA, Ireland's first high-tech success.[6] Accel, Greylock, and the Irish firm ACT, joined in the later rounds by InterWest, invested a total of $36.38 million in Cape Clear between 2001 and 2007.[7] For Greylock, a noted U.S. firm, the Cape Clear deal was its first investment outside North America. Accel led the transaction and provided day-to-day supervision from its London office. In 2008, Cape Clear was purchased by WorkDay, which was cofounded by Aneel Bhusri,[8] the very Greylock partner who had invested in Cape Clear seven years before.

Many governments welcome private equity for several reasons. As seen in the Punjab Tractors transaction, private equity firms can play an important role in privatization. By buying a company or even bidding for it, private equity practitioners set an objective price and certify the operation's value. Moreover, private equity can provide funding for infrastructure and other investments that cash-strapped governments find difficult to support. Various studies have noted the job creation record of VC firms,[9] even though the evidence for buyouts is mixed, as we discuss in Chapter 10.

Yet private equity has not been universally welcomed or universally successful in its international expansion. Months before Rubenstein's comment, Franz Müntefering, the German vice-chancellor, described private equity firms (accounts vary; some say hedge funds) as "locusts that fall on companies, stripping them bare before moving on."[10] Private equity's proportion of GDP in different countries varies dramatically. What makes a country or region more likely to adopt private equity as a financing mechanism? For most of the decade of the 1990s, emerging market returns were abysmal. What conditions predispose private equity transactions to success?

Global private equity, like that in the United States, is highly cyclical. As Figure 8.1 shows, there have been three boom-to-bust cycles since 1990. Starting in 2000, private equity has made a concerted move into emerging markets; and in 2010 (not included in the chart) the industry appears to be recovering more quickly there than in the developed world. While some of the operators are U.S.-based, domestic firms have increased their presence throughout the world—Sequoia Capital has operations in India, Israel, and China; Warburg Pincus is in China, Hong Kong, India, and Singapore; and Carlyle has twenty-six offices in twenty countries. U.K.-based operations like Candover, Apax, and 3i are active in Europe and internationally, as are Luxembourg-based CVC Capital Partners and German operations such as Early Bird. In the rest of the

---

[5] Sanatu Choudhury and Anand Krishnamoorthy, "Mahindra Agrees to Buy 43.3 Percent Stake in Punjab Tractors," *Bloomberg.com*, March 8, 2007, http://www.bloomberg.com/apps/news?pid=newsarchive&sid=aCFvMp7B2CUk, accessed May 26, 2010.

[6] For more on Accel's London office and Cape Clear, see Felda Hardymon, Josh Lerner, and Ann Leamon, "Accel Partners' European Launch," HBS Case No. 803-02 (Boston: HBS Publishing, 2003).

[7] Data from Thomson Reuters private equity database, as of May 25, 2010.

[8] Mary Hayes Weier, "SaaS Start-Up Workday Acquires Cape Clear," *InformationWeek*, February 6, 2008, http://www.informationweek.com/news/software/soa/showArticle.jhtml?articleID=206105347, accessed May 27, 2010.

[9] For some articles, see Florence Eid, "Private Equity Finance as a Growth Engine," *Business Economics* 41, no. 3 (2006), 7–22; and National Venture Capital Association, "Venture Impact: The Economic Impact of Venture Capital," March 2007, http://www.nvca.org/index.php?option=com_content&view=article&id=255&Itemid=103, accessed August 3, 2007.

[10] Tracy Corrigan, "Recession: We Need Private Equity to Weather the Storm," *Telegraph.co.uk*, November 17, 2008, http://www.telegraph.co.uk/finance/comment/tracycorrigan/3474851/Recession-We-need-private-equity-to-weather-the-storm.html, accessed July 11, 2011.

FIGURE 8.1   Private equity fund-raising outside the United States, 1989–2009

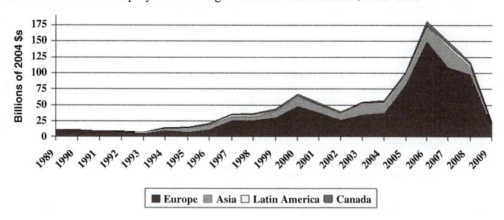

Source: Various national PEVC organizations, Thomson-Reuters, and Prequin Global.

world, examples include Abraaj Capital and Citadel Capital in the Middle East; Jerusalem Venture Partners in Israel; India's Chrysalis Capital and ICICI Ventures; and in China, Hony Capital, Gobi Partners, SAIF, and a host of others. In 2010, the Private Equity International (PEI) list of the top fifty largest private equity firms, based on the capital raised over the prior five years, for the first time included a firm not based in North America or Europe—Dubai-based Abraaj Capital. Of the top 50, thirty-four were headquartered in North American (2 in Canada), 9 in London, 2 in Sweden, 2 in France, 1 in Holland, and 1 in Greece. See Table 8.1 for the full list of 2010's top fifty and their rankings in the prior three years.

Table 8.1   PEI's Top Fifty Global Private Equity Firms

2010 Rank	Name of Firm	Headquarters	Capital Raised over Past Five Years ($ Millions)*	2009 Rank	2008 Rank	2007 Rank
1	Goldman Sachs Principal Investment Area	New York	$54,584	2	2	3
2	The Carlyle Group	Washington, DC	$47,826	3	1	1
3	Kohlberg Kravis Roberts	New York	$47,031	4	4	2
4	TPG	Fort Worth, TX	$45,052	1	3	5
5	Apollo Global Management	New York	$34,710	5	6	12
6	CVC Capital Partners	London	$34,175	7	5	10
7	The Blackstone Group	New York	$31,139	8	10	4
8	Bain Capital	Boston	$29,240	6	7	8
9	Warburg Pincus	New York	$23,000	9	11	14
10	Apax Partners	London	$21,728	10	9	7
11	First Reserve Corporation	Greenwich, CT	$19,064	11	23	22
12	Advent International	Boston	$18,180	16	13	43
13	Hellman & Friedman	San Francisco	$17,300	14	25	16

(*continued*)

Table 8.1 (*Continued*)

2010 Rank	Name of Firm	Headquarters	Capital Raised over Past Five Years ($ Millions)*	2009 Rank	2008 Rank	2007 Rank
14	Cerberus Capital Management	New York	$14,900	21	18	34
15	General Atlantic	Greenwich, CT	$14,700	18	21	18
16	Permira	London	$12,963	22	8	6
17	Providence Equity Partners	Providence, RI	$12,100	15	16	9
18	Clayton Dubilier & Rice	New York	$11,704	23	28	47
19	Terra Firma Capital Partners	London	$11,645	17	14	15
20	Bridgepoint	London	$11,203	26	27	36
21	Teachers' Private Capital	Toronto	$10,891	30	29	20
22	Charterhouse Capital Partners	London	$10,762	29	30	24
23	Fortress Investment Group	New York	$10,700	19	20	27
24	Madison Dearborn Partners	Chicago	$10,600	28	47	32
25	Oaktree Capital Management	Los Angeles	$10,562	37	36	49
26	TA Associates	Boston	$10,548	51	41	39
27	Citi Alternative Investments	New York	$10,197	48	NA	NA
28	Thomas H. Lee Partners	Boston	$10,100	31	32	30
29	Riverstone Holdings	New York	$9,800	34	NA	NA
30	Cinven	London	$9,607	32	26	11
31	AXA Private Equity	Paris	$9,535	35	34	NA
32	JC Flowers & Co.	New York	$9,300	36	40	NA
33	Silver Lake	Menlo Park	$9,300	20	17	19
34	BC Partners	London	$8,897	38	33	29
35	3i	London	$8,341	12	12	13
36	Nordic Capital	Stockholm	$8,341	41	NA	NA
37	HarbourVest Partners	Boston	$7,954	NA	NA	NA
38	PAI Partners	Paris	$7,930	25	22	35
39	Lindsay Goldberg	New York	$7,800	43	NA	NA
40	NGP Energy Capital Management	Dallas	$7,519	45	35	NA
41	Lone Star Funds	Dallas	$7,500	NA	NA	NA
42	AlpInvest Partners	Amsterdam	$7,399	46	NA	NA
43	EQT Partners	Stockholm	$7,372	27	24	21
44	Welch Carson Anderson & Stowe	New York	$7,309	40	NA	NA
45	Onex Partners	Toronto	$7,278	33	49	33
46	Marfin	Athens	$6,955	49	37	NA
47	WL Ross & Co.	New York	$6,900	42	45	NA
48	Oak Hill Capital Partners	Stamford, CT	$6,607	56	NA	NA
49	Sun Capital Partners	Boca Raton, FL	$6,500	44	38	28
50	Abraaj Capital	Dubai	$6,459	54	NA	NA

* Capital raised from January 1, 2005, to April 2010.
Source: Adapted from *The PEI 300 Executive Summary*, May 2010, http://www.abraaj.com/mediacenter; and Wanching Leong and David Snow, eds., *The Largest Private Equity Firms in the World* (Dealogic & PEI Media, 2008), 7, http://www.peim.com.

Yet overseas expansion did not occur overnight. There were several false starts as the U.S. "invaders" returned home to lick their wounds, absorb their losses, and eventually try again. Domestic efforts have similarly endured setbacks and enjoyed successes. Private equity has moved around the world in different guises. In some regions—Europe, for instance—buyouts are predominant. In others, such as most emerging markets, growth equity has been the most successful. Israel has a thriving VC industry. Why hasn't private equity of all types prospered, like the proverbial weed, evenly across the globe? What has been its history thus far?

In this chapter, we explore the larger themes of private equity globalization—its history and expansion into different parts of the world. We consider the differences between the United States and Europe, and how European countries differ among themselves. We then look at the vibrant private equity scene in emerging markets. Throughout the discussion, we consider the aspects of a good private equity market. Of necessity, this discussion is at a very high level. Extensive reports and books have been written on this topic, even on the private equity industry in a single country. We apologize in advance for any oversights.

PRIVATE EQUITY IN THE DEVELOPED MARKETS

Although elements of private equity—names like Montagu and Schroders,[11] for instance; the Venetian "carried interest" profit split; and Queen Isabella's venture funding for Christopher Columbus—appeared centuries ago in Europe, private equity became a distinct asset class there only in the 1980s. Since then, Europe has become the world's second most developed private equity market after the United States.

Historical Experience

Just as in the United States, European private equity has whipsawed between booms and busts as good returns attract additional funds, additional funds drive up pricing and depress returns, and fund inflows fall. In the late 1980s, the first VC boom occurred in Europe. Part of this mirrored activity in the United States, which had seen a modest boom cycle at that time and whose firms were going abroad in search of new, well-priced deals. European banks also drove this activity, seeing early-stage investment as a chance to found new companies that would be customers for their banking services. John Singer, head of European operations for Advent International, was quoted as saying, "The industry was staffed in completely the wrong way . . . with bankers and accountants. They were fine in terms of structuring the deals, but lacked the expertise to assess trends and technologies and to add value."[12]

This inexperience, coupled with the large amounts of money that were raised, meant that investors tended to do poor deals at high prices. They often failed to establish solid governance systems—a key part of active investing. The recession of the early 1990s annihilated the industry. Institutional investors, especially pension funds and insurance companies, fled the sector; European firms closed their VC operations; and U.S. firms closed or sharply reduced their European presence. The virtual collapse of the venture industry gave it a reputation for illiquidity that persisted into the mid-1990s.[13] This was borne out by results: large European buyouts substantially outperformed between 1980 and 1994, beating the average midsized fund by almost nine

---

[11] Schroder's was a merchant/investment bank founded in the Napoleonic Wars and eventually gave rise to Schroder Ventures and then Permira. Montagu was founded in 1853, only to go through a number of names and owners before becoming independent in 2003.

[12] Rick Butler, "Europe Comes Under Pressure to Perform," *Global Investor*, April 2000, 13.

[13] Ibid.; data from Thomson Reuters private equity database, http://www.venturexpert.com, accessed August 3, 2010.

percentage points (23.1 vs. 14.7 percent) after fees, and the average VC fund by 19 percentage points (23.1 vs. 4 percent) after fees.[14]

European VC did not shed that reputation until the late 1990s, when appetite for the asset class was whetted by the mind-boggling returns of the VC-fueled Internet bubble in the United States.[17] Overseas capital also entered Europe as U.S. venture funds moved overseas in search of better-priced opportunities, sometimes raising dedicated funds for that purpose.[18] In addition, VC performance strengthened. By the end of 1999, the ten-year performance of European VC funds (17.2 percent) was almost indistinguishable from that of buyouts (17.5 percent).[19]

3i: The Bumblebee Investment Firm

The United Kingdom's 3i is one of the earliest VC-type firms in Europe, and it is a member of a rare breed: the publicly traded private equity firm.[15] It was founded in 1945 by the U.K. government but with backing from the country's major banks in an effort to prevent a recurrence of the Great Depression of the 1930s and assist with the country's postwar rebuilding effort. 3i invented the skills for providing expansion capital, most often long-term debt, to risky firms—the small- and medium-sized organizations outside the purview of the large banks. The organization grew to twenty-nine offices throughout the United Kingdom. With a strong tradition of investing in technology, the early 3i-backed Bond Helicopters, Caledonian Airways (later British Caledonian), and Oxford Instruments, the pioneer of magnetic resonance imaging (MRI). Starting in 1982, it established offices in the United States and Europe; it then entered Australia and Japan, only to close these operations by the end of the decade. Shortly after, it went public on the London Stock Exchange in 1994,3i became a member of the Financial Times Stock Exchange (FTSE) 100, the United Kingdom's leading stock market index. Starting in 1997, management at 3i revisited the idea of international expansion; and by 2003, it had thirty-one offices in thirteen countries. It was one of the first private equity firms to grow by acquisition, purchasing firms in Finland and Germany. By 2010, the company had offices in twelve countries and had shifted its product suite from VC toward growth equity, infrastructure, and small- to medium-sized buyouts.[16]

At that point, Europe-based funds became more active in VC, and existing groups, such as Atlas Ventures, raised significantly larger funds. New firms, in many cases modeled after American groups, entered the market (examples included Amadeus in the United Kingdom and Early Bird in Germany). Finally, generalist funds returned to VC; for instance, over the late 1990s, 3i increased its allocation to technology investments from 15 to 40 percent.[20] The supply of funds also grew due to the U.K. government's authorization of VC trusts. These publicly traded venture firms provided significant tax savings to their investors and were accessible to people

---

[14] Josh Lerner and Paul Gompers, *Money of Invention* (Boston: HBS Publishing, 2001), 195.

[15] For more on 3i, see Josh Lerner, Felda Hardymon, and Ann Leamon, "3i Group plc," HBS Case No. 803-020 (Boston: HBS Publishing, 2003).

[16] Lerner et al., "3i Group plc"; and http://www.3i.com, accessed May 27, 2010.

[17] Butler, "Europe Comes Under Pressure to Perform"; data from Thomson Reuters private equity database, http://www.venturexpert.com, accessed June 7, 2002; and Datastream data services, accessed June 28, 2002.

[18] Butler, "Europe Comes Under Pressure to Perform."

[19] Venture Economics, *Investment Benchmark Reports: International Private Equity* (Newark, NJ: Venture Economics, 2000).

[20] http://www.3igroup.com, various annual reports.

without significant wealth who could buy just a few shares. Between their authorization in 1994 and 2002, 155 VC trusts had raised £1.6 billion (almost $3 billion).[21]

After the inevitable crash in 2000, many venture firms exited the business or returned to buyout activities. The historical disparity between venture and buyout returns reappeared in Europe, where venture funds returned an average of *negative* 9.6 percent between 2001 and the end of 2006 and buyout funds earned 18.5 percent.[22] Some of the difficulties accompanying VC investment may be due either to cultural attitudes that discourage entrepreneurship and risk taking or to a different set of exit opportunities—a greater tendency to exit through trade sales and secondary buyouts rather than more lucrative initial public offerings (IPOs)—but many European private equity investors may believe that early-stage investments are simply not worth the increased risk.

The persistent discrepancy in returns between buyouts and VC is one reason that later-stage investments dominate European private equity, as shown in Table 8.2. The other reason is that the structure of the European business landscape has historically favored buyouts. The Thatcher government's privatization program in the 1980s gave English buyout firms a head start in developing the skills to succeed in control transactions. As other countries began their own privatization efforts in the 1990s, English buyout firms built on their early experience to establish a

Table 8.2   Fund-Raising for European Venture Capital and Buyouts ($ Millions)

	Venture Capital	Buyouts and Other Private Equity	Total	Buyouts Percent of Total
1984	$0.12	$0.28	$0.40	71
1985	$0.27	$0.78	$1.04	74
1986	$0.32	$1.05	$1.38	76
1987	$0.39	$2.88	$3.28	88
1988	$0.51	$3.57	$4.08	88
1989	$0.46	$4.24	$4.71	90
1990	$0.45	$4.81	$5.25	92
1991	$0.40	$5.34	$5.74	93
1992	$0.36	$5.73	$6.09	94
1993	$0.23	$4.59	$4.82	95
1994	$0.37	$6.09	$6.46	94
1995	$0.41	$6.77	$7.18	94
1996	$0.55	$7.95	$8.51	94
1997	$0.80	$10.10	$10.91	93
1998	$1.82	$14.42	$16.24	89
1999	$3.45	$23.30	$26.75	87

(*continued*)

---

[21] Data from HM Revenue and Customs/National Statistics, http://www.hmrc.gov.uk/stats/venture/table8-6.pdf, accessed July 27, 2011.

[22] Data sourced from Cambridge Associates LLC, August 2, 2007.

Table 8.2 (*Continued*)

	Venture Capital	Buyouts and Other Private Equity	Total	Buyouts Percent of Total
2000	$6.15	$26.14	$32.29	81
2001	$3.74	$18.05	$21.79	83
2002	$2.76	$23.40	$26.16	89
2003	$2.40	$30.55	$32.96	93
2004	$2.96	$42.96	$45.93	94
2005	$3.02	$55.52	$58.56	95
2006	$9.24	$80.18	$89.41	90
2007	$10.73	$90.43	$101.16	89
2008	$10.05	$69.54	$79.59	87
2009	$2.40	$16.20	$18.60	87

Source: Compiled from European Venture Capital Association (EVCA), *EVCA Yearbook* (Zaventum, Belgium: EVCA, 2007 and earlier); and Thomson Reuters private equity database, accessed November 26, 2010.

pan-European presence. By the mid-1990s, the English firms of Apax and Schroder Ventures (now Permira) had become noted European buyout houses.[23]

And they had ample room to ply their trade since many large European companies were conglomerates that had been created as much for national economic and social aims as business efficiencies. Telecommunications companies, for instance, were famous for their overstaffed, unreliable, and expensive operations.[24] This began to change as the European Union (EU) pressed for a more open market and urged firms to privatize. Companies like Hoechst and Siemens started selling subsidiaries to concentrate on their core activities.[25] Generational change also played a part: transitions from father to child no longer occurred automatically, and a sale to a buyout firm was a viable option. With cash-flow-positive companies and practitioners skilled in financial engineering, buyouts flourished. Whether due to cultural attitudes or historical business structure, buyouts have generated better returns in Europe than VC—and with less volatility. It is an open question, though, if this reputation will endure after the most recent cyclic downturn.

Most European buyout firms grew out of financial institutions, although many of these have now gone through management buyouts themselves and become independent. These include Doughty Hanson (Charterhouse and Westdeutsche Landesbank), BC Partners (Barings), Industri Kapital (Skandinaviska Enskilda Banken), Permira (Schroder Ventures), both Charterhouse and Montagu Equity Partners (from HSBC in 2001 and 2003, respectively), and Cinven (the Government Coal Board Pension Fund). CVC Capital Partners and Apax Partners, on the other hand, were established as private equity investment operations from the start.

---

[23] Schroders (sometimes also referred to as Schroder Group) is a fund management group. Schroder Ventures was founded in 1983 by Schroders but gradually delinked itself and became Permira after it was spun off in 2000. For more on the evolution of Schroder Ventures, see Josh Lerner, Kate Bingham, and Nick Ferguson, "Schroder Ventures: Launch of the Euro Fund," HBS Case No. 597-026 (Boston: HBS Publishing, 1997).

[24] Michael Watkins and Ann Leamon, "Telecom Italia (A)," HBS Case No. 800-363 (Boston: HBS Publishing, 2000), 4.

[25] Andy Thomson, "European Venture Capital," *European Venture Capital Journal*, December 1, 1999, S9.

The Industry Since 2000

Overall, Europe has risen in popularity as a private equity destination. From 2000's then record of $44 billion[26] raised, the markets crashed between 2002 and 2005 and then recovered to 2006's all-time high of $141 billion, as shown in Table 8.3. Recently, though, fund-raising

Table 8.3   Total European Private Equity Fund-Raising ($ Billions)

Year	Funds Raised
1986	$1.85
1987	$3.40
1988	$4.12
1989	$5.63
1990	$5.84
1991	$5.19
1992	$5.46
1993	$4.01
1994	$7.94
1995	$5.69
1996	$9.97
1997	$22.60
1998	$22.84
1999	$27.06
2000	$44.35
2001	$35.84
2002	$26.05
2003	$30.60
2004	$34.15
2005	$89.36
2006	$141.15
2007	$111.58
2008	$117.10
2009	$18.10

Source: Compiled from EVCA, *EVCA Yearbook* (Zaventum, Belgium: EVCA, 2009 and earlier).

---

[26] Data except where noted are derived from the European Private Equity and Venture Capital Association, *2009 EVCA Yearbook* (Zaventum, Belgium: European Private Equity and Venture Capital Association & Coller Capital, June 2009) and converted using the appropriate annual average from http://www.oanda.com.

has crashed again—the $18.6 billion raised in 2009 was the least since 1996. Most of the capital went to buyouts—venture funds rarely represented more than 13 percent of the annual fund-raising total. Three countries accounted for most of the venture-targeted fund-raising: the United Kingdom and Germany each raised 25 percent of the total, and France 17 percent.[27] Traditionally, the Scandinavian countries have had a fair amount of venture investment activity as well.

Slightly more than half (54 percent) of the funds raised in 2008 (2009 is anomalous) came from within Europe, and 30 percent was raised domestically (i.e., in the firm's home country). Investors outside Europe, mostly in North America, provided the balance.[28] Private pension funds and funds-of-funds were the two largest limited partnership (LP) groups in 2008. The pension funds could take advantage of their regular cash inflows due to payroll withholding to access interesting funds and, sometimes, improve the terms of their investment. The same trends fueled the participation of funds-of-funds, which often represent pension funds.[29]

Attitudes toward private equity in general and VC in particular vary across the Continent. Europe is not a monolith. Although the euro provides a common currency, languages, business customs, tax laws, accounting regulations, and export and import rules differ from country to country. The amount of private equity funding—venture or buyout—also varies from country to country.

To demonstrate, let us compare private equity investment by nation to that nation's GDP in 2008,[30] as shown in Figure 8.2. The largest and most developed private equity market in Europe is the United Kingdom, where private equity makes up 0.73 percent of GDP. In 2008, U.K. funds raised more than half of all European private equity funds. U.S. pension funds, in particular, have been attracted by the United Kingdom's relatively familiar legal and fiscal conditions.

After the United Kingdom, based on percentage of 2008 GDP, are Sweden, Denmark, France, and, in a three-way tie, Norway, Finland, and The Netherlands. Based on funds raised, France has moved into second place behind the United Kingdom; but based on private equity investment relative to their smaller GDPs, Sweden and Denmark lead. Germany, Europe's largest economy, has risen in the rankings and tied with Switzerland for sixth place; private equity investment made up 0.22 percent of its GDP in 2008. On the smaller end of the scale lies much of Eastern Europe; this is unsurprising given the region's recent economic reforms—although Hungary, whose private equity investment makes up 0.17 percent of its GDP, leads market-driven Belgium, which has only 0.13 percent.

Sweden is an interesting case of a small country with a fairly sizeable private equity industry. As with the United Kingdom, in Sweden, a significant share of capital raised by firms is actually invested in other European countries. The allure of Sweden's private equity market is its consistently high returns, which are based on a favorable corporate tax regime, the country's educated and internationally oriented population, and the fact that companies have to be ready to compete globally almost from the moment of founding.[31]

---

[27] Ibid.

[28] Data from Preqin, *2009 Global Private Equity Report* (London: Preqin, 2009), 34; and *2009 EVCA Yearbook*, 26.

[29] *2009 EVCA Yearbook*, 26.

[30] We are using 2008 rather than the more contemporary 2009 because the recession's impact makes 2009 (we hope!) anomalous. Even so, the results for small countries can be massively swung by a single investment. Data are sourced from a country's own private equity association where possible; where this does not exist, from regional groups; and in the last resort, from global groups such as EMPEA. GDP data are from the Economist Intelligence Unit.

[31] Charlotte Celsing, "Foreign Venture Capital is Pouring into Sweden," *Sweden.se*, January 12, 2007, http://www.sweden.se/eng/Home/Business/Economy/Reading/Riskkapital/, accessed August 12, 2010.

FIGURE 8.2 Private equity investment as a percentage of 2008 GDP

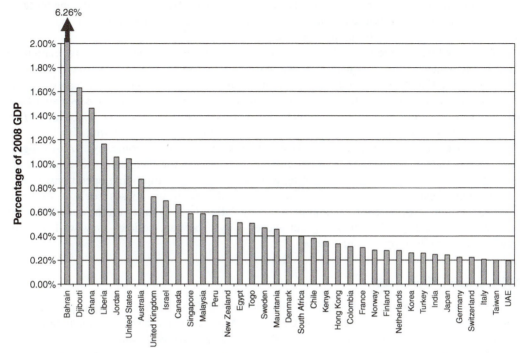

Source: National private equity/venture capital associations and regional reports. The top five results investments were due to single large deals relative to small GDPs.

Germany

Private equity has struggled to establish itself in Europe's largest economy, Germany. Müntefering's "locusts" comment, combined with the European Venture Capital Association's assessment that Germany's tax and regulatory environment is among the worst in Western Europe,[32] paint a bleak picture. Recently, however, German private equity has advanced. In 2006 and 2007, the government passed laws clarifying the tax treatment of private equity funds and several noteworthy deals occurred, including Fortress Investment Group's purchase of the entire public housing stock of the city of Dresden.[33] Although the industry stumbled there, as it did worldwide in 2008 and 2009, there was cautious optimism by 2010: almost 1,200 companies were funded, down only 10 percent from 2008. This was ascribed to the greater difficulty of obtaining bank financing. Fund-raising, however, had plummeted to levels below even 2002 and 2003, the decade's nadir, and activity in the VC market was particularly slow.[34]

---

[32] European Private Equity and Venture Capital Association, *2007 EVCA Yearbook* (Zaventum, Belgium: European Private Equity and Venture Capital Association & Coller Capital, June 2008), 151.

[33] Carter Dougherty, "The Buzz on German Private Equity," *New York Times*, October 20, 2006, http://www.nytimes.com/2006/10/20/business/worldbusiness/20iht-wblocust.html, accessed May 30, 2010.

[34] Data from BVK, the German Private Equity and Venture Capital Association in "German Companies Rely on Private Equity Even in the Credit Crunch," the German Private Equity and Venture Capital Association, March 8, 2010, http://www.bvkap.de/privateequity.php/cat/67/aid/599/title/German_companies_rely_on_private_equity_even_in_the_credit_crunch, accessed May 30, 2010.

One barrier to private equity remains Europe's fragmented regulatory environment, which greatly complicates cross-border activity. The European Commission has made reducing obstacles to cross-border investments a centerpiece of its efforts to promote private equity, but many remain skeptical of its capacity to bring about the requisite change.[35]

A further threat is the possibility of regulatory constraints. A wide range of regulation has been implemented in the Alternative Investment Fund Management (AIFM) directive recently enacted by the European Commission. While many of the details remain to be resolved as the directive is translated into the legal code of each member nation, many view this as a significant challenge to the industry's future prospects. Of particular concern has been the wide-ranging Article 30, which seeks to address concerns about "asset stripping" by restricting distributions or dividends paid in the first two years of a buyout firm's ownership of a company.[36] Assessing the state of the buyout industry in Europe, Eilis Ferran argues for balancing the economically worthwhile activity of buyouts—facilitating generational change, improving operations, streamlining conglomerates, and increasing efficiency—while curtailing abuses such as excessive leverage, conflicts of interest, and market manipulation.[37] It is unclear, however, whether regulators will manage this balancing act successfully. The new policies may well limit the industry's future development in Europe.

Why These Differences?

What helps create a strong VC market? How can the United Kingdom have a vibrant private equity market while the industry has struggled in Germany? As we consider the developing nations in the latter part of this chapter, are there any hallmarks that indicate an environment favorable to private equity?

In their seminal 2000 article, Leslie Jeng and Philippe Wells[38] explored the importance of IPOs, GDP, market capitalization growth, labor market rigidities, accounting standards, private pension funds, and government programs in determining the amount of VC funding in twenty-one developed countries. IPOs, they discovered, had the most significant impact on VC funding. Given the visibility afforded to companies that go public, along with their (usually) higher returns, this is not surprising. Austria, which ranked near the bottom of the 2008 list (private equity investment at 0.03 percent of GDP), had no exits via IPO in Jeng and Wells's analysis of 1991 to 1995; in the United Kingdom, IPOs made up an average of 35 percent of exits during that period.

In looking more closely at IPOs, Jeng and Wells find that they have little effect on early-stage investment, possibly because any exit at all appears so distant, but are very important in determining differences in later-stage VC investing across countries. This might reflect two dynamics: first, a more immediate concern about exiting via an IPO; and second, the importance of having that option to use as a bargaining chip with strategic acquirers. As one might assume, government-funded VC is not as sensitive to IPOs as funds raised from nongovernment sources.

Furthermore, the authors found that the involvement of private pension funds affected the level of VC funding *over time* but not across countries.[39] In Ireland, for instance, fund-raising increased from $32.4 million in 1993 to $232.1 million in 1994 after the government

---

[35] European Commission, *Expert Group Report on Removing Obstacles to Cross-Border Investments by Venture Capital Funds* (Brussels, European Commission, 2007).

[36] Linklaters, "AIFM Directive: Asset Stripping," July 8, 2011, http://www.linklaters.com/ Publications/ 20100218/Pages/ 15_Asset_Stripping.aspx, accessed July 26, 2011.

[37] Eilis Ferran, "Regulation of Private Equity-Backed Leverage Buyout Activity in Europe," *European Corporate Governance Institute* (Law Working Paper No. 84/2007), accessed at SSRN: http://ssrn.com/abstract=989748.

[38] Leslie Jeng and Philippe Wells, "The Determinants of Venture Capital Funding: Evidence across Countries," *Journal of Corporate Finance* 6 (2000): 241–89.

[39] Ibid., 242.

recommended that pension plans invest in private equity.[40] This is corroborated by experience in the United States—the entry of pension funds as limited partners substantially increased the funds available for investment over time. Labor market rigidities—that is, how easily workers can leave jobs without loss of prestige or benefits—worked against early-stage venture investments (seed and early stage) but had no impact on later-stage deals. This could reduce a worker's willingness to start a company but would have little impact on firms already past the crucial early stage of development.

For buyout firms, labor market rigidities represent one of the biggest challenges to the ability to restructure a portfolio company. Ant Bozkaya and William Kerr[41] built on the work by Jeng and Wells and broke down labor market rigidities into two parts: labor market expenditures (LMEs, such as unemployment insurance) and employment protection regulations (laws that restrict the firing of workers). They explored the impact of each of these on the private equity industry in various European countries, constructing an index that ranked the regulation levels in each labor market. Employment protections restricted private equity activity because they acted like a tax on the ability of private equity firms to adjust hiring at their portfolio companies and to shut them down if necessary. LMEs, on the other hand, encouraged greater private equity activity and higher investment, especially in VC.

This affects the execution of active investing. A buyout firm often relies on operational improvements to increase the company's efficiency, making staff reductions in the short term.[42] Mergers and acquisitions often reduce head count as redundancies (e.g., two chief financial officers) are eliminated. In VC, company head counts will ebb and flow as the company grows. Even if the total staff level is kept the same, a company that has moved from developing a product to marketing it will need to lay off engineers and hire marketing experts. Regulations that reduce this flexibility will reduce the investors' interest in entering the market. On the other hand, the LME cost is borne more widely and does not affect the investors' ability to change the course of the company, but simply the overall cost of employing workers.

Along with labor market regulations, many other factors that contribute to a favorable private equity climate involve the government. Tax and legal structures certainly play a significant role. Pointing to Portugal, Jeng and Wells noted that when the government legalized tax-advantaged VC corporations, private equity investments increased by a factor of thirty-eight in the span of a year.[43] Whether these were good investments, of course, is another question.

On the fund-raising side, governments also play multiple roles. When pension funds are allowed or encouraged to participate in private equity, domestic fund sources increase dramatically. For instance, after the government of Finland encouraged the country's banks and pension funds to invest in VC, their percentage participation rose from 20 percent in 1994 to 79 percent in 1995.[44] Governments can invest directly or create groups that increase the supply of either investable capital or investable opportunities, as we will see in Israel's innovation initiatives. The impact of government programs is discussed at greater length in Chapter 10.

Other governmental policies, such as those that support economic stability and the rule of law, can help create a general environment that benefits the private equity industry. Some contributing

---

[40] Ibid., 278.

[41] Ant Bozkaya and William Kerr, "Labor Regulations and European Private Equity," (HBS Working Paper No. 08-043, December 2009) (Boston: HBS Publishing Working Paper Series).

[42] This is elaborated in Steven J. Davis, John Halitwanger, Ron Jarmin, Josh Lerner, and Javier Miranda., "Private Equity and Employment," in *Globalization of Alternative Investments* (Working Papers Vol. 1: *The Global Economic Impact of Private Equity Report 2008* Davos, Switzerland: World Economic Forum, 2008), 43–64. The authors suggest that in the long term, companies that undergo buyouts create additional jobs, making up a substantial proportion of those lost.

[43] Jeng and Wells, "Determinants of Venture Capital Funding," 277.

[44] Ibid., 279.

factors can be seen as natural endowments, such as national size, a strong university system, or resource wealth that, if used wisely, can generate money for reinvestment. Yet without enabling legislation, private equity will struggle.

The literature has also explored the impact of different legal systems on VC investing. Jeng and Wells's analysis supported the finding that civil law countries such as France and Germany tended to have lower levels of venture investing as compared to contract law countries like the United Kingdom. We shall see that the influence of different legal systems on VC and buyout investment activity seems to hold throughout the world.

Yet another obstacle can be a country's management culture. While financial incentives commonly work well in the United Kingdom and the United States, they are less emphasized on the Continent, because a stockholding attitude is not as deeply embedded. Cultural attitudes also play a part; in unpublished research, practitioners noted that "in Europe, it's seen as more respectable to work for a big company or for the government. In the U.S., a mother wants her son to be the next Bill Gates; in Europe, she wants him to be the Transport Minister."[45]

THE EUROPEAN PRIVATE EQUITY CYCLE

Regardless of geography, private equity follows the same cycle of fund-raising, investment, exit, and further fund-raising. There may be regional variations in the types of limited partners (LPs), the stage focus of firms (VC or LBO), the sources of deals, and the avenues toward exit, but the general pattern is the same whether in the United States, United Kingdom, or European Union.

Fund-Raising

Sources of European private equity funds have traditionally been segmented by national boundaries. Private equity groups raised funds from banks, insurance companies, and government bodies in their own country, with little involvement of other investors. The one exception was the United Kingdom, where fund-raising had a strong international flavor, with heavy involvement by U.S. institutional investors.

These barriers are now rapidly breaking down, for two reasons. First, institutional investors—particularly in the United States—are seeking diversification through increased exposure to European funds. Second, most international private equity firms are now fully engaged in Europe and have developed local presences and networks.

Mayer et al.[46] explored the impact of different fund sources (banks, corporations, and pension funds) on the investment activities of VC funds in four developed markets—Israel, Germany, Japan, and the United Kingdom. The authors found that different fund sources are linked to different investments—for instance, venture firms backed by banks and pension funds tend to invest in later-stage firms more than do those backed by individuals and corporations. This does not, however, explain the variation in venture activity between countries.

Investing

Competition for buyout transactions is intense in Europe. As a direct result, so-called secondary deals—where one private equity fund sells a portfolio company to another—have rapidly increased. In addition, many deals are initiated through auctions. Investment banks have made the auction process very efficient, leaving little opportunity to buy firms for below their market value.

---

[45] Felda Hardymon, Josh Lerner, and Ann Leamon, "Venture Capital in Europe" (Working Paper, July 1, 2002, unpublished).

[46] Colin Mayer, Koen Schoors, and Yishay Yafeh, "Sources of Funds and Investment Activities of Venture Capital Funds," *Journal of Corporate Finance* 11 (2005): 586–608.

European private equity deals commonly involve the purchases of subsidiaries of conglomerates or family businesses rather than "take private" transactions, in which private equity firms buy publicly listed companies. In part, this stems from the stringent corporate control rules in some countries: for instance, in France, interest expense on debt can be deducted only if 95 percent or more of the equity is acquired.

Venture capital investment, too, can exhibit substantial differences between its application in the United States and in Europe, though these differences are gradually diminishing. Many European venture capitalists have traditionally had financial or consulting backgrounds rather than operating experience. Perhaps as a result, the relationships between venture capitalists and portfolio companies have tended to be more distant, with a greater emphasis on the assessment of financial performance than on active, hands-on investment.[47]

Another difference relates to the geographic distribution of investments. As in buyout investing, venture capitalists tend to invest in the country where a fund is located. Traditional reluctance to co-invest across borders reflects both the legacy of legal and regulatory barriers (now greatly reduced) and the distinct business cultures of many European nations. In Europe, one rarely finds geographic clustering of either VC firms or venture-backed entrepreneurs along the lines of Silicon Valley and Route 128 in the United States—perhaps the closest is the U.K's Thames Valley. This complicates the process of negotiating deals and managing company growth.

Exiting

A sale to a corporate acquirer—also known as a trade sale—is still the most common form of exit in the United Kingdom and on the Continent. As mentioned earlier, another popular exit method is a secondary sale, the sale of the company to another private equity firm. The United Kingdom has an advantage over the other European countries in terms of exit, since it has a well-developed capital market. In the wake of the 2002 Sarbanes-Oxley Act that tightened securities regulation in the United States, London's Alternative Investment Market (AIM) has emerged as a viable option to exits via acquisition.

On the Continent, almost every country has its own stock market. The pan-European exchange, the Euronext, merged the Amsterdam, Lisbon, Paris, and Brussels stock markets to form Europe's second-largest exchange. Listed stocks are traded both on the Euronext and on their home country exchanges. In 2005, the Euronext formed the Alternext as an alternative to London's AIM and the NASDAQ; it was acquired by the New York Stock Exchange in 2006.

OTHER DEVELOPED PRIVATE EQUITY MARKETS

While Europe is the second-largest private equity market in the world, some other developed countries have their own private equity ecosystems. We would be remiss if we did not discuss the private equity markets of Canada, Israel, Australia, and Japan.

Canadian Private Equity

For all that this volume tends to focus on the United States, there is a private equity industry north of the border. Canada's private equity industry, with C\$84.5 billion (US\$69.3 billion)

---

[47] See, for instance, the case studies presented in Gavin Reid, *Venture Capital Investment: An Agency Analysis of Practice* (London: Routledge, 1998).

under management in 2008,[48] is a fraction of the size of its southern neighbor's, but private equity investment made up an impressive 0.66 percent of the country's GDP. The industry is dominated by buyout firms with a strong international orientation;[49] in 2008, VC investment at C$1.4 billion (US$1.14 billion) was dwarfed by the C$9.1 billion (US$7.44 billion) from buyouts.[50] As occurred across the globe, 2009 saw both fund-raising and investment activity plummet, although investors sounded optimistic about renewed energy in the sector by early 2010.[51] The development of a more entrepreneurial mind-set in the country had been attributed to the success of Research In Motion, developer of the Blackberry device. Canada, like Germany, Japan, Sweden, and the United Kingdom, has implemented government programs to support VC; it also allows individuals to participate in mutual funds that invest in VC, known as Labour-Sponsored Investment Funds (LSIFs). Douglas J. Cumming and Jeffrey G. MacIntosh[52] explored the efficiency of these vehicles, only to find that they have experienced poor performance (lagging behind even low-risk Treasury bills) and incurred high fees, due largely to their organizational design. But the Canadian private equity industry is far more than government VC programs. Canada is home to some of the largest and most aggressive LPs, including the Canada Pension Plan Investment Board, Ontario Teachers' Pension Plan, and the Ontario Municipal Employees Retirement System. These institutions have mostly focused on later-stage investments, such as buyouts and infrastructure, and have shown themselves willing to co-invest or even lead transactions.

Israel: The Silicon Wadi

Israel may have the most active VC market outside the United States.[53] Private equity investment—for all intents and purposes, VC—accounted for 0.7 percent of its 2008 GDP. Government policies have helped create this market. In 1992, the government set up the Yozma program to invest directly in both funds and companies. Four years later, the industry had raised $1 billion and the government ceased its efforts, although it enacted favorable tax legislation. Israel's venture-backed companies tend to be in high technology, often staffed either by individuals who meet during their compulsory military service and find themselves in positions of authority at young ages or by engineers and scientists who have immigrated to the country. Many of the companies receive grants from the Ministry of Industry and

[48] McKinsey & Co. and Thomson Reuters, *Private Equity Canada 2008* (Toronto: Venture Capital and Private Equity Association, 2009), http://www.cvca.ca/files/Downloads/Private_Equity_Canada_2008.pdf.

[49] Robert Palter, Sacha Ghai, and Jonathan Tétrault, *Private Equity Canada 2009* (Toronto: McKinsey & Co. and Thomson Reuters, 2010), 5.

[50] Thomson Reuters and Canada's Venture Capital Association, "Canada's Private Equity Buyout Industry in 2008," January 2009, http://www.cvca.ca/files/Downloads/Final_English_Q4_2008_PE_Data_Deck.pdf; and "Canada's Venture Capital Industry in 2009," January 2010, http://www.cvca.ca/files/Downloads/Final_English_Q4_2009_VC_Data_Deck.pdf, accessed August 15, 2010.

[51] Canada's Venture Capital Association, "Venture Capital Investment in 2009 Lowest Recorded in 13 Years," press release, February 17, 2010, http://www.cvca.ca/files/News/CVCA_Q4_2009_VC_Press_Release_Final.pdf; and Pav Jordan, "Canada Venture Capital Drawing Big-Name Investors," *Reuters.com*, June 6, 2010, http://www.reuters.com/article/idUSN0414800420100606.

[52] Douglas J. Cumming and Jeffrey G. MacIntosh, "Mutual Funds That Invest in Private Equity? An Analysis of Labour-Sponsored Investment Funds," *Cambridge Journal of Economics* 31 (2007): 445–87.

[53] Jeng and Wells, "Determinants of Venture Capital Funding," 280–82.

Trade, which administers the Law for Encouragement of Industrial Research and Development. Frequently, Israeli companies go public on U.S. exchanges or are acquired by international companies, although the Tel Aviv Stock Exchange is also a viable exit avenue.

The global financial crisis dealt a significant blow to Israeli fund-raising and exits. In 2009, only three funds closed on $229 million among them, for the third lowest total in a decade. Sequoia Capital Israel's $200 million fourth fund accounted for the bulk of the total; two very early-stage efforts raised the balance. This represented a 72 percent drop from 2008's $802 million and reflected the losses suffered by foreign institutional investors, which had historically been the lead investors in Israeli funds.[54] Exit activity also slowed significantly in 2009, and only one Israeli companied went public, raising $22 million on the Tel Aviv exchange.[55]

Private Equity Down Under

The Australian private equity industry is sometimes merged with that of New Zealand and Papua New Guinea (often then termed, unmelodiously, Australasia). Because the continent so dominates its neighbors, with due respect, we will comingle the region. Australia's private equity industry raised A$17.4 billion (US$13.0 billion) in the year ending June 30, 2009, compared to A$17.6 billion (US$15.8 billion) the period before. Almost all the LPs were Australian, and pension funds represented more than half of the total.[56]

The vast majority of the capital went to buyout funds—in fact, buyouts on average accounted for 80 percent of the value and 30 percent of the deals done since 2003. Deal flow fell substantially, to thirteen in the first half of 2009 from twenty-six for the similar period in 2008; but the value almost doubled, to $6.6 billion from $3.6 billion. This, however, was due to a single $5 billion deal: Canada Pension Plan Investment Board's buyout of Macquarie Communications Infrastructure Group. Funds active in Australia included domestic operations like Pacific Equity Partners, Archer Capital, Ironbridge, and CHAMP; U.S.-based Carlyle Asia and CCMP Capital Asia, as well as European firms like CVC Asia Pacific and Catalyst.[57]

The government has introduced several programs to stimulate early-stage companies, most recently the Innovation Investment Follow-on Fund (IIFF) in August 2009 in response to the shortfall in funds for VC projects.[58] In mid-2010, the government enacted further changes to the tax code to provide tax advantages to private equity groups that set up locally managed investment trusts.[59]

---

[54] "IVC: Only $229 Million Raised by Israeli VC Funds in 2009," *Israel Venture Capital*, press release, March 8, 2010.

[55] "Israeli High-Tech Mergers and Acquisitions in 2009—$2.54 billion," *Israel Venture Capital's 2009 Exits Report,* press release, March 22, 2010.

[56] Brian Pink, "Venture Capital and Later Stage Private Equity Australia" (Canberra, Australian Bureau of Statistics, February 2010) http://www.ausstats.abs.gov.au/Ausstats/subscriber.nsf/0 /B11D2DAAD8D2B357CA2576C6001CC5 7D/$File/56780_2008-09.pdf, accessed July 12, 2010.

[57] "Regional Review: Australasia," in *Asian Buyout Review* (London: Asia Venture Capital Journal, 2009), 17–19.

[58] EIU, *Country Finance: Australia* (London: Economist Intelligencer Unit, 2009).

[59] Australian Private Equity and Venture Capital Association Ltd, "Government Introduces Revised Definition of MIT in Tax Laws Amendment (2010 Measures No 3) Bill 2010," May 26, 2010, http://www.avcal.com.au/news/details/policy-news/government-introduces-revised-definition-of-mit-in-tax-laws-amendment-2010-measures-no-3-bill-2010-/1292, accessed July 27, 2011.

Japan

Private equity has struggled to establish itself in Japan, and the first half of 2010 looked bleak indeed. In that period, a mere eleven deals were announced for a total $757.8 million, down from $8.7 billion for the same period in 2008 and a peak of $10.6 billion in 2006.[60] Venture capital investment also tumbled; 2009's annual total of $404 million was almost three times less than the amount in 2008. Japan's three largest venture firms suffered combined losses of $260 million.[61]

Private equity groups active in Japan include both domestic firms and divisions of many foreign-based global firms. The domestic groups raise funds from both domestic and foreign LPs. Japanese LPs appear much more likely to invest in domestic firms, while foreign LPs are essentially split in their preference of manager.[62] Although some of the biggest Japanese venture firms, such as SBI Holdings, JAFCO, and Japan Asia Investment, are publicly traded,[63] others are classic partnerships. Deal flow, particularly for foreign firms, has been a challenge. The U.K.-based firm 3i tried several ways to establish a presence—a joint venture, then a dedicated office—before deciding to focus on investing in domestic funds.[64]

Yet there are some positive trends. Japan has a host of companies that badly need to consolidate and a generation of post–World War II founders ready to retire, although a deep cultural resistance to outside capital and advice has tripped up many buyout firms' dreams.[65] Moreover, the government has enacted legislation to reduce the tax burden for venture-backed start-ups, and private equity funds offered to "sophisticated" investors have been granted more lenient regulation.[66] The buyout market also seems to be thawing. Kohlberg Kravis Roberts (KKR), which did its first Japanese deal in 2007, finally consummated its second transaction in Japan early in 2010 with the purchase of Intelligence Ltd., a recruitment services company, for $356 million. This was one of three deals done by global private equity firms in the first half of 2010 where the transaction size exceeded $60 million.[67] Management buyouts, virtually unheard of four years ago, have become more common as well. Lastly, even overtures from Chinese firms have been accepted as Japanese companies look for access to the vibrant market across the straits.[68]

---

[60] "The Waiting Years," *Asia Private Equity Review*, July 2010, http://www.asiape.com/aper/aper_issues/aper1007.html, accessed July 12, 2010.

[61] EIU, *Country Finance: Japan* (London: Economist Intelligencer Unit, 2010), 41–43.

[62] Coller Capital, *Global Private Equity Barometer: Japanese Snapshot* (New York: Coller Capital), 2007.

[63] EIU, *Country Finance: Japan*, 42.

[64] "3i Group plc," HBS Case No. 803-020 (Boston: HBS Publishing, 2003); and http://www.3i.com, accessed November 27, 2010.

[65] Alison Tudor, "Deal Journal: China Firms Scaling the Walls of Japan," *Wall Street Journal*, July 6, 2010, C1.

[66] EIU, *Country Finance: Japan*.

[67] "The Waiting Years," *Asia Private Equity Review*.

[68] Tudor, "Deal Journal: China Firms Scaling the Walls of Japan."

PRIVATE EQUITY IN EMERGING MARKETS

The past several years have seen a dramatic increase in private equity activity in the developing world. While China and India receive the most attention, even regions that were formerly anathema to all but the most intrepid investors and limited partners—Russia and Central-Eastern Europe, Africa, the Middle East—have become the targets not just of opportunistic investments but even of specific funds, raised both overseas and domestically. Even the 2008 financial crisis, while initially sparking a "flight to security," quickly became a "flight to growth" that drew private equity investors back to the emerging markets.

Since the 1990s, emerging markets have benefited both from actions on their own parts to enhance their attractiveness and from exogenous changes that reduced the attractiveness of developed markets. Internal reforms such as increased market orientation, heightened fiscal transparency, and reduced restrictions on foreign investment coincided with external policy shifts by developed nations that lowered barriers to trade. Growth in emerging markets has substantially outpaced that of the developed world. While the developed economies grew at an inflation-adjusted compound annual rate of 2 percent between 1999 and 2009, emerging market economies grew at 5.8 percent.[69] The growth rates of some example countries from both groups are shown in Table 8.4.

Table 8.4   Average Real GDP Growth Rates, 1999–2009 (%)

Compound Annual Growth Rate (CAGR) of Real GDP (US$ at 2005 prices), 1999–2009	
Emerging Markets	**Growth Rates**
China	10.3
Nigeria	8.7
India	7.0
Russia	5.3
Indonesia	5.1
Egypt	4.9
Pakistan	4.8
Malaysia	4.8
South Africa	3.6
Developed Markets	
Israel	3.5
Brazil	3.3
Australia	3.1
United States	1.8
Western Europe	1.5
European Union	1.4
Euro Area	1.3
Japan	0.7

Source: Economist Intelligence Unit Data.

---

[69] Data from the International Monetary Fund, World Economic Outlook Database, October 2010.

The recent attention paid to emerging markets is not the first such surge of interest, but it seems to be the most widespread. An earlier surge occurred in the early and mid-1990s, fueled by the rapid growth of many developing nations and the relaxation of curbs on foreign investment. This was compounded by the perception by many institutional investors in the mid-1990s that the returns from private equity investments in the United States were likely to fall. Over the last years of the decade, however, these two perceptions shifted. Private equity fund-raising in developing countries suffered as a result, and a recovery started only in 2003.

The second wave of private equity shares some similarities with the first but also differs in important ways. Some of the developing nations appear to have reached real inflection points in their GDP growth trajectories. In the two countries in the world with the greatest population, India and China, and to a smaller extent across the developing globe, a middle class is being created that, in the words of a venture capitalist who led his top-tier firm into India, "wants—well, what every other middle class consumer wants." Governments are also realizing that a key to their own survival is job creation, with which some research suggests private equity can assist.[70]

Realizing this, some governments have taken specific steps to increase their countries' ability to attract private equity. Some, such as Mexico, have tried to increase the transparency of their corporate governance. Many have implemented protection for minority shareholders. China inaugurated its Shenzhen and ChiNEXT exchanges to provide exit options for less established companies. Many countries have relaxed capital controls and opened sectors of the economy to foreign investment. India's real estate sector, for instance, exploded overnight when it was opened to foreign investment in March 2005, given the country's shortage of 24.7 million housing units.[71]

Emerging Market Private Equity in the Past

Private equity first appeared in the emerging markets in the 1970s,[72] often driven by government-associated development finance institutions (DFIs), such as the World Bank's for-profit financing arm, the International Finance Corporation (IFC). Loans and grants historically had made up much of this investment.

Developing a private equity market in these nations was impeded by a host of challenges. Many developing countries lacked not just financial markets but even fundamental business infrastructure. Investment opportunities were difficult to find, especially deals of a size that allowed the investor to create economies of scale. In some regions, such as Africa, the money from DFIs trying to enter the market far outstripped the opportunities to deploy it wisely. Once an opportunity was found, obtaining adequate leverage for large deals could be difficult. Management skills might be weak by developed market standards, sometimes due to lack of training, but also because the environment might value certain aptitudes—relationships and connections, for instance—more than a focus on profits. The fledgling financial markets were badly rocked by the market slide that started in mid-1990s with the Russian and Asian fiscal crises. Even in the late

---

[70] Some studies have shown that private-equity-funded companies tend to create more jobs than do companies not funded with private equity. These companies were already in operation, and not start-ups, so this data did not start from a small base. For more, see Florence Eid, "Private Equity Finance as a Growth Engine," *Business Economics* 41, no. 3 (2006); and National Venture Capital Association, "Venture Impact: The Economic Impact of Venture Capital," March 2007, http://www.nvca.org, accessed August 3, 2007.

[71] Minister for Housing and Urban Poverty Alleviation, Kumari Selja, cited in "Shortage of Housing in India? 24.71 mn only!" Rediff, February 26, 2009, http://www.rediff.com/money/2009/feb/26bcrisis-shortage-of-housing-in-india.htm, accessed May 31, 2010.

[72] This section is informed by Lerner et al., "CDC Capital Partners," 2–5.

1990s, the culture of some emerging markets discouraged the transparency that private equity required before investors were willing to commit. Observed one IFC official:

> In a country where the rule of law is uncertain, you don't want to make a lot of money because your children may be kidnapped and held for ransom. Local officials may be corrupt and think that you can afford to pay bribes. Likewise, if the tax authorities aren't very strong, financial transparency is a competitive disadvantage, because you might have to pay taxes that your competitors can avoid. In emerging markets there are a lot of good reasons to keep things quiet, and the amount of money that an entrepreneur can get through an equity investment may not outweigh the costs.[73]

Despite these differences, the basic private equity cycle followed the familiar pattern described in this book. Assets were hard to value, and the success of a company was extremely uncertain. Investors found deals, took equity stakes, and hoped to exit with appropriate returns when the timing was right. Exits were themselves difficult since many developing countries lacked efficient stock markets for IPOs, and mergers and acquisitions were complicated because the pool of purchasers was small, usually had limited means, and was aware of the investor's need to exit.

Historically, returns in emerging markets have been extremely volatile for several reasons, including currency fluctuations, political instability, inadequate legal systems, weak accounting standards, and, sometimes, competition from subsidized state-run enterprises.[74] In addition, the runaway romp of developed world markets during the late 1990s into the early 2000s far overshadowed the performance of emerging markets, making it even harder for such investments to compete. As shown in Figure 8.3, the five-year annualized returns to the public indices of

FIGURE 8.3 Five-year returns to major indices for developed and emerging markets

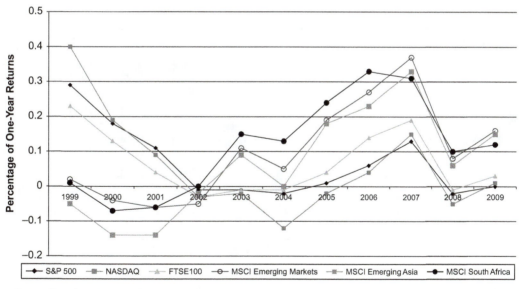

Source: Data from Datastream.

---

[73] Private communication, December 18, 2002, in Lerner et al., "CDC Capital Partners," 4.

[74] James C. Brenner, "Direct Equity Investment Funds: Public-Private Partnership Experience" (Paper prepared for the Forum for International Financial Institution Investment Fund Specialists, February 8–9, 1999), 34.

developed markets outperformed those of the emerging markets until 2003, whereupon the situation reversed. By 2009, the five-year annualized returns to the MSCI Emerging Market Index were 16 percent compared to 3 percent for the United Kingdom's FTSE 100, 1 percent for the NASDAQ, and 0 percent for the S&P 500.[75] These indices are public and thus liquid; one would expect that private investors would require higher returns to risk investing in emerging market private equity.

Emerging Markets: Private Equity Since 2000

Although emerging market investing was definitely a high-stakes game in which exposure to the wrong country or region at the wrong time (Argentina in 2002, Russia in 1998, Asia in 1997) could decimate returns, emerging markets caught fire starting in 2003. Multinational companies actively started to acquire emerging companies—IBM purchased India's Daksh in 2004, for example. Many emerging market companies also went public, whether on domestic exchanges or those of developed markets.

This activity has persisted and even intensified. Despite the huge run-up in developed market private equity fund-raising and investment between 2001 and 2009, emerging markets saw a similar or greater increase, as shown in Figures 8.4a and 8.4b.[76] In 2009, emerging market fund-raising accounted for 16 percent of the total, and investment activity in those markets made up 22 percent. In addition, the decline in activity between the peak and 2009 has been smaller, in percentage terms, for the emerging markets—fund-raising for developed markets fell 75 percent from its peak; that for emerging markets lost 66 percent.[77]

FIGURE 8.4a   Fund-raising for emerging and developed markets

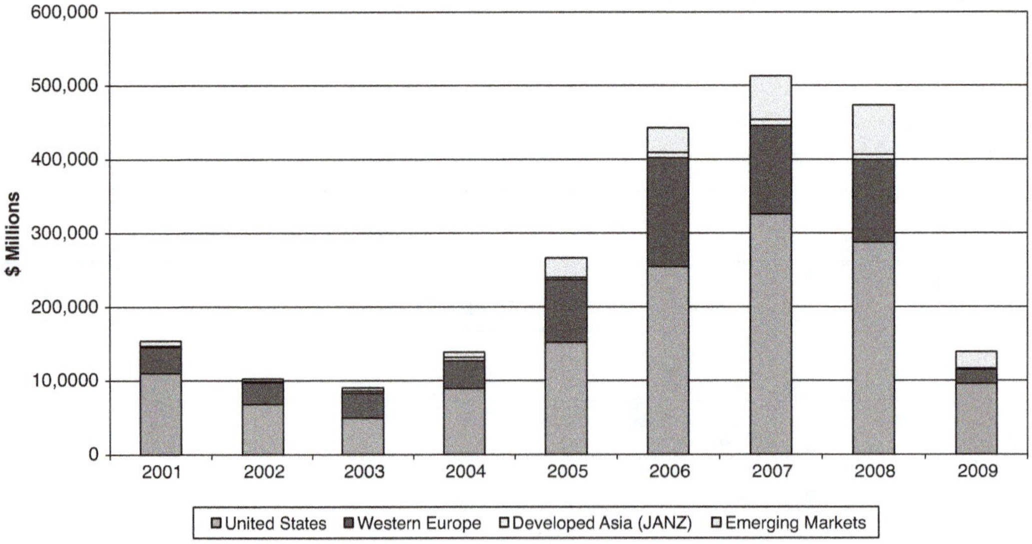

Note: JANZ: Japan, Australia, New Zealand.
Source: Data from Emerging Markets Private Equity Association, *EM PE Industry Statistics Review: Fundraising, Investment, Performance Through Q4 2009*, (Washington DC: EMPEA, 2010), updated April 7, 2010.

---

[75] Data from Datastream.
[76] Data from Emerging Markets Private Equity Association, *EMPE Industry Statistics Review: Fundraising, Investment, Performance through Q4 2009* (Washington, DC: EMPEA, 2010), updated April 7, 2010.
[77] Ibid.

FIGURE 8.4b   Investments in emerging and developed markets

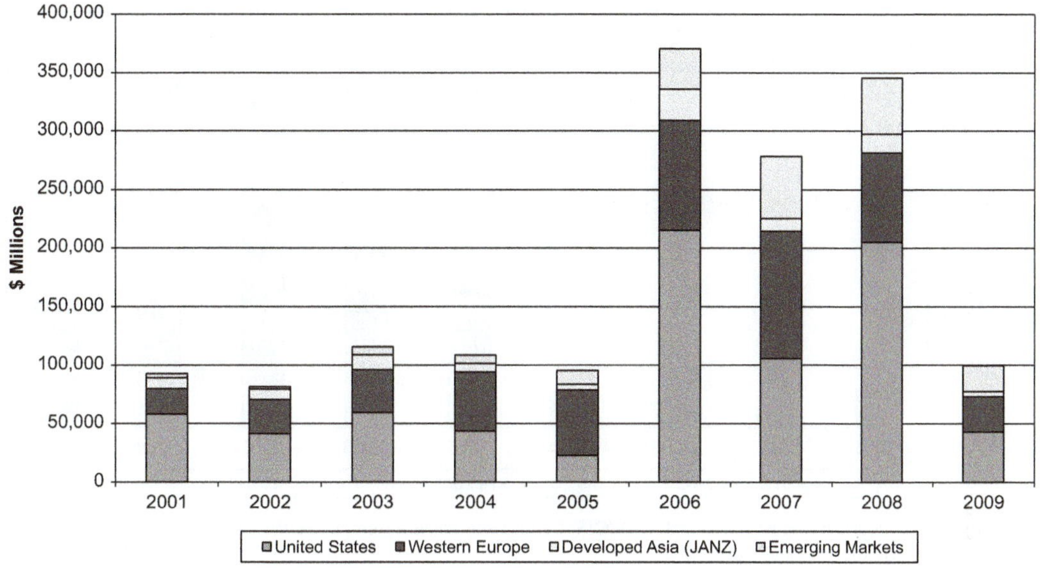

Note: JANZ: Japan, Australia, New Zealand.
Source: Data from Emerging Markets Private Equity Association, *EM PE Industry Statistics Review: Fundraising, Investment, Performance Through Q4 2009*, (Washington DC: EMPEA, 2010), updated April 7, 2010.

Emerging markets also appear to be recovering more quickly from the slump. High levels of domestic growth and the fact that the financial crash originated in the developed markets create a compelling investment story, especially for growth equity. At the end of 2009, 67 percent of 151 major institutional LPs reported that they expected their 2006- and 2007-vintage emerging market funds—those raised during the bubble—to outperform developed market funds, and a vast majority of these LPs anticipate returns in excess of 16 percent. Only 29 percent expected such performance from their developed market funds. In view of such expectations, it is not surprising that more than half of these LPs expected to increase their allocations to emerging markets and to raise the median allocation from "6%–10%" to "11% to 15%."[78]

In many emerging markets, most private equity investment occurs as growth capital. Investing in a company that already has a market and a product avoids the intense hands-on supervision necessary with a start-up and the government approval and debt availability that may be required for a leveraged buyout (LBO). As competition heightens in the middle market, private equity firms move to the ends of the spectrum. A study of emerging market-targeted funds that closed in 2008 found that growth-stage investments predominated (86 funds, 41 percent of the total number, with $18.3 billion, or 26 percent of the capital), followed by VC (64 funds, 30 percent of the total number, with $7.6 billion, or 7 percent of the capital). Last in terms of number were buyouts, which involved 32 funds or 15 percent of the total, but the bulk of the capital (45 percent and $31 billion).[79]

Since 2001, the amount of money raised for emerging markets grew tenfold, from $6.6 billion to $66.5 billion in 2008, only to fall to $22.6 billion in 2009, as seen in Figures 8.5a and 8.5b. In general, the most popular region has been "emerging Asia" (Asia excluding Japan, Australia, and New Zealand, thus primarily China and India), which was the target of 59 percent of the funds raised in 2008 and 70 percent in 2009. Of the emerging markets, China and India have received the

---

[78] Ibid.
[79] Emerging Markets Private Equity Association, *EM PE 2008 Fundraising and Investment Review* (Washington, DC: EMPEA, 2009).

FIGURE 8.5a Fund-raising for emerging markets

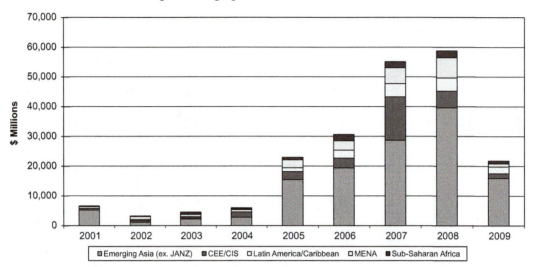

Note: JANZ: Japan, Australia, New Zealand. CEE/CIS: Central and Eastern Europe and the Commonwealth of Independent States. MENA: Middle East and North Africa.
Source: Data from Emerging Markets Private Equity Association, *EM PE Industry Statistics Review: Fundraising, Investment, Performance Through Q4 2009*, (Washington DC: EMPEA, 2010), updated April 7, 2010.

greatest amount of press coverage and have funds run by the most widely recognized firms. Data for the other emerging regions comes from a small base, which makes results sensitive to the closing of a single large fund in a particular year and obscures broader trends. Beyond emerging Asia, however, 2008 funds targeted the Middle East and North Africa (MENA), Central and Eastern Europe and the Commonwealth of Independent States (CEE/CIS), Latin America and

FIGURE 8.5b Emerging market investment

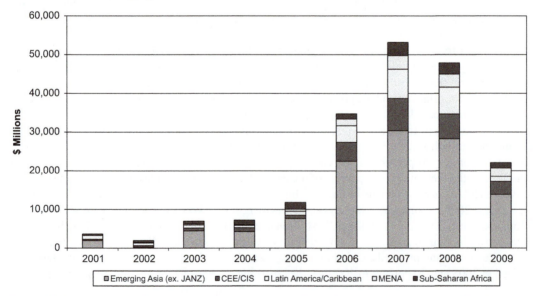

Note: JANZ: Japan, Australia, New Zealand. CEE/CIS: Central and Eastern Europe and the Commonwealth of Independent States. MENA: Middle East and North Africa.
Source: Data from Emerging Markets Private Equity Association, *EM PE Industry Statistics Review: Fundraising, Investment, Performance Through Q4 2009*, (Washington DC: EMPEA, 2010), updated April 7, 2010.

the Caribbean, and sub-Saharan Africa, along with a substantial amount to multiregion funds. In the shrunken total of 2009, MENA, CEE/CIS, and multiregion funds lost favor compared to the other emerging areas.[80]

Why has there been such interest in emerging markets?[81] Some is due to the markets themselves, some to external trends. The recent crash has many LPs looking for new arenas for investing—in fact, David Rubenstein of Carlyle said, "The U.S. dominance [in private equity] will recede during the next five years or so. Right now, all the largest private equity firms are American. That shouldn't necessarily be the case."[82]

One of the biggest reasons for the attention to emerging markets has been their substantial economic reforms. It is easy to forget that twenty-five years ago, only one billion of the world's citizens were in capitalist economies; today, only a handful of countries have centrally planned economies. Even China, the largest centrally planned economy, has adopted a host of capitalist market structures.

Due to external changes like the United States' Brady Plan—which dramatically reduced debt service payments for Latin America and strengthened those economies—and internal reforms initiated by the countries themselves, emerging market economies have largely stabilized. In many countries, capital gains taxes have been reduced along with restrictions on foreign investment, while accounting and disclosure standards have been raised, encouraging foreign investors.

Even in the face of the economic slump in 2008, emerging markets did not subside into chaos or upheaval. With leverage "no longer considered a sure thing to generate returns,"[83] LPs started seeking areas with strong domestic growth. By the end of the first quarter of 2010, a number of emerging market funds had closed, among them Advent International with $1.65 billion in its fifth Latin American fund and Carlyle with $2.55 billion for its latest Asian fund; activity that is particularly noteworthy given the difficulties that many developed market firms encountered in raising funds focused on the United States and Europe.

Private Equity Markets in Other Countries

In this section, we will take a brief tour of the state of private equity in selected countries and regions such as China, India, and Africa. Other markets do exist, but space precludes their consideration in this volume. Here we examine the key challenges and opportunities that private equity investors face in each market and how they are similar to or different from those of the developed world.

China

China's process of deregulation started in 1980 with the first market reforms.[84] The country opened its first stock exchanges in 1990, and by the mid-2000s, the IPOs of Chinese companies routinely set records as the "world's largest to date": the October 2006 IPO of the Industrial and

---

[80] Data from Emerging Markets Private Equity Association, *EM PE Industry Statistics Review: Fundraising, Investment, Performance through Q4 2009*.

[81] According to the World Bank, emerging nations are those countries that have either low- or middle-level per capita incomes, have underdeveloped capital markets, and/or are not industrialized. It should be noted, however, that the application of these criteria is somewhat subjective.

[82] David Rubenstein, address at the Swedish Private Equity and Venture Capital Association Congress, Stockholm Sweden; cited in Johan Nylander, "China to Become Biggest Private Equity Player," *Tribune Business News*, April 28, 2010.

[83] Ken McFadyen, "LPs Bullish on Emerging Markets," *Mergers & Acquisitions Report*, April 26, 2010, 5.

[84] Material drawn from Felda Hardymon and Ann Leamon, "Gobi Partners and DMG," HBS Case No. 810-095 (Boston: HBS Publishing, 2010), 2–5.

Commercial Bank of China raised $22 billion in a simultaneous Hong Kong and Shanghai listing that valued the organization at $156.5 billion;[85] the market debut of China's Agricultural Bank, also a dual listing in Hong Kong and Shanghai, raised $19.2 billion on its first trading day, an amount that valued the company at $128 billion despite a weaker global market and concerns about the bank's underlying strength.[86] In an effort to provide exit opportunities for smaller enterprises, the government established the Small and Medium Enterprise (SME) board in 2004 and the ChiNEXT exchange, similar to the NASDAQ and London's AIM, in 2009.

China is considered by some private equity investors "the most attractive . . . market in the world."[87] The sheer size of the market, with the world's largest population and record of high growth, provides the opportunity to create a world-class company simply by serving domestic demand. Growth equity is the most common type of investment.

In 2006, the Chinese government authorized the creation of funds in the local currency (renminbi or RMB), raised from local individuals or institutions and often with ties to the government. In 2009, for the first time, RMB-denominated funds overtook dollar-denominated funds, both in terms of the number of funds raised and the amount committed to them. Both domestic entities (CDH, Gobi Partners, and Hony Capital) and international firms (Carlyle and Blackstone) are raising RMB funds, although their long-term success is open to question. The domestic LP base in China is seen as fragmented, short run in its orientation, and new to the asset class.[88] New GPs of new RMB funds are frequently inexperienced, particularly in the nuances of active investing.

China's private equity environment is still evolving. Legal, regulatory, and administrative frameworks for the RMB funds and for the joint ventures that they might form with foreign-domiciled funds are still developing. Legislation can be years in the making and then implemented overnight. As one experienced China private equity investor noted, "There's a government policy website. We check it every day, like the weather."[89]

The overall Chinese private equity market, though, is viewed favorably. The growing middle class is eager for everything from cars to mobile phones to vacations.[90] As in many emerging markets, the lack of an established technology infrastructure allows China to leapfrog intermediate technology phases. Exits occur regularly, whether IPOs on foreign or Chinese markets or trade sales.[91]

The Chinese private equity market is not without its risks. In mid-2008, Carlyle Group abandoned a three-year effort to acquire Xugong Group, China's largest construction equipment maker. The firm had agreed to purchase 85 percent of the company for $375 million in October 2005, only to have the deal arouse fierce outcry (especially from Xugong's major competitor) about the sale of critical national assets to foreigners.[92] Despite two proposals from Carlyle to

[85] "China Finance: The World's Largest IPO Update," *EIU ViewsWire*, October 27, 2006.

[86] Richard McGregor and Patrick Jenkins, "China Banks Fear Falling Confidence," *FT.com*, July 11, 2010; and Michael Wines, "China Bank I.P.O. Raises $19 Billion," *New York Times*, July 6, 2010, http://www.nytimes.com/2010/07/07/business/global/07ipo.html, accessed July 26, 2010.

[87] SCM Strategic Capital Management AG, "State of the Asia-Pacific Private Equity Markets," analysis prepared by SCM Strategic Capital Management AG, April 2010, 14.

[88] York Chen, "China VC Market from 2009 to 2010" (ID TechVentures slide show, February 10, 2010), http://www.idtvc.com.cn/documents/129125770356718750.pdf, accessed June 3, 2010.

[89] Felda Hardymon, Josh Lerner, and Ann Leamon, "Gobi Partners: Raising Fund II," HBS Case No. 807-093 (Boston: HBS Publishing, 2007), 6.

[90] Suzanne McGee, "China's Open Door," *Investment Dealers' Digest*, September 11, 2006, 1; cited in Felda Hardymon and Ann Leamon, "Digital Media Group: The Shanghai Bid," HBS Case No. 810-099 (Boston: HBS Publishing, 2010), 3.

[91] Danielle Fugazy, "2008: Year of the Rat Race," *Mergers & Acquisitions*, March 2008, 50–51; cited in Felda Hardymon and Ann Leamon, "Digital Media Group: The Shanghai Bid," 3.

[92] Zachary Wei, "China SASAC Approves Carlyle's Bid to Acquire 50 pct of Xugong," *Forbes*, November 12, 2006, http://www.forbes.com, accessed December 13, 2006.

reduce its ownership and increase the valuation, government approval did not materialize.[93] Of course, this is not unique to China—the bid by the China National Offshore Oil Company (CNOOC) to acquire U.S.-based Unocal in 2005 aroused a firestorm of controversy; CNOOC eventually withdrew the offer.

Interestingly, by late 2010, the Chinese government was eagerly inviting global private equity firms to invest in the country and issuing quotas to cities such as Beijing and Shanghai that would allow the firms to bypass China's currency controls and raise offshore money for RMB funds. Said Carlyle's Rubenstein, "The Chinese government . . . recognizes how [private equity firms] can help local companies acquire western competitors and technologies and that's something they're very interested in."[94]

Private equity investors routinely cite other challenges to investing in China, which include finding and retaining management comfortable in Western-style companies, opaque company financials, and language barriers. Yet despite the challenges and uncertainties, the government appears to be strongly committed to private equity.[95] David Rubenstein's prediction of Chinese leadership in private equity does not seem far-fetched—in fact, he declared that the Chinese market in late 2010 "is more favorable for private equity capital than most other markets. More favorable even than the United States."[96]

India

India has established its own growth story separately from China's. Starting in 1991, the economy has gradually been deregulated. Since then, and despite different parties in government, India has steadily created a more hospitable business climate with a particular eye toward attracting foreign investment.[97] India also boasts the oldest stock exchange in Asia, a legal structure inherited from the British, and the widespread use of English as the language of business.

India's first private equity boom occurred in 1999 and 2000, when investments peaked at $1.16 billion in 280 companies.[98] This was primarily VC riding the tech wave of the United States and outsourcing projects, whether programming, data analysis, or call centers, to India's lower-wage but highly educated labor force. When the NASDAQ bubble burst, interest in India subsided.

India's next boom started in 2004. In 2008, private equity investors raised $7.7 billion for India,[99] much of it was invested in growth equity deals.[100] The popularity of growth equity stemmed from the risk of early-stage investing, which was mitigated by investing in companies that had successful operating records, and India's laws against borrowing to make acquisitions, which essentially ruled out LBOs.[101] Overseas funds as diverse as Carlyle, Blackstone, 3i, Sequoia, Bessemer Venture Partners, and KKR have established offices in India or raised funds targeting the country. They joined domestic investors such as Chrysalis Capital, ICICI, and India Value Fund, and foreign incumbents like Actis, Morgan Stanley, and Warburg Pincus. Moreover, new players have entered the landscape. India's major corporations and financial institutions have

---

[93] "China's Xugong Says Carlyle Investment Deal Dead," *Reuters.com*, July 22, 2008, http://www.reuters.com/article/idUSSHA32313820080722, accessed January 24, 2010.

[94] Jamil Anderlini, "China Rolls Out the Red Carpet for Private Equity," *Financial Times*, November 26, 2010, 18.

[95] EMPEA, *Insight China*, September 2009, 7.

[96] Anderlini, "China Rolls Out the Red Carpet for Private Equity."

[97] This paragraph is based on Felda Hardymon and Ann Leamon, "Motilal Oswal Financial Services: An IPO in India," HBS Case No. 807-095 (Boston: HBS Publishing), 3.

[98] India Venture Capital Association, "Venture Capital and Private Equity in India" (slide presentation, October 2007), http://www.indiavca.org/IVCA%20Presentation_October2007.pdf, accessed July 11, 2010.

[99] EMPEA, *Insight India*, July/August 2009, 1.

[100] Data from Evaluserve report; cited in "Venture Capital Stages Resurgence in India," *Asia Pulse*, September 11, 2006.

[101] KPMG, *Insight: India* (London: KPMG, July 2009), 3. If the deal was structured outside India, a certain amount of leverage might be allowed, but less than a typical Western buyout deal.

either created their own private equity operations or plan to raise outside capital to do so.[102] Domestic firms are starting to raise money internally, auguring increased competition for international firms since domestic operations can avoid the borrowing caps and sector prohibitions imposed on foreign firms.[103]

India's growth is creating additional opportunities for private equity. The middle class is eager to purchase educational opportunities for their children and financial products that were unthinkable just a decade ago.[104] Generational shifts provide opportunities to buy into or purchase outright family businesses, whose sale had previously been viewed as an admission of failure.[105]

In a sign of maturation, there has been a move toward sector-specific funds rather than funds that target the country as a whole. Infrastructure, of which India is in dire need, and technology have attracted the greatest attention. Although India's private equity scene looks promising, it still faces barriers. The country's poor infrastructure and its complicated regulatory system are particular areas of concern.

Africa

Although virtually overlooked by many investors as late as 2005, sub-Saharan Africa has become a remarkable growth story.[106] A 2010 study by Emerging Markets Private Equity Association (EMPEA) of major LPs found that 28 percent (vs. 4 percent in 2006) of them are currently investing in Africa.[107] Much of Africa's private equity funding, though, still comes through DFIs.

While part of Africa's GDP growth is due to soaring prices for oil, minerals, and commodities, internal changes have also played a significant role. The cessation of most conflicts and the enactment of internal economic reforms have created a much more stable business climate. State-owned enterprises have been privatized, legal and regulatory systems strengthened, transparency increased, and both physical and social infrastructure enhanced.[108] A growing middle class is sparking domestic consumption, and the labor force is expanding.

Africa does face challenges. Infrastructure and electricity are scarce, as is skilled labor. The reforms are fragile, and the "lost decade" of the 1990s is still a fresh memory. Yet private equity has started to target the region and is expanding beyond its historic focus on South Africa, which receives the greatest attention in recognition of its rule of law, strong economic growth, and thriving capital markets. Country-specific funds are being raised for Botswana, Nigeria, and Namibia.[109] London-based Standard Bank Private Equity established an investment team in Nigeria in early 2009, joining the Nigerian pioneer African Capital Alliance and Actis. Most funds, though, target subregions where economies are linked by culture and/or language. Local funds are also entering the market.

Continued interest in Africa must be supported by exits. Most IPOs are limited to the Johannesburg Stock Exchange, and most exits occur via share sales (sales of additional shares by an already-listed company) or share buybacks (in which the company repurchases the investors' holdings). Strategic sales, though, are starting to occur.[110] The continent still is a bit of a frontier

---

[102] EMPEA, *Insight India*, July/August 2009, 3–4.

[103] Ibid., 7.

[104] Hardymon and Leamon, "Motilal Oswal Financial Services: An IPO in India," 5.

[105] KPMG, *Insight: India*, 3.

[106] It is difficult to reduce any of these countries into a few paragraphs, but particularly so for this continent.

[107] EMPEA, *Insight Sub-Saharan Africa*, October 2009, 1.

[108] Acha Leke, Susan Lund, Charles Roxburgh, and Arend von Wamelen, "What's Driving Africa's Growth?" *McKinsey Quarterly*, June 2010.

[109] EMPEA, *Insight Sub-Saharan Africa*, 3.

[110] EMPEA, *Insight Sub-Saharan Africa*, 6.

market; but as a McKinsey report notes, "If recent trends continue, Africa will play an increasingly important role in the global economy."[111]

Middle East and North Africa (MENA)

Private equity is a recent arrival in MENA—in 2001, a mere $78 million was raised by three funds in the entire region. But private equity fund-raising in the MENA region more than tripled between 2005 ($2 billion) and 2008 ($6.9 billion).[112] Dubai-based Abraaj Capital, the largest fund in the area, made the list of Top 50 Largest Private Equity funds for 2009. Many MENA funds target mid-market growth equity deals, given the region's preponderance of family-owned businesses. The owners, however, tended to be wary of investment. Faisal Belhoul, managing partner of private equity firm Ithmar Capital and a member of a major business family, explained, "Business in the Gulf is a question of personal fulfillment, providing a means to enhance a family's social standing, rather than a purely wealth-generating market-driven activity."[113] Venture capital is very rare, given uncertainty about quality deal flow and the difficulty of successful exits.[114]

Some MENA funds focus on the Gulf Cooperation Council (GCC—Qatar, Saudi Arabia, Oman, United Arab Emirates, Bahrain, and Kuwait) countries, others include much of North Africa (Morocco, Egypt, Algeria), and yet others expand their focus to Jordan and Lebanon. Traditionally, the private equity industry has been dominated by local firms that invest across the entire MENA region. In 2009, though, the U.S.-based firms Carlyle Group and KKR and France's BNP Paribas entered the region or announced intentions to do so.

The LPs in MENA funds typically come from that region. These include sovereign wealth funds, family offices, and high-net-worth individuals, although the recent financial slump has forced many fund managers to look elsewhere for investors.

The GCC governments opened to private equity in an attempt to create jobs for their large and growing populations and create an economy that can exist in the post-oil era. The region also plans to build or privatize infrastructure assets with their necessarily high price tags.[115]

The global financial downturn dealt the GCC countries a blow, particularly Dubai with its debt woes and other concerns about accounting transparency—a key area in which private equity can contribute. Exits were still somewhat uncertain, especially in light of the drubbing delivered by the stock market slump in 2008. IPOs have been the preferred exit route, but strategic sales also provide an avenue.[116]

Central and Eastern Europe (CEE)

With their close ties to Western Europe, the CEE countries[117] tended to be the first destination for LPs looking to start investing in emerging markets. Unfortunately, these investors retreated in 2008, either fearing that Europe's financial malaise would affect CEE or preferring newer emerging markets in the rest of the world. Although funds devoted to the region grew tenfold between 2003 ($230 million) and 2008 ($2.8 billion), 2009 saw a mere $600 million raised.[118]

---

[111] Leke et al., "What's Driving Africa's Growth?" 11.

[112] EMPEA, *Insight: MENA*, March 2010; and Josh Lerner and Ann Leamon, "Ithmar Capital," HBS Case No. 809-032 (Boston: HBS Publishing, 2008), 3–5.

[113] Cited in Gulf Venture Capital Association and KPMG, *Private Equity and Venture Capital in the Middle East Annual Report* 2008 (Dubai: KPMG, 2008), 20.

[114] Ibid., 39.

[115] Ibid., 38.

[116] EMPEA, *Insight: MENA*, March 2010, 6–7.

[117] CEE countries include Albania, Bosnia & Herzegovina, Bulgaria, Croatia, Cyprus, Czech Republic, Estonia, Hungary, Latvia, Lithuania, Malta, Montenegro, Poland, Republic of Macedonia, Romania, Serbia, Slovakia, Slovenia, and Turkey.

[118] EMPEA, *Insight: CEE*, January/February 2010, 1.

Even so, there is a vast dispersion in the impact of the crisis on these countries; Poland was seeing positive growth while Latvia barely escaped bankruptcy. In general, the countries that joined the EU earliest—Poland, Hungary, and the Czech Republic—have tended to attract the greatest private equity attention, although recently Turkey has received substantial private equity investment from fund managers looking to play both CEE and MENA strategies.[119]

Unlike other emerging regions, several firms have raised funds to target distressed opportunities in CEE following the downturn, because buyouts were fairly common there and used a substantial amount of now-troubled debt. Venture capital, as in the rest of Europe, is rare; but there is a strong entrepreneurial cluster fueled by incubators and government assistance programs.

One of CEE's earliest investors, intriguingly enough, was the U.S. government, which in 1989 passed the first of two laws that authorized $1.2 billion for ten so-called Enterprise Funds throughout CEE and the former Soviet Union.[120] These funds reported to the U.S. Agency for International Development (USAID) but were supervised by private boards of directors composed of individuals with extensive experience in business and government in both the United States and the host country. The goal was to encourage free market development through loans and investments to public-private partnerships.

A number of these funds turned out to be remarkably successful. As of 2007, the Enterprise Funds had invested and reinvested more than $1.5 billion in more than 500 small and medium enterprises and also participated in the privatization of formerly state-owned companies. As of 2009, the Bulgarian-American Enterprise Fund, established in 1992 with $55 million, had generated more than $400 million in proceeds.[121] Programs included loans targeted to local needs and technical assistance such as business and financial training. The funds had assisted in establishing many now-leading banks in the region, along with their mortgage lending operations, and helped to attract foreign investors such as Euronet Worldwide, GE Capital, and Whirlpool. The Enterprise Funds also provided seed funding for other private equity funds that then raised more than $2 billion to invest in the region. These included Poland-based Enterprise Investors, the largest private equity fund manager in CEE, the Romanian-Bulgarian-focused Balkan Accession Fund, Russia's Delta Private Equity Partners, and Hungary's MAVA.[122]

In 2009, the area's largest acquisition occurred when Luxembourg-based CVC Capital Partners acquired the Czech-based operations of Anheuser-Busch InBev's CEE operations for $3 billion (assuming all earn-outs are met).[123] Strategic sales provided most of the exit opportunities in 2009. Unlike many emerging markets, secondary transactions where one private equity firm purchases an asset from another, have also occurred.[124]

Argentina: Cry for Private Equity

Until 2000, Argentina attracted the lion's share of Latin America's private equity funds. When it defaulted on its debt in December 2001 and then devalued its currency, private equity firms suffered severe losses. Hicks Muse Tate and Furst lost at least $1 billion invested in the Argentine

---

[119] Ibid., 3.

[120] Background on the Enterprise Funds comes from John P. Birklund, "Doing Good While Doing Well," *Foreign Affairs*, (Sept.–Oct. 2001): 14–20; USAID, "The Enterprise Funds in Europe and Eurasia," July 2007, http://pdf.usaid.gov/pdf_docs/PDACL255.pdf; and "Enterprise Funds in Central and Eastern Europe and Central Asia, 1990–2007," *The Enterprise Funds Exchange of Experiences*, http://www.seedact.com, accessed July 13, 2010.

[121] Ashtar Analeed Marcus, "Bulgarian-American Enterprise Fund Pays U.S. Back $27 Million," *USAID Frontlines*, February 2009, http://www.usaid.gov/press/frontlines/fl_feb09/p5_enterprise.html, accessed June 19, 2009.

[122] "Enterprise Funds in Central and Eastern Europe and Central Asia, 1990–2007," *The Enterprise Funds Exchange of Experiences*, http://www.seedact.com; accessed July 13, 2010.

[123] "Anheuser-Busch InBev and CVC Capital Partners Announce Completion of Sale of Central European Operations," press release, December 2, 2009, http://www.ab-inbev.com/press_releases/hugin_pdf%5C330959.pdf, accessed July 13, 2010.

[124] EMPEA, *Insight: CEE*, January/February 2010, 7.

technology and media companies.[125] Argentina has since failed to recover from its woes. Its ranking for "business friendliness for buyout and VC" has steadily declined over the past two years; in 2010, the country tied with El Salvador and rated tenth out of twelve countries in Latin America.[126] Problematic laws on fund formation, discouraging tax regimes, and perceived corruption have all repressed private equity, although the crowning blow was the nationalization of local pension funds in 2008, which prohibited these funds from investing in private equity. Argentina's only positives are its high accounting standards and the government's programs supporting entrepreneurship and small businesses. Unfortunately, most other countries in the region offer a more welcoming private equity environment.

Brazil

If Argentina is a case study in how not to attract private equity, Brazil has learned its lesson. Brazil dominates the Latin American private equity landscape; it received two-thirds of the region's investment between 2002 and 2008—funds raised more than quadrupled from 2004 ($6 billion) to 2008 ($28 billion).[127] As early as 1974, the country attempted to establish a private equity industry, only to have it disappear in short order due to hyperinflation and legal uncertainty.[128] Only in 1998, when the Cardoso administration privatized the telecommunications monopoly, did Brazil's private equity sector seriously reawaken.

The strengths of the Brazilian market include its favorable laws for fund formation and operation, favorable tax treatment for private equity, protection of minority shareholders' rights, bankruptcy procedures, and the government's commitment to the industry.[129] In 2004, the financial regulator enacted laws that required higher levels of corporate governance and transparency. Moreover, domestic pension funds are allowed to invest up to 20 percent of their assets in local private equity funds, thus providing a significant pool of capital.[130] From an investors' perspective, Brazil has much to recommend it—a growing middle class, restrained inflation, and the fifth-largest population in the world. Yet the country's high taxes and restrictive labor laws can be discouraging.

Brazil led EMPEA's list as the country with the greatest interest expressed by limited partners in 2008, and it ranked second in 2009, behind only China.[131] To access the country, a number of international firms have established joint ventures with Brazilian operations. Domestic firms have raised capital from domestic as well as international investors.[132]

The country's renewable energy sector has attracted significant investment. Government programs to encourage technology have supported a growing VC industry, although most investments are in growth capital. Some buyout transactions have occurred, although most of Brazil's transactions involve very little leverage.[133]

[125] Mike Esterl, "Private Equity Falls in Latin America," *Wall Street Journal*, August 21, 2002, http://www.bain.com/bainweb/Pulications/printer_ready.asp?id=8612, accessed July 13, 2010.

[126] Latin American Venture Capital Association, *2010 Scorecard: The Private Equity and Venture Capital Environment in Latin America*, http://lavca.org/wp-content/uploads/2010/05/scorecard2010-updated-for-web-1.pdf, accessed July 13, 2010.

[127] EMPEA, *Insight: Brazil*, June 2009, 7; and Spencer Ante, "Brazil: The Next Hotbed of Venture Capital and Private Equity?" *Business Week*, June 26, 2009.

[128] "Venture Capital in Brazil" (paper given at the Venture Capital Conference, Monterrey Mexico, April 21–22, 2010), http://www.mvcc.mx/wp-content/uploads/2010/04/VC-in-Brazil-MVCC2010.pdf, 1.

[129] Ibid., 8.

[130] EMPEA, *Insight: Brazil*, June 2009, 7.

[131] Coller Capital LP study, April 2009, cited in Ante, "Brazil: The Next Hotbed of Venture Capital and Private Equity?"

[132] EMPEA, *Insight: Brazil*, June 2009, 3.

[133] Ibid., 5.

Most investments have been exited via trade sale, often to multinational companies. Buscape.com, a Latin American online shopping and price comparison service, was sold to South Africa-based Naspers for $342 million in the difficult climate of September 2009. Domestic companies, however, are also proving eager acquirers. IPOs are less frequent, although Advent International listed its company Cetip SA Balcao Organizadao de Ativos e Derivativos (a provider of back-office services to financial institutions) on the Bovespa stock exchange and raised $450 million in October 2009. Secondary buyouts, while traditionally less important, have also started to offer exit options.[134]

Russia

Commitments to Russian funds reached $4.27 billion in 2008; three funds alone accounted for almost half of the total. Limited partners include both standard institutional investors such as endowments, family offices, and foreign pension funds, and DFIs such as the European Bank for Reconstruction and Development and the World Bank's IFC. The Russian government has established programs to support early-stage companies, but regulations prohibit local pension funds from investing in private equity.[135] By the end of 2008, a total of 155 funds, both buyout and VC, managed $14.3 billion. Most private equity funds are structured as limited partnerships based in a reputable tax-advantaged jurisdiction like Bermuda and have a local investment advisor in Russia.

During 2008, there were 120 reported transactions totaling roughly $2 billion. Most deals (89 percent) were expansion stage. The vast majority of exits occur via sales to strategic investors.[136]

The country's financial system and tax code are still evolving, given the recent introduction of a market economy, and private equity firms face all the classic challenges of investing in emerging markets. Management skills are scarce, accounting standards uncertain, corporate governance weak, and capital markets underdeveloped. In addition, exits are challenging and often occur on international exchanges.

Given the challenges faced by private equity in Russia, not to mention the country's somewhat uncertain political situation, it may be no surprise that the most recent EMPEA study showed Russia lagging other emerging markets in terms of attractiveness to LPs. In both 2009 and 2010, LPs ranked it last in attractiveness, and twice as many planned to reduce their allocations to the country as to increase them.[137]

THE EMERGING MARKET PRIVATE EQUITY CYCLE

In our discussion thus far, we have noted the primary sources of capital for emerging markets—generally the same as those investing in developed nations except for the presence of DFIs in some areas and sovereign wealth funds, which tend to invest in domestic vehicles. For instance, the Abu Dhabi Investment Council, the manager of domestic investment efforts for the sovereign wealth fund Abu Dhabi Investment Authority (ADIA), has invested in some funds domiciled in the United Arab Emirates.

We have also noted the types of investments pursued in emerging markets. In most of these markets, **growth equity** transactions are the most common because they reduce risk for the investors and are more acceptable to owners. For investors, the company is already operational; and in some countries, such as India, it may also be publicly listed although with little liquidity. For owners, a

---

[134] Ernst & Young, *Private Equity in Brazil: Ready for Its Moment in the Sun* (Ernst & Young, 2010), 12; available at http://www.ey.com/Publication/vwLUAssets/Private_Equity_in_Brazil/$FILE/EY_Private_Equity_in_Brazil.pdf.

[135] David Wack and Christopher Rose, "Private Equity 2010: Country Q&A—Russian Federation," in *PLC Cross-border Private Equity Handbook 2010* (London: Practical Law, 2009); accessed at http://www.practicallaw.com/privateequityhandbook.

[136] Ibid.

[137] EMPEA, *Emerging Markets Private Equity Survey* (Washington, DC: Coller Capital, 2010); available at http://www.collercapital.com/assets/images/press/Emerging_Markets_Private_Equity_Survey_2010.pdf, 9.

growth equity deal allows them to maintain control, test the idea of working with outside partners, and obtain financing that is difficult or impossible to achieve through other means. Other sources of investment opportunities are the **privatizations** of former state-owned companies, **corporate restructurings**, and **infrastructure finance**, in which investors finance projects such as bridges, docks, and highways.[138] Infrastructure projects are scarce in China but very common in India, where the government welcomes foreign investment in that sector. Least common are **strategic alliances**, through which firms provide on-the-ground guidance to major corporations that have made strategic investments (acquisitions, joint ventures, and alliances) in developing countries.

Investments

For several reasons, private equity investors in developing nations are reluctant to make the kinds of early-stage, technology-intensive investments that are characteristic of U.S. venture capitalists. First, trained technical talent and the necessary infrastructure (e.g., state-of-the-art research laboratories) are often scarce. Second, in many nations, intellectual property protection is weak, or the enforcement of these rights questionable. A third challenge is finding talented management with an understanding of private equity owners. A fourth factor is the difficulty of exiting these investments. Finally, many investors argue that investing in a developing country is already high risk. To take on additional business risk would be imprudent. Consequently, many firms concentrate on mature enterprises with established track records.

Recently, though, true VC investments have become more common in developing nations, which have fallen into three broad categories. The first set has sought to provide products or services to developing countries that are already available in the developed nations. These have included cell phone services and handsets; online games; online markets; advertising; and financial, brokerage, and travel services. The second category has sought to link the human capital in developing nations with labor-starved Western corporations. An early example of this was the U.S.-based firms' investments in Indian operations for business process outsourcing. In Russia, the Russian Corporation of Nanotechnologies manages $4.4 billion in government funds to encourage the creation of a Russian nanotechnology industry by establishing VC funds and investing directly in companies that will move to Russia.[139] The final set of transactions has sought to commercialize technology originating in developing countries for sale in the global marketplace.

Deal Identification and Due Diligence

Finding appropriate transactions is a major focus of private equity funds in both developed and emerging markets. Countries like India and China present a baffling array of opportunities. Finding good ones, though, requires an active strategy since investors exploit tight relationships among business and social groups in the region. This often gives them a first-mover advantage over competitors without such ties.

The criteria for evaluating opportunities are similar. In interviews, both sets of investors rate management as the overriding factor in the success of any venture, in addition to criteria such as market size, the threat of obsolescence, and the ability to exit the investment.

In evaluating potential deals, however, private equity investors in developing nations emphasize two sets of risks often not encountered in developed nations. The first of these is

---

[138] Recently, however, developed nation governments have also been selling their infrastructure operations, as seen in Canada Pension Plan Investment Board's acquisition of Anglian Water, a Welsh water system, and Global Infrastructure Partners' acquisition of Gatwick Airport outside London.

[139] Wack and Rose, "Private Equity 2010: Country Q&A—Russian Federation"; and James Tyrrell, "RUSNANO Attracts Nanotechnology on an Industrial Scale," *Nanoweb.org*, September 29, 2009, http://nanotechweb.org/cws/article/indepth/40545, accessed July 27, 2010.

country risk. A war might seriously affect the investment's prospects. A more common threat, however, is unforeseen regulatory changes, which can directly affect cash flows—or indeed the very viability of the transaction. Investors need to analyze the institutions, legal framework, and industry regulations carefully. One example is the Chinese government's promulgation of "Article 10" in the fall of 2006. This legislation gave the government approval powers over merger and acquisition activity funded by foreign investment groups and in certain undefined sectors of "state economic security, famous China trademarks, or old China trade names"[140] and allowed it to control the approval and timing of the foreign IPOs of domestic companies.[141]

A second concern is exchange rate risk. A major devaluation of a nation's currency, as occurred in Argentina in 2001, could lead to a sharp drop in the returns enjoyed by its foreign investors. Ways to mitigate this risk include entering into currency swaps, purchasing options based on relative currency prices, or purchasing forward currency. Since the nature and timing of the future payments are usually unknown to private equity investors, however, this poses some real challenges. While hedging tools have attracted increasing interest, their actual use by private equity investors in developing nations appears to be very limited to date.

Deal Structuring

The choice of financing vehicle also differs between developed and developing markets. Investors in developed nations use a variety of instruments, as described in Chapter 5. These financial instruments allow the private equity investors to stage investments, allocate risk, control management, provide incentives to executives, and demarcate ownership.

In many developing countries, private equity investors primarily use plain common stock. This reflects several factors. First, several countries, especially in Asia, do not permit different classes of stock with different voting powers. As a result, investors must seek other ways to control the firm. Such methods are often extremely important, since most of the companies are family owned or controlled. Such control rights may allow the investors to step in during controversies such as a dispute between two sons over who should succeed the father as president.

A study by Josh Lerner and Antoinette Schoar[142] shed light on this issue by analyzing a sample of 210 transactions from a wide variety of private equity groups in developing countries. It assessed deal structures and how they varied with the nations in which the investments were made. The paper found that emerging markets used a much broader array of securities than were found in the United States, where preferred stock is almost ubiquitous. Terms protecting private equity investor rights (such as antidilution rights), however, were less frequently employed. Moreover, the choice of security was influenced by location of both the private equity group and the investment. Investments in common law nations (such as India, whose legal system is based on the United Kingdom's) and by private equity groups based in the United States and United Kingdom were more likely to use preferred stock. Common law nations were also more likely to provide contractual protections, like antidilution provisions, for the private equity firm. In non-common law countries, the difficulty of enforcing these protections in court reduced their usefulness. In nations where the rule of law is less well established, private equity groups emphasized large equity holdings, which were often contingent on the company's performance. The deals were often structured to ensure that the firm owned most of the company's equity if it encountered difficulties. At least in part because the investors could feel more comfortable about the investment structures, common law countries were home to larger transactions with higher valuations.

---

[140] Peter Neumann and Tony Zhang, "China's New Foreign-funded M&A Provisions," *China Law & Practice*, October 2006, 1.

[141] Hardymon and Leamon, "Gobi Partners: Raising Fund II," 5.

[142] Josh Lerner and Antoinette Schoar, "Does Legal Enforcement Affect Financial Transactions? The Contractual Channel in Private Equity," *Quarterly Journal of Economics* 120 (2005): 223–46.

Another study by Steven Kaplan, Frederic Martel, and Per Strömberg[143] explored a smaller sample of 145 investments in 107 companies in 23 countries (emerging and developed) by 70 different lead venture capitalists between 1992 and 2001. Like Lerner and Schoar, Kaplan et al. found that venture capitalists investing outside the United States usually had substantially weaker liquidation and exit rights because they usually did not or could not use convertible preferred stock. This reduced their ability to become actively involved with underperforming investments. Nor did they use contingencies, such as milestones or antidilution rights, which reduced the cash-flow incentives to let the owners yield control in hopes of improved performance. The authors also reported that investments in common law countries used contracts that were more similar to standard U.S. VC contracts than those in civil law (non-common law) countries. Specific legal measures, such as creditor protection and tax treatment, did not explain these differences.

In looking at the measures employed by specific venture investors, Kaplan et al. found that larger or more experienced firms and those with more exposure to the United States were much more likely to implement U.S. contractual terms. For an experienced venture firm, the legal regime (civil or common law) did not matter. To answer the question of whether old-line firms simply imposed the contracts with which they were most familiar, rather than those that best fit the situation, the authors studied the survival of the seventy lead investors in their sample. As of August 2003, eleven had folded, and all but one of those had *never* used convertible preferred stock in their contracts. Said one of those unfortunate venture capitalists, he "did not think it [contracts] mattered."[144] All of the thirty-seven firms that had exclusively used convertible preferred stock and U.S.-style contracts had survived. Firms that had used both non-U.S.-style contracts and U.S.-style contracts switched to favor the latter over time. This, the authors concluded, argued strongly for the long-term success of U.S.-style contracts regardless of the legal regime. Contracts do matter.

Pricing

Venture capitalists' assessment of a company's value in a developing nation is often problematic. Challenges abound at many levels. For instance, many developing countries lack timely and accurate macroeconomic and financial information. Sometimes macroeconomic variables published by central banks are manipulated by governments to portray a healthier economy. These uncertainties—combined with political and regulatory risks—may make it extremely difficult to draw up reasonably accurate projections. The uncertainty increases further since many private companies, especially family-run businesses, may not have audited financial statements. Furthermore, accounting principles and practices, although improving, are still very different from Western standards.

Exits

Lately, progress has been made toward resolving the vexing issue of exits in emerging markets—despite the slowdown in the wake of the global financing crisis. Across the emerging world, public listings on either domestic or international exchanges (sometimes both) and acquisitions by foreign and domestic companies have provided exit options that are both profitable and efficient. Old Mutual in South Africa floated simultaneously on the Johannesburg and London Stock Exchanges, while the Chinese gaming company Shanda and India's Infosys floated on NASDAQ. Abraaj Capital sold its position in Egyptian Fertilizers Company to an Egyptian firm; Kuwait's MTC (now Zain) acquired the pan-African cell phone service provider Celtel. Developed nation

---

[143] Steven N. Kaplan, Frederic Martel, and Per Strömberg, "How Do Legal Differences and Experience Affect Financial Contracts?" *Journal of Financial Intermediation* 16, no. 3 (2007): 273–311.

[144] Ibid., 308.

companies also provide exit options, as seen when Amazon purchased Joyo, a Chinese online bookseller, eBay acquired the Chinese online auction house Eachnet,[145] and the Brazilian firm Gávea sold its position in Ipanema Coffee to Norway's Kaffehuset Friele.[146] This speaks to the governance and value creation that the private equity owners provide, as well as to the availability of exit avenues.

In some cases, the acquirer is itself a private-equity-backed company that has gone public, as in the case of the Chinese digital signage firm Focus Media. Backed by 3i Group and others, Focus Media went public on NASDAQ in 2005[147] and has since acquired venture-backed AllYes and Target Media, funded by the Carlyle Group.

In work that builds on Jeng and Wells and extends that of Kaplan and coauthors, Douglas Cumming, Grant Fleming, and Armin Schwienbacher[148] analyzed the impact of the quality of a country's legal system (called legality) on VC exits in an Asia-Pacific context. Using data from 468 VC-backed companies in twelve Asia-Pacific countries between 1989 and 2001, they found that the quality of a country's legal system more directly facilitated IPOs than did the size of its stock market. The major reason for this was that legality increased transparency, which was an essential component of good governance, and reduced conflicts of interest or provided an avenue for their resolution. Small increases in legality in emerging markets, they found, corresponded to a much greater increase in the likelihood of an IPO than did a similar increase in the legality index for a more developed country, indicating that small improvements in legality could create substantial increases in IPOs and, therefore, in private equity activity.

CONCLUSION

As we have toured private equity around the world, it has been clear that it has succeeded more in some countries than in others. Certainly government regulation helps and harms—laws that forbid the use of convertible preferred stock or that set high standards for accounting transparency can impede or encourage private equity investment. The result of our whirlwind tour, though, should be a sense of awe at the persistence of private equity and its practitioners and entrepreneurs. In 1999, when Warburg Pincus invested in India's Bharti Telecom, the entire country had 3.6 million cell phone subscribers and Bharti 104,000 of them. When Warburg Pincus exited its holding in 2005, Bharti's market capitalization was $15 billion, and observers estimated Warburg Pincus's total realizations at $1.6 billion.[149] In developed markets, equally transformative events occur across borders of countries that less than a century ago were trying to blow each other up. Active investing, with its emphasis on good governance, transparency, respect for the rights of minority shareholders, and the rule of law, both encourages and rewards developments toward a vibrant entrepreneurial culture. As such, it can have a positive impact on economic development, even if the investments are undertaken with purely financial motives.

Having explored the way that private equity groups work in both developed and developing markets over the past few chapters, we now turn to the consequences of these activities. In the next few chapters, we consider the impact of these investments as well as how and in what ways private

---

[145] Data from Zero2ipo; cited in York Chen, "China VC Industry at a Turning Point," (talk, October 2004, unpublished); cited in Hardymon, Lerner, and Leamon, "Gobi Ventures: October 2004," HBS Case No. 805-090 (Boston: HBS Publishing, 2005), 5.

[146] EMPEA, *Insight: Brazil*, June 2009, 6.

[147] AFX News Limited, "China's Focus Media Gains Bullish Response in US Debut," *Forbes.com*, July 14, 2005, http://www.focusmedia.tv/pdf/forbes.pdf, accessed July 27, 2011.

[148] Douglas Cumming, Grant Fleming, and Armin Schwienbacher, "Legality and Venture Capital Exits," *Journal of Corporate Finance* 12 (2006): 214–45.

[149] "Why Are Private Equity Firms Looking Hard at India?" *Knowledge@Wharton*, November 2, 2005; cited in Hardymon and Leamon, "Motilal Oswal Financial Services: An IPO in India?" 5.

equity will evolve. First, we shift our focus and examine how to assess the risk and return of private equity efforts. We then consider the management of private equity firms and the overall impact this activity has on the greater society. Finally, we address the questions that private equity faces as it looks into the future.

QUESTIONS

1. What characteristics of the European business landscape have made Europe an attractive market for buyouts?

2. What are some of the difficulties European buyout firms face when investing across European nations?

3. Why has the private equity market in Germany been challenging, even though Germany is Europe's largest economy?

4. Why are developing nations seeking to attract private equity investment?

5. What impact does a country's level of IPO activity have on its venture capital funding? How does this compare to the impact of labor market rigidities?

6. Despite the difficulties of investing in emerging markets, why have private equity firms continued to focus on these opportunities?

7. What are the advantages for funds that are denominated in local currency?

8. Why might the Chinese government have opposed the Carlyle Group's proposed buyout of Xugong Group even after the buyout firm increased its valuation and reduced its ownership?

9. What led to the success of the Central European Enterprise Funds?

10. Compare and contrast government policies for private equity in Argentina and Brazil.

11. Why have investors been reluctant to make VC investments in developing nations?

12. What are some of the risks associated with private equity investment in developing nations that are not often seen in developed nations?

13. What are the challenges of pricing deals in developing nations?

Chapter 9

Risk and Return

Up until now, we have focused on understanding the role played by venture and buyout investors, as well as the others with whom they interact. In the next two chapters, we turn to a more evaluative question: how well have these funds performed? We'll begin here with financial performance; in the next chapter, we consider the broader impacts on society.

Measuring performance in private equity is a tricky problem. To see this, consider the experience of a very real family of funds that we will call (to protect the guilty—though it should be noted, they were far from the only such offender in the venture industry at the time) Optimistic Venture Partners. This group, which had been founded in the late 1980s, specialized in telecommunications investments. In March 2001, the firm closed on an $800 million fourth fund, largely based on the track records of its second and third funds. In its private placement memorandum for Fund IV, which was dated January 2001, the firm described the internal rate of return (IRR) for its 1995 second fund as 31 percent, and that of its 1999 third fund as 11 percent. But the performance of Optimistic Venture Partners as of mid-2010 was rather different: according to the Preqin database, the second fund ultimately generated a return of 1 percent; and the 1999 fund had an IRR of –4 percent—far less impressive numbers, and far less enticing to new investors.

How can this be? How could two funds that looked so promising in 2001 have ended up with such disappointing performance? There are several reasons. First, we know that the first few years of the twenty-first century were very difficult for technology firms, particularly for young telecommunications companies. The bursting of the "NASDAQ bubble" sharply reduced revenue and profits for many of these firms as their customers fell on hard times and sharply curtailed their activity. Thus, much of the decline in Optimistic's returns may have been due to the subsequent struggles of its portfolio companies.

But there is a second, less pleasant possibility as well. Performance measurement in private equity is highly inexact, even inadequate. Groups can misstate their performance, whether inadvertently or with ill intent. The choice of a valuation approach or an end date (as we saw in the discussion of portfolio company valuation in Chapter 4) can dramatically affect these calculations. One well might well wonder whether the partners at Optimistic Venture Partners, eager to close as large a fourth fund as possible, deliberately misled their investors about the performance of their earlier funds.

A more recent example comes from the buyout industry following the September 2008 financial crisis. During the fourth quarter of 2008, private equity funds reported returns of –16 percent, according to Cambridge Associates.[1] This might seem bad enough, but many observers

---

[1] Cambridge Associates LLC, "Cambridge Associates Private Equity and Venture Capital Market Commentary for Quarter Ending December 31, 2008," press release, July 2009, http://www.cambridgeassociates.com/about_us/news/press_releases/Fourth%20Quarter%202008%20Cambridge%20Associates'%20Private%20Equity%20and%20Venture%20Capital%20Benchmark%20Commentaries.pdf, accessed August 21, 2009.

were skeptical. In particular, they pointed out that over the same period, the S&P 500 declined by nearly 22 percent and many other benchmarks did even worse. Moreover, in most cases the buyout funds' equity was highly leveraged, and thus the effect of any losses would have been magnified.

Based on these vignettes, many readers might end up agreeing with Bob Boldt, the head of University of Texas' endowment, who added the following comment to his discussion of the private equity performance numbers that the university had disclosed: "I hope when people write about these numbers, they include some sort of warning like on cigarette packages. They can be harmful to your health if you pay attention to them."[2] To be sure, the calculation of private equity returns is not easy. But it is extremely important on a number of fronts. General partners (GPs) base their compensation on such figures; limited partners (LPs) base current spending decisions for their operations as well as future investment decisions on them; even legislators refer to them when determining regulatory proposals. As we discuss later in this chapter, there are ways to look systematically at these issues.

After grappling with how to measure risk for the bulk of this chapter, we will turn at the end to risk *management*. In particular, we'll highlight the way in which the diversification of private equity stakes can help limit some of these challenges.

WHY IS ASSESSING PRIVATE EQUITY PERFORMANCE DIFFICULT?

Why should the decision to invest in private equity pose more difficulties than investing in other asset classes, such as government bonds or European equities? The crucial problem lies in the nature of the investments that GPs make. Evaluating private equity is particularly tricky to evaluate because private firms are affected by three essential problems:

1. **The Ongoing Theme of Illiquidity.** Companies that receive capital from private equity funds very often remain privately held for a number of years. As such, they have no observable market price. In addition, the private equity funds themselves, which are typically structured as private partnerships, rarely trade on an organized public market. Hence, investors cannot observe their valuations.

2. **Information Uncertainty (asymmetry) Regarding Portfolio Company Valuations.** Particularly with early-stage companies, valuations assigned by private equity firms to their own portfolio of investments often are not based on quantitative metrics (such as price-to-earnings or discounted cash flow) because the company may not have any prior earnings or reliable projections. Instead, the partners rely on complex, frequently subjective assessments of a venture's technology, its expected market opportunity, and its management team's prowess. While classic valuation data may be more available for a buyout, its reliability may also be questionable because the typical company undergoing a buyout is going through a period of substantial change.

3. **Cyclicality.** Private equity valuation levels, as a whole, appear to rise and fall dramatically in response to the fund-raising environment. For example, when considerable capital is flowing into private equity funds, the valuation levels of investments in companies rise significantly, and vice versa. Work exploring the U.S. venture capital industry makes this point explicitly, showing that every time the level of fund-raising doubled, the value assigned to new investments (or reinvestments in companies already in the funds' portfolios) increased between 7 and 21 percent. These results suggest that the more

---

[2] Dan Primack, "Opening Up a Private World: U. of Texas Invest Company Bares All, Shocking the VC World," *Investment Dealers' Digest,* September 30, 2002, 36–37 (the quote is on p. 37).

than fortyfold increase in venture fund-raising between 1991 and 2000 in the United States alone led to a sixfold increase in valuation levels.[3]

HOW IS PERFORMANCE TYPICALLY MEASURED?

Despite the difficulties in measuring investment performance, it must be done for the reasons mentioned earlier—compensation, budgeting, investment allocation, and investment choice. Limited partners, GPs, and intermediaries in the private equity industry tend to rely on two ways of assessing performance: IRRs and cash-on-cash multiples. While a few groups have pushed to employ alternative methods, little consensus exists on the preferred approach. As yet, no "industry standard" has appeared; hence the need to understand various methodologies.

Cash on Cash

Perhaps the most straightforward approach is the computation of **cash-on-cash returns**.[4] Essentially, this technique looks at the ratio of the money returned and/or currently in the fund to the money invested. More precisely, one common variant—the ratio of distributed to paid-in capital—examines the ratio of the capital returned to the LPs to the funds that they have provided. A second frequently used approach is to compute the ratio of the capital returned to the LPs *and* the current value of the fund's holdings to the funds they have provided. Based on these measures, funds can be compared to others with a similar level of maturity (i.e., those raised in the same year).

Internal Rate of Return

Most private equity investors also utilize vintage-year analyses in which the **internal rate of return** (the discount rate that sets the net present value (NPV) of the fund's cash flows equal to zero) of a specific private equity fund is compared to those of a set of similar funds raised in the same year. This provides a simple comparison, but it is prey to many difficulties stemming from peculiarities of the IRR calculation itself. (We discuss the mechanism of IRR calculation in the box below.)

The Mechanics of Internal Rates of Return

Before we consider the strengths and weaknesses of the IRR, let's review the calculation's mechanics. The IRR is closely related to the NPV approach to evaluating cash flows.

The NPV first begins with a discount rate—typically, the minimum rate of return that investors will be comfortable earning. Next, this approach identifies the timing and size of each of the "cash flows"—the flows of funds into and out of an investment.

In the private equity setting, the drawdown of capital into the fund is regarded as a negative cash flow; the return of proceeds is seen as a positive flow. Consider a case where there are three cash flows (x_0, x_1, and x_2) that take place at time t_0, time t_1, and time t_2,

---

[3] Paul A. Gompers and Josh Lerner, "Money Chasing Deals? The Impact of Fund Inflows on Private Equity Financings," *Journal of Financial Economics* 55 (2000): 281–325.

[4] Carolina Braunschweig, "LPs Consider 'Cash-In and Cash-Out' Policy," *Private Equity Week*, April 1, 2002, http://www.altassets.net/private-equity-knowledge-bank/article/nz2510.html, accessed August 9, 2009.

respectively. Computing the NPV of these cash flows at time t_0 with a discount rate (r) can be expressed as

$$NPV = x_0 + \frac{x_1}{(1+r)^{(t_1-t_0)}} + \frac{x_2}{(1+r)^{(t_2-t_0)}}$$

Essentially, the cash flows that occur in the future are discounted, or assigned less weight. This reflects the "time value of money," the fact that we could have invested the money elsewhere during this period and earned an attractive return. As long as the NPV indicated by this formula is positive, the project should be undertaken.

Calculation of the IRR can be seen as the reverse of this problem: we calculate the discount rate that sets the NPV equal to zero. Consider the preceding example. Instead of taking the discount rate r as a given and computing the NPV, we would set the NPV to zero. We would then solve for the r that makes this equation hold.

Because the calculations are so similar, it is not surprising that they give the same answer in simple cases. For example, consider a fund that has an upfront drawdown of $100 and then distributes $50 in cash at the end of year 1 and $150 at the end of year 2. To determine the IRR, we set the NPV formula equal to zero:

$$0 = -100 + \frac{50}{(1+r)} + \frac{150}{(1+r)^2}$$

(Note that the first term is negative because it is a cash flow provided *by* the investors; the other flows are *to* the investors and positive.) After trying various possible solutions, we discover that $r = 0.5$, or a discount rate of 50 percent, will solve the equation. If we were to compute the NPV, we would instead determine our discount rate r in advance and solve the equation:

$$NPV = -100 + \frac{50}{(1+r)} + \frac{150}{(1+r)^2}$$

Figure 9.1 illustrates what transpires when we solve this equation using different discount rates. As long as we use a discount rate of under 50 percent ($r < 0.5$), the NPV is positive. If we employ a higher discount rate, the discounted positive cash flows are not large enough

FIGURE 9.1   Net present value varies inversely with the discount rate

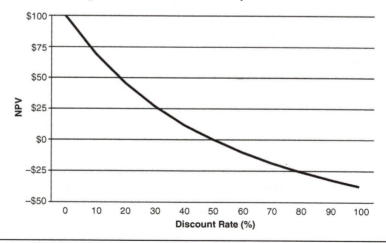

to cover the initial cost, and the NPV is negative. The crossover point, 50 percent, is exactly the same answer that the IRR calculation produced. As a result, in evaluating simple projects or funds with straightforward cash flows, the choice between NPV and IRR is not consequential.

Table 9.1 Cash-on-Cash and IRR Metrics for Different Private Equity Groups

United States	Cash-on-Cash from Inception	IRR over Different Time Periods (%)				
		1 Year	3 Year	5 Year	10 Year	20 Year
Early/Seed VC	1.50	−16.9	NA	3.0	25.5	22.1
Later-stage VC	1.49	−7.9	7.7	8.1	7.3	14.7
All ventures	1.50	−17.5	2.5	5.7	13.4	17.2
Small buyouts	1.67	−13.0	2.5	7.4	4.6	12.3
Medium buyouts	1.49	−24.1	6.4	11.1	7.5	11.4
Large buyouts	1.47	−13.7	3.4	6.8	6.1	10.6
Mega buyouts	1.12	−27.4	−1.0	6.1	4.7	8.0
All buyouts	1.21	−26.4	0.2	6.7	5.2	9.3
All private equity	1.29	−24.4	1.3	6.5	7.1	11.5

Europe	Cash-on-Cash from Inception	IRR over Different Time Periods (%)				
		1 Year	3 Year	5 Year	10 Year	20 Year
Early/Seed VC	0.91	−12.5	−2.8	−0.5	−2.5	−1.1
Later-stage VC	1.23	−18.4	0.4	3.4	2.8	6.9
All ventures	1.06	−18.4	−0.7	1.5	−0.3	2.2
Small buyouts	1.41	−3.5	7.0	8.3	8.7	12.0
Medium buyouts	1.54	−23.4	6.9	12.4	13.7	14.6
Large buyouts	1.39	−15.4	11.2	11.7	19.8	19.7
Mega buyouts	1.04	−34.2	1.2	11.3	9.2	9.1
All buyouts	1.17	−31.0	3.8	11.1	11.2	12.5
All private equity	1.16	−30.2	2.8	8.3	7.9	9.4

Notes: U.S. performance as of March 31, 2009; European performance as of December 31, 2008.
All cash-on-cash data is capital-weighted average ratio of distributions and fund value to paid-in capital.
All IRR performance data is pooled annualized IRRs.
NA = not available.
Source: Data from Thomson Reuters private equity database, accessed September 5, 2009.

The IRR has many advantages over cash-on-cash multiples as a measurement of performance. The most important one is that it allows investors to measure the performance of a series of uneven positive or negative cash flows and accounts for the time value of money.

These two measures quickly become second nature to those in the private equity industry, because they are used so often. Table 9.1 presents the performance of private equity funds of various types over different time horizons, reporting the weighted average ratio of distributed and residual fund value to paid-in capital and the pooled IRR (more on this later). These data are taken from the Thomson Reuters private equity database, one of the standard sources of performance and investment data.

Several patterns emerge from the tables. First, performance across categories and regions has differed. In particular, the data show the very low performance of European venture funds, whether measured using cash-on-cash returns or IRRs. Second, the IRRs show an enormous variation in returns over time. Some periods, such as 2008, were characterized by very poor performance; others, such as the late 1990s and the mid-2000s, were very good indeed. Third, venture capital (VC) and buyout funds have done better and worse in particular periods: VC funds thrived in the 1990s and large buyout funds in the mid-2000s. While VC has trailed the field for much of the last decade, in the longer run, U.S. venture funds have done considerably better than other categories. Among buyout groups, over the long haul, the worst performers have been the largest funds.

WHAT ARE THE PROBLEMS WITH THESE MEASUREMENTS?

Although these methodologies are widely used, all is not rosy. Both methods alas, have significant problems that we discuss in this section.

The cash-on-cash approach, while very simple, is in many respects a victim of its straightforwardness. It does not take into account the timing of the cash flows that it compares. This violates one of the central tenets of finance that "a dollar today is worth more than a dollar tomorrow." Using cash-on-cash metrics, we cannot tell whether the returns came evenly distributed over time, front-weighted, or back-weighted. Clearly, one might be preferable to another; but the cash-on-cash metric makes no judgments.

This problem is illustrated in Figure 9.2, which shows two funds that each raise $1 billion dollars. The first fund returns $3 billion to its LPs in year 5; the other returns $4 billion in year 10. If we relied on the cash-on-cash returns, we would choose the second fund. Yet this choice fails to take into account that the money returned in year 5 could be reinvested, potentially for an even higher rate of return. For instance, if we undertake an NPV calculation using a discount rate of 15 percent, the first fund generates an aggregate positive return to investors of nearly half a billion dollars. In the second fund, however, the investors actually lose money on an NPV basis. The cash-on-cash return calculation, by ignoring the time value of money, can give misleading answers. Although we may avoid unreasonably favoring the hare, we risk backing some mighty slow turtles.

Although IRR takes better account of timing differences, it is not a cure-all either. Among its drawbacks are four that we will call, for purposes of discussion, the "tortoise and hare"[5] problem; lack of systematization; the paradox of multiple IRRs; and the aggregation problem.

The Case of the Tortoise and the Hare

First, let's consider the "tortoise and hare" problem. Essentially, the IRR calculation rewards the "hares" of the private equity community, those private equity groups that quickly return capital to their investors. In principle, the idea of a rapid return of cash is a good thing: all else being equal, investors would prefer receiving the returns from their investments sooner rather than later

---

[5] Aesop's "tortoise and hare" allegory recounts a speedy but distractible hare who is beaten in a race by a tortoise's slow and steady progress.

FIGURE 9.2 Emphasizing cash-on-cash returns can lead to problematic decisions

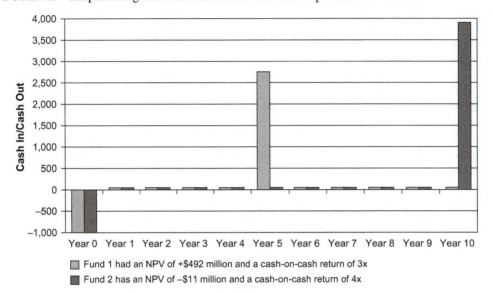

Fund 1 had an NPV of +$492 million and a cash-on-cash return of 3x

Fund 2 has an NPV of –$11 million and a cash-on-cash return of 4x

because they can then invest that capital in another fund. The drawback, however, is that the IRR can end up placing too much weight on these hares.

In virtually all contexts, the IRR favors groups that generate quick exits, even if the ultimate returns lag those of their peers. This was most evident in the fevered venture market of the late 1990s, when companies went from start-up to initial public offering (IPO) in record time.

Let's consider two private equity funds, each with $1 billion invested. In one case, the cumulative amount returned to the investors is $2 billion; in the other, it is $4 billion. In both cases, the funds are returned relatively rapidly; but the first fund has an early success (e.g., an acquisition) that allows the bulk of the money to be returned after just one quarter. The performance of these funds is described in Figure 9.3.

Most investors, seeing that the funds would be returned relatively rapidly in any case, would prefer the second fund since the capital gains are three times larger ($3 billion vs. $1 billion). Moreover, if we did an NPV analysis with a 15 percent discount rate, the second fund would come out on top (though the ratio of the NPVs is less than 3:1 because the first fund returns some cash sooner than the second fund). But the IRR calculation is so influenced by the "quick return" of the first fund that its annualized IRR is more than twice as large as that of the second fund. The key consideration must be the extent to which an investor has repeated opportunities for fast-return investments. If the investor could count on regular access to speedy returns, the first fund might be preferable because the proceeds could be quickly reinvested for another quick return.

This problem makes cash-on-cash returns such a popular alternative. Looking at who has returned funds would urge us to choose the private equity group that returned the most cash, rather than the one that made the first distribution. By looking at actual cash payments, the LPs hope to avoid the measurement problems and "gaming" that sometimes plague the assessment of IRRs.

Lack of Systemization

Our second concern with using IRRs as an industry-standard method of performance calculation is that, when all is said and done, there is no one right way to calculate an IRR. It seems fairly

FIGURE 9.3 IRR calculations may favor a quick cash return over a bigger, slower payback

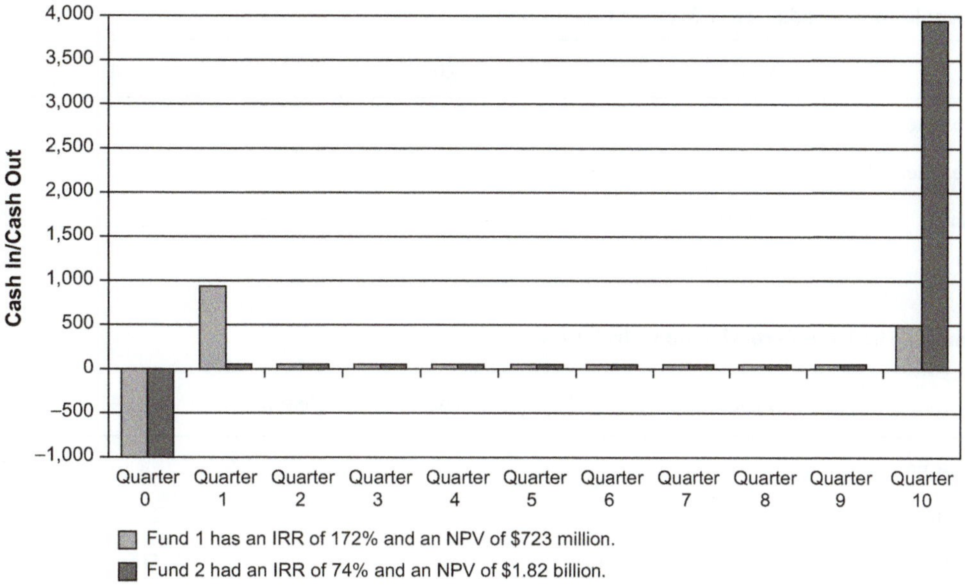

Fund 1 has an IRR of 172% and an NPV of $723 million.

Fund 2 had an IRR of 74% and an NPV of $1.82 billion.

straightforward to follow the directions in the earlier box and arrive at a defensible—even the "right"—results, but just a small change in the methodology employed can create dramatic shifts in the outcome.

Private equity groups differ sharply in their treatment of such elements as the timing and valuation of exited investments, the valuation of companies remaining in their investment portfolio, the impact of taxes, and other details of the IRR calculation. Let's focus on the timing of cash flows.

Two popular methods for calculating IRRs are the "calendar time" and the "time zero" methods. The calendar-time approach (sometimes called dollar-weighted in the private equity industry press) entails lining up all drawdowns and returns of capital in the year (or quarter, or month, or even the day) in which they occurred. If, for instance, in the third year of the fund, an IPO returned $100 million to investors while $150 million was drawn down from them, the cash hyphen;flow in that year would be recorded as −$50 million. If the investment made in the third year of the fund was ultimately harvested in the eighth year and yielded $400 million for the limited partners, that cash flow would be recorded as occurring in the eighth year of the fund.

The time-zero method assumes that all investments are made at the inception of the fund. Thus, an investment occurring in year 3 would be transferred to the initial year (year 1). Similarly, the sale would be brought forward two years, as if it occurred in year 6 (rather than year 8). These different methods, as shown in Table 9.2, can produce dramatically different IRRs. In Example 1, switching from the calendar-time to the time-zero method substantially increases the IRR, from 22 to 26 percent. In Example 2, the shift triggers a sharp decrease (from 43 to 34 percent). These unpredictable swings—and the lack of a standardized methodology for computing IRRs—make comparing the IRRs of different groups very challenging.

The Paradox of Multiple IRRs

As we noted earlier, when cash flows are simple, the IRR calculation is straightforward. If all capital flows into a private equity fund at its inception and this inflow is followed by a series of distributions, calculation of the IRR poses no problems.

Table 9.2 Calendar-Time and Time-Zero IRR Calculations

Example 1a: Calendar-Time Method Calculation

	Year 0	Year 1	Year 2	Year 3	Year 4	Year 5
Investment A	−100					
Investment B		−100				500
Total	−100	−100	0	0	0	500
IRR	22%					

Example 1b: Time-Zero Method Calculation

	Year 0	Year 1	Year 2	Year 3	Year 4	Year 5
Investment A	−100					
Investment B	−100				500	
Total	−200	0	0	0	500	0
IRR	26%					

Example 2a: Calendar-Time Method Calculation

	Year 0	Year 1	Year 2	Year 3	Year 4	Year 5
Investment A	−50			400		
Investment B		−100				
Investment C			−100			200
Total	−50	−100	−100	400	0	200
IRR	43%					

Example 2b: Time-Zero Method Calculation

	Year 0	Year 1	Year 2	Year 3	Year 4	Year 5
Investment A	−50			400		
Investment B	−100					
Investment C	−100			200		
Total	−250	0	0	600	0	0
IRR	34%					

Note: In each case, we assume the funds were drawn down from investors immediately before the investment.

A more complex series of cash flows—in particular, when we see several sequences of drawdowns and capital returns—exposes another drawback in using the IRR to measure fund performance. This situation, which is completely normal for private equity funds, often has the unfortunate side effect of generating multiple IRRs.

How Do Multiple IRRs Come About?

Consider a case where a fund with committed capital of $25 million draws down $5 million at its inception and $20 million at its second anniversary. The capital from the first drawdown is invested in a company that is acquired for $22.25 million at the end of the first year, and the proceeds of the sale are immediately returned to investors. The capital from the second drawdown, however, is invested in firms that prove unsuccessful and are ultimately liquidated for a total loss. In this case, the IRR equation to solve will be

$$0 = -5 + \frac{22.25}{(1+r)} - \frac{20}{(1+r)^2}$$

(Because the first and third cash flows are drawdowns from the limited investors, they are negative while the return of the proceeds is positive.) Unfortunately, this equation has multiple solutions: both $r = 25$ percent and $r = 220$ percent will give an NPV of zero.

How can this be? Figure 9.4 provides one way of understanding the situation. Like Figure 9.1, it shows the NPV of the cash flows that we just calculated when we employ different discount rates. At very low discount rates, the negative cash flow in the second period is given sufficient weight that it makes the entire stream of investments unattractive. At very high discount rates, events in the first and second quarter are so heavily discounted that they become inconsequential relative to the initial drawdown. Between these two extremes, however, a fund displaying this set of cash flows would actually be attractive. As the graph shows, there are two places where the NPV takes on a value of zero, and hence there are two IRRs.

FIGURE 9.4   Net present value can give multiple answers

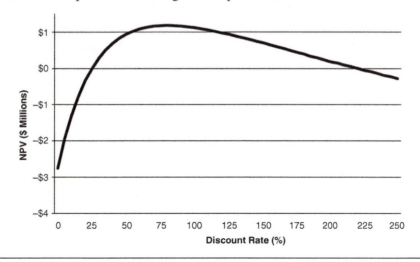

This problem of multiple IRRs is exacerbated by the manner in which spreadsheets calculate IRRs and then simply display one answer rather than alerting investors to the presence of multiple IRRs. In the example just given, if the spreadsheet starts with a default of zero, it will conclude that the IRR is 25 percent. If, however, we choose an intial IRR estimate of 100 percent, the program produces an IRR of 220 percent. As a result, a very real danger exists of drawing a false conclusion and making a disadvantageous investment decision.

This is an important problem because complex cash-flow patterns are prevalent. For instance, during the late 1990s and into 2000, many venture groups were able to exit investments very early in their funds' lives. The same thing was true for buyout funds in the mid-2000s. In many cases, cash or shares were returned to investors before the last drawdown of capital occurred, creating many possible IRRs. In these cases, the IRR really cannot serve as a guidepost. It is better to either compute the NPV of the various funds' cash flows, using a discount rate that reflects your target rate of return for private equity, or to simply look at cash-on-cash returns.

The Aggregation Problem

The last problem we'll highlight in this section has to do with the idiosyncratic way that the IRR combines information on multiple cash flows. Typically, a private equity fund will invest in a number of deals; in contrast, an institutional investor invests in multiple funds. Unfortunately, the way that IRRs handle the results from multiple funds is by no means obvious.

This problem can best be illustrated rather than described abstractly. Consider a university endowment that invests in three funds and wants to compute its rate of return, as illustrated in Table 9.3. The endowment's chief investment officer considers three ways to do this:

Table 9.3   IRRs and Multiple Funds

Fund Name	Commitment Size ($ Millions)	2002	2003	2004	2005	2006	2007	2008	2009	2010	2011	IRR (%)
Abracadabra Ventures	100	−50	−50	0	0	0	30	0	300	20	0	22
Boring Private Equity	800	−400	20	−380	50	100	150	50	75	75	0	−9
Complete Balanced Fund	500	−250	−250	0	0	100	200	250	150	300	120	14
Pooled cash flows		−700	−280	−380	50	200	380	300	525	395	120	
Average IRR												9
Weighted average IRR												2
Pooled IRR												7

1. Compute the IRR of each fund and then average them.

2. Calculate the weighted average of the IRRs, where the weights are the amount committed to each fund.

3. Add together all the cash flows, as if it were a single fund, and compute the IRR of the cash flows. This computation produces what is often known as the pooled IRR.

As the table reveals, the three calculations give very different answers. The simple average gives the highest return, because the smallest fund has the best performance. More puzzling is that the pooled IRR yields a return *four times* that of the weighted average IRR. Had we used a different set of numbers, the results might have gone another way. The IRR is a measure that can be quite sensitive to the way calculations are made, in ways that are not readily explicable.

As we saw with the example of the University of Texas, this lack of a standard can pose significant problems for investors in private equity. After all, performance assessment is a critical piece of the private equity investment decision. Although top-down asset allocation decisions are critical, the ability to gauge performance and pick the top-performing funds is also essential to the success of a private equity program.

Is There a Better Way?

Given the limitations of the cash-on-cash and IRR calculations, are there better ways of assessing private equity fund returns? While these two methodologies dominate practice, the answer is almost unquestionably yes.

A promising approach is to look at the NPV of funds, normalized by the amount of capital they have raised. The NPV, unlike cash-on-cash returns, takes account of the time value of money. Moreover, it avoids many of the problems of IRRs. For instance, it avoids the tortoise-and-hare problem because a rapid repayment of a small amount of capital will not lead to a huge NPV. The aggregation problem does not materialize. The sum of the NPV of two cash flows will not differ from the present value of the summed cash flows. Moreover, NPV is also immune to the multiple-solution problem.

The central problem with NPV is finding the appropriate discount rate. As discussed in Chapter 4, it is *not* right to use the very high hurdle rates employed by private equity investors, which comingle both the cost of capital and an adjustment for excessive entrepreneurial optimism. Rather, a discount rate that reflects the true expected return on the part of the institutions and individuals who provide the capital—perhaps somewhere between 12 and 18 percent—seems far more appropriate. We explore this issue in the next section.

COMPARING PRIVATE EQUITY TO THE PUBLIC MARKETS

So far, we have focused on comparing private equity funds to each other. Certainly, comparing performance is important when assessing performance; but many entities want to compare the results of private equity investments to other asset classes. In particular, it is natural to wonder how the performance of private equity compares to that of public equities.

Initially, we might approach this assessment by comparing returns over the same time period. For instance, Table 9.1 reported that the performance of private equity as a whole over the past twenty years was 11.5 percent. During the same period, the S&P 500 returned 7.4 percent. We might therefore conclude that private equity has performed somewhat better than public stocks.

But this comparison is somewhat misleading. In particular, as we saw in Figure 1.1 and discussed elsewhere, private equity has seen a torrent of funding over the past decade, so there is far more capital available to private equity investors than was the case fifteen years ago. To simply compare private equity performance to the aggregate public returns over a twenty-year period, where we are essentially giving each year of public market performance equal weight, might be misleading.

This approach might also be misleading if we were comparing a private equity fund to the public market. Consider a fund active between 1997 and 2009 that had an IRR of 7.5 percent. During that same period, the S&P 500 returned an average of 7.2 percent per year. We might conclude that the fund did quite well. But at the end of the fund's life, when the market was doing very poorly, only a tiny amount of capital was left in the fund. Perhaps we should really focus on the earlier years, when the bulk of the investments were made and returned to investors. What is the right way to think about this calculation?

This problem has led to the development of the **public market equivalent** (PME) methodology to compare an investment in a private equity fund with a public market index. First developed by Austin Long and Craig Nickles, this methodology compares the proceeds generated by investing in the private equity fund with those from investing the same amount in the S&P 500 (or, if one prefers, another index). If the ratio of the proceeds from the private equity investments to the public investment is greater than one, private equity is the superior investment; if the ratio is less than one, the public investment is better.

This methodology can best be illustrated with a couple of examples.[6] For instance, consider a case where a buyout fund draws down $100 million in June 2004 and returns a distribution of $200 million in April 2007. An investor alternatively could have invested in the public market, but the same investment in June 2004 in the S&P 500 would have yielded only $139.52 million if sold in April 2007. The PME of this investment of 1.43 (or 200/139.52) indicates that the private equity investment would have been superior. On the other hand, a $10 million investment in a venture fund in January 1993 that was liquidated in December 1999 for $40 million looks pretty spectacular. But since an investment at the same time in the S&P 500 would have yielded $39.16 million in December 1999, the PME is a disappointing 1.03 (40/39.16)—indicating that the investment yielded barely more than the public market securities, which allow liquidity.[7]

Table 9.4 provides Steve Kaplan and Antoinette Schoar's computation of the PMEs for private equity as well as for VC and buyout groups separately. The calculations highlight the impact of using weighted and unweighted data. When we use unweighted data (treating each fund equally), the performance of venture and buyout funds differs little. While the median fund has a PME well below one, the typical fund has a PME of almost one. This difference stems from the fact that the distribution of PMEs is skewed; some funds have very high returns that bring up the average.

The weighted data looks different. Now private equity in general has a PME greater than one. This change is driven by the venture groups, which have a PME greater than one. The PME of the average buyout group actually falls. This pattern is driven by the fact that while the largest venture funds have outperformed their peers, the largest buyout funds actually do worse (we also saw this in Table 9.1). It is worth noting, however, that this analysis consisted of 746 funds established between 1980 and 1995. During many of the succeeding years, buyout funds have done

---

[6] These examples are drawn from Steven Kaplan and Antoinette Schoar, "Private Equity Performance: Returns, Persistence, and Capital," *Journal of Finance* 60 (2005): 1791–823.

[7] These calculations can get more complex, not surprisingly, when there are many flows in and out of the fund, particularly when the private equity fund makes very large distributions over the course of the fund. The details of the calculations in these instances are explained in http://www.alignmentcapital.com/pdfs/research/icm_aimr_benchmark_1996.pdf, especially Appendix B, accessed August 21, 2009.

Table 9.4   Public Market Equivalents for Private Equity, Venture, and Buyouts

	Unweighted			Weighted		
	All Private Equity	Venture	Buyout	All Private Equity	Venture	Buyout
Mean	0.96	0.96	0.97	1.05	1.21	0.93
Median	0.74	0.66	0.80	0.82	0.92	0.83
Lower quartile	0.45	0.43	0.62	0.67	0.55	0.72
Upper quartile	1.14	1.13	1.12	1.11	1.40	1.03

Note: All data are public market equivalents.
Source: Data from Steven Kaplan and Antoinette Schoar, "Private Equity Performance: Returns, Persistence, and Capital," *Journal of Finance* 60 (2005): 1798.

significantly better than venture funds, so any conclusions about general tendencies must be cautious.

The Yardstick Problem

So far, so good. But as is all too often the case when it comes to private equity, this simple solution is too simple. These comparisons between public and private equity, and even between private equity funds, are likely not to be really fair.

The "yardstick problem" reflects the fact that private equity funds differ fundamentally—both from public equities and between each other—in many respects. These dimensions might include their investment strategies, use of debt, stages of development, geographical investment patterns, types of investment, and associated risks. Ideally, the assessment of private equity fund returns would take account of these differences, but the PME definitely does not.

This point can be illustrated by considering a private equity fund—let's call it Hotshot Capital—where the companies' overall value changes in ways that exactly mirror the market. Hotshot's investments are heavily laden with debt: for every one dollar of equity invested, nine are borrowed. For instance, assume the market goes up by 10 percent over the course of a year. The overall (enterprise) value of Acme Industries, in which Hotshot has invested its entire fund of $1 billion dollars (and borrowed an additional $9 billion), also increases by 10 percent, from $10 to $11 billion. At the end of the year, Hotshot sells its investment and gets a terrific return: after repaying the $9 billion in debt, its $1 billion has increased to $2 billion. (We assume that Acme's profits during the year are just enough to offset the interest due on the debt and the copious fees that must be paid to everyone from the investment bankers to the accountants.) A PME analysis would suggest that Hotshot had well outperformed the benchmark, with a ratio of 1.82 (= 2/1.1).

But we know this isn't right. Hotshot has done well not because it truly created value, but because it took more risks. Had the market declined by 10 percent, the investors in public equities would have lost only 10 percent of their capital, while the LPs of Hotshot Capital would have been completely wiped out. There must be a way to adjust for this!

In public markets, a standard approach is to run a regression that seeks to explain the fund's returns using one or more measures of public market performance, as well as a constant. In these regressions, there are two key items of interest. The first is the coefficient on the market returns, typically known as a beta. As we discussed in Chapter 4, a beta of one suggests that the fund is as risky as the market, a beta less than one implies it is less risky, and a beta greater than one implies it is riskier. The beta—and thus the required return before a fund is pronounced to be an outperformer—grows with the risk that the fund assumes.

The second important element of the regression equation is the constant term. The analysis seeks to determine whether, after controlling for the market's movements, the coefficient of the constant is positive, negative, or indistinguishable from zero (i.e., whether the market-adjusted performance is superior to the appropriate benchmark, inferior to that measure, or too close to the measure of market performance to discern).

In this way, analysts can avoid drawing false conclusions about the success of different investment managers. For instance, consider two mutual funds, one holding equities of small high-technology firms and one holding securities issued by utilities. While the high-technology fund may have higher absolute returns over a given period, it may not be a superior performer once the greater riskiness (higher beta) of its portfolio is controlled for. Similarly, a mutual fund that makes greater use of debt will have a higher beta and a greater required return before it is designated an outperformer.

In recent years, there has been extensive discussion in the finance literature about the measures of market performance that should be used as control variables in these regressions. A consensus has emerged around the view, first articulated by Gene Fama and Ken French, that three crucial measures should be used in such analyses: (1) the performance of the market as a whole; (2) the performance of small-capitalization stocks relative to larger securities; and (3) the performance of "growth" stocks relative to "value" stocks (i.e., the differential performance of those securities with higher and lower ratios of market value of their equity to their book equity value). In other words, it is necessary to isolate the performance of the fund from overall market changes ("a rising tide lifts all boats") and particular dynamics that might affect companies of different sizes and characteristics. Once these three aspects of the market's impact on a specific investment portfolio are controlled, the coefficient on the constant term should give an appropriate indication of the fund's relative performance.

In the private equity setting, investors do not typically attempt to adjust returns in the same way that mutual fund investors do. In other words, they are content to simply compare the IRRs and cash-on-cash returns of funds against their peers rather than against what was happening in markets more generally during the period. In part, this may be due to the private equity industry's conservatism: many investors feel that cash-on-cash returns and IRRs have worked well enough, and there is no need for change. But it can be problematic, for several reasons. If the funds are different—say, one is considerably riskier than others in its cohort—this can create misleading results. Moreover, sometimes private equity funds as a whole may do particularly well or poorly when compared to public markets. But there is another difficulty as well: because of stale prices and inconsistency, it is simply very hard to calculate the relationship between private equity and public markets.

Stale prices pose a stubborn obstacle to comparisons between funds and between asset classes over time. While the movements of public market indexes can be observed on a daily (or even minute-by-minute) basis, changes in the value of private companies can be observed only after substantial delay. Even the GP on the board might not know that a particular technology has worked until the next board meeting, and the LPs might not know the impact of this news on the company's valuation until they receive the annual report. More typically, the delay is even longer: the change in value may be reported only when the private equity firm announces the company's IPO at a great valuation increase, rather than periodically as the company gradually meets its milestones. This means that the company goes along being valued at "lower of cost or last round" (as we discussed in Chapter 4) and suddenly goes public at perhaps twenty times that value. A pleasant surprise, to be sure—but one that renders pricing models unusable. Acquisitions can be equally unexpected and may place a value on a company many times its carrying value in the portfolio.

These stale prices make comparisons of public and private equity returns very difficult. Thus it is hard to know to what extent private equity returns simply reflect public stock movements or true excess value creation. The types of analyses commonly used when assessing mutual and hedge funds are much more difficult to undertake here.

To illustrate this difficulty, consider a world in which we observe the S&P 500 on a monthly basis, but we receive reports on other assets (for the sake of illustration, we will use the shares of IBM and GE as well as the S&P 500 itself) less frequently. In addition, although we receive a monthly report on these other assets, most of the time we receive a "stale price"—the same price two months in a row—instead of the actual price. If we don't recognize that the problem of stale pricing exists, or if we disregard it, we would simply estimate the correlation between the S&P 500 and the other assets using the monthly data—certainly an imperfect solution.

Table 9.5 illustrates this problem. In this chart, we tabulate the price of a hypothetical asset and a market index for six months. In the first row, the true value at the end of each of the six months is recorded. But if the asset suffers from a stale price problem, we will only observe its true value intermittently.

For example, in the second row, we see what happens if the asset's true price is observed only every other month. Months 1, 3, and 5 show the asset's true price. Months 2, 4, and 6 report its price from the previous month (i.e., the stale price, which is not equal to the true price in that month). In the third row, we see what happens if we can observe the asset's true price only every third month. In months 1 and 4, we observe the true price, while in the other months we merely observe the stale price.

Figure 9.5 illustrates the consequences of just this type of problem. If we saw the true prices every month from January 1950 through December 2002, we would find that asset correlations were very high. Between the S&P 500 and GE, the correlation would be 0.73, while between the S&P 500 and IBM, it would be 0.60. (The correlation between the S&P 500 and itself is 1.00.) If, however, we receive the correct price for the other assets only every second month and have to make do with stale prices in between, the correlations would fall to 0.40 for GE and 0.30 for IBM. In fact, even the correlation between the S&P 500 and the "stale" S&P 500 would drop to 0.53. If we receive the accurate price only once every three months (i.e., two months of stale pricing between each month of current pricing), the correlations decline to 0.23 for GE, 0.16 for IBM, and 0.34 for the "stale" S&P 500.

Table 9.5   The Stale Pricing Problem

Return in Each Month, without Stale Price Problem (%)					
Month 1	Month 2	Month 3	Month 4	Month 5	Month 6
5	−1	3	−4	−2	4

Return in Each Month, with One-Month Stale Prices (%)					
Month 1	Month 2	Month 3	Month 4	Month 5	Month 6
0	4	0	−1	0	2

Return in Each Month, with Two-Month Stale Prices (%)					
Month 1	Month 2	Month 3	Month 4	Month 5	Month 6
0	0	4	0	0	1

FIGURE 9.5   Correlation of the S&P 500 with GE, IBM, and itself with stale pricing

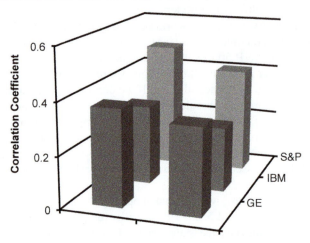

Correlation with S&P 500 with One Stale Month
Correlation with S&P 500 with Two Stale Months

    Returning to the issues we discussed in Chapter 4, the valuation of private equity companies suffers from severe stale pricing. In part, this is because the companies simply accrete value slowly and uncertainly; in part, it is because these changes are reported only sporadically. With venture-backed companies, valuations typically change when an outside investor sets the price for the new round, which happens every two or three years. We just saw the impact of prices that were only three months stale—even the S&P 500's correlation with itself fell by 66 percent. Due to the Financial Accounting Standards (FAS) 157 regulations, investors are supposed to revisit company valuations more frequently than at each financing round. But even so, how does one realistically value a company that might be the next Google or might go out of business? Buyout firms are less prone to the issue because their portfolio companies more often have revenues and profits or publicly traded comparables, but "marking the portfolio to market" is still a topic of great debate and concern. The discussion in Chapter 4 about valuation approaches notes the ongoing philosophical conversation around the subject in private equity fields. Clearly, this is an area that requires considerable research and the development of a rigorous quantitative methodology.

    Adding complexity to this problem is the inconsistency with which private equity groups value investments. The practices of the established venture groups—even after reform efforts such as the adoption of FAS 157—emphasize computing returns using conservative assumptions. At least in theory, these procedures help prevent investors from being misled by overly aggressive assumptions—and organizations—but such conservatism makes it particularly difficult for investors to compare private equity returns to returns in other asset classes. Thus, while it may be possible for private equity organizations to demonstrate that their funds have out-performed other partnerships formed at around the same time (i.e., the same vintage year), it is difficult to understand how their returns have evolved relative to the equity or bond markets. Meanwhile, less-established private equity organizations are often less conservative in their valuation practices. Differences in valuation methodology can create the appearance that certain groups have superior performance when interim returns are compared, while their long-run performance may be no different from (or even lower than) that of other organizations. Nor, as we have seen, have the efforts to establish consistency across private equity funds been particularly successful.

Solving the Yardstick Problem—Harder Than It Looks

How, then, to address the yardstick problem and compare the performance of the variety of different private equity funds among each other and against other asset classes? One solution to this problem is to "mark to market" the private equity organization's portfolio. Rather than waiting until there is a "material" event (e.g., a financing or an IPO) to revalue a company, as a private equity group might do, interested parties could periodically reexamine the valuations of all firms in the portfolio. Comparing the marked-to-market private equity fund (or the portfolio of funds) to the public market would yield an appropriate correlation.

These quarterly or annual assessments can incorporate a wide variety of information about the changes over this period. Two initial choices would be the change in the market valuations for comparable public companies over the period and the change in the company's profitability. For instance, if from 2008 to 2009, a portfolio company's profits increased by 10 percent, and the price-earnings multiple of public firms in the same industry climbed by 20 percent, we might want to increase the company's valuation by 21 percent ($= 1.1 * 1.2$).

But there are many other measures we might want to factor in as well:

- The change in valuation of private firms that were refinanced.
- The change in the relative prices of private and public equity markets as a whole.
- The change in any other company characteristics that equity market analysts commonly used to value similar firms (e.g., for young biotechnology firms, the number of patents awarded).
- The overall shifts in the market for IPOs and acquisitions.
- The market's interest in the company as reflected in its ability to raise more money.

By undertaking such a calculation, the stale-price problem can be addressed to a certain extent. These revised valuations, as well as cash inflows and outflows from the portfolio, can establish meaningful returns that can be compared to the returns from the public market during the same time interval. In this way, we can avoid the kind of biases discussed earlier when drawing conclusions about the performance of private equity in general and of specific funds.

This approach may sound simple in theory, but in practice it is far more challenging. Table 9.6 summarizes a number of academic studies that have tried to compute the risk-adjusted performance of private equity funds. The papers have differed in terms of their focus, time period examined, and methodological choices employed.

It is hard to be convinced that there is a definitive answer about the returns of private equity. In general, it is fair to say that most studies conclude that venture firms match or slightly exceed the public market benchmark, and most studies suggest that buyout funds returns lag. But few studies have included the boom period for buyout funds in the mid-2000s; thus, subsequent conclusions may differ. Moreover, the results seem incredibly sensitive to underlying assumptions when modeling how the value of private equity portfolios evolves.

THINKING ABOUT DIVERSIFICATION

Understanding the riskiness of private equity is essential for another task as well: determining the proper mix of these investments in the portfolio. In many cases, investors seem to make decisions concerning their portfolio allocations to private equity by relying more on intuition than on systematic analysis.

While this approach may not have been a problem when private equity represented only a very modest share—say, 1 or 2 percent—of an investor's portfolio, in recent years, portfolio allocations to private equity have been growing. Figure 9.6 illustrates this point by showing the changing

Table 9.6 Summaries of Studies on Risk and Return

Author and Paper	PE Class	Methodology	Beta	Alpha (or other abnormal return measure, as noted)
Reyes, "Industry Struggling to Forge Tools for Measuring Risk," 1990	VC	The data sample included 175 mature VC funds; however, it used no *correction* for selection or missing intermediate data. No α computed.	1.0–3.8	
Gompers and Lerner, "Risk and Reward in Private Equity Investments: The Challenge of Performance Assessment," 1997	VC	This study examines the risk-adjusted performance using a sample of 96 VC investments of a single fund group by marking to market each investment, in order to obtain the fund's quarterly market value. The resulting time series of gross returns is regressed on asset pricing factors.	1.08–1.40	8%
Peng, "Building a Venture Capital Index," 2001	VC	The data set included 12,946 rounds of VC financings with 5,643 VC-backed firms between 1987 and 1999. Using a propensity weighting method, reports β on the S&P 500 and on NASDAQ.	1.3–2.4 (S&P 500) 0.8–4.7 (NASDAQ)	55%
Jones and Rhodes-Kropf, "The Price of Diversifiable Risk in Venture Capital and Private Equity," 2003	VC	The data set from 866 venture funds between 1980 and 1999 included returns calculated for using GP estimates of value rather than actual cash flows.	1.11	4.68%
Jones and Rhodes-Kropf, "The Price of Diversifiable Risk in Venture Capital and Private Equity," 2003	BOs	The data set from 379 venture funds between 1980 and 1999 included returns calculated for using GP estimates of value rather than actual cash flows.	0.81	0.72%
Ljungqvist and Richardson, "The Cash Flow, Return and Risk Characteristics of Private Equity," 2003	All PE	The paper analyzes returns to investments in 73 venture and buyout funds by one large LP in funds raised from 1981 to 1993. Reported are the mean values for β and a unique risk-adjusted profitability index (PI), with ex ante and ex post values of the S&P 500 used as a benchmark and 0% represents no abnormal performance.	1.09	32.23%, 24.00% (PI)

Study	Type	Description	β	Return
Ljungqvist and Richardson, "The Cash Flow, Return and Risk Characteristics of Private Equity," 2003	VC	The paper analyzes returns to investments in 19 venture funds by one large LP in funds raised from 1981 to 1993. Reported are the mean values for β and a unique risk-adjusted PI, with ex ante and ex post values of the S&P 500 used as a benchmark, and 0% represents no abnormal performance.	1.12	28.08%, 15.11% (PI)
Ljungqvist and Richardson, "The Cash Flow, Return and Risk Characteristics of Private Equity," 2003	BOs	The paper analyzes returns to investments in 54 buyout funds by one large LP in funds raised from 1981 to 1993. Reported are the mean values for β and a unique risk-adjusted PI, with ex ante and ex post values of the S&P 500 used as a benchmark and 0% represents no abnormal performance.	1.08	33.69%, 27.13% (PI)
Woodward and Hall, "Benchmarking the Returns to Venture Capital," 2004	VC	The data set, from 1987 to 2001, continuously reinvested value-weighted portfolios of all venture-backed and similar pre-public companies.	0.86	8.5%
Kaplan and Schoar, "Private Equity Performance: Returns, Persistence, and Capital Flows," 2005	All PE	The data sample included 746 funds in the period 1980–1997. β assumed to equal 1; S&P 500 used for PME. PME = 1 denotes no abnormal performance.		1.05 (PME)
Kaplan and Schoar, "Private Equity Performance: Returns, Persistence, and Capital Flows," 2005	VC	The data sample included 580 funds in the period 1980–1997. β assumed to equal 1; S&P 500 used for PME. PME = 1 denotes no abnormal performance.		1.21 (PME)
Kaplan and Schoar, "Private Equity Performance: Returns, Persistence, and Capital Flows," 2005	BOs	The data sample included 166 funds in the period 1980–1997. β assumed to equal 1; S&P 500 used for PME. PME = 1 denotes no abnormal performance.		0.93 (PME)
Cochrane, "The Risk and Return of Venture Capital," 2005	VC	The paper analyzes 16,613 observations on 7,765 start-up firms over the period of 1987–2000.	1.7	32%
	VC		0.4–0.6	≈1%

(continued)

Table 9.6 *(Continued)*

Author and Paper	PE Class	Methodology	Beta	Alpha (or other abnormal return measure, as noted)
Hwang, Quigley, and Woodward, "An Index for Venture Capital 1987–2003," 2005		The data set reports 50,734 funding events, which include the contemporaneous valuations of 9,092 private equity firms disclosed 19,208 times over 1987–2003. Estimates β between the venture deals and NASDAQ and S&P 500.		
Phalippou and Zollo, "Performance of Private Equity Funds: Another Puzzle?" 2005	All PE	The data sample, from 1980 to 2003, includes 2,844 funds raised between 1980 and 1996. The performance is based on the aggregated cash flows across all funds.	1.3	**1.05** to **0.95** (PI when compared to S&P 500 = 1 for the same time period.)
Ewens, "A New Model of Venture Capital Risk and Return," 2009	VC	The data sample covered 1987–2007 and over 55,000 financing events and 10,000 returns.	2.4	27%
Phalippou and Gottschalg, "The Performance of Private Equity Funds," 2009	All PE	The data sample included 1,328 funds from 1980 to 1993. β assumed to equal 1.		−3% to −6%
Woodward, "Measuring Risk for Venture Capital and Private Equity Portfolios," 2009	VC	The data sample includes 51 observations after adjustments, period 1996Q1–2008Q3. Values of α per quarter.	2.2	0.5%
Woodward, "Measuring Risk for Venture Capital and Private Equity Portfolios," 2009	VC	The data sample includes 27 observations after adjustments, period 2002Q1–2008Q3. Values of α per quarter.	1.1	−0.6%
Woodward, "Measuring Risk for Venture Capital and Private Equity Portfolios," 2009	BOs	The data sample includes 51 observations after adjustments, period 1996Q1–2008Q3. Values of α per quarter.	0.96	1.4%
Woodward, "Measuring Risk for Venture Capital and Private Equity Portfolios," 2009	BOs	The data sample includes 29 observations after adjustments, period 2001Q3–2008Q3. Values of α per quarter.	1.1	2.1%

Study	Type	Description	β	α
Franzoni, Nowak, and Phalippou, "Private Equity Performance and Liquidity Risk," 2010	All PE	The data sample includes cash flows for 4,403 liquidated investments over the period 1975–2006, which are both successful and unsuccessful.	**0.7–1.3**	**≈ 0%**
Driessen, Phalippou, and Lin, "A New Method to Estimate Risk and Return of Non-Traded Assets from Cash Flows: The Case of Private Equity Funds," 2010	VC	The data sample includes 686 mature VC funds over 1980–2003. A good small sample of properties to assess the abnormal performance and risk exposure of a nontraded asset from a panel of cash-flow data. Values for β and α per annum gross of fees.	**3.21**	**−1.24%**
Driessen, Phalippou, and Lin, "A New Method to Estimate Risk and Return of Non-Traded Assets from Cash Flows: The Case of Private Equity Funds," 2010	BOs	The data sample includes 272 mature buyout funds from 1980 to 2003. A small sample of properties to assess the abnormal performance and risk exposure of a nontraded asset from a panel of cash-flow data. Values for β and α per annum gross of fees.	**0.33**	**0.49%**
Jegadeesh, Kräussl, and Pollet, "Risk and Expected Returns of Private Equity Investments: Evidence Based on Market Prices," 2010	All PE	The paper uses two samples of publicly traded firms that invest in PE from 1994 to 2008: the first sample contains 24 publicly traded funds of funds that predominantly invest in unlisted PE funds; second sample contains 155 listed PE (LPE) funds. The study uses MSCI World or S&P 500 indices as market proxies.	**≈1**	**0.5%** (for unlisted PEs) ~**0%** (for LPEs after fees)
Korteweg and Sorensen, "Risk and Return Characteristics of Venture Capital-Backed Entrepreneurial Companies," 2010	VC	The data sample includes 61,356 investment rounds for 18,237 companies from 1987 to 2005. β and α present average monthly values for the three periods: 1987–1993, 1993–2001, and 2001–2005.	**2.8**	**1.6%** (1987–1993) **5.8%** (1993–2001) **−2.7%** (2001–2005)

Source: The authors thank Vladimir Bosiljevac for his work on this table.

FIGURE 9.6 Asset allocation of major universities to private equity

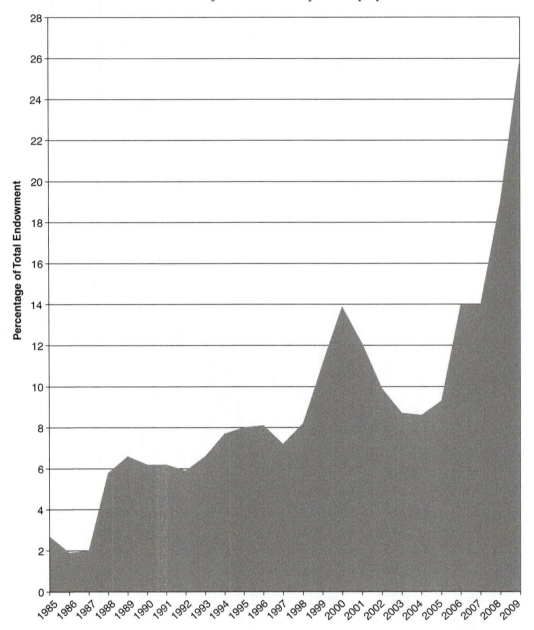

Source: National Association of College and University Business Offices, Endowment Study for appropriate years, available at www.nacubo.org.

allocation to private equity of one set of institutional investors: colleges and universities.[8] As private equity becomes increasingly important in the overall mix of investment opportunities, a thorough understanding of how it fits with the rest of the portfolio has become equally critical.

---

[8] This chart is compiled from various publications of the National Association of College and University Business Officers (NACUBO). While there has been a slight decline in the allocation to private equity, which includes both funds devoted to leveraged buyouts and venture capital investments (in recent years, they are declining in part due to distributions and write-downs by private equity groups), the level remains far above that seen historically.

While determining the overall allocations to private equity is important, we think it is necessary to point out that a successful private equity investment program consists of far more than simply getting an appropriate percentage allocated to these funds. Selecting appropriate funds across a number of years is also critical to achieving the goals of generating attractive risk-adjusted returns for investors.

The Asset Allocation Dilemma

Most institutional investors begin their money management decision process by determining their appropriate asset allocation (i.e., how much of their capital should be invested in public equities, government or corporate bonds, real estate, and private equity). Asset allocation models begin with the investor's demands for future payouts from the portfolio as well as historical information on the level of and variability of returns on various asset classes. Typically, these models use information not only on the attractiveness and variability of the returns of each asset class but also on the extent to which the returns of different asset classes move together (how they correlate with one another). This information is then run through an analytical model to determine the optimal portfolio mix. For instance, an analytical model based on the capital asset pricing model (CAPM) will seek to find the combination of high returns and low portfolio variability—expressed more technically, a portfolio that has a high "Sharpe ratio"—that most closely fits with the investors' needs.

Investors typically begin the decision process of how much to allocate to private equity by determining how much risk they want to take on. Risk in this context is generally thought of as the volatility of a given portfolio's returns. Portfolios with returns that vary more widely between extremes of loss and gain are considered riskier than portfolios whose returns move within a narrower range. In general, higher risk implies higher returns. The insights of modern finance, however, have demonstrated that the only types of risk that should lead to higher expected returns are the types of risk that you cannot reduce by diversifying them in a portfolio of assorted investments. In other words, the types of risk that lead to higher expected returns are those risks whose fluctuations are not canceled out by the movement of returns to other investments.

An example may help illustrate this point. Consider two companies, one selling umbrellas, the other sunscreen. The first company's stock price may rise during rainy spells, while the other's price falls. During sunny periods, the opposite pattern may hold. But even though each stock individually may be quite noisy, a portfolio holding both stocks together may be quite stable in value: the movement of the two stocks may largely cancel each other out. In this case, the expected return of neither stock would be very high, even though individually the stocks were quite volatile.

Because correlation between assets measures how two investments move in relation to each other, measuring correlations is a critical element of any asset allocation model. Asset allocation models use the correlation among various asset classes to determine the mix of investments that will lead to the highest potential return for a given amount of risk. (Of course, when deciding whether to invest in private equity, in addition to deciding on the level of risk that they want to bear, investors face constraints when they make any asset allocation decision. Most important are the need for liquidity, tax considerations, legal constraints, the size of the target allocation relative to the fund size, and the ability of the investor to access the desired private equity funds. We discuss these issues in Chapter 2.)

Diversification is crucial when investing because it is a critical method of attempting to reduce risk in investment portfolios. From the viewpoint of a private equity investor, the diversification benefit of a private equity investment program depends on how the return of a particular set of investments moves up or down with the return of other investments (i.e., on how correlated their returns are). If the returns of two investments have relatively low correlation with each other, combining the investments in a portfolio will reduce the variability of the overall portfolio's return. As historical data and portfolio management practice have indicated, portfolios with greater diversification have assets whose returns exhibit lower variability and, hence, lower risk.

What Not to Do: The Boston University Horror Show

Boston University's experience with VC investments shows what can happen to the portfolios of large investors that do not take a diversified approach to investing. In 1987, Boston University's endowment was $142 million. At that time, its VC subsidiary invested in a privately held biotechnology company that had been founded in 1979 by a number of scientists affiliated with the institution. The university's initial 1987 investment bought out the stakes of several independent VC investors, who had apparently concluded after a number of financing rounds that the firm's prospects were unattractive.

Between 1987 and 1992, Boston University, investing alongside university officials and trustees, provided at least $90 million—over 60 percent of the university's total endowment in 1987—to the biotech firm.[9] While the biotech company finally did succeed in completing an IPO, it encountered a series of disappointments with its products and was ultimately sold to a San Diego-based biotechnology concern for only a few million dollars. As a result, Boston University was out more than $90 million as well as the opportunity to have invested a considerable chunk of its assets elsewhere and perhaps more productively. The university's decision to concentrate its private equity investment in one company in one sector created tremendous portfolio risk that ultimately had a significant negative impact on the university's endowment. Clearly this raises the issues of appropriate asset allocation, as well as appropriate diversification within an asset class. Putting all the eggs in one basket can scramble returns.

Elements of Private Equity Diversification

With traditional public securities, diversification entails buying a set of listed stocks, bonds, and cash instruments, or their proxies, whose returns can potentially create an "optimal" portfolio. Because these investment vehicles are freely traded and are reasonably liquid, the task of diversification is generally an exercise in selecting among various choices. Research on public stocks has shown that, in general, the biggest benefit of diversification comes after the selection of the first twenty to thirty stocks in a given equity portfolio.[10] Beyond that, adding stocks may further reduce the portfolio's total risk, but the incremental reduction is much smaller.

Within private equity, however, the task of diversification requires careful thinking about the elements that affect the overall risk of a private equity portfolio. At least four features are crucial: (1) diversification across various vintages of private equity funds; (2) diversification across

---

[9] This account is based on Seragen's filings with the U.S. Securities and Exchange Commission. In a 1992 agreement with the State of Massachusetts Attorney General's Office, the university agreed to make no further equity investments. The school, however, made a $12 million loan guarantee in 1995 (subsequently converted into equity) and a $5 million payment as part of an asset purchase in 1997.

[10] M. Statman, "How Many Stocks Make a Diversified Portfolio?" *Journal of Financial and Quantitative Analysis* 22, no. 3 (1987): 353–64.

industry segments; (3) diversification across various private equity sub-asset classes (e.g., VC, buyouts, mezzanine, distressed, etc.); and (4) diversification across geography.

Diversification across Vintages

Private equity funds are commonly characterized by "vintage," or year of fund inception, because of the way they invest capital. A private equity fund receives capital commitments from investors in one specific year and then invests the capital over the subsequent several years. These investments form part of a portfolio that may be held for five to ten years until they go public, are purchased, or are liquidated. Thus an investor who commits capital to a fund in a particular year is exposed to the economic conditions and opportunities in the years that follow when the capital is tied up. These economic conditions and opportunities are likely to differ from year to year, so private equity funds of different vintages face different macroeconomic conditions. The further apart two vintages are in time, the more likely their prospects are to differ.

What factors can differ across various vintages that might affect the prospects of each fund differently? In the case of venture capital, the prospects for a given year's investments are affected quite dramatically by the new technologies that are coming to market—genomics one year, perhaps, followed by breakthroughs in wireless enterprise software the next year. Unlike public equities, the new technologies that become available in a given year may greatly affect a VC fund's diversification and hence increase the benefits of holding multiple investments across various vintage years. Because a public equity technology manager can buy and sell companies that have new and different technologies at any time, that manager can gain diversification across technology cycles. But VC funds are illiquid: they cannot freely buy and sell equity stakes in their portfolio companies. Once capital is fully invested, no new investments can be made, even if exciting and potentially profitable new technologies emerge.

As a result, investors who commit to VC funds across various vintages may gain the benefit of investing across several years when fresh technology opportunities may come to market. For example, a life sciences VC fund raised in 1991 may have invested heavily in biotechnology because of the technology opportunities available to it at that time, whereas a life sciences fund raised in 1995 may have found more opportunities in medical devices and, as a result, devoted more of its capital to such companies.

Diversification by vintage also affects buyout investments, because the underlying success of a buyout greatly depends on the deal's pricing as well as its investors' access to debt capital for financing. In addition, the valuation of buyout opportunities has historically depended on public market activity in any given field. For example, if the prices of publicly traded health-care stocks are low in one year, a buyout specialist might find attractively priced opportunities. Similarly, if small public service providers find themselves in an economic environment where the value of their stock is rapidly increasing, a buyout group that specializes in roll-ups of smaller service providers might have to pay more for a particular set of transactions. Furthermore, because public market pricing in particular sectors and opportunities may gyrate widely, public market volatility can affect private markets.

All else being equal, a buyout firm that finds attractive investment prices is likely to generate higher returns on its fund. Because the deal pricing affecting a buyout firm in one year may be very different from that for a buyout fund raised three years later, the returns of various vintages of buyout groups may have little relationship to each other: in other words, they may be relatively uncorrelated and therefore valuable to an investment portfolio in reducing idiosyncratic risk.

Much like the equity markets, the debt markets show significant variations with great volatility in interest rates. If money is tight one year or interest rates are high, investors may be less willing to borrow in order to contribute to a buyout. For example, in the late 1980s, the collapse of the high-yield debt market in the United States made it difficult to leverage the deals with the requisite amount of debt. Diversification across various buyout vintages allows an investor to commit to deals that have had varying access to debt capital and different return potentials.

Another element of vintage diversification is the simple availability of certain types of funds from year to year. The buyout funds raised in one year, for example, may have very different strategies from buyout funds raised in another: one year may see predominantly late-stage telecommunications funds coming to market, while another may be more heavily weighted toward software funds. With the variation in economic circumstances from year to year, exit opportunities may also differ markedly for investments within different fund vintages. This means that, unlike public equity managers who can buy and sell stocks in diversified portfolios whenever they decide, private equity managers who want broad-based diversification across different types of opportunities need to commit to a range of vintage years to access a variety of funds and fund types, diversify across economic cycles and the opportunities available in each, and access a wide variety of exit opportunities.

Other Forms of Diversification

As the private equity industry has matured, distinctive subclasses of private equity have developed (e.g., VC, buyouts, mezzanine, distressed, etc.). An investor can similarly benefit from diversifying across these various subasset classes.

Table 9.7 uses Thomson Reuters vintage-year data to examine the correlation of vintage-year fund returns across buyouts and VC. As the table shows, investing across the two private equity sectors results in low vintage-year correlations. In the United States, average and median correlations of VC and buyouts are around 0.5 and below. Only when we look at the lower-quartile returns for U.S. venture capital and U.S. buyouts do we find a high correlation. These results suggest a strong diversification benefit from investing in both U.S. venture capital and U.S. buyout funds.

We find similar results for European buyouts and European VC vintage-year funds. These correlations, while relatively low (around 0.4 and 0.6), are higher than the U.S. correlations. There are several possible explanations for these results. First, many European VC funds make investments in more mature companies than do comparable U.S. venture capital funds, which

Table 9.7   Correlations among Various Private Equity Asset Classes

	Correlation of U.S. Venture with U.S. Buyouts	Correlation of European Venture with European Buyouts
Equal-weighted average return	0.19	0.62
Capital-weighted average return	0.41	0.45
Pooled return	0.26	0.49
Maximum return	−0.17	0.47
Upper-quartile return	0.11	0.63
Median return	0.54	0.81
Lower-quartile return	0.85	0.45
Minimum return	0.66	0.44

Note: All figures are correlations between annualized IRRs.

means the companies in portfolios of European VC funds may have more similarities to those in European buyout funds. In the United States, the underlying companies may be more dissimilar. Second, the return series for European venture and buyout funds are shorter than the return series for the United States in this study. The higher correlations may therefore reflect the selected time period; over longer time periods, the return correlations may be lower.

Diversification strategies within private equity portfolios should also consider the potential benefits of investing in private equity funds across different geographies. In the public markets, investing in different geographies has been a widely accepted diversification practice for the past twenty years. A question to ask is whether the same geographic diversification principles apply to the world of private equity investing.

There are reasons to believe that the answer is yes. For example, VC funds in different countries may have access to different types of technology. The technology base of one market may provide opportunities that are distinct from other markets. For example, wireless usage is substantially higher in Europe than it is in the United States, so European VC funds may actually invest in more advanced wireless companies than their U.S. venture counterparts do. Similarly, software may be particularly important in the Israeli VC market, which may affect the portfolio composition of venture funds focusing on that geography.

Buyout opportunities in different geographies may exhibit similar patterns, but the risks are unlikely to be perfectly correlated. The opportunity for buyouts depends considerably on the overall economic climate, which differs from country to country. Similarly, changes in the relative inefficiencies within the corporate sectors of various countries also differ, leading to geographically variable opportunities to add value.

Let's explore the diversification benefits of investing in private equity across different markets. Consider Table 9.8, which shows the correlation of vintage-year internal rates of return for VC and buyout funds based in the United States and Europe. The correlations of U.S. venture

Table 9.8　Comparison of Different Private Equity Asset Types in Differing Geographies

	U.S. Venture with European Private Equity	U.S. Venture with European Buyouts	U.S. Buyouts with European Venture Capital	U.S. Buyouts with European Buyouts
Equal-weighted average return	0.89	0.61	0.23	0.78
Capital-weighted average return	0.89	0.4	0.45	0.72
Pooled return	0.87	0.36	0.25	0.61
Maximum return	0.71	0.5	−0.09	0.15
Upper-quartile return	0.58	0.46	0.34	0.83
Median return	0.63	0.74	0.46	0.81
Lower-quartile return	0.73	0.73	0.59	0.72
Minimum return	0.36	0.38	0.53	0.4

Note: All figures are correlations between annualized IRRs.

with European venture and U.S. buyouts with European buyouts are between 0.7 and 0.9. These correlations are high, but not surprisingly so. We also see, however, that the correlation between U.S. VC and European buyouts as well as European VC and U.S. buyouts is, in contrast, quite low. While it is clear that U.S. and European private equity markets are not completely independent, a diversification benefit from investing across funds in different geographies seems to emerge. The differences in overall economic conditions, regulatory environments, consumer needs and tastes, and the ability to exit investments all mean that the returns to private equity will differ considerably across nations and continents.

FINAL THOUGHTS

This chapter has grappled with what is in many respects the most challenging question in private equity today. There are no firmly established answers as to how risk and reward should be assessed in this industry. This arena is a rapidly changing one; new ideas and approaches are emerging every year.

Based on these discussions, we now are well aware of the shortcomings of the classic cash-on-cash and IRR metrics for judging performance. Other possibilities, such as the PME, have yet to be widely adopted and have their own shortcomings. While all measures are imperfect, it is nonetheless important to employ several methods—not to choose the most favorable answer, but to create a more nuanced view of the question. Understanding the key issues in this arena and the recent research findings will pay substantial dividends.

Likewise, the measures of and adjustments for risk in the private equity arena are imperfect and inexact. Nonetheless, the importance of the topic cannot be understated. As the recent financial crisis has underscored, an understanding of the risks that one has assumed is absolutely essential. To adequately understand that, one must also understand the composition of the portfolio, even the sectors and geographies of interest. Thus, the inexactitude of the approaches is no excuse for inattention; indeed, their imprecision calls for added attention because information is critical to a full appreciation of the risks and performance of this asset class.

QUESTIONS

1. What are the dangers of taking private equity returns information at face value?
2. Explain the occasional correlation between a private equity firm's fund-raising and valuation levels it calculates for its private equity investments.
3. What are the advantages of evaluating fund performance based on IRR? Why would an investor prefer to evaluate a fund based on a cash-on-cash return?
4. When evaluating a fund based on its cash-on-cash returns, what other considerations should you keep in mind?
5. Over the long haul, the worst-performing buyout funds have been the largest funds. Why has this been the case?
6. Explain the difference between the calendar-time and the time-zero methods of calculating IRRs. Which method is more likely to improve returns?
7. How is it possible to derive two IRRs for the same investment using the same methodology?
8. What is a pooled IRR? When would you want to use one?
9. What does the PME seek to accomplish?
10. If a buyout fund invested $300 million on March 31, 2005 and returned $800 million on June 30, 2008, calculate the PME during the same period. (Use S&P 500 as a benchmark.)

11. What is the stale-price problem, and what are the resulting issues?

12. Why are private equity firms generally conservative in valuing their investments? What would be the benefits and disadvantages if they changed to a more optimistic standpoint?

13. In 2009, in the wake of the financial crisis, some endowments indicated that they had actually increased their asset allocation to private equity. Explain.

14. What are some of the ways investors diversify their private equity holdings?

Chapter 10

The Impact of Private Equity on Society— Does This Really Matter Anyway?

Clearly, venture capital (VC) and private equity funds exert a major impact on the fates of individual companies. But to what extent does all this fund-raising, investing, governance, and exiting influence the overall economic landscape as well?

Part of the challenge in assessing this question is the sheer amount of activity—and the many variables that affect and outcome. Because the activity of private equity firms affects the outcome of their investments, it is easy to hold them responsible for outcomes both good and bad. We can certainly find many illustrations of venture and buyout groups adding value to the firms they financed, and others for which the outcome was far less happy, as shown in this chapter.

On the one hand, many case studies illustrate situations where venture investors have allowed entrepreneurs to realize value that they would otherwise not have been able to garner. Consider, for example, the story of Lingtu.[1] This Beijing Company, which makes digital maps for both individual and corporate applications, provides a particularly important service in China, where city streets are frequently a maze of winding, tiny lanes and breakneck growth renders paper maps obsolete soon after they are printed. By January 2003, Lingtu's founders decided they needed help in thinking about strategic choices. Lingtu's team met Gobi Partners, a fund that from its inception in 2001 has focused single-mindedly on financing early-stage Chinese digital media and information technology companies. After an exhaustive due diligence process, Gobi invested a little over $2 million in Lingtu. Gobi assisted the firm in a variety of ways in the next few years:

- First, it helped the firm prioritize the allocation of resources.
- Second, Gobi introduced Lingtu to a number of corporations that were its own limited partners (LPs). These included IBM, which partnered with Lingtu to develop navigation and web map-search programs and supported the young firm in its winning bid for a project with

---

[1] This discussion is based on James T. Areddy, "Venture Capital Swarms China," *Wall Street Journal*, March 14, 2006; "Chinese Startup Lingtu Collaborates with IBM to Reach New Markets," *PR Newswire*, June 28, 2006; and Felda Hardymon and Ann Leamon, "Gobi Partners: Raising Fund II," HBS Case No. 807-093 (Boston: HBS Publishing, 2007).

telecommunications provider China Unicom, as well as NTT DoCoMo, which also served as lead investor in a subsequent financing round.

- Finally, the initial and subsequent financing rounds allowed the company to expand its investment in technology and marketing.

Similarly, case studies of private equity deals note situations in which target companies achieved substantial productivity gains, often in the form of improvements to existing operations. For instance, in the Hertz buyout, the Carlyle Group, Clayton, Dubilier & Rice, and Merrill Lynch Private Equity addressed inefficiencies in preexisting operations to help increase profitability.[2] Specifically, the investors reduced overhead costs by shrinking inefficient labor expenses and cutting noncapital investments to industry-standard levels. The owners also aligned managerial incentives more closely with the return on capital. Similarly, the buyout of O.M. Scott & Sons led to substantial operating improvements in the firm's existing operations, partly through powerful incentives offered to management and partly through specific suggestions made by the private equity investors.[3] In examples like these, profitability enhancement and creation of private value are likely to go hand in hand with productivity gains.

But other cases suggest that private equity transactions generate few lasting gains for the companies they invest in, much less for society as a whole. In several cases, and for various reasons, private equity groups sometimes fail to achieve their goals for target companies. For instance, when Berkshire Partners bought Wisconsin Central Railroad, it had an ambitious plan to increase productivity.[4] Technological problems arose soon after the buyout transaction, however, and prevented the deployment of a computerized control system that was crucial to the plan. Moreover, the original business plan overlooked certain costs and greatly overestimated the target's ability to cut expenses. As a result, the numbers in the ambitious business plan were never met and the company went into technical default on its loan covenants.[5]

In other cases, such as the Revco transaction, a crippling debt load, along with management disarray, a weak and inexperienced leveraged buyout (LBO) sponsor, and a disastrous midstream shift in strategy led to a failure to achieve performance goals.[6] Inasmuch as this transaction created private value, it seems to have sprung from tax savings rather than operational improvements, and thus it is unlikely to have led to any lasting social benefits. Many other cases will doubtless emerge from the most recent buyout wave.[7]

Clearly, looking at individual case studies only takes us so far. To be able to really answer the questions of the broader impact of VC and private equity, we need to grapple with the systematic evidence. While less thrilling than single company studies, such a wider assessment is

---

[2] Timothy Luehrman, "The Hertz Corporation (A)," HBS Case No. 208-030 (Boston: HBS Publishing), 2007.

[3] George P. Baker and Karen Wruck, "Organizational Changes and Value Creation in Leveraged Buyouts: The Case of the O.M. Scott & Sons Company," *Journal of Financial Economics* 25 (1989): 163–90.

[4] Michael C. Jensen, Willy Burkhardt, and Brian K. Barry, "Wisconsin Central Ltd. Railroad and Berkshire Partners (A): Leveraged Buyouts and Financial Distress," HBS Case No. 9-190-062 (Boston: HBS Publishing, 1990).

[5] Over the next several years, however, the company and its investors managed to revise operations and performance recovered. In 1991, Wisconsin Central went public. Since then, it has expanded both domestically and internationally and was acquired by the Canadian National Railway in 2001. Whether its progress would have been smoother without private equity ownership, of course, is an open question.

[6] Karen Wruck, "What Really Went Wrong at Revco?" *Journal of Applied Corporate Finance* 3 (1991): 79–92.

[7] For one illustration (TH Lee's failed buyout of Simmons), see Julie Creswell, "Profits for Buyout Firms as Company Debt Soared," *New York Times*, October 4, 2009, A-1.

a crucial step in understanding the impact of venture and buyout funds. This wider appreciation is important for two reasons:

1. On a personal level, choosing to invest in a career in a venture or buyout firm makes sense only if the industry is likely to have real "staying power" for the decades to come. If the industry just makes money by shuffling assets, its long-term prospects are fairly limited—consider the situation of the long-term career prospects for the investment bankers who made tons of money in 2006 by securitizing subprime mortgages. Moreover, though we may be accused of idealism, there is a natural and commendable desire to pursue a career that does more than simply provide a paycheck. It is natural to ask whether private equity can be said to provide a benefit to society.

2. Policymakers are intensely interested in private equity. Whether seeking to regulate problematic practices by buyout funds that may endanger the economy or encouraging more venture funds to finance young firms, their decisions are likely to profoundly shape the industry. But without a clear understanding of how the industry shapes the economy, it is unclear that the proper policy decisions will be made.

In this chapter, we explore these important issues. We begin by seeking to understand what the literature has told us about the impact of VC for economic growth and innovation. We then explore the consequences of later-stage private equity investments. Finally, we consider the consequences of these findings for public policy because policymakers seek to restrain possible abuses by private equity firms by imposing regulations that will affect the industry—and the economy—for years to come.

THE CONSEQUENCES OF VENTURE CAPITAL

To assess the impact of VC, we must look at studies of the experience in the market with the most developed and seasoned VC industry, the United States. (Given the much smaller representation of VC in other nations, as discussed in Chapter 8, we have limited ability to say much about its influence elsewhere.[8]) Even though venture activity is most developed in the United States, the reader might be skeptical as to whether this activity could noticeably affect innovation: for most of the past three decades, investments made by the entire VC sector totaled less than the research and development (R&D) and capital expenditure budgets of single companies (such as IBM, General Motors, or Merck).

We can begin this exploration by examining the cumulative impact of venture investing on wealth, jobs, and other financial measures across a variety of industries. Though it would be useful to track the fate of *every* VC-financed company and find out where the innovation or technology ended up, in reality we can only track those companies that have gone public. Consistent information on venture-backed firms that were acquired or went out of business simply doesn't exist. For instance, how much of the growth in Microsoft's revenues and profits should we attribute to the web-mail service Hotmail (a company originally funded by venture firm Draper Fisher Jurvetson, which was integrated into Microsoft's MSN service, after its acquisition) and Visio (a diagrammatic software firm funded by Technology Venture Investors and Kleiner Perkins, which was incorporated into the Microsoft Office suite of software)? But in general, investments in companies that eventually go public yield much higher returns for venture capitalists than those in

[8] However, a small number of studies do look at non-U.S. venture markets. For a comparison of German venture-backed and nonventure start-ups, see Dirk Engeland and Max C. Keilbach, "Firm-Level Implications of Early Stage Venture Capital Investment—An Empirical Investigation," *Journal of Empirical Finance* 14 (2007): 150–67.

Table 10.1   Relative Status of Venture-Backed and Non-Venture Firms at the End of 2009

	Number of Firms	Market Capitalization	Employees	Sales	Operating Income before Depreciation	Net Income	Average Profit Margin
Venture-Backed	794	1,946,561	3,334	974,631	182,153	75,042	7.7%
Non-Venture	4,842	10,980,893	34,715	11,296,722	1,611,619	510,288	4.4%

Note: All dollar figures are in millions; all employment figures are in thousands.
Source: Compustat.

firms that get acquired or remain privately held, so focusing on this subset may paint a reasonable picture of the collective impact of VC.

Even within the limitations of our measurement, venture-backed firms have had an unmistakable effect on the U.S. economy. One way to assess the overall impact of the VC industry is to look at the economic "weight" of venture-backed companies in the context of the larger economy.[9] As Table 10.1 reports, in late 2009, some 794 firms were publicly traded on U.S. markets after receiving their private financing from venture capitalists. (This does not include the firms that went public, but were subsequently acquired or delisted.) Venture-backed firms that had gone public made up over 14 percent of the total number of public firms in existence in the United States at that time. And of the total market value of public firms ($14 trillion), venture-backed companies represented $1.9 trillion—13.7 percent.

Venture-funded firms also made up over 4 percent (nearly $975 billion) of total sales ($22 trillion) of all U.S. public firms at the time. Contrary to the general perception that venture-supported companies are not profitable, operating income margins for these companies hit an average of 7.7 percent—close to the average public company's profit margin of 4.4 percent. Finally, those public firms supported by venture funding employed 8.8 percent of the total public company workforce—and most of these jobs were high-salaried, skilled positions in the technology sector. Clearly, venture investing fuels a substantial portion of the U.S. economy.

This impact is, of course, not spread equally across all sectors of the economy. It is quite modest in industries dominated by mature companies, such as those in manufacturing. In highly innovative industries, though, the picture is completely different. For example, companies in the computer software and hardware industry that received venture backing during their gestation as private firms represent more than 75 percent of the industry's value. Venture-financed firms also play a central role in the biotechnology, computer services, and semiconductor industries. In recent years, the scope of venture groups' activity has been expanding rapidly in the critical energy and environmental field, though the impact of these investments remains to be seen. Given that the economic effects of these emerging industries in the future is likely to be particularly important, the calculations just provided actually understate the economic impact of VC.

The preceding discussion helps paint a broad picture of the wider impact of VC, but it still omits much detail. Manju Puri and Rebecca Zarutskie introduce a more precise way to look at the performance of venture-backed firms.[10] They employ the detailed information in the U.S. Bureau of the Census Longitudinal Business Database (LBD), which tracks virtually all for-profit entities

---

[9] This analysis is based on the authors' tabulation of unpublished data from SDC Venture Economics, with supplemental information from Compustat and the Center for Research into Securities Prices (CRSP) databases.

[10] "On the Lifecycle Dynamics of Venture-Capital and Non-Venture-Capital-Financed Firms," (Working Paper, Duke University, Durham, North Carolina, 2009, unpublished).

in the United States, whether publicly traded or privately held. This rich source of information allows a careful comparison between venture-backed companies and similar companies that did not get venture financing.

In their paper, the authors track the average employment and sales by firm age for all venture-backed and non-venture firms in the LBD that were founded between 1981 and 2005. The firms are followed until the year of their first exit event—a failure, acquisition, or initial public offering (IPO). Two key patterns emerge. Venture-backed firms are larger than non-venture firms, measured by both employment and sales, at each age of the life cycle before the exit event. In addition, the size difference between venture and non-venture firms becomes larger with time; that is, the average growth rate of venture-backed firms is higher.

One might wonder whether the larger scale of venture-backed firms was simply driven by a higher failure rate for these companies. If venture capitalists were simply more ruthless in shutting down small companies, we might see a similar pattern—that is, the venture-backed companies would grow faster because the laggards were truncated from the sample—without the venture capitalists doing anything particularly positive for their companies.

The analysis in the paper does not support this. Venture capitalists, the Census data show, are *less* likely to shut down firms in the first four years after the company receives funding. After more than four years, though, the pattern reverses and the venture-backed firms are more likely to be closed. The authors suggest that the venture capitalists give their companies a certain period to grow; but should the companies cross this threshold without reaching some sort of milestone, the venture capitalists' patience could be exhausted and underperforming companies are shut down relatively quickly. All in all, this analysis is consistent with the notion that venture capitalists, as active investors, do seem to have some sort of "secret sauce" that facilitates portfolio company growth and that they will cease providing it if their efforts appear to be wasted.

Indeed, Yael Hochberg provides some specific evidence as to what that secret sauce may be: better governance.[11] She considers governance in three areas: the use of discretionary accounting accruals to smooth earnings fluctuations; the adoption of a shareholder rights agreement (poison pill) to protect the managers in hostile takeover situations; and board independence. She focuses on firms that went public and looks at 2,827 IPOs between 1983 and 1994, roughly 40 percent of which were venture-backed.

She finds that venture-backed firms were more likely to pursue policies that ensured transparency and maximization of company value than were non-venture-backed companies. The earnings results of venture-backed firms were less likely to be muddled by discretionary accruals, which can be used to artificially smooth quarterly fluctuations. As a result, shareholders had a more accurate picture of these companies' performance. Likewise, the adoption of shareholder protection rules like poison pills, which can either protect incumbent management by making it harder to take a firm private or ensure that all shareholders are treated equally regardless of the size of their holding, are more likely to trigger a stock price increase in venture-backed firms. The positive reaction to the enactment of such provisions suggests that they are in the best interests of all shareholders.

Hochberg also examines board independence. An outsider-dominated board is seen as another way to protect shareholders since outsiders are thought more likely to act as a check on management, more willing to replace the CEO for underperformance, and more amenable to major restructuring events such as mergers and acquisitions. She shows that the boards of venture-backed companies had substantially more outsiders than insiders. In addition, the influential audit and compensation committees of VC-backed companies were much more likely to consist solely of outside members, further freeing them from management influence. Separation of the CEO and

---

[11] Yael V. Hochberg, "Venture Capital and Corporate Governance in the Newly Public Firm" (paper presented at American Finance Association (AFA) 2004 San Diego Meetings, December 8, 2003) available at SSRN: http://ssrn.com/abstract=474542.

chairman, also a way of providing checks and balances in a company, was more common in venture-backed companies. Thus, even after the firms went public, venture-backed firms seemed to be examples of good governance.

Thus far, the research has suggested that venture-backed companies grow faster and have better governance than do non-venture-backed operations. But we might ask if this growth and governance is to any avail. If venture-backed companies are no different from their peers, should we be celebrating the existence of these financiers? A question that is attracting increasing research is the impact of VC on innovation. If VC creates high-growth, well-run companies that can bring innovative solutions to the pressing problems that the world is likely to face over the next decades—global warming, environmental degradation, proliferating pandemics, terrorism, and the like—we can make a stronger case for its contributions to society overall.

But even if VC-funded firms cannot solve these problems, innovations have a particular social importance. Since the pioneering work of Morris Abramowitz and Robert Solow in the 1950s,[12] we have understood that technological innovation is critical to economic growth. Technological change has not just made our lives more comfortable and longer than those of our great-grandparents, it has made our nations richer as well. Innumerable studies have documented the strong connection between new discoveries and economic prosperity both across nations and over time. This relationship is particularly strong in advanced nations—that is, countries that cannot rely on copying others or a growing population for economic growth.

Some readers may think we should be able to assess the impact of VC on innovation in a more rigorous manner. For instance, we could seek to explain across industries and time whether, controlling for R&D spending, VC funding has an impact on various measures of innovation. But even a simple model of the relationship between VC, R&D, and innovation suggests that this approach is likely to give misleading estimates, because both venture funding and innovation could be positively related to a third unobserved factor—the arrival of technological opportunities. Thus, there might be more innovation at times of high VC activity not because VC caused the innovation, but rather because the venture capitalists reacted to some fundamental technological shock that led to more innovation.

The relationship between VC and innovation is indeed complex. For instance, the first silicon semiconductor was invented in 1958 at Fairchild Semiconductor, a division of Fairchild Camera and Instrument that had adopted the project only because it caught the interest of the founder, Sherman Fairchild. Silicon-based semiconductors completely changed the playing field, which had been dominated by vastly more expensive germanium-based production. Shortly thereafter, venture capitalists did get involved. The best-known venture investment in semiconductors, however, happened an entire decade later when Arthur Rock backed Intel, which was founded by Robert Noyce and Gordon Moore from Fairchild Semiconductor. So to what extent were venture capitalists responsible for innovations in the semiconductor industry?

Indeed, some venture capitalists argue that they don't make money on inventing things but on commercializing them. The Internet, for instance, was invented by U.S. government scientists at the Defense Advanced Research Projects Agency (DARPA) but only commercialized—with the help of a lot of venture investment—in the early 1990s.

The first of the papers that have attempted to address these challenging issues, by Thomas Hellmann and Manju Puri,[13] examines a sample of 170 recently formed firms in Silicon Valley. The authors examine both venture-backed and non-venture firms. Using questionnaire responses, they find evidence that VC financing is related to product market strategies and the outcomes of

---

[12] Morris Abramowitz, "Resource and Output Trends in the United States since 1870," *American Economic Review* 46 (1956): 5–23; and Robert M. Solow, "Technical Change and the Aggregate Production Function," *Review of Economics and Statistics* 39 (1957): 312–20.

[13] Thomas Hellmann and Manju Puri, "Venture Capital and the Professionalization of Start-Up Firms: Empirical Evidence," *Journal of Finance* 57 (2002): 169–97.

start-ups. They find that firms that are pursuing what they term an innovator strategy (a classification based on the content analysis of survey responses) are 69 percent more likely to obtain VC than are those pursuing an imitator strategy, and the innovators raise financing faster. The presence of a venture capitalist is also associated with a significant reduction in the time taken to bring a product to market, especially for innovators (probably because these firms can focus more on innovating and less on raising money). Furthermore, these companies are more likely to list "obtaining venture capital" as a significant milestone in their life cycle as compared to other financing events, such as obtaining a bank loan. This may well reflect the fact that receiving VC is not just a funding event for the company but also a credentialing moment in its life. The product idea and team have been assessed and found to deserve not only funding but also the advice and interaction that accompany a venture investment.

The results suggest significant interrelations between VC and innovation-heavy firms, in addition to a role for VC in encouraging innovative companies. But this does not definitively answer the question of whether venture capitalists *cause* innovation. For instance, we might observe personal injury lawyers at accident sites, handing out business cards in the hopes of drumming up clients. But just because the lawyer is at the scene of the car crash does not mean that he caused it. In a similar vein, the possibility remains that more innovative firms choose to finance themselves with VC, rather than VC causing firms to be more innovative.

Sam Kortum and Josh Lerner visit the same question.[14] Here, the study looks at the aggregate level: did the participation of venture capitalists in any given industry over the past few decades lead to more or less innovation? It might be thought that such an analysis would have the same problem as the personal injury lawyer example just described. Put another way, even if we see an increase in venture funding and a boost in innovation, how can we be sure that one caused the other?

The authors address these concerns about causality by looking back over the industry's history. In particular, as we discussed earlier, a major discontinuity in the VC industry's recent history was the U.S. Department of Labor's clarification of the Employee Retirement Income Security Act in the late 1970s, a policy shift that freed pensions to invest in various higher-risk investment strategies, including VC. This shift led to a sharp increase in the funds committed to the asset class. This type of external change should indicate the impact of VC on innovation because the policy shift (whose impact on venture financing was little anticipated) is unlikely to be related to how many or how few entrepreneurial opportunities there were to be funded.

The results in Kortum and Lerner suggest that venture funding does have a strong positive impact on innovation. In particular, they find that the policy shift seems to have triggered a substantial amount of innovation—measured by number of patents received. The estimated coefficients of their regressions vary according to the techniques employed, but on average a dollar of VC appears to be *three to four* times more potent in stimulating patenting than a dollar of traditional corporate R&D. The estimates therefore suggest that VC, even though it averaged less than 3 percent of corporate R&D in the United States from 1983 to 1992, is responsible for a much greater share—perhaps 10 percent—of U.S. industrial innovations in this decade.

A natural worry with the preceding analysis is that it looks at the relationship between VC and patenting, not VC and innovation. One possible explanation is that such funding leads to entrepreneurs to protect their intellectual property with patents rather than other mechanisms such as trade secrets. For instance, the entrepreneurs may be able to fool their venture investors by applying for a large number of patents, even though many of the patents are not particularly important ones. If this is true, it might be inferred that the patents of venture-backed firms would be of lower quality than non-venture-backed patent filings.

---

[14] Sam Kortum and Josh Lerner, "Assessing the Contribution of Venture Capital to Innovation," *Rand Journal of Economics* 31 (2000): 674–92.

This question certainly bears consideration. To address it, we can check the number of patents that cite a particular patent.[15] Higher-quality patents, it has been shown, are cited by other innovators more often than lower-quality patents because they moved the state of the industry forward. Similarly, if venture-backed patents are lower in quality, then companies receiving venture funding would be less likely to initiate patent-infringement litigation. (It makes no sense to pay money to engage in the costly process of patent litigation to defend low-quality patents.)

So, what happens when patent quality is measured with these criteria? As it happens, the patents of venture-backed firms are more frequently cited by other patents and are more aggressively litigated; thus, it can be concluded that they are of high quality. Furthermore, the venture-backed firms more frequently litigate trade secrets, suggesting that they are not simply patenting frantically in lieu of relying on trade-secret protection. These findings reinforce the notion that venture-supported firms are simply more innovative than their non-venture-supported counterparts.

Marcos Mollica and Luigi Zingales,[16] by way of contrast, focus on regional patterns instead of looking across industries. As a regional unit, they use the 179 Bureau of Economic Analysis economic areas, which are composed of counties surrounding metropolitan areas. They exploit the regional, cross-industry, and time-series variability of venture investments in the United States to study the impact of VC activity on innovation and the creation of new businesses. Again, they grapple with causality issues by using an instrumental variable: as a standard for the size of venture investments, they use the size of a state pension fund's assets. The idea is that state pension funds are subject to political pressure to invest some of their funds in new businesses in the state. Hence, the size of the state pension fund triggers a shift in the local supply of VC investment, which should help identify the effect of venture activity on innovation.

Even with these controls, they find that VC investments have a significant positive effect both on the production of patents and the creation of new businesses. An increase of one standard deviation in the VC investment per capita generates an increase in the number of patents between 4 and 15 percent. An increase of 10 percent in the volume of venture investment increases the total number of new business by 2.5 percent.

Thomas Chemmanur, Karthik Krishnan, and Debarshi Nandy look at yet another measure of innovation.[17] They focus on the growth in what economists call the firm's **total factor productivity (TFP)**, which can be defined as the change in output after accounting for the growth in various inputs (e.g., labor, materials, and energy). In other words, this measure focuses on the amount of the firm's growth that is due to doing things in a more innovative way, as opposed to simply doing more of the same (an improvement in manufacturing processes versus adding a second shift).

These authors, like Puri and Zarutskie, employ the U.S. Census dataset because it allows them to compare public and private firms. But productivity is hard to measure in many sectors—how do we realistically capture the efficiency of a consulting firm, for instance?—so they focus on manufacturing firms. Here they find several interesting patterns that are largely consistent with the results noted earlier, despite the very different measures. The TFP of venture-backed firms before receiving financing is higher than that of non-venture-backed entities, and this disparity only widens in the years after the transaction. These results suggest not only that venture capitalists are

---

[15] Patent applicants and examiners at the patent office include references to other relevant patents. These serve a legal role similar to that of property markers at the edge of a land holding.

[16] Marcos Mollica and Luigi Zingales,"The Impact of Venture Capital on Innovation and the Creation of New Business" (Working Paper University of Chicago, 2007, unpublished).

[17] Thomas Chemmanur, Karthik Krishnan, and Debarshi Nandy, "How Does Venture Capital Financing Improve Efficiency in Private Firms? A Look beneath the Surface," (Working Papers No. 08-16, Center for Economic Studies U.S. Census Bureau, Washington, DC, 2008).

able to find and fund companies that are more innovative but also that their monitoring and mentoring after the financing—governance—make a difference.

Interestingly, Chemmanur and coauthors find that the effect of venture capitalists is not the same across firms. They divide the venture firms into those that have raised a relatively larger and smaller share of funds in the previous years (they argue that by and large, the more successful funds should have raised more capital). The authors find little difference in the TFP of the companies funded by the large and small groups at the time of the deal. After the transactions, however, the growth in TFP is significantly higher for firms backed by more established venture investors compared to smaller funds. Here again we find support for the claim that not all private equity groups are equal—better firms create better outcomes in their companies, thus further enhancing their reputations.

THE IMPACT OF BUYOUTS

The growth of the buyout industry over the past decade has triggered anxiety about its impact in nations as diverse as China, Germany, South Korea, the United Kingdom, and the United States. This anxiety is reasonable given the magnitude of recent activity and the industry's somewhat checkered reputation since the "Barbarians at the Gate" era of the 1980s.[18]

These anxieties have led to a recent surge of work on the consequences of buyout investments. Some may wonder why this work is needed: after all, the leveraged buyout transactions of the 1980s were scrutinized in a number of important academic analyses. To understand the strengths and limitations of the earlier works, we can consider the two classic studies of the period, both by Steve Kaplan.[19]

Assessing the Buyouts of the 1980s

Kaplan examined a sample of 76 large management buyouts of public companies completed between 1980 and 1986, in an effort to determine the operating changes that take place in the firms after the transactions. He investigates the validity of the view that these transactions really added value to the firms—for instance, by improving operations or providing new incentives to managers—or, instead, generated value by expropriating wealth from the company's existing employees or public shareholders. To do this, he seeks to relate the value increases that the firms experienced post-buyout with the changes in company performance.

The analysis finds that the firms have noticeably better post-buyout operating performance than other firms in their industry, particularly when measured by returns on assets and sales. Most significantly, buyout companies experience a reduction in capital expenditures in the three years after the buyout, at least when compared to other firms in the same industry. These results could be interpreted in two ways: they might reflect either a curbing of wasteful expenditures by the newly

---

[18] This reference is to the last buyout boom in the late 1980s, which culminated in the acquisition of RJR Nabisco by KKR and was recounted by Bryan Burrough and John Helyar in *Barbarians at the Gate: The Fall of RJR Nabisco* (New York: Harper, 1990).

[19] Steven N. Kaplan, "The Effects of Management Buyouts on Operating Performance and Value," *Journal of Financial Economics* 24 (1989): 217–54 and Steven Kaplan, "Management Buyouts: Evidence on Taxes as a Source of Value," *Journal of Finance* 44, no. 3 (1989): 611–32 (papers and proceedings of the Forty-Eighth Annual Meeting of the American Finance Association, New York, New York, December 28–30, 1988). Other notable studies of this period include F. Lichtenberg and D. Siegel, "The Effects of Leveraged Buyouts on Productivity and Related Aspects of Firm Behavior," *Journal of Financial Economics* 27 (1990): 165–94; Chris J. Muscarella and Michael R. Vetsuypens, "Efficiency and Organizational Structure: A Study of Reverse LBOs," *Journal of Finance* 45 (1990): 1389–1413; and Abbie J. Smith, "Corporate Ownership Structure and Performance: The Case of Management Buyouts," *Journal of Financial Economics* 27 (1990): 143–64.

motivated management team or the crippling effects of heavy debt burdens. These firms also display large increases in cash flows from operations after the buyout.

In a closely related paper, Kaplan explores the possibility that the increase in buyout performance is just driven by the tax advantages provided by the interest payments on the debt, as we discussed earlier. Is it possible that much of the bought-out companies' ostensible improvement simply reflects tax savings?[20] Again looking at these large public buyouts, he showed that while the typical company did pay little federal tax in its first two years after the transaction, it generally paid taxes in the third year and thereafter. To do this, he compares the tax benefits of the transaction with the value that the market believed the transaction created, which he argues is measured by the premium over the market price before the buyout that was paid to the shareholders (i.e., the difference between the transaction and the pre-buyout valuation). This premium, on average, was 40 percent of the company's pre-buyout market price.[21] The tax benefits ranged from 21 to 143 percent of the premium paid by the buyout group. While tax advantages are an important source of value, Kaplan concludes that this is unlikely to be the sole source of the wealth created in the buyouts. In short, Kaplan concludes that the evidence supports the contention that buyouts created value in terms of operating efficiencies and/or better incentives.

But these studies, and many of their contemporaneous work, had some important limitations. First, the bulk of the older research focused on a relatively small number of transactions involving previously publicly traded firms based in the United States. But public-to-private transactions represent only a very modest fraction of all buyouts. The second limitation of the older research relates to the fact that the industry has grown and evolved tremendously since the 1980s, as we saw in Chapter 1.

Assessing Recent Buyouts

Recent research has sought to assess the consequences of buyout investments over more comprehensive and more global samples. Each study has looked at a particular consequence of the investment process.

First, Per Strömberg examined the nature and outcome of the 21,397 private equity transactions worldwide between 1970 and 2007.[22] In the most straightforward possible outcome, the author simply sought to understand the consequences of these transactions. The key findings were as follows:

- Holding periods for private equity investments have increased, rather than decreased, over the years. More than half—58 percent—of the buyout funds' investments are exited more than five years after the initial transaction. So-called quick flips (i.e., exits within two years of investment by the buyout fund) account for 12 percent of deals and have also decreased in the last few years.

- IPOs account for only 13 percent of private equity investment exits, and this exit route seems to have decreased in relative importance over time. The most common exit route is trade sales to another corporation, accounting for 38 percent of all exits. The second most common exit route is secondary buyouts (24 percent), which have increased in importance over the last decade, consistent with anecdotal evidence.

---

[20] Steve Kaplan, "Management Buyouts: Evidence on Taxes as a Source of Value," *Journal of Finance* 44, no. 3 (1989): 611–32.

[21] Steve Kaplan, "The Effects of Management Buyouts on Operating Performance and Value."

[22] Per Strömberg, "The New Demography of Private Equity," in, ed. A. Gurung and J. Lerner *Globalization of Alternative Investments Working Papers Volume 1: Global Economic Impact of Private Equity 2008* (New York: World Economic Forum USA, 2008), 3–26.

Table 10.2 Exits of LBO Transactions, 1970–2007

With a Financial Sponsor	Number of Exits	Percentage of Total
Bankruptcy	552	6
IPO	1,110	13
Financial buyer	3,366	39
LBO-backed corporate buyer	2,106	24
Sold to management	446	5
Strategic buyer	130	2
Other/unknown	948	11
No exit	12,739	60
Total exited	8,658	40

Source: Adapted from: Per Strömberg. "The New Demography of Private Equity," in ed. A. Gurung and J. Lerner *Globalization of Alternative Investments Working Papers Volume 1: Global Economic Impact of Private Equity 2008*, (New York: World Economic Forum USA, 2008), 3–26, available at www.weforum.org/pdf/cgi/pe/Full_Report.pdf.

- As Table 10.2 shows, of exited buyout transactions, only 6 percent end in bankruptcy or financial restructuring. This translates into an annual rate of bankruptcy or major financial distress of 1.2 percent per year. This rate is lower than the default rate for U.S. corporate bond issuers, which has averaged 1.6 percent per year.

This study, of course, examines only a small fraction of the possible consequences of these transactions. It cannot answer the question of whether the bulk of the firms would be worse or better off because of these transactions. Also note that these counts are computed using the number of transactions rather than their dollar sizes. Because the largest deals tend to be concentrated at market peaks, and a disproportionate number of these transactions tend to get into trouble (more about this later), the results may differ for the broader sample.

Nick Bloom, Raffaella Sadun, and John Van Reenen[23] examine management practices across four thousand private-equity-owned and other firms in a sample of medium-sized manufacturing firms in Asia, Europe, and the United States by using a unique double-blind management survey to score firms across eighteen dimensions. The main goal of the study is to determine whether private equity ownership, relative to other ownership forms, improves management practices within firms through the introduction of new managers and better practices.

As shown in Figure 10.1, the authors find that private-equity-owned firms are on average the best-managed group. They are significantly better managed across a wide range of management practices than are government-, family-, and privately owned firms. This is true even when controlling for a range of other company characteristics such as country, industry, size, and employee skills. Private-equity-funded firms are particularly strong at operations management practices, such as the adoption of modern lean manufacturing practices and the use of continuous improvements and a comprehensive performance documentation process. But because the survey

---

[23] Nick Bloom, Raffaella Sadun, and John Van Reenen, "Do Private Equity-Owned Firms Have Better Management Practices?" in *Globalization of Alternative Investments Working Papers Volume 2: Global Economic Impact of Private Equity 2009*, ed. A. Gurung and J. Lerner (New York: World Economic Forum USA, 2009), 1–23.

FIGURE 10.1   Average score on eighteen management practice questions

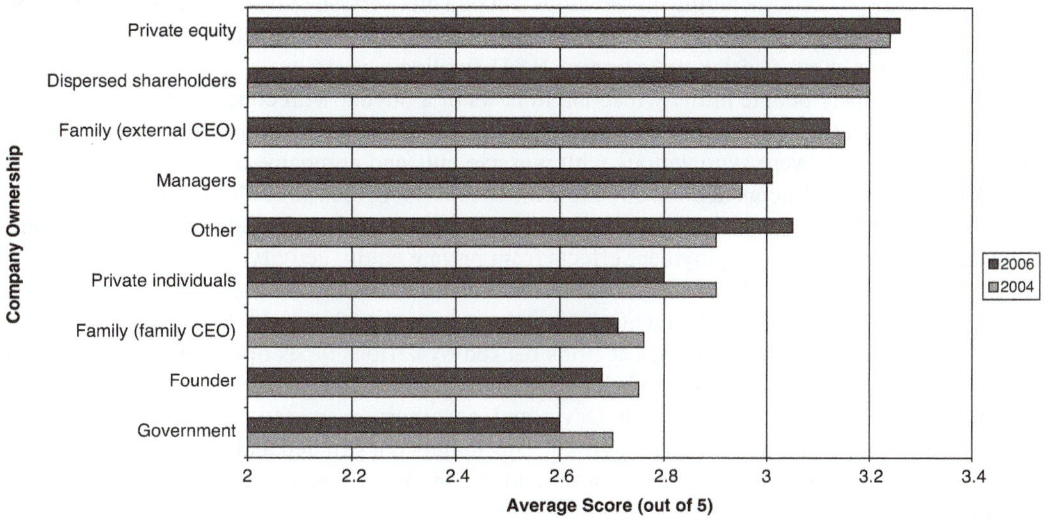

Source: Nick Bloom, Raffaella Sadun, and John Van Reenen, "Do Private Equity-Owned Firms Have Better Managements Practices?" in A. Gurung and J. Lerner (eds.), *Globalization of Alternative Investments Working Papers Volume 2: Global Economic Impact of Private Equity 2009* (New York: World Economic Forum USA, 2009).

is only cross-sectional, the authors cannot determine whether the private equity groups turned these companies into better-managed ones or simply purchased firms that were better managed in the first place. Even if the companies had better practices in the first place, it is noteworthy that the private equity owners did not degrade them.

Another question raised about private equity ownership involves the period over which buyout-owned companies enact changes. Being privately held, some argue, enables managers to implement challenging restructurings without the pressure of catering to the market's demands for steadily growing quarterly profits, which can make companies focus on short-run investments. Others, who point to practices such as special dividends to equity investors, have questioned whether private-equity-backed firms do indeed take a longer-run perspective than their public peers. To address this question, Josh Lerner, Morten Sorensen, and Per Strömberg examined long-run investments by private-equity-owned companies.[24]

This study examined one form of long-run investment: investments in innovation. Due to various factors, innovation provides an attractive testing ground for the issues described earlier. These factors include the long-run nature of R&D expenditures and their importance to the ultimate health of firms. Moreover, an extensive body of work in the economics literature has documented that the characteristics of patents can be used to assess the nature of both publicly and privately held firms' technological innovations.

The key finding was that patenting *levels* before and after buyouts are largely unchanged. Firms that undergo a buyout, however, pursue more economically important innovations, as measured by patent citations, in the years after private equity investments. The increase in the number of citations given to private-equity-backed firms' patents is quite substantial, about 25 percent. This means that the companies intensify their focus on the technologies that they have targeted historically, but improve the quality of the research that they perform. It is noteworthy to

---

[24] Josh Lerner, Morten Sorensen, and Per Strömberg, "Private Equity and Long-Run Investment: The Case of Innovation," (Working Paper No. 14623, National Bureau of Economic Research, Cambridge, MA 2009).

observe that Orangina, under the ownership of Lion Capital and Blackstone, embarked upon a number of R&D projects, including the development of a diet version of its namesake beverage. Its former corporate parent, Cadbury, had focused far more on the mainstay chocolates and biscuits business, starving the soft drink operation of R&D funding.

Of course, many people initially respond to news of a buyout with concern about job losses. The 1980s movies *Other People's Money* and *Wall Street* imparted to the popular consciousness the idea that buyouts were synonymous with massive cuts and company shutdowns. Even more recently, a German politician decried buyout firms as locusts. Critics have claimed huge job losses from buyouts, while private equity associations and other groups have released several recent studies that claim positive employment effects from private equity activity. Even many academic studies have had significant limitations, such as the reliance on surveys with incomplete responses, an inability to control for employment changes in comparable firms, the failure to distinguish cleanly between employment changes at firms backed by various types of private equity, and an inability to determine nations in which jobs are being created and destroyed.

In a pair of recent studies, Steve Davis and coauthors examined the impact of buyout investment on employment and productivity.[25] The authors constructed and analyzed a dataset in order to overcome the limitations noted earlier and, at the same time, to encompass a much larger set of employers and private equity transactions. The study is based on the LBD, which was used in two of the venture studies already described. With the LBD the authors could analyze employment at both the firm level and establishment level. Establishments in this context mean the specific factories, offices, retail outlets, and other distinct physical locations where business takes place. The LBD covers the entire nonfarm private sector and includes annual data on employment and payroll for about five million firms and six million establishments. Within that group, 5,000 U.S. firms were acquired in private equity transactions from 1980 to 2005 ("target firms"), and about 300,000 U.S. establishments were operated by these firms at the time of the private equity transaction ("target establishments").

The key results paint an interesting picture:

- Over the five years before the buyout, employment grows 2 percent faster in total at target companies than at the control group, In the year of the transaction, it jumps by a further 2.25 percent, perhaps as management tries to bolster production and avoid a buyout or compensates for insufficient capital expenditure by hiring more workers. Put another way, relative to their peers, companies that underwent buyouts were bulking up before the deal.

- As shown in Figure 10.2, employment declines more rapidly in bought-out establishments than in control establishments after the private equity transaction and it stays depressed. In the five years after the buyout, employment at the private equity-owned establishments falls a total of 6 percent relative to the controls, more than 1 percent per year on average, an effect that is particularly dramatic in public-to-private transactions.

- But in unreported calculations, companies backed by private firms have 5 percent more "greenfield job" creation in the years after the deal—that is, jobs created at new facilities in the United States—than their peer group. Thus, it appears that the job losses at already existing establishments of firms after a buyout are largely offset by substantially larger job gains in the form of greenfield job creation by these same companies.

---

[25] Steve Davis, John Haltiwanger, Ron Jarmin, Josh Lerner, and Javier Miranda, "Private Equity and Employment," in *Globalization of Alternative Investments Working Papers Volume 1: Global Economic Impact of Private Equity 2008*, 43–64; and "Private Equity, Jobs and Productivity," in *Globalization of Alternative Investments Working Papers Volume 2: Global Economic Impact of Private Equity 2009*, 25–44.

FIGURE 10.2   Net growth rates—difference between targets and controls

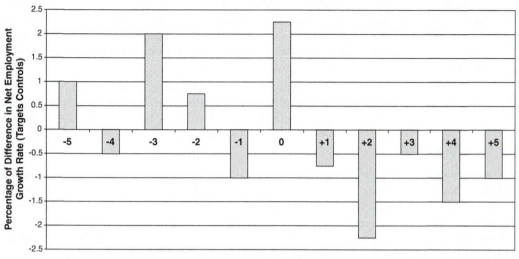

Years from Event

Source: Steve Davis, John Haltiwanger, Ron Jarmin, Josh Lerner, and Javier Miranda, "Private Equity and Employment," in *Globalization of Alternative Investments Working Papers Volume 1: Global Economic Impact of Private Equity 2008* ed. A. Gurung and J. Lerner (New York: World Economic Forum USA, 2008), 57, available at http://www.weforum.org/pdf/cgi/pe/Full_Report.pdf.

In their follow-on study, the authors focus on whether and how labor productivity changed at U.S. manufacturing firms that were targets of private equity transactions from 1980 to 2005. The authors find that while firms acquired by private equity groups had higher productivity than their peers at the time of the original acquisition (by roughly 4 percent), productivity growth in the two-year period after the transaction averages two percentage points more. About 72 percent of this differential in productivity growth after the deal reflects more effective management of existing facilities, rather than the shutting down and opening of operations. (Note that private equity investors are much more likely to close underperforming establishments at the firms they back, as measured by labor productivity.) Nor does the differential narrow thereafter; it continues to grow at roughly 1 percent per year, perhaps indicating that the good habits are retained.

As private equity has spread across the world, its impact has been scrutinized elsewhere as well. Some of the most important work has been done in the United Kingdom:

- In a pair of studies, Kevin Amess compared the productivity growth of 78 buyouts with 156 similar control firms matched along a variety of dimensions.[26] All of the firms were manufacturers of small and medium equipment and machinery. Using a variety of productivity measures, he showed that the firms that underwent buyouts seemed to use inputs more efficiently after the transaction.

- Richard Harris, Donald Siegel, and Mike Wright assessed the total factor productivity of a much larger sample of entities—over 35,000 manufacturing establishments before and after

---

[26] Kevin Amess, "The Effect of Management Buyouts on Firm-level Technical Inefficiency: Evidence from a Panel of UK Machinery and Equipment Manufacturers," *Journal of Industrial Economics* 51 (2003): 35–44; and "Management Buyouts and Firm-Level Productivity: Evidence from a Panel of UK Manufacturing Firms," *Scottish Journal of Political Economy* 49 (2002): 304–17.

management buyouts.[27] They found that these plants are less productive than comparable plants before the buyouts, but they experience a substantial increase in productivity after the transactions. The authors argued that these productivity improvements seemed to be due to measures undertaken by the new owners to reduce the labor intensity of production, in particular their much greater reliance on outsourcing various inputs to the production process.

- Kevin Amess and Mike Wright then looked at the employment consequences of leveraged buyouts.[28] They examined a sample of 1,350 LBOs, which they argued were representative of the entire population of U.K. buyouts. Buyouts, they found, had a very modest impact on employment growth; but these firms had significantly lower wage growth than did matching firms.

There are far fewer studies of the consequences of private equity outside the United Kingdom and the United States. One exception is the study of how buyout transactions affect corporate growth in France that focused on deals between 1994 and 2004. (Note that large, highly leveraged transactions did not become common in France until the mid-2000s.) During these periods, French private equity funds seemed to act as an engine of growth for small- and medium-sized enterprises. Post-LBO growth in jobs, productivity, and the sales and assets of the acquired companies was higher than in comparable firms. These effects seem higher in industries that have insufficient internal capital as well as at times when the capital markets are weak.

Some Important Caveats

So far, the consequences of the private equity and VC industry appear to be relatively positive. Both VC and buyouts do seem, in general, to create overall economic value by inculcating good governance, funding innovation, and, to varying extents, increasing job growth and productivity. We must acknowledge that net job growth is a very gross measure; a job lost is a crisis for that person, even if productivity increases as a result. We do not want to appear to minimize that experience, but simply to state the findings on a broader level.

Note also that all of these studies have important limitations. First, they consider the impact of these financing sources in the aggregate. As alluded to repeatedly in this volume, and as we explore in depth in Chapter 13, both the venture and buyout industries are very cyclical, characterized by highly "lumpy" fund-raising wherein a few years account for the peak of the fund-raising. These years are also characterized by poorer private returns and higher rates of bankruptcy among portfolio companies, which might suggest that the social returns from these periods are modest as well.

The data limitations are particularly acute in the case of the private equity studies. None of them can grapple with the consequences of the 2005–2007 market peak, which accounted for 34 percent of the private equity raised (in inflation-adjusted dollars) between 1980 and 2007.[29] We will simply have to wait until the results of that frenetic period work through the system.

Those few studies on buyout activity during the 2005–2007 peak raise questions about what goes on during these boom periods. As we discuss in Chapter 13, these periods are associated with more leverage in transactions—even if it does not seem to be justified—as well as higher failure

---

[27] Richard Harris, Donald Siegel, and Mike Wright, "Assessing the Impact of Management Buyouts on Economic Efficiency: Plant-Level Evidence from the United Kingdom," *Review of Economics and Statistics* 87 (2005): 148–53.

[28] Kevin Amess and Mike Wright, "The Wage and Employment Effects of Leveraged Buyouts in the UK," *International Journal of the Economics of Business* 14 (2007): 179–95.

[29] This figure is for the United States globally, those three years comprised 34 percent of the funds raised between 1980 and 2007.

rates and fewer operational improvements among companies. But the extent to which these periods have long-run detrimental effects on society remains hotly debated.

THE CONSEQUENCES OF PUBLIC INTERVENTIONS

In the aftermath of the economic crisis, governments have intensified their involvement in the VC and private equity industries. These efforts have taken two forms. On the one hand, public efforts to stimulate VC and growth equity for entrepreneurial firms have become widespread. On the other, the question of whether and how to regulate alternative investors, including private equity funds, has been increasingly debated. In this final section, we will take a quick look at both of these efforts.

Stimulus Efforts

When we look at the regions of the world that are emerging as the great hubs of entrepreneurial activity—places such as Silicon Valley, Singapore, Tel Aviv, Bangalore, and Guangdong and Zhejiang provinces—the stamp of the public sector is unmistakable. Enlightened government intervention played a key role in creating each of these regions. Even a review of the history of Silicon Valley shows that public funding helped build many of the critical foundations of the entrepreneurial cluster there.

But for every effective government intervention, there have been dozens, even hundreds, of failures, where substantial public expenditures bore no fruit. Examples abound from Europe, Japan, and many of the U.S. states, where literally billions have been spent in the hope of promoting VC and entrepreneurial finance more generally with no lasting benefits.

This account of the results of public investment might lead the reader to conclude that the public sector's pursuit of entrepreneurial growth is a massive casino. Some may think that the public sector is simply making bets, with no guarantees of success. Perhaps there are no lessons to be garnered from the experiences of the successful and the failed efforts to create entrepreneurial hubs.

The truth, however, is very different. In many cases, the failure of government efforts to promote venture and entrepreneurial activity was completely predictable. These efforts shared a set of design flaws that doomed them virtually from the start. In many corners of the world, from Europe and the United States to the newest emerging economies, the same classes of problems have reappeared.

Certainly, from an abstract intellectual perspective, one can offer rationales for government investment to promote VC. These arguments rest on two indisputable pillars:

1. The role of technological innovation as a spur for economic growth is now widely recognized. Indeed, government statements of policy worldwide highlight the importance of innovation in promoting and sustaining economic growth and prosperity.

2. As we discussed earlier in the chapter, academic research has highlighted the role of entrepreneurship and VC in stimulating innovation. Venture capital and the entrepreneurs it funds will never supplant other wellsprings of innovation, such as vibrant universities and corporate research laboratories (in an ideal world, these components of growth all feed each other). But in an innovative system, a healthy entrepreneurial sector and VC industry will be important contributors.

If that were the whole story, the case for public involvement would be pretty compelling. But the case for public intervention rests as well on a third leg: the argument that governments can effectively promote entrepreneurship and VC. And this, alas, is a much shakier assumption.

To be sure, entrepreneurial markets have features that allow us to identify a natural role for governments in encouraging their evolution. Entrepreneurship is a business in which there are increasing returns. Put another way, it is far easier to found a start-up if ten other entrepreneurs are nearby. In many respects, founders and venture capitalists benefit from their peers. For instance, if entrepreneurs are already active in the market, investors, employees, intermediaries such as lawyers and data providers, and the wider capital markets are likely to be knowledgeable about the venturing process and the strategies, financing, support, and exit mechanisms it requires. In the activities associated with entrepreneurship and VC, the actions of any one group are likely to have positive spillovers, or externalities, for their peers. In these types of settings, the government can often play a very positive role as a catalyst.

This observation is supported by numerous examples of government intervention that successfully triggered the growth of a VC sector. For instance, the Small Business Investment Company (SBIC) program in the United States led to the formation of the infrastructure for much of the modern VC industry. Many early VC funds and leading intermediaries in the industry—such as law firms and data providers—began as organizations oriented to the SBIC funds and then gradually shifted their focus to independent venture capitalists. Similarly, public programs played an important role in triggering the explosive growth of virtually every other major venture market around the globe.

But there are also many reasons to be cautious about the efficacy of government intervention. In particular, two well-documented problems can derail government programs. First, they can simply get it wrong by allocating funds and support in an inept or, even worse, a counterproductive manner. An extensive literature has examined the factors that affect the quality of governmental efforts in general and suggests that more competent programs are likelier in nations that are wealthier, have more heterogeneous populations, and are based on an English legal tradition.

Economists have also focused on a second problem, delineated in the theory of regulatory capture. These writings suggest that private and public sector entities will organize to capture direct and indirect subsidies that the public sector provides. For instance, programs geared toward boosting nascent entrepreneurs may instead end up boosting cronies of the nation's rulers or legislators. The annals of government venturing programs abound with examples of efforts that have been hijacked in such a manner.

The SBIR program, the largest public venture program in the United States, provides an illustration of this problem in an analysis by Josh Lerner.[30] The effect of a fairness policy can be seen by comparing the performance of program recipients with that of matching firms. (See Figure 10.3, which compares the growth of SBIR awardees and matching firms. The figure shows that the awardees grew considerably faster than companies in the same locations and industries that did not receive awards.)

Unfortunately, beneath these positive results lie some intense political pressures and conflicting interests. For one thing, congressmen and their staffers have pressured program managers to award funding to companies in their states. As a result, in almost every recent fiscal year, firms in all fifty states (and indeed every one of the 435 congressional districts) have received at least one SBIR award.

Figure 10.3 also highlights the consequences of such political pressures. In particular, it contrasts what happened to the workforce size of SBIR awardees located in regions character-ized by considerable high-tech activity (i.e., the company received at least one independent VC financing round in the three years before the SBIR award) and those elsewhere. The figure reveals that in the ten years after receipt of SBIR funding, the workforce of the average award recipient in a high-tech region grew by forty-seven employees, doubling in size. The workforces

---

[30] Josh Lerner, "The Government as Venture Capitalist: The Long-Run Effects of the SBIR Program," *Journal of Business* 72 (1999): 285–318.

FIGURE 10.3   Change in employment in SBIR and Non-SBIR awardees

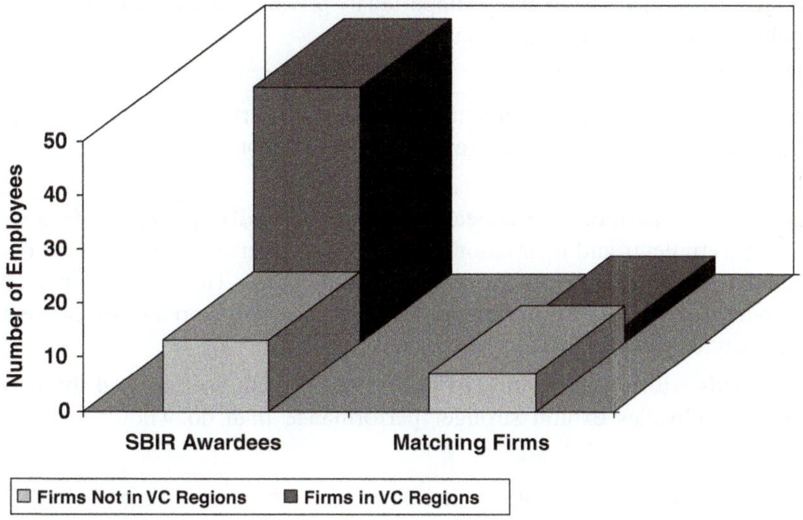

Source: Josh Lerner, "The Government as Venture Capitalist: The Long-Run Effects of the SBIR Program," *Journal of Business* 72 (1999): 285–318. © Journal of Business, University of Chicago Press, 1999.

of other awardees—those located in regions not characterized by high-tech activity—grew by only thirteen employees. Though the recipients of SBIR awards grew considerably faster than a sample of matched firms, the superior performance, as measured by growth in employment (as well as sales and other measures) was confined to awardees in areas that already had private venture activity. In the name of geographic "diversity," the program funded firms with inferior prospects.

In addition to the geographic pressures, particular companies have managed to capture a disproportionate number of awards. These "SBIR mills" often have staffs in Washington that focus only on identifying opportunities for subsidy applications. This problem has proven difficult to eliminate since mill staffers tend to be active, wily lobbyists. While mildly distressing in theory, the problem would be acceptable if mills were more efficient at innovation. Sadly, they are not; mills commercialize far fewer projects than do those firms that receive just one SBIR grant. Though a single SBIR grant does seem to encourage performance in awardee firms, the program clearly still has some work to do in eradicating waste and distortions.

A more systematic look at these issues is provided in a paper by Jim Brander, Qianqian Du, and Thomas Hellmann.[31] This paper assesses the record of government support for VC through three different channels:

1. Direct provision of VC through government-owned VC funds

2. Investment in independently managed VC funds that also rely on private investors

3. Provision of subsidies or tax concessions to venture capitalists

The researchers analyzed over 28,800 enterprises (based in 126 different countries) that received VC funding between 2000 and 2008. The enterprises cover a wide range of industries but

---

[31] Jim Brander, Qianqian Du, and Thomas Hellmann, "Governments as Venture Capitalists: Striking the Right Balance," in *Globalization of Alternative Investments Working Papers Volume 3: Global Economic Impact of Private Equity 2008*, ed. A. Gurung and J. Lerner (New York: World Economic Forum USA, 2009), 25–52.

are dominated by high-technology firms. The performance of enterprises financed by some form of government VC was compared with those supported by private venture capitalists to determine the impact of public involvement on performance.

The key findings illustrate that:

- Enterprises with moderate government VC support outperform enterprises with only private VC support and those with extensive government support, both in terms of value creation and patent creation.

- Government VC performance appears to differ markedly; public funds associated with national governments and international organizations perform better than those associated with subnational (e.g., state and provincial) governments. This may occur because broader government mandates allow the firm to choose from a larger pool of investment opportunities that may be more likely to succeed.

- Venture funds with a combination of public and private backing and those with indirect government subsidies exhibit stronger performance than do wholly government-owned funds.

Taken together, the analyses suggest that government funding may be helpful in providing certain kinds of support, including financial support. These efforts may become less useful when they have actual control over business decisions, presumably because political distortions can creep in. Government VC may be at its most effective when it remains disciplined by private funding.

Regulatory Initiatives

In 2009, as a response to the global financial crisis that began in 2007, governments worldwide began rethinking their approach to regulating financial institutions. Proposed reforms have, broadly speaking, taken two forms:

1. Reshaping regulatory bodies to avoid situations where different regulators oversee companies playing similar economic roles

2. Expanding the reach of regulation to cover unregulated (or lightly regulated) financial institutions that nonetheless pose serious risks to the economy

The debates occasioned by these proposals took center stage in 2010.

Among the financial institutions that have fallen under the gaze of regulators have been private equity funds. Traditionally, these funds have been lightly scrutinized. For instance, in the United States, funds with a limited number of "sophisticated" (i.e., sufficiently wealthy) investors have been exempt from the provisions of the Investment Company Act of 1940, which mandates extensive reporting requirements. In many cases, it appears these exceptions stem not from deliberate policy decisions, but from historical accident: many nations' financial regulatory architectures were designed when the private equity industry was in its infancy.

But in the aftermath of the global financial crisis, many policymakers have taken a closer look at the regulation of private equity. In many cases, these reexaminations have been motivated by worries that these funds increase the volatility and risk confronting national economies. For instance, the European Commission[32] has declared:

---

[32] European Commission, *Commission Staff Working Document Accompanying the Proposal for a Directive of the European Parliament and of the Council on Alternative Investment Fund Managers and Amending Directives 2004/39/EC and 2009/ . . . /EC: Impact Assessment*, COM(2009) 207/SEC(2009) 577 (Brussels: European Commission, 2009).

The activities of AIFM [Alternative Investment Fund Managers] give rise to risks for AIF investors, counterparties, the financial markets and the wider economy over and above the investment risk that is intrinsic to a financial investment. . . . Adverse market conditions have severely affected the sector and have provided evidence of the role of AIFM in exacerbating market dynamics.

As a result of these beliefs, a number of proposals have sought to systematize and increase the regulatory oversight of these institutions. Most notable for its scope and potential impact has been the "Proposal for a Directive on Alternative Investment Fund Managers," released by the European Commission in April 2009 and adopted by the European Parliament in November 2010.

Despite the intense interest in this issue, there has been almost no scrutiny of whether private equity boosts the risks that economies face. In a recent paper undertaken under the auspices of the World Economic Forum, Shai Bernstein and coauthors seek to partially address this question by examining the impact of private equity investments across twenty industries in twenty-six major nations between 1991 and 2007.[33] The paper focuses on whether private equity investments in an industry affect aggregate growth and cyclicality. Throughout the analysis, the growth rate in a particular industry is measured relative to the average growth rate across countries in the same year. In addition, the analysis uses country and industry fixed effects, ensuring that the impact of private equity activity is measured relative to the average economic performance in a given country, industry, and year. For instance, if the Swedish steel industry has more private equity investment than the Finnish one, the paper examines whether the steel industry in these two countries performs better or worse over time relative to the average performance of the steel industry across all countries in the sample, and whether the variations in performance over the industry cycles are more or less dramatic.

Overall, the analysis is unable to find evidence supporting the detrimental effects of private equity investments on industries:

- Industries where private equity funds have been active in the past five years grow more rapidly than other sectors, whether measured using total production, value added, or employment. In industries with any private equity investments, there are few significant differences between industries with a low and high level of this activity.

- Activity in industries with private equity backing appears to be no more volatile in the face of industry cycles than in other industries, and sometimes less so. The reduced volatility is particularly apparent in employment.

- It seems unlikely that these results are driven by reverse causality—that is, private equity funds selecting to invest in industries that are growing faster and/or are less volatile. Even after controlling—admittedly imperfectly—for factors that may have led to more private equity investments, the results still hold.

Of course, economic growth and volatility are only two of many questions that regulators must confront when assessing the impact of private investment. And it is still too early to assess the consequences of the economic conditions in 2008 and 2009, a period where private equity investment fell and the absolute volume of distressed private-equity-backed assets rose far more steeply than in earlier cycles. But these findings do raise questions about some of the assertions

---

[33] Shai Bernstein, Josh Lerner, Morten Sorenson, and Per Strömberg, "Private Equity and Industry Performance," in *Globalization of Alternative Investments Working Papers Volume 2: Global Economic Impact of Private Equity 2010*, ed. A. Gurung and J. Lerner (New York: World Economic Forum USA, 2010).

about the private equity industry's detrimental impact on the economy as a whole—assertions that have been motivating regulatory action.

TAKING STOCK

Assessing the overall impact of the VC and private equity industry is a challenging exercise. Funds have done many thousands of transactions to date, and some paint a positive picture of these investors' role, others an unflattering one. Large-sample studies struggle with the development of appropriate measures of economic impact and limited access to data. Even if one had perfect measures, disentangling what would have happened without the presence of venture and buyout investment is a major challenge.

But despite these difficulties, some clear conclusions seem to follow from the analyses just described:

- The impact of both VC and private equity examined in aggregate is surprisingly positive for the firms in which they invest and, to the extent it can be measured, for the economy more generally.

- The extreme cyclicality of the business seems to lead to dramatic consequences. Many of the relationships seen during more normal times may not hold during heady market peaks, and the impact of these investors on their portfolio companies may be far less positive.

- Based on what we know, it is hard to make a compelling case for broad regulatory intervention into the private equity industry.

- The magnitude of the events between 2005 and 2009 were so large that they may dramatically reshape our conclusions about the impact of the private equity industry. We will be unable to definitively assess the consequences of this period, however, for several more years.

QUESTIONS

1. Why do you think there has been such emphasis on taking successful venture-backed companies public?

2. What in the structure of venture capital firms might explain the patterns that Puri and Zarutskie observed?

3. In what ways do Hochberg's findings support or contradict those of Davis et al.?

4. Why do you think private equity firms would create good governance in their portfolio companies?

5. What would make the better governance of private-equity-owned firms persist?

6. Why is it so difficult to determine conclusively the impact of venture capital on innovation?

7. Why do you think venture-backed companies would produce more and higher-quality patents than non-venture-backed companies?

8. Why would companies backed by more-established venture firms have higher improvement in TFP?

9. What do you think accounts for the fact that the failure rates for buyouts is lower than the default rate on corporate bonds?

10. What might explain the finding observed in the paper by Lerner et al., where companies that have been bought out appear to pursue more economically important innovations?

11. What do you think explains the pattern of employment change in buyout targets relative to their peers?

12. How can government funding help create a private equity industry?

13. What are three major ways in which government funding can go awry?

14. What specific challenges might subnational governments (states, provinces, etc.) encounter that make it more difficult for them to create successful private equity industry?

15. How does the SBIR employment data (Figure 10.3) influence your answer?

16. The ruler of the country of Utopia has approached you to recommend three principles to follow in creating a government program to jump-start its currently miniscule private equity industry. The country has a robust financial system, a strong entrepreneurial tradition, and a healthy tech sector, bolstered by world-class research coming from its university system. What do you suggest?

Chapter 11

People, Positions and Culture—Management of the Private Equity Firm

$\mathbf{T}$hus far, we have been talking about partnerships and general partners (GPs), with an occasional mention of an associate or an analyst, as if they had randomly fallen into place in their firms. In this chapter, we examine more closely the inner workings of a private equity firm, the characteristics of people who work there, the way one might join a firm, and how these firms are managed. Private equity firms vary widely in size—New Enterprise Associates (NEA), one of the original U.S. venture capital (VC) firms, has 13 general partners, 12 partners, 7 principals, 8 associates, 16 venture partners, 3 managing or executive directors, 3 vice presidents, 3 advisors or special partners, 2 legal counsels, and a CFO in four offices in three countries.[1] Founder Collective, established within a year of this book's writing, has two managing partners and five founder partners.[2] In 1977 when NEA was founded, it was even smaller than Founder Collective—NEA had three partners initially. The buyout firm Blackstone has over 1,440 employees, as of 2010, most of them professionals, and yet its core business is the same as that of Brazos, which has a staff of fewer than two dozen.

Equally varied are the backgrounds of the people who have joined private equity firms. David Blitzer, a senior managing director of Blackstone Group, joined the firm in 1991 immediately after graduating from the University of Pennsylvania's Wharton School with a bachelor's degree. In 2002, he established Blackstone's London office.[3] Sean Klimczak joined Blackstone in 2005 as a senior associate with a bachelor's degree from Notre Dame, several years' experience in the European operations of Madison Dearborn, and a distinguished MBA from Harvard Business School. By 2010, he had participated in a number of deals including the Weather Channel acquisition and had been promoted to managing director.[4] Graham Gardner, a board-certified cardiologist with an MBA, joined the health-care practice of Highland Capital as a principal.[5] Kent Bennett, a vice president at Bessemer Venture Partners, was a Hollywood

---

[1] http://www.nea.com/Team/Default.aspx, accessed August 25, 2010.

[2] http://foundercollective.com/people, accessed August 25, 2010.

[3] Felda Hardymon, Josh Lerner, and Ann Leamon, "Lion Capital and The Blackstone Group: The Orangina Deal," HBS Case No. 807-005 (Boston: HBS Publishing, 2007), 22.

[4] http://www.blackstone.com/cps/rde/xchg/bxcom/hs/firm_ourpeople_sean_klimczak.htm, accessed July 31, 2011.

[5] http://www.hcp.com/graham_gardner, accessed August 24, 2010. Gardner has since founded two health-care start-ups and shifted to a venture partner role at Highland.

screen writer and a consultant for Bain & Company before earning an MBA.[6] Joseph Casey, with a background in sales for Xerox, an MBA, and experience at Intel, started his private equity career at Venrock, where he became a GP, then moved to Boston Partners as a partner, and then went to Denham Capital as managing director of strategy and development.[7] Laila Partridge majored in studio art, later earned an MBA, and then joined Intel, where she became the manager of Intel Capital's IA-64 fund, a $200 million venture fund focused on products and applications that used Intel semiconductors' full capability.[8]

Clearly, there are almost as many private equity backgrounds as there are private equity practitioners. This raises a host of questions. What qualities make a good private equity investor? While an MBA seems useful, it is not essential. An operating, consulting, and financial background all seem to have worked to make the people just mentioned attractive to and successful at private equity firms. How does an aspiring private equity investor find a firm? How do firms differ, apart from the obvious variations in size and strategy? How is a firm managed when it is composed of such disparate individuals acting in a loose partnership? Are there certain generalizations we can make about culture based on firm size?

In this chapter, we begin to answer these questions. Because private equity is an evolving industry, we cannot claim to give definitive replies—but we can lay the groundwork. First, we walk through the basic structure of a private equity firm, the various career bands, and their associated responsibilities. We then look at compensation and how that changes as a professional moves up the career ladder. Next, we explore the issue of firm culture and how that affects the types of people who are hired and succeed as well as the way the firm is likely to be structured and managed. Finally, we look at some alternative structures, particularly the challenges of affiliated operations such as corporate VC efforts.

PRIVATE EQUITY JOBS—WHAT ARE THEY, AND HOW DO YOU GET ONE?

As described in Chapter 2, nearly all private equity firms, be they in VC, growth or mezzanine capital, or leveraged buyouts, are limited partnerships (LPs). Those that are not organized in this way—for example, corporate private equity firms such as Intel Capital, Microsoft's IP Ventures, and In-Q-Tel—almost always have analogous positions to those described here. Therefore, we will assume the LP structure for our discussion.

In the last several years, despite fluctuations on the overall economy, the number of private equity firms has increased worldwide, as shown in Figure 11.1. As of 2009, Preqin estimates that there were 69,100 jobs in private equity, the vast majority in firms with head offices in the United States.[9] Increasingly, though, U.S.-based firms are opening offices in other countries—most commonly in India and China; some in Israel and Europe, often London. This shift to other countries poses logistical and organizational challenges, as we discuss later.

Within the LP, the firm is often organized as a triangle with a large number of entry-level positions supporting a usually smaller number of decision makers who also manage the firm, as shown in Figure 11.2. This arrangement is typical in many professional services firms, such as law

---

[6] http://www.bvp.com/team/kent-bennett.aspx, accessed August 24, 2010.

[7] http://www.denhamcapital.com/Team/TeamMembers.aspx?viewType=&id=42, accessed August 24, 2010.

[8] Felda Hardymon and Ann Leamon, "The IA-64 Fund," HBS Case No. 800-351 (Boston: HBS Publishing, 2000).

[9] Preqin, *The 2010 Preqin Private Equity Compensation and Employment Review*, http://www.preqin.com/docs/samples/Preqin_Compensation_Review_Sample_Pages.pdf?rnd=1, p. 4, accessed September 3, 2010.

FIGURE 11.1   Growth in private equity firms

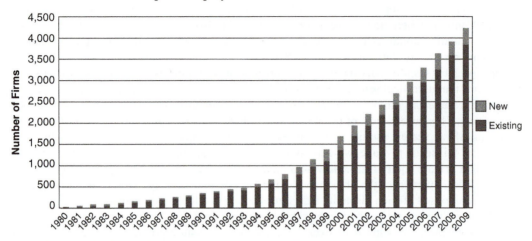

Source: Preqin, the 2010 Preqin Private Equity Compensation and Employment Review, www.preqin.com/docs/samples/Preqin_Compensation_Review_Sample_Pages.pdf?md¼41, p. 4; accessed September 3, 2010. Used with permission.

FIGURE 11.2   Structure of a typical private equity firm

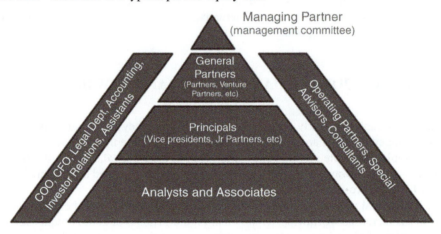

firms and consultancies. We will use the most common title nomenclature for these jobs, but note that while these positions exist in most private equity firms, they are sometimes known by different names—and are even mixed up with other typical titles. An analyst in one firm may be called an associate in another; a venture partner may also be called special partner or just partner; a principal in one firm may be a junior partner somewhere else. With that warning, we now describe each level, starting at the entry.

Analysts

The most junior person in a private equity firm is the *analyst*.[10] In today's market, analyst positions are usually "pre-MBA," that is, the educational prerequisite is an undergraduate degree.

---

[10] Occasionally the analyst and associate positions are one and the same; or what we call an associate is called an analyst, and vice versa. If you are looking for an entry-level private equity job, be sure you understand how the firm you are applying to uses the titles.

These positions often have a limited term of two to three years before the analyst moves on, departing to another job or graduate school or—less typically—through promotion to associate. The "post-MBA" associate jobs are apprenticeship positions where the main responsibility is to extend the GP for whom the associate works while gaining active investing skills and perhaps starting on the path to partner.

A private equity analyst performs two types of analysis: financial and business. One can think of a private equity analyst as someone who is equally comfortable doing the financial modeling of an investment banking analyst and the business analysis of an analyst in a strategic consulting firm, such as McKinsey or BCG. Of course, no one comes out of college ready to do all of this; so like all private equity entrants, analysts learn on the job in a sort of apprenticeship. Private equity firms look for people who are high academic achievers with major studies in areas where they have developed comfort with numbers and the analytical process. Thus engineering, science, marketing, and economics majors are frequently found among entry-level hires by private equity firms.

Practical experience, however, nearly always trumps academic credentials. Even emerging undergraduates are judged on the quality of their internships and summer jobs. Practical experience showing the candidate's facility and comfort with numbers is especially important. If the candidate has been out of school for a few years, experience gained on the first job is examined closely. Success as an analyst in investment banking or consulting firms is considered a very good indicator of the potential to be a private equity analyst or associate.

In addition to facility with numbers, an analyst must also be able to communicate the information learned and analysis performed. Communication inside private equity firms varies from the primarily informal and verbal communication of small teams to the more formal and documentary communication of large-scale firms where there is a premium on writing. All firms ultimately need to describe their decisions, and much of that writing often falls to analysts and associates. As part of the interview process, applicants are often required to submit writing samples.

Testing for financial and business analytical talent is more difficult. Many firms use business cases as part of the interview. A business case will outline a potential investment thesis, and the interviewees must describe how they would validate or analyze specific aspects of it. Usually these cases are presented verbally in an interview situation, though a few firms have written material. They vary greatly and are frequently drawn from the firm's and the interviewer's experience. For example, a business case may posit that the margins of a processed food company could be increased by certain changes in distribution and ask the interviewee how that might be verified. Alternatively, a business case may require a deep understanding of a company's competition. Interviewees will respond by describing how they would find data and analyze the competitive structure of the company's industry. On the financial side, the cases and questions may address such topics as cash-flow analysis for a company and its debt structures, along with some high-level leveraged buyout (LBO) math to test the candidate's understanding of the interplay of earnings before interest, tax, depreciation, and amortization (EBITDA) and leverage with returns.

In all of these situations, interviewees are judged more on the quality of their thinking, the process they propose for the analysis, and their confidence in their ability to complete the analysis than on the specifics of the answers themselves. Candidates are assessed on their ability to break down the key issues, the approaches they suggest to address them, and their ability to avoid red herrings (i.e., issues that could appear to be important but on inspection are not). Firms want to know if the candidate has the beginnings of good business judgment. Can they describe the attractive characteristics of a business in a specific case? Can they deduce warning signs of bad performance in a business?

Firms want to know if the candidate is a fast learner, confident in her abilities, and able to work with minimal supervision. It is more important that the potential analyst can take on the challenge, rather than being able to do the work she previously performed in a former job.

In the case of VC firms, where intellectual curiosity is especially prized, candidates are often asked to describe the blogs they read and their thoughts on new business directions. Awareness of new companies, technologies, and directions in the firm's market of interest is considered a baseline requirement in the VC world. Having started a company or been employed in an early-stage company—even if it failed—is also viewed with approval.

Beyond analytical and communications skills, the third important trait is personality. Analysts are expected to work as part of a team. The pressure of large sums of money and tight deal deadlines, and the need to coordinate with experts outside the firm—such as management, lawyers, bankers, accountants, and consultants—means that private equity teams often spend long hours together for many consecutive weeks on a single project. When considering a candidate, these questions are important: Would you want this person working day and night on your team? Is she too awkward? Too aggressive? Not team oriented? Confident enough to inspire confidence in her work but not so confident as to be obnoxious?

Judging personality traits is entirely subjective. Interviewers in private equity firms often work from lists of desired traits and note stories or instances where they see evidence of those characteristics during the interview. An interviewer's list might include:[11]

- Leadership
- Initiative
- Team player
- Ability to marshal resources
- Ability to convince others of your ideas
- Poise and grace under pressure
- Ability to develop conviction and support it

The nature of the job once landed can vary. Large firms with a large number of analysts often use a system that essentially shares analysts across projects on an assignment-by-assignment basis. In such firms, an analyst may be working on assignments from several different investors at the same time.

Often the analyst job has specific responsibilities for one aspect of deal making. Firms that systematically create deal flow by calling lists of potential investments, such as Summit Partners and TA Associates (see Chapter 3), often assign analysts to research a sector and "dial for deals." Analysts may also be assigned to monitor specific attributes of existing portfolio companies and report them in a regular format to the rest of the partnership. But in general, the analyst job is the first rung of the private equity career ladder and is characterized by the requirement to answer specific financial and business questions by finding and analyzing data.

The key to promotion from the analyst position is the ability to propose effective approaches to answering due diligence questions around an investment thesis. The successful analyst does not need a specific road map to start identifying and answering the crucial issues that must be resolved before reaching an investment decision. The analyst can redefine fuzzy problems and resolve them, one piece at a time, with limited supervision. Attention to detail is the most important quality for a successful analyst. Sloppiness, whether in defining issues around the deal, researching the answers, or communicating the results to the deal team undercuts the credibility of the entire analysis. Attention to detail often separates successful analysts from those asked to move on at the end of their terms.

---

[11] Compiled from multiple confidential interviews with private equity hiring executives.

Associates

The specific job description for an associate can vary greatly from firm to firm. In general, associates are true extenders of the deal makers. In addition to answering the type of questions confronting the analysts, they integrate the material into a coherent view of the deal and often become deeply involved in managing the transaction itself. Associate-level jobs are considered partner-track positions in most firms; the associate is expected to be promoted or leave within some period of time (often two to four years). In addition to business and financial analysis, associates are often involved in creating valuation analyses, framing negotiation options, and developing responses to potential financing options. The associate often writes the first draft of the investment memorandum.

The heart of an associate's job is doing due diligence (see Chapter 3). Successful associates develop good interviewing and note-taking skills and are well organized. Because due diligence is often done under great time pressure, deciding which of the many issues deserves more attention (so-called **materiality**) is a critical skill. Being independent, creative, and proactive in finding ways to dig deeper on due diligence issues is the best help an associate can provide.

Here the personality traits we discussed earlier are particularly important. An associate needs to be the ultimate team player, anticipating the team's needs, communicating information from various team members as it develops, and synthesizing data and analysis. An associate's intellectual curiosity and engagement becomes a great asset. For example, due diligence interviews yield much more robust information when the subject feels real engagement from the interviewer. Intellectual curiosity leads the good associate to ask questions that penetrate to the important aspects of the business problem at hand. People give more and better information to someone they like—and who is genuinely interested in what they have to say.

Associates are often responsible for building the private equity firm's financial models of potential deals and ensuring they incorporate the best estimate of the company's performance. As we have noted before, active investors invest with a detailed point of view on expected performance. This goes beyond just top-line and bottom-line estimations based on analogous companies. Typically, the models used in later-stage transactions are "bottom-up" exercises that consider the future margins of the product line, detailed sales, and marketing expenses by distribution channel; cost of sales at the most elemental level; administrative expenses; and so on. (Obviously, for very early-stage transactions such material is almost impossible to find, and the associates are more involved in assessing the feasibility of new technology and potential market adoption patterns.) Maintaining the model requires strong spreadsheet skills and the ability to read detailed findings from a host of sources (accounting, sales, marketing, and the like) and interpret its impact. Often it is the associate who pulls together separate analyses from many analysts, lawyers, bankers, and consultants into the detailed deal model.

Even after the deal is consummated, this detailed model continues to evolve—in fact, it forms the benchmark for the governance that creates value, as described in Chapter 6. The associates are usually the keepers of those models. After the investment is made, associates often collect the data to monitor the investment. Most important is the company performance data that is compared to expectations set by the model, updating and refining it to reflect new insights and changes in the business. Skills learned at consulting firms translate well into private equity, especially post-investment.

In some firms, associates screen deals, taking first meetings and culling through investment bank deal books to find the most promising deals for the firm to pursue. On the other hand, many firms believe that placing such responsibility on associates produces suboptimal results because all deals are contextual. That is, a deal's attractiveness depends as much on what's going on at the firm at that time as it does on the characteristics of the investment under consideration. As mentioned in Chapter 3, many unique features of the firm itself affect the desirability of a deal. Does the firm have capacity for *this particular* deal? Does the deal support the LPs' expectations in terms of stage, sector, and geography? *Who* in the firm has capacity, and what is her capability in relation to this deal? How does this deal position the firm with respect to other firms in the industry? How does the likely holding period fit with the next fund-raising? An associate is rarely in a position to be aware of and sensitive to all these issues.

Unlike analysts, who often work on a number of deals simultaneously, associates are more commonly assigned to a single active deal. The key to an associate's promotion is the ability to run a transaction from day to day. Over time, associates take on more and more responsibility. At some point, it is clear that the associate can handle all the project management around completing a deal. Whereas an analyst needs to prove he can break down a problem and find the answer without much supervision, an associate must do that and also show she can manage a deal case. Project management and communication skills distinguish the successful associates who are promoted to principal.

Finding a Job in Private Equity

Even a planned, organized campaign to find a job in private equity can be quite frustrating. In part, this is because there are far more small-scale firms than large ones, and small firms are generally sporadic and unsystematic in hiring. Here is advice on how to go about finding a private equity job.

1. **Prepare yourself.** Private equity job searches usually take a long time; plan ahead to have ways to support yourself and your search for the long run.
2. **Know yourself and the firm.** Understand how firms perceive the risks of hiring the wrong person, and act accordingly. Research the field and pursue only those firms whose profile you fit. Adams Capital has no associates and hires only people with an engineering background. If you don't have an engineering background or aren't qualified for a position above associate, Adams Capital should not be on your list.
3. **Follow the money.** Understand where each target firm is in its fund-raising cycle. A firm that has just raised a successful new fund is more likely to be expanding; a firm at the end of the current fund's life and in an unfavorable fund-raising climate is not a good target.
4. **Practice.** If you are looking to join a somewhat larger private equity firm where the hiring process likely involves doing business cases in the interview, find a way to practice. One of the best ways is to seek out a friend who has experience. (If you are at a business school, probably some of your classmates have been analysts in private equity firms, consulting firms, or investment banks. If you are an undergraduate, try to find a classmate who has had a similar internship or summer job.) Ask her to walk through some typical situations (within the bounds of their confidentiality obligation) to give you a feel for the kind of case you may encounter in an interview.
5. **Network.** Do everything you can to network to the partners of the firm and create a relationship. Since GPs in private equity firms are not generally interested in having long conversations about you, especially when they may not have an immediate need to hire someone, you must engage them in topics involving *their* business. For students doing a job search ahead of graduation, soliciting help on projects that promise to yield valuable information to the firm itself can be one way to accomplish this. Working with a portfolio company is another way. Asking colleagues who know both you and the private equity firm well to advocate your case is still another way.

The stakes for hiring in a small firm are high, so the more the firm feels they know you, the less risk your hiring represents.

6. **Have a backup plan.** If necessary, plan a two-step approach where you take a job that involves working with partners of a firm for which you may be appropriate. Consulting and working at a portfolio company are two examples. There are many examples of successful private equity partners who tried for many years before landing their first job in the industry.

A job seeker should imagine that there are many doors to many private equity firms with many people trying to get in. The qualified people best known to each firm are "closest to the door"—in this world, a person can be close to several doors if he is well known to several firms and an appropriate or typical hire for each. The doors open only sporadically to admit someone, and that is the one the partners feel to be least risky—usually as measured by the one best known to them. Your goal should be to position yourself as close to as many doors as possible and hang around until a door near you opens. Private equity is one of the world's most competitive fields in which to find a job—have patience and perseverance.

Principal

In most firms, a successful associate will be promoted to principal[12] as a next career step. A principal has some deal-making responsibility but generally plays a limited role in the firm's investment decision making and none in the decisions on managing the firm. Instead, a principal usually has responsibility for part of the portfolio, even sitting on boards and making investment recommendations. Generally, principals do not have carried interest across the whole portfolio; but like venture partners, to be described later, they may have carried interest in the companies for which they are responsible. A principal is a deal maker and as such can source, manage, and complete deals. It is the last step in the partnership track before becoming a full partner. Key to a principal's promotion to partner is track record—can she make money?—and ability to find and source deals—is he a rainmaker?

Special Partners

A number of other professionals may be found in some but not all private equity firms. An operating partner is a partner who generally does not have deal-making responsibility, but helps the firm manage investments once they are in the portfolio. The roles of operating partners vary from consultant to board member to interim management, depending on the situation. They are usually paid a retainer by the private equity firm, and their compensation is often supplemented by stock awarded to them by the companies with which they work. They occasionally get carried interest from the private equity firm itself. One of the most famous operating partners was Jack Welch, who retired from his career as the successful long-term CEO of GE and joined the private equity firm Clayton, Dubilier & Rice as an operating partner.[13] In this role (Mr. Welch was called a "special partner"), he advised "the firm on a wide range of issues, including changing the culture in

---

[12] In some firms, associates are promoted to senior associate, then vice president, and only then to principal. These additional levels have more to do with compensation and longevity at the firm than with significantly different job responsibilities. The principal role itself may have several levels and various titles (e.g., vice president, managing director, etc.).

[13] http://www.prnewswire.co.uk/cgi/news/release?id=74354, October 2, 2001, accessed August 25, 2010.

portfolio companies, management best practices, corporate governance, and performance improvement initiatives." He did not, however, make investments.

Venture partners are partners who do have deal-making responsibility but receive carried interest only on their own deals. Generally venture partnerships are seen as trial arrangements for senior hires coming into the firm; they allow the firm to test whether the partner will develop as a successful deal maker and, more important, to see whether the partner fits into the firm. In some cases, firms use venture partnerships as another rung on the ladder from associate to GP. Senior GPs who are trying to ease out of day-to-day activities in the firm may also become venture partners. By reducing their carry to pertain only to their own deals, they signal their reduced scope of responsibility. This can help set the stage for a clean generational transition within the firm by freeing up carried interest to be awarded to younger, more productive partners.

General Partners

At the top of the hierarchy is the GP.[14] GPs have the fiduciary responsibility to invest the LP's money carefully and abide by the charter of the partnership. They have a carried interest across the firm's entire portfolio. Since GPs are made, not born, their main qualification is a track record of successful investing.

In addition, GPs have operating responsibility for the partnership. Perhaps the most important decisions made by the GPs are those that assign the firm's resources to pursue an investment—in many ways, decisions on committing resources are larger decisions than even investment decisions. The scarcest resource in any private equity firm is not the money, but the human capital.

Yet in addition to assigning resources, the GPs must consider a host of questions that define the firm's operations and overall culture—who to hire and when? Does the firm go after deals with a team, or an individual deal maker with some help? If it is a team, is the team formed just for the particular deal, or does it stay together and do a number of transactions? Who looks after the portfolio? What is a deal maker—does it need to be a partner, or can a nonpartner be empowered to do deals? Who gets paid what? Is there a bonus scheme? How is the carry split? Who communicates with the LPs? What should the firm tell the LPs? When does the firm raise the next fund? How much capital should be held in reserve for each deal? What is the firm's strategy—what deal would the partners *not* consider? The list of goes on.

General partners do not become GPs because they can manage these firm-level operating issues well; they become GPs because of their investing track record. It is on the track record that the firm raises money (see Chapter 2), and from the track record devolves all operating power in the firm. An apt analogy is considering whether the best football players will also be the best managers and coaches. Moreover, if the best investors are running the firm, is that the best use of their talents?

A solution to this conundrum is the position of managing GP. Some firms are run by committees of partners that include GPs whose responsibility is *not* to make deals, but to manage the firm and take a firm-wide view of the portfolio. Others focus management in one senior GP, designated as managing partner, CEO, chairman, or the like. In general, even in firms that have only one titular head, that person's main job is usually to assign partners to committees to do the management functions. The variations on this theme are endless: NEA has one managing GP; Flagship Ventures has two, as does General Atlantic, which calls them CEO and COO. Vitruvian Partners has three managing GP; Blackstone is managed by a committee of four (with corporate-like titles); and Bessemer Venture Partners is managed by a committee of five. Some firms have widely distributed governance—Warburg Pincus, for example, is managed by a central group of about twenty partners.

---

[14] General partners may have the title of managing partner or, sometimes, founding partner.

Through this prism, we see that most private equity positions serve to extend the main GP investors in the firm. In addition to those on the investment side of the business, all firms also have operations staff. These may be one office manager or dozens of important and well-paid professionals who support the activity of the firm without being actual investors.

Other Professionals

Depending on the scale of the firm, the operations staff may be quite extensive and often includes a number of accounting experts, along with tax and legal professionals. They deal with the logistics of closing transactions, fund and firm accounting, and communication with LPs.

Private equity firm accounting is a particular specialty. No matter their scale, private equity firms are charged with providing market valuations of the firm's portfolio (see Chapter 4 for a discussion of FAS 157). This is a question for audit on the one hand and LP confidence on the other. Consequently, even the smallest VC firm must seek out accountants who understand the details of portfolio and partnership accounting. Outside accounting firms that audit private equity firms usually have specialty departments that assist the in-house accounting staff.

Some larger firms have their own in-house counsel for legal advice on specific issues. In general, these in-house counsels manage the outside law firms hired to actually do transactions; they rarely draft the purchase agreements. In-house counsels are invaluable during fund-raising, when they are often charged with managing multiple closings of dozens of LPs, each with their own issues. They also can assist with setting up funds, which can become extremely complex when assets are held in different countries with different tax treaties and when LPs are likewise diverse.

Managing the relationship with its LPs is one of the firm's most time-consuming, but certainly among the most important, management activities. In smaller firms, this is almost always left to the most senior partners since they are the ones who periodically raise the money from those very LPs. One GP has noted that talking with LPs takes up nearly 25 percent of the senior partners' time—a great tax on the capacity of small firms. Larger firms have investor relations staff whose job is to manage fund-raising and maintain close communication with LPs, satisfying their need to monitor and account for their investment in the firm. Since it is so important for LPs to have an accurate view of what the firm is doing and so important to the firm itself to meet the needs of its source of capital, the senior investment relations staff usually report to the top of the private equity firm and are represented on the firm's most important management committees. For example, Blackstone's management committee, which allocates the firm's resources, comprises the chairman, the CEO, the CFO, and the senior investor relationship manager.[15]

Administrative assistance is especially important in a private equity firm because scheduling and supporting active, curious, and highly committed individuals with strong egos is a talent in itself. Operations specialists in private equity firms are usually compensated more highly than their peers in other service firms. This is because they operate under intense time pressure, work long hours, and are required to be very discreet because of the sensitive information they handle.

The Special Case of Venture Capital

Venture investing requires a different emphasis in skill sets, although the positions just described all exist in the venture world. Two factors make venture investing somewhat different: (1) the venture investor is investing in companies with fewer—often intangible—assets; and (2) venture investing is almost always **minority investing** (i.e., a VC investment position is almost always for less than 50 percent of the company, often alongside a number of co-investors). Mezzanine and growth investing are also minority investing, but there are plenty of assets to value and a financial

---

[15] http://www.blackstone.com, accessed August 29, 2010.

structure that contributes to protection and return (see Chapter 5). But in the venture case, financial structuring takes a backseat to establishing a close partnership with the entrepreneur and creating governance around the young company to help it react to the swings and roundabouts of its fortunes.

So at heart, VC is a *consensus business*. The venture capitalist is trying to get the entrepreneur to sell her stock to him at his price, while competing with other venture capitalists. As the deal is being done, the venture capitalist is trying to convince his partners of the merits of the deal while also influencing his co-investors to do the deal the way he thinks best. After the deal is done, the venture capitalist may own 15, 25, even 40 percent of the company and may or may not be on the board. He becomes one of many trying to influence the company and its board to set strategy, hire personnel, and finance the enterprise in the way he sees best. When there is an unexpected issue—and there are always unexpected issues in VC projects—the venture capitalist is trying to be the CEO or entrepreneur's first call. In addition to the business skills of a consultant and the financial skills of an investment banker, the successful venture capitalist is a nimble and effective conceptual salesman—because if he isn't, then all his business skills are for naught.

More than any other kind of active investing, VC relies on the personal traits of the venture capitalist. As a result, VC investing admits a lot of styles. But due to this element of personal conceptual selling, no one style is always effective. To be successful, the venture capitalist must develop an authentic style that fits him and his background. There are numerous examples of very successful venture capitalists who are effective in very different ways. Stewart Greenfield, a founder of Oak Investment Partners, was known for his quiet, soft-spoken style as he sat on the boards of such companies as Ungermann-Bass (the first LAN company); the equally successful Fred Adler, founder of Adler & Company, was direct, urgent and sometimes profane when leading investments in Data General (one of the first minicomputer companies) and Applied Materials (the dominant capital goods supplier to the semiconductor industry). Both were effective, both were successful, both relied on styles authentic and comfortable to them.

For over two decades, the partners at Bessemer Venture Partners compiled a list of their perception of the traits of a successful venture capitalist. The list, shown in Figure 11.3, is remarkable in that it contains not specific skills but personal characteristics, none of which are readily deduced from reading a resume.

In all of private equity, financial skills are but tools of the trade. Real private equity success comes from the ability to actively influence the course of an investment, correcting problems quickly, holding management accountable, and keeping discipline while managing for maximum

FIGURE 11.3   Qualities of a good venture capitalist

<u>What Makes a Good Venture Capitalist?</u>

The ability to communicate

The ability to get mindshare

Discipline

A sense of equity

Empathy

Reputation

Perspective

Stability

...and luck

long-term value. Noted one CEO who had been backed by a very successful venture capitalist, "He's the best. You'll be up to your elbows in alligators and he's cracking jokes and solving problems. He makes you feel like it's all a grand adventure that you'll laugh about tomorrow." Private equity professionals are successful and effective businesspeople first, financiers second.

Is Operating Experience a Necessary—or Even Good—Background for a Successful Private Equity Investor?

A commonly asked question, especially in VC investing, is whether a private equity investor requires operating experience to succeed. In an informal survey of Harvard Business School graduates who became private equity professionals, Josh Lerner showed that private equity professionals came from a variety of backgrounds—operating, consulting, and financial services (with a slight concentration of financial services backgrounds among buyout professionals). Roughly half joined the private equity industry immediately upon graduation, the remainder after jobs—and sometimes whole careers—elsewhere. The statistics then says there is no success bias for or against operating backgrounds in private equity.

Yet many VC firms insist on operating backgrounds—at least in public. One might wonder if this is another case of VC being slightly different from private equity overall. Again the facts say no, that operating backgrounds do not particularly predict success. During 1997–2000, the greatest venture bubble to date, which was driven by the telecommunications equipment companies developing the hardware that eventually made up the Internet, the most active and successful telecoms investors included Paul Ferri of Matrix, Roger Evans of Greylock, David Cowan of Bessemer, Dick Kramlich of NEA, and Todd Degras of Battery. All but one of these (Roger Evans) had essentially no operating background.

The argument in favor of an operating background centers on the notion that a former operating manager best understands the problems of the entrepreneur building a company and therefore is in the best position to help. The counterargument is that past methods and solutions may not be the right answer, especially for problems in new innovative companies within industries that have just emerged. Much more important is the venture capitalist's ability to communicate and empathize with management and thereby gain influence to create governance. An operating background *may* be of help in establishing a strong and influential bond with management, but it is by no means necessary. What is necessary is a solid understanding of the start-up milieu—what it is like to be inside a company focused intensely on starting a business with limited resources and time.

Lastly, we must remember that VC is a business that admits great variation in styles. When partners hire, their two main concerns typically are (1) how well do I know this person? and (2) since I'm successful, how much is this person like me? Often new venture capitalists are recruited from successful portfolio companies or from industry role model companies (e.g., Microsoft, Hewlett Packard, Apple, Google, Cisco, etc.), and thus the operating background myth is perpetuated. As a result, people who want to get into VC may start their careers in venture-backed portfolio companies simply to remove the objection.

COMPENSATION

Compensation schemes are at the heart of the private equity operating culture, especially in small-scale firms. There are two sources of cash flow in private equity firms: fees (including transaction fees, in the case of LBO firms) and carried interest. In general, the fees are used to pay salaries and

FIGURE 11.4 Median salaries for north american private equity professionals, 2008

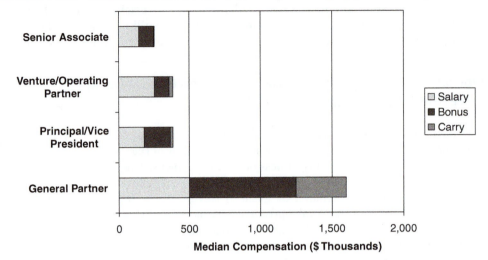

Source: Data from R. Michael Holt, *Dow Jones Private Equity Analyst—Holt Compensation Study* (New York: Dow Jones, 2008), 10.

bonuses since they can be predicted and budgeted. The carried interest is used as a long-term incentive, largely for the owners of the firm (i.e., the GPs).

Befitting what is essentially an apprenticeship dynamic, the difference between the GPs' salary and bonus structure and that of all other professionals is quite steep. Figure 11.4 illustrates the point and reflects two important principles: (1) even at lower levels, private equity compensation is heavily performance weighted; and (2) there is a dramatic increase in all components of compensation as one moves from principal to GP. Note that bonuses increase the base by 70 percent and more.[16] This reflects the apprenticeship aspect—individuals must prove their knowledge and staying power before sharing in the real spoils of the firm. Nevertheless, private equity compensation compares favorably with career track positions in investment banking and consulting and so attracts high-performing individuals.

The figure also reveals how little carry is distributed below the partner level. A typical associate package may have 20 basis points (bps) of carry (that is, the associate gets 0.2 percent of the 20 percent of total carry in the pool—for a 0.04 percent share of the net profits).[17] The principle is to give apprentices a taste of the spoils to come if they are successful.

The same study showed that larger firms paid far better than smaller firms, especially at the levels below GP. Obviously, the general scalability of the buyout business (as discussed later in this chapter and in Chapter 12) plus the additional cash flow from transaction fees allows for more compensation per professional. Moreover, the buyout business *needs* more analyst, associate, and principal support because of the time pressure to compete for deals. So paying nonpartners well but not deeply sharing the carry is a reasonable trade-off for the partners of a large-scale buyout firm.

In most VC firms, no carry is granted before at least the principal level, and most firms wait until the emerging venture capitalist reaches partner rank. This practice reflects the fact that

---

[16] Data from Jennifer Rossa, R. Michael Holt, David Smagalla, eds. *Dow Jones Private Equity Analyst—Holt Compensation Study*, 2008 ed., (Jersey City, NJ: Dow Jones & Co., 2008).

[17] Felda Hardymon, Josh Lerner, Ann Leamon, and Sean Klimczak, "Tad O'Malley: December 2004," HBS Case No. 806-024 (Boston: HBS Publishing, 2004).

venture returns tend to come in big lumps; so it is conceivable that an associate with even a small bit of carry could have a significant carry distribution because she was at the firm at the right time, while other associates may miss out altogether by being at the firm when there were few liquidity events.

There are two basic schemes when it comes to dividing up carried interest among partners; we call them the *royalty model* and the *insurance model.* In the royalty model, the senior partners on whose track record the fund was raised take the lion's share of carry. The reasoning goes that "if it weren't for me, there would be no money to invest, so my share should reflect that." Before private equity became institutionalized as an industry, this was the dominant method of distributing carry. A famous story is told of a very early Silicon Valley venture firm that had four partners. The firm had a 20 percent carried interest, which was split 17-1-1-1 among the four partners. The larger share went to the senior partner, who had convinced several large insurance companies to invest as LPs. In those days, LPs for venture funds were few and far between, so this sentiment was understandable. The firm was quite successful; and based on his acquired track record, one partner left to found his own firm. After he parted, the carry was re-split 18-1-1. Not surprisingly, two more spinout firms followed as each 1 percent partner raised his own fund based on his own record. This story explains why venture firms tended to stay small and spawn other venture firms in the decades of the 1970s and 1980s, when LPs were just discovering VC as an asset class and a premium was placed on having a record good enough to attract money.

In the insurance model, the carry tends to be split more or less evenly across the partners, although there may be some small premium for longevity. The model reflects the idea that private equity is highly cyclical and performance comes in lumps. Therefore, a senior partner is willing to give up some of his carry as insurance against the possibility that his performance might suffer in the upcoming cycle. Moreover, the system recognizes that as long as someone on the team has a good streak of successes, the firm will grow and provide better compensation in the long run. "The hot hand today may be the cold hand tomorrow" could be thought of as the motto for this approach. Obviously such a scheme assumes the firm will remain in business and continue to raise money—an easier assumption in 2010, after nearly forty years of LP interest in private equity, than in the 1970s when private equity allocations were a new concept.

The two ways carried interest is split coincide with two broad characteristics of private equity firms. Broadly speaking, firms can be classified as those that encourage and thrive on a "star system"—where the firm has one (or a few) great investors and the entire firm supports them—and those that strive to create a team ethos. Almost all new firms start as star systems, since the original money has to be raised on a previous track record. Venture capital firms in particular have this characteristic, but it is also true of any LBO firm that has a particular investor's—or group of investors'—name on the door. The named partners started as the stars of the firm, and everything, at least in the beginning, was built around them. Over time, some firms consciously evolve from a star system into more of a team format with the goals of creating a durable institution that can support new investors as they develop and can tolerate losing partners to retirement.

The approach chosen is a matter of personal temperament—not whether one model works better than another. Consider the example of Arthur Rock and Associates, founded in 1969 by Arthur Rock and Dick Kramlich. Rock is perhaps the greatest individual venture capitalist ever, with early investments in Fairchild Semiconductor, Teledyne, Intel, Apple, and many other high-tech companies.[18] Rock has continued to invest from a very small setting, essentially operating as a sole investor for decades. Kramlich went on to build NEA, one of the largest and most successful venture firms ever, with more than $11 billion under management and dozens of senior partners. NEA is a model of a firm that succeeds through teamwork and the development of new investors.

---

[18] http://www.hbs.edu/entrepreneurs/pdf/arthurrock.pdf, accessed July 15, 2011.

In essence, NEA has institutionalized itself and created a platform that will survive for many generations.

Taken together, the typical modern compensation scheme sets the operating culture in private equity. The nonpartners are considered to be earning their way in with much lower compensation packages than the partners, although those compensation packages are highly performance oriented and high percentages are devoted to bonuses. Moreover, in most cases, the long-term compensation (i.e., carried interest) is split to encourage teamwork by stressing overall portfolio performance above individual performance. All in all, private equity compensation creates a highly leveraged performance culture.

MANAGING THE PRIVATE EQUITY FIRM

Now that we have discussed the positions in private equity and the nature of the people who fill them, let's address the management issues. These are partnerships comprised of high-performing, highly compensated, fiercely independent-minded professionals—what holds them together and makes them work? For this section's discussion, we divide the private equity firms by scale since scale determines much of the operating culture in private equity.

We refer to the parameters related to size as scale attributes: amount under management, geographic dispersion, deal size, velocity (i.e., number of deals per year), and number of partners and other professionals. Whether the firm is a buyout firm or VC firm, scale is a key determinant of culture and organization. The larger the scale, the greater is the need for institutionalization such as formal reporting, fixed processes, and hierarchical organization—and for the administrative staff to support it. Chapter 12 deals with issues of scale, especially with respect to performance. Here we are just treating the management implications for the firm.

Small-Scale Firms

Small-scale firms[19] are universally flat in structure. In fact, in many small firms the only professional employees are GPs; and all major decisions, be they personnel, investments, strategy or fund-raising, take place through direct discussion—mostly informal—between partners. The culture of such firms is highly personal and based on close ties between the partners. The problem of hiring at a small-scale firm is, in effect, that the partners are looking for someone with whom they can entrust their personal checkbooks. Such small-scale and organizationally flat firms overwhelmingly comprised the private equity industry of the 1960s and 1970s and still predominate in VC today. The following list defines the management principles of these firms:

- *Decision making* is informal, often with partners working quite independently of one another and relying on the frequency of communication that a small firm permits. The decision steps described in Chapter 3 blur because steps tend to be comingled. The decision to commit firm resources to a deal is the same as a GP becoming interested in it; and deal socialization is often a running conversation that leads straight to deal approval. In fact, there can be a problem in documenting the rationale for investment decisions in such firms; many small firms lack institutional memory of the reasons that they made certain investments.

- *Investment strategy* is constrained by scale and the specific skills and interests of the GPs. Consequently, GPs in smaller-scale firms are more likely to be generalists. Nowhere is the saying that "your strategy is what you hire" truer than in firms with less than a dozen

---

[19] In general, we refer to firms as being small scale if they have a dozen partners or fewer.

professionals. Consider a small private equity firm that specializes in bank buyouts. Should the market for bank buyouts become difficult, the partners face a Hobson's choice: either go out of business or retool their investment skills to practice in another area. During the Internet/telecoms bubble of the late 1990s, many VC firms eliminated their health-care/life sciences practices in favor of their booming IT practices, only for health care to pick up as IT crashed in the early 2000s. One GP from a firm that stayed in both sectors is quoted as saying, "We IT guys used to want to exterminate the life sciences guys, now [in 2004] we wonder why they don't exterminate us." Because active investing requires domain knowledge, strategy shifts by smaller private equity firms take a long time. Also, it is difficult for small-scale firms to execute strategies of great geographical diversity. Not only must the firm manage communications among offices (see page 38 box on knowledge communications systems), but there will often be offices with just one or two partners. Consensus decision making is better than individual decision making,[20] and partners in small offices lack the sounding board of a team of professionals. In addition, members of a small team in a new office may feel that they must "earn their keep" and be tempted to do suboptimal deals to look busy.

- *Portfolio management* in small-scale firms is defined by the tension between an individual partner's opportunities and the firm's capacity to accommodate each deal. Rarely is a single person charged with worrying about the overall portfolio. It is not unusual for turf battles to erupt over the issue of whether to support a less promising deal presented by a less successful deal maker[21] who happens to have more bandwidth, or to support another deal brought in by a more successful deal maker with little free time. This is a particular issue in a small firm, where each sector may be associated with a different partner. When one sector is hot and another cold, the firm may manage the portfolio by—in effect—discouraging some partners from doing new deals. As we describe in the example of Brentwood Venture Partners and Institutional Venture Partners in Chapter 12, small-scale firms can split up over issues of different sectors following different business cycles. The irony, of course, is that diversifying across sectors should theoretically provide a natural hedge against cycles in the broader business environment; but in the world of smaller private equity firms, strategy and portfolio management are so tied to individual GPs that executing the hedge operationally is extremely difficult since it requires a culture that tolerates differential workloads among the partners.

Small-scale firms tend to be organized with fewer different positions and to look, conceptually, like an inverted triangle; that is, they are more top heavy than larger firms.[22] Associates are generally assigned to a partner or a small group of partners who work together. As the associate develops increasingly specific skills, she can more ably extend the capabilities of the partner with whom she is working. Small-scale firms typically do not have a pool of associates who can work on any given deal interchangeably; but like the partners of the firm they support, associates work in silos defined by geography, sector, and type of deal. An associate's job track in a smaller firm is narrow indeed, and this can create obstacles to a successful private equity career. To be ultimately successful as a partner in a private equity firm, she must be apprenticed in a good firm with a good

---

[20] Alan S. Blinder and John Morgan, "Are Two Heads Better Than One? An Experimental Analysis of Group vs. Individual Decisionmaking" (NBER Working Paper No. W7909, September 2000) available at SSRN: http://ssrn.com/abstract=242143; and Alan S. Blinder and John Morgan, "Are Two Heads Better Than One? Monetary Policy by Committee," *Journal of Money, Credit, and Banking* 37, no. 5 (2005): 798–811.

[21] Part of the question is also whether the partner's lack of success makes the partners less likely to judge her deal as promising.

[22] Noam Wasserman, "Revisiting the Strategy, Structure, and Performance Paradigm: The Case of Venture Capital," *Organization Science* 19, no. 2 (2008): 241–59.

partner in a good field. Here again we encounter the enduring theme of credentialing—it is far easier for an associate from a good firm to find a subsequent position in the private equity industry than it is for a person who has entered the industry in a lower-tier firm. Associates may choose to leave a firm for a host of reasons; a new firm will assume they have had good training and developed good habits if they have a good pedigree.

A typical small-scale firm, then, will have a core of GPs and a cadre of associates with an occasional operating or venture partner. Communication and reporting tend to be informal, and portfolio management is left either to a senior partner or to a firm protocol that encourages partners to raise portfolio issues when necessary. Small firms hire and develop people slowly and carefully; to do otherwise runs the risk of serious mistakes (in Chapter 12, we discuss the consequences of fast growth).

The risks of hiring make small-scale firms very leery of hiring. First, there is huge cost to the firm in finding, vetting, hiring, and training new talent—and not only is it financially expensive, but it absorbs substantial amounts of the partners' time. Small firms rely so much on chemistry and culture that only partners can really do the hiring—and that comes at the cost of time that would otherwise be spent on investments. In fact, most firms embark on the hiring process only when the pain of insufficient capacity is so great that it is worth dropping some investment activity to resolve it. Yet because a bad choice can upset the firm's culture (and lead to bad investments), the stakes for each hire are extremely high.

Therefore, small-scale private equity firms tend to hire people they know well, or people who are quite junior and represent less hiring risk, or both. These firms usually develop new professionals through long apprenticeship or by hiring executives they have worked with in portfolio companies as operating partners or venture partners. Admitting partners to and removing partners from a private equity firm is difficult, regardless of its size. Partners are equity holders in an entity comprised of illiquid and hard-to-value securities. Therefore, adding a partner involves valuing illiquid securities so the new partner can buy his share—or be bought out if the partner is being removed. Since international partnership law requires GPs to incur financial risk, transactions adding or removing partners involve cash or full recourse notes, which further raises the stakes of valuing illiquid securities. Moreover, admission and removal of GPs requires transparency to the LPs and must be done at the same values that the partnership is reporting to the LPs, which compounds the risk of a mistake. Consequently, small-scale private equity firms in particular, and all firms in general, move very deliberately in matters of personnel.

Operating procedures within small firms tend to be informal and flexible. Nearly all firms have a regular weekly meeting (usually on Monday to start the week); in the case of multilocation small firms, these meetings tend to take place through video conference. The main agenda items are investment decisions and review of the portfolio companies' progress. As described in Chapter 3, the decision making is almost always by consensus after discussion. The partner advocating the deal will have distributed an investment recommendation (or investment memo), which—depending on the culture of the firm—may be in a standard format or include certain topics like financing risk, management biographies, forecasts presented in a particular way, and the like. Since there is less capacity to swarm a deal and get a number of views on potential investments, small firms need to expose the partners directly to the new investment. Usually it is at the Monday meeting that the partnership hears presentations from the management of candidate investment companies.

The method of reviewing portfolio company progress varies enormously from firm to firm. In many cases, portfolio review is simply an informal discussion driven by the partner following each company and occurring only when the partner deems something of note has happened. On the other hand, some firms require regular written updates that cover certain required topics and include information from board meeting notes. For example, Adams Capital Management (ACM) requires each partner to report progress on five fronts as part of a systemized approach to portfolio monitoring termed *structured navigation.*[23] These benchmarks include

1. Progress in rounding out the management team
2. Obtaining corporate partner or endorsement
3. Early exposure to investment bankers
4. Expansion of the product line
5. Elimination of nonexecution business risks

Regardless of the criticism that one list cannot possibly fit all early-stage companies, the ACM partners point out that the list provides a common language to make an amorphous topic more precise. As long as the partners approach structured navigation with flexibility in applying each topic to each portfolio company, they are well served by having a common language and a set of standards to track progress within the portfolio.

Large-Scale Firms

How, then, do firms of large scale differ in these management principles? In general, while large-scale firms differ among themselves every bit as much as do their smaller brethren, there is a general difference between large and small. Whereas small-scale firms are characterized by less formal, less hierarchical management, large-scale firms operate in a more institutionalized way, simply due to the practicalities of organizing larger numbers of people.

Here are the general characteristics of large-scale firm processes:

- *Decision making* is a formal process with well-defined, well-documented steps. The deal-socialization phase in a large firm is actually a decision gate for committing the firm's resources to the pursuit of the deal. Since most large-scale firms are buyout, mezzanine, or growth equity firms,[24] they incur very large up-front costs associated with legal, due diligence, and financing costs for their deals (see Chapter 3), especially in competitive situations with substantial time pressure. Consequently the decision to *pursue* a deal is an important commitment of firm resources, both financial and precious partner time. In some firms such as Blackstone, the decision to pursue a deal is made by a central investment committee of four senior officers, while the actual investment decision is made by the team assigned to the deal (described in Chapter 3). This dichotomy reflects the earlier observation that decisions on how to invest the human capital of the firm are more critical than decisions on how to invest its financial capital.

    As a result, the decision-making organization of large firms nearly always has a committee (occasionally this may be a committee of one senior managing partner) with responsibility for approving the commitment of firm resources to pursue a transaction. That committee may or may not also make the final investment decision. But getting permission

---

[23] Felda Hardymon and Bill Wasick, "Adams Capital: March 1999," HBS Case No. 899-256 (Boston: HBS Publishing, 1999).

[24] In 1999–2000, twenty-two VC firms raised $1 billion or larger funds. By 2001, all but a handful had reduced the size of their fund as the VC market slowed down and firms realized the limits of scaling in VC. Josh Lerner, Felda Hardymon, Frank Angella, and Ann Leamon, "Grove Street Advisors," HBS Case No. 804-050 (Boston: HBS Publishing, 2004). One reason for the limit to scaling in VC funds was given by Andrew Metrick in a seminar on risk in venture investing (http://www.altassets.com/private-equity-knowledge-bank/learning-curve/article/nz9264.html). Metrick pointed out that the venture model was one of taking big risks in the hopes of the occasional very big payoff. He noted that even the largest VC firms have very few partners, allowing each to win big if a high-risk investment pays off. "These are small organizations. When they get too big, the incentives for any one person aren't so clear," said Metrick. "If someone is better than their partner, then they leave and start their own firm."

just to pursue an opportunity means that partners in large firms start each transaction as an advocate in a competitive process to obtain firm resources. Indeed, decision processes at large firms risk having more advocacy and less consensus building around transactions than may be healthy for the firm's culture. Therefore, large firms tend to separate decision making from deal making to maintain objectivity and to ameliorate the effect of deal makers who may not know one another well, nor even see each other often, competing against one another for resources.

- *Investment strategy* is less constrained in a large firm because there are more resources with more variation, creating more flexibility to add or change strategies. Indeed, many large private equity firms have defined themselves as investment managers that happen to do private equity. These firms (Blackstone, Bain, and KKR, to name three) have developed other funds as part of a broad product offering. In some cases the new businesses have synergy with the private equity practice (e.g., trading collateralized loan obligations [CLOs] or an advisory business), and in some cases they are related only insofar as they solicit funds from the same LPs (e.g., fund of hedge funds). But this flexibility requires a separate, ongoing strategy function that usually resides with senior management that does not make investments, but firm resource allocations and the firm's investment strategy.

- *Portfolio management*, like strategy, is a separate function in a large firm. Often the function is carried out by the same committees that make resource allocation and investment decisions. Because costs are so high in a large-scale firm, there is a tendency to take advantage of knowledge learned in one deal and apply it to similar companies in the same industries. As just a few examples, London-based Hg Capital did a series of deals that focused on business systems software for small- and medium-sized companies. Not only did Hg leverage its knowledge over at least five such companies (Iris Software, Addison Software and Service, Computer Software Group, Visma, and Team Systems), but it combined two of them in a secondary buyout to Hellman and Friedman, another private equity group.[25] Montagu Private Equity did three waste management deals: Lincwaste in the 1990s, Cory in 2005, and Biffa in 2008.[26] Apax Partners did three deals over two years in the hospital operations space: Sweden's Capio and General Healthcare Group in the United Kingdom, both in 2006, followed by India's Apollo Hospitals the following year.[27]

Because large firms must use expensive (usually the most expensive) partners to separately manage decision making, strategy, and portfolio management, they must be of considerable size. To afford such a structure and create enough cash flow to go around and keep professionals tied to the firm (because even though the senior managing partners are not directly making deals, they must be compensated at a level equal to or exceeding the deal makers), they must have a considerable fee flow. Private equity, like cabinet making, is one of those businesses whose operating structure allows small and large firms to thrive but makes operating a midsized firm uneconomical. Just as the cabinet maker finds he can thrive when the number of jobs is such that he can manage the business and a few helpers without appreciably cutting into his own production time, the small-scale firm can have partners who both manage and make investments. But should the cabinet maker expand, he would soon find himself forced to grow to a scale where the business can comfortably support him without his making cabinets. Similarly, once private equity firms get above a dozen or so partners, they must either curb their growth or reach a much larger scale in

---

[25] http://www.hgcapital.com/en/investments/Pages/Exited.aspx, accessed August 31, 2010; and Jeremy Kirk, "Venture Capital Firm Trumps Sage's Offer for Visma," *InfoWorld*, April 19, 2006, http://www.infoworld.com/t/data-management/venture-capital-firm-trumps-sages-offer-visma-144, accessed August 31, 2010.

[26] E-mail communication with Chris Masterson, Montagu, August 30, 2010.

[27] http://www.apax.com/sectors/healthcare/our-investments.aspx, accessed July 31, 2011.

order to afford an effective operating structure. They must be large enough to afford partners who manage rather than invest.

Communications within a large firm are, as one would expect, much more formal. The strategy and portfolio management functions are centralized, and the investment capability resides in deal teams with different domain expertise that may be domiciled in different countries. Moreover, it is simply impractical for firms with dozens of professionals to meet in regular meetings to discuss the details of day-to-day investing. So firms must rely on a strong IT platform that supports a knowledge-sharing system. Indeed, private equity is one of the few businesses where IT is regarded not as a cost but as a source of competitive advantage.

These knowledge management systems, many built on business intelligence platforms, allow professionals to find firm-wide resources such as consultants, lawyers, analysts, domain expertise from previous transactions, and the like. They also keep the deal makers informed of transactions that have been completed or are being pursued. Since investment decisions generally are made by deal teams, a strong knowledge-sharing system is essential to let the London-based team pursuing the buyout of a European financial services company know what the mezzanine team in Mumbai is doing—which would be particularly crucial if the one could assist the other. The lack of such information can contribute to the firm's eventual destruction, since different teams might feel they could succeed on their own and spin out to raise their own funds—just as happened in the very small VC firms in the 1970s.

CULTURE AND STRATEGY

Private equity firms, like all professional services firms, rely on building a culture that encompasses and communicates the firm's ethics and quality standards. Achieving understanding and consensus in service firms is difficult because professionals—in the case of private equity firms, deal makers—are busy doing deals. Top-down implementation is difficult in a private equity firm, meaning that firms rely on culture to build consensus and adherence to strategy.[28]

Culture determines strategy, particularly how the strategy is executed. Both ACM and Sequoia Capital are U.S.-based venture firms specializing in early-stage technology investments. ACM, founded in 1996, has a culture of "no one is indispensible," and it is staffed entirely by engineers at the partner level only—no associates—who use a team approach. The partners create white papers as a way to anticipate what might be the "next great thing."[29]

Sequoia, on the other hand, is one of the oldest and most successful Silicon Valley investors. Founded in 1972 by Don Valentine, the "grandfather of Silicon Valley venture capital" and an original investor in Apple and Cisco,[30] the firm has always espoused the culture of the smart individual investor following his instincts and business judgment (especially paying attention to potential market size) to create the next great company.

While the headline strategy of these two firms—early-stage technology investing—is the same, not surprisingly their execution is quite different and consistent with each firm's culture. ACM owns a significant percentage of its investee companies (often 50 percent or higher), usually with a first-time entrepreneur, in locations dispersed throughout the United States. The ACM companies are almost all business-to-business operations where the sale is based on return on

[28] Ashish Nanda, "Strategy and Positioning in Professional Service Firms," HBS Case No. 904-060 (Boston: HBS Publishing, 2004).

[29] Felda Hardymon, Josh Lerner, and Ann Leamon, "Adams Capital Management: March 2002," HBS Case No. 803-143 (Boston: HBS Publishing, 2003).

[30] Alorie Gilbert, "Legendary Venture Capitalist Looks Ahead," *CNet News*, November 27, 2004, http://news.cnet.com/Legendary-venture-capitalist-looks-ahead/2008-1082_3-5466478.html, accessed July 15, 2011.

investment (ROI) to the customer since those types of products are more easily analyzed in white-paper analyses done by venture capitalists with engineering backgrounds.[31]

Sequoia's companies are concentrated in Silicon Valley, often staffed by entrepreneurs from other Sequoia deals, and can be described as lean start-ups with high public profiles. Sequoia has had great recent success in business-to-consumer technology companies such as Google and YouTube.

In buyouts, one can think of Permira and Montagu as both being European-based leveraged buyout firms. Permira spun out of the investment banking culture of Schroders and took with it a finance and transaction mentality. Not surprisingly, most Permira partners have a finance background.[32] Montagu, on the other hand, started as the European private equity office of HSBC, which had taken over the practice from Midland Bank—a U.K. retail bank focused on middle-market businesses.[33] Moreover, many of the Montagu partners came from the U.K. publicly traded private equity firm 3i, which was involved in mid-market investments with an emphasis on operational improvement. The culture in Montagu is based on building trust with the management teams and a belief in improving operations through good management.

Despite both being European-based leveraged buyout firms, the difference in their day-to-day investment strategy is marked. Montagu does mid-market deals requiring €50 to 100 million of equity with continuity of management, usually characterized as management buyouts (MBOs), which are not highly leveraged, are located in Western Europe, and sourced through proprietary channels—usually by working with management. At Permira, the deals are typically sourced through a competitive process, dispersed throughout the world, of much greater scale, and often highly leveraged, which can accelerate returns and create significant management incentives. Both Permira and Montagu have long and successful track records. Obviously, the differences in these firms are mostly explained by strategy; but strategy is closely related to the firms' culture and management.

A SPECIAL CASE: CORPORATE VENTURE CAPITAL AND AFFILIATED FUNDS

The largest type of affiliated fund is the corporate VC operation, in which a corporation decides to fund a division that invests in early-stage companies that are of interest to the parent. Among the corporations with VC operations are life sciences companies like Johnson & Johnson, Eli Lilly, and Pfizer; technology companies like Microsoft, Intel, and Siemens; and even Disney, the media company. Banks also may run a private equity fund, usually a buyout operation, both to provide its clients with access to the asset class and to take advantage of synergies with the parent's lending operation. While the goals of these groups, especially the corporate groups, may differ from those of a classic private equity fund due to the parent's desire for new technology or exposure in certain geographies, the real difference occurs in the affiliated group's structure and compensation.

We have just described the structure of a typical VC operation—small, nimble, and with compensation highly correlated to performance. Affiliated groups often struggle with integrating these characteristics into a hierarchical bureaucracy. A captive group might lose deals if the approval process involves multiple meetings with layers of bureaucracy. Moreover, the affiliated group risks losing its staff if they are not compensated at industry norms. Many of the investors

---

[31] Hardymon et al., "Adams Capital Management: Fund IV."

[32] Josh Lerner, Kate Bingham, and Nick Ferguson, "Schroder Ventures: Launch of the Euro Fund," HBS Case No. 297-026 (Boston: HBS Publishing, 1997).

[33] Felda Hardymon, Josh Lerner, and Ann Leamon, "Montagu Private Equity (A)," HBS Case No. 804-051 (Boston: HBS Publishing, 2004).

working for Intel Capital left the company in 2000 when their investments produced $2.3 billion in gains in one quarter, and their compensation did not reflect this.[34] Observed a manager at GE, which had a well-regarded corporate venture program in the late 1970s, "How can I have a guy in the VC division landing his helicopter on the front lawn when the manager of the Peoria plant doing $100 million a year is making $60,000?" Carried interest and corporate pay grades coexist very uneasily. Often, investors received a bonus that reflected gains to the portfolio but was not commensurate to carried interest. A case in point is Xerox Corporation, which in sequence built corporate VC units in the 1970s, 1980s, and 1990s. Each time, Xerox disbanded the unit either when success led to compensation issues with the venture capitalists staffing the unit or when corporate priorities shifted. Unlike industrial corporations, most of the bank-affiliated buyout operations are structured to operate with almost complete independence, and compensation issues are less severe because the compensation culture in financial services tolerates the profit-sharing ethos of private equity.

FINAL THOUGHTS

In this chapter, we have explored characteristics of private equity professionals themselves and looked at what it takes to succeed in the industry. We have then moved into the question of the private equity firm and how it is structured to encourage these individuals to perform. In addition, we have noted the special challenges presented to VC investors as compared to the other types of private equity practitioners.

Like all professional service firms, private equity firms are an uncertain combination of high-performing individuals ranging from "individual cowboys sharing office space and support" to a closely integrated team that nonetheless strikes a balance between individuality and process. The heart of the firm is the talent of the small group of GPs, and the firm itself is structured to extend and support them. We've seen in this chapter that firms use a combination of compensation, apprenticeship, and culture to manage the process of recruiting, training, retaining, and promoting individuals. A key characteristic regarding an organization's final form is its scale. A firm's scale and its ability to grow are influenced by whether the firm is run by the star system or the team system, and this tends to determine the form of the compensation system. In the difficult period of 2008, for instance, GPs in some firms took lower bonuses or none at all to ensure that their more junior staff received a reward.[35]

As has become apparent in this chapter, the organization and management of a private equity firm depends vastly on informal interaction. That can be extended to a certain degree through regular off-site meetings, teleconferences, and knowledge management systems. Yet when does this become insufficient for organizational cohesion? It is possible to have firms with far-flung offices that work well and others where the structure eventually topples and implodes due to its weight or intractability. At the same time, an international presence has become increasingly important as buyout activity (and to a lesser extent, VC) becomes global. Chapter 12 explores the way that private equity firms, these small groups with their delicate balance of autonomy and collegiality, have addressed the limits, dangers, and difficulties of scale and what the quantitative data tells us.

---

[34] The VC industry norm would be 20 percent of the gains. While Intel provided the Intel Capital staff with enhanced salary and stock benefits, many left for VC industry-standard compensation. See Paul A. Gompers and Josh Lerner, *The Money of Invention* (Boston: Harvard Business School Press, 2001), 164.

[35] Data from a conversation with R. Michael Holt, Holt Private Equity Consultants, December 4, 2009, referencing data from 2009 *Private Equity Analyst/Holt Compensation Survey*; cited in Josh Lerner, Matthew Rhodes-Kropf, and Ann Leamon, "Iris Running Crane: March 2009," HBS Case No. 810-073 (Boston: HBS Publishing, 2010).

QUESTIONS

1. Is there an ideal background for a private equity professional? In particular, for a venture capitalist? A buyout investor?

2. What are the key characteristics a private equity firm looks for when evaluating an entry-level hire?

3. Describe the typical organization of a private equity firm. What are the main motivating factors that result in this type of organization?

4. What are the three main traits required of an analyst? What are the keys to promotion for an analyst?

5. How does the associate job differ from the analyst job? What are the keys to promotion for an associate?

6. How does the principal job differ from the associate job? What are the keys to promotion for a principal?

7. What are venture partners and operating partners? What are their roles in a private equity firm?

8. Besides investment decisions, what other critical decisions must GPs make?

9. How does minority investing differ from majority investing? In particular, how do the investors' skill sets differ?

10. Describe the main principles of the compensation structure in private equity firms. How are the firm's cash-flow sources matched to the elements of compensation?

11. How does compensation vary by level in a private equity firm? When is carry granted?

12. What are the basic ways carry is divided in private equity firms? What are the rationales for the basic schemes?

13. Describe the main operating management characteristics of small-scale firms. Why have they developed in this way?

14. Describe the main operating management characteristics of large-scale firms? Why have they developed in this way?

15. Describe the role of culture in the management of private equity firms.

Chapter **12**

Scaling and Institutionalization

$\mathbf{P}$robably no aspect of running a private equity firm is more challenging than the management of growth and the challenges that come with it. This claim might initially seem surprising—after all, don't most firms grow because they are doing well? Moreover, haven't many of the best-known groups expanded dramatically over the past decade? Consider a few examples:

- Between 2001 and 2007, the Blackstone Group grew its assets under management—including private equity, real estate, and hedge funds—at a 41 percent annualized rate, from $14 to $88 billion.[1]
- In 2009, after a decade of rapid growth, the Carlyle Group managed $84.5 billion in 64 funds. Nearly 500 investment professionals operated out of offices in 20 countries.[2]
- Even in venture capital, the past decade saw expansion: for instance, growing through acquisition and organic expansion, Silicon Valley-based Sequoia Capital opened offices in Israel, China, and India.[3]

It may seem puzzling that this process of growth can be characterized as a challenge, rather than a source for celebration. After all, it is the fund's success that permits it to raise additional funds. But while a relationship between past success and growth undoubtedly exists, the process of growth can pose substantial issues to private equity groups. Growth necessitates changes for private equity groups along many dimensions. For instance, it may require that they move from doing one type of transaction successfully to another arena in which they often are less experienced, and it can change the way that investment professionals are selected and rewarded. Chapter 11 described the intense amount of personal interaction that occurs in private equity firms in assessing, hiring, and training investment professionals and making investment decisions. Does an ability to raise more money necessarily imply that the team can manage it with the same skill?

This caution can be illustrated through the experience of many groups that were once illustrious but are now forgotten. In many cases, while a variety of ill fortune led to the group's

---

[1] The Blackstone Group, "Prospectus," June 25, 2007, http://files.shareholder.com/downloads/BX/1029469720x0x252012/9eb40a28-196e-4146-a19d-4807d14baebf/prospectusfiledpursuanttorule424.pdf, accessed September 5, 2009.
[2] http://www.carlyle.com/Company/item1676.html, accessed September 5, 2009.
[3] http://www.sequoiacap.com/, accessed September 5, 2009.

difficulties, the pursuit of growth made the firm particularly vulnerable. Consider, for instance, the story of the Buenos Aires-based Exxel Group.[4]

Exxel was established in 1991 by Juan Navarro, a veteran of Citibank, who had first led the bank's efforts to swap its troubled Argentine loans for equity and then maximized the value of these stakes. His first-time fund raised $47 million from sophisticated investors and deployed the money in small buyouts, such as a $22 million consolidation of consumer cleaning product firms, a $15 million stake in a paper products company, and other modest-sized transactions. Exxel closed its $150 million second fund in 1995, and continued with deals that followed the same template.

Shortly thereafter, however, the firm started aggressively pursuing larger transactions, including the $136 million Argencard transaction and the $440 million purchase of Norte Supermarkets. Exxel used three methods to finance these deals. First, it raised special-purpose funds that provided equity for individual transactions; second, it raised progressively larger and more frequent funds, most notably the $867 million Exxel Capital Partners V, which closed in 1998; and finally, it borrowed from banks and the bond markets. On the equity side alone, Exxel raised seven partnerships totaling over $2 billion in special-purpose and traditional funds in the four-and-a-half years through 2000.

With the benefit of hindsight, the timing for this fund-raising binge was problematic. In the early 2000s, Argentina experienced an economic cataclysm: a dramatic economic collapse, a wrenching devaluation, and hyperinflation. This set of circumstances pushed many of the nation's best-run firms into bankruptcy, let alone companies that had been recently acquired in highly leveraged transactions. Indeed, Exxel's pursuit of growth in many respects accentuated the difficulties that the portfolio suffered. Among the problems was the need to finance transactions with dollar-denominated debt, which meant that the amounts the companies owed exploded when the peso was devalued, along with the fact that the portfolio's size and complexity exceeded the fund managers' ability to shape it. There was a strong likelihood that in their eagerness to do deals, Exxel's investors may have overpaid for many of the portfolio companies. While it is impossible to know how well Excel would have done had it grown at a more modest rate, it is hard not to feel they would have far exceeded the rate of return of –45.4 percent that Preqin recorded for Exxel Capital Partners V as of September 30, 2010.

In this chapter, we explore the challenging issues associated with managing the growth of private equity funds. We proceed in two very different ways. First, we consider the quantitative evidence. We present the key facts regarding the ways that the performance of private equity funds changes over the time, and the impacts that growth can have. We begin by highlighting the fact that the performance of private equity funds differs dramatically, with greater variation than that of the managers of other financial assets. We then show that these differences are not random: not only do more established groups have better returns, but there is a lot of persistence; the same groups perform better in fund after fund. But we show the dark side of success as well: raising a substantially larger fund is associated with lower returns. We then turn to understanding why growth may be harmful to private equity returns and explore how choices about a firm's personnel and scope can affect performance.

---

[4] This account is based on Alex Hoye and Josh Lerner, "The Exxel Group: September 1995," HBS Case No. 297-068 (Boston: HBS Publishing, 1997); Alberto Ballve and Josh Lerner, "The Exxel Group: March 2001," HBS Case No. 9-202-053 (Boston: HBS Publishing, 2001); http://www.exxelgroup.com/site/index.html, accessed September 1, 2009; and various press accounts.

We then consider the evidence from in-depth interviews and case studies of private equity groups, highlighting three lessons that emerge. First, growth can create very real strains. Even groups with a long track record of collaboration can encounter many pressures if they dramatically increase fund sizes or broaden their range of offerings. Second, there is no one right approach to institutionalization and scaling. The groups that have successfully navigated this process have taken different routes, although certain shared elements have been present. Finally, despite the natural concerns of the limited partner (LP) community, the process of institutionalization and growth can be managed in a way that benefits everyone.

KEY FACTS ABOUT GROWTH AND SCALING: QUANTITATIVE EVIDENCE

In this section, we look at the quantitative evidence of six dimensions of the scaling and institutionalization of private equity funds. While there is a considerable amount of diversity between the performances of individual funds, the patterns presented here offer a compelling picture of the challenges that growth poses for these organizations. This is a fairly new topic of research—and an exciting one with far-reaching consequences for the industry—so a step-by-step examination of the current findings will inform our later discussion of approaches to managing growth and its implications.

Dispersion

The first key point is that there are extreme disparities in performance between private equity funds, far more so than in other asset classes.

The evidence presented in Chapter 9 might lead one to conclude that private equity returns are, on the whole, pretty unattractive. The average return for private equity barely exceeds the public markets, where one can always just sell the stock. But despite these modest *average* returns for private equity funds (particularly when adjusted for risk and for missing data on poorly performing funds), many private equity sponsors have delivered truly excellent returns. The reason for this apparent paradox is that, when compared to public equity and bond fund managers, there is an extreme dispersion in returns across private equity funds: the differences between the top performers and the underperformers are huge indeed. This difference is masked, of course, in the average.

These points can perhaps be best illustrated by several simple tabulations. Figures 12.1a through 12.1c show the distribution of private equity fund performance from their establishment through 2003. (We eliminate more recent funds because we want to be sure to examine the performance of mature funds. As we have repeatedly highlighted, due to accounting conventions and the inherent difficulty of valuation, assessing the performance of immature funds is challenging. The panels show the performance for all U.S. venture funds, all U.S. buyout funds, and all European private equity funds, as identified by Thomson VentureXpert.)

These figures highlight the range of performance. When we consider U.S. venture capital (VC) funds over their history, the difference between a fund performing at the seventy-fifth percentile (i.e., that is, better than 75 percent of all funds) and one in the twenty-fifth percentile (better than only one-quarter of its peers) is 19 percent (19 vs. 0 percent). The disparities in other classes of private equity, while slightly more modest, are also substantial: for both European and U.S. buyout funds, the relevant difference is 16 percent. The extremes of performance are particularly dramatic for U.S. venture funds, where the top 10 percent of funds are far more successful than their peers. But the wide dispersion of returns seems to be a defining characteristic of private equity worldwide.

This dispersion in private equity returns is particularly unusual compared to other classes of investments. For instance, Yale's Investment Office computed the dispersion of returns among

FIGURE 12.1a Performance of U.S. venture funds

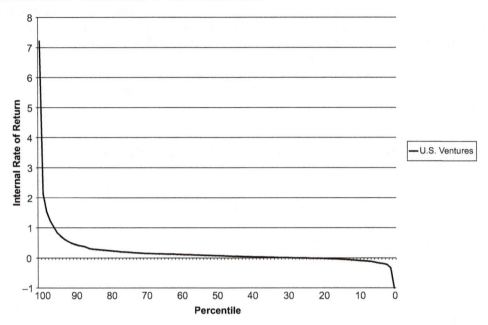

active managers over the decade ending in 2005.[5] (The results are shown in Figure 12.2.) They found that, for most asset classes, the inter-quartile range (the difference between the seventy-fifth and twenty-fifth percentile managers) was far lower than in private equity. For instance, the dispersion for U.S. fixed-income managers was only 0.5 percent—about one-fortieth that of

FIGURE 12.1b Performance of U.S. buyout funds

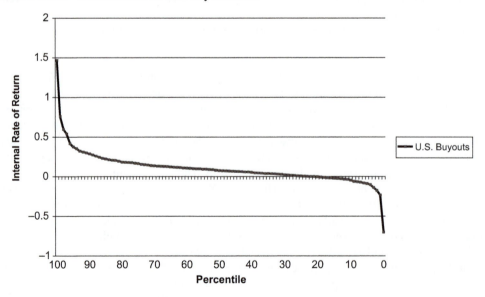

---

[5] Yale University Investments Office, *The Yale Endowment—2006* (New Haven, CT: Investments Office, 2007).

FIGURE 12.1c   Performance of european private equity funds

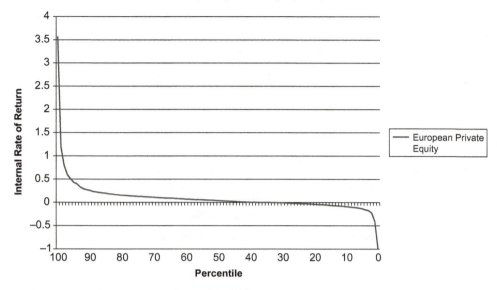

Source: Data from Thomson Reuters, accessed October 15, 2010.

private equity funds. Among U.S. and global stock managers, the differences were still modest. Even in hedge funds, which boast a plethora of investment types and approaches, the difference in performance—just over 7 percent—was considerably lower than in private equity.

Thus, just because the return of the average private equity fund has been modest, that does not mean we should regard private equity funds as questionable performers. The dramatic

FIGURE 12.2   Dispersion of active management returns, decade to June 30, 2005

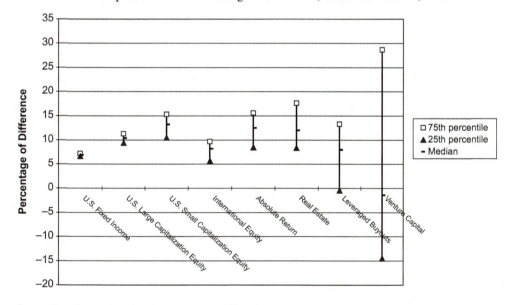

Source: Data from Yale University Investments Office, The Yale Endowment 2005, http://www.yale.edu/investments/Yale_Endowment_05.pdf, p. 36.

FIGURE 12.3 Realized IRR by fund sequence number

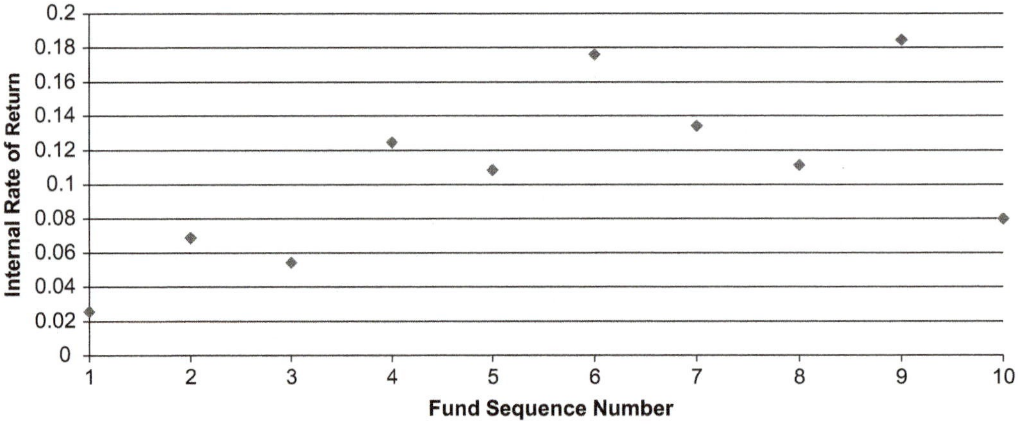

Source: Josh Lerner and Antoinette Schoar, unpublished analysis of Preqin data, 2009.

performance dispersion among funds is so great that it creates opportunities. Whether an entrepreneur is seeking venture funding or a pension fund is looking to invest in a good buyout fund, accessing a good firm makes an enormous difference in the outcome. As noted throughout this book, the source of the money matters. Success begets success—if one can access the successful funds on a consistent basis. This, of course, is a big "if."

Maturity

The second key point is the improvement in fund performance over time: first-time funds are the weakest performers, while others do better. There is, in essence, a learning component to private equity. Just as an investor goes through an apprenticeship, the general partners (GPs) running a fund learn to work together.

This pattern is illustrated in Figure 12.3, which shows the performance of different funds.[6] We compare the performance of first-time funds, second funds, and so forth.[7] We once again limit the analysis to mature funds (those raised through 2003), and use information on all funds in the Preqin database. Clearly, the basic pattern is a steady increase in performance although there is some variation, as we see in Fund VIIIs, which seem to have lower performance. This underperformance might, however, simply reflect the fact that there are a relatively few higher-numbered funds. If the bulk of Fund VIIIs were raised and then invested in a difficult period for investing, the average for all these funds might be depressed.

As the earlier comment suggests, these results do introduce a few concerns. These patterns might be driven by the type of funds or by when they were raised. For instance, if the most mature fund families are venture groups (reflecting the fact that venture capitalists have been around the longest), the differing performance of more mature funds might be driven by the changing mix of funds raised, rather than something inherent about more mature funds. To

---

[6] This analysis, as well as those in the "Getting Big" and "Increasing Capital Intensity" sections below, is based on an unpublished study by Josh Lerner and Antoinette Schoar, as updated by the authors.

[7] One complication is introduced by groups who raise funds of many different types. We consider each fund type that a group raised to be a first fund; thus, although Carlyle has raised many funds in the past, we still count the first Asian buyout fund it raises as a first-time fund.

FIGURE 12.4 Predicted IRR by fund sequence number

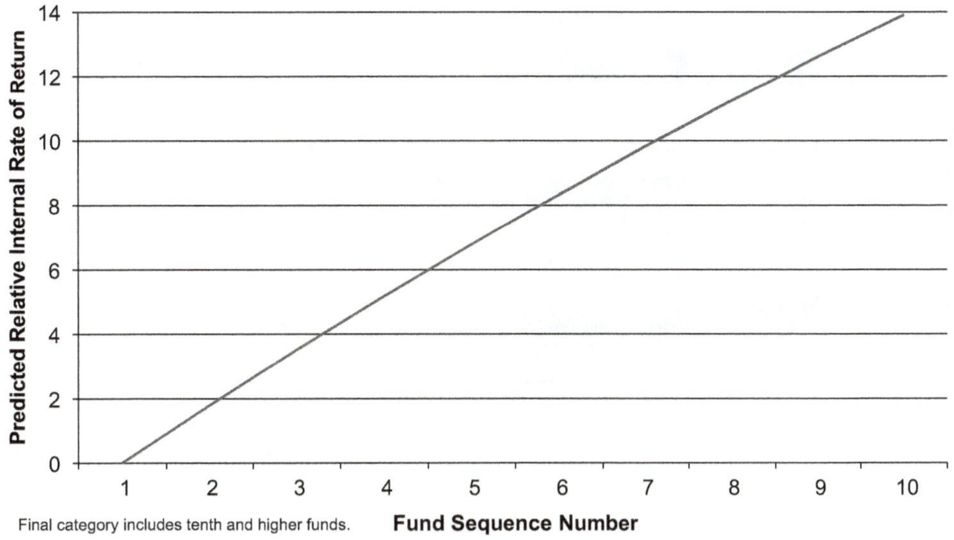

Final category includes tenth and higher funds. **Fund Sequence Number**

Source: Josh Lerner and Antoinette Schoar, unpublished analysis of Preqin data, 2009.

address this concern, we ran a regression whereby we can simultaneously control for a variety of attributes of the funds:

- The type of fund (venture, buyout, growth equity, etc.)
- The year it was raised
- The fund's location (e.g., Europe or Asia)
- The fund's size

Figure 12.4 presents the "bottom line": how, after controlling for these features, performance changes with fund maturity. The fitted line represents the average performance for second, third, and so on funds, all relative to first-time funds. Overall, there is a clear association between maturity and better performance. While the relationship weakens as we move outward, the association is strongly positive.

What this analysis cannot distinguish, however, is *why* this pattern appears. One possibility is that the private equity investors become more effective over time—the apprenticeship model. For instance, greater experience may provide them with better judgment about what makes an attractive investment or deeper relationships with entrepreneurs, investment bankers, and corporate executives that allow them to structure attractive deals and help their portfolio companies. Alternatively, a "Darwinian" effect may be at work. The improvement in performance may be due less to any improvement in the surviving groups than to the inability of many ineffective groups to raise a second or third fund.

Persistence

The third key pattern is persistence—the best managers outperform again and again. An unusual feature of private equity performance returns is that private equity groups with superior performance repeat this in fund after fund. Unlike virtually any other kind of investing, private equity has a tremendous degree of persistence.

FIGURE 12.5 Performance of the next fund based on current fund

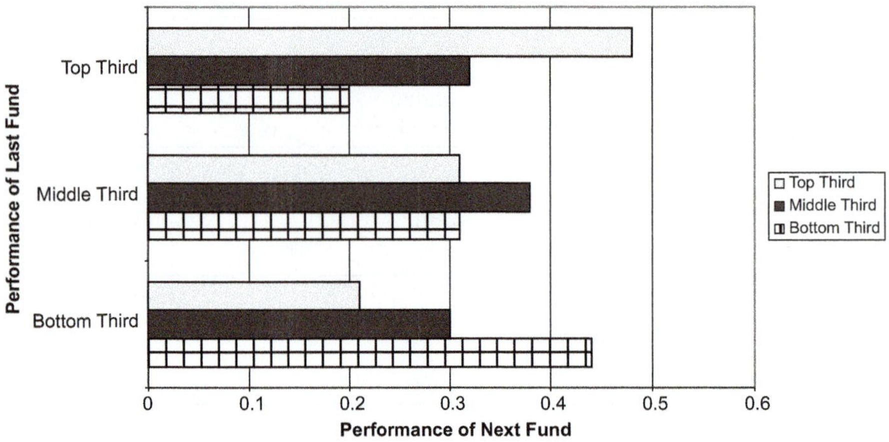

Source: Adapted from Steve Kaplan and Antoinette Schoar, "Private Equity Returns: Persistence and Capital Flows," *Journal of Finance* 60 (2005): 1791–823.

This pattern was documented by Steve Kaplan and Antoinette Schoar, who examined the extent to which outperformance in a sponsor's private equity fund predicted superior returns in subsequent funds.[8] Looking at 746 funds raised between 1980 and 1994, they saw a pattern of strong persistence: a fund that outperformed its peers by 1 percent annually could be expected to beat its rivals in its next funds by somewhere between 0.5 and 0.7 percent per year.

We illustrate these authors' findings in Figure 12.5. Here, they divide the performance of each private equity fund by whether its rate of return was in the top, middle, or bottom third of funds relative to its peers. These are arranged along the vertical axis. They then look at the return of the next fund raised by the group to see whether it was in the top, middle, or bottom third relative to its peers. If there was no persistence of performance, then the bars of the graph would read 33 percent and they would all be even—the probability of being good, bad, or mediocre would be the same, regardless of how well the last fund did. In fact, much of the activity matches the current fund's performance. Private equity groups that have previously outperformed are disproportionately likely (a probability of 48 percent, rather than 33 percent) to do so in their next fund—note the longer white bar for "Top Third," while the laggards, on average, continue to perform poorly (a probability of 44 percent), as seen in the longer checked bar for the bottom group.

One might argue that this persistence was driven only by venture funds. As we discussed in Chapter 11, top venture capitalists have powerful networks of connections and relationships, which help them outperform in fund after fund. Kaplan and Schoar find that while these patterns are strongest among venture funds, they are also present among U.S. buyout groups. In subsequent research, similar patterns have been seen in funds outside the United States and even in more specialized groups such as real estate private equity funds.[9]

---

[8] Steve Kaplan and Antoinette Schoar, "Private Equity Returns: Persistence and Capital Flows," *Journal of Finance* 60 (2005): 1791–823.

[9] See, for instance, Christoph Kaserer and Christian Diller, "What Drives Private Equity Returns?—Fund Inflows, Skilled GPs, and/or Risk?" (CEFS Working Paper No. 2004-2), http://ssrn.com/abstract=590124, accessed September 1, 2009; and Thea C. Hahn, David Geltner, and Nori Gerardo-Lietz, "Real Estate Opportunity Funds," *Journal of Portfolio Management* 31, no. 5 (2005): 143–53.

It is worth noting how unusual these patterns are relative to other categories of investment assets. A substantial literature has examined the persistence of performance in mutual funds—or lack of it. Although financial economists initially believed that mutual fund managers had "hot hands" (i.e., groups that did well in one year were likely to continue to do so in the following years), more sophisticated analytical techniques revealed these as statistical flukes.[10]

Even among hedge funds, which rely on the development of proprietary analytical tools, financial researchers have been able to find little evidence of long-run persistence.[11] There has been some evidence of persistence on a quarterly basis; that is, a hedge fund with superior performance in a given quarter may continue for a second quarter but has no higher performance a half year (two quarters) or one year later. The contrast with private equity—where superior performance has predicted outperformance in funds raised many years later—could not be more dramatic.

Getting Big

The previous two sections might suggest that identifying superior private equity funds is "easy"— all one needs to do is look for established groups with excellent track records. Alas, the answer is not that straightforward, due to one important limitation: sponsors that have been successful in the past frequently expand their capital under management too rapidly. And as we saw in the introduction, a rapid growth in fund size can result in a significant deterioration of investment returns.

The complex relationship between fund size and returns is shown in the next three figures. Figure 12.6 shows the aggregate relationship between fund size and internal rate of return (IRR). Once again, we look at all mature private equity funds raised through 2003 and control for

FIGURE 12.6 Predicted relative IRR and fund size

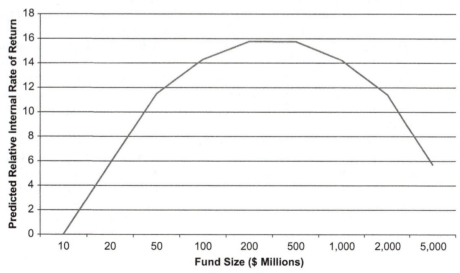

Source: Josh Lerner and Antoinette Schoar, unpublished analysis of Preqin data, 2009.

---

[10] A classic analysis is Mark Carhart, "On Persistence in Mutual Fund Performance," *Journal of Finance* 52 (1997): 57–82.

[11] See, for instance, Stephen J. Brown, William N. Goetzmann, and Roger G. Ibbotson, "Offshore Hedge Funds: Survival and Performance, 1989–95," *Journal of Business* 72 (1999): 91–117.

FIGURE 12.7 Predicted IRR and fund size

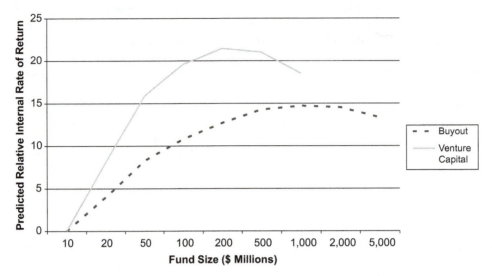

the type of fund and the year the fund was raised. We show how the predicted return changes (relative to an extremely small $10 million fund) as funds get larger, holding everything else the same. The basic relationship is an "inverted U" shape with midsized funds outperforming small ones, but with a deterioration of performance for the very largest funds. The analysis suggests that peak performance occurs for a midsized fund with roughly $300 million under management.[12]

So does that mean we should find a successful group raising $300 million and beg to invest with them? Not entirely—one objection to this analysis is that it conflates many different types of funds: can we really consider regard a seed venture fund and a mega buyout found in the same analysis? Indeed, when we separate venture and buyout funds and predict the relationships between fund size and performance for each, we see that fund size seems to have a greater impact on performance for VC organizations than for buyouts. The inverted U relationship in Figure 12.7 is sharper and more statistically significant for the venture funds. The level of fund size predicted to be associated with peak performance is higher for buyout funds: $1.2 billion versus $280 million for the venture funds.

While there is a noticeable effect of fund size on returns, its magnitude must be said to be modest: a buyout fund of $5 billion, for instance, has a predicted return only 1.2 percent, less than a buyout fund of $2 billion. A firm that consistently raises $5 billion funds would, according to the data, do reasonably well. The problem, according to our analysis, comes from *changes* in fund size, as illustrated in Figure 12.8. Here, we look at the impact of changes in fund size, controlling for the features and skills of each firm and the year and focus of the fund. We find that growth has a substantial negative effect on returns: a doubling of fund size, all else being equal, leads to a drop in IRR of –5.3 percent. This analysis suggests that a group with a 25 percent IRR in its $1 billion third fund could expect a return of less than 20 percent if it raised a $2 billion fund next.

---

[12] Remember we are looking only at funds raised before 2000, in order to have accurate performance data. As a result, our sample contains relatively few very large funds. If these funds are not representative, or if private equity groups have become much better at managing large funds, these results may not hold for more recent periods.

FIGURE 12.8   Change in IRR with change in fund size

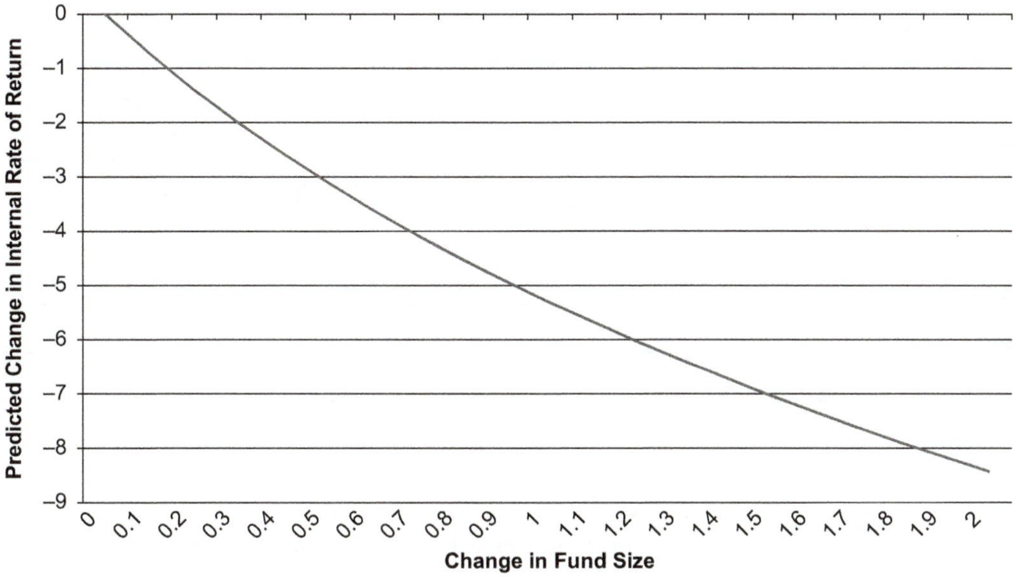

Source: Josh Lerner and Antoinette Schoar, unpublished analysis of Preqin data, 2009.

While our interpretation of this effect's magnitude must be cautious, the implications about the impact of growth seem clear. Large funds do not necessarily perform dramatically worse than small funds, but the process of *getting larger* seems to be associated with a deterioration of returns. Because many of the firms that have grown rapidly have been successful in the past, this pattern limits the persistence documented by Kaplan and Schoar. Were it not for this tendency, they would likely find an even stronger relationship between size and performance.

Human Resource Challenges

The previous section suggests a negative relationship between private equity fund growth and performance but does not explain why this comes about. Normally, we are used to thinking of growing businesses as a good thing: growth allows us to exploit economies of scale by spreading our fixed costs over a larger base of activity. Why is private equity different? While we cannot answer this question definitively, we can provide two clues about what might be behind this relationship, both of them relating to the human dimension of private equity.

More Dollars per Investor

The first of the clues about the relationship between private equity fund growth and performance relates to the investment professionals at the private equity firm. As we have emphasized repeatedly, private equity is very much a "people business," where the connections and experience of the managing partners drive a group's success. In this industry, growth frequently entails more and more money being managed by a slowly growing number of partners. For instance, a buyout fund that has raised a $200 million first-time fund with three partners not uncommonly raises a

FIGURE 12.9 Senior professionals related to fund size

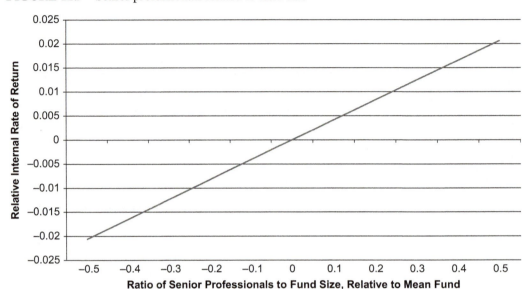

$1 billion third fund with five partners. Given what we saw in Chapter 2 about the economics of fund partnerships—if the two funds have the same level of success, the third fund will generate considerably more income per partner from management and transaction fees as well as from carried interest—the temptations to grow capital per partner are totally understandable. But, as we will see, such a move may not be in the best interest of the LPs or even of the long-term health of the private equity organization.

Figures 12.9 and 12.10 present one way of looking at the impact on returns of the relationship between the number of partners and fund size. The first figure looks at the impact of changing the ratio of senior professionals (which we define here as people with senior investment professional titles, such as managing director, senior executives with roles as operating partners, and the fund's chairman) relative to the size of the latest fund. (Once again, we control for the focus of the fund, the year it was raised, and other factors that may drive fund performance.) As we move from the senior-professional-to-capital ratio of the average fund (0.09) to a ratio that is 25 percent higher (0.11), the expected performance climbs by 1 percent. Similarly, as the ratio of partners to fund size falls, performance deteriorates. We look at buyouts and venture funds separately—as well as large and small funds—in analyses that we do not depict here, and we find similar patterns across the board. That is, with more senior people involved in investment assessment and portfolio company management at the firm, performance improves.

But what if we look at the other levels below senior professionals? After all, as we discussed in Chapter 11, private equity firms have a number of junior investment professionals and even operations staff, all of whom are supposed to extend the senior partners and improve fund performance. Indeed, we did explore that question. In general, having more staff is a good thing, but the effects are very uneven. Funds with more senior partners have sharply higher returns, but the impact of more junior staff seems much lower (and statistically insignificant): the ratio of the two coefficients is nearly 30 to 1. To illustrate this effect, consider the impact of new staff for a modest-sized private equity group consisting of four senior professionals and four other staff (e.g., three analysts and a CFO). Adding one senior professional boosts the expected returns by roughly 2 percent, but adding a junior staff member increases the predicted IRR by only 0.1 percent. Thus, while having more staff seems to translate into higher returns, the critical part of the recipe seems to be the involvement of senior investment professionals.

Some real-world confirmation of this result stems from the experience of a leading venture group during the late 1990s and early 2000s.[13] The last years of the millennium saw fantastic financial success for seasoned VC funds as they quickly "flipped" various Internet and communication deals to eager public investors. Many groups responded by raising funds more frequently (sometimes only twelve months apart, rather than the usual three to five years) and by rapidly increasing fund size. Naturally, many LPs wondered whether these groups could successfully manage such growth.

As they grew, many VC groups responded to LP concerns by expanding their ranks of support staff. One such effort was CRVelocity, launched by one of the leading venture firms, Charles River Ventures. Inaugurated in 2000, CRVelocity provided a variety of business services to the firm's portfolio companies, helping them address financial, marketing, legal, human resources, and information technology issues. The group was staffed by twenty new recruits, professionals who were experienced in their own domains—marketing, accounting, and the like—but not traditional investment professionals. Other venture groups, such as Battery, Mayfield, and Sequoia, launched similar initiatives at the time.

Within two years, however, Charles River Ventures and many of its competitors abandoned these efforts. First, there was the matter of the substantial direct cost of the programs, particularly after the market for venture-backed initial public offerings (IPOs) declined in late 2000 and the frenetic pace of venture investment ebbed. In addition, the implementation of this strategy raised a variety of challenges, particularly how to define the roles of each party, ensure timely and accurate information flows, and provide the proper incentives for everyone involved. In many cases, for instance, start-ups wanted to use their existing outside counsel, or the one with particular expertise, rather than the in-house lawyers hired by the venture groups. In this case, although the addition of in-house support staff initially seemed to make perfect sense, the move probably decreased returns to the LPs.

Increasing Scope

A second reason that growth may be associated with decreased returns is a loss of focus at private equity groups. Even for very seasoned private equity professionals and groups, transferring the skills that made them successful in one area to another arena may be difficult. Examples abound of venture capitalists in a narrow niche, such as alternative energy and advanced materials, who moved into more general investing without much success. Even in the buyout realm, groups who built their reputation on one type of deal may find it hard to transfer their skills elsewhere.

One cautionary illustration is the experience of Hicks, Muse, Tate & Furst (HMTF).[14] Despite an enviable track record and the presence of Thomas Hicks (one of the legendary private equity investors) as lead partner, the group stumbled badly when it expanded.

HMTF was founded after Hicks's success in partnership with Robert Haas as Hicks & Haas, best known for its purchase of Dr Pepper's Texas bottling operations for an enterprise value of

---

[13] The next three paragraphs are based on Paul Gompers, Ann Leamon, and Josh Lerner, "CRVelocity," HBS Case No. 201-092 (Boston: HBS Publishing, 2001).

[14] The next four paragraphs are based on Josh Lerner, "Acme Investment Trust: January 2001," HBS Case no. 9-202-055 (Boston: HBS Publishing, 2002).

$100 million in 1985. When combined with subsequent acquisitions, this enterprise was sold to Cadbury Schweppes in 1995 for $2.5 billion. HMTF employed the then-uncommon "buy and build" strategy. The fund would acquire a well-run "platform" company, typically far from the northeastern United States where many buyout firms concentrated, and then add smaller acquisitions. The buyout of DuPont's electronics supplier business (subsequently renamed Berg Electronics) illustrated the group's approach. The buyout group, working in conjunction with management, made eight add-on acquisitions over five years. During this period, the firm's earnings before interest, tax, depreciation, and amortization (EBITDA) increased nearly four times over, and its equity value increased more than thirteenfold.

But in the late 1990s, HMTF aggressively moved into new lines of business, and trouble soon followed. First, it embarked on an international strategy. The private equity group had raised a Latin American fund with committed capital of $960 million in 1998, and a €1.5 billion European fund in 1999. While the European group thrived, the Latin group made a series of investments that provided a major source of distraction. Secondly, even at home in the United States, its larger investment size involved the firm in other deals that encountered difficulties; most notably, its investment with Kohlberg, Kravis, Roberts & Co. (KKR) into Regal Cinemas, the third-largest movie chain in the United States, ended in bankruptcy.

But the bulk of HMTF's troubles had stemmed from investments made in 1999 and 2000 that differed from those it had made previously. In particular, the firm had invested approximately $1.2 billion in broadband communications and technology service firms. Not only were the industries different, but these were private investments in public equities (PIPE) transactions, which involved the purchase of minority stakes in publicly listed companies. As the technology market collapsed, most of these investments rapidly fell in value. This series of disappointments— and the fact that they appeared to grow out of the firm's deviation from its previous focus—led to a dramatic restructuring, including the wholesale replacement of key partners and a sharp reduction in capital under management.

Like so much in private equity, though, these are merely anecdotes. Interesting as they are, can we actually generalize from them? Paul Gompers, Anna Kovner, and Josh Lerner sought to test these anecdotes by examining how the specialization of firms and performance affects the performance of VC funds.[15] In a departure from analyses like those discussed earlier in the chapter, the authors focused on the performance of individual transactions rather than the returns of funds as a whole. Using a database of 11,000 investments made up to 2003 by more than eight hundred VC organizations, they determined the degree of specialization or generalization of each by examining the diversity of deals across nine broad industry categories. More precisely, they computed for each organization and partner the sum of the squares of the percentage of all previous investments in each industry.

The authors found that generalist firms tend to underperform relative to specialist firms. Generalist firms appear to fail on two fronts: they do not appear to allocate capital well across industries (e.g., picking "hot" sectors to invest in), and they also underperform in their investments within an industry. Importantly, however, this underperformance is far less if the individual venture capitalists in generalist firms are industry specialists. Thus, if 50 percent of the transactions of a generalist firm with generalist people were acquired or went public in a typical year, the success rate of an equivalent firm with more specialized people would be 52.7 percent in that year. Meanwhile, a specialized firm with specialized people would have the most exits, with a success rate of 54.2 percent.

Despite this pattern, venture groups tend to become *less* specialized over time, as do the individual partners. This result is shown in Figure 12.10, which displays the shifting specialization

---

[15] Paul Gompers, Anna Kovner, and Josh Lerner, "Specialization and Success: Evidence from Venture Capital," *Journal of Economics and Management Strategy* 18 (2009): 817–44.

FIGURE 12.10   Venture capital firm specialization over time

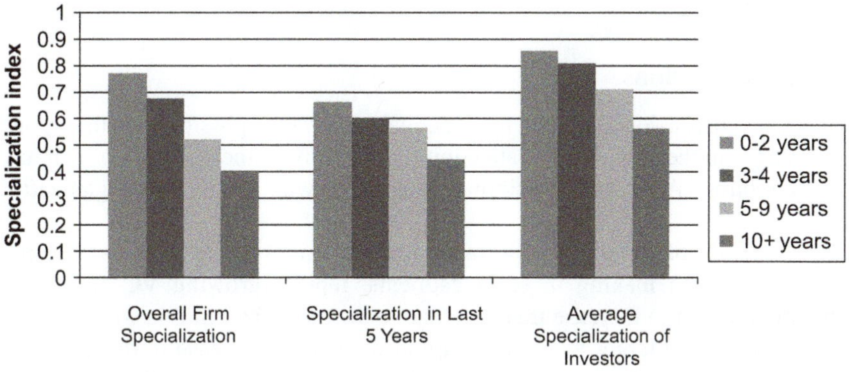

Source: Paul Gompers, Anna Kovner, and Josh Lerner, "Specialization and Success: Evidence from Venture Capital,"
Journal of Economics and Management Strategy 18 (2009): 817–44.

of venture groups. On a scale of zero (least specialized) to one, the typical fund under two years old
has a specialization index of 0.77; the same group when ten years or older has a specialization
index of 0.40.[16] That is, if the partner focused solely on companies in a single industry, the index
would be 1.0; if the partner split his investments equally between three industries, the index would
be 0.33. We see the same pattern when we look at investments over the past five years and at the
specialization of individual partners. This pattern likely reflects the consequences of growth—as
groups struggle to deploy more capital, the partners move into sectors, deal types, or transaction
sizes further from their original expertise.

KEY FACTS ABOUT GROWTH AND SCALING: CASE STUDY EVIDENCE

Previously, we have focused on the statistical evidence. We have shown that there is an enormous
difference across the performance of funds as well as clear patterns behind this diversity. More
mature funds tend to do better; in particular, these are seasoned funds that have done well in the
past. But this tendency is limited by the effects of growth: in a sort of Faustian bargain, if firms take
advantage of their success to raise dramatically larger funds, their performance is likely to decline.
The data suggest that this decline is associated with an increase of dollars managed per partner as
well as a loss of focus.

But this kind of statistical evidence can give us only the broad patterns. Given that this is so,
how do firms react? To better understand how groups effectively manage growth, we need to turn
to the "real world." Although we must refer to case studies rather than statistical evidence, they can
give a better sense of the trade-offs associated with scaling and institutionalization.

In looking over the experience of many groups, three lessons are obvious:

1. Growth can introduce severe strains on organizations, even if they have been working
   together successfully before.

2. While there are shared best practices across successful private equity groups, there are
   many different ways to implement such practices successfully.

---

[16] These indices are again the sum of the squared industry shares (more technically, Herfindahl indices) described earlier.
  This pattern holds whether one looks at all investments by the funds or only the ones they have made recently.

3. Despite the fears of LPs, the process of institutionalization and growth can be managed in a way that benefits everyone.

Growth Can Introduce Tensions

Why might the adjustment costs associated with more capital occur? One possibility is that growth frequently leads to changes in the way that private equity groups invest their capital, which has a deleterious effect on returns. A second possibility is that growth strains the organizations themselves.

First, consider the types of pressures that rapid growth imposes on the private equity investment process. Rather than making more investments, rapidly growing VC and buyout organizations frequently attempt to increase their average investment size. In this way, the same number of partners can manage a larger amount of capital without an increase in the number of portfolio companies on whose boards each must serve. But as the Exxel case in the introduction suggests, this change can bring with it many costs as the organization moves away from its "sweet spot" where it has the most access to transactions and ability to add value.

The shift to larger investments often entails changes in the structure of transactions as well. For instance, many VC groups, eager to put money to work more quickly, will make larger up-front capital commitments to companies in lieu of staged investments. This change can potentially reduce the investor's ability to control the firm using staged capital commitments. Similarly, venture firms often syndicate less with their peers during times of rapid growth. By not syndicating, venture groups can put more money to work more quickly. As the sole investor, each partner can invest more capital but restrain the number of companies for which he is responsible to a manageable level. But as we saw in Chapter 3, sharing a deal with other firms (syndication) can have a number of advantages, such as helping to reduce the danger of costly investment mistakes by providing a second opinion and expanding the network of contacts that the company can access. By increasing the number of sole investments, a firm and the particular portfolio company lose these advantages.

Other tensions around growth relate to pressures on the organization. Limited and general partners may underestimate the consequences of expanding the scale (and the scope) of the fund. An essential characteristic of VC and buyout organizations has always been the speed with which decisions can be made and the parallel incentives that motivate both parties. Expanding the fund can weaken the bonds that tie the partnership into a cohesive whole. These issues can be particularly severe if a private equity group expands into different product lines, such as mezzanine, hedge fund, or real estate investing. The compensation practices, deal assessment and approval processes, and time frames of these various asset classes are likely to be very different, thus increasing the challenge of managing the investment group.

One dramatic illustration of these challenges is the experience of Schroder Ventures.[17] Schroder's private equity effort began in 1985 with funds focused on British VC and buyout investments. Over time, however, the firm added funds focusing on other markets, such as France and Germany, and on particular technologies, such as life sciences. The venture capitalists—and the institutional investors backing them—realized that there were substantial opportunities in these other markets.

But as the venture organization grew, substantial management challenges emerged. In particular, it became increasingly difficult to monitor the investment activities of each fund. This was a real concern since the parent organization served as the GP of each fund and thus was ultimately liable for any losses. Each fund saw itself as an autonomous entity and, in some cases,

---

[17] This account is derived from Kate Bingham, Nick Ferguson, and Josh Lerner, "Schroder Ventures: Launch of the Euro Fund," HBS Case No. 9-297-026 (Boston: HBS Publishing, 1996), and assorted press accounts.

resisted cooperating (and sharing capital gains) with the others. The informal ties that held the partners together in the firm's earliest days began unraveling as many new staff members were added and the pace of business reduced personal interactions. While the organization eventually restructured and raised a single fund for all of Europe, the process of change was slow and painful.

These tensions are by no means confined to international private equity organizations. Very similar tensions have appeared in rapidly growing U.S.-based groups between GPs specializing in different domains—life sciences and information technology—and even between those located in different regions. In some instances, one of these groups has become convinced that the other is getting a disproportionate share of rewards in light of their relative investment performances. In others, it has become difficult to coordinate and oversee activities. As noted earlier in the book, the degree to which these differences can be accommodated is influenced by whether the firm shares carry on the royalty model or the insurance model described in Chapter 11, and whether it is organized to support a star or a team.

In some cases, these tensions have broken groups apart. For instance, in August 1999, Institutional Venture Partners and Brentwood Venture Capital—venture funds that had each invested about $1 billion over several decades with a dual life sciences and information technology strategy—announced their intentions to restructure. The information technology and life sciences venture capitalists from each firm would join with each other to form two new VC groups. Palladium Venture Capital would exclusively pursue health-care transactions, while Redpoint Ventures would focus on Internet and broadband infrastructure investments. Press accounts suggested the decision was largely driven by the dissatisfaction of some of the information technology partners at the firms, who felt that their stellar performance had not been appropriately recognized.[18]

In other cases, a key partner—often dissatisfied with her role or compensation—has departs from a venture or buyout group, entailing a substantial disruption to the organization. Frequently, such departures can trigger a "key man" clause in the agreement between the LPs and GPs. The resulting negotiations can impel the remaining GPs to offer concessions to the LPs (e.g., reduced management fees) to mollify their concerns about the fund's ability to perform as promised in the private placement memorandum (PPM). In some cases, investors may successfully demand that the fund return their capital and cease investing. For instance, Foster Capital Management returned $200 million after several junior partners departed in 1998.[19] In other cases, groups can survive a departure—but only after tense times, such as when Jon Moulton departed Alchemy Capital in 2009. Before he founded Alchemy, Moulton had previously departed Apax, CVC, and Permira on strained terms. In a letter to LPs, Moulton announced his intention to step down thirteen months earlier than planned and urged them not to support his handpicked successor and to close the firm he had established in 1997.[20]

To a great extent, these personnel challenges reflect the fact that in private equity, the role of certain individuals is critical, to an extent that is much greater than in other professional service firms. It would be hard to imagine one or two partners defecting from Goldman Sachs, for instance, and competing effectively against their old employer in most lines of business. The lack of capital reserves, a deep research department, and much of the other infrastructure of a global investment bank would pose too much of a hurdle. In private equity, however, because a few deal makers are critical to the investment process, defecting groups can soon emerge as formidable competitors.

---

[18] David G. Barry and David M. Toll, "Brentwood, IVP Find Health Care, High Tech Don't Mix," *Private Equity Analyst* 9 (1999): 1, 29–32.

[19] "Foster Management Moves to Dissolve Consolidation Fund," *Private Equity Analyst* 8 (1998): 6.

[20] James Mawson and Marietta Cauchi, "Moulton Resigns from Alchemy Partners," *Wall Street Journal*, September 4, 2009.

One Size Does Not Fit All

A second crucial point is that there is no one right approach to managing the process of institutionalization. Private equity groups have tried numerous approaches to fund management—and succeeded.

This comment should not be construed to imply that successful private equity groups do not share certain characteristics. Throughout the chapters in this volume, we have highlighted features that characterize effectively run private equity organizations. One way to summarize the features of effective private equity is to highlight a broad set of four features:

1. *Mission and governance (see Chapter 11).* The organization has a well-defined, explicit mission that is communicated and understood throughout the organization. The key sources of competitive differentiation are understood by LPs and internally; and the roles for such factors as the executive committee, the investment committee, the deal teams, and the advisory board are clearly defined.

2. *Investment philosophy and strategy (see Chapter 3).* An overarching philosophy drives the choice of investment themes and strategies, which shapes not just strategic decisions to allocate capital but also the evaluation of new investments and existing deals against this philosophy. The firm's competitive positioning is widely understood and appreciated, and strong networks have been developed with entrepreneurs, co-investors, and others.

3. *Structure and processes (see Chapters 3 through 6).* The investment process is well defined with full accountability and transparency; the firm has the ability to tap into internal and external research resources; there is ongoing monitoring of the workload on team members as well as a clear risk management role (whether quantitative or qualitative). Functions such as human resources and information technology support are well developed.

4. *Culture and compensation (see Chapter 11).* The firm seeks to develop a portfolio of human talent, combining deal-making and operating skills; the incentives are high-powered and aligned with the firm's long-run goals; performance assessments have well-defined and agreed criteria for promotion; and the firm is a meritocracy, but with a collegial culture and honest and transparent communication.

Within these broad guidelines, though, room exists for many variants, and very successful private equity organizations can end up looking very different from each other.

One illustration of how different groups can be, and still be very successful, is the private equity firm Warburg Pincus.[21] Warburg Pincus grew out of E.M. Warburg & Co. (a very small private investment counseling firm founded in 1939 by Eric Warburg), which merged in 1966 with Lionel I. Pincus & Co. The merged company took the name E.M. Warburg, Pincus & Co. and, with John Vogelstein's arrival in 1967, set out to bring a "professionalized approach" to private equity. Between 1971 and 2010, the firm had raised twelve funds and over $40 billion, and for all but two funds, performance had exceeded the benchmark.

Warburg Pincus invests across the spectrum of company stages, divided roughly equally among VC, growth capital, and buyouts. Geographically, it is also diversified, with offices in Beijing, Frankfurt, Hong Kong, London, Mumbai, Menlo Park, New York, Shanghai, and Tokyo. The target sectors are diverse and include real estate, media, communications, financial services, information technology, health care, energy, industrials, consumer goods, and retail.

The firm has developed several organizational features that differ sharply from those of many other successful "mega groups." In particular, it is characterized by an extremely flat structure.

---

[21] This discussion is drawn from Felda Hardymon, Ann Leamon, and Josh Lerner, "Warburg Pincus and EMGS: The IPO Decision (A)," HBS Case 9-807-092 (Boston: HBS Publishing, 2007).

A seventeen-member executive team coordinates activities across sectors and geographies on a macro level. The idea is to take advantage of geopolitical trends and economic growth in specific areas, thus positioning the firm to move on interesting opportunities.

But Warburg Pincus's deal approval process occurs in a decentralized way. The partners involved in a particular area oversee the decision unless the investment is difficult or of particularly large scale. The executive group discusses each deal early in the process at a high level, but senior partners are involved primarily in a consultative role. Although the deal team partners are responsible for the decision, they do not work alone. The team involves other investment professionals in the firm in everything from informal "hallway conversations" to formal meetings with the company as deemed necessary. Only *after* the investment has been made does the investment team publish a detailed memo to the rest of the firm describing the specific investment and highlighting its upside potential and downside risks. In most other large-scale private equity firms, the deal approval process is much more centralized and the investment memo is written before the deal is approved.

Another area in which Warburg Pincus differs substantially from its peers is compensation structure. The firm has never taken deal and other transaction fees, which it believes keeps partner interests closely aligned with those of the management teams. Moreover, compensation is remarkably flat throughout the organization: partners invest in each fund but not in individual deals, and carry is not paid by office or sector. Rather, carry comes "off the same plate." All the partners have a strong incentive to help each other because their compensation is inexorably linked.

Certainly, many of Warburg's peers would argue that this approach might not work successfully for other firms. For instance, many groups believe the discipline of a formal review by an investment committee before a deal is completed prevents chaos, that providing deal-specific rewards allows them to retain high-achieving investment professionals more effectively, and that transaction fees are necessary to ensure the economics of the funds (though the evidence presented in Chapter 2 might lead us to approach this final claim somewhat skeptically). Clearly, the Warburg Pincus model would not work for every successful group. But the truly essential point is that it works for Warburg Pincus.

DESPITE LIMITED PARTNER FEARS, GROWTH CAN BE HELPFUL

Given these anecdotes, it is not surprising that LPs are wary of plans by private equity groups to expand their fund sizes and lines of business. Typically, it is clear how the GP benefits from such changes: more capital under management, more fees, and more carried interest. But are the changes an appropriate way to treat the LPs, many of whom may have backed the group from its earliest days?

Many of the LPs' concerns revolve around the organizational challenges highlighted in the previous section. The process of growing a private equity group poses real problems, which are likely to absorb a lot of management attention. Given how so much fund performance is driven by a few actors, their distraction with internecine conflicts can substantially affect returns. If the star investor shifts her focus from investing to supervising, isn't this likely to degrade performance?

A second worry is that growth may lead to an even more one-sided relationship between LPs and GPs. As we highlighted in Chapter 2 and elsewhere, many LPs feel that while VC and buyout investments may generate substantial value, most of the wealth created through this process ends up in the hands of GPs rather than LPs. By acquiescing to a process of expansion, LPs may be making this disparity worse:

- In many cases, as groups expand, the dollars managed per partner increase, as we noted earlier. These additional funds translate into more fee income per partner. Many LPs worry that this increased income will blunt the incentives of carried interest to create fund-wide value.

- In a number of cases, LPs have felt obliged to invest in new product offerings, lest they jeopardize their access to the group's flagship fund. To cite one example, Yale declined to invest in some funds launched in the past few years by the top-tier venture firm Sequoia, including a 2005 fund focused on Chinese companies. In response, Sequoia later "oust[ed] Yale from its partner group," according to a September 2006 internal Yale review of the endowment's private equity portfolio.[22] Many worry that such pressures represent another "tax" on LPs that will further drag down their returns.

- LPs worry about cross-subsidization issues. For instance, to boost a new fund focusing on later-stage investments, the parent fund might let its subsidiary co-invest at very modest valuations in some transactions done by its early-stage fund. Such transactions would not only be unfair to the LPs in the earlier-stage fund but also might introduce dissension into the partnership.

These worries are only compounded by the historic track record of groups that have expanded. One often-discussed case is Bain Capital, which had built a spectacular track record over the decades after its founding in 1984. By 1994, the firm had $500 million under mangement, almost fifteen times its original $37 million fund. With such successes as Staples and the spin-out of Gartner Group to its credit, Bain claimed annual returns in excess of 50 percent in its first decade. Four years later, after executing 115 investments in 14 years, the firm had an average annualized return of 113 percent, and 60 of those transactions produced returns in excess of 200 percent. With such performance, Bain raised a $1.5 billion fund that closed in July 1998 with a 30 percent carried interest, 50 percent higher than the industry standard 20 percent.[23] But over time, the firm established a wide variety of satellite operations. In addition to affiliates in Asia, Europe, and India, it launched a variety of funds including

- Absolute Return Capital, Bain's absolute return affiliate, which manages assets in fixed income, equity, and commodity markets

- Bain Capital Ventures, the VC arm of Bain Capital, which focuses on seed through late-stage growth equity investing

- Brookside Capital, the public equity affiliate of Bain Capital

- Sankaty Advisors, the fixed-income affiliate of Bain Capital, and a market-leading private manager of high-yield debt obligations

While assigning causation is always tricky—many factors may lead to disappointing returns in the short run—some critics have attributed the decline in Bain's relative performance to the distractions brought about from managing such a complex array of funds. For instance, Bain's Fund IX, which closed on $8 billion plus a $2 billion co-investment fund in April 2006, produced an IRR of –46 percent as of 2010 compared to a benchmark of –9.97 percent; and in April 2009, Bain wrote down the value of its portfolio by 46 percent from the level a year before. Bain's 2008-vintage $10 billion Fund X, while still early in its life, had written down 15 percent of its value year over year as of April 2009.[24]

Thus, there are certainly grounds for concern about the diversification efforts of private equity groups. But at the same time, there are also compelling reasons for firms to expand. Perhaps the

[22] Rebecca Buckman, "Venture Firms vs. Investors: Yale and the Like Quietly Cite Pressure to Back Offbeat Funds," *Wall Street Journal*, August 28, 2007.

[23] Erica Copulsky, "Gadzooks!—The Super LBO Players Increasingly are Those That are Expanding Their Reach," *Investment Dealers' Digest*, August 17, 1998, 1; and David D. Kirkpatrick, "Romney's Fortunes Tied to Business Riches," *New York Times*, June 4, 2007, http://www.nytimes.com/2007/06/04/us/politics/04bain.html, accessed November 26, 2010.

[24] Data from Pitchbook, http://www.pitchbook.com, accessed November 26, 2010.

most important is the possibility of synergies. Blackstone's real estate group, for instance, can help its private equity group when assessing a potential investment in a property-rich company or when working with management after the transaction. The real estate group, if properly incentivized, can bring a fresh perspective on adding value to the firm, as well as additional connections that can be valuable. More generally, product extensions may allow a private equity group to translate a set of market insights into positive investment opportunities in a variety of settings. Growth can also enable the firm to gain greater scale, allowing it to make investments in research and information technology that might not have been possible otherwise.

There are some additional rationales for expansion. Some LPs—particularly some of the larger ones—desire a "one-stop shop," where they can deploy a large amount of money in one fell swoop. Other institutional investors disagree; they liken such offers to buying "the multi-pack at Costco when you only like one flavor" and state their preference for investing in the "best of class" in each asset type rather than suboptimizing for the sake of transactional efficiency. Yet such efficiency may be quite attractive to entrepreneurs. For instance, a growth equity group with an in-house mezzanine fund or credit facility may be more appealing to a manager who would otherwise have to establish a relationship with two separate organizations. Another advantage of expansion is that it can address many of the difficult personnel issues discussed in Chapter 11. In a rapidly growing firm, the desire of the younger partners for a significant share of the economics can be accommodated without engendering (hopefully) too much resistance from the more senior partners. Moreover, from the firm's perspective, growth allows it to accommodate brighter people rather than training them and losing them to competitors. Finally, if the new fund is counter-cyclical to the existing one (for instance, a distressed debt fund would likely be active at times when private equity was depressed), it can help the group survive fallow periods without painful layoffs.

Whatever the virtues of these arguments, there are clearly right and wrong ways to approach product extensions. Several areas can be highlighted as best practices:

- Product extensions work best when they naturally support the group's current product line. In these cases, the synergies highlighted earlier are most likely to exist, and the firm's reputation from its existing activities is more likely to carry over to the new activities. Examples include the successful efforts by a number of British private equity groups to invest in continental Europe as well as the United Kingdom, and a number of emerging market growth equity groups moving to offer products that involved public market investments. In each case, the differences between the old and new activities were relatively modest, and the groups could build a plausible case for how their existing skill sets could give them a competitive advantage in this new arena. Moreover, these funds are often the easiest to raise since the private equity group's existing activities may illustrate its ability to add value in this new arena.

- Activities that represent a departure from the firm's existing ones should be located in a separate fund. Not only does this limit the danger of conflicts of interest, but it allows for compensation to be customized if practices differ across the groups. Such a stand-alone structure also allows the group's existing investors to opt out if they are uncomfortable with the new fund. To maintain goodwill and trust with the firm's LPs, these new funds should be raised without pressuring the existing investors.

- The fund's expansion must be accompanied by a substantial rethinking of the firm's internal structure to ensure that it supports the process.

- Acquisitions of other groups represent a plausible way to expand into other product lines. In recent years, we have seen not just acquisitions by large funds (e.g., Blackstone acquiring $3.2 billion in debt funds from Allied Capital in 2010) but also numerous smaller transactions, including many by funds based in emerging markets.[25] These transactions enable a group to "hit the ground running" by beginning with a team, a track record, and a number of LPs in the new area. As a result, the process can be considerably less disruptive than attempting to build a new product line from scratch.

- Coupling expansion of the private equity fund with the introduction or strengthening of LP-friendly partnership terms. The concerns of the institutional investors about the expansion of private equity groups were discussed at length earlier in this chapter. One way to head off these issues is to combine an expansion initiative with the addition of provisions that are likely to please the LPs. These include economic terms perceived to be LP-friendly, such as rebating of all the transaction and monitoring fees to the investors and stronger clawback provisions that ensure timely adjustment of the LPs' distributions if investments prove to be subsequently disappointing (see Chapter 2 for a discussion). Governance provisions, particularly the establishment of empowered advisory committees for each fund where the investors can meet in executive sessions and have access to independent legal and accounting advice, are also important. More generally, an emphasis on clear communication and accountability can go a long way toward addressing investors' concerns.

FINAL THOUGHTS

We have focused in this chapter on the process by which VC and buyout firms grow, and the implications of these changes for performance. The picture that emerges is of a process that, although quite challenging, can be managed effectively with enough careful thought and planning.

The quantitative evidence paints a two-sided picture. On the one hand, the performances of individual private equity funds display a great deal of diversity, far more than is seen in other classes of investments. Also unlike other arenas, a considerable amount of persistence is seen from fund to fund: the same groups tend to outperform (or underperform) over many years. Moreover, all else being equal, established groups tend to outperform their newer peers.

But we then show that all else is *not* equal. Many successful groups raise considerably larger funds over time on the basis of their track records. And being big is not only hazardous to returns—midsized venture and buyout funds outperform their larger and smaller peers in general—but *getting big* is frequently associated with disappointment: raising a substantially larger fund seems to lead to lower returns. Much of this deterioration in performance is associated with the fact that the partners in rapidly growing firms seem to try to do too much. Performance falls particularly sharply as each partner manages more capital and the individual investment professionals' scope of investment broadens—two patterns frequently associated with firm growth.

We also drew in this chapter on conversations and case studies about institutionalization and growth in VC and buyout funds. This evidence highlights the very real strains that can emerge as private equity firms grow. At the same time, the evidence indicates that there is room for optimism: firms can address their investors' fears and grow in an intelligent manner that is likely to be much less disruptive to their mission. While there is not a one-size-fits-all recipe for growth—firms have taken very different approaches to growing successfully—certain common hallmarks characterize the firms that have managed the expansion process without major disruptions.

To make this process even more challenging, expansion decisions are frequently taken against the backdrop of a rapidly evolving private equity market. The changing environment, and

---

[25] Walden Siew, "Blackstone to Take over Some Allied Capital Funds," Reuters News Service, January 21, 2010. For an example of an emerging market transaction, see "Abraaj Capital to Buy Riyada Ventures, Focus on SME investments," http://www.altassets.com/private-equity-news/by-region/middle-east-israel/middle-east/article/nz17381.html, accessed June 7, 2010.

particularly the sequence of booms and busts as investors rush into and out of particular areas, makes the management of firm growth considerably harder. These issues are the focus of Chapter 13.

QUESTIONS

1. Why are there extreme disparities in performance among private equity funds relative to disparities in performance among other asset classes?

2. The evidence indicates that first-time funds tend to be the weakest performers; why would someone want to invest in one?

3. Why do subsequent funds tend to outperform their predecessors? Is there a correlation between performance and maturity?

4. If performance persists, why would anyone ever invest in a mid- or bottom-tier fund?

5. If you were a GP in a mid- or bottom-tier fund, how would you position yourself to raise funds?

6. As a lower-tier fund, how would you go about improving your performance?

7. Explain why private equity groups that have outperformed their peers are more likely to continue to do so in subsequent finds. How is this different for VC and buyout funds?

8. Relative to other asset classes, are private equity fund performances more predictable? How is this different for the overall asset class?

9. What are some of the reasons that private equity firms that grow too quickly often see deterioration in their returns?

10. From an LP's perspective, when does it make sense for a private equity firm to grow?

11. What happens to the compensation structure of a partner (as it relates to the traditional 2 percent fee and 20 percent carried interest) as the assets under management per partner grows? What happens to the alignment of interests among LPs and GPs?

12. What key missteps were made by Hicks, Muse, Tate & Furst as the firm expanded? What happened to their fund performance, and how did their LPs react?

13. Over time, why do VC groups tend to become less specialized? Is this more common for funds focused on certain sectors than others?

14. What are some common characteristics of successfully run private equity firms? Which do you view as the most important?

15. How does the Warburg Pincus model differ from that of other mega funds? What are some of the barriers to other firms replicating this model?

16. Provide an example of how synergies may be possible for private equity groups across funds.

Chapter 13

Boom and Bust

As the short history in Chapter 1 suggested, booms and busts have been part of the landscape of venture capital (VC) and buyouts since their earliest days. In many senses, cycles can be seen as a defining element of the private equity landscape. In this chapter, we try to understand the causes and consequences of these cycles as well as the appropriate responses to these shifts.

To briefly review, in the United States the late 1960s, the early 1980s, and the late 1990s all saw VC booms, the last of which was felt worldwide. Each boom saw dramatic increases in the amount of funds raised, along with the entry of numerous new venture funds and a flurry of financing activity. Each boom was followed by a painful correction that led to a sharp reduction in the level of financing, the failure of numerous firms, and predictions that the days of the venture industry were numbered. More recently, venture markets have boomed in markets such as China and India, and it is hard not to feel that same process of adjustment must inevitably follow.

On the buyout side, the patterns have been similar, but the stakes are much larger due to the size of the funds involved. The 1980s saw a dramatic increase in transaction activity and size in the United States and Western Europe (particularly Great Britain); the mid-2000s saw a worldwide explosion in activity. These ended in ugly corrections that were driven both by economic downturns and a realization of the extent of the excesses that had come before.

The problematic legacy of the most recent buyout boom is perhaps best captured by the story of Simmons Mattress, a century-old Wisconsin-based bedding company.[1] It was owned by a series of private equity groups over a twenty-year period: first, in 1986, the firm was purchased by Wesray, which sold it to the employees in 1989; then, in 1991, it was purchased (at a substantial discount) by Merrill Lynch Capital Partners, which in 1996 sold it to Investcorp; and in 1998, it was sold to Fenway Partners. As it moved from owner to owner, the firm took on increasing levels of debt (see Figure 13.1).

But the level of indebtedness spiraled upward after 2003, when TH Lee purchased the firm from Fenway for $1.1 billion, of which $327 million was equity and the remainder debt. While the company had hits and misses in its operation over the ensuing years, its debt load steadily climbed, from $750 million at the time of the buyout to over $1.25 billion in 2008. This level of indebtedness raised concern from analysts even at the time of the transaction. Much of the proceeds from these loans went to its owner: during its tenure, TH Lee reviewed special dividends totaling $375 million and nearly another $30 million in fees. While none of these transactions was unusual at the time, it led to the inability for Simmons to cope once the economic downturn hit. In 2008, after extensive layoffs, the company filed for bankruptcy.

---

[1] This account is based on Julie Creswell, "Profits for Buyout Firms as Company Debt Soared," *New York Times*, October 4, 2009, and filings with the U.S. Securities and Exchange Commission by Simmons Mattress.

FIGURE 13.1 Simmons bedding's owners and debt load

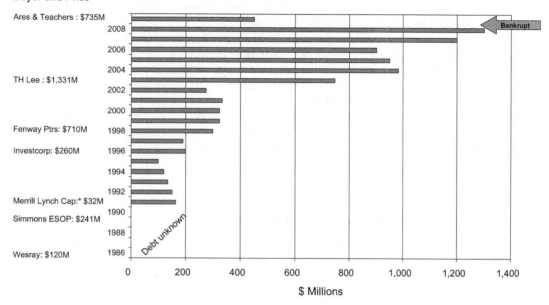

Buyer and Price

Boom periods have often seen a breakdown of investment discipline; but for the VC industry, the Internet bubble was in a league of its own. This period saw venture capitalists embrace ever-sketchier ideas, which often lacked even a vaguely plausible economic foundation. Let's sell large bags of pet food on the Internet at a discount to retail prices and offer free shipping! Let's offer one hour free delivery of books, meals, and CDs in Manhattan—again for free! Meanwhile, entrepreneurs seemed intent on burning through as much venture money as quickly as possible.

Probably the apotheosis of this period was Pixelon.[2] The start-up was founded with the claim to offer technology that brought high-quality video to computer monitors. It quickly signed partnerships with a variety of dot-com players and attracted interest from venture capitalists. The company's technology struck a chord with early-stage investors. Their support was enough to persuade Advanced Equities, a self-styled "venture capital investment bank," to raise $31 million of funding for the new venture.

The firm rapidly spent $12 million on—you guessed it—a launch party. And not just any party: a weekend-long Las Vegas bash at the MGM Grand, which featured performances by, among others, The Who, the Dixie Chicks, and Tony Bennett. (Admittedly, they did save some money by convincing some of the more gullible artists to take payment in Pixelon stock.) The party's publicity led to the revelation that the founder, Michael Fenne, was really David Stanley, a West Virginia con man who had been on the lam since bilking the parishioners of his father's Baptist church a decade earlier. Mr. Stanley ended up behind bars for an extended period. Needless to say, the story did not end on a much happier note for Pixelon's shareholders.

In this chapter, we begin by exploring the nature of boom and bust in the private equity industry. We highlight that the drivers of the cycles seem quite different: while venture investing

---

[2] This account is based on, among other sources, Dan Goodin, "The Great Internet Con," *The Standard*, June 26, 2000; Justin Hibbard, "And of Course, the Anti-Entrepreneur," *Red Herring*, August 31, 2000; and Patricia Jacobus, "Pixelon Issues Sweeping Layoffs after Founder's Arrest," *CNET News¸* May 12, 2000.

seems to boom as public markets climb, particularly the market for new issues, the buyout market responds to changes in debt availability. But in both cases, an up cycle looks the same: acceleration in the investment pace, higher valuations and (in many cases) lowered standards for investing coupled with a greater ease of fund-raising.

We then consider a simple framework for understanding these cycles. Using the long-familiar notions of supply and demand, we show how these tools can capture periods where private equity returns both rise and fall after an increase in activity. These simple tools can also explain why we tend to see "overshooting" and "undershooting" in the amount of private equity raised relative to the existing opportunities.

Finally, we turn to understanding the implications of these cycles. We discuss how private equity investors and the entrepreneurs they back must adjust their strategies in response to these changes. We also highlight the implications for government officials and others who seek to shape public policy.

THE NATURE OF INDUSTRY CYCLES

A natural starting place for our discussion is the nature of cycles in the private equity industry. The literature has suggested at least three broad areas where cycles appear in VC and buyout funds: in the amount of funds raised, in the volume of investments made, and in the performance of these investments. These patterns are explored in this section.

Cycles and Fund-Raising

Of course, many factors are involved in determining the overall level of private equity across countries, as we explored in Chapter 8. But when it comes to the fluctuations in the amount raised by venture and buyout funds, researchers have pointed a finger to one key consideration: the impact of the public markets.

There are several reasons for thinking that the public markets should matter in driving the level of private equity fund-raising. Periods with soaring stock prices are associated with more initial public offerings:[3] as a result, it is easier for private equity groups to take companies public. In addition, high stock prices are often associated with more acquisitions of private firms by public companies, often using their own stock. Such felicitous environments should boost private equity investment in three ways:

1. **The limited partners (LPs) accelerate their investment rate.** As Chapter 7 described, private equity groups will typically sell the shares of their exited firms shortly after the initial public offering (IPO) and return the cash to their investors. Alternately, they simply distribute the shares of newly public firms to their LPs. Thus, during "hot" periods with large numbers of initial public offerings and acquisitions, LPs receive large flows from venture funds. If institutional investors are trying to keep a fixed percentage of their assets in private equity (and as we discussed in Chapter 2, many have fixed targets), they will need to invest more to maintain that level. As a result, the LPs—both institutions and individuals—must accelerate their rate of investment.

2. **The investors all pursue the same "hot" sector.** Investors may infer (as we'll see, mistakenly) that the good times will last forever, and they rush into the category that has done best in the past. Such trend chasing—or investing while looking in the rearview mirror—

---

[3] See, for supporting evidence, Michelle Lowry and G. William Schwert, "IPO Market Cycles: Bubbles or Sequential Learning?" *Journal of Finance* 57 (2002): 1171–200.

seems to be an enduring behavioral characteristic of many institutions and has driven surges in assets as diverse as Indian stocks and American collateralized loan obligations.[4]

3. Let the good times roll! If an individual group has had some recent exits at attractive valuations, it often wants to raise a new fund to take advantage of its attractive track record.

During periods when stock market valuations are falling, on the other hand, the reverse dynamics come into play. If an institution's public equity portfolio has fallen sharply in value, it may seek to scale back its new commitments to private equity to maintain a set allotment to the asset class. The behavior—sometimes called the denominator effect—is prevalent during downturns due to the reluctance of private equity groups to sharply revalue their portfolios (as we discussed in Chapters 4 and 9). Similarly, individual private equity groups may have little to boast about and may opt to defer fund-raising until there is better news.

The basic relationships can be captured in the three-part Figure 13.2. Part (a) depicts the relationship between U.S. VC fund-raising and the NASDAQ index; part (b) between U.S. buyout funds raised and the Standard & Poor's 500 large-capitalization stock index; and part (c) between aggregate European private equity fund-raising and the Financial Times Stock Exchange (FTSE) 100 index. In each case, a strong positive correlation is apparent.

We will discuss two papers that look at these patterns and demonstrate these relationships in a rigorous way. The first is by Paul Gompers and Josh Lerner.[5] This analysis looks at the raising of venture funds only in the United States, at both the aggregate and individual group levels. The authors

FIGURE 13.2   Fund-raising and public markets

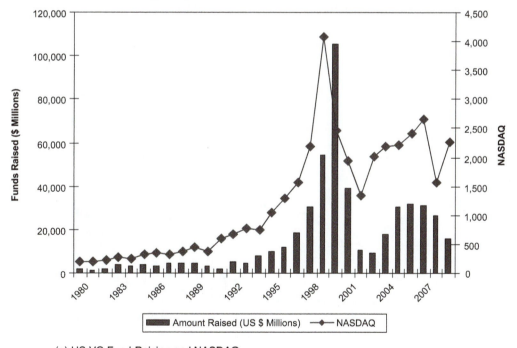

(a) US VC Fund-Raising and NASDAQ

---

[4] A number of pieces have made these arguments. Among the first (and most influential) is David S. Scharfstein and Jeremy C. Stein, "Herd Behavior and Investment," *American Economic Review* 80 (1990): 465–79.

[5] Paul Gompers and Josh Lerner, "What Drives Venture Capital Fundraising?" *Brookings Papers on Economic Activity, Microeconomics* (July 1998): 149–204.

FIGURE 13.2 (*Continued*)

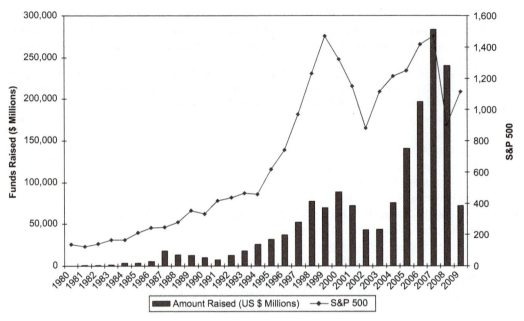

(b) US LBO Fund-Raising and S&P 500

Source: Data from Thomson Reuters VenturExpert, accessed November 6, 2010, and Datastream.

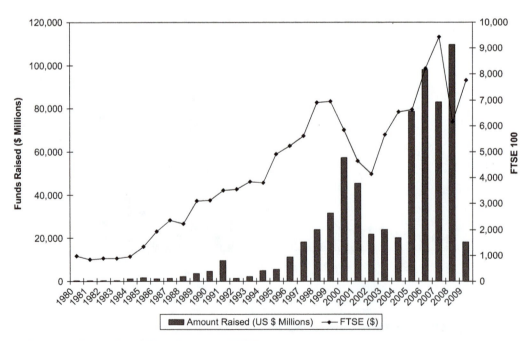

(c) European Private Equity Fund-Raising and FTSE 100

find that fund performance—in particular, taking companies public—is an important determinant of a venture fund's ability to raise new capital. Firms that hold larger equity stakes in companies that have recently gone public are more likely to raise new funds, and to raise larger funds. Both the value of equity held in companies taken public by the VC firm in the current year and in the previous year have a positive effect on the probability of raising a new fund and on the size of the fund raised. The effect of the previous year's IPO volume is about three times as large as the current year's. This might reflect the time it takes to raise a new fund (which, as we saw in Chapter 2, can often take many months).

The second analysis is the paper by Steve Kaplan and Antoinette Schoar,[6] which we discussed in part in the last chapter. These authors focus their fund-raising analysis exclusively on the formation of first-time funds, looking at both VC and buyouts. They examine the relationship between the number and amount raised by first-time funds in each year and past performance of private equity funds and other controls over twenty-six years. In periods when recent returns are higher—whether of public market indexes or venture and buyout funds themselves—more first-time funds and larger debut funds are likely to be raised.

Cycles and Investment Levels

A second body of closely related work has sought to explore the investment cycles that characterize the activity of later- and early-stage investors as they invest in companies. The ebbs and flows of the debt market appear to be a crucial driver in the buyout case, while in the venture world, the enthusiasm of the public markets for initial public offerings is often critical.

We will start with the buyout world. One way to capture the nature of cycles in the buyout world is to begin with Figure 13.3, which shows the difference between interest rates paid for

FIGURE 13.3   Spread between highest and lowest investment-grade rates

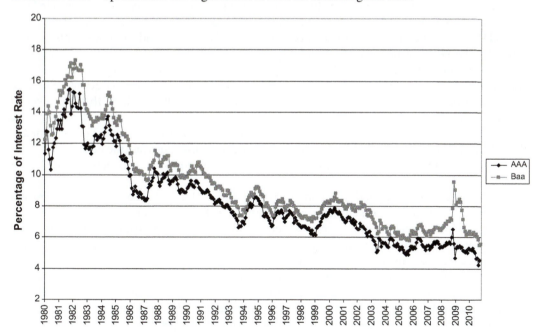

Source: Data from Moody's. Baa is the lowest investment-grade rating.

[6] Steve Kaplan and Antoinette Schoar, "Private Equity Returns: Persistence and Capital Flows," *Journal of Finance* 60 (2005): 1791–823.

FIGURE 13.4 Ratio of enterprise value to EBITDA, 1980–2009

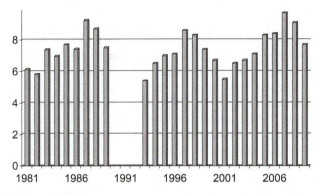

Note: 1981 deals include those in 1980.
Source: For 1980s data, Steve Kaplan and Jeremy Stein, "The Evolution of Buyout Pricing and Financial Structure in the 1980s," *Quarterly Journal of Economics* 108 (1993): 313–57; Standard & Poor's data is for large buyouts only.

corporate bonds rated AAA and Baa over time; that is, between the safest debt and the lowest investment-grade bonds (i.e., one notch above "junk debt"). The figure shows that while interest rates have fluctuated in general over time—they were much higher in the 1980s than in the 2000s, for instance—the spread between these two rates has also varied dramatically. During periods of economic prosperity, such as the mid-1980s and the mid-2000s, the spread between the two rates has been modest. During periods of uncertainty, such as the recessions of the early 1990s and the late 2000s, the gap has become very large indeed.

Buyout investments have also shown a great deal of variation over time. Figure 13.4 shows the changes in the ratio of the enterprise value (the purchase price, including equity and debt) in large U.S. buyout transactions to earnings before interest, taxes, depreciation, and amortization (EBITDA) over time. The rise of valuations during the late 1980s and the mid-2000s—which were also the peaks of the two major global buyout waves—is apparent.

Ulf Axelson and coauthors look at these patterns more carefully, seeking to document the ways in which cycles in leverage affect buyouts.[7] Using a sample of 1,157 transactions completed by major groups worldwide between 1985 through 2008, the authors show that the level of leverage is driven by the overall cost of debt rather than the more industry- and firm-specific factors that affect leverage in publicly traded firms (such as the inherent riskiness of the firm and the industry). The cheaper debt is, more it is used in buyout transactions and the more transactions are completed. Moreover, the availability of leverage seems to be strongly associated with higher valuation levels in deals.

Their argument is captured in Figure 13.5. This figure shows, first of all, how the greater ability to access debt—measured here by the ratio of debt to the transaction's EBITDA—is associated with a greater volume of transactions. Second, the companies' valuation—here measured using the ratio of enterprise value to EBITDA—tracks on a nearly one-for-one basis the leverage that the buyout group could obtain.

From a finance perspective, these results are initially puzzling. Why should a change in interest rates inspire investors to pay dramatically more for companies? One possible mechanism is that cheaper debt leads to more activity in the buyout market, which translates into more intense competition for transactions, and higher prices result from the competition. Another explanation is that the debt markets may be pricing bank loans too cheaply. If the buyout groups see that debt is

---

[7] Ulf Axelson, Per Strömberg, Tim Jenkinson, and Michael Weisbach, "Leverage and Pricing in Buyouts: An Empirical Analysis," (Working Paper, EFA 2009 Bergen Meetings, February 15, 2009), available at http://ssrn.com/abstract=1344023.

FIGURE 13.5   Debt to enterprise value and debt to EBITDA in buyouts

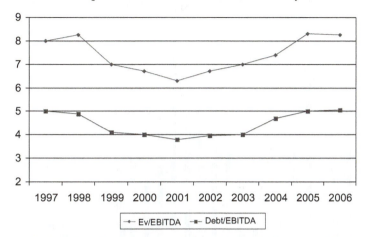

Source: Ulf Axelson, Per Strömberg, Tim Jenkinson, and Michael Weisbach, "Leverage and Pricing in Buyouts:
An Empirical Analysis," (Working Paper, EFA 2009 Bergen Meetings February 15, 2009), available at http://ssrn.com/
abstract¼1344023, 39.

misvalued, they may be able to pay more for companies; in short, they are giving up some of their
savings from the underpriced debt to the equity holders in the form of higher prices.

Although not as well documented, other patterns repeat themselves during cycles as well. For
instance, the work of Victoria Ivashina and Anna Kovner[8] suggests that one of the most critical
covenants in buyout transactions—the limitation of how much debt the company can take on
(again expressed as a multiple of EBITDA)—also shows a cyclical variation. Not only do banks
lend more money during booms, but they waive their own ability to step in if things go badly.

Perhaps the most dramatic illustration of the change in deal structures during booms occurs in
the payable in kind (PIK) provisions that appeared at the height of the 1980s and 2000s buyout
booms. These provisions essentially allowed buyout groups to repay their interest obligations not
in cash, but by simply providing the banks with shares of equity. Such generous provisions, which
can greatly ease the financial pressures that troubled leveraged firms face, have rarely been used
except at the peak of a market frenzy.

It should be noted, though, that history does not mechanically repeat itself. Some learning
takes place from one boom to the next. For instance, as noted in Chapter 5, the extreme levels of
leverage (often as high as 90 or 95 percent of the capital structure seen in 1980s buyout boom) have
not been repeated even at the most ebullient peaks of the 2000s.

Shifts in the level of financial market activity also dramatically affect VC investments.
Because few venture firms have much debt—they are too uncertain and risky to attract the interest
of banks—debt market cycles have relatively little impact on the industry. Instead, the market's
appetite for IPOs—which, as we discussed earlier, are closely tied to the valuations of small-
growth stocks—is closely related to activity in the venture market.

Figure 13.6 illustrates this relationship in the United States over time. The figure displays the
aggregate time series of venture financing provided (in billions of dollars), annual changes in the
NASDAQ stock index, and the aggregate number of entrepreneurial IPOs.[9] During hot markets,
more companies go public. Venture capital investment does seem to increase but with a bit of a lag,

---

[8] Victoria Ivashina and Anna Kovner, "The Private Equity Advantage: Leveraged Buyout Firms and Relationship
Banking," (Working Paper, 2010, unpublished).

[9] That is, we exclude from our totals closed-end funds, real estate investment trusts, cross-listings of foreign firms
(American Depository Receipts), reverse leveraged buyouts (LBOs), and corporate spin-outs. These data are taken from
the Thomson's Securities Data Company and VentureXpert databases, and from Ibbotson Associates.

FIGURE 13.6 VC investment, entrepreneurial IPOs, and NASDAQ change

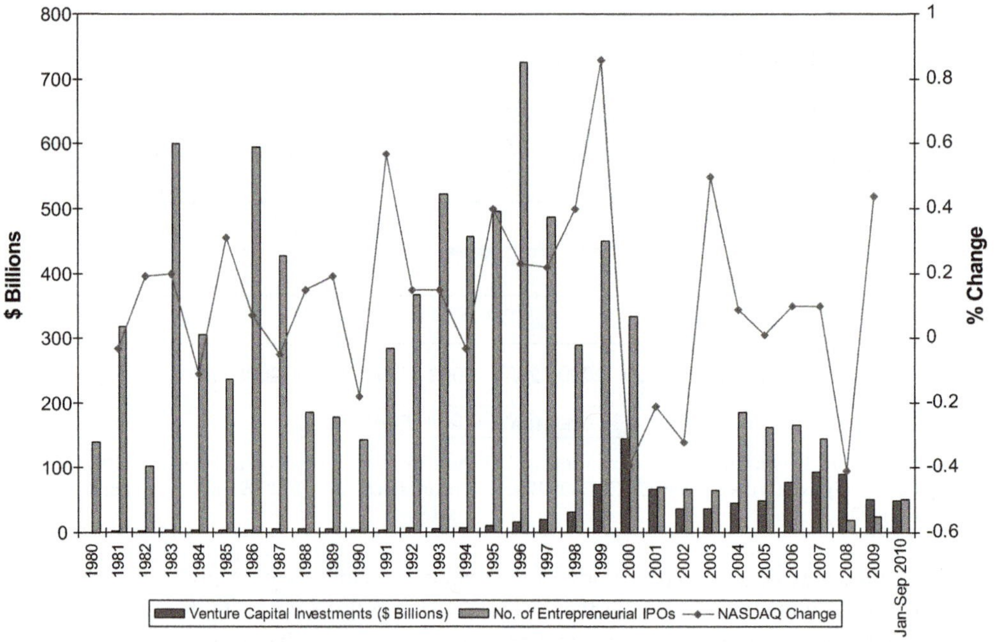

Source: Data from Thomson Reuters private equity database and Datastream.

perhaps due to the time required to raise and close a fund—investment hit its peak in 2000, just as the number of IPOs and the NASDAQ cratered.

This pattern also manifests itself in the number of transactions at the industry level. Figure 13.7 displays the relationship between the number of IPOs and volume of venture investments (in millions of dollars) in four sectors: Internet and computer, biotechnology and health care, communications, and energy. While the extent of the relationship varies by sector, there appears to be a strong positive association once again.

These patterns are explored in greater length in the work of Paul Gompers and coauthors.[10] The authors start by showing what the graphs suggest: that VC investment activity at the industry level is very sensitive to public market signals of industry attractiveness. To measure this, they look at the ratio of the market-to-book ratio of all firms' equity in a given industry. If this ratio is higher than average, venture capitalists are far more likely to invest: a shift from the bottom to the top quarter in the market-to-book ratio increases the number of investments in that industry by more than 15 percent. Similarly, venture investment in an industry increases in response to a surge of IPOs of such companies.

The authors then look at which venture capitalists are most responsive to the signals. Interestingly, this relationship is driven largely by VC firms with the most experience—particularly experience doing deals in that industry—undertaking more transactions. Presumably, these groups are better able than their less seasoned rivals either to understand these opportunities or to take advantage of them (e.g., by pushing investment banks to take their companies public at a time when many investors are seeking IPOs for their firms). In short, they either recognize the shift more quickly or act on it more effectively. Thus trend chasing is not a game confined to marginal or inexperienced funds, but a strategy that the best and most successful employ. This reinforces the importance of a firm's strategy, as seen in Chapter 3, and also the findings in Chapter 12 about the

---

[10] Paul Gompers, Anna Kovner, Josh Lerner, and David Scharfstein, "Venture Capital Investment Cycles: The Impact of Public Markets," *Journal of Financial Economics* 87 (2008): 1–23.

FIGURE 13.7   VC investments and IPOs

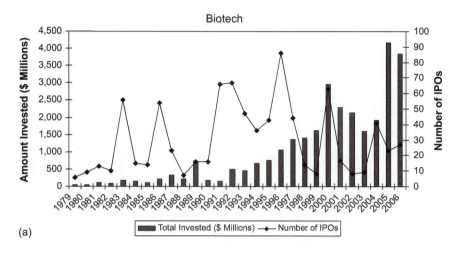

(a)

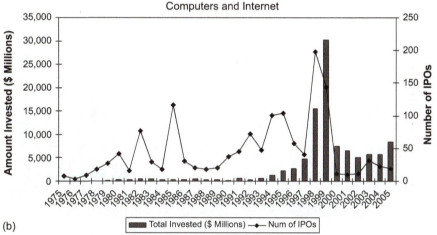

(b)

Source: Data from Thomson Venture Economics, accessed October 21, 2010. Adapted from analysis in Paul Gompers, Anna Kovner, Josh Lerner, and David Scharfstein, "Venture Capital Investment Cycles: The Impact of Public Markets," *Journal of Financial Economics* 87 (2008): 1–23.

performance of specialized firms and specialized partners. Knowing the general landscape allows a firm to seize on positive changes.

Cycles and Investment Performance

Another line of research has looked at the performance of investments made at different points in the investment cycle. A strong pattern has emerged: generally, investments made during market peaks (whether of fund-raising or investing) appear to have underperformed. These patterns have been seen both at the individual transaction and aggregate levels as well as in both the VC and buyout realms.

This result is perhaps not surprising given the earlier discussions in this chapter. If firms completing buyouts at market peaks employ excessive leverage and overpay for transactions, we may expect years and industries with heavy buyout activity to experience more intense subsequent downturns. As seen in the story of Simmons Mattress, high levels of debt leave a company more vulnerable to any changes in the broader economy. Moreover, the effects of this overinvestment would be exacerbated if buyout investments drive rivals with such financing to invest aggressively

FIGURE 13.7   (*Continued*)

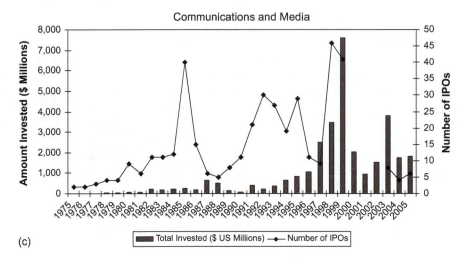

(c)

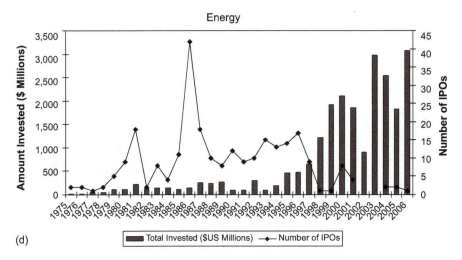

(d)

and take on high leverage themselves. For instance, around the time of the mid-2000s, buyout boom (which featured, as one of the largest transactions, the buyout of the Tribune Corporation by Sam Zell), the family owners of the New York Times Company engaged in a debt-fueled orgy of their own, repurchasing several billion dollars of equity from the public markets.[11] (The *Tribune* filed for bankruptcy in December 2008; the *Times* has fared a little better, staving off distress at least for now by undertaking a quasi-usurious loan from Mexican billionaire Carlos Slim[12]). In a more systematic study, Judith Chevalier shows that in regions where many supermarkets received buyout investments during the 1980s, rivals responded aggressively, entering into the markets and expanding existing stores.[13] Thus it would not be surprising if a market downturn were felt particularly acutely in industries where buyout firms had been most active.

---

[11] For a short history, see Ed Pilkington, "Turbulent Times," *The Guardian*, March 2, 2009, 7.

[12] Robert Macmillan, "New York Times Falls on Slim's Expensive Loan," *Reuters,* January 20, 2009, http://www.reuters.com/article/idUSN2039256320090120, accessed November 23, 2010.

[13] Judith Chevalier, "Capital Structure and Product-Market Competition: Empirical Evidence from the Supermarket Industry," *American Economic Review* 85 (1995): 415–35.

A number of high-profile examples support these claims. Perhaps most dramatic was the crash that followed the buyout wave of the late 1980s. While overall the rate of failure of buyout backed firms is rare—as noted earlier, the Strömberg study shows that only 6 percent of exited deals over the history of the industry worldwide have ended in a bankruptcy or a distressed reorganization—the failure rates appear to be far greater for mega deals concluded at the peak of buyout booms. A study by Steve Kaplan and Jeremy Stein concludes that of the sixty-six largest deals done at the peak of the 1980s buyout boom (i.e., between 1986 and 1988), fully twenty-five (or 38 percent) experienced financial distress by the end of 1991, where *distress* is defined as default or an actual or attempted restructuring of debt obligations due to difficulties in making payments.[14] Of those, eighteen (27 percent of the total) actually did default on debt repayments, often in conjunction with a Chapter 11 filing.

Similarly, Davis and coauthors[15] find that the positive productivity growth at firms undergoing buyouts (relative to controls) that we discussed in Chapter 10 varies with industry cycles, as shown in Figure 13.8. The productivity advantage is larger in periods with an unusually high interest rate spread between AAA-rated and BB-rated corporate bonds (such as characterized the early 1990s and late 2000s), and virtually nonexistent during periods with low spreads (as was the case during the "go-go" days of the mid-2000s). One interpretation of this pattern is that buyout groups are committed to adding value to their portfolio only during periods when making money through other means (e.g., through leverage and financial engineering) is not feasible—that is, during periods when the debt markets are relatively quiescent.

Examining Figure 13.8 in more detail helps explain this point. The figure compares the productivity growth of companies between 1990 and 2005, matching buyout-owned companies with those that were not, based on industry, age, size, and structure. Along the horizontal axis is the annual average of the difference between high-yield bonds, those that the buyout groups rely upon to finance their transactions, and investment-grade (AAA) bonds, relative to the mean difference throughout that period. The graph shows that as the market becomes tougher for buyout

FIGURE 13.8   Difference in annual productivity growth, private-equity-backed and other firms, and interest rates

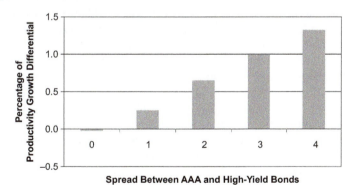

Source: Steve Davis, John Haltiwanger, Ron Jarmin, Josh Lerner, and Javier Miranda, "Private Equity, Jobs and Productivity," in A. Gurung and J. Lerner (eds.), *Globalization of Alternative Investments Working Papers Volume 2: Global Economic Impact of Private Equity 2009* (New York: World Economic Forum USA, 2009), 25–44. Available at www.weforum.org/pdf/cgi/pe/Full_Report2.pdf.

---

[14] Steve Kaplan and Jeremy Stein, "The Evolution of Buyout Pricing and Financial Structure in the 1980s," *Quarterly Journal of Economics* 108 (1993): 313–57.

[15] Steve Davis, John Haltiwanger, Ron Jarmin, Josh Lerner, and Javier Miranda, "Private Equity, Jobs and Productivity," in *Globalization of Alternative Investments Working Papers Volume 2: Global Economic Impact of Private Equity 2009*, ed. A. Gurung and J. Lerner (New York: World Economic Forum USA, 2009), 25–44.

funds—that is, as the spreads widen between the two interest rates and debt is less available—the productivity gains increase. When the two interest rates differ by no more than the average amount, productivity increases very little if at all. This can be interpreted to mean that firms will invest more time and effort in improving operations at their companies when the costs of input (debt) is more expensive and thus they cannot rely upon debt-fueled special dividends or "quick flips," that is, speedy exits to either the public markets or other buyout firms, for gains. This indicates that the frequent buyout firm claim of adding value to their operations might be viewed somewhat more cynically, with the coda "when we don't have a choice."

But the magnitude of the detrimental effects of industry cycles remains under debate. A counterargument, originally proposed by Michael Jensen,[16] is that the high levels of debt in buyout transactions force firms to respond earlier and more forcefully to negative shocks to their businesses. As a result, buyout-backed firms may be forced to adjust their operations earlier at the beginning of an industry downturn, enabling them to better weather a recession. Even if some buyout-backed firms eventually end up in financial distress, their underlying operations may thus be in better shape than their peers, which facilitates an efficient restructuring of their capital structure and lowers the deadweight costs on the economy.

Consistent with this argument, Gregor Andrade and Steven Kaplan study thirty-one distressed leveraged buyouts from the 1980s and found that the value of the companies post-distress was slightly *higher* than the value before the buyout. They argued that this suggested that the costs of excessive leverage were not too large and that even the leveraged buyouts most severely affected by adverse shocks created some economic value.[17]

Venture capital investments made during booms also appear to perform more poorly. One way to see this is to look at individual transactions, as do Paul Gompers and Josh Lerner.[18] During periods when more money is flowing into venture funds—which, as we saw above, are associated with more robust public markets for growth—venture capitalists are willing to pay more for transactions. Even after controlling for all the key features of the firm (e.g., its location and stage of development), there is a strong relationship: doubling inflows into venture funds increases the valuations that venture capitalists will pay for transactions between 7 and 21 percent.

Moreover, these effects are not even. Venture capital inflows appear to increase the valuations of California and Massachusetts companies more than others. This may reflect the fact that while regions like Silicon Valley and Route 128 near Boston are characterized by a concentration of entrepreneurial ventures, the representation of venture capitalists is even more disproportionate.

Higher valuations alone are not sufficient to prove that the venture investments underperform. It might be, for instance, that these valuation increases reflect better prospects for firms funded in this period. To assess this, the authors look at the investments' outcomes. The companies funded during boom periods are neither any more likely to go public—as we have seen in Chapter 7, this is typically the way most successful venture investments are exited—nor more likely to be acquired at a valuation twice or more than that of the original investment round. Thus, venture investments during booms are characterized on average by considerably higher prices with little justification.

Kaplan and Schoar examine how inflows of capital into new funds affect the aggregate returns of private equity funds. They show that, in general, years that see the entry of both more venture and buyout funds experience lower returns. This pattern holds even after controlling for the performance of public markets in the ensuing years. The effect is particularly interesting in the VC industry: the returns of more experienced firms are relatively unaffected by the entry of new funds, while those of younger funds are severely and negatively affected. Moreover, many of the new

---

[16] Michael Jensen, "The Eclipse of the Public Corporation," *Harvard Business Review* 67 (1989): 61–74.

[17] Gregor Andrade and Steven Kaplan, "How Costly is Financial (Not Economic) Distress? Evidence from Highly Leveraged Transactions That Became Distressed," *Journal of Finance* 53 (1998): 1443–93.

[18] Paul Gompers and Josh Lerner, "Money Chasing Deals? The Impact of Fund Inflows on Private Equity Valuations," *Journal of Financial Economics* 55 (2000): 281–325.

venture organizations that raise funds during these periods never raise another fund, which suggests their own performance was poor. Taken together, these patterns suggest that the kind of problematic behavior seen during booms (e.g., the frequent entry of funds and overpriced deals) does not affect the more seasoned funds to nearly the same extent as others.

WHAT IS BEHIND THE CYCLES?

We have established that private equity is prey to significant boom and bust cycles and explored some of their outcomes. It is less obvious, however, what drives these patterns. In the section that follows, we consider some explanations.

A Simple Framework

To understand the dynamics of the private equity industry, it is helpful to employ a simple framework.[19] The two critical elements for understanding shifts in private equity fund-raising are straightforward: a demand curve and a supply curve. Just as in markets for commodities like oil and semiconductors, shifts in supply and demand shape the amount of capital raised by private equity funds. Shifts in supply and demand also drive the returns that investors earn in these markets.

The supply of private equity is determined by the willingness of the LPs—the investors—to provide funds. Their willingness to do this, in turn, depends on the expected rate of return from these investments relative to the return they expect to receive from other investments. Higher expected returns lead to a greater desire on the part of investors to supply private equity. As the return they expect to earn from their venture and buyout investments increases—that is, as we go up the vertical axis—the amount supplied by investors grows (we move further to the right on the horizontal axis).

The number of entrepreneurial companies seeking private equity determines the demand for capital. Demand is also likely to vary with the rate of return that investors anticipate. As the minimum rate of return sought by the investors increases, fewer entrepreneurial companies can meet that threshold. The demand schedule typically slopes downward: higher return expectations lead to fewer financeable companies because fewer entrepreneurial projects can meet the higher hurdle.

Together, supply and demand should determine the level of private equity in the economy. This is illustrated in Figure 13.9. The level of VC should be determined by the intersection of the two lines—the supply curve (S) and the demand curve (D). Put another way, we would expect a

FIGURE 13.9   Steady-state level of private equity

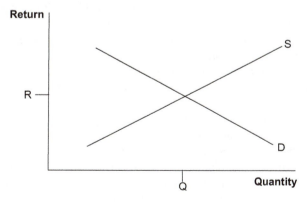

[19] The "supply and demand" framework for analyzing VC discussed here was introduced in James M. Poterba, "Venture Capital and Capital Gains Taxation," in *Tax Policy and the Economy*, ed. Lawrence Summers (Cambridge, MA: MIT Press, 1989), and refined in Gompers and Lerner, "What Drives Venture Capital Fundraising?"

FIGURE 13.10 Impact of demand shock

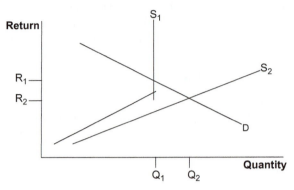

quantity Q of private equity to be raised in the economy, while the funds earn a return of R on average.

It is natural to think of supply and demand curves as smooth lines. But this is not always the case. Consider, for instance, the private equity market before the Department of Labor's clarification of the Employee Retirement Income Security Act's (ERISA) "prudent man" rule in 1979. The willingness of investors to provide capital before the clarification of ERISA policies—the supply curve—would have been distinctly limited: no matter how high the expected rate of return was for these funds, the supply would be limited to a set amount, as Figure 13.10 depicts. The vertical segment of the supply curve resulted because pension funds, a segment of the United States financial market that controlled a substantial fraction of the country's long-term savings, were simply unable to invest in venture and buyout funds. Consequently, the supply of private equity may have been limited at any expected rate of return.

The Impact of Shifts

The "supply and demand" curves just described are not fixed. For instance, the shift in ERISA policies led to the supply of funds for private equity moving outward. Similarly, major technological discoveries, such as the development of genetic engineering, led to an increase in the demand for venture capital.

But the quantity of private equity raised and the returns it enjoys often do not adjust quickly and smoothly to the changes in supply and demand curves. We can illustrate this by comparing the private equity market to that for snack foods. Companies like Frito-Lay and Nabisco closely monitor the shifting demand for their products, getting daily updates on data collected by supermarket scanners. They restock the shelves every few days, adjusting the product offerings in response to changing consumer tastes. They can address any imbalances of supply and demand by offering coupons to consumers or making other special offers.

By way of contrast, in the venture and buyout market the quantity of funds provided may not shift rapidly. The adjustment process is often quite slow and uneven, which can lead to substantial and persistent imbalances. When the quantity provided does react, the shift may "overshoot" the ideal amount and lead to yet further problems.

This point can be illustrated again by using our framework. It is important to distinguish here between short- and long-run curves. While in the long run the curve may have a smooth upward slope, the short-run curve may be quite different. The long-run supply curve (SL) may have a smooth upward slope. But the supply in the short run may be essentially fixed, if investors cannot or will not adjust their allocations to VC funds. Thus the short-run curve may instead be a vertical line (SS).

This difference is illustrated Figure 13.11, which explores the short- and long-run impact of a positive demand shock. For instance, the discovery of a new scientific approach, such as genetic

FIGURE 13.11   Impact of a demand shock in the short and long run

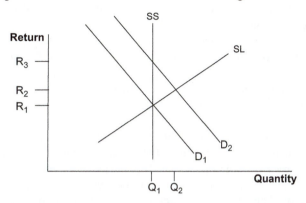

engineering, or the diffusion of a new technology, such as the semiconductor or the Internet, may have a profound effect on the VC industry. As large companies struggle to adjust to these new technologies, numerous agile small companies may seek to exploit the opportunity. As a result, for any given level of return demanded by investors, there now may be many more attractive investment candidates.

In the long run, the quantity of VC provided will adjust upward from Q_1 to Q_2. Returns will also increase, from R_1 to R_2. In the months or even years after the shock, however, the amount of VC available may be essentially fixed. Instead of leading to more companies being funded, the return to the investors may climb dramatically, up to R_3. Only with time will the rate of return gradually subside as the supply of VC adjusts.

At least two factors might lead to such short-run rigidities. These are the structure of the funds themselves and the time lag with which information on performance is reported to investors. We explore how each factor serves to dampen the speed with which the supply of private equity adjusts to shifts in demand.

The Nature of Private Equity Funds

Increasing an allocation to public equities or bonds is easily accomplished. These markets are "liquid": shares can be bought and sold easily, and the level of holdings can be readily adjusted. The nature of VC and buyout funds, however, makes these kinds of rapid adjustments much more difficult.

Consider an instance where a university endowment decides that private equity is a particularly attractive investment class and decides to increase its allocation to these investments. From the time this new target is agreed upon, it is likely to be several years before the policy is fully implemented. Since venture firms raise funds only every two or three years, even if the endowment simply wants to increase its commitment to existing funds, it must wait until the next fund-raising cycle. In many cases, it may be unable to invest as much in the new funds as it wishes.

This difficulty stems from the fact that the number of experienced venture capitalists often adjusts more slowly than the swings in capital. Many of the crucial skills of an effective private equity investor cannot be taught formally, as noted in Chapter 11; rather, they are developed through a process of apprenticeship. Furthermore, as we discussed in Chapter 12, the organizational challenges associated with rapidly increasing a partnership's size are often wrenching, and many venture groups have resisted rapid growth, even if investor demand is so great that they could easily raise many billions of dollars.

If indeed the endowment decides to undertake a strategy of investing in new funds, potential candidates for the university's funds will need to be exhaustively reviewed. Once the firms are chosen, the investments will not be made immediately. Rather, the capital that the university commits will be drawn down in stages over a number of years. If the endowment wishes to access a particular small group of firms, it may have to wait through several fund-raising cycles before it can deploy a sufficient amount of money.

The same logic works in reverse. Scaling back a commitment to private equity also usually takes a number of years. An illustration of this stickiness was seen following the stock market correction of 1987. Many investors, noting the extent of equity market volatility and the poor performance of small high-technology stocks, sought to scale back their commitments to VC. Despite the correction, flows into VC funds continued to rise, not reaching their peak until the last quarter of 1989.[20]

Another contributing factor is the self-liquidating nature of private equity funds. When firms exit investments, they do not reinvest the funds, but rather return the capital to their investors. The pace of distributions varies with the rate at which the firms can liquidate their holdings. During those "cold" periods when investors most wish to reduce their allocation to this asset class, they receive few distributions. Thus it is often difficult to achieve a desired exposure to private equity during periods of rapid change in the market.

The Role of Information Lags

A second factor contributing to the stickiness of the supply of private equity is the difficulty in discerning the current status of the private equity market at any given time. While mutual and hedge funds that hold public securities are "marked to market" on a daily basis, the delay between the inception of a venture investment and the discovery of its quality is long indeed.

The information lags can have profound effects. For instance, when the investment environment becomes far more attractive, the market can take a number of years to fully realize the fact. While investments in Internet-related securities in the mid-1990s yielded extremely high returns, it took many years for the bulk of institutional investors to realize the size of the opportunity. Similarly, when the investment environment becomes substantially less attractive, as it did during the spring of 2000 and the summer of 2007, investors often continue to plow money into funds.[21]

Some of these information problems stem from the firms themselves. The types of companies that attract private equity are surrounded by substantial uncertainty and information gaps—in fact, an ongoing theme in this book has been the role of information gaps (or asymmetries) in the industry. But these inevitable difficulties are exacerbated by the manner in which fund performance is typically reported, as we discussed in Chapter 9.

An Illustration of Slow Adjustment

The discussion of supply and demand adjustment thus far ignores many of the complex institutional realities affecting the ebbs and flows of VC fund-raising in particular. But even such simple tools as a "supply and demand" graph can be quite helpful in understanding overall movements in VC activity, as can be illustrated by considering the recent history of the VC industry.

---

[20] This claim is based on an analysis of an unpublished Venture Economics database. Limited partners can sell their stakes in the secondary market, but often only at substantial discounts, particularly during periods when they are likely to be most eager to do so (such as late 2008 and early 2009).

[21] See, for instance, the discussion in Laura Kreutzer, "Many LPs Expect to Commit Less to Private Equity," *Private Equity Analyst* 11 (2001): 1, 85–86; and AltAssets, "LPs Shun Large Buyout Funds . . . ," *AltAssets.com*, January 20, 2009, http://www.altassets.com/private-equity-news/article/nz15074.html, accessed November 23, 2010.

As discussed earlier, the supply of venture funding began growing rapidly in the mid-1990s. Many practitioners at the time viewed this event glumly, arguing that a boost in venture activity must inevitably lead to a deterioration of returns. Yet the investments during this period enjoyed extraordinary success. How could these seasoned observers have been so wrong?

The reason is that these years saw a dramatic shift in the opportunities available to VC investors. The rapid diffusion of Internet access and the associated development of the World Wide Web ushered in an extraordinary period in the U.S. economy. The ability to transfer visual and text information in a rapid and interactive manner was a powerful tool, one that would transform retail activities as well as the internal management of firms.

Such a change led to an increase in the demand for VC financing. Thus, for any given level of return that investors demanded, there should have been a considerably greater number of opportunities to fund. Far from declining, the rate of return to venture investments actually rose. Much of this rise reflected the fact that the supply of effective and credible venture organizations adjusted only slowly. As a result, those groups who were active in the market during this period enjoyed extraordinary successes.

Why Does the Private Equity Market Overreact?

Another frequently discussed pathology in the private equity market is the other side of the same coin. Once the markets do adjust to the changing demand conditions, they frequently go too far. The supply of VC and buyout funds ultimately will rise to meet the increased opportunities, but these shifts often are too large. Too much capital may be raised for the opportunities outstanding. Instead of shifting to the new steady-state level, the short-term supply curve may shift to an excessively high level.

The same problem can occur in reverse. A downward shift in demand can trigger a wholesale withdrawal from the industry by LPs. Returns rise dramatically as a result. While such over-reactions will not last forever—ultimately, the supply of VC and buyout funds will rise to meet the demand—in the interim, promising companies may not be able to attract funding. In this section, we explore two possible explanations for this phenomenon.

One possibility is that institutional investors and private equity investors may overestimate the shifts that have occurred. They may believe that there are tremendous new opportunities and consequently shift the supply of private equity to meet that apparent demand.

This suggestion is captured in Figure 13.12. A positive shock to the demand for private equity occurs, moving the demand curve out from D_1 to D_2. Limited and general partners, however, mistakenly believe that the curve has shifted out to D_3. The short-run supply curve thus shifts from SS_1 to SS_3, leaving excessive investment and disappointing returns in its wake.

Such mistakes may arise because of misleading information from the public markets. Examples abound where private equity investors have made substantial investments in new sectors, at least partially responding to the impetus provided by high valuations in that sector. Understanding why public markets overvalue particular sectors is still somewhat of a mystery. Certainly, though, it seems in some cases that investors fail to take into account the impact of competitors: firms appear to be valued as if they are the sole firm active in a sector, and the impact of competitors on revenues and profit margins is not fully anticipated.

Whatever the causes of these misvaluations, historical illustrations are plentiful. One famous example was during the early 1980s, when nineteen disk drive companies received VC financing.[22] Two-thirds of these investments came in 1982 and 1983, as the valuation of publicly

---

[22] For detailed discussions, see Josh Lerner, "An Empirical Exploration of a Technology Race," *Rand Journal of Economics* 28 (1997): 228–47; and William A. Sahlman and Howard Stevenson, "Capital Market Myopia," *Journal of Business Venturing* 1 (1986): 7–30.

FIGURE 13.12   Overshooting

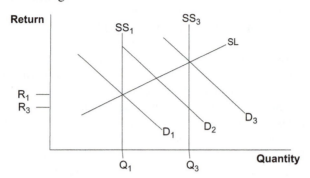

traded computer hardware firms soared. Many disk drive companies also went public during this period. While industry growth was rapid during this period (sales increased from $27 million in 1978 to $1.3 billion in 1983), it was questioned at the time whether the scale of investment was rational given any reasonable expectations of industry growth and future economic trends. Indeed, between October 1983 and December 1984, the average public disk drive firm lost 68 percent of its value. Numerous disk drive manufacturers that had yet to go public were terminated, and venture capitalists became very reluctant to fund computer hardware firms.

A second explanation for the overshooting phenomenon is the failure of private equity investors to consider the costly adjustments associated with the growth of their own investment activity. As we saw in Chapter 12, the very act of growing the pool of private equity under management may cause distractions and introduce organizational tensions. Even if demand has expanded, the number of opportunities that a venture or buyout group—or the industry as a whole—can address may at first be limited. Rapid growth puts severe pressures on private equity organizations. Even when the problems do not result in an extreme outcome such as a group's dissolution—as has happened in some cases—resolving such issues places substantial demands on the partners' time. Thus, during periods of rapid growth, VC and buyout groups may correctly observe that there are many more opportunities to fund. Rapidly expanding to address these opportunities may be counterproductive, however, and lead to disappointing returns.

EFFECTIVELY MANAGING CYCLES

How, then, can these cycles be addressed? Certainly, many of the booms and busts in the private equity industry have been truly global in scope. These have often been beyond the ability of any government—much less any individual entrepreneur or private equity group—to control. But that does not mean that private equity groups and policymakers are helpless, and unable to respond effectively to market cycles. In this final section, we review some of the implications for private-equity-backed firms, for investment groups, and for policymakers.

Implications for Private Equity Groups

The presence of investment cycles is a profound challenge for many private equity groups. To underscore the effect that investment cycles have on funds, consider any of the recent protracted booms, such as Internet investing during the late 1990s or the credit bubble in the mid-2000s. The groups that were highly exposed when the music ended—with portfolios of overvalued and difficult to liquidate holdings—may have wished with the benefit of hindsight that they had never played the game at all. Perhaps they should have sat out all the craziness?

Of course, that is usually not a viable option. Such a step would have translated into the group's returns lagging the competition's for an extended period. Such underperformance would have reduced the group's ability to raise new funds and may have inspired key investment professionals to defect to the competition. Few groups would have the discipline to stick to a contrarian strategy in the face of these pressures. Moreover, resisting these trends may not even be in the best interest of the firm's investors. As we discussed earlier in the chapter, established groups are actually among the most aggressive in responding quickly to booms and investing in areas that are enjoying public market favor.

Thus, to ignore the opportunities that hot markets present for raising capital and exiting investments can be suicidal. At the same time, to ignore the old rule that "what comes up must go down" is also a recipe for disaster. Consequently, private equity groups must follow a balancing act. But a variety of steps—ranging from philosophic principles to specific tactics—can be taken to limit the detrimental effects of cycles, downturns in particular.

The first response is more a set of beliefs or an attitude than anything else. There is much to be said for the "power of contrarian management." Maintaining a constant appreciation of the prevalence of cycles as well as a general skepticism about inevitable "trends" and "new paradigms" is necessary. In other words, while periods of overvaluation and excessive enthusiasm open the door for exiting investments at attractive valuations, avoiding going overboard on the assumption that the trend will last forever is also essential.

A contrarian philosophy has very real implications for fund strategy. This approach should translate into staging investments, so the fund has the option to abandon a given strategy if market conditions shift radically, and diversifying the portfolio of companies to limit exposure to a single sector, stage of investment, or geography. Similarly, encouraging portfolio companies to maintain options and alternative strategic routes is an appropriate response to an overheated market Put another way, it is important to think about what can go wrong, not just about what can go right.

A related philosophic and practical principle is to think carefully about incentives and how they may affect the behavior of funds, managers, and others. While the power of incentives has been discussed at length in the economic, psychological, and popular literature, it is still easy to underestimate their power. As Warren Buffet's long-standing lieutenant, Charlie Munger, has observed: "I've been in the top 5% of my age cohort all my life in understanding the power of incentives, and all my life I've underestimated it. And never a year passes but I get some surprise that pushes my limit a little farther."[23] In particular, it is essential to be keenly aware of (and react to) situations where compensation is not linked to performance, or where it creates a conflict between the general partners (GPs) and LPs or between the GPs and the entrepreneurs. When risk and the creation of long-term value are being ignored in favor of short-term rewards, it is a recipe for disaster.

There are also a variety of implications for financing choices. Perhaps the most essential of these is the need for a "cookie jar" philosophy: that you should take some cookies from the jar when it is passed to you, whether you are hungry or not, because you never know whether it is going to be empty when it comes back. Money is hardest to raise when it is needed the most, so investors should take advantage of financing windows when they can, rather than holding off in the hopes of getting a higher valuation for their portfolio company at some future time.

A related point has to do with what kind of financing to raise. The 2008–2009 crisis exposed many parties—from portfolio companies to institutional investors—as being hopelessly over-leveraged. Thinking carefully about what kind of debt exposure companies and institutions have

---

[23] Munger speaking before Harvard Law School on the psychology of human misjudgment: http://www.intelligentinvestor.com.au/articles/233/The-power-of-incentives.cfm, accessed May 29, 2010.

and how they would handle an abrupt change of economic conditions is critical. Just because a bank will lend a large amount of debt to a portfolio company does not mean that such a step is reasonable. It is also important to think about exposure to "hidden" debt that does not show up on the balance sheet but represents real liabilities nonetheless.[24]

The cookie-jar rule also has implications for exiting investments. Often, groups are tempted to hold onto investments because of the possibility of additional upside. There is a lot to be said, however, for taking advantage of opportunities to exit at a profit, especially during periods where markets appear to be frothy or uncertain. Giving up some of the potential for future gains can be a modest price to pay for avoiding catastrophic losses. Thinking carefully about exits from the day of the initial investment can help ensure that opportunities to sell out at attractive prices are not lost.

The final set of implications has to do with communicating about the market conditions. Too often, when markets are booming, private equity groups are inclined to simply take credit for their investment successes. It is not surprising, then, that when things turn south, the LPs meet their efforts to blame market conditions with some skepticism. Conveying where the fund sees itself in the private equity cycle, and how the firm is responding, can be an important success factor. Even if the firm's investments subsequently suffer when the markets do turn south, the fact that the LPs were engaged in and acquiesced to the decision to invest aggressively can limit the damage to the firm's reputation.

Implications for Public Policy

Intense investment cycles also have implications for policymakers. Far too often, policymakers have intervened to seek to boost VC financing. (A focus on encouraging buyouts, given their more complicated reputation, has been much rarer.) But these efforts to encourage venture activity have tended to happen at exactly the wrong times, exacerbating overheated booms.

Government officials and policy advisors are naturally concerned about spurring innovation. Encouraging VC financing is an increasingly popular way to accomplish these ends: numerous efforts to spur such intermediaries have been launched in many nations in Asia, Europe, and the Americas. But far too often, these efforts have ignored the cycles discussed in this chapter.

As we have highlighted, VC is an intensely cyclic industry. Moreover, we have discussed how the impact of VC varies: during peak periods, much of the funding seems duplicative and is far less likely to have a favorable impact on innovation. Yet government programs have frequently provided the most funding during those very periods when VC funds have been most active, and they often have targeted the very same sectors favored by venture investors.

This type of behavior reflects the manner in which such policy initiatives are frequently evaluated and rewarded. Far too often, the appearance of a successful program is far more important than actual success in spurring innovation. For instance, the administrators of many "public venture capital" programs prepare glossy brochures full of "success stories" about particular firms. The prospect of such recognition may lead a program manager to decide to fund a firm in a "hot" industry whose prospects of success may be brighter, even if the sector is already well funded by venture investors (and the impact of additional funding on innovation quite modest). To cite one example, the Advanced Technology Program in the United States launched

---

[24] Hidden liabilities are also a real concern for many LPs. Many endowments, for instance, found themselves with dire financial strains after the onset of the financial crisis in 2008. Many of their problems stemmed from the fact that they had made commitments to too many private equity and real estate funds, confident that these funds would be returning a steady stream of capital to fund future commitments. Once the funds' steady flow of realizations back to the endowments dried up, the schools had to scramble to make good on their ongoing commitments. These commitments were not treated as debt on the schools' balance sheets, and as a result, the investment committees were surprised by the hidden liabilities they faced.

major efforts to fund genomics and Internet tools companies during periods when venture funding was flooding into these sectors.[25]

A far more successful approach would be to address the gaps in the venture financing process. As noted earlier, venture investments tend to be very focused into a few areas of technology that are perceived to have great potential. Increases in venture fund-raising—which are driven by factors such as shifts in capital gains tax rates—appear more likely to lead to more intense competition for transactions within an existing set of technologies than to greater diversity in the types of companies funded. Policymakers may wish to respond to these industry conditions by focusing on technologies that are not currently popular among venture investors and by providing follow-on capital to firms already funded by venture capitalists during periods when venture inflows are falling.

Two other U.S. programs seem to have done a better job of adhering to these strategies. The Central Intelligence Agency's In-Q-Tel fund has more effectively addressed gaps in traditional venture financing by placing strong emphasis on finding technologies that address the agency's particular needs.[26] The Small Business Innovation Research program provides another contrasting example.[27] Decisions about which companies to finance are not made by centralized bodies, but rather devolved in many agencies to program managers who seek to address very specific technical needs (e.g., an Air Force research administrator who wants to encourage the development of new composites). As a result, this program has funded many unconventional technologies that are not of interest to traditional venture investors.

Of course, public programs can also create an overheated venture market if they are too big for the market to accommodate. Not only can such programs lead to the problems we discussed, but if public programs become too large, they can even crowd out or discourage private funding. Public funds may become so extensive that they discourage venture capitalists from investing in a given market because all attractive opportunities have been financed already by the public funds.

The experience of the Canadian Labor Fund Program in the 1990s provides a good illustration of this latter danger.[28] A number of provincial governments, seeking to encourage venture capital, established these funds in the 1980s and 1990s. But in doing so, they adopted some very peculiar elements, such as the decision that these funds would managed by labor unions. Predictably, unions were unfamiliar with the venture process, leading to a "rent a union" dynamic where outsiders curried favor with unions to get permission to run their funds. Not surprisingly, the unions often turned to cronies and fast-buck operators rather than experienced investors to manage the funds. But most troublingly, the amount of capital investors put into labor funds grew spectacularly: the investment pool climbed from $800 million in 1992 to $7.2 billion in 2001, while private independent funds grew from $1.5 billion to $4.4 billion over the same period (all figures in billions of 1992 Canadian dollars). Not surprisingly, the funds that were established and raised capital were far from inspiring, and the program actually set the industry back.

---

[25] Paul Gompers and Josh Lerner, *Capital Market Imperfections in Venture Markets: A Report to the Advanced Technology Program* (Washington, DC: Advanced Technology Program, U.S. Department of Commerce, 1999).

[26] Business Executives for National Security, *Accelerating the Acquisition and Implementation of New Technologies for Intelligence: The Report of the Independent Panel on the CIA In-Q-Tel Venture* (Washington, DC: Business Executives for National Security, 2001); and Kevin Book, Felda Hardymon, Ann Leamon, and Josh Lerner, "In-Q-Tel," HBS Case No. 9-804-146 (Boston: HBS Publishing, 2004).

[27] For evidence illustrating the positive impact of the SBIR award program, see Josh Lerner, "The Government as Venture Capitalist: The Long-Run Effects of the SBIR Program," *Journal of Business* 72 (1999): 285–318.

[28] This account is based on, among other sources, Canadian Auto Workers, *Labour-Sponsored Funds: Examining the Evidence* (Toronto: CAW Research Department, 1999); Douglas Cummings and Jeffrey MacIntosh. "Crowding Out Private Equity: Canadian Evidence," *Journal of Business Venturing* 21 (2006): 569–609; and Katrina Onstad, "Nothing Ventured, Tax Break Gained," *Canadian Business* 70, no. 11 (1997): 47–52.

More generally, the greatest assistance to VC may be provided by government programs that seek to increase the demand for these funds, rather than the supply of capital. Examples would include efforts to facilitate the commercialization of early-stage technology, such as the Bayh-Dole Act of 1980 and the Federal Technology Transfer Act of 1986, both of which eased entrepreneurs' ability to access early-stage research, particularly that funded by governments at universities and other research facilities. Similarly, efforts to make entrepreneurship more attractive through tax policy (e.g., by lowering tax rates on capital gains relative to those on ordinary income) may have a substantial impact on the amount of VC provided and the returns that these investments may yield. These less direct measures may have the greatest success in ensuring that the venture industry will survive the recent upheavals.

In short, while some government programs aimed at spurring VC and entrepreneurial innovation likely have experienced a positive social rate of return, the most effective programs and policies seem to be those that lay the foundations for effective private investment. Our analysis suggests that the market for VC may be subject to substantial "imperfections" and that these imperfections may substantially lower the total social gain achieved by venture finance. Given the extraordinary rate of growth (and now retrenchment) experienced by VC over the past decades, the most effective policies are likely those that focus on increasing the efficiency of private markets over the long term, rather than providing a short-term funding boost during the current period of transition.

Yet another side of public intervention has been a tendency to try to "fix" the industry's shortcomings through problematic regulations during periods when a downturn leads to poor returns and high-profile bankruptcies of private-equity-backed firms. Interventions often appear to be inspired by the discontents brought about by downturns and can in turn intensify them.

Among the financial institutions that have fallen under the gaze of regulators have been private equity funds, especially buyout funds. These funds have traditionally been lightly scrutinized. For instance, in the United States, funds with a limited number of "sophisticated" (i.e., sufficiently wealthy) investors have been exempt from the provisions of the Investment Company Act of 1940. In many cases, it appears these exceptions stem not from deliberate policy decisions, but rather from historical accident: many nations' financial regulatory architectures were designed when the private equity industry was in its infancy.

But in the aftermath of the global financial crisis, many policymakers have taken a closer look at the regulation of private equity. In many cases, these reexaminations have been motivated by worries that these funds increase the volatility and risk that their economies face. For instance, the European Commission[29] has declared:

> The activities of AIFM [Alternative Investment Fund Managers] give rise to risks for AIF investors, counterparties, the financial markets and the wider economy over and above the investment risk that is intrinsic to a financial investment. . . . Adverse market conditions have severely affected the sector and have provided evidence of the role of AIFM in exacerbating market dynamics.

As a result of these beliefs, several proposals have sought to systematize and increase the regulatory oversight of these institutions. This legislation—taken up by European Parliament in 2010—called for a wide variety of changes, such as limits on leverage and disclosure for any private equity firm investing, or potentially even raising funds, in the European Community.

While this effort may have been well intentioned, it involved two fundamental problems. First, it hardly seems rational to target buyout for special curbs on leverage and requirements for disclosure when others doing similar investments in companies—from individual investors like Richard Branson to sovereign wealth funds, and even corporations themselves—have no limits.

---

[29] European Commission, *Commission Staff Working Document Accompanying the Proposal for a Directive of the European Parliament and of the Council on Alternative Investment Fund Managers and Amending Directives 2004/39/ EC and 2009/ . . . /EC: Impact Assessment,* COM(2009) 207/SEC(2009) 577 (Brussels: European Commission, 2009).

These rules simply seem to "tilt the table" to favor some investors and hobble buyout funds. Moreover, the legislators seem to have been motivated by sweeping claims about the detrimental effects of private equity, claims that—as we saw in Chapter 10—are really not justified by the evidence. While the desire by policymakers to "do something" during downturns is understandable, the responses may not always be appropriate.

TAKING STOCK

Private equity is a business characterized by cycles. Periods of boom and bust have been a feature of the industry since its earliest days, and they show little sign of abating. To be effective, venture and buyouts groups must take advantage of—and limit the danger from—these fluctuations.

In this chapter, we explore this important but challenging territory. We show that in both the venture and buyout markets, periods of intense fund-raising and investing are commonplace. The determinants of these market upturns, though, appear to be different. While venture booms seem to be associated with buoyant public markets—and particularly, the market for IPOs—an important driver of buyout booms appears to be the availability of debt on favorable terms for these transactions.

After seeking to understand these cycles through the lenses of supply and demand, we turn to the implications for private equity groups and private-equity-backed firms. We argue that it is at once important to take advantage of the opportunities the cycles pose, while defensively positioning oneself to avoid getting caught in the inevitable downdrafts. We also discuss the challenges that these cycles pose for policymakers, and the frequency with which policy interventions, however well intentioned, actually make these cycles worse. Cycles are an unavoidable fact of private equity life. Reader, ignore them at your peril.

QUESTIONS

1. How do the drivers of venture capital and buyout cycles differ?

2. How is the level of private equity fund-raising correlated with the public markets? Why is this the case?

3. How have the spreads of AAA and B corporate bonds changed over time? What impact do these spreads have on buyout activity?

4. Why are experienced VC and buyout firms more active than their less seasoned peers during periods of public market attractiveness?

5. During which market cycles would it be advantageous to be a "net seller" or a "net buyer"?

6. Why would private equity firms be willing to pay higher prices for enterprises during boom periods when they are no more likely to go public or be sold for higher valuations than enterprises purchased in other periods? Why not sit on the sidelines until valuation expectations come down?

7. Draw the shift in supply and demand for private equity capital from the peak of the boom in 2007 to the immediate recession that followed in 2008 to the period of recovery in 2009.

8. Despite the poor performance of private equity funds over the past couple of years, explain why some endowments and pension funds have increased their allocation to this asset class.

9. How would you critique a private equity fund's strategy of investing 20 percent of its capital per annum? (Assume a five-year investment horizon.) What are the potential advantages and disadvantages of this type of strategy?

10. How do you balance over-leveraging a portfolio company while taking advantage of attractive financing markets? Should there be controls in place to avoid over-leveraging?

11. What are some of the ways that public capital can better address the gaps in venture funding? What are some examples?

12. How would you respond the European Commission's declaration that "Adverse market conditions have severely affected the sector and have provided evidence of the role of alternative investment fund managers in exacerbating market dynamics"?

Chapter 14

Wrapping Up

This volume is intended to provide an understanding of the workings of the private equity industry today. Because the large-sample studies and cases we draw on must of necessity look at events in the past, they may provide less guidance about the future of the private equity industry than we might like.

The question of how the venture and buyout industries will evolve over the next decade is particularly critical because its growth in the recent past was so spectacular, the downturn was so dramatic, and the industry's effect on the overall economy has become significant. It is natural to ask whether the increase in activity seen over the past decades can be sustained, or whether private equity will join a long list of financial fads—from portfolio insurance to securitized subprime debt obligations—that had their moment in the sun and then faded away.

A related set of questions relates to the geography of the venture capital (VC) and private equity business. As we have seen in Chapters 1 and 8, what was originally an industry focused in the United States and Great Britain has become increasingly global. The extent to which the private equity model will translate overseas remains an open issue. Certainly, VC has had little success globally outside of a few geographic pockets: on average, the performance of most funds outside the United States has distantly lagged the U.S.-based funds. Even though there have been successful later-stage deals in many more regions, whether the venture model will work on a sustained basis in many nations remains uncertain, given the relative youth of the activities there.

Our concerns may be exacerbated by the wrenching changes that have taken place in private equity since the inception of the economic crisis in mid-2007:

- Some of the highest-profile transactions of the mid-2000s boom have undergone bankruptcies or distressed restructurings. These include Chrysler, Extended Stay America, Linens 'n Things, and Readers' Digest.

- A number of the investors who popularized private equity investing, including the endowments of Harvard and Yale Universities, experienced very negative returns in the 2009 fiscal year. Moreover, the heavy representation of alternative investments in their portfolios, which could not be easily sold, created significant liquidity challenges when the schools came under financial pressure.

- Many private equity groups were forced to lay off staff and scale back activities as a result of the downturn.

These are fair questions. Given the unprecedented changes in the private equity industry, it is natural to ask whether the industry as described in this volume is likely to survive, or whether it will transform itself into something entirely different.

In this chapter, we explore these issues. We begin by considering four scenarios along which the industry may evolve in its major market. We then turn to the special challenges facing private equity funds in emerging markets.

SCENARIOS

Given the uncertainty in the private equity industry today, it is hard to predict what its future will look like. Rather, we will lay out a range of possible scenarios, each of them plausible.

One way to organize these scenarios—in a tried-and-true business school manner—is as a two-by-two matrix, as depicted in Table 14.1. On the horizontal axis, we contrast cases where the investor base—the limited partners (LPs)—remains basically the same against situations where it shifts sharply. The vertical axis distinguishes between scenarios where the returns to private equity funds going forward are fair—that is, they are commensurate with the risks that investors take on—and those where they are disappointing.[1]

Recovery

Scenario 1 in Table 14.1, which we call "Recovery," envisions a return to the conditions that have characterized the industry over the past two decades.

As was highlighted in Chapter 13, short-run shifts in the supply of or demand for VC and private equity investments have been a feature of the industry since its inception. And these shifts can have dramatic effects. For instance, periods with a rapid increase in capital commitments have historically led to fewer restrictions on private equity investors, larger investments in portfolio companies, higher valuations for those investments, and lower returns for investors. Lower returns discourage investors who then invest elsewhere; fewer or smaller investments occur in portfolio companies. In fact, some of the evidence discussed in Chapter 10 suggests that private equity investors do a better job of adding value to firms during the market troughs, which would again lead to a recovery. Eventually returns rise, and the cycle continues.

These patterns have led many practitioners to conclude that the industry is inherently cyclical. In short, this view implies that periods of rapid growth generate sufficient problems that periods of retrenchment are sure to follow. Intense competition between private equity groups leads to a willingness to pay a premium for certain types of companies. This is not sustainable in the long run: private equity groups that persist in such a strategy will earn low returns and eventually be unable to raise follow-on funds. The events of the decade of the 2000s can be seen as a classic boom-and-bust cycle, only in more dramatic form than previously.

At the same time, it is also important to consider the *long-run* determinants of the level of private equity, not just the short-run effects. In the short run, as we have highlighted, the ebb and flow of returns and the state of the public and debt markets are likely to be critical. But the types of

Table 14.1   Future Scenarios for the Venture Capital and Private Equity Industry

	Constant Investor Base	Turnover in Investor Base
"Fair" returns	Scenario 1: Recovery	Scenario 2: Back to the future
Disappointing returns	Scenario 3: A broken industry	Scenario 4: The LPs' desertion

---

[1] Of course, as we discussed in Chapter 9, what constitutes a fair return is subject to debate.

Table 14.2 **Drivers of Venture Capital and Private Equity Activity**

	Short Run	Long Run
Supply	Asset allocations	Deal-sourcing strategy
	Change in other asset values	Value-added for portfolio firms
	Distributions	Incentive schemes
	Track record	Addressing generational transitions
Demand	Investment strategy	Innovation
	Mix of personnel	Supply of management and labor
	Group's concerns about growth and reputation	Economic dynamism
		Regulatory environment

factors that determine the long-run, steady-state supply of private equity in the economy are more fundamental.

These long-run drivers are likely to include the degree of dynamism in the economy (whether new innovations or corporate restructurings), which creates investment opportunities; the ability of venture and buyout investors to add value to portfolio firms; the willingness of highly skilled managers and engineers to work in entrepreneurial environments; and the presence of liquid and competitive markets where private equity investors can sell their investments (whether markets for stock offerings or acquisitions). However painful the short-run adjustments are, these more fundamental factors are likely to be critical in establishing the long-run level of activity. This distinction between short- and long-run drivers is highlighted in Table 14.2.

Upon examining these more fundamental factors, a compelling case can be made that in many respects substantial changes for the better have occurred over the past decade. We have already discussed in Chapter 10 the evidence regarding the effects of private equity groups on the companies in which they invest. Other favorable indicators include the increasing willingness of boards of directors—who even a few years ago frequently viewed private equity groups as "barbarians"—to consider the sale of an underperforming division or even an entire company to a private equity fund. The increasing number of professionals and managers familiar with and accustomed to the employment arrangements offered by private-equity-backed companies (such as a heavy reliance on stock options) has also been a major shift. The increase in the number of patent filings and awards (depicted in Figure 14.1), though partially a consequence of changes in patent policy, suggests that venture capitalists are unlikely to run out of innovations to fund. In addition, even in the face of the current downturn, the pool of prospective investors in private equity funds has broadened beyond the small circle of U.S.-based endowments and pensions that drove much of the activity during the 1980s and 1990s. Finally, the efficiency of the private equity process has been greatly enhanced by the emergence of other intermediaries familiar with its workings. The presence of such expertise on the part of lawyers, accountants, managers, and others—even real estate brokers—has substantially reduced the transaction costs associated with forming and financing new companies or restructuring existing ones.

In short, the increasing familiarity with the private equity process has made the long-term prospects for such investments as attractive—or even more attractive—than they have ever been before. It is also worth emphasizing that despite its growth, the private equity pool today remains relatively small. For every one dollar of private equity in the portfolio of U.S. institutional

FIGURE 14.1 U.S. Patent applications and awards

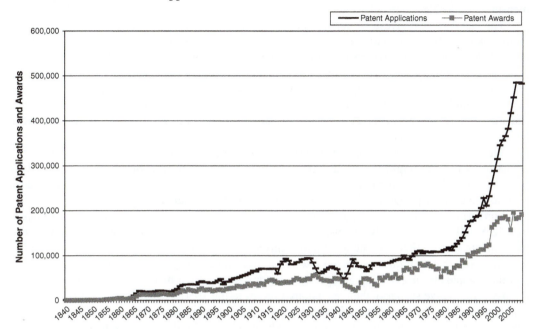

Source: U.S. Patent Office data, accessed November 6, 2011.

investors at the end of 2009, there were almost six dollars of publicly traded equities.[2] The ratios are even more uneven for overseas institutions. At the same time, the size of the foreign private equity pool remains far below that of the United States. The disparity can be illustrated by comparing the ratio of the private equity investment to the size of the economy (gross domestic product). In 2008, this ratio was about 6.8 times higher in the United States than in China, and 3.3 times higher in the United States than in Western Europe.[3] At least to the casual observer, these ratios seem modest when compared to the economic role of new firms, products, and processes in the developed economies.

Taken together, these facts suggest the first scenario: that the level of private equity is likely to rebound in the years to come. The fact that the industry has experienced periods of boom and bust in recent years is nothing new and indeed is more the rule than the exception. The private equity model has many inherent strengths, and the disruption of the recent market crash is not likely to be persistent.

Back to the Future

An alternative possibility, Scenario 2 in Table 14.1, is rooted in the inequality of VC and private equity returns discussed in Chapter 9. As we highlighted, the returns to different classes of private equity investors has been highly uneven; the bulk of the "goodies" go to endowments, particularly the top third of performers. Moreover, as Chapter 9 documented, private equity in aggregate has done little better—or maybe slightly worse—than public equity investments. Taken together, these

---

[2] Data from the Federal Reserve Board and VentureXpert.

[3] We use 2008 for comparison because 2009 was such an anomalous year in terms of private equity investment. These statistics are taken from the European Venture Capital Association, *EVCA Yearbook 2009* (Zaventum, Belgium: European Venture Capital Association, 2009); Zero2IPO, *China Venture Capital Report, 2009*; and Thomson Reuters private equity database.

two facts suggest that for most investors, private equity has been—if performance is properly measured—a losing game.

The fact that most investors garnered poor returns from private equity may have been true for many years, but the appreciation of this fact may have received increased attention only recently. Many LPs initially may have been willing to dismiss the poor returns from their private equity programs, attributing them to the program's youth. More generally, with the inception of the economic crisis, many are turning a skeptical eye to the financial community as a whole and have begun to wonder whether many of the claims of outperformance over the past two decades were illusionary. Thus the recent debates at many investment committees about the suitability of private equity should come as no surprise.

This scenario suggests that many of these conversations will convince investors to exit private equity investing. We might anticipate that this fall-off in interest would not be universal: LPs with better returns might remain in the industry while others might decide that the returns generated by such an investment program may not be worth the trouble of managing the effort.

Furthermore, we might anticipate that the largest and smallest investors would be the most likely to exit. Small funds are likely to conclude that they do not have the critical mass to make these investments, that the time and energy requirements are simply too great. The largest pools of capital may conclude that their choices are too few—that given the amount of capital they need to deploy and the complexity of assessing groups, they can invest in only a handful of very large groups.

One alternative scenario, then, envisions a return to the 1980s, when private equity investing was dominated by midsized, sophisticated investors such as corporate pensions and endowments. The exit of numerous other investors is likely to be good news for these remaining investors: there will be less competition from other LPs for access to top-tier funds, and given the resulting difficulty in fund-raising for their competitors, these funds will have less competition when making investments. Reflecting the dynamics we discussed in Chapter 13, this environment should see the surviving funds and institutional investors enjoying superior performance.

The Limited Partners' Desertion

The second pair of scenarios from Table 14.1 anticipates that VC and private equity funds do not generate the rate of return that investors expect—and paints a gloomier picture. In the Scenario 3, we anticipate that continuing poor returns and a problematic organizational structure may drive away many investors.

Why might the exit of many LPs not lead to improving returns, as the second scenario suggested? One possibility is that the wedge between gross and net returns introduced by management fees may be too great to overcome. As Chapter 2 discussed, the same fee structures are in place today as in the early days of the industry, even though funds are many times larger. Thus, even if a shrunken private equity industry leads to gross returns recovering smartly, the net returns that the LPs receive may still be unsatisfactory.

It is worth pointing out that LPs have sought to address high fee levels in the past without success. In the aftermath of the private equity crash of the early 1990s, nine large public pension funds commissioned a study by the consulting firm William M. Mercer, Inc. The report, which was released in November 1996, argues that much of the underperformance experienced by these investors to date was driven by the terms of private equity compensation. The report recommended that management fees be reduced and based on actual expenses; that the carried interest shift to less than 20 percent; and that the general partners (GPs) contribute more capital to their funds. But the proposals were "dead on arrival," and were never taken seriously by the GPs. A similar earlier effort by British LPs fared no better.

A pessimist might argue that the lack of success of these efforts was not just simply a matter of bad timing or inappropriate arguments. Rather, the issue of compensation for private equity investors may be fundamentally unaddressable—a "third rail," as it were. The LP community is fractured across different types of institutions in different geographies. As much as LPs espouse solidarity, they compete fiercely with each other to get into top funds: as we saw in Chapter 9, the extreme skew in performance makes accessing the proper funds critical to success. Moreover, maintaining cohesion among the LP community is difficult when key leaders are frequently lured away to higher-paying positions at funds-of-funds or at private equity groups themselves.

All these factors may lead to a dramatic shrinkage in the pool of limited partners. General partners may be forced to exit the business or raise dramatically smaller funds. Executives at start-up or growth firms may be forced to turn increasingly to informal sources of capital (e.g., family members or angel groups) to support their ventures.

Lest the reader consider this scenario too far-fetched, historical precedents do exist. To cite one example, oil and gas LPs were popular among endowments and other forward-thinking LPs in the 1970s and 1980s. When these vehicles lost their advantaged tax status and the price of crude oil plummeted, sharply reducing gains and hence dividends, investors became disillusioned and cut their commitments to such funds. The industry shifted dramatically as only conservative partnerships survived, generating bond-like returns attractive mostly to retail investors.[4]

A Broken Industry

The final possibility, Scenario 4, suggests that while returns for VC and private equity funds will be disappointing, the sector may continue to gather substantial amounts of funds. Due to some of the measurement issues highlighted in Chapter 9, as well as the organizational dynamics that are likely to make private equity specialists at many large institutional investors unwilling to recommend abandoning their own specialties, these groups may continue to raise capital, even if in the absence of returns. Such a state might continue for a decade or longer.

Again, the skeptical reader may question whether such a scenario could really transpire—after all, it is far removed from the standard notions of market efficiency. But the recent past suggests that such scenarios are not entirely implausible. The recent history of the U.S. venture capital industry provides one illustration.

Figure 14.2 depicts the ratio of distributed to paid-in capital—that is, the ratio of money paid out to LPs compared to money received—for various vintage years of venture funds.[5] (We do not include the most recent vintage years in this graph: given the long gestation of venture investments, as was discussed in Chapters 6 and 7, it is unreasonable to expect that they will have yielded much by way of actual returns to their investors yet.) A value of two for a given vintage implies that the investor in the average (or median) venture fund received twice its original capital back. Looking from the vantage point of late 2009, the last vintage year where investors in the average and median venture funds were returned their money was 1997—fully a dozen years prior. In subsequent years, the typical investor has received a multiple below one. While these portfolios may have investments yet to be harvested, and they may still be exited for a gain—increasing the ratio of distributed to paid-in capital—investors have certainly been waiting a long time for their returns.

One possible root of the problem may be seen in Figures 14.3a and 14.3b, which depict the funds invested and exited on a monthly basis by U.S. venture funds.[6] If we ignore the bubble years of 1998 to 2000, we see that there has been a dramatic change in the investment rate from the years

---

[4] James J. Murchie, "Master Limited Partnerships—Lessons from History," *Investment Management Association*, March/April 2008, http://www.imca.org/cms_images/file_462.pdf, accessed November 24, 2010.

[5] These data are compiled from various Thomson Reuters private equity databases.

[6] These data are taken from the records of the consulting firm Sand Hill Econometrics. The compilations use the date that a firm goes public as the date it exits from the venture capitalist's portfolio, rather than the date the shares are distributed to investors or sold in the open market (see the discussion of exits in Chapter 7).

FIGURE 14.2 Distributed to paid-in ratio by vintage year for u.s. venture capital funds

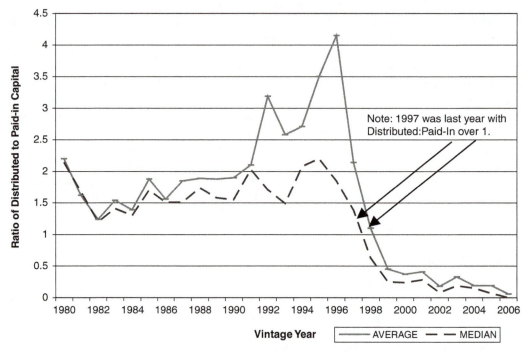

Source: Data from Thomson Reuters private equity database, accessed October 15, 2010.

FIGURE 14.3a Venture money invested, december 1991–june 2010

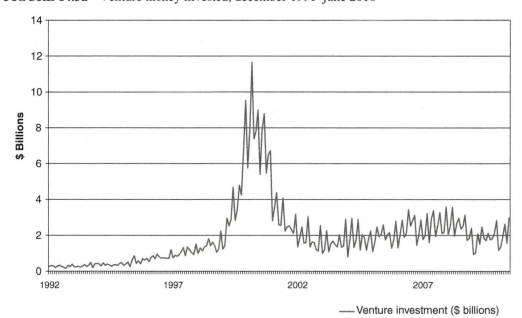

Source: Data from Sand Hill Econometrics. Used with permission.

FIGURE 14.3b   Venture exits, december 1991–june 2010

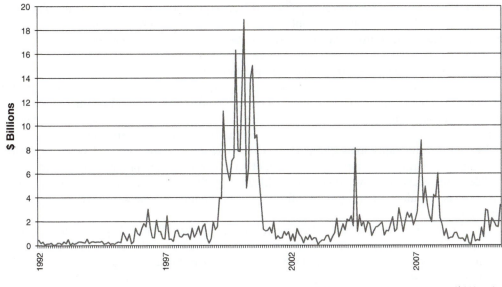

——Exit value of venture investments ($ billions)

Source: Data from Sand Hill Econometrics. Used with permission.

before the bubble. The investment rate has increased by roughly tenfold: it has gone from an annual rate of about $2 billion to above $20 billion. When we look at the exit rate, we see that with a few exceptions (such as August 2004, the month of the Google IPO, and the first half of 2007, which saw a flowering of venture-backed IPOs), we see few changes. Despite the rapid acceleration in investments, roughly the same amount of initial public offerings and acquisitions are taking place. This is a recipe for low realized returns and unhappy investors.[7]

This scenario suggests a very unhappy result. LPs will continue to place money into venture and buyout funds, whether out of stubbornness, self-interest, or misleading data. Yet the returns will not be there. While this might be good news for GPs who can stay in business, it is hard to feel that society as a whole will benefit from such an outcome.

Taking Stock

Distinguishing between the four scenarios just presented is challenging. A reasonable case can be made for each of them. We tend to see somewhere between the Scenario 1 and Scenario 2 as being the most likely, but perhaps we are simply optimists.

SOME SPECIFIC PREDICTIONS

Whatever the overall arc of the private equity industry, we believe it is possible to make some more specific predictions that are likely to transpire regardless of how the industry evolves. In this section of the chapter, we review a few of these calls.

---

[7] Of course, during the post-bubble period, the public markets were also languishing. Venture capital's return during this period looks much less problematic if compared to public benchmarks.

The Growing Importance of Emerging Markets

In future years, much of the growth of VC and private equity activity is likely to take place in the developing world. As we saw in Chapter 8, the trend toward increasing interest in emerging economies was evident from the first days of the twenty-first century. We believe that the aftermath of the financial crisis of 2008 and the attendant recession, while negatively affecting private equity funds everywhere, is likely to accelerate this trend.

Our prediction stems from several sources. In part, this reflects the internal situation of the developing nations themselves: there was a lot of pain to go around in the aftermath of the financial crisis; but clearly, the recovery occurred more quickly in the advanced emerging markets. Moreover, given the likelihood that debt will be unavailable for a considerable period of time, the kind of growth equity transactions that characterize developing country VC are likely to be especially popular. Finally, the need for the tool kit that venture and private equity investors can provide—the mechanisms we reviewed in Chapters 2 through 6—is clearly greatest in many emerging economies, where (often informally run) family businesses have dominated the economies.

At the same time, it is important to acknowledge that there will be challenges in this movement of VC and private equity into the developing markets. This claim can be supported by the low returns produced by many pioneering funds. For instance, venture, growth, and private equity funds active in the developing world—defined here as everything other than Canada, the United States, Western Europe, Australia, Japan, and New Zealand—have garnered very disappointing returns over the past two decades. If we take the simple average of the rates of return of these funds, they have generated an annual return of 3.8 percent.[8] The weighted average (i.e., when we count larger funds more) is even grimmer: –1.5 percent. These returns are less than those that would have come from holding the safest Treasury bills, much less public stocks.

A natural interpretation of these patterns is that they reflect the difficulties of undertaking successful investments in markets such as China and Russia, where regulatory uncertainties, inexperienced entrepreneurs, and a problematic judiciary present substantial challenges. Indeed, the returns from the early days of the U.S. VC industry provide a similar picture. The pioneering VC fund American Research & Development Corporation (ARDC) had an annual return of only 14.7 percent despite its "home run" return from Digital Equipment.[9] While this may seem respectable, we must recall that this is only one fund, which we are comparing to an average. There were many dozens of funds during the decades in which ARDC was active, and today most of them are forgotten. Given that the vanished funds were in all probability far less successful than ARDC, the returns of the U.S. VC industry during its early years are likely to have been no better than those seen in the emerging-market funds during their initial years. This pattern suggests that no matter how promising the ultimate returns of entrepreneurial activity may be, low returns are likely in a VC market's early years. Too many funds in the early days of the U.S. industry were too small, and they were run by inexperienced investors. In other cases, the market was simply too under-developed—it was difficult to recruit employees or obtain protection for the nascent firms' ideas.

In the same way, we should not expect an easy ride for emerging-market VC. Even in the absence of the financial crisis, inexperienced groups and those operating in immature markets would have encountered many challenges. But despite these disappointments, and the need for caution, it is hard not to be optimistic about the longer-run prospects for VC in many emerging markets, from Turkey to Latin America to Africa. In addition, we believe that growth equity, with its ability to fund risky expansion of larger companies, and buyouts, which can help conglomerates

[8] These calculations are the authors'. These calculations are based on an updated version of the database described in Josh Lerner, Antoinette Schoar, and Wan Wongsunwai, "Smart Institutions, Foolish Choices: The Limited Partner Performance Puzzle," *Journal of Finance* 62 (2007): 731–64.

[9] Patrick R. Liles, *Sustaining the Venture Capital Firm* (Cambridge, MA: Management Analysis Center, 1978), 83.

rationalize and family businesses survive generational transfers, will also find their footing and establish an important presence in these markets.

The Renewed Attention to Incentives

Another open question relates to the governance of private equity firms. The model of loose governance by LPs, who rely on incentive compensation to ensure that the GPs "do the right thing," may have reached its limits. Today, there is a changing, broader LP base that may require more assurances that its money is being managed prudently. The disappointments brought about by the bursting of the bubbles in the late 1990s and mid-2000s have opened the door to tough questions. There is also a rapidly expanding base of private equity professionals who do not have the history and culture that was shared among many of the industry's pioneers. And, as noted earlier, regulatory authorities, accustomed to scrutinizing public firms with detailed governance structures, are increasingly interested in private equity.

All of these factors point to an increased attention to—and perhaps a fundamental rethinking of—the way in which private equity groups are governed. It is distressing that, although private-equity-owned firms are rated highest in terms of governance, the private equity groups themselves must be rated very low, given their overall lack of transparency. As we pointed out earlier in this chapter, powerful forces make it difficult to change the ways in which private equity and venture groups are compensated. But it is our hope—and cautious prediction—that the industry will see movement along at least two dimensions:

1. The aggregate level of compensation that GPs receive may not change, but hopefully the way that it is received will evolve. The increased attention being paid to transaction and board fees may transform into a broader shift toward incentive compensation. Today, buyout funds almost universally receive 20 percent of the profits, while venture funds receive between 20 and 30 percent, as we saw in Chapter 2. One might wonder why we regard a higher carried interest rate—which clearly reduces the payments that the LPs receive—as a good thing. Our belief is that shifting payments from fees to carry will create a much great alignment of incentives between the LPs and GPs, and that the industry as a whole will benefit.

2. As we discussed in Chapter 7 and elsewhere in this volume, the need to raise new funds can profoundly distort the behavior of private equity funds, leading them to take a variety of steps that make their investments look good at the time of fund-raising, even if it hurts performance in the long run. Fund-raising is clearly an essential part of the process. But to the extent that funds move to a model like that of General Atlantic—which instead of raising one large fund every few years, raises capital every year from a rotating group of partners (essentially, a series of mini-funds, rather than a big fund)—these distortions can be reduced.

As we have acknowledged, figuring out an appropriate compensation scheme for private equity funds is a major challenge for the industry. But we are certain that there are better ways to reward investors than the approaches used to date, and we are cautiously hopeful that the industry is moving in this direction.

The Increased Public Footprint

As we highlighted in Chapter 10, the public sector is likely to shape the direction of the VC and private equity industry in the years to come. In part, this trend may have been inevitable, given the increased size and role of alternative investment funds in the economy. But it is clear that the financial crisis of the late 2000s opened the door to governmental involvement in the economy on a level not seen for many decades.

The public involvement is likely to have two faces. On the one hand, the continuing challenges that the VC industry may face in many nations and regions worldwide will lead to increased subsidization of venture funds, in addition to direct financing of entrepreneurs. On the other hand, the perceived necessity of preventing another financial meltdown—combined with the lack of public support for the private equity industry in many nations—will increase efforts to regulate buyout funds.

The consequences of these efforts remain difficult to predict. As we highlighted earlier, the legacy of public attempts to encourage venture investment has been mixed. The recent wave of programs, which exhibit a wide diversity that runs the gamut from thoughtful efforts to others that simply repeat the mistakes of the past, continues this legacy. We hope that governments will learn from and share successes, gradually increasing the impacts of these programs.

The consequences of the regulatory wave that is likely to sweep buyout and even venture funds in some nations are similarly difficult to foretell. Increased transparency may actually be beneficial to the industry in terms of limiting the kind of extreme cyclicality we discussed in Chapter 13. But the history of financial regulation is littered with examples of draconian policies that have had unintended consequences and, in some cases, sectors that public officials sought to regulate out of business. One conclusion is clear: the private equity industry will need to do a much better job of explaining its economic role to legislators and bureaucrats as well as making a case for the importance of its contribution to society.

The Challenge of Institutionalization

We believe that the institutionalization of the industry discussed in Chapter 11 and especially in Chapter 12 will continue to be a focus of debate and discussion. With the concentration of assets and the growth of portfolios, portfolio management will be an increasingly important issue in private equity. This is the natural result of a more efficient market with more competition, transparency, training, and knowledge.

This trend is likely to interact with the industry's rapid globalization. But given the importance of hands-on involvement by experienced individuals, the process of institutionalization across geographies is unlikely to be smooth. Active investing is at the heart of industry returns, but there is no clear template for what active investing means in different industries in different places around the world. The extent to which the U.S. model will spread overseas and the degree to which the American model will—or can—be successfully adapted during this process are particularly interesting questions. In the decade to come, private equity managers will have to determine what is universal and what is local.

Scaling private equity firms is a natural result of growth and globalization. But the inflow of money has preceded organizational development, and firms are already straining the limits of their organizations to invest the assets they have. In venture capital, the early 2000s provided a dramatic illustration of the limits of scaling in venture capital: 19 of the 22 VC firms that raised more than a billion dollars in a single fund reduced their fund sizes. It would not be surprising to see the largest buyout funds facing similar challenges in upcoming years. Solving the problem of managing multiple locations, large amounts of money, and scores of independent investment professionals is a top priority for the industry, but easy answers are likely to be elusive.

FINAL THOUGHTS

As we saw from the brief history presented in Chapter 1, and in many other places in this volume, private equity is a young industry. Over its relatively short history, it has been prone to dramatic changes and great reversals. Instability and change have been its hallmarks.

Despite this legacy of change, it is hard not to conclude that we are in a particularly great period of change today. Investors are questioning many of the assumptions about the industry and what kind of returns it can generate. The types of deals that characterize the industry are changing rapidly, moving from mega deals to small-growth equity transactions, many in emerging markets. The players that dominate the business may change more in the next few years than they did in the decades before.

Change is disconcerting. But at the same time, it creates great opportunity, whether one is seeking to join the industry, launch a new fund, or even invest successfully in the sector. While the next few years are likely to see both disappointment and triumph, the single certainty is that the private equity industry—whether venture capital or buyouts—will be a very interesting place to be.

QUESTIONS

1. How would you structure a government program in a new geography aimed at spurring venture capital and entrepreneurial innovation?

2. Assume you are a seasoned private equity professional setting out to start your own firm. What challenges might you face as a first-time fund and how would you overcome them? How would you want to structure your firm, and how would you attract talent?

3. Assume your private equity firm has successfully invested two funds, and you are looking to expand. What is your firm's growth strategy, and what are the potential pitfalls?

4. As a limited partner looking to invest in private equity and venture capital for the first time, how would you structure your portfolio? How might this change over time?

5. In your opinion, what is the future of private equity; how will it evolve? Will there still be opportunities to make outsized returns? Will there be more or fewer players in the industry? Will private equity investors—and LPs—learn from their mistakes? Why or why not?

6. What do you think are the most important positive benefits from a vibrant private equity industry? How does your answer change when you consider venture capital and buyouts separately?

7. What are the greatest risks of private equity, and how do they change when you consider venture capital and buyouts?

Glossary

Acceleration   A provision in employment agreements that allow employees to exercise all or some of their stock options before the vesting schedule allows, typically in the event of the acquisition of the company.

Accredited investor   Under the Investment Company Act of 1940, an individual or institution who satisfies certain tests based on net worth or income.

Adjusted present value (APV)   A variant of the net present value approach that is particularly appropriate when a company's level of indebtedness is changing or it has past operating losses that can be used to offset tax obligations.

Advisory board   A set of limited partners or outsiders who advise a private equity organization. The board may, for instance, provide guidance on overall fund strategy or ways to value privately held comapnies at the end of each fiscal year.

Agency problem   A conflict between managers and investors, or more generally, an instance where an agent does not intrinsically desire to follow the wishes of the principal that hired him.

Agreement of limited partnership   *See* Partnership agreement.

Angel   A wealthy individual who invests in entrepreneurial companies. Although angels perform many of the same functions as venture capitalists, they invest their own capital rather than that of institutional and other individual investors.

Anti-dilution provision   In a preferred stock agreement, a provision that adjusts upward the number of shares (or percentage of the company) held by the holders of the preferred shares if the company subsequently undertakes a financing at a lower valuation than the one at which the existing preferred investors purchased the shares. *See* Full ratchet and Weighted average.

As-converted basis   A calculation of a company's outstanding stock assuming that all the debt and equity that can be converted into common stock has indeed been converted.

Asset allocation   The process through which institutional or individual investors set targets for how their investment portfolios should be divided across the different asset classes.

Asset class   One of a number of investment categories—such as bonds, real estate, and private equity—that institutional and individual investors consider when making asset allocations.

Associate   A professional employee of a private equity firm who is not yet a partner.

Asymmetric information problem   A problem that arises when, because of day-to-day involvement with a situation, one party to an agreement has deeper knowledge than another. This can occur between an entpreneur and an investor, strategic partner, or customer; between current and prospective investors in a company; or between a local office and a remote head office.

Bank book   A description of a company for sale, prepared by the investment bank handling the transaction. Also called a *confidential information memorandum* (CIM).

Basis points (bp or bps)   One hundredth of 1 percent, or 0.01 percent. Interest rates are frequently specified as "LIBOR plus a certain number of basis points."

Beauty contest   The process by which the private equity investors and management of a company that is planning to go public will choose an investment bank. The banks will present their credentials, their ideas for marketing the company, the similar companies they have taken public, their expectations about price, and the analysts who will provide coverage.

Benchmarks   Metrics for the performance of a fund or a company that compare it to other similar funds or operations.

Best efforts   A situation in which an investment bank agrees to do its best to sell a company's stock to the public, but does not purchase the securities outright and therefore is not responsible for any unsold inventory of shares.

Beta   A measure of the extent to which a company's market value varies with an index of overall market value. For instance, a stock with a beta of zero displays no correlation with the market, that with a beta of one generally mirrors the market's movements, and that with a beta greater than one experiences more dramatic shifts when the index moves.

Bogey   *See* Hurdle rate.

Book building   As part of an IPO, the process through which an investment bank discovers the price purchasers would be willing to pay for the stock. After reading the preliminary prospectus, investors submit the amounts of stock they would be willing to purchase at various prices, essentially creating a demand curve for the stock.

Book-to-market ratio   The ratio of a company's accounting (book) value of its equity to the value of the equity assigned by the market (i.e., the product of the number of shares outstanding and the share price).

Bulge bracket   A term frequently used to refer to the top tier of the most reputable and established investment banks.

Buyout   *See* Leveraged buyout.

Call option   The right, but not the obligation, to buy a security at a set price (or range of prices) in a given period.

Callable   A security that the security issuer has an option to repurchase from the security holder.

Capital expenditure (Also known as capex)   Expenditures made by companies to upgrade their business operations.

Capital structure   The mixture of equity and debt that a company has raised.

Capital under management   *See* Committed capital.

Carried interest   The substantial share, often around 20 percent, of profits that are allocated to the general partners of a private equity partnership.

Cash flow available for debt service (CFADS)   An accounting metric considered by banks when funding LBO transactions. CFADS differs from EBITDA in cases where there are noncash earnings or where pools of cash must be reserved for other uses.

Cash-on-cash return   A simplified method for calculating return by dividing the total amount of money received from an investment (or the combination of cash returned and the current value of the portfolio) by the amount initially committed. If an LP receives a total of $200 million after fees from a $50 million investment in a fund, the cash-on-cash return is 4x. Sometimes also called a multiple.

Catch-up   A provision in limited partnership agreements often used in conjunction with a preferred return. The provision allows the general partners to receive all or most of the distributions after the limited partners receive their capital and the preferred return. Such a catch-up typically remains in force until the general partners have received their contractually specified share of the distributions (e.g., 20 percent).

Certification   The "stamp of approval" that a reputable private equity investor or other financial intermediary can provide to a company or individual.

Claw back   A provision in a limited partnership agreement that requires general partners to return funds to the limited partners at the end of the fund's life, if they have received more than their contractually specified share.

Closed-end fund   A publicly traded mutual fund whose shares must be sold to other investors (rather than redeemed from the issuing company, as is the case with open-end mutual funds). Many early venture capital funds were structured in this manner.

Closing   The signing of the contract by an investor or group of investors that binds them to supply a set amount of capital to a private equity fund. Often a fraction of that capital is provided at the time of the closing. A single fund may have multiple closings.

Co-investment   Either *(a)* the syndication of a private equity financing round (*see* Syndication), or *(b)* an investment by an individual general or limited partner alongside a private equity fund in a financing round.

Collar   A combination of an equal number of call and put options at slightly different exercise prices.

Commercial banker   A provider of retail banking services (checking, savings, loans) as opposed to investment banking services (stock underwriting and merger and acquisition advice).

Committed capital   Pledges of capital to a private equity fund. Typically, this money is not received all at once, but rather taken down over three to five years starting in the year the fund is formed.

Common stock   The equity typically held by management and founders. Typically, at the time of an initial public offering, all equity is converted into common stock, which usually holds no special rights. Also known as common equity.

Community development venture capital   Venture capital funds organized by non-profit bodies, often with the twin goals of encouraging economic development and generating financial returns.

Companion fund   A fund, often raised at the same time as a traditional private equity fund, that is restricted to close associates of a private equity group. These funds often have more favorable terms (e.g., reduced fees and no carried interest) than traditional funds.

Consolidation   A private equity investment strategy that involves merging several small comapnies together and exploiting economies of scale or scope.

Conversion ratio   The number of shares for which a convertible debt or equity issue can be exchanged.

Convertible equity or debt   A security that under certain conditions can be converted into another security (often into common stock). The convertible shares often have special rights that the common stock does not have.

Cooperative Research and Development Agreement (CRADA)   A collaborative arrangement between a federally owned research facility and a private company. These were first authorized by the U.S. Congress in the early 1980s.

Corporate venture capital (CVC)   An initiative by a corporation to invest either in young companies outside the corporation or in business concepts originating within the corporation. These are often organized as corporate subsidiaries, not as limited partnerships.

Corporate restructuring   The process of redesigning a company to improve its competitiveness. Usually this occurs in a leveraged buyout although it can occur with a growth capital investment.

Covenants   Items in an agreement that stipulate or restrict certain activities.

Credit crunch   A period when, due to regulatory actions or shifts in the economic conditions, a sharp reduction occurs in the availability of bank loans or other debt financing, particularly for small businesses. The early 1990s were one such period in the United States. The period of 2008-2009 was another.

Cumulative redeemable preferred stock   *See* Redeemable preferred stock.

Depreciation   The process by which the value of an asset with a long but limited life is gradually reduced.

Dilution   The reduction in the fraction of a company's equity owned by the founders and existing shareholders that is associated with a new financing round.

Direct investment   An investment by a limited partner or a fund of funds into an entrepreneurial or restructuring company.

Disbursement   An investment by a private equity fund into a company.

Distressed debt   A private equity investment strategy that involves purchasing discounted bonds of a financially distressed company. Distressed debt investors frequent convert their holdings into equity and become actively involved with the management of the distressed company.

Distribution   The transfer of shares in a (typically publicly traded) portfolio company or the transfer of cash from a private equity fund to each limited partner and (frequently) each general partner.

Down round   A financing round where the valuation of the company is lower than that in the previous round.

Draw down   *See* Take down.

Due diligence   The review of a business plan and assessment of a management team prior to a private equity investment.

Earnings before interest and taxes (EBIT)   A measure of the company's profitability before any adjustment for interest expenses or tax obligations. This measure is often used to compare companies with different levels of indebtedness.

Earnings before interest, taxes, depreciation, and amortization (EBITDA)   A measure of the company's profitability before any adjustment for interest expenses, tax obligations, or noncash charges associated with acquisitions and capital expenditures. This measure frequently serves as a proxy for free cash flow and is used to evaluate a business's ability to handle debt.

Employee Retirement Income Security Act (ERISA)   The 1974 legislation that codified the regulation of corporate pension plans. *See* Prudent man rule.

Endowment   The long-term pool of financial assets held by many universities, hospitals, foundations, and other nonprofit institutions.

Equipment takedown schedule   In a venture leasing contract, the time when the lessee can or must draw down funds to purchase preapproved equipment.

Equity kicker   A transaction in which a small number of shares or warrants are added to what is primarily a debt financing.

Evergreen fund   A fund that has a permanent pool of capital and does not need to raise funds on a regular basis. The private equity operations of old family offices were essentially evergreen funds, in that the family trust supplied capital as needed.

Exercise price   The price at which a share of stock can be purchased (in a call option) or sold (in a put option). This price is set at the time the contract is written. Thus an employee's stock options have an exercise price, usually set at the time the individual joins the company. To exercise the option, the employee must buy the stock at the exercise price and then can sell it at the market price (if the company has gone public) or to another acquirer.

Expansion capital   *See* Growth capital.

External corporate venture capital   A corporate venture capital program that invests in entrepreneurial companies outside the corporation. These investments are often made alongside other venture capitalists.

Financing round   The provision of capital by a private equity group to a company. Since venture capital organizations generally provide capital in stages, a typical venture-backed company will receive several financing rounds over a series of years.

Firm commitment   An underwriting where the underwriter guarantees the company a certain purchase price, by buying the securities from the company and then reselling them. In actuality, the transaction is not finalized until the night before the transaction, so the risk the underwriter runs is usually very low.

First closing   The initial closing of a fund. At this point the firm can usually begin making investments from the new fund.

First dollar carry   A provision in limited partnerships that allow general partners to receive carried interest once the capital actually invested has been returned to the limited partners. The more traditional alternative is that both the invested capital and the management fees must be returned to the limited partners before the general partners receive carried interest.

First fund   An initial fund raised by a private equity organization; also known as a first-time fund.

Float   In a public market context, the percentage of the company's shares that is in the hands of outside investors, as opposed to being held by corporate insiders.

Follow-on fund   A fund that is subsequent to a private equity organization's first fund.

Follow-on offering   *See* Seasoned equity offering.

Form 10-K   An annual filing required by the U.S. Securities and Exchange Commission from each publicly traded company, as well as certain private operations. The statement provides a wide variety of summary data about the company.

'40 Act   *See* Investment Company Act of 1940.

Free cash flow problem   The temptation to undertake wasteful expenditures often posed by the presence of cash not needed for operations or investments.

"Friends and family" fund   *See* Companion fund.

Full ratchet anti-dilution   A system of compensating investors in earlier rounds for a lower price in a subsequent round based on the difference between the price of each round, ensuring that the investor's ownership percentage remains the same as if it had occurred at the new lower price.

Fund   A pool of capital raised periodically by a private equity organization. Usually in the form of limited partnerships, private equity funds typically have a ten-year life, though extensions of several years are often possible.

Fund of funds (FOF)   A fund that invests primarily in other private equity funds rather than operating companies, frequently organized by an investment advisor or investment bank.

Gatekeeper   *See* Investment advisor.

General partner (GP)   A partner in a limited partnership who is responsible for the day-to-day operations of the fund. In the case of a private equity fund, the venture capitalists or buyout experts are either general partners or own the corporation that serves as the general partner. The general partners assume all liability for the fund's debts.

Glass-Steagall Act   The 1933 legislation that limited the equity holdings and underwriting activities of commercial banks in the United States.

Grandstanding problem   The strategy, sometimes employed by young private equity organizations, of rushing young companies to the public marketplace in order to demonstrate a successful track record, even if the companies are not ready to go public.

Green Shoe option   A provision in an underwriting agreement that allows the underwriter to sell an additional amount (typically 15 percent) of shares at the time of the offering.

Growth capital   The sale of equity in a (typically) privately held operating company, frequently one that is profitable, to raise funds to increase production capacity, supply working capital, or further develop the product. Both venture capital funds and mid-market buyout funds do growth capital investing.

Growth equity   *See* Growth capital.

Hedging   A securities transaction that allows an investor to limit the losses that may result from the shifts in value of an existing asset or financial obligation. For instance, a farmer may hedge his exposure to fluctuating crop prices by agreeing before the harvest on a sale price for part of his crop.

Herding problem   A situation in which investors, particularly institutions, make investments that are more similar to one another than is desirable.

Hot issue market   A market with high demand for new securities offerings, particularly for initial public offerings.

Hurdle rate   Either *(a)* the set rate of return that the limited partners must receive before the general partners can begin sharing in any distributions, or *(b)* the level that the fund's net asset value must reach before the general partners can begin sharing in any distributions.

Implicit rate   Also known as the implicit yield, the implicit rate in venture leasing is the annual percentage rate of return before considering the impact of the warrants included as part of the transaction.

In the money   An option or a warrant that would have a positive value if it was immediately exercised.

Inadvertent investment company   An operating company that falls by accident under the '40 Act's definition of an investment company.

Infrastructure fund   A fund raised to invest in infrastructure, usually projects like toll roads, water systems, or port facilities (among others) that have characteristics of steady but low returns with low risk over long periods.

Infrastructure investment   The process by which private equity firms invest in infrastructure (*see* Infrastructure fund). A private equity firm does not have to raise an infrastructure fund to invest in such assets.

Initial public offering (IPO)   The sale of shares to public investors of a company that has not hitherto been traded on a public stock exchange. An investment bank typically underwrites these offerings.

Insider   A director, an officer, or a shareholder with at least a certain percentage (often 10 percent) of a company's equity.

Intangible asset   A patent, trade secret, informal know-how, brand capital, or other nonphysical asset.

Intellectual property (IP)   Creations of the mind (patents, processes, and the like) that have value in the market and can be legally protected.

Internal corporate venture capital program   A corporate venture capital program that invests in business concepts originating inside the corporation.

Internal rate of return (IRR)   The annualized effective compounded return rate that can be earned on the invested capital; the investment's yield. For both venture capital and buyout firms, the longer the money is tied up in the investment, the higher the multiple of the original investment that must be returned to have an adequate IRR.

Intrapreneuring   A corporate venture capital program that invests in business concepts originating inside the corporation. The term often is applied specifically to efforts in which the corporation intends to reacquire its new ventures.

Investment advisor   A financial intermediary who assists investors, particularly institutions, with investments in private equity and other financial assets. Advisors assess potential new private equity funds for their clients and monitor the progress of existing investments. In some cases, they pool their investors' capital in funds of funds.

Investment bank   A financial intermediary that, among other services, may underwrite securities offerings, facilitate mergers and acquisitions, and trade securities for its own account.

Investment banker   A financial expert who works at an investment bank and may, among other services, underwrite securities offerings, facilitate mergers and acquisitions, and trade securities.

Investment committee   A group, typically consisting of general partners of a private equity fund, that reviews potential and/or existing investments. This may also refer to a group of individuals that advise or monitor the activities of an institutional investor's investment staff. Sometimes referred to as a board of trustees.

Investment Company Act of 1940   Legislation that imposed extensive disclosure requirements and operating restrictions on mutual funds. A major concern of publicly traded venture funds has been avoiding designation as an investment company as defined by the provisions of this Act.

Investment trust   *See* Closed-end fund. This term is commonly used in Great Britain.

Investor buyout (IBO)   *See* Management buy-in.

Key performance indicators (KPIs)   Measurement of those changes that are deemed critical to the company's success.

Lease line   Similar to a bank line of credit, a credit that allows a venture lessee a certain amount of money to add equipment as needed, according to a preapproved takedown schedule.

Lemons problem   *See* Asymmetric information problem.

Lessee   The party to a lease agreement who is obliged to make monthly rental payments and can use the equipment during the lease term.

Lessor   The party to a lease agreement who has legal title to the equipment, grants the lessee the right to use the equipment for the lease term, and is entitled to the rental payments.

Leveraged buyout (LBO)   The acquisition of a company or business unit, typically in a mature industry, with a considerable amount of debt. The debt is then repaid according to a strict schedule.

Leveraged buyout fund   A fund, typically organized in a similar manner to a venture capital fund, specializing in leveraged buyout investments. Some of these funds also make venture capital investments.

Leveraged recapitalization   A transaction in which the management team (rather than new investors as in the case of an LBO) borrows money to buy out the interests of other investors. As in an LBO, the debt is then repaid.

Licensee   In a licensing agreement, the party who receives the right to use a technology, product, or brand name in exchange for payments.

Licensor   In a licensing agreement, the party who receives payments in exchange for providing the right to use a technology, product, or brand name that it owns.

Limit order   In an underwritten IPO, the price-dependent orders made by individual or institutional investors: for example, the agreement by an investor to purchase 10,000 shares, conditional on the price of the offering being under $12 per share.

Limited partner (LP)   An investor in a limited partnership. Limited partners can monitor the partnership's progress but cannot become involved in its day-to-day management if they are to retain limited liability.

Limited partnership   An organizational form that entails a finitely lived contractual arrangement between limited and general partners, governed by a partnership agreement.

Limited partnership agreement (LPA)   The written contract setting forth the terms and conditions that govern the relationship between the limited partners and the general partners in a particular fund.

Liquidation   The process of selling an investment and achieving liquidity for a fund's investors. Liquidation events can be either positive and generate profits, or negative and create losses.

Liquidation preference provision   In a preferred stock agreement, a provision that insures preference over common stock with respect to any dividends or payments in association with the liquidation of the company.

Lock up   A provision in the underwriting agreement between an investment bank and existing shareholders that prohibits corporate insiders and private equity investors from selling at the time of the offering.

Look back   *See* Claw back.

Management buy-in (MBI)   A European term for an LBO initiated by a private equity group with no previous connection to the company.

Management buyout (MBO)   A European term for an LBO initiated by an existing management team, which then solicits the involvement of a private equity group.

Management fee   The fee, typically a percentage of committed capital or net asset value, that is paid by a private equity fund to the general partners to cover salaries and expenses.

Managing general partner   The general partner (or partners) who is ultimately responsible for the management of the fund.

Mandatory conversion provision   In a preferred stock agreement, a provision that requires the preferred stock holders to convert their shares into common stock. Typically, holders are required to make such exchanges in the event of an initial public offering of at least a certain size and at least a certain valuation.

Mandatory redemption provision   In a preferred stock agreement, a provision that requires the company to purchase the shares from the private equity investors according to a set schedule. Typically used in the case of redeemable preferred stock investments.

Market maker   The service provided by an investment bank or broker in insuring the liquidity of trading in a given security. As a part of its duties, the market maker may accumulate a substantial inventory of shares in the company.

Market-to-book ratio   The inverse of the book-to-market ratio.

Market risk premium   The difference between the return on a publicly traded portfolio and the risk-free rate (usually long-term government bonds).

Materiality   The degree to which a particular issue or detail affects the broader question at hand. For instance, a CEO's birthplace may be irrelevant unless it inclines him toward emotionally driven and sub-optimal expansion decisions in that region.

Mega-fund   One of the largest leveraged buyout funds, measured by the amount of committed capital.

Merger and acquisition (M&A)   An exit method through which one company purchases another. Although often combined, each method differs: in a merger, the two companies are combined into a new entity and issue a new stock; in an acquisition, one company purchases the other and pays for it in cash and/or its own stock. The acquired company ceases to exist, becoming a division of the new parent. In a merger, both participants cease to exist as independent entities and instead operate as a merged entity.

Mezzanine   Either *(a)* a private equity financing round shortly before an initial public offering, or *(b)* an investment that employs subordinated debt that has fewer privileges than bank debt but more than equity and often has attached warrants.

Mid-market   Companies somewhere between "small" and "large," variously defined in terms of ownership (most often, family-owned), employees, revenues (e.g., between $200 and $600 million), enterprise value, and equity investment (e.g., between $25 and $200 million).

Milestone payments   In a licensing agreement, the payments made by the licensee to the licensor at specified times in the future or else when certain technological or business objectives have been achieved. Some venture capital investments may also involve payments tied to the achievement of milestones upon which all parties (investors and entrepreneurs) have agreed.

Minority position   A situation in which an investor purchases less than a majority control of a company. Frequently this occurs in venture capital and in growth or expansion capital investments; less frequently with buyouts. Also known as *minority investing*.

Multiple   A comparison of one number to another. It can be the returns from a fund or a company (total money returned compared to total money invested) or the consideration paid for a company (total price compared to EBITDA or revenues).

Naked short   In the context of a security underwriting, a case where the underwriter sells more shares than agreed upon (and those allowed under the Green Shoe option). In this case, the underwriter must buy back shares in the open market after the offering is completed to close out the short position.

NASDAQ   The U.S. stock exchange where many IPOs are listed and most companies that were formerly backed by private equity investors trade.

Net asset value (NAV)   The value of a fund's holdings, which may be calculated using a variety of valuation rules. The value does not include funds that have been committed but not drawn down.

Net income   A company's profits after taxes.

Net operating losses (NOLs)   Tax credits that are compiled by companies that have financial losses. These credits generally cannot be used until the company becomes profitable (or returns to profitability).

Net present value (NPV)   A valuation method that computes the expected value of one or more future cash flows and discounts them at a rate that reflects the cost of capital (which will vary with the cash flows' riskiness).

Operating lease   In venture leasing, a short-term lease in which the customer uses equipment for a fraction of its useful life. Obligations of ownership may remain with the lessor, including maintenance, insurance, and taxes.

Option   The right, but not the obligation, to buy or sell a security at a set price (or range of prices) in a given period.

Option pool   Shares in a private company that have been set aside for possible issuance to employees at a later date.

Out of the money   An option or a warrant that would have a negative value if it was immediately exercised.

Participating convertible preferred stock   *See* Participating preferred stock.

Participating preferred stock   Convertible stock where, under certain conditions, the holder receives both the return of his original investment and a share of the company's equity.

Participation   The quality of having participating preferred stock.

Partnership agreement   The contract that explicitly specifies the compensation and conditions that govern the relationship between the investors (limited partners) and the venture capitalists (general partners) during a private equity fund's life. Occasionally used to refer to the separate agreement between the general partners regarding the internal operations of the fund (e.g., the division of the carried interest).

Patent   A government grant of rights to one or more discoveries for a period, based on a set of criteria.

Phantom stock A form of compensation, sometimes used in internal corporate venture capital programs, where employees receive payments that imitate those received from holding stock options, but where they do not actually hold equity. These compensation plans often have negative tax and accounting consequences.

Placement agent A financial intermediary hired by private equity organizations to facilitate the raising of new funds.

Point One percent of a private equity fund's profits. The general partners of a private equity fund are often allocated 20 points, or 20 percent of the capital gains, which are divided among the individual partners.

Pooled IRR A method for calculating the returns from a number of funds in which an IRR is calculated from the aggregatred cash flows of all the funds.

Pooled preferences A situation in which the liquidation preferences of preferred stock acquired in different investment rounds are calculated proportionately (by face value to the total liquidation preferences in the pool).

Portfolio management The process of ensuring that the risk in a portfolio of investments is balanced along a variety of dimensions, which can include geography, stage, sector, and/or partner time requirements.

Post-money valuation The product of the price paid per share in a financing round and the shares outstanding after the financing round. As a rule of thumb, the pre-money value plus the new money raised. This is true only if there are no stock redemptions or warrants issued.

Preferred return A provision in limited partnership agreements that insures that the limited partners receive not only their capital back, but also a contractually stipulated rate of return on their funds before the general partners receive any carried interest.

Preferred stock Stock that has preference over common stock with respect to any dividends or payments in association with the liquidation of the company. Preferred stockholders may also have additional rights, such as the ability to block mergers or displace management.

Pre-money valuation The product of the price paid per share in a financing round and the shares outstanding before the financing round. As a rule of thumb, the price of the company before the new money goes in.

Price-earnings ratio (P/E ratio) The ratio of the company's share price to its earnings per share (net income divided by shares outstanding).

Primary investment An investment by a limited partner or a fund of funds into a private equity partnership that is raising capital from investors.

Private equity shares of a company that are not traded on a public market.

Private equity fund Organizations devoted to venture capital, leveraged buyout, consolidation, mezzanine, and distressed debt investments, as well as a variety of hybrids such as venture leasing and venture factoring.

Private placement The sale of securities not registered with the U.S. Securities and Exchange Commission to institutional investors or wealthy individuals. These transactions are frequently facilitated by an investment bank.

Privatization A situation in which a company becomes privately owned. This happens in two different ways:
  a. A state-owned company is sold off. In some situations, it is sold to a private equity group; in others, it is listed on a public exchange (as has occurred in China) or shares are distributed to citizens (as occurred in Russia).
  b. A publicly traded company is acquired by a private entity, usually a private equity firm. In this case, its shares are no longer listed.

Pro forma Financial statements that project future changes in a company's income statement or balance sheet. These often form the basis for valuation analyses of various types.

Pro rata Proportionately to existing ownership.

Prospectus A condensed, widely disseminated version of the registration statement that is also filed with the U.S. Securities and Exchange Commission. The prospectus provides a wide variety of summary data about the company or fund.

Proxy statement   A filing with the U.S. Securities and Exchange Commission that, among other information, provides information on the holdings and names of corporate insiders.

Prudent man rule   Prior to 1979, a provision in the Employee Retirement Income Security Act (ERISA) that essentially prohibited pension funds from investing substantial amounts of money in private equity or other high-risk asset classes. The Department of Labor's clarification of the rule in that year allowed pension managers to invest in high-risk assets, including private equity.

Public market equivalent (PME)   A methodology for calculating returns to investing in a private equity fund relative to those from investing the same amount in a public index. If the ratio of the proceeds from the private equity investments to the public investment is greater than one, private equity is the superior investment; if the ratio is less than one, the public investment is better.

Public venture capital   Venture capital funds organized by government bodies, or programs to make venture-like financings with public funds. Examples include the Small Business Investment Company and Small Business Innovation Research programs.

Put option   The right, but not the obligation, to sell a security at a set price (or range of prices) in a given period.

Putable   A security which the security holder has an option to sell back to the issuer.

Qualified investor   Under the 1996 amendments to the '40 Act, an individual or institution who satisfies certain tests based on net worth or income. The minimum amounts for attaining such a status are higher than those for accredited investors.

Recapitalization (Recap)   An investment that essentially eliminates the company's existing capital structure and restarts the company, often with a new set of investors and always with a new set of preferences and a simplified structure.

Red herring   A preliminary version of the prospectus that is distributed to potential investors before a security offering. The name derives from the disclaimers typically printed in red on the front cover. Also known as a preliminary or pathfinder prospectus.

Redeemable preferred stock   Preferred stock where the holders have no right to convert the security into common equity. The return to the investor, like that of a bond, consists of a series of dividend payments and the return of the face value of the share, which is paid out at the contractually specified time when the company must redeem the shares.

Registration right provision   In a preferred stock agreement, provisions that allow the private equity investors to force the company to go public, or to sell their shares as part of a public offering that the company is undertaking.

Registration statement   A filing with the U.S. Securities and Exchange Commission (e.g., an S-1 or S-18 form) that must be reviewed by the Commission before a company can sell shares to the public. The statement provides a wide variety of summary data about the company, as well as copies of key legal documents.

Residual value   In venture leasing, the fair-market value of the leased equipment at the end of the lease term.

Restricted stock   Shares that cannot be sold under U.S. Securities and Exchange Commission regulations or that can only be sold in limited amounts.

Reverse claw back   In a limited partnership agreement, a provision that requires limited partners to return funds to the general partners at the end of the fund's life, if they have received more than their contractually specified share.

Reverse leveraged buyout (RLBO)   The situation when a company that is taken private in a leveraged buyout returns to the public markets.

Right of first refusal   A contractual provision that gives a corporation or private equity fund the right to purchase, license, or invest in all opportunities associated with another organization before other companies or funds can do so. A weaker form of this provision is termed the "right of first look."

Road show   The marketing of a private equity fund or public offering to potential investors.

Roll-up   *See* Consolidation.

Round   *See* Financing round.

Royalties   In a licensing agreement, the percentage of sales or profits that the licensee pays to the licensor.

Rule of 99   A provision in the '40 Act that exempted funds with fewer than ninety-nine accredited investors from being designated investment companies. This rule was relaxed in a 1996 amendment to the '40 Act.

Rule 10(b)-5   The U.S. Securities and Exchange Commission regulation that most generally prohibits fraudulent activity in the purchase or sale of any security.

Rule 16(a)   The U.S. Securities and Exchange Commission regulation that requires insiders to disclose any transactions in a company's stock on a monthly basis.

Rule 144   The U.S. Securities and Exchange Commission regulation that prohibits sales for one year (originally, two years) after the purchase of restricted stock and limits the pace of sales between the first and second (originally, second and third) year after the purchase.

Run rate   A company's results if the performance of the current period were to be extrapolated to a full year. This can be a useful approach in fast-growing companies; it can be misleading if the company is distinctly seasonal and the base period corresponds to a seasonal peak.

Seasoned equity offering   An offering by a company that has already completed an initial public offering and whose shares are already publicly traded.

Secondary buyout   A situation in which a company owned by a buyout firm is sold to another buyout firm. Also called a *sponsor-to-sponsor transaction.*

Secondary investment   The purchase by a limited partner or a fund of funds of an existing limited partnership holding from another limited partner.

Secondary offering   An offering of shares that are not being issued by the company, but rather are sold by existing shareholders. Consequently, the company does not receive the proceeds from the sale of these shares.

Seniority   An investor's place in the capital structure of a company. Investors in a financing round with seniority will receive any returns from a liquidation event first.

Service providers   Professionals who provide ancillary services to private equity funds. These can include accountants, lawyers, human resource professionals, and others.

Shares outstanding   The number of shares that the company has issued.

Small Business Innovation Research (SBIR) program   A federal program, established in 1982, that provides a set percentage of the federal R&D budget to small, high-technology companies.

Small Business Investment Company (SBIC) program   A federally guaranteed risk capital pool. These funds were first authorized by the U.S. Congress in 1958, proliferated during the 1960s, and then dwindled after many organizations encountered management and incentive problems.

Social venture capital   Either community development venture capital or public venture capital (see definitions).

Special limited partner   A limited partner who receives part of the carried interest from the fund. In many cases, the first investors in a new fund are given special limited partner status.

Sponsor-to-sponsor transaction   See Secondary buyout.

Staging   The provision of capital to entrepreneurs in multiple installments, with each financing conditional on meeting particular business targets. This provision helps ensure that the money is not squandered on unprofitable prospects. Also known as a "tranched" investment.

Stapled fund   A fund raised at the same time as another private equity fund, which invests on *pro rata* in a subset (defined in advance) of the fund's transactions. Sometimes the term is used to refer to funds that invest in all transactions by the fund, but are raised from a different class of investors (e.g., international limited partners).

Stock appreciation rights   One type of phantom stock compensation scheme.

Stockbroker   A regulated professional who buys and sells shares and other securities.

Straight preferred stock   *See* Redeemable preferred stock.

Strategic alliance   In private equity, a situation in which a private equity firm teams up with a major corporation that has made an investment in a developing country. Also a collaboration between companies, one or both of which are private-equity backed

Strike price   *See* Exercise price.

Subordinated (sub) debt   Debt that ranks below senior debt in the capital structure. Sub debt holders will be paid after the holders of senior debt but before the equity holders if the company is liquidated. Sometimes called "junior debt."

Super majority voting provision   In a preferred stock agreement, a provision that requires that more than a majority of the preferred stock holders approves a given decision.

Syndication   The joint purchase of shares by two or more private equity organizations or the joint underwriting of an offering by two or more investment banks.

Take down   The transfer of some or all of the committed capital from the limited partners to a private equity fund.

Takedown schedule   The contractual language that describes how and when a private equity fund can (or must) receive the committed capital from its limited partners. In venture leasing, the period after the lease begins when the lessee can or must draw down funds for the preapproval equipment to be purchased.

Tangible asset   A machine, building, land, inventory, or another physical asset.

Target capital structure   The mixture of debt and equity that a company wishes to achieve. This may differ substantially from the current capital structure if the company wishes to increase or decrease its indebtedness.

Term of lease   In venture leasing, the duration of the lease, usually in months, which is fixed at its inception.

Term sheet   A preliminary outline of the structure of a private equity partnership or stock purchase agreement, frequently agreed to by the key parties before the formal contractual language is negotiated.

Terminal value   The value of an investment at the end of a certain period of time.

Time zero   A method for calculating IRRs in which all the investments are assumed to be made in the first year of the fund and all exits correspondingly brought forward in time.

Tombstone   An advertisement, typically in a major business publication, by an underwriter to publicize an offering that it has been underwritten.

Total Factor Productivity (TFP)   A variable that accounts for changes in total output not caused by inputs—that is, the amount of growth due to an economy's long-term technological change or vitality.

Trade sale   A European term for the exiting of an investment by a private equity group by selling it to a corporation. Usually called a merger or an acquisition in the United States.

Tranched investment   An investment where money is released contingent upon the company's achievement of specific milestones. *See* Staging.

Triple-net full-payout lease   In venture leasing, a long-term lease in which the lessee's lease payments cover the entire cost of the leased equipment and the lessee assumes all responsibilities of ownership, including maintenance, insurance, and taxes.

Uncertainty problem   The array of potential outcomes for a company or project. The wider the dispersion of potential outcomes, the greater the uncertainty.

Underpricing   The discount to the projected trading price at which the investment banker sells shares in an initial public offering. A substantial positive return on the first trading day is often interpreted by financial economists as evidence of underpricing.

Underwriter   The investment bank that underwrites an offering.

Underwriting   The purchase of a securities issue from a company by an investment bank and its (typically almost immediate) resale to investors.

Unrelated business taxable income (UBTI)   The gross income from any unrelated business that a tax-exempt institution regularly carries out. If a private equity partnership is generating significant income from debt-financed property, tax-exempt limited partners may face tax liabilities due to UBTI provisions.

Unseasoned equity offering   *See* Initial public offering.

Up-front fees   In a licensing agreement, nonrefundable payments made by the licensee to the licensor at the time the agreement is signed.

Valuation rule   The algorithm by which a private equity fund assigns values to the public and private companies in its portfolio.

Venture capital   Independently managed, dedicated pools of capital that focus on equity or equity-linked investments in privately held, high-growth companies. Many venture capital funds, however, occasionally make other types of private equity investments. Outside of the United States, this phrase is often used as a synonym for private equity and/or leveraged buyouts.

Venture capital method   A valuation approach that values the company at some point in the future, assuming that it has been successful, and then discounts this projected value at some high discount rate.

Venture capitalist   A general partner or associate at a private equity organization, usually one that invests in early-stage companies.

Venture debt   A loan for companies that do not meet traditional banking requirements for revenue and assets. Venture debt requires standard repayment with interest and may also include warrants. It can be used by venture-backed companies to extend their cash without further diluting equity.

Venture factoring   A private equity investment strategy that involves purchasing the receivables of high-risk young companies. As part of the transaction, the venture factoring fund typically also receives warrants in the young company.

Venture leasing   A private equity investment strategy that involves leasing equipment or other assets to high-risk young companies. As part of the transaction, the venture leasing fund typically also receives warrants in the company.

Venture returns   The general range of returns expected from venture capital firms, usually between 15 percent and 20 percent. This expected return may have little correlation to returns actually generated.

Vesting   A provision in employment agreements that restricts employees from exercising all or some of their stock options immediately. These agreements typically include a schedule specifying the percentage of shares that the employee is allowed to exercise over time, known as a vesting schedule.

Vintage year   The group of funds whose first closing was in a certain year.

Volatility   The standard deviation of returns around the mean, or the degree to which portfolio performance may vary over time.

Warrant-based lease   In venture leasing, a lease that requires the lessee to grant equity participation to the lessor, usually in the form of warrants.

Warrants   An option to buy shares of stock issued directly by a company at a certain price in the future.

Weighted average anti-dilution   A method of compensating investors in earlier rounds for a lower price in a subsequent round based on the averaged price of each round weighted by the number of shares. *See also* Full ratchet anti-dilution.

Weighted average cost of capital (WACC)   A calculation of the company's cost of capital that takes into account the costs of all capital sources (debt, common stock, preferred stock, and so forth) and weights them proportionally.

Window dressing problem   The behavior of money managers of adjusting their portfolios at the end of the quarter by buying companies whose shares have appreciated and selling "mistakes." This is driven by the fact that institutional investors may examine not only quarterly returns, but also end-of-period holdings. It can also occur among private equity firms when GPs buy shares in late-stage companies that have received substantial press attention to demonstrate to their LPs that they had a position in a popular company.

Withdrawn offering   A transaction in which a registration statement is made with the U.S. Securities and Exchange Commission but either the company writes to the Commission withdrawing the proposed offering before it is effective or the offering is not completed within nine months.

Index

423